Ex Líbris

CIVIL WAR TIMES ILLUSTRATED

PHOTOGRAPHIC HISTORY OF
The Civil War

FORT SUMTER TO GETTYSBURG

Shadows of the Storm

The Guns of '62

The Embattled Confederacy

EDITED BY WILLIAM C. DAVIS AND BELL I. WILEY

UNDER THE DIRECTION OF THE NATIONAL HISTORICAL SOCIETY

WITH A NEW INTRODUCTION BY WILLIAM C. DAVIS

BLACK DOG & LEVENTHAL PUBLISHERS
NEW YORK

Editor

William C. Davis

Senior Consulting Editor

Bell I. Wiley

Photographic Consultants

William A. Frassanito
Manuel Kean
Lloyd Ostendorf
Frederick Ray

Editorial Assistants

Deborah A. Berrier
Karen K. Kennedy
Denise Mummert
James Rietmulder

Originally published in three separate volumes as:

The Image of War 1861-1865, volume One:
Shadows of the Storm

The Image of War 1861-1865, volume Two:
The Guns of '62

The Image of War 1861-1865, volume Three:
The Embattled Confederacy

This edition published by arrangement with Cowles Magazines, Inc.

Published by Black Dog & Leventhal Publishers, Inc.
151 W. 19th Street
New York, NY 10011

Distributed by Workman Publishing Company
708 Broadway
New York, NY 10003

Manufactured in the United States of America

ISBN 1-884822-08-8

LC CIP data TK

Contents

The Guns of '62

The Embattled Confederacy

Introduction

WILLIAM C. DAVIS

THE ORIGINS of the *Civil War Times Illustrated Photographic History of the Civil War* are just about as obscure and unlikely as they could be. At their remotest distance, they date from 1960 in a cramped two-bedroom bungalow in Sebastopol, California, in the heart of the redwood and wine country. Not exactly a place one associates with the Civil War.

But there I was, aged almost fourteen, having read perhaps two books on the "late unpleasantness," and vaguely aware that I found the general subject interesting. Then I saw an advertisement in the now long-defunct *True Magazine*. It was for a book titled *Campfire and Battlefield of the Civil War,* and emphasized that the volume included almost 1,000 photographs from the conflict. In fact, though the ad did not bother to say so, it was a reprint of one of the very first Civil War photographic books, put together by Rossiter Johnson and first published around the turn of the century when the development of the halftone printing process made it practical to reproduce photographs in books and magazines.

To a typical fourteen-year-old—meaning one with no job and no money—the terms were alluring. The book cost $15.00 plus postage and handling, could be ordered on approval with no money down, and paid for in four installments of $3.95 each. Remember, this is 1960, and begging even $3.95 a month from financially hard-pressed parents was no easy feat. As I recall, I ordered the book unilaterally, trusting that I would find the money somewhere later on.

When the book arrived I experienced something like unto an epiphany. Day after day I poured over the book. I never read the text then or later. To this day I have not read it, nor would I advise anyone else to do so, for intervening years of experience have taught me how unreliable was most of the material being written at that time.

But the photographs transfixed me. The reproduction was awful. Even the originals were not too clear, for halftone printing was still fairly primitive when *Campfire and Battlefield* first appeared. The reprint I bought was merely photographed from an original copy, and with little care given to quality. Nevertheless, it was what was *in* the photos, and not their quality, that seized me. Here were the actual faces and figures of the men and women of the Civil War, their weapons, their homes, their forts and railroads. These were not just stilted paintings or the crude woodcuts of the time, but the faces of the Civil War exactly as they appeared to each other.

I treasured that book, and have it still. It was the very first Civil War book I ever bought (eventually *someone* made those $3.95 payments, though I cannot remember who). More to the point, it inaugurated a fascination with the photographic record of the conflict that has lasted to this day, and that along the way has produced some of the most exhilarating moments of my life, and with them these new volumes of the *Civil War Times Illustrated Photographic History of the Civil War.*

No one is interested in the life stories of historians, and wisely, I might add, so I will skip the next eighteen years and pick up the story in 1978. Through a series of acci-

dents, fortuitous circumstances, and only occasional design, by then I was editor of *Civil War Times Illustrated,* the nation's largest and leading magazine devoted to the conflict, and living in central Pennsylvania where it was published. One of the happiest aspects of editing that magazine was that almost every week, thanks to its wide circulation and reputation, the magazine's editorial offices received letters out of the blue regarding new discoveries in Civil War photography. Collectors sent in copies of the treasures they uncovered in flea markets and antique stores. Dusty attics disgorged long hidden images of the great and small. And in the course of researching illustrations for articles, our editors and art director constantly found overlooked rarities in public archives.

With no particular object in mind, I filed all of this in the back of my mind along with all the rest of the clutter that a historian carries around. Then in 1978 the thunderbolt struck. At nearby Carlisle sat the United States Army Military History Institute, the Army's chief repository of books and documents. In that year the Institute received an incredible bequest. A defunct Civil War veterans organization, the Massachusetts commandery of the Military Order of the Loyal Legion of the United States, seeking a secure home for its fabulous collections of documents and artifacts before they were vandalized into oblivion, turned most of the material over to the Army. Among the donations were some photographs.

About 40,000 to be exact! The Massachusetts MOLLUS commandery—the acronym by which the group was known—had accumulated in the last two decades of the nine-teenth century the greatest collection of Civil War photographs in existence, yet for years it had been virtually unknown outside the MOLLUS membership. Even the people at *Civil War Times Illustrated,* which by then had been publishing for almost two decades, had never heard of the collection. I'll never forget the day the 100 and more leather-bound volumes arrived at the Institute. Colonel George Pappas, then director of the Institute, piled them on a metal trolley and wheeled load after load into the archives room, where I and a couple of other expectant Institute staff attacked them greedily. Almost every page yielded something new, something never-before-published. Here were portraits of generals

we had never known to exist, regiment after regiment standing at attention for the camera, nurses at work in the hospitals, even photos of the photographers themselves at work. The magnitude of the collection was staggering, dwarfing by several multiples the largest known holdings of the time.

As near as I can recall, that same evening, stunned by what I had seen, I lay awake most of the night turning over in my mind just what could be done with that collection. It was out of that sleepless night, whose own roots went all the way back to a fire lit in 1960, that the *Civil War Times Illustrated Photographic History of the Civil War* eventually emerged.

At the end of the long road, Samuel Cooley photographs a soldier in the ruins of Fort Sumter at the war's close. The soldier and the camera have come a long way together.

Shadows of the Storm

The Coming of the War

T. HARRY WILLIAMS

America goes mad, and to war with itself

THE MOST SENSATIONAL NEWS in the big city newspapers of the United States in 1855 and 1856 concerned events in far-off Kansas Territory. There, according to reports of correspondents, settlers were committing widespread acts of violence on other settlers, burning and destroying property and engaging in wholesale murder. A certain amount of violence occurred in every frontier area undergoing settlement, and although this was duly recorded in the press, it did not attract special attention. What set the disorders in Kansas apart was that they resulted from, or seemed to result from, a difference in ideology between contesting individuals and groups. Kansans were not killing each other in a spirit of passion or lawlessness but in a mood of crusading zeal. They were fighting to make Kansas a free state—or a slave state. As the turmoil mounted and the deaths increased, the term "Bleeding Kansas" became a national byword.

The question of whether slavery should be permitted to enter the territories was an old one in American politics. It had first arisen in 1819 when Missouri applied for admission as a state with a constitution establishing slavery, and northern opponents of slavery and southern influence in the federal government had attempted to block admis-

sion. Although Missouri won entrance in the following year, the bulk of the then existing national domain was declared closed to slavery in the Missouri Compromise. The issue slumbered for years thereafter, but criticism of slavery continued; indeed, beginning in the 1830s more and more persons in the North began to say that slavery must be eradicated, be either abolished immediately or phased out gradually. The territorial issue reappeared in 1848 at the close of the Mexican War. As a result of that conflict, the United States had acquired a huge region to the southwest of the existing boundary, and hardly was the ink dry on the peace treaty when men in the North and the South began to argue about the status of slavery in the new possession.

As the dispute deepened, three proposals to solve the situation were advanced. Most Southerners contended that slaveholders had a constitutional right to take their human property into the recently acquired territory, or for that matter, into any part of the national domain, and to be protected in holding their property by the federal government. The most confirmed antislavery Northerners held that Congress had a constitutional power and a moral duty to exclude the institution from the new territory, or from any other territory;

"Let Freedom Ring." Symbols of American independence—Congress Hall, the Pennsylvania State House, and Philadelphia's old City Hall, in 1855. Here began the epic of American nationhood. Here, too, the Founding Fathers planted unknowingly the seeds of dissolution. (FREE LIBRARY OF PHILADELPHIA)

It is a thriving, bustling nation, full of itself and its ever-stretching power and prosperity. Already in 1860, Broadway in New York City is one of the busiest streets in the world. (U. S. ARMY MILITARY HISTORY INSTITUTE, CARLISLE BARRACKS, PA.)

they believed that if slavery was prevented from expanding, it would ultimately die a forced death. In between these diametrically opposed views was a third formula that drew its strongest support from Democrats in the northwestern states. Known as popular sovereignty, it recommended that Congress should make no pronouncement on the status of slavery in the Mexican cession territory nor, by implication, in any other territory. Slaveholders should be permitted to enter, and the position of the institution would be determined by the territorial legislature, or, as advocates of the doctrine liked to say, by the people themselves. Although popular sovereignty did not formally exclude slavery, it was actually a subtle exclusion prescription—the majority of settlers in a territory would undoubtedly come from the more populous North.

Popular sovereignty found enough support to be enacted into law as a part of the Compromise of 1850, which attempted to settle the territorial dispute and other issues which had arisen between the sections. Comparative calm prevailed for several years after passage of the compromise act. But in 1854 Senator Stephen A. Douglas of Illinois offered a measure that stirred fresh and even more bitter controversy. The leader of the northwestern Democrats, Douglas was a believer in popular sovereignty and in the future of the West. Both principles influenced the provisions that he put into his bill. To speed settlement of the western region, he proposed to organize two new territories, Kansas and Nebraska, which lay north of the line proscribing slavery in the Missouri Compromise. But to get southern support for the bill, he had to insert a section that repealed the exclusion clause of the old and revered Missouri law, leaving the determination of the condition of slavery in the proposed territories to their legislatures. The whole North seemed to blaze with fury at passage of the Kansas-Nebraska Act. Antislavery leaders cried that the South had used its malign influence to extend its immoral institution and that this latest threat to freedom must be checked—Kansas, the southernmost of the two territories, must be settled by people from the North who would vote to make it a free state. Southern leaders responded to the challenge by urging their people to immigrate to the territory to vote for slavery. Kansas was about to become a prize to be contended for by the sections.

Many of the settlers who went to Kansas did so for the reasons that usually impelled families to move to a new area—they were looking only for a better life. But others entered to support a cause—dedicated enemies of slavery from the northeastern states and dedicated adherents of the institution from the neighboring state of Missouri who were willing to become transitory and illegal voters. Some men on both sides were not content to rely on voting to decide the issue, and soon the intimidation and the shooting started. Violence was superseding the normal democratic process.

The Kansas question stirred men to passion everywhere, including on the floors of Congress. In May 1856 antislavery senator Charles Sumner of Massachusetts delivered a bitter speech attacking various southern colleagues for supporting what he called "The Crime Against Kansas." Representative Preston Brooks of South Carolina, a younger kinsman of one of the senators attacked, was so enraged at the speech that he armed himself with a cane and went over to the other chamber and beat Sumner into bloody unconsciousness. The episode was but one of many examples of actual or threatened violence in Congress. Some members came to sessions bearing thinly concealed pistols, several fist-swinging brawls occurred between individual Northerners and Southerners or between groups, and challenges to duels were freely passed. The violence in halls dedicated to debate, like the violence in Kansas, was a symbol dark with portent for the future. Americans were becoming so aroused about the question of slavery in any of its manifestations that they were not satisfied to discuss it or to vote on it. They could relieve their feelings only by committing physical harm on those who disagreed with them. Their anger flowed in part from the contradictions in American society, a society that was homogeneous but also diverse, that was experiencing an expansion of wealth and power but was being torn apart by ideological division.

The United States in 1860 was a land of imposing physical dimensions. The writ of American authority ran from the Atlantic Ocean to the Pacific Ocean, from the Canadian border to the Mexican border. A large part of the expanse west of the Mississippi River was as yet unpeopled except by Indian tribes. A tier of states just beyond the river marked the farthest line of settlement, and beyond them was wilderness stretching to California and

Oregon on the Pacific coast. But already emigrants were pushing into the distant areas—the movement to Kansas was one example—and a constant increase in the population of the older regions gave promise that the eruptions would continue and that more states would soon be added to what popular orators liked to call "the galaxy of the Union."

The population of the thirty-three states then in the Union was approximately 31,000,000 persons, almost double the number of inhabitants in 1840. Nearly half of these lived west of the Appalachian mountain chain, a distribution that revealed the newer states were growing in influence at the expense of the older ones. Another demographic development, and at the moment a more ominous one, was the disparity in population between the free states and the slave states. The former numbered about 22,000,000 persons and the latter 9,000,000 persons of whom one third were black slaves. The South was becoming a minority, losing strength in the House of Representatives and the Electoral College every decade.

Most Americans lived, as their fathers and grandfathers had lived, in rural surroundings, on farms or in small towns. But beginning in the 1840s a significant shift of population toward cities occurred. New York City, the largest urban center, counted over 800,000 persons in 1860; Philadelphia, 565,000 persons; and Boston, 165,000. The most sensational growth was experienced by Chicago, which in little more than twenty years grew from 250 to over 100,000 inhabitants. Not participating in the trend toward urbanism was the South. If Baltimore, with its 200,000 people, is excepted as a border town, the region could boast of but one large city, New Orleans, whose 165,000 population was small in comparison with the teeming northern centers. Richmond and Charleston, next greatest in numbers, had only 40,000 each.

An increasing population was but one manifestation of national growth. Also expanding was the economy, the most dramatic and significant inflation occurring in industry. Textile, iron, and other plants dotted the Northeast, and manufacturies were beginning to spread into the Northwest and, although to a lesser extent, into the South. Accompanying the revolution in production was a revolution in transportation and communication. Railroads, superseding other means of conveyance,

laced the eastern half of the country, the greatest concentration of lines being in the Northeast and the Northwest. The effect of the coming of the railroads on American life was like that of the great technological innovations of the twentieth century —a conquest of time and space had occurred. In the 1830s a traveler required three weeks to go from New York to Chicago or St. Louis; by 1860 he could complete the trip in two to three days. The transportation revolution bound the various parts of the country into a greater if uncomfortable unity.

The section least affected by the transforming changes of the time was the South. The region below the Potomac and the Ohio stood apart, or wanted to stand apart, from the mainstream of progress. The South was still distinctive—rural, agricultural, conservative, maintaining an ordered and orderly social structure, and boasting in its plantation lords the closest approach to an American aristocracy. Above all other differences, the South was the only part of the country that contained in large numbers a race of another color than white, a race held in slavery. Southerners of all classes stood determined to uphold slavery and the system of race relations based on it against all outside attacks. Their peculiar culture, they proclaimed, was superior to that of the North. One spokesman, denouncing free society as a "monstrous abortion," described his own society as a "healthy, beautiful and natural being." The refusal of Southerners to consider any modification of their system was a key to the conflicts that rent the nation during the last half of the 1850s.

The presidential election of 1856 took place against this backdrop of continuing violence in Kansas and continuing debate over the status of slavery in the territories. The Democrats nominated James Buchanan of Pennsylvania as their candidate and offered popular sovereignty as a formula to settle the territorial question. Their opposition was a new party, the Republicans, just two years of age. The Republican organization had been formed in the anger that swept the North after the enactment of the Kansas-Nebraska Act and had absorbed most northern members of the former Whig party and some antislavery northern Democrats. The Republicans nominated as their candidate John C. Frémont of California, famous as an explorer of the Far West, and submitted as

*On Saturday, October 13, 1860, J. W. Black of the firm of Black & Batchelder
loaded his camera into a balloon operated by Professor Samuel A. King, and
up they went, several hundred feet above Boston. There below them they
captured the image of one of the principal trading cities of the world.
Washington Street runs diagonally from lower right, Old South Meeting House
at its other end.* (U. S. AIR FORCE)

It is a nation moving west, leaving in train thousands of rural still lifes such as this unidentified scene. (JOE M. BAUMAN)

their platform congressional exclusion of slavery from all national territories. A one-idea party, they were also a sectional party, having their main strength in the North with only a smattering of support in the border slave states.

The Democrats, although troubled by sectional division, were still a national party, and they elected Buchanan and a majority to Congress. However, the young Republican party had made a surprising showing. Frémont carried eleven of the sixteen northern states and rolled up a large popular vote. A slight shift of votes in a few states would have made the sectional party the majority party.

James Buchanan was a dignified "elder statesman," almost sixty-six years of age at the time of

his inauguration, and an amiable and well-meaning public servant. But he lacked resolution of character and flinched from taking strong action in a crisis. Enjoying the company of Southerners, he was inclined to let himself be guided by southern leaders. Cast into office in a period of storm, he could not have controlled all events; he rarely tried to control any of them.

Most of the crises of his administration were concerned with the issues in controversy between the sections and every outcome exacerbated sectional bitterness and moved the nation closer to dissolution. In Kansas the turmoil between the contesting factions continued unabated, with efforts now concentrated on electing a convention to write a state constitution. Buchanan used his influence to aid the proslavery side, which was clearly a minority. His action enraged Republicans and disgusted popular sovereignty members of his own party, and Congress refused to accept the con- stitution presented by the slavery adherents. Kansas remained a territory, and an issue of discord.

At the height of the Kansas dispute the Supreme Court handed down a pronouncement on the ques-

To St. Joseph, Missouri, where immigrant trains jumped off into the Great Plains for the trek to Oregon and California. Albert Bierstadt took this 1859 view of the "Pike's Peak Passenger & Freight Express Co." (KANSAS STATE HISTORICAL SOCIETY, TOPEKA)

tion of whether slavery could enter a territory in *Dred Scott* v. *Sanford*. The case had a complicated background, but in the broadest meaning it involved the exclusion clause in the Missouri Compromise. The majority opinion (seven of the nine justices were Democrats) held that this clause was in violation of the constitutional provision that forbade Congress to take property without "due process of law." The Congress of 1820 had acted illegally in barring slavery, and no Congress could exclude the institution. Translated into the language of current politics, the decision declared the platform of the Republican party to be unconstitutional. By implication it also disallowed popular sovereignty, for if Congress could not prohibit slavery in the territories neither could a territorial legislature that was created by Congress. The voice of the highest tribunal did not calm but rather excited sectional passions. A typical Republican effusion denounced the Court as the "last resort behind which despotism is sheltered," and Republican leaders proclaimed that when their party gained control of the government they would reconstitute the Court and retry the case.

Northern anger at the Dred Scott decision was more than matched by southern rage at an event occurring in 1859. John Brown, a fierce foe of slavery who had migrated to Kansas and participated in the killings there, reappeared in the East full of a plan to strike at slavery in the South itself. With encouragement and monetary support from certain abolitionists, who realized his general purpose, he proposed to seize the Federal arsenal at Harpers Ferry in western Virginia, and from this base to incite an armed slave insurrection. In October he and eighteen followers descended on the town and captured the arsenal. No slaves came in to join him, and he was pinned down in his position by attacking citizens and local militia. News of the raid alarmed official Washington, and President Buchanan, reacting with unusual vigor, dispatched a contingent of marines under Colonel Robert E. Lee of the Regular Army to Harpers Ferry to deal with the crisis. Brown resisted the onslaught of Lee's force, but with ten of his men killed he finally had to surrender. The national government handed him over to Virginia to be tried for treason against the state.

Brown's raid aroused fury in the South, and also horror. The whites lived in constant fear of a slave uprising, and now it seemed that outside agitators, abolitionists or Republicans, had attempted to incite an insurrection. Southern suspicions were heightened by the praise heaped upon Brown by abolitionist leaders who hailed him as a saint, an "angel of light" in the words of New England writer Henry David Thoreau. Thoreau and others hoped that Brown would not escape hanging and would become a martyr to the cause of freedom. They need not have feared. Brown was duly tried and executed. In his last message to the world he wrote that he was certain the crimes of "this, guilty land" would never be purged away "but with Blood." The stage was set for the fateful presidential election of 1860.

All the boiling tensions in the country came to a head in 1860. The election in that year marked the apogee of sectionalism. Parties represented largely sectional interests, and the result prompted the South to withdraw from the Union. It is the only contest in American history in which the losing side felt that it could not live with the consequence of defeat.

The Democrats were the first to meet in convention. Gathering in historic Charleston in April, they plunged into angry debate on the issue of slavery in the territories. Southern delegates demanded that the platform affirm the right of slaveholders to take their chattels into any part of the national domain, and northern delegates held out for a popular sovereignty plank. When the latter triumphed, a number of southern delegations walked out of the hall. The managers thereupon adjourned the convention to meet again in Baltimore in June, hoping that time would cool the passions of the opposing factions. However, at Baltimore anger was even more intense, and another southern exodus occurred. The remaining delegates nominated Stephen A. Douglas to run on a popular sovereignty platform. The bolters nominated John C. Breckinridge of Kentucky to stand for the rights of slavery in the territories. There were now two Democratic parties in the field, and although each had adherents in the other section, one was a northern party and one was a southern party. The only national political organization in the country had at last split on the rock of sectionalism.

The Republicans met in bustling Chicago in May in a huge building, the Wigwam, built by the Republicans of the city to house the convention.

*To Illinois expansion spread, to Galena, and a leather store run by Grant &
Perkins. Ulysses S. Grant.* (CHICAGO HISTORICAL SOCIETY)

Elated at the promise of victory held out by Democratic division, the party managers were determined to present a platform and a candidate that would appeal to the broadest spectrum of northern opinion. They were especially concerned that the party should not appear to be a collection of wild-eyed crusaders who had no other objective but to attack slavery. Now the Republicans were to stand before the voters as men of moderation whose vision embraced many issues. The platform embodied the new strategy. Although reaffirming their opposition to slavery's expansion into the territories, the Republicans declared that they had no intention of interfering with the institution in the states where it already existed. Other planks emphasized economic issues. The party endorsed a high protective tariff, internal improvements (national financial support to transportation projects), and a homestead bill (free land to settlers in the West). In a shrewd bid for victory the Republicans had combined the idealism of the antislavery impulse and the aspirations of the principal economic groups in the North.

The party showed the same sense of practicality in choosing a candidate. Passing over the best-known leaders who had records that might alienate some voters, the convention nominated Abraham Lincoln of Illinois. Lincoln was, in the language of politics, an "available" candidate. He had a national reputation, but he had not been on the national scene long enough to accumulate a list of enemies. He had spoken out against the Kansas-Nebraska Act, but he was not thought to be a "radical" antislavery man. His views on slavery squared with those of the mass of Republicans. He believed that the institution was wrong and that it should persistently be labeled as wrong. He would not interfere with the institution where it existed, but he would uncompromisingly oppose its expansion with the purpose of bringing about its demise. The opponents of slavery, he said, must "place it where the public mind shall rest in the belief that it is in the course of ultimate extinction."

The appearance of three major parties indicated an unusual splintering of popular opinion. And this was not the end of it. Still a fourth party entered the lists, the new and hastily formed Constitutional Union party. Composed of former Whigs, it nominated John Bell of Tennessee as its candidate and presented as a platform only support of the Constitution and the Union. The apparent softness in its position was a deliberate strategy. The leaders thought that with so many candidates dividing the vote no one of them would gain a majority of the electoral vote and that the election would be thrown into the House of Representatives. There their conservative nominee might emerge as the victor.

The result of the election in November reflected the division of parties and populace. Although Lincoln had a minority of the popular vote, about 40 per cent of the total, he rolled up a clear electoral majority, 180 votes. His margin was the conse-

quence of success in the northern states with large electoral votes; he carried every free state except New Jersey, which he divided with Douglas. (The Republican sweep did not, however, bring in a majority in Congress.) Breckinridge carried the Lower South and three border slave states and stood second in the electoral vote. Bell took three border states and came in third. Douglas won only one state, Missouri, and divided New Jersey with Lincoln. However, his popular vote was second to Lincoln's, about 30 per cent of the total. If it is assumed that his popular sovereignty followers were voting against the expansion of slavery, 70 per cent of the voters had registered a verdict to pen up slavery where it was.

During the campaign, extremist leaders in the Lower South had tried to impress upon their people that if the Republicans won the contest, the interests of the South would not be safe in the Union. The "Black Republicans" would sooner or later be driven to attack slavery, that is, to interfere with the prevailing racial patterns, and to prevent this dire eventuality southern states should secede from the Union. One of the loudest sounders of the cry to get out was Robert Toombs of Georgia, and he became even more strident after the election. Addressing the Georgia legislature in November, he urged secession before the Republicans, "your enemies," took office on March 4, 1861. "Then strike," he thundered, "strike while it is yet time." Leaders in other states reechoed his demand.

The threats of secession were heard in the North with mixed feelings. Many persons refused to believe that the danger was serious, thinking that the South was only bluffing to wring concessions from the national government. Other men were acutely alarmed, realizing that the Union was threatened with dissolution. One who was especially concerned was lame-duck President Buchanan.

In his message to Congress in early December, Buchanan took note of the gathering sentiment behind secession in the Lower South. He denied that a state could constitutionally leave the Union, but he also denied that the federal government could force a state that had left to return, or, as he put it, could "make war against a state." To avert secession, he urged Congress to frame an amendment to the Constitution that would guarantee the existence of slavery, ensure the right of slaveholders to enter the territories, and guarantee the privilege

*West to Nebraska spread the tentacles of a voracious America, taking root in
the rich farmlands that produced abundant grain for sale in the East.
Steamboats like the* Colorado *here at Omaha brought the produce to the
railhead for the Hannibal & St. Joe and other new railroads to move speedily
to market.* (NEBRASKA STATE HISTORICAL SOCIETY, LINCOLN)

of owners to recover fugitive slaves. In pleading for
compromise Buchanan thought that he was acting
the part of a patriot. He did not seem to realize
that his idea of compromise was weighted heavily
in favor of the South.

Both houses of Congress took Buchanan's advice,
appointing separate committees to frame an
amendment. The House committee was never able
to come up with a complete plan; it agreed on an
amendment guaranteeing the existence of slavery,
but arrived at no accord on the question of slavery
in the territories. The Senate committee gave earnest consideration to a proposal submitted by Senator John J. Crittenden of Kentucky and known
therefore as the Crittenden Compromise. This
measure also ensured the existence of slavery and
contained a provision to satisfy southern demands
as to fugitive slaves. Most important, Crittenden
attempted to deal with the troublesome territorial
problem. His solution was to establish the demar-
cation line of the Missouri Compromise, the thirty-
sixth parallel, in all of the territory of the United

To Minnesota's Castle Rock it spread.
(MINNESOTA HISTORICAL SOCIETY)

To the mining camps and burgeoning cities of the mountains like Central City, Colorado. (DENVER PUBLIC LIBRARY, WESTERN HISTORY DEPARTMENT)

States then held or thereafter acquired—slavery would be prohibited north of the line and permitted south of it. Southern members of the committee indicated that they would accept this division if the Republicans as a party would support it. Before returning an answer, Republican leaders sought the reaction of President-elect Lincoln, waiting in Springfield to come to Washington. Lincoln returned a negative answer. There could be "no compromise" on the question of extending slavery, he said. "The tug has to come & better now than later," he wrote in one letter. The Senate committee had to abandon its labors.

The attempts at compromise failed for various reasons. Many men on both sides felt that they could not yield their beliefs, either out of devotion to principle or to party. Some men on both sides would have been willing to give way if they had thought war would follow, but they convinced themselves that they could have their desires without war. And there were some in each section who did not care if war came, who, in fact, welcomed it, if for no other reason than to relieve tensions that were becoming unbearable.

While the efforts to compromise were dragging to a sad conclusion in Washington, in the deep South states the adventure in secession got off in a mood of gaiety and exultation. South Carolina, long the leader of southern separatism, acted first. A convention elected to consider the course the state should take proved unanimously secessionist. Meeting in Charleston, the convention voted on December 20 to take the state out of the Union. The news of its action was greeted in the city with wild rejoicing. An English newspaper correspondent visiting in Charleston a short time later caught the spirit of the citizens. "Secession is the fashion here," he wrote. "Young ladies sing for it; old ladies pray for it; young men are dying to fight for it; old men are ready to demonstrate it."

Six other states soon followed the example of South Carolina. They were, in the order of their leaving, Mississippi, Florida, Alabama, Georgia, Louisiana, and Texas. Not all of them went out rejoicing as South Carolina had done. In some conventions there were men who opposed secession, not the right but the need to secede; they counseled delay and cooperative sectional action rather than individual state action. And there were other men who accepted secession reluctantly, and with heavy hearts voted to sever relations with the Union. But the seceders were in control in every convention and carried their will. The process was completed by February 1.

To the once barren wastes of Utah, where Salt Lake City sprang from the desert and Brigham Young's dream. (UTAH STATE HISTORICAL SOCIETY)

The secession leaders realized that their states could not exist separately. Their intention from the first had been to create a new and a southern Union. Accordingly, representatives of the seven states met in February at the little city of Montgomery, Alabama (population, 8,800), to write a provisional constitution and form a provisional government. They called their nation the Confederate States of America and chose as its president Jefferson Davis of Mississippi. Davis came to Montgomery to be inaugurated on February 18. In his address he affirmed unrelenting devotion to the cause of southern independence.

Less than a month later Abraham Lincoln was inaugurated President of what had been the United States in a Washington tense with rumors of impending civil conflict. Although in his address he pled with the seceded states to return, he made it clear that he would not offer any concessions to induce them to come back. He denied that any state could lawfully leave the Union, repudiating secession as the "essense of anarchy." The portion of his remarks that most angered Southerners was the announcement that he would "hold, occupy, and possess" Federal properties within the confines of the Confederacy. He did not have to identify the places that he was referring to, offshore forts that the seceding states and the Confederate government had not been able to seize. Two of these forts

particularly occupied public attention, Sumter in Charleston harbor and Pickens near the coast at Pensacola, Florida. The Davis government was mounting military preparations to assault them if this was necessary to secure them, and Lincoln was letting Davis know that they would be defended.

Lincoln's policy, although stated subtly, was nevertheless plain—he hoped that the Union could be restored peaceably but if this was not possible, he was willing to employ force, to resort to war. Davis's policy was also clear—the seceded states would not voluntarily return to the Union and the Confederacy would maintain its independence by force if it had to. The policies of both men and both governments accorded with the feelings of the northern and the southern people. Most Northerners valued the Union and would fight to keep it inviolate. Most Southerners valued the political and social system represented by the Confederacy and would fight to defend that. A martial spirit was rising in both sections. It could be seen in the bellicose declarations of leaders, in the cry for action from ordinary people, and, in a picturesque but dangerous manifestation, in the many volunteer and militia groups of young men that were springing into being throughout the once united land and that were loudly eager to demonstrate their manhood.

Only an incident was needed to touch off war.

Northwest to Oregon went America, to Table Rock City, on stirring stories of the Oregon Trail. (SOUTHERN OREGON HISTORICAL SOCIETY)

And with "California or Bust," they completed the conquest of a continent, drawn by land, adventure, and gold. This early daguerreotype by Shaw & Johnson shows a gold claim in the early 1850s. (CALIFORNIA HISTORICAL SOCIETY LIBRARY)

It was a nation thriving on commerce, whose fast clipper ships traded with the world and turned the docks at the end of New York's Wall Street into a forest of masts. (NEW-YORK HISTORICAL SOCIETY)

*Trade between the states flourished, borne on iron rails and man-made
waterways like the Chesapeake & Ohio Canal.* (NATIONAL ARCHIVES,
WASHINGTON, D.C.)

*The barons of industrial expansion
discovered the riches beneath the earth,
and profits came to be measured in barrels.
Oil Creek Valley, near Rouseville,
Pennsylvania—already the scars of
industry blotted the landscape.* (DRAKE
WELL MUSEUM, TITUSVILLE, PA.)

And the factory came to America, the sweatshop, the women and child labor, the endless days at machines producing textiles. There was great prosperity, but it cost great toil. (USAMHI)

Yet there were two Americas. While the northern states and their people pushed and built and traded and manufactured, another America took a slower pace. The South, too, had its major trading cities like Charleston, South Carolina, and to be sure, its skyline evidences a few factory smokestacks. (NYHS)

*But Southerners preferred to think of themselves in
a different way, as the last outpost of a more
graceful, pastoral mode of life that existed more
in myth than in actual memory. They thought
of the beauty of Wade Hampton's garden at his
plantation in Columbia, South Carolina.* (USAMHI)

*. . . of their river cities like Vicksburg on the mighty Mississippi. H. J. Herrick
took this view from the Louisiana side of the river, Vicksburg's courthouse
towering over all.* (OLD COURT HOUSE MUSEUM, VICKSBURG, MISS.)

Their pride lay not in capitalism, but in cotton, piled in bales on Charleston's wharves awaiting shipment to northern and European textile mills. (WRHS)

They grudgingly gave credit to Yankee Eli Whitney's invention of the cotton gin for making possible the large-scale production and harvest of the fiber. Gin houses like this one on Edisto Island in South Carolina hummed with activity throughout the 1850s. (WRHS)

Whitney made only part of the work easy. The rest, the picking, must be done by hand, by slaves, the captive labor force of the South, the legacy of a problem the Founding Fathers chose not to solve. Timothy O'Sullivan photographed this slave family on a South Carolina cotton plantation in 1862. (LIBRARY OF CONGRESS, WASHINGTON, D.C.)

Slaves became not only a work force, but a measure of wealth as well. These blacks of all ages and sex are gathered in Baton Rouge, Louisiana. (OCHM)

They planted the fields on Pope's Plantation at Hilton Head, South Carolina. (USAMHI)

Slaves were bought and sold, and between transactions were often kept in pens like this one at Alexandria, Virginia, almost within sight of the Capitol in Washington City. (USAMHI)

They picked the cotton under the eye of their white overseers, as in this postwar image. (NA, WOMEN'S BUREAU)

And they brought their day's pickings in every evening to put it through Mr. Whitney's machine. George N. Barnard's postwar photograph was taken near Charleston, South Carolina. (NYHS)

Despite differences in their economies and ways of life, North and South still managed to accommodate each other peaceably enough in the first half of the century. Both rejoiced in the young nation's expanding horizons, and celebrated their common heroes on days like the July 4, 1859, celebration at New York Harbor. (USAMHI)

Over the nation loomed the haunting specter of sectionalism, of slavery, of southern pretensions for a nationhood of its own. South Carolina's John C. Calhoun, ardent champion of states' rights and secession, might lie dead in his tomb in Charleston, but what he stood for still lived. (USAMHI)

Sectional schism was seemingly averted in 1856 when the contest for the presidency first saw a young Republican party, northern for the most part and antislavery in character, defeated at the polls. Democrats in the South paraded horse-drawn "ships of state" in their streets. They elected their candidate, routed Republicanism, and, so they thought, ensured peace. (JMB)

Of all the men ever to hold presidential office, the people chose the one least suited. James Buchanan lacked almost everything necessary in a President, most of all a firm will and resolution. The collapse of the Union began almost at once. (NA)

Kansas came to be "Bloody Kansas" as it sought statehood. Antislave men flocked to the territory while proslave interests, fearing that the slave states would soon become a minority in Congress, did likewise. Each hoped to provide a majority to bring Kansas into statehood. The conflict between them led to open warfare on the plains, fought by units like this Free-State Battery at Topeka in 1856. (KANSAS STATE HISTORICAL SOCIETY, TOPEKA)

Violent men like James Lane led bands of marauders who proved little better than ruffians in the quest to wrest control of Kansas from their opposition. (USAMHI)

The conflict reached the floor of the United States Senate when Charles Sumner of Massachusetts, decrying the "Crime Against Kansas" in a violent antislave speech, was attacked and caned senseless by Preston Brooks of South Carolina. For three years Sumner's chair remained empty, itself a powerful symbol for the abolitionist forces. (USAMHI)

Many in the North refused to abide by the Fugitive Slave Law, part of the Compromise of 1850. When this slave, "Old Peter," nearly one hundred years old, escaped to the home of Slater Brown in Lancaster, Pennsylvania, the Quaker refused to return him to his former master. (JMB)

The celebrated trial of Dred Scott focused even more attention on the growing rift between North and South over slavery. Despite able representation by the influential Montgomery Blair of Missouri, Scott lost his case, and his freedom. (USAMHI)

In 1858 the battle continued in Illinois, where Stephen A. Douglas and
Abraham Lincoln vied for a Senate seat. Douglas won the election, but Lincoln
won nationwide prominence thanks to their celebrated series of debates.
Photograph by Calvin Jackson of Pittsfield, October 1, 1858. (USAMHI)

Then violence erupted at Harpers Ferry, Virginia, and the North and South were so polarized that there seemed no cementing them back together. John Brown of Ossawatomie, a free-state fighter from Kansas, led a band of men across this bridge on the Potomac, turned right, and . . . (USAMHI)

. . . *swarmed down this street to the United States Arsenal. Here they hoped to capture arms to lead a slave uprising in the South that would end slavery forever. Instead, the townspeople quickly organized against them, and Brown and his men found themselves cornered across the street* . . . (CHESAPEAKE & OHIO RAILROAD CO.)

. . . *in an engine house.* (CHESAPEAKE & OHIO RAILROAD CO.)

Here the old man, who had grown a beard since this 1856 photograph was made, fought desperately, even while his sons were being killed beside him. (KANSAS STATE HISTORICAL SOCIETY, TOPEKA)

(WILLIAM A. ALBAUGH)

In Richmond, Virginia's governor issued the call for troops to suppress this outrage, and many stepped forward. The 1st Virginia Militia, the "Richmond Grays," answered the call. They did not take part in the final capture of Brown, but they did arrive in Charles Town, Virginia, in time to form a hollow square around a gallows where old John Brown was hanged after his trial. One of their number present was John Wilkes Booth, an actor, who rather pitied Brown, "a brave old man," he said. These four views, two of them not previously published, show the Richmond Grays at the time of Brown's trial and hanging.

(VALENTINE MUSEUM, RICHMOND, VA.)

(VM)

(VM)

The man who led the capture of Brown, Colonel Robert E. Lee—a photo taken in 1851. (CHS)

Never was there greater pressure on the leaders in Washington to compromise, to lead. Yet, just as they could not agree to finish the monument to the nation's first President, so could they not agree on a course to save the country from disunion. (NA)

Leadership from the Executive Mansion, the "White House," was nonexistent. Here Montgomery C. Meigs, the engineer supervising the expansion of the Capitol building, used his stereo camera to provide a deceptively peaceful image. (LC)

*Buchanan and his Cabinet proved hopelessly ineffectual. The two members
seated at left, Jacob Thompson and John B. Floyd, were suspected of financial
malfeasance. Both would become secessionists. Secretary of State Lewis Cass,
behind them, had long since ceased to be a potent force in public affairs.
Howell Cobb of Georgia, standing just right of Buchanan, would support
secession as well. Only Joseph Holt, standing at far right, and Jeremiah Black,
seated far right, were men of real force and strong Union sentiment. Isaac
Toucey, seated to the left of Black, remained an unknown quantity. A divided
administration could hardly unite a country. (LC)*

The situation was worse at the opposite end of Pennsylvania Avenue. The Congress, like the building in which it met, seemed to be in pieces. Montgomery Meigs's photograph shows the old Capitol dome, which he would soon replace, and the partially completed new Senate wing. (LC)

The Capitol from Pennsylvania Avenue in 1860. There is still much work to be done—on the building and the Union. (LC)

Meigs's camera captures Secretary of State Cass standing at a table, and his own image in the mirror in the background. (LC)

Here compromise failed. The old House of Representatives chamber about 1861. (LC)

*There the once powerful voice of Henry Clay had managed compromise from
discord. But Clay's voice was stilled, and none stepped forward to take his
place.* (NYHS)

*Instead the hotbloods took the floor, the
"fire-eaters" like Senator William L. Yancey of
Alabama. Dazzled by the idea of a southern
nation, and perhaps their own political ambitions
within it, they spurned compromise.* (NYHS)

Buchanan's Secretary of the Treasury Howell Cobb gave the secessionists tacit support. (LC)

Virginia's governor Henry A. Wise, from his experience with John Brown's raid in his own state, felt more keenly than most the fear of slave uprising and northern aggressions against slavery. (JACK MCGUIRE)

Alexander H. Stephens, congressman from Georgia, one-time friend of Lincoln, spoke for those who interpreted the Constitution so strictly that secession seemed justified, if not actually legal. (CHS)

Not all Southerners were fire-eaters, though. The old hero of the Texas
Revolution, Sam Houston, spoke out against secession and for the Union, even
at personal risk. (NA)

The fiery W. G. "Parson" Brownlow of Tennessee
made strident exclamations for the Union, and
published his newspaper called the Rebel
Ventilator. (USAMHI)

In the midst of the sectional agitation, and largely stimulated by it, a martial spirit grew rapidly North and South. Cadets at the United States Military Academy at West Point, New York, found themselves divided, often in heated argument. From their practice batteries overlooking the Hudson . . . (LC)

. . . to their field exercises at Camp Walker, they argued and took their sides.
(LOUISIANA STATE UNIVERSITY, DEPARTMENT OF ARCHIVES AND MANUSCRIPTS, BATON ROUGE)

A bitter reminder to the southern cadets were the cannon captured during the war with Mexico a decade before. Southern soldiers contributed considerably to that war, and they had hoped to bring much of the conquered territory into the Union as slave states.

Now young men, like these members of the class of 1864, pondered just what their budding military careers held for them, and who their first battles would bring against them. Standing at left is Ranald MacKenzie, soon to be a general, and in years to come a noted Indian fighter in the West. (USAMHI)

The old Regular Army was undermanned, ill equipped, and officered largely by men with no real combat experience, and those that did know battle were acquainted with a kind of war that would never be fought again. Colonel Joseph Plympton and his black orderly. (PEARL KORN)

*Even less experienced were the volunteer and militia units springing up
everywhere. What they lacked in field knowledge, they made up for in natty
attire and precision at drill. Here officers of the 6th New York State Militia
and, standing second from the left, E. Elmer Ellsworth, in July 1860. A
favorite of Abraham Lincoln, Ellsworth led one of the North's finest drilled
units, his "Fire Zouaves."* (CHS)

Cincinnati, Ohio's "Guthrie Grays," ready for the foe, whoever it might be.
(CINCINNATI HISTORICAL SOCIETY)

And in the South men like Hamilton McDevit Branch of the Oglethorpe Light Infantry paraded in their military finery. (HERB PECK, JR.)

The Mobile Cadets from Alabama refined their marksmanship. (HP)

*And in Louisville, Kentucky, in August 1860, the State Guard held a much
publicized encampment. The holiday atmosphere of it all, with a refreshment
stand and ice cream, barely concealed the rattling sabers.* (KENTUCKY HISTORICAL
SOCIETY, KENTUCKY MILITARY HISTORY MUSEUM, FRANKFORT, KY.)

By 1860, the last remaining hope of
maintaining the Union was the
Democratic party. Friendly to southern
interests, it could keep the South in the
nation if it stayed united and defeated
the Republicans in November. Instead,
the party fragmented. The chiefly
northern wing nominated Stephen A.
Douglas, the "Little Giant" of Illinois.
Immensely popular, he still came in last
in the electoral ballot. (USAMHI)

The more conservative Northerners and
the southern rights men nominated
Buchanan's Vice-President, John C.
Breckinridge of Kentucky. The only
candidate with nationwide appeal, his
popular vote was evenly divided between
North and South, but he placed second
in the Electoral College. (LC)

The Republicans, in the face of a Democratic split, were ensured of success. New York's William H. Seward, standing at left, had hoped for the nomination, but he lost it to Douglas's old foe from Illinois . . . (NYHS)

. . . Abraham Lincoln. In June 1860 photographer Alexander Hesler of Chicago captured Lincoln just after his nomination. Friends regarded it as the best portrait of Lincoln ever made. In November he became the sixteenth President of the United States. (KEAN ARCHIVES, PHILADELPHIA)

Elected with him, as Vice-President, was Hannibal Hamlin of Maine. (USAMHI)

Shortly after his nomination for the Presidency, a still beardless Lincoln unbends his lanky frame for a full-length portrait in his home town of Springfield, Illinois. (LC)

Their election brought jubilation in much of the North, as in Mohawk, New York, where the "Mohawk Wide Awakes" and their band paraded in honor of the victory. (LLOYD OSTENDORF COLLECTION)

*But there was no rejoicing in Charleston, South Carolina. Despite Lincoln's
earnest promises not to interfere with slavery where it already existed,
Southerners saw in his election a dagger poised at their labor system, their way
of life, and their honor.* (NYHS)

*Animated by years of heated rhetoric, exaggerated
fears and hatreds, irresponsible politicians, and an
impulse for southern nationalism, South Carolina
called a convention here in Secession Hall. The
outcome was never in doubt. In December 1860
they adopted here an ordinance of secession. The
broadsides on the streets the next day read "The
Union Is Dissolved."* (USAMHI)

Six other states did the same in the weeks to follow, and on February 18, 1861, in Montgomery, Alabama, new capital of the Confederate States of America, they inaugurated their first President, Jefferson Davis of Mississippi. A. C. McIntyre of Montgomery sensed something historic taking place, and set his camera to capture the scene. The Alabama statehouse clock says 1 P.M. Davis and Howell Cobb stand at the doorway between the center columns. The Confederacy is begun. (NA)

Jefferson Davis, photographed in 1859 by Montgomery Meigs. An unpublished portrait which shows him with a hint of a smile. After 1860 he would rarely smile again. (LC)

*In the North, four days after Davis's inauguration, President-elect Lincoln
arrived in Philadelphia. Here, on Washington's birthday, he symbolically raised
the flag at Independence Hall. The Union, he promised, would be preserved.
Frederick D. Richards caught the scene with his camera while the dignitaries
stood at prayer. Lincoln is visible directly above the star on the left of the flag,
while men view the scene from trees.* (LO)

*And on March 4, 1861, a crowd gathered before the stands on the Capitol steps
in Washington. Meigs set his camera to record the scene.* (LC)

*Then Lincoln took the oath of office and told the nation that the Union must
be preserved. "We are not enemies, but friends," he told the South. "We must
not be enemies." "In your hands, my dissatisfied fellow-countrymen, and not in
mine, is the momentous issue of civil war." Meigs certainly could not have
heard the President, but his camera caught the moment forever.* (LC)

*The word spread across the nation, to a host of men then little known and not
likely to be remembered. In Cairo, Illinois, to a man standing just left of the
post office pillar, Ulysses S. Grant . . .* (CHS)

. . . to three friends from West Point days, Philip H. Sheridan in the center, and George Crook at left. (U. S. MILITARY ACADEMY ARCHIVES)

. . . to a captain in the United States Topographical Engineers, George G. Meade. (USAMHI)

. . . to an adjutant general in the Army, Lieutenant Colonel Don Carlos Buell. (USAMHI)

. . . to a firebrand Unionist in Missouri, Nathaniel
Lyon. (USAMHI)

. . . to a professor at the Virginia Military
Institute, seen here in Mexican War uniform,
Thomas Jonathan Jackson. (USAMHI)

. . . to a young southern officer, Ambrose Powell
Hill. (MUSEUM OF THE CONFEDERACY)

. . . to a dashing Virginian who had helped Lee
corner John Brown, James Ewell Brown Stuart.
(CONFEDERATE MUSEUM, NEW ORLEANS)

. . . to a sour, humorless, Mexican War veteran,
Braxton Bragg. (SOUTHERN HISTORICAL
COLLECTION, UNIVERSITY OF NORTH CAROLINA,
CHAPEL HILL)

. . . to men like Captain A. W. Reynolds.
(USAMHI)

And to Charleston went the word. It was in their hands, said Lincoln. (LC)

In the hands of Brigadier General Pierre G. T. Beauregard, commanding the Confederates gathered in Charleston. (OCHM)

And in their hands were guns trained on an island of masonry in the middle of Charleston Harbor, Fort Sumter. (LOUISIANA HISTORICAL ASSOCIATION, SPECIAL COLLECTIONS DIVISION, TULANE UNIVERSITY)

The Guns at Fort Sumter

W. A. SWANBERG

A Charleston April shatters America's innocence

"I HAVE THE HONOR TO REPORT," Major Robert Anderson wrote on December 26, 1860, after his night-shrouded move across a mile of water to Fort Sumter, "that I have just completed, by the blessing of God, the removal to this fort of all my garrison." The anger which this clandestine shift of a mere seventy-odd men caused in the South, and the joy it aroused in the North, bespoke the sectional strife of which the major and the Charleston forts had become a symbol.

President Buchanan saw in it none of God's work. "Are calamities never to come singly!" he lamented. Yearning to finish his nine remaining weeks in office and to leave the secession crisis in the lap of the man who had caused it, Lincoln, he had said that there would be no "hostile act" in the harbor. Three South Carolina commissioners, just arrived in Washington to parley about the forts, said Anderson's move *was* a hostile act. Mississippi Senator Jefferson Davis, soon to be Confederate President, told the President, ". . . you are surrounded with blood and dishonor on all sides." Exultant headlines in the North and outraged ones in the South told the real significance of the major's action. Secretary of War John B. Floyd telegraphed Anderson in anger:

Intelligence has reached here this morning that you have abandoned Fort Moultrie, spiked your guns, burned the carriages, and gone to Fort Sumter. . . . Explain the meaning of this report.

But Floyd was a Virginian who had been implicated first in a financial scandal and then in an effort to ship cannon from Pittsburgh to southern points, where they would be useful to the new Confederacy if it came to war. Buchanan had asked him to resign. Floyd had not yet got around to it. His continued presence in the Cabinet was one of the errors of a lame-duck President whose power to govern had virtually become paralyzed. Floyd had sent Anderson to Charleston in the first place because of the major's background as a Kentuckian who had married a Georgia girl, had until recently owned a few slaves, and expressed a sympathy for the South equaled only by his reverence for the Union. At Moultrie he had been deserted by the secretary—left in an untenable fort without reinforcements, his requests for instructions usually ignored. Moultrie, in the midst of extensive repairs, had gaps in its walls entered by neighborhood dogs, children, or secessionist leaders who watched, took notes and photographs, and called the Union presence there "coercion." From secessionist homes overlooking the fort it would be possible for snipers to pick off cannoneers. A well-armed force could overpower the garrison. Anderson's father, Major Richard Clough Anderson, had defended Moultrie against the British in 1779 and been captured— one particular footstep the son preferred not to follow in. He was aroused by Charlestonian threats and insistence that the forts be handed over, noting, "They are making every preparation (drilling nightly, &c) for the fight which they say must take place and insist on our not doing anything."

Indeed, few outsiders could gauge the Carolinian intensity. Francis W. Pickens had learned this when he returned from a recent tour as minister to Russia, talked with his good Democratic friend Buchanan in the White House, agreed that the Palmetto people were being hasty, and said he would quiet them when he got home. But Pickens, immediately running for governor of the state, found his moderating speeches so disdained that he quickly became a hotspur and was elected. Now, with Anderson in Sumter, the governor seized Moultrie, the United States arsenal (with 22,000 muskets), the customs house, and post office.

That was an error, for the chances were good that if Pickens had only protested, Buchanan would have ordered Anderson back to Moultrie. Now, if the President did such a thing, he would be hanged in effigy in a hundred northern cities and probably impeached. And now he was confronted by Secretary Floyd, whom he considered already fired, coming to him and resigning because of the President's "dishonorable" acceptance of the move to Sumter—a wily exit indeed. And when the South Carolina commissioners left after calling Buchanan lying and deceitful, he seemed more affected by this insult to his person than by the various discourtesies to the Union. Anderson, he said heavily, would have to be reinforced.

At Sumter, Chaplain Mathias Harris led a prayer of thanksgiving. Major Anderson raised Old Glory with slow dignity. The band played "Hail, Columbia" as the battery presented arms, then the men broke into spontaneous cheers, both in enthusiasm for their leader and in relief at escaping Moultrie. Yet, while it was true that Sumter was entirely surrounded by water, four times as big as Moultrie, and planned for three tiers of 146 guns served by 650 men, it was anything but impregnable in its present condition. Work on the fort had been im-

peded by the current quarrels. The barracks were unfinished, only fifteen guns had been mounted, many embrasures were wide open, the parade was choked with building materials as well as 5,600 shot and shell and sixty-six unmounted guns. The place could have been taken by a few hundred men with scaling ladders. Luckily, this was not known in town. "Twenty-five well-drilled men could hold it against all Charleston," said the Charleston *Courier* in dismay.

The garrison began mounting more guns. Abolitionist officers such as Captain Abner Doubleday and Captain John G. Foster, who had suspected Anderson of excessive southern sympathies, praised the skillful move to Sumter, and morale was high until the *Star of the West* arrived from New York on January 9 with two hundred men and supplies for the garrison. It was typical of the confusion and irresolution in government that the men were sent in a rented, unarmed merchantman rather than a Navy warship, and that Major Anderson had not been informed of its dispatch whereas the Charlestonians had. Buchanan's secessionist Secretary of the Interior, Jacob Thompson of Mississippi, had telegraphed the news to Governor Pickens and then resigned his post. Anderson was utterly perplexed when the vessel hove into view and was fired on by one of the Carolina batteries— arguably the first shot of the War Between the States, fired by a young cadet named George E. Haynsworth. Other batteries let fly, with aim mostly poor. Anderson, whose orders had been to act "strictly on the defensive," had his gunners ready but so longed for an amicable settlement between the states that he was loath to give the order to fire. As he pondered, the *Star* took two minor hits and fled. Doubleday and others were incensed at this failure to defend the flag, whereas soldiers with southern sympathies, such as Lieutenant R. K. Meade, thought Anderson's restraint wise. As for the fire-eating Robert Barnwell Rhett's Charleston *Mercury*, it hailed the striking of the first blow, saying, "It has wiped out a half century of scorn and outrage."

Governor Pickens was in the odd position of heading a self-styled South Carolina republic that still used United States stamps. Its congressmen were using their franking privileges to propagandize for the new Confederacy, and Pickens himself was asking for a $3,000 balance due him as min-

The ghostly face of Fort Sumter in Charleston Harbor, almost lost in this scratched and faded ambrotype. It is the only known photo of the fortress before its bombardment. (VM)

ister to Russia, although he had forbidden the U. S. Subtreasury in Charleston to cash any more drafts from Washington. That cost him dearly when Washington, with intentional irony, sent him a $3,000 draft on the Subtreasury whose payments he had stopped. Pickens sent out his secretaries of state and war, Judge A. G. Magrath and General D. F. Jamison, under a flag of truce to urge Anderson to look to his own safety and evacuate Sumter peacefully since, they said, the United States government itself was crumbling. The major declined, urged diplomacy with Washington, and kept his men at the task of mounting more guns. Meanwhile, Colonel Samuel Colt of Hartford was shipping thousands of firearms south and building himself a mansion, and a Connecticut munitions firm sold 300,000 pounds of powder to Governor Pickens. Treason? Not at all. Did not the President himself declare that the seceded states were still part of the Union?

"The people of the South are mad," old Lewis Cass said; "the people of the North are asleep. The President is pale with fear. . . . God only knows what is to be the fate of my country!"

With South Carolina spending $20,000 daily for defense, and shipping now avoiding its greatest harbor, bankruptcy became a threat. Yet other southern leaders urged Pickens to go slowly, arguing that northern Democrats would sustain Buchanan whereas if a confrontation could be delayed until Lincoln took office, the Democrats would oppose him and the North would be divided. A new voice in Washington was that of William Henry Seward, Secretary of State–designate for Lincoln, who let it be known that he had plans (as yet unspecified) to resolve the whole quarrel and save the Union too. Other voices rumored that secessionists plotted to seize the capital on February 13, when the electoral votes would be officially counted and Lincoln formally declared the winner. They inspired the aged, Virginia-born General Winfield Scott, head of the Army, to colorful utterance:

> I have said that any [such person] should be lashed to the muzzle of a 12-pounder and fired out of a window of the Capitol. I would manure the hills of Arlington with fragments of his body. . . . It is my duty to suppress insurrection—*my duty!*

The day passed without incident. Buchanan's severity had given way once more to caution. He had swallowed the *Star of the West* affront. He wavered about reinforcing Anderson at all. He hoped that the new Confederate government would be less demanding than Pickens, that the crisis could be put off for his remaining days in the White House. On the complaint of Southerners that it was "warlike," he was ready to cancel a Washington's Birthday parade of six hundred soldiers until the spirited New York Congressman Daniel Sickles exploded that Washington was a Virginian, a national hero. The President was, critics said, ready to "give up part or even the whole of the Constitution to save the remainder."

Lincoln arrived quietly next day, having taken an earlier train to foil a rumored plot to assassinate him. The delegates from the seceded states had already met in Montgomery, elected Jefferson Davis president, and taken pains to remove the question of the forts from the excitable Pickens, who was now only a governor again. The men at Sumter froze in a heatless fort and ran low on tobacco while the aristocratic Carolinians enjoyed madeira, champagne, Spanish cigars and spoiled for a fight. Major Pierre Beauregard, U.S.A., recently deprived of his post as commander at West Point because of his southern allegiance, arrived in Charleston to take charge as Brigadier General Beauregard, C.S.A. He had been Anderson's pupil when the latter taught gunnery at West Point. He respected his one-time teacher but soon realized that he could overpower or starve out the meager Sumter garrison if he could prevent its reinforcement. Anderson, the man of honor, was wrestling also with the problem of what he should do in case his own state of Kentucky seceded, in which event it seemed to him that no matter what course he took there would be dishonor involved. A popular ditty in the North ran:

Brigadier General Pierre G. T. Beauregard, commanding Confederate forces in and around Charleston. He appears in his uniform as colonel of engineers in the Provisional Army of Louisiana, shortly after the time he served briefly as superintendent of the Military Academy at West Point. Filled with grand ideas of warfare—and his potential part in it—this Creole officer looked forward to firing on Fort Sumter as soon as the authorities gave him the word. (USAMHI)

> James is in his Cabinet
> Doubting and debating;
> Anderson's in Sumter,
> Very tired of waiting.
>
> Pickens is in Charleston,
> Blustering of blows;
> Thank goodness March the Fourth is near,
> To nip Secession's nose.

On the fourth, Lincoln gave his inaugural in a city bristling with police and soldiers against a threatened secessionist coup, saying among other things, ". . . no state, upon its own mere notion, can lawfully get out of the Union," and "The power confided in me will be used to hold, occupy and possess the property and places belonging to the government." He had earlier said more colorfully that the Union was not a "free love arrangement" which any state could repudiate at will. The new Confederate commissioners arrived in Washington to parley with Lincoln through an intermediary, since the President would not recognize the C.S.A. Secretary Seward launched into an irresponsible and unauthorized course, letting the commissioners know that Lincoln was untutored in national affairs but that he, Seward, would soon bring him around and that Sumter would be peacefully evacuated. Seward's policy was based on his certainty that there was great innate love for the Union in the South and that if the states were permitted to secede, this love would combine with loss of trade and internal bickering to make them clamor to rejoin the Union within a year or so.

A message from Major Anderson staggered the new administration, for it told of the steady buildup of Confederate forces, the fact that Sumter had supplies for less than forty days, and gave an estimate (in which Anderson's officers substantially agreed) that it would take reinforcements of 20,000 men to hold the fort.

Twenty thousand men! No such force was available, nor were there enough Navy men-of-war to carry them if there had been. General Scott, much under Seward's influence, agreed with Anderson's estimate and told Lincoln, "Evacuation seems almost inevitable."

The idea was repugnant to the President. It would violate his "hold, occupy and possess" promise in his inaugural. It would begin his administration with a surrender which not even the irresolute Buchanan had contemplated. It would outrage the North and subject him to the contempt of the South—indeed, the whole watching world. Seward pressed him with the evacuation idea and the theory of an affectionate South which, if given its way, would spring back into the Union as if on a rubber band—a theory Lincoln deeply suspected. Determined to get the facts, he sent Gustavus Vasa Fox, a former Navy captain who yearned to lead an expedition to reinforce Anderson, to Charleston to confer with the major and find the actual condition of the fort and garrison. He dispatched Ward Lamon and Stephen Hurlbut separately to Charleston to sound officials and private citizens

His antagonist, Major Robert Anderson, commanding in Fort Sumter. A native of Kentucky, Anderson's sympathies were severely torn by the sectional crisis, but he saw his duty to the Union as paramount. (USAMHI)

and see if they were, as Seward supposed, affectionate Unionists in a temporary fit of bad temper.

There were signs of spring in Charleston, ladies and gentlemen were promenading on the Battery, and the rumor that Sumter would soon be evacuated—which had appeared in the local papers—added spice to the air. The Army in South Carolina now numbered ten regiments of 8,835 men. Local photographers did a large business perpetuating the likenesses of these young men in their new uniforms. One photographer, George Cook, went to Sumter and persuaded the officers to sit for a group portrait despite Doubleday's conviction that he was a spy. In the city there was a magnificent St. Patrick's Day parade, and the feeling toward Anderson and his tobaccoless and short-rationed men softened enough so that cigars and several cases of claret were sent out for the officers. Captain Fox was permitted to visit Anderson and to observe, without mentioning it to the major, that reinforcement of the fort appeared feasible if done skillfully in darkness. Ward Lamon, Lincoln's close friend, apparently believed that there was now no choice but to quit Sumter, for he clearly gave Governor Pickens that impression and, on visiting Anderson at the fort, left him with the conviction that he would be withdrawn. Hurlbut, a native of Charleston who was now an Illinois lawyer, devoted himself to a survey of relatives and friends he had in the city. He decided that Seward's theory was absurd, that "there is a unanimity of sentiment" against the Union that was deep and unrelenting.

It is doubtful that there was ever so important an issue on which there was so much disagreement, so many misinterpretations and errors, so many men at cross purposes, often utterly mistaken and snarled in confusion.

Anderson was relieved that the issue, as he now believed, was to be settled by his withdrawal and that war would be averted. But as the days passed in Charleston (where there were rumors that the major had resigned his commission and that Captain Doubleday had gone insane and was in irons), impatience grew at the failure of the garrison to decamp. General Beauregard, hearing talk that

Castle Pinckney in Charleston. Here and at other works like this, the Confederate volunteers gathered during the early months of 1861, to train and await the time of their taking the Yankee fort that taunted them in their own harbor. (VM)

demolition charges might be left in Sumter, wrote Anderson to suggest discreetly that the fort be left undamaged when he departed. The Confederacy in Montgomery was angry at the delay. In Sumter, the garrison was ready to pack and go north where pork chops, apple pie, and beautiful women were realities instead of dreams. Sumter was down to its last barrel of flour, as Anderson reported on April 3 to the new Secretary of War, Simon Cameron, urgently asking instructions. No instructions came.

The Confederate commissioners in Washington now found through an intermediary that Seward was no longer certain that Sumter would be evacuated. The secretary had done his best to impose his policy on the new President and, in failing, had caused misunderstanding and provoked accusations of bad faith. On April 8, a messenger from Lincoln handed Governor Pickens a paper whose single sentence exuded blunt honesty:

> I am directed by the President of the United States to notify you to expect an attempt will be made to supply Fort Sumter with provisions only, and that if such attempt be not resisted, no effort to throw in men, arms or ammunition, will be made, without further notice, or in case of an attack upon the Fort.

At the same time, Anderson received his first instructions from the new administration: an expedition would attempt to supply him "and, in case the effort is resisted, will endeavor also to reinforce you." He had reconciled himself to his mortifying failure to defend the *Star of the West* on the ground that he had saved the peace. Now he had mortification and war too. As for Sumter's men, to whom their fort had become a prison, they reacted with a kind of glorious cussedness and cheered lustily at the news that they would have a chance to throw iron at the Carolinians who had made their lives so difficult.

Anderson declined a last offer by Beauregard permitting him to salute his flag if he would leave peacefully. With food left for perhaps sixty hours, he put his men on stern rations. The Carolinians now had at least thirty guns and eighteen mortars bearing on Sumter from six widely separated emplacements, some of which Sumter could not touch. To save his men, the major ordered them to serve only the guns in the more protected casemate tier, which limited them to twenty-one guns, most

Probably Confederates lounging inside Castle Pinckney, ready to fill its cannon with the shot stacked all about them and send the missiles on their way to Sumter.
(SOUTH CAROLINA HISTORICAL SOCIETY)

of them only 32-pounders, and not a single mortar.

The first shot on Fort Sumter was fired from Fort Johnson on James Island at 4:30 A.M. April 12, 1861. It woke up Doubleday, who commented, "[It] seemed to bury itself in the masonry about a foot from my head." He stayed in bed as the firing became an intermittent roar. Sumter did not answer until after 6 o'clock reveille and a breakfast consisting of fat pork and water. "Be careful of your lives," Anderson cautioned, ordering his men to stay in the casemates as much as possible. Doubleday, his second in command, was given the honor of firing the first shot against the rebellion—one he accepted with zest, reflecting, "To me it was simply a contest, politically speaking, as to whether virtue or vice should rule." Private John Carmody, knowing that the bigger barbette guns above were loaded and aimed at Moultrie, disobeyed orders, stole up there, and fired them one by one, making a great noise but with little effect on the well-protected Confederate batteries. It was an unequal battle, what with Sumter's lack of mortars and inability to fire shell (there were no fuses), not to mention the poor provender. Enemy fire, gaining in accuracy,

The Charleston Zouave Cadets in Castle Pinckney, smart, well equipped, and anxious. (USAMHI)

cleared the parapet and started fires in the wooden barracks inside, which took smart work to extinguish. Sumter's most visible achievement was a ball that crashed into the large frame Moultrie House hotel, which sent dozens of battle-watchers scurrying.

Early in the afternoon a Sumter watchman saw a United States man-of-war far out beyond the bar. Reinforcements and food! A shout of joy went up from the exhausted gunners—all in vain. The expedition led by Captain Fox had been broken up by confusion in New York and by a storm that drove two of its fighting ships and its tugs off course. The tugs were the heart of Fox's careful plan for reaching the fort, and the guns were essential to protect the tugs. Fox was waiting for help that never came.

The Sumtermen loosed curses the next morning when they saw the "rescue" vessels still waiting in the distance. Cartridges got so low that they restricted their firing to one gun every ten minutes. The barracks took fire again so that there was no

putting it out. Flames crept slowly toward the magazine where 275 barrels of powder were stored. The magazine was banked with earth for protection, but flying embers touched off stockpiles of shells and grenades that had been placed at strategic spots along the gorge wall, sending down showers of sparks and broken masonry. The main gates were now ablaze. Smoke poured into the casemates, choking the men serving the guns. From the shore the smoke and flame made it seem impossible that Sumter could continue the battle, and there was Carolinian admiration when its guns kept firing. Texas Senator Louis Wigfall, now a Confederate colonel, who had damned the Union and cheered the attack, marveled at this display of courage but thought it had gone far enough. He got a boat and was rowed to the fort, unseen by the smoke-blinded defenders. He entered an open embrasure, carrying a white flag on his sword, and came upon a sooty-faced Major Anderson, whose coolness astonished him.

"You have defended your flag nobly, sir," Wigfall shouted. "It's madness to persevere. . . . General Beauregard wishes to stop this, and to ask upon what terms you will evacuate this work."

Anderson at length agreed to parley. Only three cartridges remained. His men were spent. The larder was all but empty. There was danger of explosions in the fort. The effort to reinforce him had somehow collapsed. It would indeed be madness to persevere.

After thirty-three hours of bombardment, the Sumter flag went down at 1:30 P.M. April 13. A few men on each side had been injured by flying debris, but the only fatality of battle was a horse killed on Morris Island by a Sumter ball. Charleston was in transports over the victory. Headlines in the North used the word "WAR." Young men, North and South, began flocking to the banners. It was, as Horace Greeley said later, a comparatively bloodless beginning for the bloodiest conflict America ever knew.

Lieutenant R. C. Gilchrist, standing second from the left, carries a sword more like a scimitar than a saber, but the cadets in their pipe-clayed crossbelts dare not smile. Neither do their black orderlies at the rear. A year before most southern states had statutes on their books preventing slaves from reading or gathering together. Now they were uniformed and sometimes even trusted with arms as they came to the front to see to life's amenities while their masters met the enemy. (VM)

Some military organizations that existed before the war, as much fraternal groups as real armed units, readied for the coming fight. Prominent were the men of Charleston's own Washington Light Infantry. They bivouacked in Camp Truesdale on the east end of Sullivan's Island. This faded old print shows their officers before their tent, equipped in a manner that two years hence would be only a fond memory. (WASHINGTON LIGHT INFANTRY)

*Another group of Confederates in Charleston, fully equipped for the field, their
knapsacks on their backs, their Harpers Ferry rifles on their shoulders.* (VM)

*Simon Cameron, Lincoln's Secretary of War, was
slow in appreciating Anderson's helpless situation
at Sumter, and slower still in doing anything about
it.* (USAMHI)

Reminder of an earlier brave, now buried at Fort Moultrie. Osceola, the Seminole leader, effectively defeated the U. S. Army's attempt to subdue his people until the government admitted that it had lost the contest. His example was hardly lost on the high-spirited Southrons gathered at Charleston. (VM)

Secretary of State William Seward played several ends against the middle in attempting to avoid the outbreak of hostilities in Charleston. In so doing he lied, overstepped his authority, and severely tried the patience of Lincoln. (USAMHI)

*Hurt most by Seward's interference was septuagenarian Lieutenant General
Winfield Scott. Once the foremost soldier of the young republic, he was now an
obese old man, a picture of ruined magnificence. Yet his mind was as active as
ever, and he appreciated at once the hopelessness of reinforcing Anderson in
Sumter without precipitating war. He advised that the fort be evacuated.
Lincoln would not have it. (KA)*

*And that left Major Robert Anderson caught
squarely in a trap. Charleston photographer George
Cook took his camera out to Sumter in February
1861 and persuaded Anderson and his officers to
sit for him. A tongue-in-cheek broadside soon
appeared describing how "Col. George S. Cook, of
the Charleston Photographic Light Artillery,"
stormed Sumter, "heroically penetrated to the
presence of Maj. Anderson, and levelling a
double barrelled Camera, demanded his
unconditional surrender." The broadside appeared
under the headline, "MAJOR ANDERSON TAKEN!"
It looked like war was going to be fun. (VM)*

*Anderson and his officers "captured" by Cook. Most of them would be heard
from in the war to come. Seated from the left are Captain Abner Doubleday,
Anderson, Surgeon Samuel W. Crawford, and Captain John G. Foster.
Standing from the left are Captain Truman Seymour, Lieutenant G. W.
Snyder, Lieutenant Jefferson C. Davis, Lieutenant R. K. Meade, and Captain
T. Talbot. All but Snyder, Meade, and Talbot will become generals.* (USAMHI)

Talbot, Crawford, and Seymour posed separately, enjoying the distinction of being "captured" twice. (USAMHI)

There were those who would help Anderson, and finally a relief expedition was sent, led by Gustavus V. Fox, Assistant Secretary of the Navy. But it could not dare Charleston's guns, and so it sat on the horizon, within sight but not reach of Anderson's exhausted command. (NAVAL PHOTOGRAPHIC CENTER)

The Confederates, from their lookout tower at Fort Washington, expected Fox's coming. Several of them are here waving their caps in celebration, perhaps at the Union fleet's failure to test their batteries. (WASHINGTON LIGHT INFANTRY)

And finally came war. At 4:30 A.M., or shortly after, April 12, 1861, a signal gun was fired from Fort Johnson. Seconds later Edmund Ruffin, fire-eating secessionist from South Carolina, jerked a lanyard . . . (NA, BRADY COLLECTION)

. . . on one of these eight-inch columbiads in the Iron Clad Battery moored off
Morris Island, and launched one of the first hostile shots of the war against
Sumter's parapet.

   A rare, previously unpublished photograph by Osborn & Durbec of
Charleston showing the interior of the Iron Clad Battery, taken April 17, 1861,
just five days after the firing. One of these guns, or a third not shown, fired
Ruffin's hostile shot. (CHS)

The first answering Federal shot of the war was fired by Captain Doubleday, who gladly sent a ball toward the Iron Clad Battery, though it bounced harmlessly off its roof. (USAMHI)

The Surgeon Crawford began firing his gun, sending his shells toward an unusual and ungainly apparition . . . (USAMHI)

The iron-sheathed Floating Battery at Sullivan's Island mounted two 42-pounder cannon and two 32-pounders, and proudly flew the flag of the new Confederacy overhead. A photograph taken on April 16, 1861, by an unidentified photographer, shows the Floating Battery in position off the island. This print has not been published in nearly seventy years. (VM)

After thirty-three hours of bombardment, former Senator Louis T. Wigfall of Texas, aide to Beauregard and an ardent secessionist, carried a truce flag to Sumter and asked Anderson to surrender. Seeing the hopelessness of further resistance, the major gave up. (CIVIL WAR TIMES ILLUSTRATED)

On April 14, Anderson and his command left the fort to its conquerors. The flag of the Confederate States of America went up a makeshift staff, and the next day photographer F. K. Houston of 307 King Street in Charleston became the first to bring a camera into Fort Sumter. Elated soldiers feigned action poses while he made his slow exposure, but the proud new flag would not stay still. (USAMHI)

That day and in those following, several cameramen came to the fort. The names of some are now lost, but thankfully not their photographs. One of them, probably Osborn & Durbec, made a panorama from three separate images of Sumter that shows vividly the damage done by Beauregard's batteries. They claimed to have made these shots the very day of the surrender.
(USAMHI)

Sumter's eastern terreplein and parapet, April 15, 1861. Just over the wall can be seen a steam sidewheeler that transported more and more Confederates into the captured fort, and sightseers from Charleston as well. One such is the top-hatted man standing at right. The man at left is Major Nathan G. Evans, who will shortly be a brigadier general at Bull Run. The man in the middle is Lieutenant Robert Pringle. (CHARLESTON LIBRARY SOCIETY)

But Anderson's men did some damage, too, and the camera artists were not loath to show it. Here on April 16 the soldiers' barracks at Fort Moultrie showed the effect of Sumter's fire. (CHARLESTON *Post-Courier*)

So, too, did Moultrie's northwest angle. (CHARLESTON MUSEUM)

April 15, the interior of Sumter, showing the destroyed western barracks and, in the right foreground, columbiads that Anderson had mounted in the ground to use as mortars. (VM)

April 15, the southwest angle of the fort, a panorama formed of two separate images. Dressed smartly on parade, the conquering Confederates line up for the camera, while their flag floats gently overhead. Anderson built the earth bank at left to protect the lower tier of soldiers' quarters. The fort's beacon lantern, removed from its place on the parapet, rests in the parade ground. These two images have never before been juxtaposed to give this wide view of the interior of the fort. (VM)

April 15, another view of the southwest angle showing officers' quarters and soldiers' barracks. Elated Confederates stand in groups retelling their experiences while watching the bombardment. (VM)

The main sally-port into Sumter, showing the confusion of rubble and the damage done by Beauregard's cannon. (NYHS)

Another view, April 17 or later, showing the effects of the fire from Charleston upon the mortar and masonry of the fort. (USAMHI)

On April 17, 1861, and probably for two or three days thereafter, two special photographers visited not only Fort Sumter, but also all of the Confederate installations that fired against it. They were James M. Osborn and F. E. Durbec of "Osborn & Durbec's Photographic Mart" at 223 King Street in Charleston. They operated a rather extensive establishment, advertising their "Cheap Photographs! Cheap Ambrotypes! Cheap Daguerreotypes! Cheap Ivorytypes! Cheap Melainotypes!"

and advised that strangers visiting Charleston "would do well to give us a call before going elsewhere." They sold views of Egypt, photo cases in some five thousand different patterns, and even carried cameras for sale. They are today forgotten, but on those days in April 1861 they took a place beside Brady and Gardner and Edwards and the rest of the war's immortal chroniclers.

Their stereo camera captured over forty scenes in Sumter and the Charleston batteries, the most

The only known photograph of the interior of Sumter's casemate, and the guns that Doubleday, Crawford, and others manned in defense. (TU)

complete record ever made of the site of a Civil War engagement. Apparently they later attempted to market their stereo views, but the war and the Federal blockade probably prevented their ever getting sufficient chemicals and supplies to manufacture the prints. As a result, very few of their images survive in more than one copy, and all but a few have been entirely lost to view until now.

What follows—in addition to the Osborn & Durbec views already presented in this and the previous chapter—is a nearly complete collection of their work. Two thirds of these images have never before been published and are newly discovered.

As for Osborn & Durbec, their partnership did not survive the war. By 1866 they had gone their separate ways. They left behind a priceless record of the first sad evidence of war between the states.

A group of Confederate dignitaries in front of the shot furnace on Sumter's parade ground. Beside them is one of the columbiads that Anderson mounted to use as mortars against Charleston. They were never fired. The tall figure in the center has long been believed to be Wade Hampton. Others probably include Governor Francis Pickens. (TU)

The sally-port at Fort Sumter seen from the wharf. Already the conquering Confederates are at work cleaning out the rubble and rebuilding. (TU)

The southwest face of the fort, showing the damage done by Edmund Ruffin and members of his Palmetto Guard as they fired the columbiads in the Iron Clad Battery. (CHS)

Damage done by Confederate guns firing from Cumming's Point. (TU)

The southwest corner, and the effects of shots fired from Morris Island and the Floating Battery. The opening at left is an embrasure for one of Sumter's guns. (CHS)

The southeast side of the parade, the hot-shot furnace, and the soldiers' east barracks. (CHS)

The ruins of the sally-port at right, and to its left the officers' quarters. (CHS)

Cleaning up the parade ground in front of the sally-port. (MHS)

The ruined officers' quarters on the southwest side, and a row of cannon
Anderson did not emplace. (CHS)

The stair tower at an angle in the perimeter, and jaunty Confederates atop their captured guns. (TU)

Damage done by the Iron Clad Battery on the interior of Sumter. (CHS)

In the left rear, the powder magazine, protected by an earth traverse. It is on the side facing Charleston, since Sumter was built to withstand an attack from the sea, not the land face. (TU)

Behind the makeshift flagstaff can be seen the effects of Fort Moultrie's fire on the officers' quarters and sally-port. (NA, BRADY COLLECTION)

The shot furnace and, to the right, Anderson's flagstaff, which was shot off during the bombardment. The new flag of the victors flutters overhead. (CHS)

More of the cleanup, with two men working while the others watch. (TU)

Sumter's parapet. Fort Moultrie is in the distance, while the guns shown are trained on the Iron Clad Battery. The gun in the foreground has been dismounted by Confederate fire. (CHS)

The rear of the same parapet, another dismounted gun, and a traverse built of sand bags to protect men from the fire from Sullivan's Island. (CWTI)

*Confederates on Morris Island, very
probably men of Colonel J. H. Trapier's
Mortar Battery.* (SOUTH CAROLINA
HISTORICAL SOCIETY)

*The Trapier Mortar Battery on Morris Island and, in the right background,
Osborn & Durbec's pyramidal portable darkroom.* (TU)

Another view of the Trapier Battery, this time manned for action. At the very
right of the image, behind the dimly seen man at the edge, is a corner of the
portable darkroom. (CHS)

A view of the Iron Clad Battery at Morris
Island from the rear. The railroad "T"
iron cladding has been removed from its
wooden beamed roof. One of the
columbiads with which Ruffin sent the
first shots against Sumter can be seen
within. (SOUTH CAROLINA HISTORICAL
SOCIETY)

The harbor face of Fort Moultrie, its shot furnace in the foreground. Since it was assumed that any attacker would come from the sea in wooden ships, the U. S. Army, when building these coastal forts, provided for sending red-hot shot like fireballs into attacking vessels. Just above the gun at the right can be seen a long dark object. It is Fort Sumter. These guns no longer bear upon it. (TU)

Another view of Moultrie's shot furnace, with the officers' quarters behind it. Heated shot from here set ablaze the wooden roofs in Sumter and caused fires that threatened the powder magazine. (TU)

The eastern angle of Moultrie, on Sullivan's Island. Damage done by Sumter's
return fire can be seen in the roof of the right wing of the large house. (TU)

Moultrie's northwestern angle. (TU)

Moultrie's western barracks overlooking the parade ground, and the damage done by Captain Doubleday. (TU)

More of Doubleday's handiwork on the western barracks. It was small recompense. (TU)

A house on Sullivan's Island riddled by Surgeon Crawford's shot as he fired on the Floating Battery (TU)

Empty gun emplacements on Sullivan's Island and, in the harbor beyond, Fort Sumter. The bloodless beginning to a bloody war. (TU)

The Boys of '61

BELL I. WILEY

Euphoric thousands enlist before they miss "the fun"

THE TREMENDOUS WAVE of patriotism that swept over North and South in the wake of Fort Sumter produced an epidemic of volunteering. Very few of the recruits had any prior military experience. Conversion of the hordes of civilians into effective soldiers presented an enormous challenge, but authorities on both sides rose to the occasion and the results proved better than might have been expected.

Since governors usually took the lead in mobilization, most recruits had a brief stint of state service before they were sworn in as Federal or Confederate troops. First came a physical examination, usually a perfunctory test consisting largely of responses to questions put by the doctors concerning the recruits' medical history. Then came formal muster into national service—inspection by the muster officer, pledging allegiance to the United States or the Confederacy, promising to obey orders, swearing to abide by the 101 articles of war to which recruits listened while standing in company formation, and signing the company muster roll.

On both sides recruits chose their officers. As a rule the rank and file elected only their company officers (lieutenants and captains), who in turn chose the field grade officers (majors, lieutenant colonels, and colonels), but in some units soldiers elected all officers, from corporals to colonels. Those who took the lead in raising units were generally chosen to command them, but when, as was sometimes the case, more than one candidate vied for a position, lively campaigns ensued. Victors in these contests sometimes celebrated their success by hosting drinking parties.

During the first weeks in camp, recruits within the various companies organized themselves into informal groups known as messes. These varied in size from six to a dozen men, drawn together by similarity of inclination and interest. Members took turns in drawing rations, gathering wood, and cooking. Ties became very close with continuing association. An Illinois soldier wrote early in 1862: "Cap wanted to take some more men in our mess but we told him we would rather not, we wanted mess No. one to remain as it was. . . . Ours . . . is the most intelligent mess in this Reg[iment], the best fellows, the bravest boys, can kill more Secesh & Eat more hard Crackers & stand more hard marching, waid deeper mud & do less grumbling than any other mess in the Northern army."

As the time approached for departure from home for "the seat of war," volunteers took part in a series of farewell activities. One of these was the presentation of a flag by one of the feminine patriots who had helped to make it. As the pretty donor made the presentation, she delivered a flowery speech, extolling cause and country and calling on the recipients to protect the emblem from the vile creatures who sought to defile it. The officer receiving the colors, usually a colonel, responded in words glowing with patriotism and pledging himself and his associates to defend the banner with their lives.

On the day of departure friends and neighbors gathered at the railway station or steamboat wharf or some other place of rendezvous to bid the soldiers farewell. After a prayer by a local minister, the recruits took their leave amid a chorus of good-byes and best wishes. The volunteers joked and laughed to mask their sadness, and loved ones left behind did their best to fight back the tears that filled their eyes.

The trip to the fighting zone, made sometimes by train and sometimes by boat, was a boisterous experience. Troops traveling by rail sometimes obtained better ventilation and visibility by knocking holes in the sides of boxcars; many rode on top of

As Lincoln and Davis issued their calls for the boys of '61, the first to be ready were those already enrolled in the scores of active militia units in North and South. New York photographer Charles D. Fredericks turned his camera out his own studio window on July 4, 1860, to catch this resplendent unit at parade. The bearskins would soon disappear. (USAMHI)

The Kentucky State Guard encampment at Louisville in August 1860 proved a training ground for several future Confederate companies. Commander of the Guard was Brigadier General Simon Bolivar Buckner, soon to be a trusted commander of the Confederacy. This group, the Lexington Rifles, was raised and captained by John Hunt Morgan. In the fall of 1861 he would lead them into the rebellion, to become a part of his famed cavalry. For now they are content to pose and drink and feast on watermelon. (KHS)

the cars, despite the admonitions of the officers. Escape from home restraints and the prospect of new and exciting experiences brought a holiday attitude. So did the hearty cheering of pretty girls who greeted them along the way. Many volunteers added to their joviality by taking generous swigs from liquor bottles which they had slipped into their baggage before taking leave of their loved ones. The first casualties experienced by some units came not from hostile bullets but from tipsy soldiers falling from trains. The congestion and filth of some of the trains and boats that transported soldiers were enough to provoke excessive drinking. In March 1862 an Illinois Yank wrote home from West Tennessee: "We was aboard the steamer

Memphis 8 or 9 days. We was in dirt, lice, shit, grease & Hard crackers."

Arrival at the front, whether in Tennessee, Kentucky, Missouri, Maryland, or Virginia, brought a change in the character of soldiering. During the initial period of service when the men were near their homes, discipline was lax and duties relatively light. Recruits frequently called their superiors by their first names or addressed them as "sarge" or "cap." Leaves were easy to obtain, and officers and men spent much of their time in nearby towns or cities. But the proximity of the enemy and the certainty of combat gave serious and urgent purpose to training. Recruits and their officers came under the control of hard-bitten professionals like Jo-

Buckner's own unit, the Citizen Guard, and more bearskins. (KHS)

seph E. Johnston, Braxton Bragg, U. S. Grant, and George B. McClellan. These commanders knew that the novices flowing in from farms, shops, and factories had to undergo a swift and drastic transformation before they could win battles. And they set themselves to effecting the change with determination and vigor. Men who previously treated soldiering as a lark now complained of the hardness of their lot. "I don't believe God ever intended for one man to pen up another and keep him in this manner," wrote a Reb to his homefolks; he added, "Dam Old Abe and Old Jeff Davis. Dam the day I 'listed." Another Reb wrote from a camp near Richmond in May 1861, "A man may come here with as much devil in him as they please, but they will soon tame him." A Georgian, after his transfer to Virginia in the fall of 1861, wrote his father: "I love my country as well as any one but I don't believe in the plan of making myself a slave. . . . A private soldier is nothing more than a slave and is often treated worse. I have during the past six months gone through more hardships than anyone of ours or Grandma's negroes; their life is a luxury to what mine is sometimes." But this soldier came to realize the value of discipline, and while he never completely gave up the cherished practice of grumbling, he eventually accepted and approved the new order. The same was true of most of his comrades and of the men they fought.

In the fighting zones, platoons, companies, and regiments had to be fitted into larger organizations. Two platoons, each commanded by a lieutenant, comprised a company, led by a captain; ten companies formed a regiment, commanded by a colonel; two or more regiments comprised a brigade, led by a brigadier general; two or more brigades combined to make a division, commanded by a major general; two or more divisions comprised a corps, commanded by a lieutenant general on the Confederate side and a major general on the Union side; and two or more corps made an army, commanded by a full general on the Confederate

But militia were not enough. New volunteer armies must be raised. Though defeated by Lincoln in 1860, Stephen A. Douglas stood firmly behind his antagonist's administration, and now took to the stump in speaking to raise support and volunteers. He wore himself out in the process, and died that summer. The last words of his final public address declared his stand for the Union: "United, firm, determined, never to permit the Government to be destroyed." (USAMHI)

side and a major general on the Union side. In the artillery, the battalion, consisting of four batteries, each containing four to six guns, was a standard organization. The squadron (known also as the troop and the equivalent roughly of the infantry company) consisting of two or more platoons was a distinctive feature of the cavalry organization. Combination of arms normally began with the attachment of artillery (usually a battery) and cavalry to an infantry brigade. Engineer, signal, and other supporting elements were added on the corps or army level.

The basic unit on both sides was the infantry company, which at full strength numbered some-

thing over one hundred officers and men. But, after the first few months of service, companies commonly dwindled to about half their authorized strength and subsequently some experienced even greater attrition. Long and intimate association and the sharing of perils and hardships of soldiering promoted a relationship among company officers and their men very much like that of a family. The captain was the father who supervised daily routine, saw that his men were equipped, fed, clothed, and sheltered, heard their complaints, administered punishment for minor offenses, looked after their health, and led them in combat. He knew every man by name and had some acquaintance with the soldier's home circumstances. He sometimes mediated domestic squabbles, wrote letters for illiterates, supervised religious worship, buried the dead, and wrote letters of sympathy to bereaved wives and mothers. The lieutenants and noncommissioned officers were the captain's helpers and their role was very much like that of the elder children in a large family. A key member of the group was the company's first or orderly sergeant, who called the roll, kept the records, and translated the captain's wishes into orders.

On the Confederate side, and to an increasing

Lincoln's old friend Senator Edward Baker of Oregon helped raise a regiment. He would lead it to destruction, and his own death, at Ball's Bluff in October. (RICHARD C. OSTERHOUT)

extent among the Federals, blacks were obtained to help clean quarters, launder clothing, clean boots and shoes, cook, and perform other menial chores. Early in the war some enlisted men even had one or more Negroes, usually body servants, to lighten the burdens of camp life, even to the extent of standing guard under the supervision of their masters. But after a few months most of these servants went home; those who remained were usually the personal aides of officers, or blacks assigned to companies and regiments as hostlers or teamsters. The blacks encountered in northern camps were ex-slaves hired for a pittance to relieve officers and men of some of the more burdensome aspects of army service. Home letters of many Yanks in 1861 and later told of the writer's good fortune in having obtained the service of black menials. Private Andrew Rose of an Ohio regiment stationed in middle Tennessee wrote his parents in 1863: "The captain got two nigers for our company; every company has got them; all we do when we want nigers is to send a company after them." In 1862 a Maine captain wrote from Louisiana: "Officers & men are having an easy time. We have Negroes to do all fatigue work, cooking and washing clothes." In both armies black servants were often called on to dance and provide music for the entertainment of officers and soldiers. The Negroes sometimes sought diversion for themselves by gambling and drinking. During the last two years of the war, about 200,000 blacks were recruited by the Federals for service as soldiers. Inspection reports show that colored troops were often required to do more than their share of labor and that sometimes their white commander treated them more like menials than as fighters.

The training received by Johnny Reb and Billy Yank was very much alike. *Hardee's Tactics*—written by William J. Hardee, a Confederate general—was the most widely used infantry manual on both sides. In accordance with rules prescribed by Hardee for "the school of the soldier" recruits mastered such fundamentals as saluting or standing erect; facing left and right; marching forward, to the rear, by the flank, and obliquely; shifting arms to the various positions; parrying and thrusting with the bayonet; and loading and firing their guns standing, kneeling, and lying down. Most Yanks and Rebs were armed either with the Springfield or the Enfield rifled musket. Since both were muzzle-

Colonel E. Elmer Ellsworth, once a denizen of Lincoln's Illinois law office, brought his New York Fire Zouaves, composed chiefly of New York City firemen, to Washington soon after the crisis came to shots at Sumter. (NYHS)

loaders, much time and patience were required for their effective use. For loading the gun Hardee specified nine movements, each initiated by the instructor's command. At the order "Load!" the soldier dropped the butt of his gun to the ground, grasped the barrel with his left hand and with his right hand reached for the cartridge box hanging from his belt. In response to subsequent commands he bit the end from the paper cartridge; poured the powder into the barrel; inserted the bullet, with hollow base down, into the muzzle and with a ramrod pushed it to the other end of the barrel; returned the ramrod to its place beneath the barrel;

took a percussion cap from a leather pouch on his belt and placed it on the nipple of the tube extending from beneath the hammer into the barrel; and shifted the gun to his right shoulder. Firing was then accomplished by movements executed at the commands "Ready," "Aim," "Fire." Despite the complexity of the procedure, a well-trained infantryman could load and fire his gun twice a minute.

After obtaining proficiency in the use of their rifles, soldiers were taught progressively to march and maneuver in squads, companies, regiments, brigades, and divisions. However, drills by units larger than brigades were infrequent and "sham battles," with infantry, artillery, and cavalry functioning together, were almost unknown until after the first year of the war, and even then they were rare.

Other branches followed a training routine comparable to that of the infantry. In the artillery much practice was required for each member of the gun crew to become proficient in his duties; the most widely used field piece on both sides was the 12-pounder smoothbore called the Napoleon. Functioning by numbers, from 1 to 10, each crew-

man not only had to make the specific movement associated with his number, such as removing the shell from the ammunition chest, passing it on to another, placing it in the muzzle, and ramming it down, but he also had to learn the movements assigned to all the other numbers so that when casualties were experienced shifts could be made without loss of efficiency.

While learning to drill and to use their weapons, recruits had to adjust to the regimented routine of army life. The soldier's day was ordered by drum or bugle calls, which ordinarily ran to about a dozen. First came reveille, sounded about dawn, to wake the soldiers and summon them to roll call. After lining up and responding to their names, they were dismissed until a second call a half-hour later ordered them to breakfast. The third call sent the ailing to the regimental surgeon and the well to such duties as cleaning quarters, tidying company grounds, and cutting wood. About eight o'clock, the musicians sounded the call for guard mounting, at which the first sergeant of each company turned out his guard detail for the next twenty-four hours' duty, inspected them, and marched them to the regimental parade ground. There the guards were

To the War Department in Washington fell the task of organizing, equipping, training, and assigning the largest army ever raised in the hemisphere. No one had any experience in dealing with such numbers. (CHS)

formed into line, inspected by the adjutant, and sent to their respective posts. Details were so arranged that each member stood guard only two hours out of every six.

Next came the call for drill, which ordinarily lasted until drummer or bugler signaled "roast beef," which was the call for lunch. Following a brief post-luncheon period of relaxation, soldiers were summoned to another drill which normally lasted from one to two hours. Then the men returned to their quarters, brushed their uniforms, blacked their leather, polished buckles and buttons, and cleaned their weapons in preparation for retreat, which consisted of roll call, inspection, and dress parade. Both officers and men took pride in the dress parade, held sometimes by regiment and sometimes by brigade, and always to the accompaniment of music. Dress parades were the occasion for reading orders and making official announcements.

Supper call came shortly after retreat, followed not long after dark by tattoo, which brought another roll call, after which the men returned to their quarters. The final call of the day required the cessation of noise and the extinguishing of lights. In the course of the war this call became "taps."

This was the typical routine of an infantry regiment in camp during a season of quiet. Practices varied to some extent in different camps and with changing situations. Sunday routine differed from that of other days. The major event on the Sabbath was a general inspection of quarters, grounds, personnel, and equipment. After a preliminary check by the units' own officers, the regiment or battalion formed by companies. The inspector, usually the brigade commander or one of his staff, proceeded up and down the open ranks, carefully observing clothing, weapons, and other equipment. The soldiers were then required to stack arms, unsling and open their knapsacks, and lay them on the ground for examination. The inspector checked the contents of the knapsacks, and if he found a dirty garment he rebuked the offender. Further reproof for this and any other faults discovered by the inspector was given by the unit commander after the men returned to their quarters. The inspecting officer made the rounds of guardhouse, hospital, sutler's shop, kitchen, and such other facilities as he chose to examine. He concluded the

Officers like Brigadier General George Cadwallader did their best to hold precarious states like Maryland and Kentucky in the Union when Lincoln's call for volunteers to put down the rebellion aroused their southern sympathies. Cadwallader defied Chief Justice Roger B. Taney himself in carrying out Lincoln's suspension of the writ of habeas corpus in Maryland, for fear of seeing it secede. (USAMHI)

inspection shortly before noon by going through the company quarters and checking floors, bunks, and walls. Soldiers usually spent Sunday afternoons writing letters, playing games, reading, or gambling. Those of religious inclination might attend prayer meetings or listen to sermons delivered by the regimental chaplain or by one of their comrades.

Every other month soldiers were mustered for pay. Standing in company formation, each soldier certified his presence by responding "here" when his name was called. After the mustering officer

The courthouse at Natchez, Mississippi, long thought to show Confederates enlisting in 1861. The photo, by Henry Gurney, more likely depicts Federal soldiers sometime after 1862, but the scene would be much the same if they were wearers of the gray. (JOAN AND THOMAS GANDY)

had accounted for every man listed on the roster, he forwarded a copy of the muster roll to the adjutant general in Washington, or Richmond. At the beginning of the war the monthly pay on both sides was $11 for infantry and artillery privates and $12 for cavalry. Early in the conflict the Union government increased the pay of privates in all three branches to $13 a month and in May 1864 to $16. Confederates received only one raise and that was on June 9, 1864, when the monthly stipend of infantry and artillery privates was increased to $20 and that of cavalry privates to $21; by that time the gold value of the Confederate dollar had shrunk to about five cents. Pay was often in arrears, sometimes as much as four months on the Union side and six to twelve months among Confederates.

An essential part of the transition from civilian to soldier was getting accustomed to military clothing. On both sides the first uniforms worn by some soldiers were those in which they had paraded as militiamen. These varied considerably in color and design. Concerning troops whom he observed in Washington in the early summer of 1861, General William T. Sherman stated: "Their uniforms were as various as the cities and states from which they came." When Northerners wore gray militia uniforms into battle and Southerners wore blue, as was the case in some of the early engagements, they had the unhappy experience of being fired on by their comrades. In 1861 and later, both sides had some Zouave units that wore fezzes, red bloomers, gaily colored vests and sashes, and white gaiters. Considerable variation in dress persisted throughout the war, but a fair degree of standardization was achieved in both armies before the end of 1861.

The usual outfit of a Federal infantryman was a long woolen dress coat of dark blue with a high stiff collar; a dark blue jacket or blouse which for field service was much preferred to the dress coat; light blue trousers; black brogan shoes; a flannel shirt; long flannel drawers; socks; blue cap with black visor; and a long blue overcoat with cape. Artillery and cavalry dress was the same as for the infantry except the coats were shorter and boots were normally worn instead of shoes. In both armies each branch had distinctive trimmings (red for artillery, blue for infantry, and yellow for cavalry). Branch was also indicated by insignia worn on the front of the headgear; Union officers below the grade of generals wore crossed cannons for artillery, a bugle for infantry, crossed sabers for cavalry, turreted castle for engineers, and flaming shell for ordnance, along with a brass numeral designating regiment and, when applicable, a brass letter specifying company. Union privates wore brass letters and numerals on their caps to indicate company and regiment; on the Confederate side, branch was designated by the color of the cap crown.

Confederate Army regulations specified a double-breasted coat for both officers and enlisted men, but among enlisted men this garment was rarely seen after the first few months of the conflict. In its stead a short, gray single-breasted jacket was worn, thus giving to Johnny Rebs the nickname "gray jackets." Confederate Army regulations also specified trousers of dark blue, but from the beginning, until the use of homemade dyes produced a yellowish brown or "butternut" hue, trousers, like coats, were of gray. Confederate shoes and socks at first were very much like those worn by Yanks, but after the northern blockade became effective, inferior shoes made of home-tanned leather had to be used, though many Rebs equipped themselves with sturdier footwear by appropriating the shoes of Yankee battle casualties. Some Confederates, especially those of rural background, regarded drawers as superfluous. Regulations of both armies listed leather stocks or ties as standard items of issue, but these were rarely worn. Many soldiers in both armies wore soft hats instead of caps. Well-meaning relatives North and South frequently loaded the soldiers down with "extras" such as havelocks to protect necks from sun and rain, sleeping caps, scarfs, and mittens, but these were usually discarded soon after the recruits arrived in camp, if not before.

The soldier's prescribed equipment included a haversack for his food, a canteen, a knapsack for extra items of clothing, stationery, toilet articles, and other personal items, a leather cartridge box, and a small leather pouch for percussion caps. But comfort, convenience, and other considerations led to a shedding of some of this equipment. Knapsacks were frequently discarded and the contents rolled in a blanket which the soldier threw over his left shoulder and tied at the ends above his right hip. Many Rebs and Yanks regarded tin cups and small skillets as essential items of equipment. These they suspended from their belts. The cups sometimes were used for boiling coffee over the coals of the campfire.

During their period of breaking in as soldiers, Yanks and Rebs frequently had to sleep on the ground under the open skies. Those fortunate enough to have shelter usually were occupants of either Sibley or "A" tents. The Sibley tent, shaped like a bell or wigwam and supported by a vertical center pole, was eighteen feet in diameter and twelve feet high. Its twelve or more occupants slept with their feet to the center and heads near the outer edge, like spokes in a wheel. Guns were stacked around the center pole and other equipment arranged according to comfort and convenience. "A" tents, known also as wedge tents, consisted of a large sheet of canvas draped over a long horizontal bar supported by upright poles, placed at each end. Front and rear were covered by two other pieces of canvas which, when tied together, had the shape of an "A." Each tent housed from four to six men; occupants could stand upright only when directly beneath the center ridgepole, and in sleeping they found maximum comfort when arranged in spoon fashion; but this meant that when one turned over, all had to do likewise. Officers normally were housed in wall tents, which, in effect, were "A" tents elevated two to four feet from the ground and walled with canvas. They were much more commodious and comfortable for their one or two occupants than were the Sibley and wedge tents.

After 1861 Sibley and "A" tents generally were replaced by lighter and less expensive dwellings known as shelter tents, or dog tents. These were two-man habitations made by buttoning together the rectangular pieces of canvas known as half shelters which each soldier carried as a part of his equipment. These halves, when combined, were made into a miniature wedge, with both ends open. Sometimes four soldiers would combine their

*A recruiting scene in an unidentified town. These men, perhaps, are
Confederates. Certainly they have the rugged look of those rough-edged, tough
men of the trans-Appalachian west who, North and South, proved to be the
fiercest fighters—and worst disciplined—of the war.* (JMB)

half shelters to make a larger covering. Lacking a
partner, a soldier could stretch his half shelter horizontally over a framework of four horizontal sticks,
one placed at each corner. Ingenious Rebs and
Yanks arranged their shelters in various other ways
to satisfy their tastes and comforts.

In seasons of cold, when the military situation
was quiescent, soldiers winterized their tents or
built log cabins. A winterized tent was a rectangular log pen, about four feet high, roofed with
sloping canvas and with the interior dug out perhaps to a depth of two feet to provide more standing room and warmth. Log cabins were one-room
huts, chinked and daubed like frontier dwellings.
Roofs were of boards, grass, or canvas. Spacious-
ness of the huts was sometimes increased by digging out the interiors. Both huts and winterized
tents were heated by fireplaces with chimneys built
of logs and chinked and lined with clay. Often
chimneys were topped with barrels or kegs to increase the draft, provide better combustion, and
keep the dwellings free of smoke. Sometimes chimneys would catch fire and cause a great commotion
in the soldier community.

Many soldiers laid wooden floors to increase the
comfort of their winter residences. They drove nails
or pegs around the walls for the hanging of hats,
haversacks, and cartridge boxes. They made stoves
and tables of boxes or barrels obtained from the
commissary or of boards taken from nearby barns
or residences. Some built double- or triple-deck
bunks along the walls to converse space. Bayonets
were stuck into floors or walls and candles inserted
in the sockets to provide illumination. Photographs,
books, and writing materials were conveniently
arranged on shelves and tables. Some soldiers
added a humorous touch by placarding the entrance of their huts with designations such as
"Buzzard Roost," "Astor House," "Howlers," and
"Growlers." Many Yanks and Rebs boasted to
their womenfolk about the comfort and attrac-
tiveness of their winter quarters. A Texan stationed
in Virginia wrote his mother on January 14, 1862:
"Our house is about 12 feet square. . . . Our guns
are in racks on the walls; our utensils consist of one
skillet, a stew kettle, a bread pan, a frying pan, & a
large kettle. Our china ware is a half dozen plates
and the same number of forks & spoons (silver of

They came in whole families, like these four brothers in blue with their target rifles. (LO)

They spoke in strange tongues, like men of this all-German artillery unit. Tens of thousands of Germans marched behind the Federal banners, often induced to volunteer by high rank being given—sometimes unwisely—to prominent Germans. (AMERICANA IMAGE GALLERY)

They came in baggy pants, the uniform of the French Chasseur. (USAMHI)

area. A New Englander stationed near Falls Church, Virginia, wrote his homefolks in January 1862: "The 2nd Maine have erected arches and other fancy works over the entrance to each avenue. These are made of cedar boughs and trees set in and around their camps. Nor has the 17th N. Y. been behind in beautifying their grounds. Over the entrance is placed the name of 'McClellan'—below and on the right is 'Porter' (commanding division), on the left Butterfield (commanding brigade)." Because of the comfort of their winter dwellings, and the respite from marching and fighting that came with cold weather, most soldiers came to regard winter as the most tolerable of their wartime seasons.

For many recruits the most undesirable feature of breaking in to army life was being "put through the measles." Troops from rural areas, largely because they had not been exposed to this malady in childhood, were more susceptible to it than were those from towns and cities. Measles usually struck during the first few months of military service and with devastating consequences. In the summer of 1861, one out of every seven Confederates of the Army of Northern Virginia had measles, and in one camp of 10,000 recruits, 4,000 men were stricken with the disease. Early in 1863 a soldier of Grant's army wrote from near Vicksburg: "Mesles . . . is what kilde the most of our boys—thay would take the measels and haf to lay out in the rain and storm and thay wod only laste abot 2 days." Comparatively few men died from measles alone, but the tendency to get up too soon often led to complications which proved fatal. A soldier of the Army of Northern Virginia wrote in August 1861: "We have some 5 or 6 that is very sick ones in our company. . . . They all had the measles, & were getting well & they turn out to drill too soon after it and they all have relapsed." Recruits of 1861 also had dysentery, malaria, typhoid, pneumonia, and other diseases that plagued Civil War armies, but the incidence of measles was much greater among new soldiers than among veterans.

Yet sickness, discomfort, drill, and discipline paled in comparison to the real business of soldiering, and all too soon these boys of '61 would mature in fire and blood to become the men of Bull Run.

course), our cups are of tin, 4 quart cups and two pint cups. Just above the fireplace you will see something which we call a mantle piece. . . . There are only four of us in this house." A member of the 16th Maine Regiment wrote from near Fredericksburg, Virginia, in January 1863: "Max and I built generously, and inside our finished house, in the warmth of a roaring blaze, we set up bedsteads and overlaid them with pine boughs for mattresses, and covered the boughs with blankets for counterpanes. How proudly we gazed upon those beds!"

Members of some regiments, after completing their huts, built ornate entrances to their camping

They came magnificently equipped, like Sergeant Dore of the 7th New York State Militia. (USAMHI)

They came, like Lieutenant A. Kintzing Post of the 45th Massachusetts, enlisting for and expecting a nine-month war. (USAMHI)

They came like these two brothers of Company I, 2d New Hampshire Volunteers, with their deceptively light colored blouses and rather distinctive headgear. (HP)

And they came young. This unknown boy wears the fatigue blouse and cap, common dress for most Federal infantry. (ROBERT MCDONALD)

And younger still they came. A photograph taken in 1861 by Lieutenant Henry Digby of Ohio, of drummer boys William Ambrose and Jimmy Carvill. (AMERICANA IMAGE GALLERY)

And still younger. David Wood, aged ten. The children came to be drummers, but many, the larger ones, often passed for beyond their years and took their place in the battle. The veterans sometimes sang nursery songs in camp when they spied these boys of '61. But it was a young man's war. Some "boys" would be generals before they were old enough to vote. (RICHARD E. WOOD)

The Southrons flocked to their country's call, too. At Fredericksburg, Virginia, in June 1861, these confident young Virginians posed in a mixture of military and civilian dress. For many it was the best they would ever get. (JOHN A. HESS)

C. C. Taylor, J. D. Jackson, and a man named Porter, all from Georgia, enlisted in the 3d Georgia Infantry, but did not leave for war before posing for this ambrotype. The numbers were against them. In this war, nearly one of every three Confederates would die. (MC)

They came to photographers who supplied them with props like Roman short swords and sometimes ungrammatical patriotic expressions. (PRIVATE COLLECTION)

They came with boyish bravado and clowning. (C.D.W. NELSON)

They came with double-barreled shotguns, huge bowie knives, and a look of wild determination. (HP)

Some looked rather bemused by it all. (WILLIAM A. ALBAUGH)

They came looking ready and alert, like Henry Kelley of the 1st Virginia, with his Colt revolving rifle. (RONN PALM)

And they came without spit or polish or posture. (LES JENSEN)

They came with poise and dignity, obviously the sons of the first families. (WENDELL W. LANG, JR.)

And they, too, came young. Brother privates, William E. Spach and Bennett Spach, of the 1st Battalion of North Carolina Sharpshooters. (JOHN T. SPACH)

North and South, the departure of the volunteers for the front was a major occasion. With great ceremony the town fathers or state officials presented the regiments with their colors. Here the 1st Michigan Infantry receive their flags in Detroit on May 1, 1861. (BURTON HISTORICAL COLLECTION, DETROIT PUBLIC LIBRARY)

Then it was off to the war. In April 1861, the 1st Rhode Island Infantry marched to the railroad depot in Providence to ride to the South, their governor, William Sprague, at their head. (RHODE ISLAND HISTORICAL SOCIETY)

Camps of instruction like Camp Chase outside Columbus, Ohio, appeared all over the divided nation, as volunteers poured in to be made into soldiers. (OHIO HISTORICAL SOCIETY)

Hasty makeshift bivouacs sprang forth in most major cities, crowding even major public buildings and filling the square in front of Philadelphia's Independence Hall. (LO)

"I have seen Him in the watch-fires of a hundred circling camps," wrote Julia Ward Howe. The camp of the 1st Connecticut Artillery, near Washington. (CHS)

The 7th New York State Militia on review in 1861 at Camp Cameron. The drill and review were all too new to the recruits of 1861. It would become all too familiar in the years to come. (MHS)

The 9th Mississippi on parade near Pensacola, caught by J. D. Edwards in April 1861. They, too, however rustic in appearance, learned the intricacies of the drill manual, though it often baffled them. They fought back by giving to the evolutions their own peculiar appellations. A right wheel soon became a "stauchendicilar to the right." (MC)

Exposed for the first time to large numbers of their fellow countrymen in close quarters, the boys of '61 were as well exposed to their germs. Hospitals and camps went in tandem all across the land. Here a tent hospital at Kendal Green, near Washington. (LC)

The best respite from the drill and fatigue duty attendant to training came at meal times. Everyone took a hand, though early in the war tasting the soup could be as dangerous as an enemy bullet. At least there were women in camp to do the laundry. And others followed the camps, tending the men's needs of the flesh. (USAMHI)

The officers dined together and fought in imagination the battles and triumphs they would visit upon the enemy. Here the officers of Company F, 8th Massachusetts Infantry, at Camp Brightwood in the District of Columbia. (USAMHI)

The men in the ranks looked forward to their boxes from home, the letters and liquor and delicacies sent by mothers and sweethearts. Men of the 8th Massachusetts. (USAMHI)

Men of the 5th Company, Washington Artillery of New Orleans, at Camp Lewis, near Carrolton, Louisiana. This new camp life was for them, as for their Yankee counterparts, a lark in the days when the war was young and bound only to last a few months. A photograph by J. W. Petty of New Orleans. (CM)

The soldiers read, relaxed, played cards, tickled each other in the ear with feathers, and even stacked the deck for the camera. The gambler to the left holds a "full house," kings and twos. Even a passing bird stops to perch on the cannon's sponge for the photographer. The 1st Massachusetts Light Artillery. (USAMHI)

Swords and pistols must be polished bright. The man seated burnishes and cleans his Starr revolver, while his mates of the 1st Massachusetts Light Artillery squint at the camera. (USAMHI)

For some in these first days of the war, campaigning was no reason to dispense with the luxuries of home life. The Washington Light Infantry of Charleston, South Carolina, lounge contentedly before their tent, awaiting baskets of food and wine served in glass goblets by their black servants. (WASHINGTON LIGHT INFANTRY)

Many Confederates, even private soldiers, appeared for muster with their bodyservants in tow. Andrew Chandler brought his slave Silas Chandler with him, and both armed for a fight. Men who once feared arms in the hands of slaves now thought little of handing them knives and shotguns. (STERLING CHANDLER AND RICHARD S. YOUNG)

*Yankees, too, enjoyed the services of blacks when they could get them. Here is
the little servant of Captain Aspinwall of the 22d New York.* (USAMHI)

*Most of all the men North and South did as American soldiers have done in all
wars, make the best of it. Confederates of the Washington Artillery relaxed,
indifferent to what lay ahead. When they left New Orleans they were told,
"May the Lord of Hosts be round about you as a wall of fire, and shield your
heads in the day of battle!"* (JAN P. REIFENBERG)

They and their foes to the north, like the 7th New York, will be ready, or think they will. None of them, in their bright uniforms . . . (USAMHI)

. . . their gaily festooned quarters for "Phunny Fellows" . . . (USAMHI)

. . . *their striped trousers, their blouses decorated with flannel badges and galloping horses* . . . (USAMHI)

. . . *none of them, for all their pretended preparedness, really know what is coming.* (USAMHI)

Instead, they smile and pose. The 23d New York Infantry. (USAMHI)

They pose in little groups. The 33d New York Infantry, the man at right armed with a "Volcanic" repeating pistol in his belt. (USAMHI)

They pose by companies, their lady friends often with them. The 22d New York State Militia. (USAMHI)

They gather around the colors they expect to lead to glory, and defend with their lives if need be. The colors of the 7th New York State Militia, at right and left the general guides, at left center the regimental banner, and right center the national colors. (NA)

*The officers and men join together for the camera. Colonel William Wilson,
center, and men of his 6th New York Infantry, "Wilson's Zouaves."* (USAMHI)

They clowned indoors at mock battle. (LO)

With bread and cider and camaraderie, they passed the summer days of soldiering. But it would not last. These militiamen are guarding the Chain Bridge over the Potomac at Washington in 1861. (RINHART GALLERIES INC.)

Washington was a threatened capital. With Virginia across the Potomac hostile, and Maryland filled with southern sympathizers who attempted to block Federal communications and reinforcement from the North, Lincoln and his city were almost blockaded. Then Benjamin F. Butler, a Massachusetts Democrat and now an ardent supporter of the war, acted under his major general's commission and led an expedition to secure . . . (MICHAEL J. MCAFEE)

. . . the Baltimore & Ohio Railroad junction at Relay House, Maryland, thereby holding open a rail route for troops to reach Washington. From May 6, 1861, onward, troops like these flowed through Relay House and on to the capital.
(MHS)

The First Bull Run

JOSEPH P. CULLEN

Reality at last in the heat and dust and blood of Manassas

IT WAS ALREADY HOT that morning of July 16, 1861, when they marched out of the camps around Washington to fight the first major battle in what has been called the last of the old wars and the first of the new. And the camera would be there, or not far behind, to record for posterity the men of the armies and the scenes of battle—a hill, a stream, a field, a copse of woods; a bridge, a church, a house, a barn. Ordinary everyday things in ordinary, everyday life, but these simple things assumed importance beyond their functional purposes. They became landmarks to show where men fought and died; landmarks to be photographed and recorded for future generations.

Since April, when the guns of Fort Sumter roared out their message that North and South were at war, troops had poured into the Washington area until the surrounding heights blossomed white with tents in a care-free, carnival atmosphere. And the untrained, undisciplined citizen-soldiers, with their gaudy, multicolored uniforms—the flamboyant 11th New York Zouaves in their blue and scarlet shirts and jackets and white turbans; the checked flannels of Michigan lumberjacks; the colorful Garibaldi Guards—added a picturesque touch. A few were army regulars, some state militia, but most were three-month volunteers

with romantic ideas about wars in general and battles in particular, who fully expected to end the war with one battle and be home at the end of their brief enlistment.

Many tried to bring the comforts of home with them into the field. One volunteer admitted that his knapsack held "a pair of trousers, two pairs of drawers, a pair of thick boots, four pairs of stockings, four flannel shirts, a blouse, a looking glass, a can of peaches, a bottle of cough-mixture, a button-stick, chalk, razor and strop, a Bible, a small volume of Shakespere, and writing utensils," in addition to a "tailor's shop," usually made of leather or cloth and "containing needles, pins, thread, buttons, and scissors." He also carried a rubber blanket and a woolen blanket and "a belt bout the body, which held a cartridge-box and bayonet, a cross-belt, also a haversack and tin drinking cup, a canteen." The cartridge-box held forty rounds of ammunition and the haversack three days' rations of "salt junk, hardtack, sugar and coffee." Altogether a load to challenge a mule.

There was an air of excitement, a feeling akin to a sudden unexpected holiday, a welcome break in the humdrum monotony of everyday living. And that feeling was very much in evidence that morning as 35,000 men in their colorful uniforms, carry-

THE FIRST BULL RUN

ing the stiff new flags clinging to their shiny staffs, marched off to battle with bands blaring and drums rolling. They knew nothing of wars or battles or any of the realities of actual combat. They expected to march for a few days and then line up somewhere in formation and shoot at the enemy from afar. Then when the Southerners ran back to Richmond it would be over and they could all go home as heroes. So they went to war as if to a picnic.

After a few days of marching in the brutal heat and choking dust, however, many of these civilian-soldiers began to have second thoughts about the glorious adventure ahead of them. "My canteen banged against my bayonet," one recruit noted, "both tin cup and bayonet badly interfered with the butt of my musket, while my cartridge-box and haversack were constantly flopping up and down." Blistered feet and aching muscles soon dictated that loads had to be lightened, so various pieces of equipment were surreptitiously dropped along the way. Thus would they learn the hard way—by experience.

In command of this ragged mass of men marching out of Washington was Irvin McDowell, a native of Ohio recently promoted to brigadier general of volunteers. A graduate of the U. S. Military Academy, McDowell was forty-three years old, a robust, heavy-set man with dark cropped hair and an iron-gray beard. He had served creditably in the Mexican War in staff positions, but had never commanded a large body of troops in the field. A quiet, introverted person who neither smoked nor drank, he was too reserved to be popular with his fellow officers, and definitely not the type to inspire men. Still he was a professional and as such recognized the weaknesses of his raw recruits. He did not want to fight until the men had been trained sufficiently to at least act like soldiers rather than civilians. "This is not an army," he told his superiors. "It will take a long time to make an army." But the times were against McDowell. The enlistments of most of the three-month volunteers was about up and the people of the North became impatient. "Forward to Richmond" screamed the newspaper headlines. And the government listened to the voice of the people. McDowell was ordered to move against a lesser Confederate force at Manassas, Virginia, about twenty-five miles southwest of Washington. To be sure, there was another

Confederate force to the west in the Shenandoah Valley, but it was to be pinned down by other Federal troops and thus prevented from reinforcing the Confederates at Manassas. "You are green, it is true," President Lincoln told the reluctant McDowell, "but they are green also."

And green they were. A few days after the firing at Fort Sumter, Virginia seceded from the Union. In Richmond there was dancing in the streets and bonfires burned to celebrate the historic event. Cannon were dragged by hand from the state arsenal to Capitol Square to fire a salute. The new Confederate flag fluttered proudly atop the capitol building. Virginians by the thousands flocked to the newly opened recruiting stations, fearful the fighting would end before they could play a part in it. Then in May the Confederate Congress, in session at Montgomery, Alabama, voted to move the Confederate capital to Richmond. Now the city underwent a dramatic change. When hundreds of regiments from farther south streamed in, Richmond took on the appearance of a vast military camp. At night the glow from thousands of campfires lit the sky. One observer noted, "One of the remarkable features of the times is that men of all classes and conditions, of all occupations and professions, are of one mind."

Although a Richmond newspaper could bluster, "There is one wild shout of fierce resolve to capture Washington City, at all and every human hazard," that was not the immediate objective of the new government. If the South could not secede from the Union peacefully, then it was determined to defend every acre of territory and maintain its independence to the last. As Confederate President Davis proclaimed: "All we ask is to be left alone." With this philosophy there was nothing to be gained by invading the North. Rather, the South wanted to exploit the advantages of a defensive posture, which would require fewer men and allow it to use its interior, or shorter, lines of communications and supply to best advantage. In addition, all the various government departments, as well as an army, had to be created, organized, and staffed to carry on a war, while at the same time a government had to be set up to pass laws governing what was hoped would be a new nation.

So thousands of young men streamed into Richmond to prepare to defend their independence, and like their counterparts in Washington, their uniforms exhibited an amazing variety. The various state militia colors mixed with fancy homemade uniforms, while some regiments had nothing but civilian clothes. Some of the higher ranking officers still wore the dress of the United States Army. And like the Northerners, the new recruits posed stiffly for portraits, followed the bands down the springtime streets, waved to the cheering girls, and set about, they thought, getting the war over with in a hurry. As one lady recorded in her diary, "There was much music and mustering and marching, much cheering and flying of flags, much firing of guns and all that sort of thing."

With Richmond now the Confederate capital, the area of Manassas, about seventy-five miles to the north, became strategically important to the defense of the city. The central point was Manassas Junction, a small railroad settlement consisting of a handful of decrepit buildings scattered carelessly about the railroad crossing. Here two railroads joined. The Orange & Alexandria, running north and south, connected with both Washington and Richmond; and the Manassas Gap Railroad, which extended westward through the Blue Ridge mountains to the rich, fertile valley of the Shenandoah. There were many good roads also, east and west, north and south, the main one being the Warrenton Turnpike, which led through the town of Centreville to Alexandria and Washington. The surrounding area was a gently rolling country of soft ridges, small farms, rail fences, crooked creeks, and quiet woods. About midway between Manassas and Centreville, Bull Run Creek meandered peacefully through the plains, the trees along its banks forming a leafy tunnel with the sun sifting through to form lacy gold patterns on the water, while picturesque arched bridges spanned it.

In June the South moved to protect this vital point. In command was Brigadier General P. G. T. Beauregard, hero of the firing on Fort Sumter. A

In the wake of Fort Sumter, the pressure on Lieutenant General Winfield Scott—shown here with his staff—became intense. The Union must strike back, put down the Rebellion. (NA)

First Washington must be made secure and troops brought in from the North.
Benjamin F. Butler's occupation of Relay House on the vital Baltimore & Ohio
ensured that. (USAMHI)

classmate of McDowell's, his last United States Army assignment had been as Superintendent of the Military Academy at West Point, New York. A small, graceful man in his early forties, Beauregard was a proud Creole from Louisiana who had distinguished himself in the Mexican War as a staff officer but, like McDowell, had never commanded a large body of troops in the field. Outspoken and critical of others, yet sensitive to criticism himself, he generally found it easier to make enemies than friends. But he too was a professional, and now with about 22,000 raw civilian-soldiers he set his line of defense along Bull Run. Although the creek itself was a formidable obstacle to any attacking force with its steep wooded banks, there were many fords and two bridges to be defended. On his right flank he destroyed the railroad bridge at Union Mills; built fortifications at McLean's, Blackburn's,

and Mitchell's fords; and stationed other forces at Ball's Ford, Lewis Ford, and the Stone Bridge on the Warrenton Turnpike, his extreme left flank. At Manassas Junction itself massive fortifications were erected running out in different directions from the little station. And across Bull Run he established advance guard posts at Centreville and Fairfax Court House and several strategic crossroads to warn of the approach of the enemy. Sixty miles away to the west across the mountains sat another force under Brigadier General Joseph E. Johnston. If Beauregard was outnumbered and attacked, he hoped to be reinforced by Johnston's troops. They would come on the cars of the Manassas Gap Railroad.

While these preparations were being made, the recruits were constantly marshaled and drilled in a desperate attempt to give them some training be-

With men of the 7th New York and other regiments garrisoning the camps around Washington, the capital was safe. That done, it was time to press the war and end the Rebellion. Within weeks these boys of '61 would become men in battle. (WRHS)

behind Bull Run. McDowell spent the next two days probing for a weak spot in the Confederate line. A reconnaissance in force was repulsed in the center at Mitchell's and Blackburn's fords, and no suitable terrain for attack appeared on the right. On the Confederate left, however, two unguarded fords, Popular and Sudley, were discovered. A crossing here would put the troops on the Sudley road, which led to the Warrenton Turnpike near the Stone House, and behind the Confederate left.

So on the afternoon of July 20, McDowell issued his battle order for the attack the next morning. His plan was simple but sound. Realizing the center of the Confederate line was too strong for a frontal attack by inexperienced troops, he ordered just a feint there, and then a long flanking march to the right to Sudley and Popular fords to circle and crumple the enemy left. Although McDowell could not know it, the two-day delay in preparing his plan was to prove fatal. Even as he issued his orders the first of Johnston's troops from the valley arrived on the railroad cars at the Junction. When they all got there the Confederates would have about 32,000 men.

Word that the battle would be fought the next day, a Sunday, quickly reached Washington and hundreds of people made frantic preparations to get there to see it. "Every carriage, gig, wagon, and hack has been engaged by people going out to see the fight," wrote an English newspaper reporter. "The French cooks and hotelkeepers, by some occult process of reasoning, have arrived at the conclusion that they must treble the prices of their wines and of the hampers of provisions" the people were ordering to take with them. "Before the battle," wrote a congressman from Ohio, "the hopes of the people and of their representatives are very elated and almost jocosely festive."

The next morning the road to Centreville jammed with nervous horses and handsome carriages, pretty ladies in bright crinoline dresses carrying picnic baskets filled with cool wines and tasty snacks. Senators and congressmen, foreign digni-

fore the battle they knew must come. Yet the camps, like the ones in the North, had a gay, festive atmosphere about them, with constant visitors at all hours of the day and night. In them could be found well-prepared meals, "caddies of tea, barrels of sugar, and many articles better suited for a picnic or a party in a summer house than to soldiers in the field." A young lady visitor wrote that they "were able during those rallying days of June to drive frequently to visit 'the boys' in camp, timing the expeditions to include battalion drill and dress parade, and taking tea afterward in the different tents. Then were the gala days of war, and our proud hosts hastened to produce home dainties dispatched from far-away plantations."

Such was life in the Confederate camps when McDowell left Washington that July 16. Beauregard received word at once that he was coming from a female spy in Washington. Not that it was any secret anyway—everyone in Washington and in the Army knew where they were going. Beauregard immediately requested that Johnston's troops in the valley be sent to him. Two days later the Union Army concentrated on the heights of Centreville overlooking the plains of Manassas as the Confederate outposts fell back to their main line

The first move was to occupy Alexandria, Virginia, just across the Potomac from Washington. Confederate flags flying over the city taunted Lincoln, and on May 24 Colonel Elmer Ellsworth led his Fire Zouaves, now the 11th New York, across the Potomac. (USAMHI)

There Ellsworth saw a Rebel banner flying above the Marshall House. He personally went to the roof and removed it from the staff still visible. On his way to the ground floor, he was met by the house's proprietor, who murdered him on the spot. Ellsworth became the nation's first great martyr, and Lincoln grieved sorely for his dead young friend. (USAMHI)

With Winfield Scott too old to take active field command, a member of his staff, Irvin McDowell, was elevated to brigadier general and given the unenviable task of molding an army and advancing to meet the enemy in Virginia. (USAMHI)

taries, bureaucrats, and reporters, dressed in their light summer clothing and carrying spyglasses and revolvers and flasks of Bourbon, rushed to Virginia to watch the great event, greeting friends, laughing and joking.

To the men in the Union ranks the occasion was not so festive, however. Since two-thirty that morning the flanking march had been taking place under bright moonlight. Across the Turnpike, over Cub Run Creek, through the woods and fields, heading for the Sudley fords. About three hours later, as the first gray streaks of dawn turned the landscape from brown to green, they heard the roar of a Union cannon near the Stone Bridge shatter the early quiet. The first major battle of the

Civil War had begun. By seven o'clock they should have been crossing Bull Run at the fords, but these civilians in uniform could not march that fast. They were still more than two hours away, and already the heat was oppressive. Now they were hot and tired, the fancy uniforms covered with choking dust. Even though the maneuver was already several hours behind schedule, the recruits still straggled after ripe blackberries, stopped for a refreshing drink, or just rested in the shade of the trees. It was about nine-thirty before they reached the fords, and then a Confederate officer high atop a signal tower spotted the glint of the sun on a brass cannon. The surprise was lost.

Quickly the Confederates swung their left flank back to Chinn Ridge behind the Stone House and rushed up reinforcements to counter the threat. Shortly after ten o'clock the Union troops came charging out of the woods into the fields on either side of the Sudley road and drove the Confederates back across the Turnpike to a new position on the plateau around the Henry and Robinson houses. The battle had opened with frightening reality. Yellow sheets of flame flashed along both lines as regiment after regiment exploded into action with a metallic roar. Gigantic crashes of artillery split the air. Shells screamed overhead, exploding in clouds of earth, horses, and men. The noise roared to a crescendo that left men dazed and confused, as the fighting surged back and forth, the issue in doubt, into the afternoon.

On a hill just below Centreville overlooking the plains of Manassas, the carriages from Washington were drawn up as if at a country horse race. Surprisingly, their presence did not seem to bother the troops who saw them. "Near Cub Run we saw carriages and barouches which contained civilians who had driven out from Washington to witness the operation," one soldier remembered. "We thought it wasn't bad idea to have the great men from Washington come out to see us thrash the Rebs." The visitors had a panoramic view of the lovely wooded country, dotted with green fields and cleared lands. According to one observer, "undulating lines of forest marked the course of the streams which intersected it and gave by their variety of color and shading an additional charm to the landscape which, enclosed in a framework of blue and purple hills, softened into violet in the extreme distance, presented one of the most agreeable

*The engineer company of the 8th New York in Arlington, Virginia, in June
1861. Photograph by Brady or an assistant.* (LC)

*Colonel Ambrose Burnside and officers of the 1st Rhode Island Infantry formed
a part of McDowell's developing army.* (USAMHI)

Men of the 1st Rhode Island at Camp Sprague, outside Washington, well trained and ready. (LC)

displays of simple pastoral woodland scenery that could be conceived." Somehow it was difficult to believe that men would actually shoot at and kill each other across this beautiful scene. But then the woods echoed to the roar of cannon, thin lines of dirty gray haze marked the angry muttering of musketry, white puffs of smoke burst high above the treetops, bayonets flashed in the glaring sun, and clouds of dust shifted constantly back and forth across the landscape. One lady spectator with an opera glass "was quite beside herself when an unusually heavy discharge roused the current of her blood—'That is splendid. Oh, my! Is not that first-rate? I guess we will be in Richmond this time tomorrow.'"

All afternoon the battle lines surged back and forth across the plateau, around the Henry House and the Robinson House, on Chinn Ridge, and along the Turnpike as men died by the hundreds in the woods, in the fields, on the banks of Bull Run, in a nightmare battle of mistakes fought by untrained volunteers led by inexperienced officers. Then when the last of Johnston's fresh Confed-

erate troops reached the field late in the afternoon, because the Federal force had failed to hold them in the Shenandoah Valley as planned, McDowell realized any chance of victory was gone and ordered a withdrawal. The exhausted troops started an orderly retreat from the field. The battle was over. "There was no confusion or panic then," one soldier remembered, but the men cursed their generals because they did not have fresh reinforcements as the enemy did. The orderly retreat quickly turned to confusion and then panic when the Confederates pursued, while the civilian spectators and their carriages and buggies created a frenzied jam among the army wagons, caissons, guns, and ambulances. "Infantry soldiers on mules and draft horses with the harness clinging to their heels, as much frightened as their riders," wrote a reporter. "Negro servants on their masters' chargers; ambulances crowded with unwounded soldiers; wagons swarming with men who threw out the contents in the road to make room, grinding through a shouting, screaming mass of men on foot who were literally yelling with rage at every

The camp of the 1st Minnesota, near Edwards Ferry, Maryland. They were
eager to march south and put down the Rebellion. (MHS)

The 2d Michigan came a long way to be in on the one battle that would surely
end the war. (THE BURTON HISTORICAL COLLECTION, DETROIT PUBLIC LIBRARY)

McDowell marched his arriving regiments across the Long Bridge and others leading from Washington to the Virginia side, and trained and organized his army in and around Arlington. (USAMHI)

He made his headquarters in the stately mansion, Arlington House, that, until a few weeks before, had been the home of Robert E. Lee. Mrs. Lee was still there when he moved in, and he took great care not to discomfort her. Here he planned his campaign. (USAMHI)

halt." No longer under any effective control, many of the soldiers headed for Washington, a confused mob with little semblance of order or discipline. By sundown it was a question of whether or not they should try to make a stand at Centreville. McDowell decided against it. "The condition of our artillery and its ammunition," he reported, "the want of food for the men, and the utter disorganization and demoralization of the mass of the army seemed to admit of no alternative but to fall back."

For miles the roads leading into Washington became strewn with the paraphernalia of war—caps, coats, blankets, rifles, canteens, haversacks. "I saw the beaten, foot-sore, spongy-looking soldiers," a reporter wrote, "officers and all the *debris* of the army filing through mud and rain, forming in crowds in front of the spirit stores." Muddy, hungry, and scared, they staggered through the streets begging food and buying liquor, dropping in exhaustion on porches, lawns, and sidewalks. Many of the younger officers, completely demoralized, filled the hotel barrooms and cheap saloons. One of the civilian casualties who walked forlornly back to Washington was a photographer, already noted for his portraits, who would later become famous, Mathew Brady. He and his assistants had lost the wagon with his camera and all his equipment in the panic, or so he claimed.

And on the plains of Manassas the soul-searing moans of the wounded and dying echoed through the still night air. Motionless forms covered the ground in grotesque positions, as if someone had carelessly heaved them from a wagon. The Federals suffered almost 3,000 casualties in killed, wounded, and missing; the Confederates almost 2,000. All through the night the stretcher-bearers, doctors, friends, and even relatives worked tirelessly among the dead and wounded, the flickering flames from the candles and lanterns casting weird shadows among the dark, silent trees.

"The capture of Washington seems now to be inevitable," a frightened government official declared. "The rout, overthrow, and utter demoralization of the whole army is complete." This, of course, was an exaggeration. A more sober, realistic view of the situation was made by another close observer of the events. "We have undertaken to make war without in the least knowing how," he wrote. "We have made a false start and we have discovered it. It only remains to start afresh." A

Old General Robert Patterson was to keep the Confederate Army of Joseph E. Johnston occupied in the Shenandoah Valley so that it could not reinforce Confederates around Manassas when McDowell attacked them. If Patterson failed, McDowell could be in grave danger. (USAMHI)

lesson had been learned—a hard lesson. It was not going to be a short, easy war. The politicians now realized that all the powerful resources of the North would have to be organized and directed in preparation for a long, bitter struggle. And the war was not going to be won by the theatrical heroics of untrained three-month volunteers and comic opera officers. Large armies would have to be raised, trained, and equipped, with the enlistments for three years or the duration, not three months. Washington would have to be adequately protected against the slightest chance of capture, for if the capital fell there would be no United States as such.

Charles P. Stone, inspector general of the District of Columbia militia, would command one of Patterson's brigades. (USAMHI)

Manassas," a clerk in the War Department in Richmond recorded in his diary. The articulate and observant wife of an aide to President Davis put it more succinctly. "That victory did nothing but send us off into a fool's paradise of conceit, and it roused the manhood of the Northern people." Indeed, there was much indignant criticism of the generals because they did not immediately follow up the victory by marching into Washington right then and there to end the war. But the fact was, as General Johnston tried patiently to explain, that "the Confederate army was more disorganized by victory than that of the United States by defeat." In addition, the men were near exhaustion, they were short on rations and ammunition, the raw troops lacked proper discipline and training, stragglers were numerous, the Federals had erected powerful fortifications around Washington, and the broad Potomac River would have had to be crossed. Also, many of the soldiers now believed the war was just about over anyway. "Exaggerated ideas of the victory among our troops cost us more men than the Federal army lost by defeat," Johnston reported. "Many left the army—not to return." Despite this premature complacency, the South was determined to resist to the bitter end, thus assuring the nation of a long, bloody struggle.

A young lady from Virginia wrote after Manassas:

> A few days later we rode over the field. The trampled grass had begun to spring again, and wild flowers were blooming around carelessly made graves. From one of these imperfect mounds of clay I saw a hand extended. . . . Fences were everywhere thrown down; the undergrowth of the woods was riddled with shot; here and there we came upon spiked guns, disabled gun-carriages, cannon balls, blood-stained blankets, and dead horses. We were glad enough to turn away and gallop homeward.

For the men in the armies, however, that homeward turn lay distant years ahead in the uncertain future.

While the North thus learned a vital lesson from this first major defeat, the South seemingly was lulled into a false sense of security by the victory. "We are resting on our oars after the victory at

On July 16, 1861, McDowell's army moved out of its camps on the road toward Manassas and the Rebel Army. This image of the 8th New York was taken that same day as they prepared for the march. (MJM)

As they marched they passed historic Falls Church, where George Washington had worshipped. (USAMHI)

They passed by Taylor's Tavern, outside Falls Church, Virginia. (WRHS)

*On July 17 the Federals skirmished with the enemy around Fairfax
Court House.* (NA)

*And the next day McDowell occupied Centreville, until that morning a
fortified Confederate camp.* (USAMHI)

From Centreville, McDowell sent Colonel
Daniel Tyler forward with his division to
reconnoiter the enemy positions along Bull
Run. He was ordered not to bring on an
engagement. (USAMHI)

Instead Tyler and his chief lieutenant,
Colonel Israel B. Richardson, became
engaged in a hot fight at Blackburn's Ford,
and were repulsed. (PENNSYLVANIA—
MOLLUS COLLECTION, WAR LIBRARY AND
MUSEUM, PHILADELPHIA)

Three days later, McDowell launched his battle plan, sending his marching columns toward Bull Run, shown here in a July 1862 image by Timothy O'Sullivan. (LC)

McDowell's coming was detected well in advance by men in signal towers built and supervised by Beauregard's signal officer, Captain Edward Porter Alexander, a Georgian who graduated from West Point four years before. He appears here in his cadet uniform, probably in 1857. (LSU)

By contrast, McDowell's signal officer, Captain A. J. Myer, spent most of the day unsuccessfully attempting to launch an observation balloon from which to spy enemy movements. (LC)

July 21, 1861, was Brigadier General David Hunter's fifty-ninth birthday. As he led McDowell's flanking column that was to assail the Confederate left via Sudley Ford, he received a birthday present in the form of a serious wound that put him out of the battle. (USAMHI)

Hunter's men passed the Thornton House, shown here in a March 1862 image by George N. Barnard. (LC)

Then they passed the Sudley Springs Ford and crossed over Bull Run to move toward Beauregard. Photograph by Barnard, March 1862. (USAMHI)

Sudley Church, above Bull Run. The Federals swarmed past it on their way to the first major engagement of the war. (WRHS)

Burnside led his brigade in the initial assaults against Confederate defenders on Mathews' Hill. (USAMHI)

One of Burnside's regiments, the 2d Rhode Island Infantry, was the first of Hunter's column to engage the enemy. They fought bravely, even after their colonel was killed and many of their officers put out of the fight. They are shown at drill here in a photograph taken several months following the battle. (USAMHI)

*Colonel Andrew Porter was next into the fray with his brigade. He felt that
Burnside had attacked with "perhaps, too hasty vigor," but he immediately
moved to Burnside's support and took command of the division after Hunter's
wound. Porter stands at center in this image taken prior to the battle.* (P-M)

*The 8th New York, perhaps the most resplendent of regiments in McDowell's
army, went into battle with Porter.* (TERENCE P. O'LEARY)

They were fighting an army led by the hero of Fort Sumter, P. G. T. Beauregard, now a brigadier general in the Confederate Army. (LC)

William Weir's house Liberia was not far from the home of Wilmer McLean, where Beauregard made his headquarters. McLean himself was so disturbed by the war's coming to his very doorstep that he moved where he thought it would never find him again. Appomattox. (WRHS)

Major Samuel Jones was Beauregard's chief of artillery, but, in fact, Confederate cannon would play a minor role in the battle unfolding. (LC)

George Barnard's March 1862 photograph of the battlefield at Bull Run, looking over the Warrenton Turnpike. (USAMHI)

The man who stopped the initial assault by Hunter's column, and several
succeeding attacks, thus buying time for Beauregard to rush troops to the
threatened left, was another veteran of Fort Sumter. Brigadier General Nathan
G. Evans, called "Shanks" by friends, was a rough, uncouth braggart whose
orderly always stood behind him with a "barrelita" of whiskey. He would later
claim that he alone, with the aid of the Almighty "and a few private
gentlemen," won the battle. (SOUTH CAROLINIANA LIBRARY)

A few of those "private gentlemen" who held the line with Evans. Major
Roberdeau Wheat's battalion of Louisiana Zouaves, commonly called Wheat's
Tigers. They are photographed here in New Orleans in 1861. (LC)

As the battle between Hunter's and Evans's troops developed, Brigadier General Samuel P. Heintzelman's division came into the fight. He, too, would be wounded, but acted heroically in attempting to hold his command together in the confusion of its first fight. (USAMHI)

Soldiers like this rugged-looking woodsman from the 4th Michigan went into the action in Orlando Willcox's brigade of Heintzelman's division. The Michiganders fought like demons, the first Westerners to do battle in the East. (HP)

While the battle raged on the Confederate left, Colonel William T. Sherman led his brigade across a ford near the Stone Bridge in the center of the line and assailed Evans's depleted command. Sherman is shown here as a major general in an 1865 photo. (NYHS)

Colonel Michael Corcoran, center, and officers of the 69th New York crossed with Sherman. (MJM)

So did Colonel James Cameron of the 79th New York. The son of Secretary of War Simon Cameron, he would not recross Bull Run. He died in battle. (USAMHI)

Battery E, 3d United States Artillery, commanded by Captain Romeyn B. Ayres. Called Sherman's Battery because it was formerly led by Thomas W. Sherman, this unit was greatly feared by the Confederates because of its mighty Parrot rifles. This image shows the battery on July 24, 1861, in Washington, three days after the battle. (BRUCE GIMELSON)

Erasmus D. Keyes, like Sherman, a colonel of a brigade in Tyler's division, also crossed Bull Run, but played a lesser role in the fighting along the Warrenton Road. (USAMHI)

The 3d Connecticut of Keyes's brigade. Their gallantry, he believed, "was never surpassed." (LC)

The fighting raged first around the Matthews' House on Matthews' Hill, where the advancing Federals slowly forced Evans and his outnumbered command back to the Warrenton Turnpike. (USAMHI)

Evans's command retreated past the Stone House on the Warrenton Road, shown in this March 1862 photo by Barnard and James F. Gibson, and up the slopes of Henry Hill. (USAMHI)

And on Henry Hill the fighting raged for most of the rest of the day. Soon after Evans's arrival, sharp fighting took place on the right of the hill near the Robinson House, where Sherman attacked the line held by yet another veteran of Fort Sumter . . . (USAMHI)

. . . Colonel Wade Hampton, commanding Hampton's Legion. Hampton himself was wounded, but he held his line. (VM)

*Lieutenant Thomas M. Logan of Hampton's
Legion played a conspicuous part in the fighting
around the Robinson House. In February 1865
he would become a brigadier general.* (MC)

*Colonel Francis S. Bartow of Georgia exposed
himself recklessly on the battlefield in leading his
brigade against the Federals. It cost him his life.*
(VM)

The fighting became even more fierce in the center of the Confederate line on Henry Hill. There Brigadier General Barnard E. Bee of South Carolina fought desperately against several enemy assaults. His very presence on the field was a harbinger of victory, for he and his brigade had been sent to Beauregard from the Shenandoah. Johnston had eluded Patterson, and even as the battle raged, more of his regiments were on their way. Bee would fall with a mortal wound, but not before bestowing on another of Johnston's brigade commanders an immortal sobriquet. Attempting to rally his men after a charge, he pointed to a brigade of Virginians behind them and said . . . (VM)

. . . "There stands Jackson like a stone wall." It was the brigade of General Thomas J. Jackson, shown here in a 1855 daguerreotype. A man of inordinate peculiarities, he would become the greatest legend of the war. (NATIONAL PORTRAIT GALLERY, SMITHSONIAN INSTITUTION, WASHINGTON, D.C.)

Officers of the Washington Artillery of New Orleans, who helped Jackson stand like a wall. They are brothers, Miles Taylor Squires, Samuel Smith Squires, and Charles W. Squires. (W. H. T. SQUIRES, JR.)

The battle raged for hours on Henry Hill, often around the Henry House itself, where poor old widow Henry, who refused to leave, was blown out of her bed by a shell that severed her foot and mortally wounded her. An 1862 view by Barnard. (USAMHI)

In desperate fighting on the forward slope of Henry Hill, Captain James B. Ricketts of Battery I, 1st United States Artillery, was wounded four times and captured along with all six of his cannon and forty-nine horses. He would recover to become a brigadier general in less than a year. (USAMHI)

Nearly as badly used up as Ricketts's battery was Battery D, 5th United States Artillery. Captain Charles Griffin obeyed orders to take it nearly to the brow of the left of Henry Hill. Once there, Griffin mistook an enemy regiment dressed in blue for his own troops, and discovered the mistake too late. All of his cannoneers were shot down and only three of his six guns escaped, and two of them had to be abandoned later. (P-M)

Former Governor of Virginia William "Extra Billy" Smith, now colonel of the 49th Virginia, took a place in the Confederate line just in time to assist in the destruction of Ricketts's and Griffin's batteries. He is shown here in the uniform of a brigadier general, probably in 1863. (USAMHI)

*Patterson's failure in the Shenandoah allowed Brigadier General Joseph E.
Johnston to bring almost his entire army to assist Beauregard. Johnston arrived
on the field and took overall command of operations the day before the battle.
This rare photo of Johnston has never before been published.* (VM)

*The unexpected arrival of Johnston's last brigade to reach the field, led by
Colonel Arnold Elzey, threw McDowell's right flank into a panic.* (VM)

Colonel Oliver O. Howard, commanding a brigade of Heintzelman's division, was at the right flank when Elzey arrived. Heroic efforts by him brought few results, and before he received orders to retire, his men were doing it on their own. He stands at left here, shortly after his promotion to brigadier general. (WRHS)

While his right crumbled into a disorganized retreat, McDowell found his left threatened when Confederates like Colonel Micah Jenkins led the 5th South Carolina across Bull Run. There was little left for McDowell but a general retreat. For Jenkins there would be a brigadier's promotion a year and a day later. (LC)

With the enemy on the run, Brigadier General Milledge L. Bonham's South Carolina brigade took over the pursuit. He would leave the Army in a few months to go to the Confederate Congress, then serve as governor of his state, then don his uniform again in the war's last days. (VM)

Colonel Joseph B. Kershaw spearheaded the pursuit with his 2d South Carolina and, along with old Edmund Ruffin, helped turn retreat into rout when they managed to disable the main bridge over Cub Run that led to safety for the Federals. (SHC)

McDowell's chief of staff, Colonel James B. Fry, made extraordinary efforts to control the retreat, but to no avail. Most of the army did not stop until it reached Centreville, and many soldiers fled all the way to Washington. (P-M)

McDowell had a reserve division commanded by Colonel Dixon S. Miles stationed at Centreville, but Miles took no part in the battle. In fact, he got drunk and could not give coherent orders to his officers. (USAMHI)

Miles's soldiers, like flamboyant Colonel Louis Blenker, shown here with men of the 8th New York, chafed at being left out of the battle. Standing just left of Blenker is Lieutenant Colonel Julius Stahel. In two weeks Blenker will be a brigadier . . . (NA)

. . . and Stahel will get his first star in November. These German and Hungarian officers were enormously popular, and the Lincoln Administration hoped that giving them high command would encourage the thousands of their nationality in the North to enlist. It also put great responsibility in the hands of men with little ability. (USAMHI)

Another popular foreigner, Colonel Frederick G. D'Utassy (third from the right) and the staff of his 39th New York, the "Garibaldi Guard." They, too, sat out the battle at Centreville. (MJM)

And for some who missed the fight, the war was already over. The 4th New Jersey and its officers shown here mustered out of service ten days after the battle. (USAMHI)

*Still, there were many heroes of the battle. One was the son of amateur
photographer—and now quartermaster general of the Union
Army—Montgomery C. Meigs. John R. Meigs served as a volunteer aide to
Colonel Israel Richardson. "A braver and more gallant young man was never
in any service," said Richardson. Here his father photographed him and his
sister on his return from the battle, perhaps looking at the elder Meigs's own
stereo photographs. Three years later, in the Shenandoah, Confederate
guerrillas would kill him.* (LC)

The famous "Sherman Battery" came through the battle with all of its guns, and was the object of much curiosity afterward. Here, again, it was photographed in Washington. (MHS)

For many of the Bull Run regiments, defeat or not, there was a triumphal welcome when they returned home to muster out of service. Many of these were three- and nine-month regiments. They will be replaced by regiments enlisted for three years or the war. The North now knew that it would not be over quickly. The return of the 1st Michigan for mustering out in Detroit, August 7, 1861. (BURTON HISTORICAL COLLECTION, DETROIT PUBLIC LIBRARY)

For many of the men of Bull Run, however, there was no welcome home. Hundreds were captured and sent south to makeshift prisons. Many, like these men of Corcoran's 69th New York, were placed in Castle Pinckney at Charleston. They kept their spirits high, lightheartedly decorating their quarters with a sign reading "Music Hall 444 Broadway." (USAMHI)

Men of Cameron's 79th New York suffer the same fate. (VM)

And Irvin McDowell will not go unscathed. Not entirely to blame for his loss, still he must be replaced. A new general from the west comes to take over, a man with Napoleonic pretensions and the nickname "Little Mac," Major General George B. McClellan. For the next year the war in the East will be his war. He stands at center here, hand in blouse, with the principal generals of the Army in August 1861. From the left they are Brigadier General William F. Smith, Brigadier General William B. Franklin, Heintzelman, Porter, McDowell, McClellan, Major General George McCall, Brigadier General Don Carlos Buell, Blenker, Brigadier General Silas Casey, and Brigadier General Fitz John Porter. They pose with hats on . . . (LC)

. . . and with hats off. (AMERICANA IMAGE GALLERY)

But many will never pose again. Barnard's 1862 photograph of the rude graves of Federal soldiers buried by the Confederates at Bull Run. (KA)

Barnard's 1862 image of a "hecatomb" where 100 Union soldiers sleep below the Sudley Church. For them the war was over. (KA)

The Navies Begin

VIRGIL CARRINGTON JONES

Improvisation and innovative technology clash on the water

EVEN BEFORE the Confederate triumph at Bull Run, the Civil War enhanced the stature of Stephen Russell Mallory, Confederate Secretary of the Navy. He took office and accepted the seemingly impossible task of sending against the enemy a fleet that did not exist. At the end of 1861, however, he had things so well organized that he was posing a threat which caused the Union to try to find effective ways to stop him.

Little about Mallory as an individual explained why the President of the new-born Confederate States of America, Jefferson Davis, so quickly singled him out for the job he held. He was rather naive and had dabbled at various occupations— town marshal, real estate dealer, admiralty lawyer, county judge, customs collector, newspaper correspondent, political leader. At age twenty-four he had had a touch of soldiery in the Seminole War. And then, in 1851, he was elected to the United States Senate from Florida, serving in that capacity for ten years and rising in time to the chairmanship of the important Naval Affairs Committee, a responsibility that unquestionably drew Davis's attention to him.

As his record shows, he was in no sense a quitter. This was demonstrated in his wooing of a Spanish beauty who was bored by his manners at first, but later accepted his proposal of marriage. It was a trait that stood him in good stead when the burden of creating a navy was placed upon his shoulders. While participating in a losing cause, he strove so diligently to succeed that he helped revolutionize the field of naval science. Under his guidance, the Confederacy took part in history's first battle between ironclads, produced the first submarine to sink a ship, and developed the underwater mine or torpedo as an effective weapon of defense.

The war still was nearly two months away when Mallory took office, but the threat was strong. Ominously, the widely scattered ships of the Union began sailing homeward, some of them steering for southern ports. At the mouth of the Mississippi River, vessels passing up or downstream were searched. Floridians surprised and captured the United States Coast Survey schooner *Dana*.

Some of the seceded states demanded that Union ships within their ports be turned over to them. Among the commanders who refused to do so and fled with their vessels were John Newland Maffitt, later an outstanding Confederate naval officer, and David D. Porter, equally as staunch a Unionist.

Leaders who formed the nucleus of the Confederacy gathered in early February at Montgomery,

The U.S.S. Constitution, *symbol of past naval glory, and of an out-of-date United States fleet in 1861.* (LC)

Alabama. Even before the government was organized, a committee was named to summon "all such persons versed in naval affairs as they may deem advisable to consult with." Only a few United States Navy officers of high rank—five captains and four commanders—had "gone South" at this time, their action hinging on the secession of their respective states. Nevertheless, telegrams were immediately sent to all officers thought to be southern in their sympathy. The response was favorable. By June, a fifth of the officers so contacted had resigned, among them sixteen captains, thirty-four commanders, and seventy-six lieutenants.

One of these officers was Commander Raphael Semmes, a member of the Lighthouse Board at Washington and only a short period away from one of the most outstanding privateering careers in history. Another was John M. Brooke, already recognized for the banded guns of his own design he was having manufactured at the Tredegar Iron Works in Richmond. Still another was John Taylor Wood, Naval Academy instructor and grandson of President Zachary Taylor.

When the Confederate Navy was created by formal act, it was soon announced that it was to be headed by chubby-faced, side-whiskered Mallory. He took office immediately, heading a fleet that existed only on paper. He had little to draw from. The South possessed virtually no merchant bottoms, no large force of skilled mechanics, and only a few seamen, for seafaring pursuits were not a favorite among its people. It had only two navy yards, one at Pensacola, Florida, and one at Norfolk, Virginia; only three rolling mills, two in Tennessee and one in Georgia, the latter unfitted for heavy work; and no machine shops of superior workmanship. Its sole foundry capable of casting heavy guns was at Richmond, soon to replace Montgomery as the capital of the Confederacy. The only raw material available was standing timber. All else, including iron, would have to be acquired. Only seven steam war vessels had ever been built in the South, and the engines of only two of these had been contracted for in the states involved.

Confronting Mallory as Union Secretary of the Navy was Gideon Welles, described as a small-town politician. His task would be one of organization, for the fleet at his disposal was recognized as third in world power. It consisted of eighty-nine vessels, forty-two in commission, twenty-six available but not in commission, and twenty-one rated unserviceable. Although considered very slow, Welles took immediate action for the purchase of 136 vessels, to be altered and commissioned, and the construction of fifty-two others.

Abraham Lincoln's inauguration on March 4 added to the burden Mallory faced, for the new President announced a policy of reoccupying and holding the forts in the South. As the approach to the most important of these was by water, it meant the Confederacy must do something promptly about its deficiency in naval armament. Water mines were settled upon as the answer.

Along with the South's plans for a navy also came the original move for the training of personnel. At Montgomery on March 16, the Congress passed an act providing for a Confederate States Naval Academy, but it would be 1863 before steps actually were taken to bring such a facility into service. At this later period, an academy was actually set up in Richmond and the steamer *Patrick Henry,* formerly of the James River squadron, was used as a schoolship. The Union in the meantime took action to protect its important Naval Academy at Annapolis, Maryland. Because of its proximity to southern soil, it was transferred, along with its training ship, to Newport, Rhode Island.

On April 1, Commander Semmes, who had been sent North on a buying tour, detrained at Montgomery. He had had little success, finding no ships available which were suitable for service on the high seas. The only purchase he had made was a large amount of ordnance stores. Meanwhile, James D. Bullock, captain of the United States mail steamer *Bienville,* and another who had resigned to side with the South were dispatched to England to make arrangements for the construction of ships.

The fall of Fort Sumter was simultaneous with one of Lincoln's most important decisions, for on this same date, April 14, 1861, the sailing frigate *Sabine,* equipped with forty-four guns, began a blockade at Pensacola. Soon it would be extended along the entire southern coast—more than 3,500 miles, the longest ever attempted by any nation—and eventually would rank as one of the North's most effective steps of offense.

Two days later, Lincoln issued a call for 75,000 troops. A counter proclamation came from Presi-

The Navy Department in Washington, faced with the herculean task of building quickly a new navy to blockade the southern coast and conquer its rivers. To organize and run this mammoth undertaking, Lincoln selected . . . (LC)

dent Davis on April 17, an offer of letters of marque under the seal of the Confederate States against ships and property of the United States. This was a direct strike against the Union's extensive merchant fleet.

The seventeenth brought other important action. Virginia seceded, affording an answer as to what was to be done with the Gosport Navy Yard at Norfolk, one of the largest in the nation. For weeks, the North had been undecided, withholding action in the hope that Virginia would remain in the Union. When the state seceded, officials at Washington decided to abandon the yard. This was one of the greatest strokes of luck that Mallory would have in his efforts to build a navy.

While ships and buildings at the yard were set afire before they were abandoned, Southerners moved in time to salvage much of what was at hand. Six ships, among them the *Merrimack,* the drydock, large supplies of ammunition and food, and more than a thousand guns were recovered. Without these guns, the Confederacy would have had to wait for months to arm some of its posts. And on April 18, the *Sumter,* a passenger ship con-

verted into a raider, slipped out of the port of New Orleans. At its helm was Raphael Semmes, commencing the career that would afford him his place in history. Before the end of the war, he would capture 305 ships, bond ten of them and burn fifty-five, making a contribution in money and destruction valued at more than $5,000,000.

By May, the South had the nucleus of a navy— ten vessels carrying fifteen guns. Some had been seized, some purchased, and some were captured slavers. The Confederacy was not alone in its quest for additional craft. The United States was just as persistent and soon acquired every available steamer in Canada.

Mallory became more and more convinced that ironclad ships would help substantially in offsetting the South's fleet discrepancy. On May 8, he wrote: "I regard the possession of an iron-armored ship as a matter of the first necessity. Such a vessel at this time could traverse the entire coast of the United States, prevent all blockades, and encounter, with a fair prospect of success, their entire navy."

His reference to the blockade was at the moment no exaggeration. All along the Atlantic coast it

. . . a Connecticut newspaperman, Gideon Welles. He wore an ill-fitting wig, lacked humor, and proved to be one of the most capable and loyal members of Lincoln's Cabinet. (NA)

was mostly a matter of bluff. Lincoln realized this and appointed an overall commander to strengthen it. The assignment went to Commodore Silas H. Stringham, a born seaman and experienced officer. Almost at the same time, the North took steps to block the Mississippi River. They were encouraged by James B. Eads, a veteran shipbuilder thoroughly familiar with the western rivers, who came to Washington to propose blocking the Mississippi to commerce, thereby shutting off a main artery by which the Confederacy could get food, as well as an important route by which it could move cotton to sea. Commander John Rodgers, capable and

efficient, was assigned the task of developing a naval force along that major stream.

By July, Mallory was able to report:

The frigate *Merrimack* has been raised and docked at an expense of $6,000, and the necessary repairs to hull and machinery to place her in her former condition is estimated by experts at $450,000. The vessel would then be in the river, and by the blockade of the enemy's fleets and batteries rendered comparatively useless. It has, therefore, been determined to shield her completely with three-inch iron, placed at such angles as to render her ball-proof, to complete her at the earliest moment, to arm her with the heaviest ordnance, and to send her at once against the enemy's fleet. It is believed that thus prepared she will be able to contend successfully against the heaviest of the enemy's ships, and to drive them from Hampton Roads and the ports of Virginia.

The *Merrimack* was only one phase of the Confederacy's program to provide its navy with ironclad ships. As it was considered impracticable to purchase these in Europe, plans were pursued to build them in the waters of the South. Contracts were let for a supply of all classes of iron. In this connection, it was learned that the Union was preparing an ironclad fleet of gunboats at St. Louis, Missouri. The Navy Department at Richmond sent reliable mechanics to that city to obtain employment on the vessels and to report on their strength and fighting character, as well as the progress made on them. In time, this information was made available to Mallory, influencing him to concentrate on the defense of New Orleans against an attack from above rather than from the Gulf of Mexico.

The first attack would come elsewhere, however. By August, the North was ready to launch a naval blow against the South. So far as the blockade was concerned, the seat of troubles was at Hatteras on the North Carolina coast. Since May, it had developed into a haven for both runners and privateers, creating such a threat to northern commerce that newspapers referred to it as "a nest for pirates." Hampered by a succession of gales, a fleet for an expedition against Hatteras slowly assembled in

War of 1812 frigates like the Santee *and* Constitution *were still in service and totally unsuited for the war to come. They are shown here at Annapolis, Maryland, at the United States Naval Academy.* (USAMHI)

had suffered defeat in the Battle of Bull Run. Prisoners included 670 officers and men. Guns found in the forts had been a part of the armament made available to the Confederates on the abandonment of the Gosport Navy Yard.

The moral effect of the victory was most important, for there were indications that the South was moving ahead in its efforts to build a navy, as well as to arm its troops. The United States consul at London reported the Rebel agents, with more funds at their control than previously, were buying at random. He revealed that the ship *Bermuda* had sailed from England with a million-dollar cargo made up of cannon, rifles, powder, cartridges, and other munitions of war. Her destination was Savannah, Georgia.

Also, the South's shipbuilding program had been stepped up considerably. Construction of two warships, the *Arkansas* and the *Tennessee,* had been started at Memphis, while two others, the *Missis-*

Many of the personnel were even older and more out of date. Captain William B. Shubrick had been in the Navy since 1806 and served aboard the Constitution *in the War of 1812.* (USAMHI)

Flag Officer Charles Stewart, senior officer in the Navy, had been born in 1778, and commanded the Constitution *when Shubrick served aboard her. He was eighty-three years old when war broke out and still on the active list.* (NYHS)

Hampton Roads under the direction of Major General John E. Wool, commanding at Fort Monroe. Foremost among the vessels it consisted of were the flagship *Minnesota,* the *Wabash, Cumberland, Monticello, Pawnee,* and *Harriet Lane,* as well as three troop carriers, the steamers *Adelaide* and *George Peabody,* and the tug *Fanny.* The frigate *Susquehanna* would join it at its destination. On August 26, the ships started moving southward. At four o'clock the next afternoon, they were sighted off Hatteras.

Early on the morning of the twenty-eighth, the signal for a landing was given. The South had nothing on hand with which to combat such a fleet, and Forts Clark and Hatteras, defending the point, lowered their flags within a matter of hours. The surrender gave the North a foothold along the southern coast and put it in possession of the main passage to the North Carolina sounds. It was the first sizable victory for the Union since its troops *sippi* and the *Louisiana,* were under way at New Orleans. Lieutenant Bullock, meanwhile, was meeting with success in England. He had arranged for the building of two vessels, the *Florida* and the *Alabama,* that would eventually become grave threats to the North's ocean-going commerce. In addition, individual states were forming their own navies, later to be turned over to the Confederacy. South Carolina in March had prepared for sea the first ship she had launched since the Revolution.

As Mallory hurriedly pressed forward, October found the North ready for its second naval expedition. This time the destination was Port Royal Sound, a body of water on the coast of South Carolina. Early in the war, the Union Navy Department listed it as one of three points that would serve as bases from which to combat blockade running. So easily could it be defended that the Federals feared the Confederates would make it impregnable before it could be taken over.

Again the starting point was Hampton Roads. There, under the command of Commodore Samuel Francis du Pont, head of Lincoln's Naval Advisory Board, a fleet of fifty ships assembled. The expedition sailed on October 29 amid much secrecy. But within a matter of hours after the fleet started moving, the Confederacy's Acting Secretary of War, Judah P. Benjamin, was able to wire military authorities at Savannah that the destination was Port Royal. This warning did little good. The Confederates again had nothing to stop a powerful fleet. The forts at Port Royal quickly fell.

While the North now had two naval victories to its credit, it still aimed no decisive blow at the South. By November, the blockade runners were nearing the peak of their activity. Eight out of every nine were getting into port, picking their destinations at random and using every trick to avoid the blockaders. It was not long before lanterns went out of style among the Union vessels standing guard off the southern coast, for it was found these lights at night were like buoys to the ships trying to make shore. Meanwhile Mallory, by December, had a fleet he no longer could count on his fingers. Thirty-five ships and sailing craft of various classes and armaments had been equipped by the Confederacy. Twenty-one of these were steam vessels, most of them small and built for speed rather than power. A majority had fewer than five guns. Some were protected by bales of cotton. He had entered into thirty-two contracts for the construction of forty gunboats, floating batteries, and vessels of war. In addition, the Navy Department had vessels under construction at its own direction. Progress was made in other quarters. A powder mill, engine mill, boiler mill, machine shops, and ordnance workshops were erected. Also completed was a ropewalk capable of making all kinds of cordage, from a rope yard to a nine-inch cable, with a capacity of 8,000 yards a month.

At Washington, Navy Secretary Welles also had been busy. By December, the Union fleet consisted of 264 vessels, carrying 2,557 guns and manned by 22,000 seamen. But the imbalance between the two navies was not the point of interest at this stage of the war. Rather, attention focused on the blockade runners. They brought the guns and ammunition, the vital items needed to make the Confederacy's armies more formidable, more able to repeat their early victories. The runners would have to continue to bear this responsibility until the South could further expand its facilities. Mallory had started office with appropriations of only $17,300. In the first eighteen months of operations, he would have available $14,605,777.

In the offing, he gained a reputation of doing much with nothing. But time would bring a kaleidoscopic pattern as the Union armies marched southward and the Union fleets gave them much-needed support in times of desperation. And after the initial Union successes at Hatteras and Port Royal, the focus of attention, land and water, turned to the West.

But there was new blood, and wood, in the Navy as well. The U.S.S. Hartford
was a powerful 24-gun sloop launched in 1858, shown here after her
commissioning at the Boston Navy Yard in 1859. (LC)

And promising younger officers like David D.
Porter, son of an earlier naval hero and brother of
"Dirty Bill" Porter, who would serve on the
Mississippi. (USAMHI)

As in all navies in all times, Welles would find more than enough eager young officers hoping to see action after he retired the men now too old to command. (NAVAL HISTORICAL CENTER)

Sailors must be enlisted to crew the growing fleet. A naval recruiting station at the Battery in New York City. They advertised a bounty of $400 to those who would enlist. (WENDELL W. LANG, JR.)

Time did not allow the building of a complete fleet. To have a Union naval presence in the South's waters as soon as possible, Welles bought merchant steamers and even New York ferry boats like the Commodore Perry *and converted them quickly into river gunboats.* (USAMHI)

There was also the safety of the Naval Academy to consider. At Annapolis it was too exposed and vulnerable to Confederate sympathizers in Maryland. (USAMHI)

Welles moved it temporarily to Newport, Rhode Island, where it continued to produce officers for the Union, as this class in 1863. (RP)

And this group of stern-faced young Nelsons. (RP)

The midshipman of 1861 could affect a jaunty air, but many felt grave fears that there would not be enough action for them in this war. (USAMHI)

They learned the art of naval gunnery . . . (NA)

And practiced aboard the old Constitution, *which moved to Newport as well.*
(USAMHI)

One hundred miles to the south of Washington, another naval secretary grappled with the problems of creating a navy. Stephen R. Mallory of Florida displayed a talent for innovation which left his personal stamp on the whole course of Confederate naval operations. It was he who would implement the building of the first ironclad. (SHC)

A stroke of good fortune was the seizure of the Gosport Navy Yard at Norfolk, shown here in Timothy O'Sullivan's image taken in the spring of 1862 after its recapture. Battlefield artist Alfred R. Waud sits in the foreground. (USAMHI)

Captain French Forrest, a hero of the old United States Navy and himself sixty-five years old, was put in charge of salvaging the priceless equipment at Norfolk. (USAMHI)

Lieutenant John Mercer Brooke, shown here in United States uniform around 1852, went to work for Mallory developing the strong and powerful naval guns that would be a major addition to the new navy. He, too, was responsible for much of the concept for the new ironclad Virginia, *converted from the* Merrimack *found at Norfolk.* (GEORGE M. BROOKE)

Commander George N. Hollins, in prewar uniform, made the Confederate Navy's first capture, the St. Nicholas, *on the Potomac in June 1861. The next month Mallory sent him to oversee naval defenses at New Orleans.* (OCHM)

Raphael Semmes, another former officer in the United States Navy, went to the North before Sumter and actually purchased naval supplies for Mallory. Soon he would outfit and command the C.S.S. Sumter, *first of the South's great commerce raiders. This photograph was probably taken in England in 1864. Semmes rests his arm on an early Confederate flag.* (NAVAL PHOTOGRAPHIC CENTER)

Mallory depended on what was captured at United States installations at the war's outset. The Warrington Navy Yard at Pensacola yielded much, as well. This superb J. D. Edwards photograph, taken in April 1861, hints at what the Confederates seized. Row upon endless row of solid shot, ship's parts; and being refitted, the sidewheeler Fulton. *A previously unpublished image recently discovered.* (SHC)

The Confederacy, too, needed a naval academy for training new officers. Hubbard T. Minor was one of its cadets, shown here in an 1864 photo by Howell & Brown of Savannah, Georgia.
(KENNETH HATHAWAY)

The sons of the South's notables attended the new academy, located aboard the C.S.S. Patrick Henry. General John C. Breckinridge's son attended, and here, at left, is Daniel M. Lee, nephew of Robert E. Lee. (TU)

Welles quickly put as many ships as possible at sea to implement Lincoln's declared blockade. The U.S.S. Pensacola had to pass Confederate batteries on the lower Potomac to reach Alexandria in early 1861, but she helped open the river. (USAMHI)

Soon the wharves at Alexandria saw all manner of vessels coming and going, on all kinds of missions. The mail steamer State of Maine. (USAMHI)

The U.S.S. Sabine, *a frigate that took thirty-three years in the building, was one of the first to go on station in the Atlantic blockade. She also carried relief to the garrison at Fort Pickens at Pensacola in April 1861.* (NA, U. S. BUREAU OF SHIPS)

One of Welles's first captures, the Confederate steamer Thomas Collyer, *taken at Alexandria on May 25, 1861, by the U.S.S.* Pawnee. (USAMHI)

The deck of the Hudson, *the first blockade runner captured in what would be a four-year game of cat and mouse.* (NA)

*The tiny Marine Corps was also the Navy's responsibility, and Welles
augmented that arm somewhat. Here a battalion of Marines drill at the
Philadelphia Navy Yard.* (USAMHI)

And here at the Washington Navy Yard. An 1864 image. (NYHS)

They will play a minor role in this conflict, and chafe at their inactivity.
(USAMHI)

The Naval Observatory in Washington. Every branch of the Navy's operations was enhanced during Welles's tenure. (USAMHI)

The Washington Navy Yard, launching and refitting site for much of the burgeoning Union fleet. (LC)

The sail loft at the Boston Navy Yard. Though this was the era of steam, many of the Union's lesser ships still relied on the wind, and even steam vessels were equipped with sails to augment their speed. (USAMHI)

Captain Joseph Smith, chief of the Bureau of Navy Yards and Docks, ran the commission which made the commitment to go ahead with ironclad design and building. (USAMHI)

The officers of the Bureau of Steam Engineering, and seated at center, Chief Engineer Benjamin F. Isherwood. They supervised the Union's construction program for steam war vessels. They designed and built the engines that drove the Federal Navy. (USAMHI)

September 17, 1864, the launch of the frigate U.S.S. Franklin *at the Portsmouth, New Hampshire, Navy Yard—a common scene in the years after Welles took command. This screw frigate itself never saw action.* (NA)

Then came the time for offensive action. Commodore Silas H. Stringham, one of Welles's most trusted confidants, commanded the Atlantic blockading squadron and planned and led the successful attack on Fort Hatteras. (USAMHI)

Captain Samuel Barron, the unsuccessful Confederate defender at Hatteras, spent eleven months in prison after his capture. (CHS)

The steam frigate Minnesota, *Stringham's flagship in the attack on Forts Clark and Hatteras.* (NA)

Port Royal, South Carolina, the next scene of Union naval victory. A Timothy O'Sullivan photograph, probably taken in early 1862. (USAMHI)

The U.S.S. Wabash, *flagship of Captain Samuel F. I. du Pont, standing in the center of the group of three officers. In it he led the attack on Port Royal.* (USAMHI)

*Captain Charles H. Davis, fleet captain of
Du Pont's seventeen ships as they attacked Forts
Walker and Beauregard.* (USAMHI)

The deck of the U.S.S. Pawnee, *an early veteran of the attempt to relieve
Sumter, and the attacks on Hatteras Inlet and Port Royal. The screw sloop will
be part of the backbone of the blockade in the years to come.* (CHS)

O'Sullivan's photograph of the Coosaw Ferry to Port Royal Island. (USAMHI)

A Federal pontoon wharf at Coosaw Ferry after the capture of Port Royal. (NYHS)

Confederate Fort Walker on Hilton Head, seen from the rear, by O'Sullivan.
(USAMHI)

Fort Beauregard, showing ten heavy guns within its earthworks. From its commanding position on Bay Point, it still could not deter Du Pont's fleet. (USAMHI)

The interior of Fort Beauregard, the Union's first strong foothold in South Carolina. (USAMHI)

O'Sullivan's 1862 photograph of one of the Confederate guns inside Fort Beauregard. (USAMHI)

The Mills Plantation on Port Royal Island, where life went on much as usual. (USAMHI)

Members of the 79th New York, veterans of Bull Run, could be happy about a victory for a change. After the battle they built this mock battery at Seabrooke Point on Port Royal Island. (USAMHI)

Quickly the Union took advantage of its capture, and enhanced it. The wharf at Hilton Head that fed a constant stream of supplies to the South Carolina Federals. (USAMHI)

A man torn by conflicting loyalties. Commander Percival Drayton was a native of South Carolina, yet he stayed with the Union. He commanded the U.S.S. Pocahontas in the attack on Hilton Head. The commander of the Confederates defending Hilton Head was . . . (USAMHI)

. . . his brother, Brigadier General Thomas F. Drayton. (USAMHI)

*The boat landing at Beaufort began to
bustle with Federal craft.* (USAMHI)

*Private homes like the Fuller House
became officers' headquarters.* (USAMHI)

The generals, like Isaac I. Stevens seated here for O'Sullivan, were a commonplace sight. (SOUTH CAROLINA HISTORICAL SOCIETY)

Workshops and barracks sprang up on the sand. (USAMHI)

Guns came aboard ships, ready to renew the offensive against the enemy. (USAMHI)

Hilton Head would soon become an area of great importance for repair of the Navy's blockade fleet. The chief engineer's quarters at Bay Point. (USAMHI)

And the photographer could once again look for scenic beauty rather than the scars of war. (USAMHI)

And the price of any great gain in this war, the graves of the dead. Eight men were killed aboard Du Pont's ships. They are buried here on Hilton Head. Photograph by O'Sullivan. (USAMHI)

By November 16, 1861, with two significant successes to its credit, the Union Navy could justifiably preen for its President. The men of the U.S.S. Pensacola man the yards in honor of a visit in Alexandria by Abraham Lincoln. (WRHS)

The War Moves West

ALBERT CASTEL

Names like Grant and Sherman and Shiloh emerge in battle

IN THE PREDOMINANTLY RURAL WEST the camera, like the war itself, was still a novelty in 1861. Moreover, just as more words were printed about military operations in the East, so were more photos taken. The majority of western photographers remained in their studios. Only a few ventured forth to the battlefields.

Perhaps this was because of the different character of the war in the West. In the East combat took place in a small area and it was comparatively easy for Brady and Gardner and others to haul their cumbersome paraphernalia to the scene. Out West, on the other hand, the fighting sprawled from the Appalachians to the Mississippi, from the banks of the Ohio to the Gulf of Mexico. Furthermore, it was hard to predict where or when a battle would occur. In fact, for a long time after the bombardment of Fort Sumter there were no battles of consequence at all.

The western soldiers, Union and Confederate alike, were eager enough. Brandishing flintlocks, butcher knives, and a hodge-podge of other impractical weapons, they looked most bellicose. However, they had to wait awhile to hear the bullets buzz and the cannons roar. First of all both North and South at the outset concentrated most of their forces near Washington in expectation that one big battle there would decide the war. Then, when the western armies did begin building up after Bull Run, they could not get at each other because of Kentucky.

As with other slave-holding border states, public opinion in Kentucky was fragmented. Many Kentuckians favored the Confederacy. Many more adhered to the Union—more or less. But in 1861 the majority preferred neutrality. Realizing this, both Lincoln and Davis refrained from sending troops into their native state for fear of pushing it into the enemy's camp. As Lincoln commented, for the Union to lose Kentucky would be to "lose the whole game." On the other hand, should the North secure control of the state, it would be in a position to penetrate the southern heartland.

Hence during the summer of 1861, increasingly strong Federal and Confederate forces stood poised on Kentucky's borders, neither daring to be the first to cross them. Meanwhile Kentucky Unionists and Secessionists formed military units which sometimes drilled simultaneously in different parts of the same town! Also at Camp Andrew Johnson, Lieutenant Samuel P. Carter of the United States Navy, acting on Lincoln's orders, organized regi-

The broad Tennessee River cut through the South like a crooked knife, from Paducah, Kentucky, to Knoxville. (WRHS)

ments of Unionist refugees from East Tennessee. Lincoln was anxious to liberate that region from Confederate rule.

Sooner or later the Bluegrass impasse had to end. It did so on September 3 when Confederate General Leonidas Polk seized Columbus on the Mississippi River. He claimed that the Yankees had planned to do the same thing, but his real purpose was to obtain a stronger position from which to resist a Union thrust down the Mississippi.

In any event he made the first and greatest of his numerous contributions to southern defeat. His incursion outraged most Kentuckians and transformed hosts of neutralists into Unionists. At the same time it provided the Federals with a legitimate excuse to invade Kentucky also. On September 6, Brigadier General Ulysses S. Grant countered Polk's move by occupying Paducah. Other Union forces soon took control of the northern two thirds of the state. General Albert Sidney Johnston, top Confederate commander in the West, sent troops up from Tennessee to block their further advance.

Still, no serious fighting occurred. Each side grossly overestimated the other's strength and so held back from a confrontation. Brigadier General William Tecumseh Sherman, commanding the center of the Union line south of Louisville, was so sure that the Rebel army at Bowling Green would overwhelm him that he nearly suffered a nervous breakdown.

It was Grant who struck the first blow. Earlier in the war, while chasing guerrillas in Missouri, he learned that the enemy was just as scared as he was, and that the secret of military success was to make his foe more scared. Applying that lesson, on November 7 he loaded 3,000 troops onto transports at Cairo, Illinois, steamed down the Mississippi, and attacked an outpost Polk had established at Belmont, Missouri, across the river from Columbus. Superior Confederate numbers finally drove him away, but he gave the Southerners a jolt and strengthened their belief that the main Union offensive would be down the Mississippi.

On the night of the day after the fight at Belmont, bands of Unionists burned five railroad bridges in East Tennessee. This strike had been approved by Lincoln, who hoped thereby to cut a vital southern supply line and at the same time set the stage for the liberation of East Tennessee. The Confederate authorities rushed troops into the area, declared martial law, jailed scores of "Tories," and hanged suspected bridge burners. Hundreds of Unionists fled northward to escape persecution; others remained to wage a ruthless guerrilla war against their persecutors.

The movement of a Federal army commanded by Brigadier General George H. Thomas toward East Tennessee led to the next important battle in the West a little over two months later. This time

For over two years the course of the war in the West would follow its meanderings, its water stained red with the blood of America. (USAMHI)

Simple places with names like Shiloh and Chickamauga would, in years to come, assume a symbolic importance, as would rude churches, and humble dwellings marked by the war. Here in Washington, Kentucky, is the birthplace of Albert Sidney Johnston, a romantic figure who became a general in the Texas revolution of 1836, fought in the Mexican War, and on the plains as colonel of the 2d United States Cavalry. (WRHS)

the scene was eastern Kentucky and the Confederates were the aggressors. Early on the morning of January 19, 1862, at Logan's Crossroads near Mill Springs, some 5,000 of them under Major General George B. Crittenden made a surprise attack on Thomas's somewhat smaller force. At first driven back, Thomas's troops rallied, then routed the ill-armed Southerners who were demoralized by the death of their popular second-in-command, Brigadier General Felix Zollicoffer. The ragged, famished remnants of Crittenden's army retreated into East Tennessee, which now lay open to northern occupation. However, much to Lincoln's frus-

tration, supply problems prevented the Federals from pushing further southward.

Thomas's victory wrecked the right wing of Johnston's long line across Kentucky. The following month Grant and the United States Navy smashed the left wing. First, on February 6, Commodore Andrew H. Foote's gunboats captured Fort Henry on the Tennessee River. Five days later Grant marched his army to the Cumberland River, where on February 13 he invested the large Confederate garrison at Fort Donelson. An attack by Foote, who had steamed back down the Tennessee to the Ohio and then up the Cumberland, failed

*With war coming to the West, troops must be raised. Existing units, like the
Kentucky State Guard, provided many companies already trained and
equipped for the Confederacy. Standing at center, in the top hat, is Kentucky's
governor, Beriah Magoffin, in this August 1860 photograph. When called on to
furnish volunteers to suppress the Rebellion, he refused to aid "the wicked
purpose" with Kentucky soldiers.* (KHS)

on February 14. The following day the Confederates almost broke out to the south—indeed, probably would have had not their commander, Brigadier General John Floyd, lost his nerve. On the
other hand, Grant, again applying the lesson he
had learned in Missouri, promptly counterattacked
and drove the Rebels back into their fortifications.

On February 16 Brigadier General Simon Bolivar Buckner, who had succeeded Floyd as commander, asked Grant for terms. Grant replied:
"No terms except unconditional and immediate
surrender. . . . I propose to move immediately
upon your works." Buckner had no choice except

to comply. Close to 12,000 Confederates became
prisoners of war.

It was the biggest Union victory so far in the
war. Along with the fall of Fort Henry it opened
middle Tennessee to Federal invasion via the Cumberland and Tennessee rivers, made Polk's position
at Columbus untenable, and forced Johnston to retreat hastily from Kentucky all the way to Corinth,
Mississippi.

There he began concentrating his hitherto scattered forces. By April he had 40,000 troops organized into four divisions commanded by generals
Polk, Braxton Bragg, William J. Hardee, and

John C. Breckinridge. On April 3 he set out to attack Grant at Pittsburg Landing on the Tennessee. His plan, which had been devised by General P. G. T. Beauregard, who had been posted from Virginia to serve as second-in-command in the West, was to surprise and destroy Grant's 42,000-man army before it was joined by another large Union force under Major General Don Carlos Buell heading down from Nashville. If successful, central Tennessee would be redeemed and the tide of the war in the West reversed.

It was only twenty miles from Corinth to Pittsburg Landing. But the roads were bad and the march discipline of the raw Rebel troops worse. Hence, instead of striking Grant on the morning of April 5 as planned, the Confederates found themselves on the evening of that day still several miles from their objective. Beauregard, despairing of achieving surprise, advised returning to Corinth. However, Johnston, believing that a retreat would be more demoralizing than a defeat, ordered the attack to be made at dawn on April 6.

And so it was—and with great success. Despite the fact that some of their patrols had heard, seen, and even clashed with advance units of Johnston's army, most of the Federals were taken by surprise. Grant, who had been promoted to major general for Fort Donelson, simply had not expected Johnston to bring the battle to him. Furthermore, he had posted his troops with a view to drilling rather than defense—nor, as usual during the early period of the war, had they bothered to entrench. Consequently the Confederates, charging with a ferocity that henceforth would be their trademark, drove back Grant's men, thousands of whom fled in wild-eyed panic. It seemed that Johnston's prediction to his staff as the battle got under way, "Tonight we will water our horses in the Tennessee River," would come true.

However, most of the Northerners fought with a

Officers of the Kentucky State Guard at Louisville in August 1860. Almost all of them will become Confederates. The officer at right shaking hands with a civilian is Colonel Thomas H. Hunt, who would later command the 9th Kentucky Infantry in the celebrated Orphan Brigade. (KHS)

stubbornness equal to the Southerners' dash. In particular several thousand of them under Brigadier General Benjamin Prentiss, stationed in a sunken road which soon and ever after was called The Hornets' Nest, repulsed assault after assault. Nearby, scores of wounded from both sides mingled as they sought to quench their thirst in "The Bloody Pond." At 2:30 P.M., Johnston, while urging his men on against the Yankee strongpoint, bled to death when a bullet severed an artery in his right leg. Not until late in the afternoon, after surrounding him, did the Confederates force Prentiss to surrender. By then Grant had been able to form a compact defense line around Pittsburg Landing with his 7,000 remaining effectives, who were bolstered by massed artillery, gunboats, and several regiments from the vanguard of Buell's army. When at twilight a few thousand exhausted Rebels —the most Beauregard, who had replaced Johnston, could muster—made a last desperate effort to drive the Federals into the river, withering fire flung them back.

It was a hideous night of torrential rain falling on thousands of untended, moaning, screaming wounded. During the night 5,000 Union troops under Brigadier General Lew Wallace, who had been encamped to the north of Pittsburg Landing, belatedly joined Grant's army. More importantly, 20,000 of Buell's men also arrived. In the morning Grant counterattacked. Beauregard, who had no more than 20,000 muskets in his firing line, slowly gave way. Finally, late in the afternoon, seeing that victory was impossible and defeat inevitable, he ordered a retreat back to Corinth. The Federals, happy to see the Confederates leave, did not pursue.

Pittsburg Landing, as the North called it, or Shiloh, as the South named it after a log church around which much of the fighting centered, was the biggest and bloodiest battle of the war to that time. Nearly 11,000 Confederates and over 13,000 Federals were killed, wounded, captured, or missing—a loss for each army of 25 per cent of the troops actually engaged. Strategically it clinched

The Federals flocked to the banners in even greater numbers; here a group of Iowa volunteers pose in their training camp. (MISSOURI HISTORICAL SOCIETY)

Officers of the 1st Minnesota gather at the home of the commandant at Fort Snelling in May 1861, ready to go to war. (MHS)

the Union gains resulting from Forts Henry and Donelson. Psychologically it was a tremendous blow to Confederate morale and gave the northern soldiers of the West something of the same sense of superiority that the Southerners in Virginia derived from Bull Run. Yet if Johnston had been able to attack on the day planned, probably he would have destroyed Grant, although it is unlikely that his army would have been in condition to follow up the victory.

As it was, the Federals failed to exploit fully their success. After the battle Major General Henry W. Halleck, overall Union commander in the West, took personal charge of operations. He soon revealed himself to be more at home at a desk than in the saddle. Although he accumulated over 120,000 men, he moved with excessive slowness and caution on Corinth, where Beauregard, despite reinforcements from the Trans-Mississippi under Major Generals Earl Van Dorn and Sterling Price, mustered barely 50,000. Then, when he finally forced Beauregard to evacuate Corinth on June 7, he neither pursued nor struck for Vicksburg, which

as a result of the Union captures of Island No. 10, Fort Pillow, and Memphis during the spring was the last remaining major Confederate stronghold on the Mississippi north of Baton Rouge. Instead he broke up his host into a number of separate armies spread between Memphis and the approaches to Chattanooga. By so doing he gave the Confederates, now commanded by Bragg, a breathing spell which they put to good use.

Kentucky and Tennessee were not the only western states to witness a Confederate rollback during the early months of 1862. The same occurred from the opposite direction in Louisiana and Mississippi. On the night of April 24, in a daring surprise move, Flag Officer David Farragut, United States Navy, ran his wooden warships past Forts St. Philip and Jackson guarding the mouth of the Mississippi. A Confederate attempt to stop him with gunboats, rams, and fire rafts failed, and on the afternoon of April 25 he seized New Orleans, the South's largest city and main port. He then proceeded up the river to capture Baton Rouge on May 12 and Natchez six days later.

"We are coming, Father Abraham," they sang. The 28th Wisconsin, bound for Kentucky. (NA)

However, strong fortifications and the powerful ironclad *Arkansas* foiled him at Vicksburg during June and July.

Meanwhile, Union troops commanded by Ben Butler, a political general from Massachusetts, garrisoned New Orleans. There some of the women expressed their resentment of the Yankee presence by spitting on blue-clad soldiers. In retaliation Butler on May 15 issued an order declaring that "hereafter when any female shall by word, gesture, or movement insult . . . any officer or soldier of the United States she shall be regarded and held liable to be treated as woman of the town plying her vocation." This order enraged Southerners, who denounced Butler as a "beast." But it stopped the spitting.

Numerous male Louisianans expressed their opposition to northern rule by forming guerrilla bands which harassed Federal outposts and shipping. On May 28 forty of these bushwhackers fired on a boat from Farragut's flagship *Hartford,* which was putting ashore at Baton Rouge. Outraged, Farragut promptly opened up with his heavy cannons, wrecking the state capitol along with many other buildings.

Not all Louisianans resisted Yankee domination.

Hundreds of free blacks—many of whom were in fact white-skinned—joined the 1st Louisiana Native Guards, the formation of which had been authorized by Butler on August 22, a full month before Lincoln issued the Preliminary Emancipation Proclamation. Mustered in at New Orleans on September 27, it was one of the first Negro regiments to serve in the Union Army.

Baton Rouge suffered further devastation on August 5 when 2,600 Confederates under Breckinridge tried to retake it. At first they drove the 2,500-man Union garrison toward the river. But then they came under heavy fire from gunboats and eventually retreated. Plans had called for the ironclad *Arkansas* to assist Breckinridge's assault, but owing to engine trouble she failed to arrive in time and on the following day her crew blew her up in order to prevent her capture by Federal warships. Both sides lost heavily at Baton Rouge, with the northern commander, Brigadier General Thomas Williams, being among the slain.

Six days after the battle the Federals evacuated the town, which was given over to pillaging and burning by Negroes and convicts released from the state prison. As for Breckinridge, he withdrew to Port Hudson, where he fortified the bluff overlook-

The status of Kentucky, key to Union and Confederate war plans, was precarious. Declared neutral, she had to depend on both sides to honor that stance. Neither did. Major General George B. McClellan, commanding Ohio state forces in April and May, refused to recognize that neutrality, and thereby helped hold Kentucky in the Union. An 1861 photograph by the Brady studio. (USAMHI)

ing the Mississippi. The approximately 150-mile-stretch between that point and Vicksburg constituted the last link between the eastern and western halves of the Confederacy.

In northern Mississippi Bragg spent the early part of the summer reorganizing and training the army he had taken over from Beauregard. His men hated his harsh discipline and him for it, but they became better soldiers and, perhaps, even better fighters. By late July he was ready to launch an offensive which had as its object nothing less than the liberation of Tennessee and the occupation of Kentucky. Leaving behind 15,000 men under Sterling Price to keep an eye on Grant in West Tennes-

see and another small army under Van Dorn to guard Vicksburg, he transferred his remaining 35,000 troops by rail from Tupelo through Mobile and Atlanta to Chattanooga. By this maneuver, the most brilliant of its kind during the war, he outflanked the entire Federal front in the West. In addition, raids by the hard-riding gray troopers of Frank Armstrong, Nathan Bedford Forrest, and John Hunt Morgan caused Buell's army, which had been slowly advancing on Chattanooga, to fall back to Nashville, thus opening a path into Kentucky.

On August 28 Bragg began marching north. "Fighting Joe" Wheeler's cavalry led the way; the infantry jubilantly sang "Dixie." Two days later another Confederate army, 7,000 men under Major General Edmund Kirby Smith, who had moved up from Knoxville, routed 6,500 Federals at Richmond, Kentucky, then occupied Lexington. Expecting to be attacked next, the people of Cincinnati frantically constructed fortifications as thousands of Ohio and Kentucky militia hastened to their aid. But Kirby Smith neither advanced northward against Cincinnati nor moved westward to reinforce Bragg: He was too cautious to do the former and too reluctant to give up his quasi-independent command to do the latter.

All the while Buell, believing that Bragg was aiming for Nashville, remained at the Tennessee capital with his 50,000 troops. Not until September 7 did he realize that the Confederate objective was Kentucky and so set out in pursuit.

Given his long lead, Bragg by rapid marching might have taken Louisville—a stroke which would have panicked the Northwest. However, Davis had instructed him not to take unnecessary risks, and he feared being caught between the forces protecting that city and Buell's army moving up from Tennessee. Therefore, after capturing a 4,000-man Federal garrison at Munfordville, Kentucky, on September 17, 1862 (the same day as the Battle of Antietam), he swerved eastward to link up with Kirby Smith. Ten days later Buell reached Louisville, where he began readying a counteroffensive. His preparations were somewhat disrupted when on September 29 Brigadier General Jefferson C. Davis murdered Brigadier General William "Bull" Nelson after the three-hundred-pound Nelson slapped him during an altercation at a hotel.

Back to the south: Price, having been instructed

By the fall, Federal recruiting and training camps appeared in the Bluegrass, at places like Camp Nelson, complete with bakeries . . . (NA, U. S. WAR DEPT. GENERAL STAFF)

. . . well-supplied workshops . . . (NA, U. S. SIGNAL CORPS)

. . . and even reservoirs with picket fences. (NA, U. S. SIGNAL CORPS)

by Bragg to enter middle Tennessee, advanced to Iuka, in northeastern Mississippi, on September 14. Grant countered by sending a column under Major General William S. Rosecrans to strike Price from the south while Major General E. O. C. Ord's army hit him from the north. However, owing to an atmospheric freak condition, neither Ord nor Grant (who accompanied him) heard the sound of battle when Rosecrans assaulted Price on September 19. Consequently they did not attack, and Price, after beating off Rosecrans, slipped out of the trap that night.

Late in September Van Dorn came up from Vicksburg to join Price at Ripley, Mississippi. Taking command of their combined force of 22,000, he marched for Corinth, which was held by 23,000 Federals under Rosecrans. On October 3 he drove Rosecrans from his outer fortifications but the next day suffered hideous losses in an attempt to storm the town. A column sent by Grant blocked his retreat, but thanks to Armstrong's cavalry he managed to escape. Shortly after the battle a photographer took pictures of Texans killed assaulting a

Union redoubt known as Battery Robinette. They are among the most grim photos of the war. Any civilian viewing them would immediately realize that real-life—or rather real-death—battlefields bore little resemblance to the scenes depicted in Currier and Ives prints.

Bragg and Kirby Smith had expected swarms of recruits in Kentucky—indeed without them they could not hope to hold the state. Instead only about 2,500 joined their ragged legions. Disgusted, Bragg decided to resort to conscription. To that end he arranged for the installation of Richard C. Hawes as Confederate Governor of Kentucky. But the inauguration ceremonies, held at Frankfort, the state capital, on October 4, were abruptly terminated by Union shellfire. Buell had launched his counteroffensive—and sooner than Bragg had anticipated, with the result that he caught the Confederates badly scattered.

Bragg fell back, planning as he did so to regroup his units for a stand west of Lexington. However, on October 8, being pressed by advancing Federals near Perryville, he lashed back at them. Charging through sheets of cannon and rifle fire, 15,000 of Polk's and Hardee's veterans hurled back the Union line, which was held by 14,000 troops, many of them raw. Then, after being reinforced, the Northerners rallied, counterattacked, and regained much ground. Ferocious but indecisive fighting continued until nightfall. The Confederates lost 3,400 and the Federals 4,200 of the 22,000 men they had engaged.

Bragg thought that he faced at Perryville only a portion of Buell's army, most of which he believed heading for Lexington by way of Frankfort. In actuality Buell had threatened Frankfort with a small column of 7,000 while his main force, 54,000 strong, had advanced on Perryville. Furthermore, Bragg's assault fell on Buell's left wing alone. Fortunately for the Confederates, Buell was so far to the rear that he did not even know a battle was taking place until two hours after it started! And then, again through ignorance plus poor staff work, he failed to exploit a splendid opportunity to crush Polk's and Hardee's divisions by striking them in the flank and rear with his virtually unopposed center and right. In brief, both Bragg and Buell were lost in the fog of war.

That night Bragg, belatedly but in time, realized that he faced Buell's concentrated power at Perryville, whereas his and Kirby Smith's forces still were dispersed. He also learned of Van Dorn's debacle at Corinth, which meant that he could not expect any help from him but that Grant was free to aid Buell—or else sweep southward. Consequently he at once retreated, first to Harrodsburg, then to Bryantsville. There on October 12 he and Kirby Smith decided to return to Tennessee before the Federals cut them off from Cumberland Gap.

Twelve days later the last of the foot-sore Confederates trudged through Cumberland Gap on the way to Knoxville. Their invasion of Kentucky, like Lee's of Maryland the month before, had ended in failure after a brilliant beginning. Many Southerners then and afterward denounced Bragg for abandoning Kentucky without an all-out battle. Bragg, however, saw no point in risking his army fighting for the Confederate cause in the Bluegrass State when so few of the Kentuckians themselves were willing to fight for it.

Lincoln urged, indeed expected, Buell to follow the Confederates to Knoxville, defeat them, and liberate East Tennessee. Instead Buell headed for

Even larger camps of instruction like Camp Butler, near Cairo, Illinois, began to produce the regiments that would fight the western war. (ILLINOIS STATE HISTORICAL LIBRARY)

*And in came the volunteers. The 52d Illinois paraded through Elgin, Illinois,
on its way to put down rebellion.* (ILLINOIS STATE HISTORICAL LIBRARY)

Nashville. Lincoln thereupon replaced him with Rosecrans—who completed the move to Nashville, then remained there through November and most of December despite repeated orders and even pleas from Washington to advance. Like Buell he believed that a winter invasion of mountainous, thinly populated East Tennessee would be logistically impractical and strategically barren. He preferred instead to accumulate a large stockpile of supplies before doing battle with Bragg, who in the meantime had shifted his forces—now and thereafter known as The Army of Tennessee—to Murfreesboro, thirty miles southeast of Nashville.

Both Buell and Rosecrans were not without justification in their concern about supplies. Late in December cavalry raids by Van Dorn and Forrest caused Grant to abandon an attempt to capture Vicksburg by marching south through Mississippi. Similarly Morgan and Wheeler snipped away at Rosecrans's communication lines in Tennessee and Kentucky, delaying thereby his preparations.

Finally, on the day after Christmas, Rosecrans moved out from Nashville with 45,000 troops and an immense wagon train containing twenty days' rations. Bragg waited for him west of Murfreesboro, his 40,000 men straddling easily fordable Stones River. The Federals arrived in front of the Confederate position on December 29, having been slowed by Wheeler's cavalry. Each commander made preparations to attack with his left. The only difference was that Bragg struck first. On the morning of December 31 the redoubtable southern infantry, spearheaded by Irish-born Patrick Cleburne's division, rolled back Rosecrans's right wing until it was at a 90-degree angle to his left. However, the Federals, whose defense was anchored by Irish-descended Phil Sheridan's division, managed to hold just short of the Nashville Pike, their lifeline to the north. A gallant but foolish Confederate attempt to break the Union center at the "Round Forest" failed and the mutual slaughter—for such it was—ceased with the coming of darkness.

That night Rosecrans asked his generals if he

should order a retreat. Bearlike George H. Thomas, awakened from a doze, said, "This army doesn't retreat," then went back to sleep. The army stood.

Both sides spent the first day of 1863 (the date the Emancipation Proclamation went into effect) recuperating and redeploying. Then on January 2 Bragg threw Breckinridge's division at Rosecrans's left. The blue infantry broke, but massed Federal artillery tore Breckinridge's ranks to pieces. During the night of January 3 Bragg, who had lost 10,000 men, retreated. Rosecrans did not pursue beyond Murfreesboro. He had suffered 13,000 casualties and Wheeler had destroyed many of his precious wagons. Although actually a draw, the battle was hailed as a victory in the North, where it revived morale that was flagging badly after Burnside's bloody fiasco at Fredericksburg.

Thus ended the first year of fighting in the West. Clearly the North had gained much, the South lost much. Indeed, it would scarcely be an exaggeration to say that while the South had been winning *battles* in the East, in the West the North had been winning the *war*.

But the western Confederates remained undaunted and dangerous. Union Colonel Abel D. Streight found this out the hard way. On April 11, 1863, he invaded Alabama with 1,500 mounted infantrymen, intending to destroy factories and railroads in North Georgia. Forrest, with 1,000 cavalry, pursued. Guided part of the way by sixteen-year-old Emma Sanson, who rode with him on his horse, he overtook Streight, harried him relentlessly, and finally captured his entire command on May 3.

Meanwhile Rosecrans's Army of the Cumberland, as it was now called, and Bragg's Army of Tennessee, lay motionless throughout the winter and spring, recuperating, skirmishing with cavalry, and steeling themselves for the fighting to come. That there would be more fighting—a great deal more—was obvious to all. It was just that no one knew when it would be, or where—although probably some general, gazing at the map, had already noted a stream, not far away in Georgia, with a strange name: Chickamauga, an Indian word meaning "River of Death."

Members of the 9th Missouri try to look their best on the street in St. Joseph, but these western soldiers will ever appear unkempt . . . and rugged as hell itself. (STATE HISTORICAL SOCIETY OF MISSOURI)

Friends and families saw them off to war in front of their courthouses, as here at Paris, Illinois, in April 1862. While the speeches were made and the colors presented, the wagons loaded with their gear awaited the march to Dixie.
(EDWARD STEERS)

From farther west they came by river steamer, like these Nebraska soldiers aboard the Henderson *at Bellview, Iowa, in 1861.* (NEBRASKA STATE HISTORICAL SOCIETY)

A troop transport loaded with soldiers lands at Cairo, Illinois, where the men will train for the war. These men come aboard the Aleck Scott, unaware that before the war she was piloted briefly by a writer who will take his pen name from the cry of a steamboat leadsman, "Mark Twain." At the moment, he is still Samuel L. Clemens, and now a young and very scared Confederate soldier. (LO)

But these Confederates are not at all frightened. Officers all, their cigars and miniature flags proclaiming their bravado, they look forward to the coming fray. (LSU)

Southerners who remained loyal to the Union enjoyed wide popularity in the North, and often obtained high rank. Samuel P. Carter of East Tennessee outdid them all. A graduate of the United States Naval Academy, he was commissioned a brigadier general in the Army in 1862, simultaneously holding that rank and a commander's commission in the Navy. He was invaluable in stirring Union sentiment in Tennessee, and in 1862 was leading loyal Tennesseans in raids against their enemies. (NA)

The first scene of conflict was Missouri, soon to be one of the most hotly contested areas of the war. The Federal commander there was a man of international stature, native of Georgia, California's first senator, unsuccessful Republican presidential candidate in 1856, and a man of almost no military capabilities—Major General John C. Frémont, the celebrated "Pathfinder" of the West. He proved to be a martinet and constant thorn in Lincoln's side. (NYHS)

The first action came bloodlessly on May 10 when a body of secessionist Missouri militia training at Camp Jackson near St. Louis was seized by the man who almost single-handedly saved Missouri for the Union. (MISSOURI HISTORICAL SOCIETY)

Captain Nathaniel Lyon. A Unionist firebrand who brooked no obstacle to his single purpose of keeping Missouri out of the hands of the secessionists. When meetings with Missouri Confederates looking toward compromise produced nothing, he stated to them laconically, "This means war." A previously unpublished portrait probably taken after his promotion to brigadier. (NA)

Missouri Confederates did not give in peacefully. The flamboyant Colonel M. Jefferson Thompson, in 1860 mayor of St. Joseph, marched on Cape Girardeau with nearly 5,000 men when Frémont took command in the state. Later, after the general issued an ill-advised and unauthorized proclamation of emancipation, Thompson promulgated his own proclamation countermanding Frémont's. He would remain throughout the war one of the most colorful figures of the western Confederates. (JM)

*Lyon was right when he said there must be war. In attempting to rid the state
of Confederates, he led his little army against that of General Benjamin
McCulloch at Wilson's Creek, near Springfield, on August 10, 1861. It was
war, and here, where the numeral "2" rests on the horizon, Lyon fell in battle.
Probably an early postwar photo.* (WRHS)

*Lyon's foe was a Tennessean commanding
Arkansas troops, Brigadier General Ben
McCulloch, a man who disdained a uniform
and went into battle attired, as here, in a black
velvet suit. In 1835 he went to Texas with Davy
Crockett. In March 1862 he would die in battle
at Pea Ridge, Arkansas.* (VM)

*Mosby Monroe Parsons, former Missouri attorney-
general and a commander of Confederate Missouri
state guardsmen at Wilson's Creek.* (LSU)

*Men of Missouri's Union State Guard. No other state, even Kentucky, would
suffer as much from divided loyalties and families.* (MISSOURI HISTORICAL
SOCIETY)

The next month Confederates led by Sterling Price besieged and captured Lexington, Missouri, defended by Colonel James A. Mulligan and his 23d Illinois "Irish Brigade." (USAMHI)

By early 1862, Missouri still had not been firmly taken by either side. On March 7–8, the largest battle west of the Mississippi took place at Pea Ridge, Arkansas, its outcome deciding the fate of Missouri. Ben McCulloch would die in the battle. Brigadier General Alexander S. Asboth, leading a Union division, would be wounded. (USAMHI)

Brigadier General Daniel M. Frost, a native of New York who sided with the South, was offered command of a brigade at Pea Ridge, but refused to accept such a small command and instead watched the battle "from a convenient height." (LSU)

Confederate Brigadier General Albert Pike was a native of Boston, Massachusetts, but raised Indian troops for the South in Arkansas and led them ingloriously at Pea Ridge. A fellow general said he was "either insane or untrue to the South." He resigned soon thereafter, and spent much of the rest of his life writing the ritual and dogma for Masonry. (NYHS)

Brigadier General William Y. Slack was mortally wounded on the first day at Pea Ridge and died two weeks later. It was nearly a month later that the Confederate Senate promoted him to brigadier, the news of his death not having reached them. The uniform in this photograph has been painted on. (VM)

A Confederate commander whose capabilities were as grand as his name, John Sappington Marmaduke. Educated at Yale and Harvard, he graduated from West Point in 1857, when this photograph was taken. Colonel of Missouri and Arkansas troops, he fought gallantly at Prairie Grove, Arkansas, in December 1862, and rose steadily in ability. He was the last Confederate to win promotion to major general, on March 18, 1865, and was later governor of Missouri. (LSU)

While the war west of the Mississippi dragged on in its bloody and tragic course, one of the Union's first victories came in January 1862 at Mill Springs, Kentucky. Brigadier General George H. Thomas, a native of Virginia, led part of his division against the Confederate command in southeast Kentucky. (USAMHI)

Native of Kentucky, Brigadier General James F. Fagan also distinguished himself in the Confederate defeat at Prairie Grove. (JM)

The Confederates Thomas faced were
led by Major General George B.
Crittenden. His father was Senator
John J. Crittenden, who unsuccessfully
attempted a last-minute compromise
between North and South in 1861.
His brother was a major general in the
Union Army; so were Kentucky families
divided. This previously unpublished
photograph shows him probably in 1862.
He was forced to give battle to Thomas
at Mill Springs, thanks in part to
disobedience to his orders from a
subordinate . . . (LSU)

. . . Brigadier General Felix Zollicoffer
of Tennessee, who was killed when he
accidentally rode into Union troops
during the battle. (JM)

Mill Springs destroyed the right of the Confederate defensive line in Kentucky. Now a new general, Ulysses S. Grant, went to work on the left of the line. (USAMHI)

Assisted by Federal gunboats under the command of Flag Officer Andrew H. Foote, Grant moved against Confederate bastions on the Tennessee and Cumberland rivers. (LC)

Foote had four new river ironclads, among them the U.S.S. Cincinnati, one of the powerful "city class" gunboats. (NHC)

Another was the U.S.S. Carondelet, heavily armed and armored, and here tied at the bank on one of the western rivers. (NHC)

A markedly different ironclad was the U.S.S. Essex, *a converted centerwheel steamboat whose arming was personally overseen by her commander . . .* (USAMHI)

. . . William David Porter. Called "Dirty Bill" because of his unlikable manner and sometimes less-than-honest methods, he was the son of Commodore David Porter of the original Essex. *His brother was Admiral David D. Porter, his half-brother Admiral David Farragut. He would be badly scalded by steam when a shot from Confederate Fort Henry penetrated the* Essex's *boiler.* (USAMHI)

One of Foote's three wooden gunboats, the U.S.S. Tyler. It would do
workhorse duty on the western waters, though even great warships still had to
dry their laundry now and then. (USAMHI)

Grant and Foote first moved against Fort Henry
on the Tennessee River. They set the attack for
February 6, 1862, but mud slowed Grant's
soldiers and it was all Foote's affair. He soon
forced Confederate Brigadier General Lloyd
Tilghman to lower his flag, after sending most of
his garrison to Fort Donelson. (SHC)

Donelson would be a different matter entirely. Commanding there was General John B. Floyd, who a year before was Buchanan's Secretary of War. On February 13, Grant launched his land attack with the division of Brigadier General Charles F. Smith, his one-time teacher at West Point. (NA)

Two days later, facing a hopeless situation, Floyd decided to escape, abandoning his command to General Gideon J. Pillow. A man of reprehensible character, Pillow, too, chose to flee rather than share the fate of his soldiers. In January 1863, at the Battle of Stones River, he would be seen hiding behind a tree while his brigade went into battle. Thereafter he gave perjured testimony against fellow generals in the political infighting that would always plague the Confederate Army of Tennessee. (VM)

Unidentified western Confederates, probably from Louisiana, men of the stamp of those who gallantly defended Donelson until it was hopeless. (CM)

Men of the 2d Kentucky Infantry almost cut a way out of Grant's trap, but they were called back before they could take advantage of it. Some of these members of the National Blues, Kentucky State Guard, made up the 2d Kentucky. (KHS)

Refusing to abandon his men as did Floyd and Pillow, the dashing Brigadier General Simon B. Buckner, formerly commander of the Kentucky State Guard, stayed with them and finally asked his old friend Grant for terms. (SHC)

*Major George B. Cosby of Kentucky carried
Buckner's request for surrender terms to Grant.
He would later become a brigadier. A previously
unpublished portrait.* (SHC)

*Gallant defenders of Donelson like Colonel
Adolphus Heiman and his 10th Tennessee were
downcast at the prospect of going to a northern
prison. Heiman would die as a result of his
confinement.* (HP)

Bushrod R. Johnson of Ohio was one general who would not stay captured. After the surrender he escaped. (VM)

And there was another Confederate who would not accept surrender. A lieutenant colonel of the 7th Tennessee Cavalry, a rich man before the war, Nathan Bedford Forrest would be heard from in this conflict. (LC)

*Then came Albert Sidney Johnston and
his surprising attack on Grant's army
at Pittsburg Landing on April 6. It was
Johnston's first and last battle of the war.
Shot in the leg, he bled to death, dying in
the arms of his brother-in-law . . .*
(USAMHI)

*. . . Colonel William Preston, former
Kentucky congressman and Buchanan's
minister to Spain. He would become a
general in another week.* (VM)

Upon Johnston's death, command of the Confederates at Shiloh passed to the seemingly ubiquitous hero of Sumter and Bull Run, General P. G. T. Beauregard. He consolidated the gains of the first day's fighting, aided largely by his confidant and adjutant . . . (NA, U. S. SIGNAL CORPS, BRADY COLLECTION)

. . . Thomas Jordan, who will be made brigadier for his gallantry in this battle. (LC)

Others, too, won laurels. Benjamin Franklin Cheatham a brigadier from Tennessee, will be promoted to major general in recognition of his service at Shiloh. (MC)

Colonel James B. Walton ably commanded his . . . (THE HISTORIC NEW ORLEANS COLLECTION)

. . . *Washington Artillery of New Orleans in the fight, the first for this branch of the famed organization that also sent several companies to the Virginia front.* (CM)

Private John Rulle of the 2d Tennessee Infantry came to Shiloh ready for a fight, from the look of him. His unit were mostly Irishmen from Memphis. (HP)

*The officers and noncommissioned officers of Captain A. M. Rutledge's
Tennessee Battery, photographed on July 4, 1861. Their guns at Shiloh would
severely discomfit the Federals.* (TENNESSEE HISTORICAL SOCIETY)

*A magnificent photograph, taken May 10, 1861, of the "Clinch Rifles," men of
the 5th Georgia. The variety of clothing and pose, with their black servant in
the background, are among the most interesting to be found in Confederate
images. They were to be far less relaxed at Shiloh.* (JOSEPH CANOLE, JR.)

The peach orchard at Shiloh. Through here swarmed the Confederate corps of Brigadier General . . . (CHS)

. . . John C. Breckinridge, formerly Vice-President and a presidential contender. No believer in secession, and almost certain that the Confederacy could not win, he was forced out of the Union and nevertheless took a command from President Davis. (NA)

Breckinridge's corps and others were bottling up the Federal division of Brigadier General Benjamin M. Prentiss in a place called . . . (USAMHI)

. . . the Hornets' Nest. It was in one of their attacks that A. S. Johnston fell mortally wounded. (CHS)

It was a bitter fight. Westerners like these used their Colt revolving rifles to deliver heavy fire power against the Confederates. (RP)

Brigadier General Daniel Ruggles, a native of Massachusetts, retaliated by massing some sixty-two cannon against the Hornets' Nest. (USAMHI)

In the final encirclement of Prentiss, Kentuckians of the Orphan Brigade closed the final trap. Colonel Thomas Hunt, standing eighth from the left here, commanded one of the Kentucky regiments that sealed the Federals' fate. (KHS)

More of the Kentuckians, photographed in August 1860, who would eventually man the Orphan Brigade. (KHS)

Finally Prentiss could not hold out longer, and beneath this tree he surrendered.
An early postwar photo. (CHS)

Meanwhile dour Major General Braxton Bragg continually pushed the Federals back toward the Tennessee River. (CM)

On the Federal right, Brigadier General William T. Sherman, like Beauregard a veteran of Bull Run, fell back under heavy Confederate attacks. (USAMHI)

*Finally, as evening approached, a last line was established by Grant and
Sherman. These 24-pounder siege guns were a part of it, and here the Federals
stood.* (USAMHI)

*They held on stubbornly, men like Colonel Madison Miller of the 18th
Missouri.* (LC)

Men of the 7th Illinois Infantry, armed with their Henry repeating rifles.
(ILLINOIS STATE HISTORICAL LIBRARY)

Even bandsmen, usually noncombatants, took arms in holding the last line.
(CHICAGO PUBLIC LIBRARY, SPECIAL COLLECTIONS)

And boys like Johnny Clem, the "drummer boy of Shiloh," acted like men. (LC)

The arrival of a relief column under Brigadier General Don Carlos Buell late that evening finally ensured that Grant would not be pushed into the Tennessee. (USAMHI)

The next day, April 7, thanks to Buell's troops arriving here at Pittsburg Landing, and the exhaustion of the Confederates, Grant forced Beauregard to retire from the field. This photograph was taken a few days after the battle. The steamer at right is the Tycoon, *sent by the Cincinnati Sanitary Commission with stores and medical supplies for the wounded. Next to it is Grant's headquarters boat, the* Tigress. *(USAMHI)*

At right, the Universe *unloads more supplies for Grant's command. The*
Tigress *is at the center, and across the stream stands the wooden gunboat* Tyler.
*The guns from Foote's fleet played a large part in halting the Confederate drive
on April 6. Shiloh was not exactly a victory for Grant, but not a defeat either,
and in the aftermath of several Union disasters, that was more important.*
(USAMHI)

*Four days after Shiloh, Major General
Henry W. Halleck took command from
Grant. Called variously "Old Brains" and
"Old Wooden Head," he was an able
administrator, and a miserable general.
Outnumbering Beauregard two to one, he
still could not catch the Confederates at
Corinth.* (MJM)

Brigadier General Daniel Tyler, of Bull Run and Blackburn's Ford fame—or ill repute—was sent west to command a brigade in the "siege" that Halleck laid to Corinth. The Federals finally moved into the town the day after the enemy escaped them. (LC)

Later in the year, with a Federal command under Major General William S. Rosecrans stationed in and around Corinth, the Confederates were not so slow. Major General Sterling Price led his little army to Iuka on the way to Corinth, and was there attacked by Rosecrans on September 19. A previously unpublished portrait of Price in 1862. (TU)

Price's most trusted subordinate, Brigadier General Lewis Henry Little, was killed at Iuka while talking with Price by a bullet that first passed under Price's arm. (CHS)

Two weeks after Iuka, the armies collided again at Corinth, on October 3–4, 1862. (CHS)

It was an important railroad depot and supply center for Rosecrans and his growing army of 21,000 men. A Howard & Hall photograph taken before the battle. Their tent studio appears just left of the Tishomingo Hotel. (USAMHI)

Rosecrans's army were western men, men of the 47th Illinois . . . (WILLIAM M. ANDERSON)

. . . and the 2d Minnesota, which bore much of the brunt of the fighting. (MHS)

Their commander, Major General William S. Rosecrans, was himself a western man, born in Ohio. He is seen here, with a hint of a smile, taken by Corinth photographer George Armistead of Armistead & White, sometime prior to the battle. (LC)

His opponent was the colorful Major General Earl Van Dorn of Mississippi, the loser at Pea Ridge. (MISSISSIPPI DEPARTMENT OF ARCHIVES & HISTORY)

For two days they fought. The 8th Indiana Artillery was heavily engaged for the Union. (RP)

*Fifty-two-year-old Brigadier General
Thomas J. McKean led one of Rosecrans's
divisions, even though he was considered
too old for active command. He is seated
here with members of his staff.* (NYHS)

*Samuel Jones, like many of these men in
Mississippi in 1862, was another veteran of
Bull Run. He commanded a division under
Van Dorn, and was also in the process of
making himself the second most
photographed general of the Confederacy.*
(VM)

*Major General Mansfield Lovell, a native
of Washington, D.C., joined Van Dorn
after he lost New Orleans to Farragut, and
skillfully commanded the Confederate
retreat from Corinth.* (CHS)

*It was a costly battle. Here in front of Federal Battery Robinette, the
Confederate dead and their horses were piled deep. This photograph, taken the
day after the battle, shows the horse of Colonel William P. Rogers in the center,
and to the left of it, the body of Rogers himself.* (WRHS)

Several of the Confederate dead in front of Robinette. Colonel William P. Rogers of the 2d Texas lies at left, and to his right, leaning on his shoulder, is the body of Colonel W. H. Moore, who led a brigade of Missouri and Mississippi troops in futile assaults against Robinette. (ALABAMA STATE DEPARTMENT OF ARCHIVES AND HISTORY)

*The Confederate threat gone, Corinth became undisputedly a Union town, and
the men of Rosecrans's army enjoyed it as they could. Supplies came in
regularly, and Howard & Hall expanded their gallery next to the Tishomingo.*
(CHS)

*Officers like Brigadier General Grenville Dodge established their headquarters in
the better homes of the city.* (CHS)

Life returned to normal for the inhabitants. (CHS)

The soldiers patronized the local business establishments. (CHS)

They built their winter quarters like Camp Davis, home for the 66th Illinois, south of the city. (ROBERT YOUNGER)

Their bands tuned for the season's demands for entertainments. Here the 97th Indiana musicians. (CHS)

*And their earthworks and tents dotted the landscape for the winter ahead,
while the firms of Armistead & White and Howard & Hall kept busy with their
captive clientele. Winter quarters could mean a small fortune to a
photographer.* (CHS)

*But it would not be a peaceful winter in
Mississippi and Tennessee, nor in
Kentucky. Brigadier General Jefferson C.
Davis, once an officer in Fort Sumter, in
late September shot and killed his superior,
William Nelson, after an altercation. It
could not have come at a worse time, for
after a year of seeming security, Kentucky
was being invaded by the Confederate
Army of Tennessee, commanded now by
Beauregard's successor . . .* (LC)

. . . General Braxton Bragg. This previously unpublished image of Bragg was made by McIntyre of Montgomery, Alabama, just a few weeks prior to his launching of the Kentucky campaign. (CM)

*Commanding the Federals who would
resist Bragg was Major General Don
Carlos Buell, of Shiloh.* (USAMHI)

*Bragg's offensive was spearheaded by a
Floridian, Major General Kirby Smith,
who had been wounded leading a brigade
at Bull Run. At Richmond, Kentucky, he
defeated Nelson in the only real
Confederate battle victory of the
campaign.* (LC)

Leading Bragg's cavalry was a young brigadier who turned twenty-six during the campaign, Joseph Wheeler. He would become one of the war's premier cavalrymen. (LC)

Bragg and Buell finally met at Perryville, Kentucky, along Doctor's Creek. Probably an early postwar view. (USAMHI)

The H. P. Bottoms House near the position of Brigadier General Lovell Rousseau, who gallantly led a division against repeated enemy attacks. (USAMHI)

Rousseau aligned his command beside a 100-year-old tree that, miraculously, survived the battle. (USAMHI)

*Federal artillery placed on this high ground, plus numerical superiority, finally
gave the battle to Buell.* (USAMHI)

*Brigadier General J. Patton Anderson of
Tennessee led one of Bragg's divisions to
no avail.* (USAMHI)

*Losses were heavy. General S. A. M.
Wood took a serious wound from Federal
fire.* (VM)

*Union Brigadier General William R.
Terrill of Virginia was struck in the side
by a piece of shell and died that night. His
brother was a general in the Confederate
Army, and would die in the war as well.*
(USAMHI)

Brigadier General James S. Jackson was a native of Kentucky, and at Perryville he died on his home soil. (USAMHI)

Heavy fighting along this lane cost Buell even more casualties, but the battle was his. (USAMHI)

Bragg watered his army at this spring, and retreated into Tennessee, his dream of conquering Kentucky gone in smoke. (USAMHI)

In December the armies meet again, this time at Murfreesboro, Tennessee, and the Federals are once again commanded by Major General William S. Rosecrans. He is seated fourth from the left in this pose with his staff. The man sitting next to him on the right is Brigadier General James A. Garfield, who will become his chief of staff after the battle and, years later, President of the United States. To the far right sits Philip H. Sheridan who, as a brigadier, commands a division at Murfreesboro, and wins promotion. (USAMHI)

The courthouse in Murfreesboro. The town remained in Confederate hands during the battle. (USAMHI)

The telegraph office from which Bragg boastfully—and prematurely—wired President Davis that he had won a great victory. (USAMHI)

Rosecrans fought a largely defensive battle, letting Bragg hurl his divisions against tough fighters like the 38th Indiana, shown here in Murfreesboro in April 1863. (JMB)

Those attacks were overseen by Bragg's corps commanders. Lieutenant General William J. Hardee of Georgia was known widely in both armies, thanks to his authorship of Hardee's Tactics, *a standard manual North and South.* (LC)

Lieutenant General Leonidas Polk of North Carolina commanded Bragg's other corps. Episcopal Missionary Bishop for the Southwest, he traded clerical robes for a uniform when the war came. He would disappoint almost everyone. (VM)

Some of the greatest infantry assaults of the war took place at Murfreesboro, and they were terribly bloody. Brigadier General Roger Hanson of Kentucky, commander of the Orphan Brigade, fell mortally wounded when the fuse from an exploding shell struck his leg. While being carried from the field he cheered his men, telling them that it was a glorious cause to die for. (JM)

Brigadier General James E. Rains was killed leading his division of Hardee's corps into a charge. His last word was "Forward!" (USAMHI)

Determined resistance by Sheridan and others finally forced Bragg to abandon the field and retreat into the interior, leaving the Federals the field and the victory. (USAMHI)

The Federals occupied Murfreesboro for most of the rest of the war. Here the headquarters from which Rosecrans sent Lincoln the good news of a victory for the New Year, 1863. (USAMHI)

Photographer of the Confederacy: J. D. Edwards

LESLIE D. JENSEN

Prolific yet unknown chronicler of rustics in rebellion

BEFORE the war guns really roared, East or West, on May 14, 1861, the citizens of New Orleans, reading the military columns of their newspapers, came across the following advertisement:

THE WAR!
Views of Pensacola, Forts Barancas, McRae and Pickens; of the Companies there— "Orleans Cadets" "Crescent Rifles" "Chausseurs a Pied," Mississippi and Alabama Regiments and of the U.S. Fleet—39 different Photographic Views, taken by an accomplished artist on the spot, will be on sale tomorrow at the Book Stores, Picture and Looking Glass Stores. They are very large and taken superbly. Price $1 per copy.

The "accomplished artist" was J. D. Edwards, a shadowy figure who remains obscure to this day, yet a man who had accomplished a feat that would not be repeated in the Confederacy. Edwards had produced a comprehensive photographic panorama of the forts, guns, barracks, shipyards, and most importantly, the men who comprised the Confederate Army. Were it not for Edwards, photographic coverage of Confederate military events would be limited to a mere handful of isolated pictures, many of them taken in northern prison camps.

Little is known about Edwards personally or of his life before his Pensacola views went on sale, and practically nothing is known of him afterward. In 1860, he was working in New Orleans. Edwards was twenty-nine years old at the time, had been born in New Hampshire, and gave his occupation as "Ambrotype Portrait." His wife, Mary, a Missourian by birth, was twenty. The Edwardses could not have been in New Orleans long, for their son Edouard had been born in Massachusetts only eight months before. The remainder of the household consisted of Eliza Zeigler, a nineteen-year-old German servant, and Edwards's two assistants, B. Barker, a twenty-nine-year-old native of Massachusetts, and a twenty-four-year-old Canadian named Johnson. Edwards valued his personal estate at $3,000.

Yet, though a newcomer to New Orleans, Edwards must have made an impression of being innovative and willing to take on unusual business assignments. When the U. S. Treasury Department and Custom House and the Marine Hospital were under construction in June 1860, Edwards took twenty-three views of the former and twelve views of the latter for the U. S. Army Engineer in charge of the work, a native Louisianan named P. G. T. Beauregard. This assignment may well have started a tradition for both men, outdoor photography for Edwards, and the inclusion of photographs with reports for Beauregard, a practice he continued during the 1861 and 1863 Charleston operations.

By 1861, Edwards operated a studio at 23 Royal Street, yet, though he was listed in the alphabetical section of a city directory, he was still not established enough to be included in the separate section devoted to photographers. Later in the year he moved to 19 Royal Street, occupied when the directory was put out by a photographer named E. J. Newton, Jr. It is not known whether Edwards bought out Newton's operation or went into business with him.

After the firing on Fort Sumter, only one major U.S. bastion remained in the Confederacy: Fort Pickens, guarding the harbor of Pensacola Bay, Florida. The importance of Fort Pickens has often been overshadowed by other events, and particularly because no major battles were fought to control it. Yet, in April 1861, it was one of the most important areas of potential trouble. As the last Union stronghold on Confederate soil, it was not only irritating to southern pride, but it blocked the bay to southern shipping and restricted the use of the splendid former U. S. Navy Yard at Warrington, just across the bay from the fort. Moreover, it could, and in time did, become a base for operations against the Confederacy. Whoever controlled Fort Pickens controlled the use of one of the best anchorages on the Gulf Coast.

Theoretically, the Confederates, vastly outnumbering the Union troops in the area, should have had little trouble taking control of the bay, but the unexpected stubbornness of Lieutenant Adam Slemmer's tiny Union command, supported by an ever growing Union fleet, kept the Confederates at bay until Union reinforcements arrived. By late April, Confederate volunteers poured into the area, preparing for what everyone thought would be the next big showdown of the war. Many of the Confederates headed for Pensacola were from New Orleans, and J. D. Edwards apparently saw in this an opportunity to create a pictorial record of the war, make a reputation for himself, and turn a profit by selling his products to the soldiers and the folks back home. Accordingly, sometime in late April, he too headed for the scene of the war's next battle.

Happily, because Edwards numbered at least some of his negatives in the order he took them, it is possible to follow his work pattern in the Pensacola area with a fair degree of certainty. He seems to have started at the Navy Yard itself, where General Braxton Bragg had his headquarters and where Edwards probably had to go to get permission to take his photographs. He took pictures looking across the bay toward Fort Pickens and photographed the steamer *Fulton* in dry dock, surrounded by the vast quantities of shells the Confederates had both captured and were making in the yard's foundry. From there, he moved west, photographing Coppens's Louisiana Zouave Battalion at drill on the grounds of the Marine Barracks. He spent a great deal of time at Fort Barrancas, photographing it inside and out, including its old Spanish half-moon battery. From there, Edwards photographed some of the sand batteries and then found himself drawn to the lighthouse. Its 165-foot height provided a perfect view of the coast, and Edwards took his camera to the top, photographing the forts and camps below. He spent considerable time in the camps themselves, mostly in those of the 1st Alabama and 9th Mississippi regiments, before moving on to the Confederate bastion on the right flank, Fort McRee. On the way back, Edwards may have taken additional camp scenes, and at some point, probably toward the end of his stay, he went to Bayou Grand, just north of Warrington, where he photographed the camp of the Orleans Cadets. Exactly how long Edwards stayed in the Pensacola area is unknown, but given the volume of work that he did and the probable work and travel time, he may have been there a week or more.

The photographs went on sale in New Orleans on May 15, but curiously, Edwards only ran his notice for three days. The various newspapers made some editorial comment on the photographs, but beyond confirming that the advertisement indeed refers to the work of J. D. Edwards, they tell us little. The New Orleans *Bee*, however, suggested that the photographs would "make an interesting souvenir for the parlor, particularly in the event, considered now so near at hand, of the capture of Fort Pickens."

Some of the photographs made their way north with surprising speed. On June 15, a woodcut appeared in *Harper's Weekly* entitled "INTERIOR OF A SAND-BAG BATTERY BEARING ON FORT PICKENS." *Harper's* claimed that it was the work of their special artist, Theodore Davis, but close comparison with Edwards's photograph No. 33, "Perote Sand Batteries 10 inch Columbiads," reveals the woodcut to have been pirated from Edwards. It is entirely possible that Davis, who had been in Pensacola with William Howard Russell at about the time Edwards was photographing, knew Edwards's work and either made a sketch from the photograph or simply sent the photograph on to *Harper's,* who incorrectly captioned it. A week later, *Harper's* ran another woodcut with the caption "BIVOUAC OF REBEL TROOPS AT GENERAL BRAGG'S CAMP AT WARRINGTON, FLORIDA," and this time admitted that it was from a photograph, although they did not identify the photographer. The scene was the well-known one of men cooking around a campfire in the 9th Mississippi's camp, but *Harper's,* not content with the original photograph, rearranged the figures.

Edwards's photographs seem to have been rather widely distributed at the time. Some ended up in the hands of S. H. Lockett, an officer in the 1st Alabama, and somehow Charles Allgower, a member of the 6th New York and an occasional artist for *Harper's,* also acquired some, probably while his regiment was stationed in the Pensacola area. Despite Edwards's claim that he produced thirty-nine views, it is now clear that the actual total was much higher. Known views, many of them published in 1911 but since lost, total forty-four. However, Edwards's negative numbers run as high as sixty-eight, and there is at least one photograph numbered "2B." Thus, despite the large number of Edwards photographs which are presented here for the first time, there may be as many as twenty or more yet unaccounted for, including at least two, those of the Crescent Rifles and the Chausseurs à Pied, referred to in the ad.

One wonders whether the appearance of the woodcuts in *Harper's Weekly* may have been a spur to another photographer, the nation's finest, Mathew B. Brady. The Confederates had already scooped him in the early coverage of the war, and the fact that their photographs were appearing in northern papers, competing with his own portrait work, may well have helped to inspire Brady to take his camera teams into the field.

The fact that the Pensacola front never produced any major battles and was eventually abandoned by the Confederates may have hurt the long-term sales of Edwards's work, but in any case, after the appearance of the photographs, he slipped once more into obscurity. Two of his negatives were seized by U.S. authorities after the fall of New Orleans, and prints from them were turned over to the U. S. Engineers office in Washington in 1863. Unfortunately, we do not know the circumstances of the seizure, and while the prints survive, the negatives have disappeared. Francis Trevelyan Miller claimed that Edwards later worked for the Confederate secret service, but no hard evidence to support the claim has come to light. Yet, there is one tantalizing clue which may indicate that Edwards was an even more important photographer than his Pensacola series indicates. Roy M. Mason, one of the searchers sent by Miller to locate Confederate photographs for the 1911 *Photographic History of the Civil War,* recalled his experiences in the armory of the Washington Artillery in New Orleans. He noted that the one-armed armorer, Sergeant Dan Kelly, "said that there were no photographs, but consented to look in the long rows of dusty shelves which line the sides of the huge, dark armory. From almost the last he drew forth a pile of soggy, limp cardboard, covered with the grime of years. He passed his sleeve carelessly over the first, and there spread into view a picture of his father sitting reading among his comrades in Camp Louisiana forty-nine years before. The photographs were those of J. D. Edwards, who had also worked at Pensacola and Mobile. Here were Confederate volunteers of '61 and the boys of the Washington Artillery which became so famous in the service of the Army of Northern Virginia." Some Washington Artillery photos were by J. W. Petty of New Orleans, but if Mason's implication is correct, Edwards may have continued to photograph Confederate troops at least as late as early 1862, when the 5th Company, Washington Artillery was photographed just before Shiloh. If so, Edwards may be responsible for a larger body of Confederate photographs than he has been given credit for.

Yet, if early 1862 was the last time that Edwards may have been at work, it is also the end of any documentation on his Civil War work. The man simply disappears for the next two decades. In the late 1880s he reemerges, working his trade in Atlanta, and there he dies in 1900. How much more wartime work he did, if any, and how much more of it survives, is a mystery.

Miller called Edwards a "pioneer camera man," but apparently even Miller was not aware of just how much of a pioneer Edwards was. In this country there was virtually no tradition of war photography, and while the Crimean War photographs of Roger Fenton and others were known, there was no one who could set the pace in this new art. While enterprising Confederates in Charleston were the first on the scene of America's bloodiest war, their job was made easier by the fact that they were photographing local events. The established photographers remained in their studios, content to take the portraits of the generals and soldiers who would fight the war. Into this scene stepped J. D. Edwards, packing his equipment over miles of swamps and bayous and into a war zone, taking pictures at least as good as Brady's and then marketing them with little apparent financial backing other than his own. At the time Edwards's work was of a far wider scope than anything any other photographer was producing, and while he was eclipsed by the superior resources of Brady, Gardner, and hundreds of others, it was J. D. Edwards, whether known by name to these other photographers or not, who showed the way a war could be photographed. In the Confederacy, no one else would match his work for innovation and sheer importance. If there was anyone who could claim the title Photographer of the Confederacy, it was the obscure Yankee from New Orleans, J. D. Edwards.

With only four exceptions, all of the J. D. Edwards photographs reproduced here are published for the first time. Several others were published in 1911, but the originals from which they were reproduced have since disappeared. The images that follow are all taken from surviving original prints newly unearthed.

The ever-frowning brow of General Braxton Bragg. He commanded the regiments of rustics forming at Pensacola when Edwards made his historic visit in April 1861. (CHS)

First Lieutenant Adam J. Slemmer of the
1st United States Artillery, the thorn in
Bragg's side who refused to give up Fort
Pickens, thus ensuring the mighty bastion
for the Union as a base deep in
Confederate territory. Edwards never
captured Slemmer as Cook did Major
Anderson and his men at Fort Sumter, but
more than once he turned his camera
toward the low, brooding profile of
Pickens, a constant reminder of Federal
power and determination. (USAMHI)

Fort Pickens photographed from Fort Barrancas, across Pensacola Harbor. The
ship is probably the Federal flag-of-truce boat U.S.S. Wyandotte. (SHC)

Guns in the old Spanish part of Fort Barrancas, trained on Fort Pickens in the distance. "I was rather interested with Fort Barrancas," wrote William H. Russell, "built by the Spaniards long ago—an old work on the old plan, weakly armed, but possessing a tolerable command from the face of fire." (SHC)

The rear of Fort Barrancas and a Confederate regiment camped beyond, probably the 1st Alabama. The variety of tents, the makeshift nature of the camp, and lack of uniformity in the dress of the Confederates drawn up in line, all attest to the informal and inexperienced nature of the Southrons who flocked to Pensacola in 1861. (GULF ISLANDS NATIONAL SEASHORE)

A side view of part of Fort Barrancas as Bragg's men move yet another cannon into place. (SHC)

A water battery at Warrington. In the distance to the right is the lighthouse. Bragg did not wish to open fire on Pickens, and the Englishman Russell believed him right. "The magazines, of the batteries I visited did not contain ammunition for more than one day's ordinary firing," he wrote. "The shots were badly cast, with projecting flanges from the mould, which would be very injurious to soft metal guns in firing." One of these rustics, standing at the wheel of the front gun, holds a shot in his hand, while his mates sham preparing to fire. The poor man at the second gun, seeing his chance for immortality about to be blocked by a cold iron cannon, had to stoop to present his face to the camera. In the right center is a hot-shot furnace for heating incendiary projectiles. (NA, OFFICE OF THE CHIEF OF ENGINEERS)

The sand battery at Fort Barrancas, and a stand of the ill-formed shot. Despite the seemingly strong positions of these guns, Russell believed that if Bragg opened fire on Slemmer, Fort Pickens "ought certainly to knock his works about his ears." (SHC)

Edwards captioned this a "View of two Sand Batteries, showing subterranean passages connecting them together, with Fort Pickens in the distance." Pickens has now disappeared from this faded print, but the crude board shoring of the tunnels is visible in the foreground. Much work remains to be done, but Russell did not find the summer soldiers anxious about it. "The working parties, as they were called—volunteers from Mississippi and Alabama, great long-bearded fellows in flannel shirts and slouched hats, uniformless in all save brightly burnished arms and resolute purpose—were lying about among the works, or contributing languidly to their completion." (TU)

The lighthouse west of Fort Barrancas. Built in 1859, it quickly attracted Edwards's eye, and he and his camera were soon at its top taking the first "aerial" photos of the war. (PENSACOLA HISTORICAL SOCIETY, PENSACOLA, FLORIDA)

Looking east from the lighthouse. Barely visible on the shore in the right center is a two-gun sand battery. Just above the right-hand row of tents is another. And just above the tents at left, distinguishable by the straight horizontal line of its parapet, is Fort Barrancas. The buildings to its left are the Barrancas Barracks, while the tall building with cupola in the distance to the right of the barracks is the Marine Hospital. This is, arguably, the first "aerial" photograph in military history. (SHC)

*Confederate camps and a four-gun sand battery immediately below the lighthouse. The "subterranean passages" connecting the guns are clearly visible, as are several Confederates lounging in the vicinity. These are Alabama troops. In the distance on the low spit of sand dune is Fort McRee, "weak and badly built," thought Russell, and "quite under the command of Pickens." (*GULF ISLANDS NATIONAL SEASHORE*)*

A Confederate encampment just south of Bayou Grande, near Pensacola, probably the Orleans Cadets. This may be the finest Confederate camp scene to survive, excellent not only for its clarity, but for what it shows as well. Almost every aspect of camp life is depicted. A bugler with his instrument to his lips, a soldier with fishing pole in hand, men reading letters and newspapers, others cleaning their rifles, a fatigue detail with shovel on shoulder, two Johnnies feigning a spar, and at right, pipe in mouth, a company officer handing orders to a saluting corporal. To the left are piled boxes of fresh rations. In this image Edwards outdid himself. (STATE PHOTOGRAPHIC ARCHIVES, STROZIER LIBRARY, FLORIDA STATE UNIVERSITY)

The encampment of the Louisville Blues, the 1st Alabama, near the lighthouse. There is a definite lack of order in this camp, blankets and clothing and equipment hanging wherever convenient. These men would learn a lot about soldiering in the years ahead, and about sanitation, too. A trench, perhaps a latrine, is just a few feet to the left of their tents and mess area. Disease, in this war, will kill far more men than bullets. (RP)

Camps of Mississippi regiments behind the lighthouse. (TU)

*Edwards did not move his camera after capturing the Mississippi camps.
Instead, he moved the Mississippians. Here they parade in all their sartorial
chaos. Top hats, stovepipes, slouch and military caps, hunting shirts, bow ties,
flannel checks, and their captain in front in a decidedly unmilitary vest. Yet
they all have rifles, and an unshakable determination. Nowhere in the world
was there another soldiery like them.* (PHS)

*The 9th Mississippi in camp, and for an Edwards photo, an unusually clear
surviving print. Rarely can one see such a brilliant representation of the
Confederate soldier of 1861. Especially eye-catching is the soldier crouching to
the left of the stand of rifles at left. The significance of the numeral "4" on his
shirt is unknown, but his resplendence is unarguable. They all have the lean,
hardened look of the American backwoods. Such men could be unbeatable.* (RP)

One of Bragg's five big siege guns, a 10-inch columbiad, and, to its right, a tunnel passage to the next gun. There are more uniforms here, more of a military look, but the same posturing for the camera of all these Southrons of 1861. The war was still a lark to them. Most had never been this far from home in their lives. They expected to be home again before the fall. (TU)

The second 10-inch columbiad in this Perote sand battery. It is manned by more Mississippians, the Quitman Rifles. (PHS)

A quiet moment in camp for men of Company B, 9th Mississippi, the Quitman Rifles. These are men from Holly Springs, Mississippi, and at least one of them is probably writing home. His tent mate reads a book, while their friend in the shadows behind their rifles appears to be peeling potatoes. Three years from now the Confederate soldier will regard this simple tent and its furnishings as unimaginable luxury. (PHS)

Company B of the 9th Mississippi again. The man stooping over the frying pan is Kinlock Falconer. One day he will serve on Bragg's staff. For the moment, he is about to serve some fried pork. The closest thing to a uniform for this company would appear to be checkered pants. (LC)

*A mortar in the water battery just west of the lighthouse, which can be seen
above the trees at left. Some of the projecting flanges William H. Russell
mentioned can be seen on the shot stacked at right. There is much evidence of
work, but apparently it was not necessarily done with perfect harmony.
"Considerable improvements were in the course of execution," found Russell,
"but the officers were not always agreed as to the work to be done. Captain A.,
at the wheelbarrows: 'Now then, you men, wheel up these sandbags, and
range them just at this corner.' Major B.: 'My good Captain A., what do you
want the bags there for? Did I not tell you, these merlons were not to be
finished till we had completed the parapet on the front?' Captain A.: 'Well,
Major, so you did, and your order made me think you know darned little about
your business; so I am going to do a little engineering of my own.'" Such was
American democracy in action.* (NA, OFFICE OF THE CHIEF OF ENGINEERS)

*The Orleans Cadets and their leader, Captain Dreux, a well-uniformed unit for
a change. New Orleans was particularly anxious to know the doings of her
native sons at Pensacola, and Edwards was aware of the commercial
possibilities of selling photographs of them at home. "Any of them will form an
interesting souvenir for the parlor," read his advertisement for the prints in
New Orleans, "particularly in the event, considered now so near at hand, of the
capture of Fort Pickens." (TU)*

*But the only Confederate who would capture Fort Pickens would be Edwards
himself, and here he takes not only the fort, but a Federal ship as well, the
U.S.S. Macedonian. His epic task done, J. D. Edwards, truly the
"Photographer of the Confederacy," would take back with him to New Orleans
a priceless record of Southerners in the early days of their bid for nationhood.
Yet his images would be all but lost, and Edwards a forgotten man. He and
they deserved better. He was truly a man with vision. (USAMHI)*

The North at War

MAURY KLEIN

Life in a country in conflict, yet still growing

UNLIKE THE SOUTHERNERS captured by
J. D. Edwards and others, for most Northerners the
Civil War was a distant event. They did not witness its carnage firsthand, and their cities and
farms escaped the devastation that blighted large
areas of the South. Seldom did the din of combat
reach their ears or the menace of invading troops
disturb their daily routines. Life went on, if not as
usual, at least with a minimum of disruption.

But distance from the battlefield could not protect Northerners from the effects of a long and
bloody war. The ordeal of sustaining so massive a
struggle intruded upon people's lives in countless
ways. The most obvious of these was, of course, the
absence of friends and kinfolk in the service. Every
town and hamlet watched its young men depart
for the front, some to die and others to return
home with bodies maimed or spirits broken. Concern for the safety of loved ones permeated households throughout the North, aggravated by the
slowness with which accurate details or casualty
lists reached home after a major battle. Thus did
distance from the seat of war breed anxiety as well
as security.

The presence of men in uniform, whether home
on leave or forming into newly organized units,
also served as constant reminders to civilians. Sol

diers could be found on the streets of cities and villages everywhere. Returning wounded brought
home stark evidence of their ordeal in combat.
Rare was the town that did not welcome home a
veteran minus an arm or leg or worse. Army camps
and prisoner-of-war compounds were opened in
many towns, and by 1862 conscription officers had
begun to replace recruitment drives and became
objects of loathing wherever they appeared.
Through all these agents the war came home to
every northern community.

Those who did not join the army found their lives
affected in other ways. The northern war effort
depended not only upon its advantage in men and
guns but also upon its superior industrial and agricultural might. In terms of productivity the war
was fought as much at home as on the battlefield,
and the fight enlisted men, women, and children
alike. The drain of manpower for military service,
coupled with increased demand for goods, meant
simply that there were fewer people to do more
work. Farm and factory alike responded to this
need in two ways: by increasing their use of machinery to replace human labor and by putting
more women and children to work.

The North relied upon its staple crops both to
feed its people and army and to produce surpluses

*The North at war was a bustling place. The great cities grew greater, frontiers
moved farther west, business and industry expanded. An early postwar view
of New York and, in the foreground, its city hall.* (USAMHI)

which could be sold abroad for sorely needed gold.
As thousands of men left the farms to fight the
war, women, children, and older men took up the
heavy field work. At the same time the use of agricultural machinery spread rapidly, a fact which
delighted manufacturers who sniffed bonanza
profits. As Cyrus McCormick reminded one of his
salesmen in Illinois, "Don't be so blue over the
prospects. Remember 20,000 militia have to leave
this state . . . and these men will have to come,
many or a large share of them, from the farms."

Mowers and reapers were still relatively new
machines in 1860; by 1864 production of them exceeded 70,000, or twice the output of 1862. These
wondrous devices saved human labor and could be
operated even by women and children. Other ma-

chines, including the horse-rake, cultivators, new
harrows, corn planters, steam threshers, and grain
drills were also devised and marketed. The use of
machinery increased the scale of agriculture and
enabled farmers to bring more land under cultiva-
tion, especially in the West.

The results of this effort were impressive. Northern farmers produced large enough corn, oat, and
wheat crops during the war years—including record crops in 1862—to fill domestic needs and still
sell large quantities to England, which experienced
three straight years of crop failures. Hog and cattle
output also increased dramatically, and wool production jumped from 60 million pounds in 1860 to
140 million pounds in 1865. During that same period the number of sheep in the North doubled, an

Fifth Avenue, looking north from the southeast corner of Twenty-eighth Street,
New York, 1865. (NYHS)

important gain since wool offered the most common substitute for the cotton supply diminished by the South's secession.

Apparently photographers, like other Northerners, took great pride in this record of productivity; at least they delighted in capturing scenes showing the new machines at work. But when they turned their attention to the factories, something more than productivity caught the eye. Pictures of giant machines sweeping across fields, or of fishing boats plying the waters of Nantucket, conveyed a sense of majesty, even charm. However, scenes of women and small children toiling in a factory, although they might suggest the sacrifice and pro-

ductivity so vital to the war effort, were utterly lacking in beauty or nobility. Unlike the sight of a man or woman astride a reaper, no charm attached to the spectacle of people young and old harnessed to machines inside dingy mills.

But the mills and factories played a major role in carrying the North to victory. From their bustling, clanging interiors came a swelling stream of muskets, cannon, equipment, locomotives, rails, wagons, tools, uniforms, shoes, and thousands of other items. Wartime needs spurred the development of other industries besides agricultural implements and armaments. The demand for uniforms and shoes prompted increased use of sewing machines. One by-product of this work was the discovery that uniforms and shoes manufactured in a few basic sizes would fit most men. This standardization simplified the production of uniforms and shoes in quantity and after the war stimulated the rise of the ready-made clothing industry. Military needs also lent a strong impetus to the canned food industry, including Gail Borden's canned milk. The desire to produce canned food quickly and in quantity led to improvements in canning techniques and machinery.

As its farms and factories responded to the war effort, an aura of prosperity settled across the North. Newspapers and politicians alike waxed elo-

quent over the nation's material well-being. The New York *Times* noted in 1864 that Northerners were better housed, clothed, and fed than ever before "in the midst of the most gigantic civil war . . . yet seen." Wholesale farm prices doubled during the war years while nonagricultural wages rose 43 per cent. Farm land values soared, as did real estate values in general.

For most Northerners, however, this prosperity proved more apparent than real. As always, wartime brought a sharp inflationary trend which in many cases erased gains in wages or income. Wholesale prices more than doubled while the consumer price index increased from 102 to 177. Ac-

Chestnut Street in Philadelphia just before the war. Hotels, booksellers, typesetters, engravers—the North bustled with the work of tradesmen and artisans. (FREE LIBRARY OF PHILADELPHIA)

Away from the eastern coast, the market towns and county seats continued to thrive as before the conflict. Indeed, the presence of large-scale armies boosted business in many communities. The market square in Carlisle, Pennsylvania, in 1862. (LC)

cording to one recent calculation, the real wage index actually declined from 102 in January 1861 to 67 in January 1865.

Wage earners suffered most from the ravages of inflation, but attempts to improve their lot through organization made little headway during the war. Most wartime trade unions began at the local level, primarily in New York, Pennsylvania, and Massachusetts, and boasted some 300 locals with an estimated 200,000 members by 1865. City federations, begun in Rochester in March 1863, soon sprang up in most major industrial centers. Intended only as advisory bodies, the federations as-

sumed such tasks as organizing trades and boycotts, generating publicity during strikes, and opposing the importation of strikebreakers. They also founded labor newspapers and in thirty-six cities and towns helped establish cooperative stores.

Attempts to revive national trade associations made some gains, but the national organizations were loose bodies with little effective power over their locals. In general the labor movement remained weak during the war. Unskilled workers, especially women, children, and blacks, endured starvation wages and sweatshop conditions with little hope of improving their lot.

Hanover Junction, Pennsylvania, around November 1863. Like hundreds of minor railroad towns, its townspeople saw little of the war and felt its effects even less, except when the trains came through loaded with soldiers going to the front. (USAMHI)

Wartime conditions imposed unusual hardships upon workers. According to a Senate report, industrial workers provided the Union Army with about one third of its troops. The Conscription Act of 1863, with its provision that service might be evaded by hiring a substitute or paying a three-hundred-dollar commutation fee, especially rankled laborers. On several occasions resentment against the draft boiled into bloody riots. The most spectacular of these occurred in New York City in July 1863 when a mob wrecked the recruiting station, demolished rail and streetcar lines and shipyards, closed factories, attacked the homes of leading Republicans, and killed several blacks. Similar riots engulfed other cities in turmoil but brought no relief to workers.

Strikes proved equally futile in wartime. The public regarded them as disloyal and the government sometimes responded with troops. On several occasions President Lincoln felt obliged to inter-

vene in an attempt to salve the feelings of workers and preserve their loyalty to the war effort. At the same time the government took steps to increase the labor supply diminished by military service and a decline in immigration. In both 1861 and 1862 immigration, which had averaged 281,455 people a year during the 1850s, fell off to slightly less than 92,000. The figure rose to 176,282 in 1863, but the following year Congress, prodded by Lincoln and concerned industrialists, passed a law which permitted the importation of contract laborers. Whatever the effect of this act, immigration rose to 193,418 in 1864 and 248,120 in 1865.

But if workers found prosperity elusive, many businessmen reaped fat profits from wartime opportunities. Alert contractors were quick to take advantage of the government's needs. Some were content to earn legitimate fortunes while others resorted to dishonest means to make their killings. Never had the nation created so large an army or required armaments and equipment on so vast a scale. The scale of operations, as well as the urgency of purchasing so much so quickly, invited corruption of unprecedented dimensions. Revelation after revelation rocked the public, prompting the New York *Herald* in June 1864 to denounce the "gross corruption prevailing in nearly every department of the government." Large commissions went to men whose only service was to procure lucrative government contracts for firms.

On the stock and gold exchanges, speculators thrived on the uncertainties of wartime. Good news from the front boosted the prices of gold and stocks; bad news sent them crashing downward. Hordes of speculators, including some women braving ridicule in a traditionally male arena, plunged into the treacherous currents of Wall Street seeking a quick fortune. One crafty manipulator, Daniel Drew, recalled that "Along with ordinary happenings, we fellows in Wall Street had the fortunes of war to speculate about. . . . It's good

An apple seller in Cincinnati, Ohio, typical of the street vendors that every large city spawned. (LO)

fishing in troubled waters." Young Jay Gould went one step further: he devised an ingenious system whereby he obtained by telegraph advance information on Union victories or defeats and shifted his speculations accordingly.

Not all northern businessmen were corrupt or dishonest, and not all made fortunes. But the war created a free-wheeling, opportunistic atmosphere that proved irresistible to many people. It is important to remember that not all Northerners bothered to fight the war or even tender it active support. Some people lacked strong interest in the conflict and either ignored it as best they could or resented it as an intrusion into their private affairs.

Among this group were men who found the wartime situation a golden opportunity for self-advancement. Their activities escaped the camera's eye, as did those of the plungers on Wall Street and the hustlers of government contracts, but their ultimate importance rivaled anything that took place on the battlefield. These ambitious young entrepreneurs used the war years to establish themselves in business while their peers were caught up in the clash of arms. Some made their fortunes even before the war ended, while others planted the roots of what were to be long and prosperous careers.

Within this group could be found a surprising number of the business titans who were to dominate the economy, and therefore much of American life, during the half century between the Civil War and World War I: Andrew Carnegie, J. P. Morgan, John D. Rockefeller, George F. Baker, James J. Hill, Gustavus Swift, Charles A. Pillsbury, George M. Pullman, Mark Hanna, Marshall Field, Jay Gould, John Wanamaker, and Peter Widener, to name but a few. Each of these men, and others like them, ignored the call to arms and concentrated instead upon the windfall business opportunities bred by wartime conditions. Few of them even tried to enlist, fewer still stayed home because of disability, and several (Carnegie, Gould, Morgan, Rockefeller, and Philip D. Armour among them) hired substitutes.

In later years some of these men grew defensive about their failure to enter the service. "I was represented in the army," Rockefeller insisted. "I sent more than twenty men, yes, nearly thirty. That is, I made such arrangements for them that they were able to go." The majority, however,

St. Paul, Minnesota, a city that grew largely from the speculations in the 1850s of Washington politicians and bankers, several of them now Confederates. (MHS)

seemed content to concentrate on the business at hand. One son of banker Thomas Mellon begged his father for money to speculate in wheat. Writing from Wisconsin, he observed that people "continue growing richer and don't care when the war closes." Mindful of the educational value afforded by prevailing conditions, the elder Mellon flatly forbade another son from enlisting:

> I had hoped my boy was going to make a smart intelligent businessman and was not such a goose as to be *seduced from duty* by the declamations of buncombe speeches. It is only greenhorns who enlist. *You can learn nothing in the army.* . . . In time you will come to understand and believe that a man may be a patriot without risking his own life or sacrificing his health. There are plenty of other lives less valuable or ready to serve for the love of serving.

To most of these men, wartime opportunities brought financial nest eggs from which huge fortunes later hatched. For them, and for many others

who advanced their prospects during those turbulent years, prosperity was anything but illusory.

Social activities reflected this mood of rising affluence, especially in the cities. As the war dragged on through month after weary month of bloody battles that produced defeat or indecision, Northerners sought diversions to dispel the gloom of uncertainty that clouded the future. So frenetic did the quest for amusement and gaiety become that stern observers periodically denounced the populace for their indifference to the suffering and hardships endured by soldiers at the front.

In rural areas, where the workday was always long and sources of amusement few, life went on much as it had before the war. There were church socials, husking bees, country fairs, and occasional barn dances. Young men played baseball or competed in foot races, wrestling, and shooting matches. A religious revival or camp meeting, accompanied by picnics and other festivities, might enliven a farm community for a week or more. Many a small town possessed an "opry house" that never saw an opera but welcomed touring lectures, dramatic companies, or minstrel shows. Occasionally too a traveling circus might wend its way through the countryside, thrilling farm folk with its menagerie of strange animals and exotic freaks. No event rivaled the celebration of national holidays like the Fourth of July, for which families gathered from miles around to enjoy barbeques, games, fireworks, oratory, and dancing, usually accompanied by liberal swigs from jugs of whiskey or hard cider.

City life offered far more varied and sophisticated amusements. As always the upper class set the standards and indulged themselves most freely. Dinners, receptions, and elegant parties occupied the fashionable in every city, especially Washington and New York. Roller-skating made its appearance in 1863 and New York's social denizens seized upon it as a pleasure which they hoped to confine to "the educated and refined classes." Ice-skating parties lightened the tedium of winter while periodic visits to fashionable resorts in Newport, Narragansett Pier, or upstate New York helped pass the summer months. Every major city had its lyceums and lecture halls, and in New York the Academy of Music offered the cultured elite a sampling of grand opera imported from Europe.

Crowds flocked to the theaters of every city in unprecedented numbers. Comedies were the staple fare, both in the high-tone playhouses and in lower-class theaters like those in New York's Bowery, where huge crowds gathered to yell and whistle, cheer and hiss, chew peanuts and spit tobacco juice. Although the emphasis upon comedy reflected a desire to escape the war, at least for a few hours, dramas based upon recent battles also proved popular. One energetic producer opened a play about Bull Run within a month of the battle, and later engagements were put on the boards by adapting a standard script to each occasion.

Besides theater, northern urbanites patronized minstrel shows, burlesque, dance halls, winter gardens, prizefights, cockfights, and the saloons. In New York, P. T. Barnum's American Museum drew enormous crowds, as did imitation counterparts in other cities. To the rest of the North Barnum sent his traveling circus, the Grand Colossal Museum and Menagerie, with curiosities borrowed from the American Museum and animals gathered from every corner of the world.

As always in wartime, amusements offered a counterpoint to anxiety and uncertainty. To out-

ward appearance, at least as the photographer captured it, life in the North hewed as closely to its normal patterns as was possible in an era of great duress. The camera recorded with an unblinking eye scenes of a wartime society clinging to its familiar habits while adjusting to changes imposed by the conflict. In so doing it portrayed the landscape of northern society unembellished and often unadorned. This fidelity freed later generations from the illustrator's imagination. Unlike the artist's drawing, the photograph offered viewers not an interpretation of a scene but some raw materials of a scene which one might interpret for himself.

More than this the camera could not do. For one thing the technology of photography was still in its infancy. Photographers still relied upon the wet-plate collodion process, a cumbersome and complicated business which required a wagonload of equipment, including a traveling dark tent for immediate developing, for all work done outside the studio. In effect the photographer could not operate abroad without carrying his laboratory with him. Even then he could not take action pictures with the equipment at his disposal.

In a real sense, then, the camera could capture little more than the bare surface of northern life during the war. On one hand, most of what was important took place beyond the photographer's— or anyone else's—eye; on the other, the technology of photography was unprepared to record the dynamism that was the essence of life in the North during these years.

War is not a still life, either on the battlefield or on the home front. The camera could preserve the residue of battle but not battle itself, the portraits of heroes but not their heroic deeds. Similarly, it might depict the stage, scenery, and characters of northern life, but not the dramatic action or inner moods and conflicts of the play itself. That realm still belonged to the writers, the painters, and the illustrators.

It is not possible to reconstruct the North at war through photographs or any other artifacts. Through the camera's eye we may look down Broadway in New York or inspect a prison in Chicago or pause at a corner in Hanover Junction. We can feel the heat and drabness of a textile mill or watch track layers at work or fishing boats casting their nets off Narragansett Bay. Each of these pictures represents neither an action nor a scene but a single-frame, a fleeting moment of time frozen and preserved for our imaginations to mull over.

Nothing before the camera had the power to do even that. To those who possess an insatiable appetite for knowledge of the past and of our ancestors, these frozen fragments remain a towering achievement and a precious legacy. Previously it was scarcely possible to preserve intact even the faces, structures, and artifacts of history. In that sense the advent of the camera divides the historical record into two distinct epochs: that about which we have read or heard or viewed the remains of, and that which we have glimpsed with our own eyes, if only fleetingly and in part.

It is fortunate indeed that the Civil War lies, if only barely, upon the latter side of that division. Without these photographs our sense of what life was like in those terrible years would be much the poorer.

Travel and sightseeing increased, even among the notables, and especially among the soldiers and foreign observers and dignitaries. Here Secretary of State William Seward entertains a host of diplomats in a pastoral setting. Those seated are, from the left, Molena, Nicaraguan minister; Seward; Baron de Stoeckel, Russian minister; and Mr. Sheffield, the British legation attaché. Standing from the left are Donaldson of Seward's State Department, a man unidentified, Secretary Bodesco of the Russian legation, Swedish minister Count Piper, Italian minister Bertenattie, Hanseatic minister Schleider, French minister Henri Mercier, and Lord Lyons, minister from Britain. (NA)

Main Street in Salt Lake City, Utah, October 24, 1861. Western Union, impelled largely by the war, completes the first transcontinental telegraph. Beneath the backdrop of the mighty mountains, a simple ceremony marks the occasion. With great good fortune, Western Union's "Telegraph Office" is right next to a combination liquor store and "Ambrotype Gallery." The result was this ambrotype of an historic moment. (LO)

The people of the Union played, and baseball became more and more a pastime. The New York Knickerbocker Nine in 1864. (NATIONAL BASEBALL LIBRARY)

Russian sailors like these were a new sight in New York and San Francisco, where the czar's fleet made showings of support for the Union. (WRHS)

Of course, there was no escape from the war entirely. Guns were everywhere. A mammoth Rodman smoothbore, photographed by Montgomery C. Meigs. (LC)

The mode of transporting a Rodman by rail, suspended from a bridge truss. (LC)

Federal commanders did rule over certain threatened parts of the country. Major General John A. Dix exercised considerable authority over largely secessionist Maryland. (USAMHI)

Governors like Andrew Curtin of Pennsylvania initiated calls for volunteers for the Army, Curtin calling for 50,000 in 1862 and 60,000 the next year. Unlike most northern governors, he also faced the trauma of Confederate invasion of his state at Gettysburg. (CHICAGO PUBLIC LIBRARY, SPECIAL COLLECTIONS)

Recruiting offices appeared in every city of any size, as here on New York's State Street. The three main buildings house the United States Quartermaster's office, but the partially obscured house on the far right has a flag in front, and a broadside offering a three-hundred-dollar bounty to men who enlist. (USAMHI)

Even on Broadway in New York the recruiters worked, and at right, behind the flag, stands the evidence of their success, an army barracks in the heart of the city. No wonder an enterprising vendor selected this spot to sell his sarsaparilla and beer at 3 cents per glass. (USAMHI)

Photographer Fuller of Madison, Wisconsin, visited his local recruiter, not to enlist, but to shoot. "Enlist—Veteran Regiment" reads the broadside. Perhaps more than a few boys were induced to join after sampling the bottles and jugs, but the significance of the fencing match is, alas, lost. (USAMHI)

*All through the war the United States Military Academy at West Point
continued to produce officers for the armies.* (NA, U. S. SIGNAL CORPS)

*The cadets were eager to get to the fighting before it was ended. Many did.
Some, like Ranald Mackenzie, seated at left, would become generals. An 1862
photograph.* (USAMHI)

Two cadets of the class of 1864. They will have their chance for glory. (USAMHI)

They, like many of the generals North and South now battling all across the country, learned their military science from Professor Dennis Hart Mahan. His alumni formed a register of nearly all the high command of both armies. (USAMHI)

The Army's military posts in the North continued their functions as before, only now incredibly more busily. The second oldest post in the nation was Carlisle Barracks, Pennsylvania. Here we see guard mounting at the cavalry school of practice in 1861. Portions of the barracks behind them will be sacked by Jeb Stuart's cavalry in 1863. (T. SCOTT SANDERS)

The evidences of a nation at war were not hard to find. Fort Ellsworth in Alexandria, Virginia, named for the Union's first martyr. (USAMHI)

*Forrest Hall Military Prison in Georgetown, D.C. Next door a candy store,
with jars of peppermint sticks in the window.* (USAMHI)

Industry for the war. A Du Pont powder mill near Wilmington, Delaware.
(E. I. DU PONT DE NEMOURS & CO.)

The Schuylkill Arsenal in Philadelphia. (KA)

The blacksmith and wagon repair shop at Camp Holt, near Jeffersonville, Indiana. (INDIANA HISTORICAL SOCIETY LIBRARY)

While fighting all along its southern "borders," the Union also had to cast a careful eye to its northern boundaries, should Great Britain decide to aid the Confederacy. Then Canada would be a natural launching place for invasion. Major General John J. Peck commanded the troops along the North's Canadian frontier in 1864–65. (P-M)

*In all the major cities and ports, the barracks. Fort Richmond on Staten Island,
New York. June 29, 1864.* (USAMHI)

Gunboats like the U.S.S. Michigan, *the Navy's first iron-hulled warship, built in 1844, cruised the Great Lakes during the war.* (NAVAL PHOTOGRAPHIC CENTER)

But for most Northerners, the most common war experience was seeing the ever-present soldiers, either going or coming, in city and country. Hanover Junction, Pennsylvania, in November 1863, saw several, some obviously recuperating from wounds and walking with canes. (USAMHI)

In the larger cities the churches and civic groups operated entertainment centers for the soldiers home on leave or recovering from their wounds. Here the "Union Volunteer Refreshment Saloon" in Philadelphia catered to the soldiers' tastes for food and beverage, if not ladies. (LO)

Sometimes when whole regiments came home on leave, their townsfolk entertained them royally. G. H. Houghton caught the scene in Brattleboro, Vermont, when the city welcomed home the 7th Vermont Infantry in September 1864. Arms stacked outside, the soldiers are in the Brattleboro Hotel, the building with white columns at the end of the street. While the veterans tried to forget the war for a while, the boys flocked to the street to rub their fingers over the shining bayonets of their brothers and fathers. Surely they had ventilated many a Rebel. (VERMONT HISTORICAL SOCIETY)

Happy were the men of the regiment whose enlistment expired. The 45th Massachusetts, at Readville, July 7, 1863, the day before they muster out. (MICHAEL J. HAMMERSON)

Homecoming for all too many, however, meant crepe and tears and the cold ground. It was a sight the North would become used to. (NA)

*The guard of honor for the funeral of Lieutenant Colonel George E. Marshall
of the 40th Massachusetts, killed at Cold Harbor, Virginia, in June 1864. Here
at home in Fitchburg, even the eagle above him is draped in mourning.*
(USAMHI)

The Ottawa, Illinois, home of Brigadier General W. H. L. Wallace, mortally wounded at Shiloh. His portrait, his riderless horse, the flag for which he died tell the whole story. (CHS)

Finally they will come in such numbers that the government must set aside special sanctuaries for its honored dead. A. J. Russell's photograph of the military cemetery at Alexandria. (NEIKRUG PHOTOGRAPHICA, LTD.)

There, in rank upon rank, they will sleep through the ages. (NEIKRUG PHOTOGRAPHICA, LTD.)

Only on a few occasions will the North actually feel the sting of the enemy's sword, and nowhere more than in Chambersburg, Pennsylvania. In July 1864, Confederates set the torch to the town when it could not raise a ransom. The fire devastated much of the town. This view by the Zacharias brothers looks down Queen Street. (MAURICE MAROTTE, JR.)

The center of Chambersburg. Rebuilding has begun already. (MAURICE MAROTTE, JR.)

Greater crises faced the nation than enemy raids. The men of the Supreme
Court had to deal constantly with the limits of authority in an emergency, with
habeas corpus, and the safety of the nation versus the rights of the individual.
(NA)

In December 1864, this military commission tried and convicted Indiana
dissenter Lambden P. Milligan of treason and sentenced him to death. Two
years later, in ex parte Milligan, the Supreme Court would reverse that
conviction. (INDIANA STATE LIBRARY)

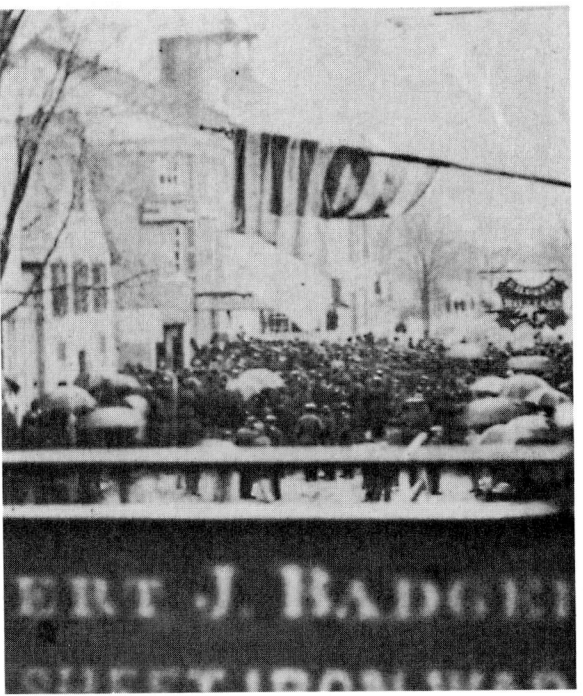

"Copperhead" newspapers, those
seemingly disloyal or opposed to the war
on whatever grounds, were often mobbed
and destroyed. In Portsmouth, New
Hampshire, a mob gathers in front of the
States & Union office angrily denouncing
its editorial stance. The sudden
appearance of rain dampened their ardor,
and the newspaper was not molested.
(USAMHI)

Riots against the military draft in 1863 turned
New York City into a bedlam, and left over 100
people dead. Lieutenant Commander Richard W.
Meade, Jr., nephew of General George G. Meade,
subdued the rioters. (USAMHI)

*In the North, war news came chiefly from the press, and the industry
capitalized whenever possible on the salability of the most recent news. Here on
June 9, 1862, the Pittsburgh* Dispatch *office advertises* "LATER FROM RICHMOND
& MEMPHIS, *Genl McClellan's Report of the Battle, Our loss in killed wounded
& missing 5,134." Three days before, thirteen Union and Confederate ships
met in the last fleet battle of the war at Memphis. On June 1 the Battle of Fair
Oaks in McClellan's Peninsula Campaign concluded. The* Dispatch *was
reporting both, and its billboard sign probably lists Pittsburghers injured in the
battles. The editor, Joseph Singerly Lare, appears in top hat seated at the right
on the second-floor ledge.* (MRS. ALBERT MCBRIDE)

The Dispatch *took offices above J. M. Fulton's Drug Store on Fifth Avenue.
Interested citizens gathered outside on the sidewalk for the early edition with
the latest news from the fronts.* (MRS. ALBERT MCBRIDE)

The most notorious copperhead of all was Ohio's Clement L. Vallandigham, pictured here in the center. Expelled from the Union, he went south, but Jefferson Davis did not want him either. He spent some time in Canada, then returned to Ohio in 1864, hoping vainly to cause an uprising of antiwar feeling that would defeat Lincoln at the polls. (LC)

Running against Lincoln was his one-time general, George B. McClellan. Virtually shelved after Antietam in the fall of 1862, "Little Mac" accepted the Democratic nomination in 1864. There was no beating Lincoln. (USAMHI)

Momence, Illinois, like most other towns in the Union, saw large demonstrations for Lincoln. He won handily. (CHS)

Meanwhile, the people of the North watched and waited. The ladies sewed mammoth flags for the soldiers. These are the ladies of the Pennsylvania Academy of Fine Arts. (LO)

*Mammoth exhibitions were held to benefit soldiers' relief organizations, like the
Union Avenue fair held in Philadelphia in 1864 by the Sanitary Commission.
All manner of war relics were displayed, including ship's wheels from famous
vessels, cases of bullets, flags, and even photographs.* (KA)

Art exhibited at the Sanitary Fair, including Emanuel Leutze's heroic depiction of Washington crossing the Delaware. (NA)

New York's great Metropolitan Fair, the largest of its kind, attracted thousands. (NA)

They saw a wondrous array of relics, displayed in that cluttered fashion so beloved of the Victorians. Here the uniform of the martyr Elmer Ellsworth, stained with his holy blood. (NA)

Captured enemy flags and relics of the battlefields. (NA)

Suppliers of military hardware displayed their stock. Here a complete exhibit of the pistols and accessories made by the Colt firearms company of Connecticut. The war made Samuel Colt a millionaire, and he sold to both sides. (NA)

Giant projectiles, swords, rifles, axes, even items totally unrelated to the war, and much of it for sale to a souvenir-hungry public. "Relics from Vicksburg Sold Here." (NA)

All manner of weapons, and even soldier art works, like miniature churches fashioned during the long hours in winter quarters. (NA)

And for those not interested in the current war, a little something from an earlier era. (NA)

For those who could not see the great fairs, the photographers provided ample souvenir cartes de visite of soldiers celebrating victories. Fetter of Logansport, Indiana, captured these two sailors, one of them a double amputee, carrying a box marked "Remember Fort Fisher." For such men, pity would be their only livelihood.

(DAVID FINNEY)

*Another popular image, the old bugler and his
dog. A Brady gallery photo taken at West Point in
1864.* (LO)

*Young girls shammed at soldiering for the camera,
often to send to boyfriends in the Army.*
(WENDELL W. LANG, JR.)

And a few women who actually passed for men or otherwise served the Army, made capital of it at home. Actress Pauline Cushman (not a very good actress) publicized widely her activities as a spy (not a very good one) in Bragg's army. (LO)

The North lived through the war and rejoiced at its end. When July 1865 came, and soldiers of Battery B, 2d United States Artillery, came to the new Soldiers National Cemetery at Gettysburg, they could look back upon the epic thus ended with some pride in their contribution to it behind the lines. (LC)

And they looked back on one who told them this time would come, and that they should look ahead "with malice toward none." Abraham Lincoln's second inauguration, March 4, 1865. Lincoln is seated, hands in his lap, just to the left of the small white lectern. On his right is Vice-President Andrew Johnson. (WRHS)

The Photographers of the War

FREDERIC E. RAY

Historians with cameras and their journey for posterity

WHEN AMERICA WENT TO WAR, the camera went with it, and by 1861 neither was a stranger to the other. Photography, as an art and an industry, had already marked its first quarter century before the guns sounded. It had come a long way.

A Frenchman, Joseph-Nicéphore Niépce, experimented with the camera obscura in the 1820s and in 1826 produced probably the first successful photograph on a polished pewter plate. The exposure took eight hours. Nine years later an Englishman, Henry Fox Talbot, developed the first practical imaging process. He called it the calotype and produced it by using paper sensitized with silver salts.

But it remained for another Frenchman, one-time partner of Niépce, to make the photograph truly attainable. Louis-Jacques-Mandé Daguerre announced his "Daguerreotype" in 1839. He used a sensitized, silver-coated copper plate to capture light images in less than one half hour. Unlike Talbot, Daguerre made his methods public and the daguerreotype quickly found enthusiastic acceptance in Europe.

Thanks to two remarkable men of genius, it also found its way to America almost from the moment of creation. Samuel F. B. Morse, inventor of the

telegraph, visited Daguerre in Paris in 1839 and brought back with him the process. The next year he and John W. Draper, a noted New York physicist, began experiments which led shortly to a reduction in exposure time from half an hour to half a minute. At once a lucrative portrait business mushroomed in the country, and one of the principal proponents of this new process was upstate New Yorker Mathew B. Brady, whose fashionable New York and Washington studios would soon attract the notables of the day. Before long a "Brady" became the commonplace term for a portrait.

In 1851, seven years after Brady went into business, another Englishman, Frederick Scott Archer, developed the collodion or wet-plate process. By recording his image on a glass plate, thus producing a negative, he and his revolutionary invention enabled the multiple duplication of photographs printed on salt- or albumen-treated paper, whereas the daguerreotypist could make one image, and one only. Archer's soon became the accepted process for portrait photographers, and their profession spread throughout America. By 1860 there were 3,154 photographers, ambrotypists, daguerreotypists, calotypists, melainotypists, and practitioners of other varieties of the art, spread from New York to San Francisco, from Chicago to New Orleans. The image took America by storm.

By the early 1860s almost every middle-class family owned an album, filled not only with portraits of their own, but also with copies of mass-produced images of their presidents, public figures, even actors and actresses. The carte de visite, a calling card-sized photograph ideally suited for albums—and for calling cards—became a rage. And for those wanting more realism, there was the stereoscopic view. The camera made two images simultaneously from two different lenses. They were mounted side by side on a card which, when viewed through a hand-held stereoscope, produced a three-dimensional picture. Thousands were sold to the parlors of America in the late 1850s.

With this market burgeoning just as the nation went to war in 1861, the economic potential of supplying war scenes to the public became self-evident. And others had already led the way in previous conflicts. Fifteen years before, an anonymous daguerreotypist went to Saltillo during the war with Mexico and made at least four outdoor military images that have survived. One shows Major General John E. Wool and his staff astride their horses in the streets of the city and is remarkable for its clarity. Several years later, during the Crimean War, a British artist turned photographer, Roger Fenton, employed the collodion process to capture over 350 images of the war in the Crimea.

And then the Civil War. In fact, the first artists to recognize and attempt to exploit its possibilities were southern photographers, and it is a happy thing for posterity that they did. Just a few months later the blockade so restricted the necessary imported chemicals and supplies that Confederate artists could no longer afford the highly speculative business of taking outdoor war views. After 1861 they almost exclusively used their carefully husbanded materials for the indoor portrait work that made their livelihood.

Simultaneously they descended on Charleston and Pensacola. Within days after the surrender of Fort Sumter, F. K. Houston of 307 King Street in Charleston set his camera within the parade ground of the fortress and captured it himself on his wet plates. On April 17 arrived James Osborn and F. E. Durbec of Osborn & Durbec's Southern

Stereoscopic & Photographic Depot on 223 King Street, at the "sign of the Big Camera." Their epic coverage of the fort and its environs would not be surpassed during the rest of the war. And at the same time, far away in Pensacola, Florida, J. D. Edwards of New Orleans began his own epic. Others, George S. Cook of Charleston and J. W. Petty of New Orleans, for instance, made less ambitious forays from their studios, but after the first spring of the war, they rarely did so again. Only Cook took one brief sortie in 1863, again to Sumter. For the rest of the war they would not be heard from again.

Then came Brady. "I can only describe the destiny that overruled me by saying that, like Euphorion, I felt that I had to go." So he said, and so he did. Perhaps he was urged by the example of Edwards and the others—for he and the North knew of their work—but more likely he and they had the same idea at the same time. In July 1861, excited by the prospect of capturing scenes of the then three-month-old war, he claimed to have accompanied McDowell's army on the road to Bull Run.

"I went to the first Battle of Bull Run with two wagons," he said. His innovative portable darkroom, a wagon hooded in black, was dubbed the "what-is-it" wagon. Clad in linen duster and straw hat, Brady says he "got as far as Blackburne's Ford." "We made pictures and expected to be in Richmond next day, but it was not so, and our apparatus was a good deal damaged on the way back to Washington." So Brady claimed thirty years later. In fact, no verifiable images from the first expedition have survived. Some that Brady later said were taken then, actually date months later, calling into question his entire account of his first trip to the front. Brady was first and foremost a businessman, a promoter, and his stories of many of his war exploits are highly colored by exaggeration.

Brady's eyesight was failing and he relegated the actual camera work to his assistants. He appears frequently in front of the camera in a number of his war views, but it is probable that he did not expose any images in the field himself. Throughout the war years, he only occasionally ventured to the armies, and instead spent his time in New York and Washington, supervising his flourishing portrait business and amassing the collection of views taken

A burgeoning industry begins. In the years immediately prior to the Civil War, the homes of Europe and America discovered the photograph. Here, in an English shop, workers cut and mount stereoscopic views for home consumption, and the public's appetite was voracious. The raw prints hang in the background. The man in the white vest seated at the center is cutting them. Ladies at the table prepare the mounting boards and glue the prints to them, while the two boys standing at the left run the finished pieces through a press. And even here the camera captures not just a scene, but history. Times are starting to change. Men and women are working together in the same shop. Yet some things have not changed, for children are working with them, too, and the clock in the background shows it is nearly 6 P.M., with the day's work not yet done. (NYHS)

by his assistants and others that he would produce as "Brady's Album Gallery" and other series. In addition, his views were widely published by the illustrated weeklies of the day, *Harper's* and *Frank Leslie's,* whose artists rendered the images into woodcuts.

The men actually following the armies for Brady were a remarkable array of artists: Alexander and James Gardner, Timothy O'Sullivan, William Pywell, George N. Barnard, David Woodbury, E. Guy Foux, James F. Gibson, Stanley Morrow, James Reekie, and several others. Some were outstanding. O'Sullivan would produce many of the best-known war scenes. Alexander Gardner and O'Sullivan together were unequaled in their coverage of the Army of the Potomac and both captured

America, even more than Europe, fell in love with the camera. All across the land the photographers and their apparatus set to work. By 1860 there were over three thousand plying the trade, like this dour fellow, lens cap in hand, recording America and Americans. It is noted Oregon artist Peter Britt. (SOUTHERN OREGON HISTORICAL SOCIETY)

many scenes which transcended photography to become genuine art. Gibson would become Brady's partner late in the war. Woodbury and others would journey to Gettysburg in November 1863 to preserve for the future the historic gathering at the dedication of the National Cemetery. Lincoln can be discerned on the speakers' platform from which he would deliver his now famous address. Gardner, too, would capture Lincoln in the field, during his visit to General McClellan at Antietam in 1862. Several, most notably Gardner and O'Sullivan, eventually leave Brady when he refuses them credit for their work.

In fact, there were several varieties of photographers with and around the armies during the Civil War. Very few enjoyed a truly official posi-

tion. Indeed, probably only one, Captain A. J. Russell, can be called a genuine Army photographer. Working for the U. S. Military Railroad, he operated the War Department's only photographic laboratory. His images are among the best that survive from the war.

Far more common were the artists who occasionally took contracts from the War Department for special assignments. George N. Barnard is the most notable for his series of views of the fortifications around Atlanta following its capture. Samuel A. Cooley was paid to photograph government warehouses and other installations at Hilton Head, South Carolina, in 1864. And several, among them Alexander Gardner, worked at enlarging and photographically copying maps for distribution in the armies.

Yet most of the war photographers, like Brady and his assistants, enjoyed no connection at all with the authorities. Rather, they were businessmen looking for profits. If they could obtain a pass from the generals commanding, they might travel freely among the troops, capturing scenes for their stereo and carte de visite series to sell in the North, and doing a lucrative trade in selling portraits to the soldiers. And many of them simply happened to be in the right place at the right time. The war came to them. When the armies reached Corinth, Mississippi, Howard & Hall and Armistead & White were there ready to take their trade. When the Federals occupied Baton Rouge, McPherson & Oliver and the prolific Andrew D. Lytle happily accommodated them, doing a brisk business not only in studio portraits, but also in outdoor views. At New Bern, North Carolina, J. L. Dowling gladly obliged the Massachusetts troops occupying the town by accepting their custom. Of those who took their operations where the soldiers were, Samuel Cooley proved the most ambitious. He operated four separate galleries, three in South Carolina and one in Jacksonville, Florida. And surely no one surpassed the flair for scenic backdrop of R. M. Linn. Perched atop Lookout Mountain, his "Gallery Point Lookout" offered the grandeur of the valley of Chattanooga as background for the portraits he made. A few northern artists made special trips to the field just to capture the doings of home state boys for civilian consumption. G. H. Houghton of Brattleboro, Vermont, made scores of outstanding images with the Vermont regiments in McClellan's army on the Peninsula, then took them home to sell to friends and loved ones.

By contrast, as already noted, Confederate field photography almost ceased to exist after 1861. Thus, the photographic record of the Confederacy is limited largely to formal studio portraits of its statesmen and military figures. Charles Rees of Richmond did venture outdoors in 1863 or 1864 to capture two images of the infamous Libby Prison, and another of Belle Isle in the James River. A. J. Riddle of Georgia took his camera to Andersonville in 1864 and there made a handful of poignant scenes of the thousands of Union prisoners in captivity. And at Brownsville, Texas, A. G. Wedge of Matamoros, Mexico, took his camera across the Rio Grande to photograph the Confederate evacuation. But these were the exceptions.

As the war stretched on, photographers followed the armies through most major campaigns, capturing nearly everything in sight. The most trivial things seemed to fascinate them, and they dearly loved to catch themselves at their work as well. A time exposure of several seconds was necessary for the successful transmission of light on the collodion plate, and the pictures thus necessarily resulted in somewhat frozen "still life" images. There are no real "action" pictures from the war. Artists deceptively posed many of their views to appear to be action scenes—cannoneers positioned at their guns, troops on parade and drill field. And at times the camera came close to battle, as at Antietam and in front of Petersburg. George Cook actually recorded accidentally the explosion of a Federal shell inside Fort Sumter in 1863. Yet for most practical purposes, the darkroom wagon could only be deployed behind the lines because of the time-consuming procedures required for taking such pictures.

These operations were tedious and exacting. The usual medium for the images was a supply of clear glass plates varying in size, but usually eight by ten inches or about four by ten inches for stereo views, carried in dust-proof boxes. When ready to expose, the artist carefully coated a plate with collodion made of a solution of gun cotton in equal parts of sulphuric ether and 95 proof alcohol. Bromide and iodine of potassium or ammonia were then added, sensitizing the surface of the plate. After letting the ether and alcohol evaporate to the right texture, the plate was immersed for three to five minutes in a bath holder solution of silver nitrate. This must be done in absolute darkness, or at best a dull amber light. The sensitized plate then went into a holder for insertion in the camera, which had already been aimed and focused. Uncapping the lens permitted an exposure of from five to thirty seconds, depending on available sunlight. Then the operator had just a few minutes to remove the plate from the camera, return it to the darkroom wagon, and develop it in a solution of sulfate of iron and acetic acid. Then it was washed to remove surplus silver with a solution of cyanide of potassium, and finally washed again, dried, and varnished.

Considering the conditions under which the war photographers worked, and the attendant chances of spoiling their plates during any one of the thirteen separate steps, the degree of quality and clarity achieved in their images is truly remarkable. A century later the best techniques could hardly do better.

The darkroom wagons in which they worked, and which so often appear in the background of their images, were well described by photographer George Rockwood some years after the war as "an ordinary delivery wagon of the period."

> [It] had a strong step attached at the rear and below the level of the wagon floor. A door was put on at the back, carefully hung so as to be light-proof. The door . . . came down over the step which was boxed in at the sides, making it a sort of well within the body of the wagon rather than a true step.
>
> The work of coating or sensitizing the plates and that of developing them was done from this well, in which there was just room enough to work. As the operator stood there the collodion was within reach of his right hand, in a special receptacle. On his left also was the holder of one of the baths. The chief developing bath was in front, with the tanks of various liquids stored in front of it again, and the space between it and the floor filled with plates.
>
> On exceptional occasions in very cold weather the life of a wet plate might be extended to nearly an hour on either side of the exposure, the coating or the development side, but ordinarily the work had to be done within a very few minutes, and every minute of delay

resulted in loss of brilliancy and depth in the negative.

To be sure, other processes were used as well. Most of the portraits of private soldiers that were made in the camps were ambrotypes, or tintypes, cheap processes within reach of the lowly private's pocketbook. The image on a tintype was caught on a small iron sheet plated with tin and coated with black lacquer. The ambrotype was a glass negative mounted against a dark background to produce a positive image. Unlike the true print derived from the collodion negatives, daguerreotypes, ambrotypes, and tintypes, were almost always mirrored copies of the subject. This reverse image called for some simple ingenuity on the part of the photographer in posing his subjects. Accoutrements were often reversed on the person of the sitter to present them correctly in the finished picture. Even belt plates bearing the letters "US" were turned upside down, presenting a perfect "S" to be sure, but a somewhat peculiar "U."

With these hundreds of photographers traveling the country, there was little that they missed, and most of what they caught has survived. Yet, there are still the "might have been's." A Chambersburg, Pennsylvania, photographer named Bishop is supposed to have arranged his camera in a window in anticipation of the arrival of General Lee during 1863's Gettysburg Campaign. The camera at-tracted the attention of Confederate soldiers and teamsters along the curbstones who arose to get into the image, thereby blocking Bishop's view of their general and robbing posterity of a memorable moment in time. Off Cherbourg, France, in 1864, the photographer François Rondin set up his camera and made an exposure of the battle raging at sea between the U.S.S. *Kearsarge* and the dreaded Confederate commerce raider C.S.S. *Alabama*. Seen widely at the time in the window of Rondin's Cherbourg shop, the priceless print has disappeared. A dozen or more wartime images of Abraham Lincoln are known to have been taken, but are now lost. A much rumored photograph taken from aloft in a Federal observation balloon has yet to surface, if indeed it was ever really taken.

Yet what does survive is truly staggering. An enormous debt is owed for the legacy left by those enterprising men with their little wagons, rolling over rutted roads with their fragile contents, hauling their clumsy cameras in camp and battlefield, occasionally risking their lives, and recording history as it had never been done before.

Mathew Brady, as usual, speaks for all of them, and largely it was through his energy and initiative that they all preserved for generations to come the image of the war and its people. "I felt that I had to go," he would say. "A spirit in my feet said 'Go' and I went."

*Alexander Gardner's own 1863 image of his gallery on 7th and D streets,
N.W., in Washington, D.C. Here one of the foremost photographers of the war
made his headquarters when not in the field with the armies. Here he thumbed
his nose at his one-time employer, Mathew B. Brady, whose own gallery stood
nearby. While proclaiming his magnificent "Views of the War" being available
on one side of his building, Gardner was a good enough businessman to devote
even more advertising to the real bread and butter for all cameramen of the
era, the portrait work in cartes de visite, ambrotypes, and a variety of other
techniques.* (LC)

*Brady and Gardner had the big studios, but hundreds of others like Bowdoin,
Taylor & Company's gallery at 204 King Street in Alexandria, Virginia,
operated the studios that most Americans saw. Always there was the large
opening in the roof to let in the sunlight essential for the camera, and always
the case of samples displayed outside the front door.* (T. SCOTT SANDERS)

And once the war came, the photographers proved nearly as fascinated by themselves at their work as they were with the conflict itself. Just as the Confederates fired the first shots of the war, so, too, did Confederate photographers take the first shots, both of the war and themselves. Even before the pioneering J. D. Edwards went to Pensacola, the remarkable Osborn & Durbec of King Street in Charleston captured Fort Sumter as surely and completely as did Beauregard.

Among their host of images stands this faded stereo print. It is unique, from a photographic viewpoint perhaps the most important Confederate picture from the entire war. The chief focus of attention are the men and two guns of the Trapier Mortar Battery on Morris Island, guns that bombarded Sumter. But what makes this photo so important is what lies hidden in the background. Lost for over a century and here published for the first time, this is the only known view of Confederate photographic apparatus in the field. Behind the mortar on the right stands a large pyramidal object, and just faintly visible on it are the words "Osborn & Durbec 223 King St." This is their portable darkroom, required for the speedy development of the emulsions of the era.

One of the great misfortunes of a tragic war is that the scarcity of chemicals and materials prevented artists of the caliber of Edwards and Osborn & Durbec from doing for their side of the conflict what Brady and others did for his. (TU)

Mathew B. Brady, the entrepreneurial genius who so identified himself with Civil War photography that for over a century afterward almost every Civil War image was just naturally assumed to be a "Brady." This somewhat retouched image purports to show him in field costume on July 22, 1861, the day he returned to Washington from the battlefield at Bull Run. Brady's whole story of his trip to the battle with McDowell's army is highly suspect, but the evidences of his showmanship in this photo are undeniable. Already he had begun to make Americans believe that he was the war photographer. (USAMHI)

*Thanks to his failing eyesight, Brady probably spent little if any time behind the
camera during the war. But he certainly spent a lot of time in front of it. In
top hat he poses next to General Samuel P. Heintzelman and with members of
the general's staff on the steps of Arlington House, the former home of Robert
E. Lee, in Arlington, Virginia. It is the late summer of 1861, following the
debacle at Bull Run.* (LC)

*At Blackburn's Ford, by the waters of Bull Run, two photographers pause for a
glass in March 1862.* (LC)

At Sudley Springs on the Manassas battlefield, the cameramen left their equipment wagon across the stream, then waded over to capture the scene, and with it their footprints in the mud. (LC)

One of the war's finest young photographers was Timothy O'Sullivan, among the first northern cameramen to return to South Carolina with the invading Federals. At Beaufort, in April 1862, he recorded an outstanding series of images, and this one probably includes himself, seated second from the right, at his "mess." (USAMHI)

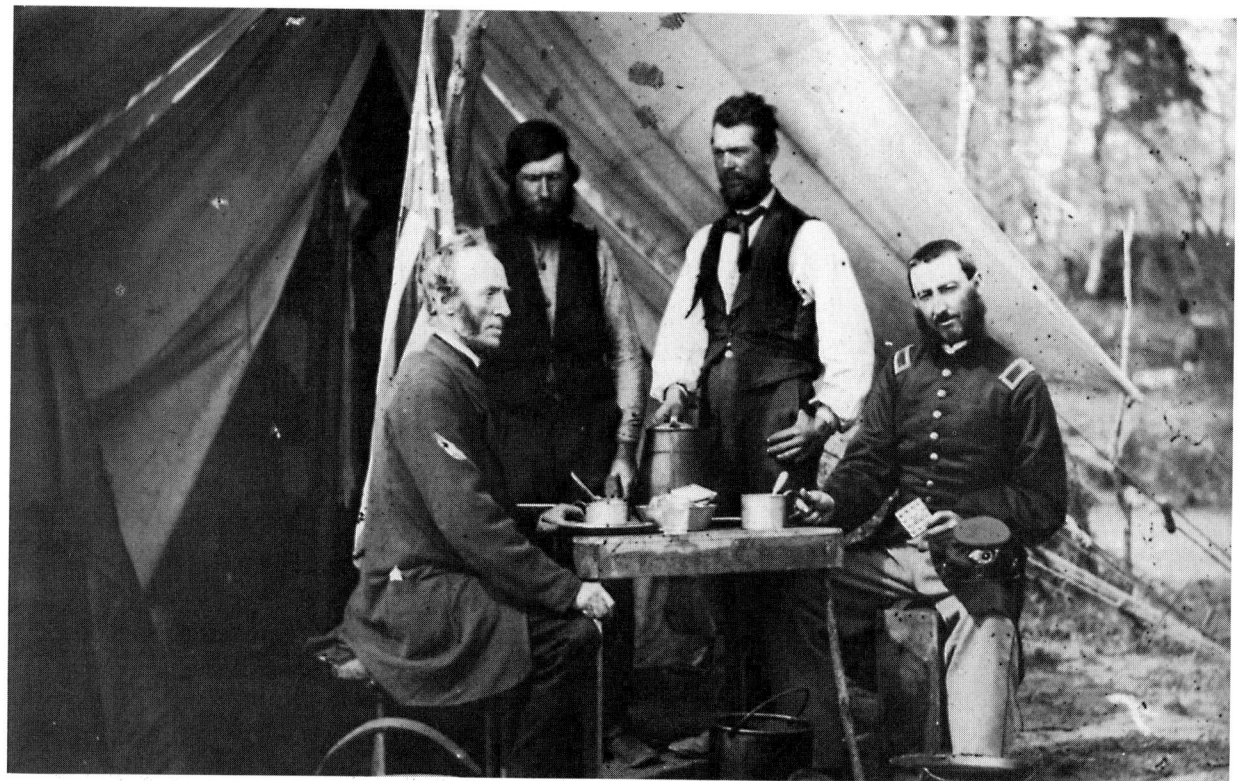

Photographers went with the army of McClellan to Yorktown in May 1862.
(LC)

*Their portable darkroom intrigued a boatload of soldiers at White House on
the Pamunkey River.* (WRHS)

When the armies returned to Manassas in July 1862, so did O'Sullivan, who pauses here for a drink beside his "what's it" wagon on the Fourth of July. (LC)

Timothy O'Sullivan, "Our Artist at Manassas," the brilliant and energetic cameraman who covered most of the Civil War in the East, and later took his lenses to the West and to Central America. (LARRY J. WEST)

The equipment box in the front of the wagon says "Brady's Washington." The men are two of his numerous assistants, the one seated at left probably being David B. Woodbury, arguably the best of the artists who stayed with Brady throughout the war. (LC)

Timothy O'Sullivan's wagon stands at the end of a bridge built by McDowell's engineers across Bull Run in August 1862, just before he met defeat for the second time on the same ground. (LC)

The men who made the pictures. The first publication of a remarkable image taken at Berlin, Maryland, October 28, 1862. Standing at right is Mathew Brady. David B. Woodbury crouches to the right of him. The other assistants are, left to right, Silas Holmes, a cook named Stephen, E. T. Whitney, Hodges, and a teamster named Jim. No other surviving image from the war shows Brady and his assistants in such detail, and their equipment as well. These are some of the men who did the real work for which Brady took credit. (KA)

*Brady surveys the ruins of the United States Arsenal at Harpers Ferry in
October 1862. He stands at right in this image by his assistant David B.
Woodbury.* (USAMHI)

*Brady, standing at right, again by Woodbury. He looks across the Potomac
River, with the Arsenal ruins in the background.* (LC)

Major General Ambrose Burnside had no idea this shot of him was being taken. He just finished posing for Brady's camera operator and had sat down on a sack of oats to read a newspaper. Brady, in the straw hat, instructed his assistant to take another shot and then sat in the chair facing the general. He loved to pose with the generals. (USAMHI)

O'Sullivan's photograph of his winter quarters with telegraphers at Brandy Station, Virginia, in 1863. (LC)

When the armies came to Gettysburg, so did the cameras. William H. Tipton sits aboard the Tyson Brothers' darkroom wagon in front of the house that served Union General George G. Meade as headquarters during the battle. (DONALD TYSON)

The tent of an army photographer in camp along the Rappahannock in 1863. (DON W. MINDEMANN)

Whenever the armies went into winter quarters, the Gardners and O'Sullivans continued their work of recording outdoor views, while others, men now largely unknown, suddenly appeared to live with the troops through the cold months. These were the pure businessmen who came to sell portraits to thousands of soldiers anxious to send their images to friends and loved ones at home. They and their makeshift studios appeared everywhere.

In Virginia's Dismal Swamp near Suffolk in December 1863. (USAMHI)

At Chattanooga, Tennessee. Morse from Huntsville, Alabama, and his "Gallery of the Cumberland." (USAMHI)

*Jefferson Rock at Harpers Ferry, overlooking the Shenandoah River, and the
"Jefferson's Rocks Photographs" establishment. A soldier poses on the rock
while the artist aims the camera out the window of the "gallery."* (RP)

At Chattanooga again. (USAMHI)

*And at Lookout Mountain, near Chattanooga, in 1864. Royan M. Linn was
the "Brady" of itinerant portrait photographers. He sold himself almost as well
as he sold his carte de visite portraits taken at his "Gallery Point Lookout."
Establishing himself on the summit of this scenic promontory, Linn sold
thousands of images of generals and soldiers posing on the point. Here "Linn of
Lookout" himself sits, cane in hand, beside a stereo camera. Over his shoulder
is spread the majesty of the Tennessee River. Here was a man with an eye for
grandeur. (*NA*)*

Linn once again at Pulpit Rock, another favorite posing place for his subjects. (KA)

Disdaining Brady's taste for notables, when Linn posed with others he selected commonplace people. Brady would never have been seen in a stovepipe hat aboard an ox-drawn wagon. (TERENCE P. O'LEARY)

Linn fascinated himself. Here he or an assistant photographs Brigadier General Thomas Sweeny, standing above the group of soldiers at left. (USAMHI)

Western photographers, though less numerous than those in the East, still made their mark, and put themselves in the picture.

A landmark of the western campaigns was Corinth, Mississippi's Tishomingo Hotel. Usually unnoticed in the war images of the hotel is the rather considerable establishment to its left, "Howard & Hall Photographers." They could boast no less than three sunlights in their roof. (CHS)

Competition among these western artists was sometimes stiff. When Brigadier General Grenville Dodge and his staff posed beside their campaign maps for Howard and Hall . . . (MICHAEL J. HAMMERSON)

*. . . photographers Armistead & White of Corinth took almost exactly the
same image, probably Howard & Hall's also, and published it under their own
imprint.* (LC)

*Vicksburg's "Washington Photograph Gallery," headquarters of Joslyn &
Smith.* (JOHN A. HESS)

A. D. Lytle of Baton Rouge, Louisiana, one of the most prolific of the western artists. Besides extensive portrait work, he took his camera outdoors and captured a remarkably complete record of a southern city under Union occupation. It was erroneously believed after the war that he used his camera to furnish information via photographs to the Confederates. (LSU)

Little Rock, Arkansas, in 1863 went onto emulsion for posterity in a splendid series of views taken by "White's Photograph Gallery." The studio appears at the lower right, its awninged sunlight extended toward the Arkansas River. Unusual for their striking clarity and quality, White's photographs have never been published before. (NA)

*In 1864, with the main focus of the war in the East, so was the chief focus of
the cameras. Stanley J. Morrow, a soldier stationed at the Point Lookout,
Maryland, prison camp, learned the trade—from Brady himself he would
claim—and opened his own studio. If his sunlight cover looks rather makeshift,
how much more so is his business sign. Hopefully Morrow planned his
darkroom operations better than he did the lettering for his "Picture Ga . . ."*
(STANLEY J. MORROW COLLECTION, W. H. OVER MUSEUM)

*James Gardner, brother of Alexander, one of the
many unsung true photographic artists of the war.*
(LJW)

Timothy O'Sullivan caught on June 13, 1864, this almost ghostly scene of a photographer and his camera, just beneath the tree at left, about to shoot a private soldier at Charles City Court House, Virginia. (LC)

Timothy O'Sullivan again, like his profession, a little older and experienced in war. (LJW)

"Bergstressers' Photographic Studio." Attaching themselves to the V Corps of the Army of the Potomac, three brothers, A. J., S. L., and J. Bergstresser, took their tintype or "melainotype" establishment to the front and flourished. The Pennsylvanian artists stayed with the Army for two years or more and took, said an observer, "the Lord only knows how many thousand portraits." Operating more than one gallery, and charging one dollar for a portrait, they sometimes took 160 in a day. "If anybody knows an easier and better way of making money than that," said a New York newspaper, "the public should know of it."

The Bergstressers were not only enterprising, but also innovative. Rather than building a permanent sunlight into this rude log studio, they put in a sliding roof. (USAMHI)

The interior of a photographer's winter quarters. On the wall behind him to the right hang several of the brass or copper frames used for cased ambrotypes. (RP)

One of Brady's wagons at Cold Harbor in June 1864. The photographer could develop his negatives at the back of the wagon, under the black hood. (LC)

Soldiers posing for the camera are joined by a one-eyed visitor, the camera on the ground at lower left. (NA)

*June 1864, Bermuda Hundred, Virginia. The signal tower built by General
Benjamin F. Butler, a flag-holding signalman atop it, seems almost an extension
of the Brady wagon and operator.* (LC)

A photographer's printing room at Bermuda Hundred. (JOHN A. HESS)

Sherman's great photographer during the Atlanta Campaign, George N. Barnard, posing for Brady's camera. One of the very few artists to be paid by the United States Army, Barnard was commissioned to record photographically Atlanta and its defenses. (KA)

Barnard's portable darkroom, chemicals, and other equipment attract the attention of several of Sherman's "bummers" in abandoned Confederate trenches southeast of Atlanta. (LC)

Henry P. Moore opened his "DAGTYPS" gallery on Hilton Head, South Carolina, in 1862, and concentrated his efforts chiefly on the men of the 3d New Hampshire. Outdoor views like this one, however, were not daguerreotypes but wet-plate photographs. (LC)

"Robbers' Row" in Hilton Head. Here the sutlers and camp followers set up their wares to lure the soldiers' money. Moore was one of them, and his gallery stands second building from the left, the simple sign "PHOTOGRAPHS" stating his business. (USAMHI)

"Sam A. Cooley. U.S. Photographer. Department of the South." That is how he billed himself, never hesitant to make capital on his quasi-official position as a contract artist for the Army in South Carolina. Hucksterism aside, he proved to be one of the most talented camera artists of the war. (WRHS)

"COOLEY'S," *headquarters in Beaufort, South Carolina, for the enterprising*
Samuel Cooley. (WRHS)

Cooley, center, with his associates and his own improved version of the "what's
it" wagon. It paid to advertise. (USAMHI)

*Paid by the War Department to photograph government supply buildings,
Cooley occasionally got himself into the picture. Here is Commissary Store
House No. 3 on Hilton Head Island, South Carolina, September 16, 1864. And
in the foreground stands the shadow of Cooley and camera.* (USAMHI)

For many of the war's photographers, their images of themselves at work are all
by which we can remember their names. Take J. L. Dowling of New Bern,
North Carolina. He made a remarkable series of prints of the Federal troops
occupying his town in 1862 and 1863; yet, while they survive, he is totally
forgotten. His recognition depends entirely on this one photograph of his
"Ambrotype & Daguerreotype Gallery" situated on a second floor above a drug
store. The focus may seem to be the men of the 25th Massachusetts lounging
below. But the real attraction is in the window above Dowling's sign. There,
standing beside his camera, is the artist himself. This was a man with style.
(USAMHI)

George S. Cook, the Confederate photographer who, in 1863, braved Federal fire to take his camera out onto Fort Sumter to record the ruin caused by the enemy's bombardment. Two years before, he made the same trip to capture the images of Major Robert Anderson and his officers as they were about to become the targets of the first shots of the war. (VM)

One of Brady's photographic wagons at City Point, Virginia, during the Siege of Petersburg. A familiar sight by now, the "what's it" wagons no longer attracted the attention they once enjoyed. (NA, U. S. SIGNAL CORPS PHOTO, BRADY COLLECTION)

Three photographers lie asleep in the shade of their tent near Petersburg, their wagon in the background, while a fourth writes a letter and a Zouave private apparently wanders into the picture. (LC)

Alexander Gardner established a great reputation in the Civil War, then enhanced it by going to the Far West immediately afterward to record the opening of the new country. (LJW)

Some artists' chief official services for the War Department came in copying maps for the Topographical Engineers Corps. Here in March 1865, in front of Petersburg, a camera is ready to shoot a map for reproduction. (USAMHI)

"Photographic Wagon, Engineer Department." Perhaps part of Gardner's equipment, shown amid the bomb proofs at Petersburg in the fall of 1864. (LC)

*The goal of four years at last attained. Richmond, taken from the south side of
the James River, in April 1865. In the foreground stands a portable darkroom
and operator at work, which explains the blur of the cameraman who is
developing his image. Across the river, the large brick building, painted white
on its lower stories, is the infamous Libby Prison. An Egbert G. Foux image, an
associate of A. J. Russell. (WRHS)*

Richmond in Federal hands, and a stereo camera ready to complete the conquest. (THE MESERVE COLLECTION)

April 8, 1865, while Grant is cornering Lee at Appomattox, Brady is already in Richmond posing for his own cameras. Here at Pratt's Castle on Gambler's Hill, he stands in top hat, the war that made him great almost done. (USAMHI)

A heavily retouched photo of Messrs. Levy & Cohen of 9th and Filbert streets, Philadelphia. Their series of photographs taken in Richmond immediately after its fall are among the best produced by anyone. Levy's untimely death six months later from a heart attack prevented the firm from publishing and distributing their prints. Instead, their negatives were sold, and never presented to the public until now. (KA)

Federal artists were quick to make use of captured Confederate photographs, and one of their favorites was southern photographer Charles Rees's print of Libby Prison in Richmond, taken probably in 1863. It was found after Richmond's fall, and several northern operators published it over their own copyright. This print was part of "Levy & Cohen's Views of the Rebel Capital and Its Environs." It is one of the very few photographs showing Confederate men and officers outdoors. Libby's commandant, Richard Turner, stands third from the left in the foreground. (KA)

At the end of the long road, the war and the camera have come full circle. Here at Fort Sumter they meet again in April 1865, four years after the beginning. Samuel Cooley prepares to photograph the remnant of a once mighty parapet. The guns are now stilled. The war's final shots belong to the camera. (LC)

Samuel Cooley photographs a soldier in the ruins of Fort Sumter in April 1865.
(LC)

*June 10, 1865, the battlefield of the first great scene of conflict, Bull Run.
Federal soldiers have come back to dedicate a monument to the memory of
their brothers who fell there four years before. The photographers came with
them. Sensing perhaps that this was for them, too, the end of an epoch,
Alexander Gardner has had assistant W. Morris Smith capture this scene of
photographers and members of the press at their liquor and cigars after the
ceremonies. Gardner is seated at far left, his hand stroking his beard. S. M.*

Carpenter of the New York Herald *is just to the right of him, a barrel on his knee. Standing in the center in white shirt, a dipper in his hand, is L. A. Whiteley of the* Herald. *And lying on the ground in front of him is James Gardner, brother of Alexander. Well might they celebrate, for they had seen and helped their industry come of age and, by their efforts, left a priceless record of America's most crucial moment for posterity.* (LJW)

The Guns of '62

Part of the ruin of 1862. Rolling stock of the Orange & Alexandria Railroad, once used to supply a Union Army marching to Manassas, and now destroyed by it to deny it to the victorious Confederates. It, like so many other scenes this year, is indicative of the almost constant defeat suffered by the North.

(U.S. ARMY MILITARY HISTORY INSTITUTE, CARLISLE BARRACKS, PENNSYLVANIA)

The Guns of '62

Yorktown: The First Siege

WARREN W. HASSLER, JR.

A "Napoleon," a "Prince John," and other dignitaries do battle for Richmond

YORKTOWN! Mere mention of the Virginia river port could conjure heroic images of great historical moment to both Northerners and Southerners at the start of the Civil War.

Both sides knew that it was at this quaint town on the south bank of the York River that Lord Cornwallis had surrendered his British Army to General George Washington's Continentals and their French allies, thereby virtually terminating the Revolutionary War with America triumphant. To Abraham Lincoln's Federals, it was well remembered that Washington had been a staunch nationalist, one who had gainsaid the particularism preached by the states' rights doctrinaires. To Jefferson Davis's Confederates—who naturally hoped to be able to retain control of the grass-covered redoubts still remaining at Yorktown—there was still fierce pride in the fact that Washington was a native son of the Old Dominion, a stalwart who had been the one indispensable man of the patriots' struggle to establish an independent nation.

And Virginia was destined to be a central battle arena of the Civil War. Even though they had occupied the great National naval base at Norfolk and had emerged victorious over the Union Army at the First Battle of Bull Run on July 21, 1861,

the Southerners were well aware of Federal pressure on their seaward littoral. From the start of hostilities, blue-clad soldiers had maintained control of the most powerful Gibraltar in North America—Fort Monroe, located at Old Point Comfort at the tip of the historic Peninsula between the York and James rivers—a stronghold their forces would hold throughout the war.

Yorktown was a charming, staid village of tree-lined streets and neat, impressive houses. It was a prize the North coveted. Even though Confederate forces under John Bankhead "Prince John" Magruder and Daniel Harvey Hill had easily repulsed the inept and feeble attacks on June 10, 1861, of Benjamin Franklin Butler's troops at Big Bethel, a few miles from Old Point Comfort, by early 1862 the Union garrison at Fort Monroe under John E. Wool would be enlarged to some 12,500 soldiers. And the strategic offensive would remain with the Federals, now near Washington, D.C., being molded by the "Young Napoleon," George B. McClellan, into the truly superb Army of the Potomac.

"Little Mac," as the latter was called—a West Point graduate, a twice-brevetted hero of the War with Mexico, an official observer in the Crimean War, and a railroad president—argued long and hard with Lincoln and Secretary of War Edwin M. Stanton over what route the Army of the Potomac should take to move against the Confederate capital of Richmond. The administration favored the overland route through Manassas, but McClellan strongly recommended taking advantage of superior National sea power by moving his force down the Chesapeake Bay and landing it at Urbana on the lower Rappahannock River, or, as less desirable but nonetheless viable alternatives, disembarking it at Mobjack Bay or Fort Monroe. A quick move to West Point on the Pamunkey River —a tributary of the York—would bring the Federals to the point where they expected to employ the Richmond & York River Railroad to supply their short land march upon Richmond. After much disputation, McClellan was authorized to move with approximately 150,000 men on his amphibious operation. However, when the immense movement—one of the largest amphibious ones in warfare up to that time—actually unfolded in late March 1862, the Union commander's force was reduced—against his strenuous objections—to some 100,000 men.

The Confederate victor of Bull Run, Joseph E. Johnston, had gotten warning of the Federal plans and pulled his army back from Manassas to Fredericksburg on the Rappanhannock River. This rendered inoperative McClellan's scheme to debark at Urbana, so he determined to go ahead with the plan to land at Fort Monroe and advance up the Peninsula via Yorktown and Williamsburg toward Richmond. Further, and, McClellan would claim later, crippling to his strategy, was Lincoln's sudden insistence at the beginning of the operation on withholding Irvin McDowell's I Corps of some 38,000 men near Washington to assure the safety of the National Capital (although McClellan believed he had left Washington perfectly secure). The Union commander had earmarked McDowell's force as a flying column to move swiftly by water up the York to land on the Peninsula across from West Point so as to outflank and take in the rear the Confederate forces under Magruder on the lower Peninsula near Yorktown, where the Southern general had established his headquarters. Additionally, 10,000 of John E. Wool's troops which had been pledged to McClellan were now withdrawn from his use.

Also hampering the Union commander initially

was the presence near Hampton Roads of the Confederate ironclad warship CSS *Virginia* (formerly the *Merrimack*), which was neutralized by the USS *Monitor* in the classic battle of March 9, 1862. The Federal naval authorities assured McClellan that he could now proceed with his Peninsular campaign, and they even promised naval assistance in reducing and running past the enemy artillery batteries and fortifications being

Major General John E. Wool, a hero of the Mexican War, turned seventy-seven just before the outbreak of war. Yet he showed no lack of energy in immediately ensuring the safety of Fort Monroe at Hampton Roads, Virginia, a vital base in Confederate territory, and in the course of the war a staging area for more than one major campaign. In the coming campaign for Yorktown . . . (U. S. ARMY MILITARY HISTORY INSTITUTE)

. . . *Fort Monroe would play a significant part. The exterior of the officers'*
quarters. (USAMHI)

constructed by "Prince John" at Yorktown and across the river, which at that point narrows to less than a mile in width, at Gloucester Point. But Lincoln so lacked faith in McClellan that he not only withheld McDowell's corps but also demoted "Little Mac" from General-in-Chief of all the Union armies, a vote of no-confidence which left him in command of just the Army of the Potomac and not even of his base of supplies and communication. The President did not agree with McClellan's contention that the best defense of Washington was the heavy pressure McClellan was

about to apply against Richmond. Lincoln was concerned about Rebel forces under "Stonewall" Jackson lurking in the Shenandoah.

Delays in assembling the vast shipping slowed the movement of the Union amphibious force to Fort Monroe, and once the troops began landing there—in the heaviest rains known to the region in twenty years—a shortage of supply wagons further impeded the advance. Only 42,000 men could be initially landed; several more weeks would be required for the rest of the army of about 100,000 to arrive and disembark. And McClellan was a most

The house at Fairfax Court House where McClellan made his headquarters. Here he planned his campaign for the Virginia Peninsula. A Timothy O'Sullivan image taken in June 1863. (USAMHI)

circumspect general, seldom one to take chances—especially since he was convinced time and preponderant resources were on the side of the North.

So colossal was the Federal undertaking that a foreign observer hailed it as "the stride of a giant." But Fort Monroe lacked sufficient wharf facilities for so gigantic a movement; therefore, a secondary landing place was brought into use at Ship Point, nearer Yorktown. Without the flying column of the I Corps sweeping up the York to West Point, McClellan—now informed by the navy that it would not be able to join in attacking the Confederate batteries at Gloucester Point and Yorktown, or to run past them—was obliged to slog through

the seas of mud and lay siege to the latter stronghold.

Meantime, the Confederates had not been idle. The local commander, John Magruder—a native Virginian—was a tall, erect, dark-haired general of fifty-one who had won brevets in the Mexican War and who, as a master of bluff and legerdemain, could make his 15,000 defenders look much more numerous than they were. There were few more colorful Civil War figures than "Prince John." A dandy dresser, he was an artillerist who had gained a wide reputation in the old army as a bon vivant and bountiful host at a myriad of social functions. Magruder never wearied of penning entreaties to his superiors for more reinforcements of men and artillery. He would in due time be joined by Johnston's main army which would, with Magruder's own force, total some 56,000 troops. The limited wharf facilities in the old river port of Yorktown made it difficult to enlarge his force rapidly, as there was no railroad down the Peninsula from Richmond or Williamsburg, and the few roads, upon which the Southern troops had to march, were infamous in this unusually heavy rainy season.

For many months, Magruder had been working steadily on the fortifications to defend Yorktown and the lower Peninsula. The earthworks immedi-

ately around the town were fairly strong, and Magruder incorporated with his own new ones some of the old Revolutionary War British redoubts. The water batteries, down low near the York River, as well as the field entrenchments, were buttressed by cotton bales, used also as breastworks. Similarly, Gloucester Point, across from Yorktown, was fortified, though less strongly so.

Noting that the Warwick River ran across the Peninsula at right angles to McClellan's line of advance from Fort Monroe, Magruder determined to erect defenses behind this stream. To make the Federal advance and expected attacks more difficult, the Confederate commander built five

Major General George B. McClellan and his staff in the Yorktown operations. "Little Mac" was well named, standing a full head shorter than the rest. Immediately to his left is his chief of staff, Brigadier General Randolph B. Marcy, who also happened to be McClellan's father-in-law. To the left of Marcy stands Brigadier General Stewart Van Vliet, quartermaster. (CHICAGO HISTORICAL SOCIETY)

Secretary of War Simon Cameron, his administration tainted by charges of corruption, resigned his portfolio on January 11, 1862. This left McClellan working with a new war secretary, . . . (NATIONAL ARCHIVES)

headquarters a little less than a mile west of the Farnholt House, on the Federal right, and began the slow process of a siege of the Yorktown-Warwick River defenses by regular approaches. This meant miners and sappers would dig parallels encompassing earthworks and wooden platforms for the cannon, with bombproofs for soldiers and ammunition.

The Federals were assisted by a large captive observation balloon, in the basket of which such high-ranking officers as Fitz John Porter ascended to examine the Confederate lines through their field glasses. Aloft almost daily, the Union air force suffered a near-catastrophe on one occasion when it slipped loose from its moorings "and sailed majestically over the enemy's works; but fortunately for its occupants it soon met a counter-current of air which returned it safely" to friendly lines.

dams which backed up water from the Warwick to such an extent that it inundated the countryside. This flooding allowed for only a few dry crossings at such points as Lee's Mill on the Confederate right and Wynn's Mill toward Yorktown, and where these roads passed, the Southerners erected batteries and rifle-pits.

Even to the experienced McClellan and other Union Army engineers, these enemy fortifications looked stronger than they actually were. Moreover, the Federal maps of the area were inaccurate, showing erroneously that the Warwick ran parallel to the York and James and therefore comprised no military obstacle. A probing attack on April 16 at Lee's Mill on the Federal left was repelled by the grayclads. So the Union commander set up his

. . . Edwin M. Stanton, a Democrat who opposed Lincoln's election, but who now became the President's strong right arm. (NA)

*Like McDowell before him, McClellan built his army in and around
Washington and northern Virginia while he formulated his plan of campaign.
Several familiar faces from the Bull Run debacle are with him. General Samuel
P. Heintzelman stands bearded in front of the pillar on the right, with his staff.
Robert E. Lee's Arlington House was a favorite posing place.* (USAMHI)

Owing to the dearth of experienced engineering officers, McClellan, who in the mid 1850s, had personally witnessed the siege of Sevastopol in the Crimean War, felt obliged to make many personal reconnaissances himself at the front lines of his besieging forces. He was often accompanied by his large and glittering staff, which included several volunteer aides from the French nobility, namely, the Orléans princes, including the Prince de Joinville and the Comte de Paris. On one of these occasions, while observing from a redoubt at the front, McClellan and his aides were spotted by Confederate gunners who opened fire upon them. As an eyewitness described it, when several enemy artillery projectiles struck close by, the startled

prince "jumped and glanced nervously around, while McClellan quietly knocked the ashes from his cigar."

The strained relations between the Union commander and the administration in Washington continued during the one-month siege of Yorktown in April 1862. As a petulant McClellan related one such incident in a letter to his wife, "The President very coolly telegraphed me yesterday that he thought I had better break the enemy's lines at once! I was much tempted to reply that he had better come and do it himself." On the Confederate side, when Johnston arrived, his rapport with Davis was not at all good, but the Southern commander was at least blessed in having a general—

*McDowell, too, was to cooperate with McClellan, but when a threat appeared
in the Shenandoah Valley, Lincoln held him back to protect Washington.
McDowell and staff at Arlington House.* (MINNESOTA HISTORICAL SOCIETY)

the masterful Robert E. Lee—positioned in Richmond as a buffer between himself and the Confederate President. Lee could and did get along amicably with both Davis and Johnston, and he was responsible in a large degree for amassing the force on the Peninsula that Johnston and Magruder had deployed at the Yorktown-Warwick River line.

As April waned, both sides worked feverishly to strengthen their positions. McClellan—who excelled at this sort of thing—laboriously wheeled into position some 114 big guns, howitzers, and mortars. Some of these were impressive pieces of siege weaponry. For example, close to the Farnholt House near the York River, a Federal battery was established which comprised five 100-pounder Parrotts and one monster 200-pounder Parrott. Others included 10-inch and 13-inch siege mortars. The Confederates, on the other hand, while possessing some large, modern, rifled pieces, also had to make do with older and less effective 32-pounder naval smoothbores and columbiads. After completing a

4,000-yard-long first parallel, McClellan's troops then began a second parallel much closer to the main Confederate defenses. All these activities were slowed by continuing torrential rains, execrable roads, and shortages of supply wagons.

But Joe Johnston saw the writing on the wall. He knew his troops and defenses could not stand up to the greatly superior weight of metal that the mushrooming Union batteries would be able to throw when they were ready to open fire. "We are engaged in a species of warfare," Johnston acknowledged in a message to Davis and Lee on April 30, "at which we can never win. It is plain that General McClellan will adhere to the system adopted by him last summer, and depend for success upon artillery and engineering. We can compete with him in neither." Lee and the Confederate President concurred.

Finally, on May 4, just as the massed Federal artillery was about to open a mammoth bombardment of Yorktown, Johnston wisely withdrew his troops and as many of his guns as he could, blew up some of his powder magazines, and retreated precipitately toward Williamsburg and Richmond. "Yorktown is in our possession," McClellan telegraphed Washington triumphantly. So was Gloucester Point. Only then could the Union commander speed troops up the York River to Eltham's Landing, near Brick House Point, opposite West Point, to speed the Confederate retreat— a retreat that was made possible by a partially successful rearguard stand made by the graycoats on May 5 at Williamsburg.

As McClellan's Army of the Potomac moved into the evacuated Warwick River and Yorktown fortifications, they captured some seventy-seven heavy guns that Johnston had been unable to remove in his hasty retrograde movement—a loss the Confederates could ill afford. But the Federals also discovered, at the cost of some fatalities, a new engine of destruction in the form of primitive but effective land mines, then called "torpedoes." These were apparently innovated and ordered to be placed in positions around wells, springs, and elsewhere by Gabriel J. Rains. These land mines were regular 8-inch and 10-inch columbiad shells buried a few inches in the ground, and rigged with

The always ready-to-pose Brigadier General Louis Blenker, with hand in coat, at his brigade headquarters near Washington. After being left out of the fight at Bull Run, he, too, would be withheld from McClellan. On his left stands Brigadier General Julius Stahel; on his right Prussian nobleman Prince Felix Salm-Salm. (WESTERN RESERVE HISTORICAL SOCIETY)

the ordinary cannon friction primer, or fulminate of mercury, so that they detonated when moved or stepped upon. So angered was McClellan at these devices that he ordered Confederate prisoners to discover the torpedoes and remove them. Some Southerners also considered the use of the "torpedoes" unethical, and James Longstreet directed Rains to halt the practice. But later in the war both sides employed land mines efficaciously.

Following the capture of Yorktown, McClellan moved up the Peninsula via Yorktown to close in on Richmond. Yorktown was held by the Federals throughout the remainder of the war, its dockage facilities being used, along with those at Fort Monroe and later of City Point, in the final campaigns of the war against Richmond and Petersburg. Yorktown was the first major operation of the initial massive campaign of the Civil War in the eastern theater of operations, and it drew to the scene a number of photographers who were attracted there not only by the large military movements then unfolding, but also because of the historical associations of the place during the final and pivotal campaign of the revolution which had paved the way for the birth of the republic.

The skillful defense of the Yorktown-Warwick River line by first Magruder and then Johnston, combined with McClellan's caution, enabled Lee to take steps to better defend Richmond with fortifications and additional troops so as to hold the capital of the Confederacy through three more years of grim warfare before the final ennobling scene took place at Appomattox Court House.

On to the Peninsula. Shipping the siege train for the 1st Connecticut Heavy Artillery, at the lower wharf at Yorktown. A Brady & Company photo from May 1862. (SOPHIA SMITH COLLECTION, SMITH COLLEGE)

More of the wealth of ordnance and ammunition shipped to the Peninsula to help subdue Johnston and Magruder. A Brady & Company image taken after the fall of Yorktown. (USAMHI)

Flattered by the attention from European commanders, the Federal officers delighted in posing with them. Brigadier General William F. Barry with British officers and two French noblemen. (NATIONAL LIBRARY OF MEDICINE)

Several pose here on May 1, 1862, at headquarters in Camp Winfield Scott.
Seated in the front row, left to right, are Captain L'Amy of the Royal Army
and the Duc de Chartres. In the center row, seated, are Colonel Fletcher of the
Royal Army, the Prince de Joinville, and Stewart Van Vliet. Standing from the
left are Colonels Beaumont and Neville of the Royal Army, an unidentified
man, the Comte de Paris, and another unidentified civilian. (USAMHI)

*Louis Philippe Albert d'Orléans, Comte de Paris
on the left, and Robert Philippe Louis d'Orléans,
Duc de Chartres, on the right. Both wear the
Union uniform in their capacity as aides to
McClellan.* (CHS)

*James F. Gibson's May 3, 1862, image of, from the left, the Duc de Chartres,
the Prince de Joinville, and the Comte de Paris on the day of Yorktown's fall.*
(WAR LIBRARY AND MUSEUM, MOLLUS-PENNSYLVANIA)

The Prince de Joinville, a familiar sight in McClellan's army. (USAMHI)

Colonel V. DeChanal, French military observer. (USAMHI)

Gibson's photo of several of the British observers. (LIBRARY OF CONGRESS)

Lieutenant George T. Munroe, Royal Canadian Rifles. (USAMHI)

The commander of Royal Army forces in Canada, Lieutenant General Sir John Michel, K.C.B. (USAMHI)

H. M. Hippisley of the Royal Navy. (USAMHI)

And best known of all, Colonel Arthur Fremantle of the Royal Army, who wrote of and published his experiences with both Union and Confederate armies. (THE NEW-YORK HISTORICAL SOCIETY)

But this campaign was for the Americans. McClellan's topographical engineers,
photographed by Gibson on May 2, 1862. The use of the pistols to hold the
corners of the map was a bit melodramatic of the engineers, but their services
were invaluable in an area for which reliable maps were not available. (LC)

A special feature of McClellan's army was Colonel Hiram Berdan and his United States Sharpshooters, men selected and trained for their marksmanship and equipped with special rifles.
(USAMHI)

McClellan's antagonist looked every inch a great general. The resplendent Major General John Bankhead Magruder—"Prince John." He managed to completely mislead McClellan about his strength in the works at Yorktown, thereby delaying the Federals for precious days while Richmond forwarded more Confederates to the front. (LOUISIANA STATE UNIVERSITY, DEPARTMENT OF ARCHIVES AND MANUSCRIPTS)

Isaac M. St. John was Magruder's chief engineer at Yorktown, responsible largely for the defenses that so intimidated McClellan. (USAMHI)

Brigadier General Samuel R. Anderson was nearly sixty but still exercised active command of one of Magruder's brigades. Ill health forced him to resign just one week after the evacuation of Yorktown. (USAMHI)

At Lee's Mill, soon after McClellan began his investment of Yorktown,
Magruder stood off an engagement on April 16. Here is McClellan's
uncharacteristically unpretentious headquarters during the battle. Brattleboro,
Vermont, photographer G. W. Houghton, who accompanied Vermont troops
to the Peninsula, made this image as part of his excellent series of unpublished
photographs. (VERMONT HISTORICAL SOCIETY)

Houghton's portrait of Brigadier General William F. Smith, commanding a division that included the Vermonters. It was taken in April 1862, at the Gaines House. Seated at left is Captain Romeyn B. Ayers, later a noted general. (VHS)

Magruder made his headquarters in the large house on the left in this photo of Yorktown made by Brady's company within days of the evacuation. (USAMHI)

George N. Barnard's photograph of Magruder's headquarters in June 1862. "Prince John" not only dressed in style but lived that way as well. (USAMHI)

The sally port into the defenses around Yorktown, just after McClellan occupied the quiet town. (USAMHI)

The ravine behind the defenses where the Confederates placed their powder magazine. These huts were occupied by Magruder's command until a few weeks before Barnard caught this scene. (LC)

*Both North and South drew inspiration from the American successes in the
Revolution, and Yorktown was a storied place indeed. Here on the right the
building that served as headquarters for Charles Lord Cornwallis during
Washington's siege of Yorktown. Magruder used it as a hospital, as would
Dorothea Dix shortly afterward. Brady & Company's May 1862 image.* (KEAN
ARCHIVES)

*The front line of the works Magruder and St. John built to hold back
McClellan.* (USAMHI)

*Making the best use of the materials at hand, St. John sometimes
employed bales of cotton along with sandbags in building his earthworks.
When hit, the bales really showed what they were made of.* (USAMHI)

*Barnard's June photo of a Confederate battery, with McClellan's Battery No. 1
in the distance. The Confederates liked to name their cannons for their
generals. As seen by the remnant of an ammunition box in the foreground, this
gun—now gone—was named after Major General D. H. Hill.* (USAMHI)

A naval battery near the Nelson church in Yorktown, shown on George N. Barnard's July 1862 image. At left are arranged loads of canister—tin cans filled with lead or iron balls—and stands of grapeshot, clusters of a dozen or more larger iron projectiles fired like a scatter-load from the cannon. (LC)

Magruder also erected defenses at Gloucester Point, including this large Dahlgren smoothbore. (USAMHI)

The much-touted Water Battery, strongest of the Confederate works preventing McClellan's easy conquest of Yorktown that he expected. (USAMHI)

The Water Battery became a favorite place for the Federals to pose after Magruder evacuated. Barnard was happy to catch them as they lounged in the works . . . (USAMHI)

. . . and walked the parapet overlooking the York. (USAMHI)

Part of Magruder's defenses, with the York River in the background.
(USAMHI)

These Rodman guns in the Water Battery bear Magruder's name on their carriages, probably put there when they were being shipped to him from elsewhere in the Confederacy. (LC)

Gloucester Point, with Yorktown in the distance, and more Dahlgren naval guns. (NLM)

Magruder took as many of his cannons with him as possible when he evacuated. Others had to be abandoned to the enemy, and this one, at least, he did not mind leaving. An exploded gun at one of the inland batteries. By Barnard. (USAMHI)

McClellan's Battery No. 1 below Yorktown, taken by Gibson in May 1862.
McClellan's earthworks are masterpieces. (LC)

Gibson's photo of Battery No. 4, whose eight mortars lobbed shells into Yorktown constantly. The barge holds their powder and shells. Built into the earth itself are the gunners' quarters, a "bombproof" protecting them from enemy fire. (LC)

Another view of Battery No. 1. The works are made of gabions—wicker baskets filled with earth, piled around built-up soil, and topped with sandbags. (USAMHI)

The Farnholt House behind Battery No. 1, seen at left. Gunners used the roof to observe the effect of their shells. (USAMHI)

McClellan's headquarters, Camp Winfield Scott, taken by Gibson on the day Magruder evacuated. (USAMHI)

"Little Mac's" tent in the center, the day of his "victory" over Magruder. (LC)

Always the tourists, Federal soldiers visit "Cornwallis' Cave," the small cavern where the British general reputedly took refuge from Washington's artillery in 1781. (NLM)

Magruder used the cave as a powder magazine. Brady's assistants used it as a backdrop for images like this. (USAMHI)

And officers of the 1st Connecticut Artillery pulled enemy shells from within the cave for jaunty poses like this one, published by Brady & Company. (LC, FITZ JOHN PORTER PAPERS)

Magruder's evacuation was not a simple affair, even given the superb deception he had worked on McClellan. Brigadier General Lafayette McLaws was largely responsible for capably covering the retreat. It won him a promotion. (MUSEUM OF THE CONFEDERACY, RICHMOND)

Brigadier General Gabriel J. Rains also contributed his part. One of D. H. Hill's brigade commanders, he laced the roads out of Yorktown with hidden shells triggered to explode when stepped upon. "Infernal machines" they were called, or "torpedoes." He had just pioneered the antipersonnel mine. Even many Confederates thought it a barbarous concept. (USAMHI)

Major General Gustavus W. Smith attacked McClellan's pursuing Federals at Eltham's Landing on May 7 while he covered the withdrawal of Magruder's army. It was effectively the end of the Yorktown campaign. (TULANE UNIVERSITY)

The New Ironclads

WILLIAM N. STILL

Invention went wild in the race for newer
and more powerful iron behemoths

ON MARCH 9, 1862, occurred what has rightly been called one of the most important naval engagements in American history. Two iron-armored warships, the USS *Monitor* and the CSS *Virginia,* met in mortal combat, the first such battle in history. Although not the first ironclad warships completed and battle-tested, they were the first completed in North America and the first that fought against each other. They were responsible for the decision by both Abraham Lincoln's and Jefferson Davis's governments to create a powerful naval force of armored vessels.

The Confederates took the first step. Perhaps this was inevitable considering the fact that the South lacked both a navy and the potential to keep pace with their opponents in building warships. On May 9, 1861, Confederate Secretary of the Navy Stephen R. Mallory wrote in an oft-quoted report, "I regard the possession of an iron-armored ship as a matter of the first necessity. . . . If we . . . follow their [the United States Navy's] . . . example and build wooden ships, we shall have to construct several at one time; for one or two ships would fall easy prey to her comparatively numerous steam frigates. But inequality of numbers may be compensated by invulnerability; and thus not only does economy but naval success dictate the wisdom and

expediency of fighting with iron against wood." That same day the Confederate Congress appropriated $2,000,000 for the purchase or construction of ironclads in Europe. Although the Confederacy would contract for several powerful armored vessels in England and France, initial efforts were unsuccessful. Secretary Mallory then determined to construct ironclads within the Confederacy. In the middle of July the decision was made to convert the *Merrimack* into the *Virginia,* and six weeks later contracts were awarded for the construction of two ironclads later named the *Arkansas* and *Tennessee* to be built in Memphis; a fourth one, the *Mississippi,* was to be built in New Orleans. In September the *Louisiana* was also laid down in New Orleans. These five initial armorclads were designed to operate on the open sea as well as on inland waters. They were designed not only to break the blockade, but as Secretary Mallory wrote, to "traverse the entire coast of the United States . . . and encounter, with a fair prospect of success, their entire Navy." In other words, Mallory's initial ironclad strategy was offensive in nature.

The strategy was a failure. Only three of the vessels, the *Arkansas, Louisiana,* and *Virginia,* became operational; the other two were destroyed while

500

To his credit, Secretary of the Navy Gideon Welles, ridiculous wig and all, supported the ironclad idea from the first. Despite his lack of naval experience he saw what many could not, that wooden ships were things of the past. (NA)

still under construction. Of the three that were commissioned only the *Arkansas* was used for offensive purposes. During its brief career, it achieved some dramatic success, despite poor design and construction. It was 165 feet in length and carried a battery of ten guns. Its armor was made up of railroad T-rails, and it was powered by inadequate riverboat machinery. The casemate, unlike those found on the other Confederate ironclads, was perpendicular rather than slanted. On July 15, 1862, this awkward-looking warship ran through a large fleet of Union vessels anchored above Vicksburg and successfully resisted several planned attempts to destroy it. In August the *Arkansas* was to participate in a combined operation on Baton Rouge, Louisiana, but because of a breakdown in the machinery, the ironclad was blown up by its crew.

The *Louisiana's* career was briefer and less successful. As envisioned by its builder, E. C. Murray, the armor-clad was to be 264 feet in length, 64 in beam, with a battery of twenty-two guns and propelled by two paddle wheels and two 4-foot propellers. The most unorthodox feature in his design

was twin wheels along the centerline, one abaft the other in a well. The ship was still being fitted out when Admiral Farragut's squadron began its ascent of the Mississippi River. The large Confederate ironclad was towed down the river and moored near Fort Jackson. Here as a floating battery it engaged the Union vessels and was destroyed by its crew when the fort surrendered.

The *Virginia* achieved the most notable success of the initial ironclads. It was converted from the captured and partially destroyed sloop-of-war *Merrimack* at the Gosport Navy Yard in Norfolk. Frequently considered to be the prototype of all the Confederate ironclads, it was in fact an experimental vessel constructed only because the Confederacy needed to get a powerful ironclad operational as quickly as possible in that part of the South. The 262-foot vessel had a casemate 170 feet long, inclined on the sides with the ends horizontally rounded. The rounded ends along with the bow and stern of the hull being submerged were unique; no other Confederate ironclad incorporated these features. The armor, rolled at Tredegar Iron Works in Richmond from railroad iron into plates, was 4 inches thick attached in two layers. The ironclad carried a battery of ten guns, four to a side and a pivot rifle at each end. On March 8, 1862, it attacked units of the North Atlantic Blockading Squadron in Hampton Roads and destroyed the frigate *Congress* and the sloop-of-war *Cumberland*. The following day it fought the *Monitor* and for over a month successfully defended the entrance to the James River. Early in May, Norfolk was captured. With no base to return to and a draft too deep to allow it to ascend the James, the ship was destroyed by its crew to prevent its capture.

With the destruction of the *Arkansas, Louisiana,* and *Virginia,* the first Confederate ironclad program ended. Mallory's vision of a few powerful armored vessels to sweep Union warships from the seas was a failure. Unlike the Confederates', the Union Navy's initial ironclad program was tentative; professional opinion differed over the type of armored vessel to build. Early in August 1861, Congress appropriated $1,500,000 for the "construction or completion of iron or steelclad steamers or steam batteries," and authorized the creation of a board of naval officers to examine proposals and make recommendations. Then in

The Union Navy granted contracts for three radically different ironclad vessels at first. Here the USS New Ironsides, *powerful and effective, though largely conventional in design.* (SMITHSONIAN INSTITUTION)

September the board recommended that contracts be awarded for three vessels; a seagoing broadside type of vessel commissioned *New Ironsides,* a lightly armored wooden vessel, the *Galena,* and a revolving turret vessel, the *Monitor.* While the board of naval officers deliberated, the army had already contracted for seven ironclads for service on the Mississippi River and its tributaries.

These seven ironclads have been called "Pook turtles" after their designer, Samuel M. Pook, or the "city class," because they were named after western river ports. They were commissioned the *Cairo, Carondelet, Cincinnati, Louisville, Mound City, Pittsburg,* and *St. Louis* (later *Baron De Kalb*). Pook designed wooden, flat-bottomed light draft and low freeboard center-wheelers measuring 175 feet in length. Each gunboat was to be armed with ten 8-inch shell guns. With slanted casemates covered with 2½-inch armor, they were similar in appearance to Confederate ironclads. These ironclads had defects found on nearly all of the armored vessels of this type built by both sides during

the war—they were underpowered, too heavy, and vulnerable to high, arched "plunging fire" directed at their roofs. Nevertheless, they saw more service than any other class of river ironclads, fighting in various engagements from Fort Henry to Vicksburg and beyond. Three of them (*Cairo, Cincinnati,* and the *Baron De Kalb*) would be sunk.

The army was also responsible for the conversion of four large river vessels into ironclads. A snag boat was converted into the casemated ironclad *Benton* while the *Essex,* also casemated, was a rebuilt center-wheel ferryboat. The *Benton* carried sixteen heavy guns while the *Essex* carried six. Two side-wheelers named the *Lafayette* and the *Choctaw* were purchased in St. Louis and converted under the supervision of navy Commander William "Dirty Bill" Porter. Although the *Lafayette* would have a sloping casemate, the *Choctaw* would have a stationary turret with inclined sides and a curved top—"a war dome, like the dome on the Court House in St. Louis"—and be pierced to hold four guns. Just forward and aft of the wheels

The USS Galena *was not a success, its thin iron sheathing proving easily*
vulnerable to Confederate shore batteries at Drewry's Bluff in May 1862.
James Gibson's photo taken in July. (USAMHI)

But very effective, and very revolutionary, was the
design for the USS Monitor. *Much of the vessel*
was constructed here on Long Island. (U. S. NAVAL
HISTORICAL CENTER)

were two small casemates. On top of the forward casemate, which housed two howitzers to sweep the decks if the enemy should board, was located a conical pilothouse, covered with 2 inches of iron. Commander Porter designed the armor himself. The *Choctaw* had two 1-inch layers of iron and a 1-inch layer of vulcanized India rubber cushions, while the *Lafayette*'s sloping casemate was covered with 1-inch iron over 1-inch India rubber. The navy took over the eleven ironclads after they were completed, and they operated as units of the Mississippi Squadron throughout the war.

The navy also contracted for ironclads on the western rivers. Three of them, the *Chillicothe, Tuscumbia,* and *Indianola,* were built by Joseph Brown in Cincinnati. Each had a small casemate forward containing two 11-inch rifled guns and a casemate astern between two paddle wheels. All three were regarded as inefficient. The *Chillicothe*'s first commanding officer pronounced it a "cumbersome scow," and after the battle of Grand Gulf in April 1863, the *Tuscumbia*'s captain referred to his vessel as "a Disgrace."

These river ironclads were all laid down or converted during 1861 and early 1862, months before the engagement between the *Monitor* and the *Vir-*

And here it rests in Gibson's July 9, 1862, photograph, taken on the James River. The turret shows the indentations made by the Virginia's *solid shot during their epic battle at Hampton Roads.* (USAMHI)

ginia. The *Galena* was also under construction at Mystic, Connecticut, during these months.

The *Galena* was, according to Commodore Joseph Smith, senior officer of the Ironclad Board, "a Lighter boat . . . intended to have more speed than other ironclads to work in part under canvas." It resembled the wooden steam warships of that day except that the upper part of its sides was rounded inward or "tumbled home" at an angle of about 45 degrees to deflect projectiles. A battery of six guns was mounted on a gun deck protected by armor not quite 4 inches in thickness. It had two 1-inch plates of armor on its sides separated by an air space in which there were iron bars. Although it was rigged as a schooner, all the masts, except the fore lower mast kept for a lookout position, were removed. It was built by C. S. Bushnell and Company and commissioned in April 1862. In May, the *Galena* was one of the vessels of the North Atlantic Blockading Squadron that ascended the James River and engaged the Confederate batteries at Drewry's Bluff. It was badly damaged; its thin armor penetrated thirteen times. Later the armor was removed, and the *Galena* completed the war as a wooden-hulled ship.

The *New Ironsides* was a traditional broadside type warship, but 170 feet of its 230-foot hull were covered with iron armor 4½ inches in thickness. The armor belt covered the sides and deck, generally amidship, with bow and stern unarmored. This citadel protected the main battery of sixteen 11-inch Dahlgren guns. Classified a frigate, this large (more than 4,000 tons displacement) and powerful ironclad was built by Merrick & Sons in Philadelphia. *New Ironsides* spent its entire Civil War career with either the South Atlantic or the North Atlantic blockading squadrons. In April 1863 the armored warship participated in Admiral Samuel F. Du Pont's attack on Confederate positions in Charleston harbor, and in this and subsequent attacks it was hit repeatedly by enemy fire without suffering any damage. In October it was slightly damaged by the Confederate torpedo boat *David,* but after repairs it participated in Admiral David D. Porter's attacks on Fort Fisher. *New Ironsides* was the most powerful ironclad completed by the Union during the war and undoubtedly the most effective in the combined operations along the Southern coastline. It was the only seagoing armored cruiser to be completed during the war. An improved armored cruiser, the *Dunderberg,* was laid down but not completed until after Appomattox. The board of naval officers who had recommended the three original armored vessels wrote that "ocean going [armored] cruisers are for the time being impracticable." This report may have had some effect on Union policy concerning armored vessels, but the major factors were the influence of Assistant Secretary of the Navy Gustavus Fox and the *Monitor*'s designer, John Ericsson, and the impact of the battle between the *Monitor* and the *Virginia* on Northern public opinion.

As early as December 1861 the Navy Department had requested $12,000,000 to construct twenty additional turreted vessels. As designed, they were to mount a type of turret developed by Captain Cowper Coles of the British Royal Navy. Ericsson, however, persuaded the navy to substitute a turret designed by him for the Coles turret. The *Monitor*'s success was primarily responsible for this decision.

The *Monitor* was a unique warship. Designed as a harbor defense vessel, instead of a standard ship hull it had a large armored "raft" 172 feet by 41 feet, 6 inches supported by a lower section of wood 122 feet long and 34 feet wide. The "raft" was designed to increase stability in a seaway and protect the hull from ramming. The vessel's power plant consisted of two boilers and two engines that were of Ericsson's design, as was the revolving turret, which was the armor-clad's most novel feature. The *Monitor* incorporated numerous technical advances for that time including forced ventilation of living spaces, a protected anchor which could be raised and lowered without it or the crew members being exposed to enemy fire, and a protected pilothouse. The turret carried two 11-inch Dahlgren smoothbores. The *Monitor* was completed in early February 1862, and a month later it left under tow to join the North Atlantic Blockading Squadron. Its fortuitous arrival at Hampton Roads in time to challenge the *Virginia* is well known. The *Monitor* won a tactical victory in preventing the destruction of Union vessels in the Roads, and in doing so it produced such an intense enthusiasm in the North that a "monitor fever" swept the Union. From then until the end of the war the Union would concentrate on building monitor-type vessels. It is ironic that the Union Navy which obviously had to

While monitors would become a mania in the East, on the western waters a different sort of ironclad came about. The first river ironclads were converted snag boats, like the Benton. *With sixteen guns mounted on its deck, it was the most powerful vessel on the Mississippi and flagship of Foote's fleet at Island No. 10 and Davis's fleet in the battle at Memphis.* (KA)

assume an offensive strategy in order to win the war, adopted as its principal ironclad a type of vessel that was basically defensive in nature.

On March 21, three weeks after the battle, Ericsson received contracts for six enlarged and improved versions of the *Monitor* while four additional ships of the same class were ordered from other builders. These were the ten *Passaics*—the *Passaic, Montauk, Catskill, Patapsco, Lehigh, Sangamon,* (later renamed *Jason*), *Camanche, Nahant, Nantucket,* and *Weehawken.* Like the original *Monitor,* each had a single turret, increased thickness of armor, a permanent stack, and a more powerful battery. These vessels as a class were to see more service than any others of the monitor fleet. They were the major ironclad units of both

the South Atlantic and North Atlantic blockading squadrons. Monitors of this class participated in the combined operations against Charleston and Savannah, and in the James River.

In 1862 the Navy Department also initiated the construction of double-turreted monitors. The *Onondaga* was built at Continental Iron Works, Greenpoint, New York, under contract with George W. Quintard. Commissioned early in 1864, it was 226 feet long and carried a battery of two 15-inch Dahlgren smoothbores and two 150-pounder Parrott rifles. This vessel spent its entire war career in the James River and was decommissioned after the war. Four additional double-turreted monitors were built in navy yards—*Miantonomoh, Monadnock, Agamenticus* (later

Soon new ships were under construction, however, at places like the Carondelet Marine Railway at Carondelet, Missouri. Here two "city class" ironclads are being built. Their builder, James B. Eads, could construct one in forty-five days, start to finish. (NA, U. S. WAR DEPARTMENT GENERAL STAFF)

renamed *Terror*), and *Tonawanda* (later renamed *Amphitrite*). These vessels were twin-screw, wooden-hulled ironclads over 258 feet in length. Of these four, only the *Monadnock* was completed prior to the end of the war, but it saw no combat. This class, however, was considered the most efficient of the monitor type built during the war and these vessels remained in service for many years afterward.

In September 1862, orders were given to various builders for nine more Ericsson monitors. *Canonicus, Catawba, Oneonta, Mahopac, Manhattan, Tecumseh, Saugus, Manayunk* (later *Ajax*), and *Tippecanoe* (later *Wyandotte*) were similar to the *Passaics*, but with certain significant improvements —a defensive slope around the base of the turret to prevent jamming, a stronger hull, and a heavier battery of 15-inch guns. Five of this class were commissioned in time to see Civil War service, and the *Tecumseh* was sunk during the Battle of Mobile Bay.

The last of the coastal monitors contracted for in 1862 were the two giant single-turret monitors, *Puritan* and *Dictator*. Displacing more than 3,000 tons each and with large fuel capacities, these vessels were intended as oceangoing vessels. They were built in New York under contract with John Ericsson. Their 312-foot hulls were to be protected by 6-inch side armor. The single turrets would carry two 15-inch Dahlgren smoothbores each. The *Dictator,* after being commissioned in December 1864, joined the North Atlantic Blockading Squadron but saw no action. The *Puritan* was never completed.

The largest single class of monitor-type vessels was the *Casco* class. In the spring of 1863, contracts were signed for the construction of twenty of this type. However, during the war only eight were completed, and they were considered unseaworthy. Five of them were converted to torpedo boats, but none saw action.

Monitors were also constructed for operations on the western rivers. Shortly after the Hampton Roads engagement, James B. Eads received a contract to build three single-turreted monitors of his own design, although the Navy Department insisted that Ericsson's turret be used instead of one designed by Eads. The three river monitors, named *Osage, Neosho,* and *Ozark,* were unlike other monitors in that they were propelled by stern wheels. Unfortunately, the wheels (protected by armored casings) made it impossible for the turrets to turn a full 360 degrees. The *Ozark* was larger and carried additional armament of questionable value—four pivot guns located upon the open deck. They were unusual-looking vessels with virtually nothing

Here the finished products rest at anchor at Cairo, Illinois. These "Pook turtles" were the backbone of the Mississippi fleet. At left the USS Baron De Kalb, *in the center the USS* Cincinnati, *and on the right the USS* Mound City. *The* De Kalb *was formerly the USS* St. Louis, *the first of Eads's boats to launch.* (NYHS)

Another converted snag boat became the USS Essex, *an unfortunate vessel that would be much damaged and beset with difficulty throughout the war. A photograph by Dr. J. T. Field taken while the ship lay moored off Memphis in 1864. Mortar boats lie to its left bow.* (CIVIL WAR TIMES ILLUSTRATED COLLECTION)

showing above the waterline but the turret, the iron-plated house for the stern paddle wheel, and the tall, thin stacks.

Eads received a second contract for monitors. The four vessels built under this contract—*Chickasaw, Kickapoo, Milwaukee,* and *Winnebago* —were double-turreted ironclads, with one turret by Ericsson's design and one by Eads's design. The Eads turret was more sophisticated than Ericsson's. The guns in the turret were mounted on a steam-operated elevator which dropped them to a lower deck where they were loaded and then hoisted and run out through ports opened by automatic steam-operated shutters. These vessels carried four guns each—two per turret—and were the only monitors ever built with triple screws and rudders. They were principally employed with the West Gulf

Blockading Squadron operating in Mobile Bay and its vicinity and were generally considered the most serviceable of the river monitors.

The monitor-type had the great advantage of achieving a maximum of impenetrability through two radical factors—low freeboard and the concentration of guns in the armored turret. The guns could be aimed without moving the ship. In confined and sheltered waters the monitors were excellent defensive ships, but they had serious defects that affected Union naval operations. A majority of them were essentially floating batteries that had to be towed from port to port; even in the rivers they could rarely stem the current. They were unseaworthy and had so little reserve buoyancy that a leak could be fatal. For these reasons they were unsuitable for blockade service, the primary mission of the Union Navy. In anything but a flat calm a monitor's deck was awash. The crew had to remain below with hatches battened down. As Admiral Du Pont wrote: "How can such vessels lay off ports . . . and protect the wooden vessels."

The western rivers were generally more suitable for the monitor type, but even here there were problems. The gunboats' maneuverability was poor, and they had little protection from plunging shot, a serious defect considering the many miles of bluffs along the waterways.

Even more important was their unsuitability for offensive operations. Loading their guns usually required from six to eight minutes. "This delay," as one authority has written, "violated the cardinal principal of naval gunnery, volume of fire." In the attack by the *New Ironsides, Keokuk,* and seven monitors on Fort Sumter in April 1863, only 139 rounds were fired by the combined batteries of the ironclads' guns. At the same time 76 guns in the Confederate forts rained some 2,206 shots on the Union vessels. As Admiral Du Pont wrote Secretary Welles, "I . . . remind the Department that ability to endure is not sufficient element wherewith to gain victories, that endurance must be accompanied with a corresponding power to inflict injury upon the enemy . . . that the weakness of the monitor class of vessels . . . is fatal to their attempts against fortifications."

The most unusual turreted vessel commissioned during the Civil War was the converted wooden sloop-of-war *Roanoke.* Like her sister ship, the *Merrimack,* converted by the Confederates into the *Virginia,* she was cut down, and three center-line turrets were installed. With a high freeboard, she was not a monitor-type vessel. Because of instability and a deep draft, she was considered unsuitable for active service and spent the war defending New York harbor from possible attack by Confederate cruisers.

While the Union ironclad building program after 1861 emphasized the monitor type of vessel, the Confederate program on the other hand would change from one which stressed offensive vessels in 1861 to one emphasizing defensive vessels. The apparent unseaworthiness of the *Virginia* and the ironclads built in New Orleans and Memphis, the lack of adequate facilities and qualified technical expertise, the belief that powerful armor-clads

William "Dirty Bill" Porter designed the conversion of the Essex *and commanded her, while also taking a hand in the fashioning of the ungainly* Lafayette *and* Choctaw. (LC)

could be obtained in Europe, and most important, the growing threat to the Confederacy from invasion and amphibious assault all contributed to this change in policy. From 1862 until the end of the war, the Confederate naval construction program would concentrate on small, shallow-draft harbor-defense armored vessels. Approximately forty of these vessels were laid down, and half of them were completed.

These small defense ironclads were designed by naval constructor John Porter. He developed a standard design which was sent to builders and contractors throughout the Confederacy. The original plan was for a 150-foot flat-bottomed vessel with hull to be partially armored and casemate to be completely covered with iron armor. The ironclad would carry a battery of six guns and be screw-

Then came the behemoth ironclads, designed by "Dirty Bill" Porter and built by
Eads. The USS Lafayette *carried eight heavy guns and a shield of iron laid*
over rubber, intended to make shot bounce off the casemate. In practice, it did
not. (USAMHI)

propelled. Although this design was utilized by the shipbuilders, it is, nevertheless, almost impossible to generalize about the Confederate armor-clads. There were noticeable differences because of modifications in size, machinery, armor, and battery. In size they ranged from the *Albemarle* and the *Neuse* (139 feet) up to several under construction during the latter months of the war that were over 250 feet in length. The 310-foot *Nashville* was the largest of this class.

The thickness of armor measured from 2 to 8 inches, but all of it was 2-inch laminated iron plate. On several vessels such as the *Arkansas* and *Louisiana* railroad iron—T-rails—was substituted because rolled plates were not available. The marine engines and boilers varied from ship to ship. Some of them were manufactured in the South;

more of them were salvaged from other vessels. The method of propulsion consisted of either wheel or screw or a combination of both, as in the *Louisiana*, which had two wheels and two screws. A majority of them were screw steamers with either one or two propellers, but several such as the *Nashville* and *Missouri* were paddle-wheelers because of the accessibility of that kind of machinery. The machinery and propulsion units were notoriously inadequate and inefficient.

The Confederacy had more success in arming its ironclads than in providing motive power for them. There was really never a shortage of heavy guns although some of the ships' initial batteries consisted of a variety of guns. Smoothbores were carried at one time or another by nearly all of the armor-clads, but in contrast to the Union Navy, which advocated smoothbores during and after the war, the Confederate Navy concentrated on rifled guns. The standard rifled gun used on the Confederate ironclads was the Brooke gun, a cast-iron banded cannon developed by John Brooke, who headed the Confederate Navy's Bureau of Ordnance and Hydrography. The principal types used on the ironclads were 7-inch and 6.4-inch guns. The Confederate Navy also equipped its ironclads in 1863 with spar torpedoes, egg-shaped copper vessels containing from fifty to seventy pounds of powder, fitted to a long pole attached to the bow of the vessel. Although Union naval officers universally referred to the Confederate ironclads as "rams," only a few of them actually had rams built on.

The 150-foot *Richmond*, laid down at the navy yard in Norfolk and completed in Richmond, was the first of Porter's harbor defense vessels com-pleted. Other 150-foot ironclads commenced included the *Chicora, Raleigh, Palmetto State, North Carolina, Huntsville, Tuscaloosa,* and *Savannah*. Larger vessels included the *Jackson* (renamed *Muscogee*), *Fredericksburg,* and *Milledgeville* (175 feet); the *Virginia II* and *Charleston* (180 feet); *Missouri* (183 feet); the *Columbia, Texas,* and *Tennessee* (216 feet); and the *Nashville* (310 feet). Porter also designed a smaller vessel of this class to be used in the North Carolina sounds. Only two of these 139-foot ironclads, the *Albemarle* and the *Neuse*, were completed.

Although the casemated ironclad remained the standard "home water" vessel constructed within the Confederacy, two double-ender ironclads with two octagonal casemates were laid down in Richmond and Wilmington. They were similar in appearance to the Union double-turreted monitors,

Equally formidable in appearance was the USS Choctaw, *it, too, carrying eight heavy cannons. Both ships were ready to ply the rivers by late 1862.* (KA)

but since the casemates were not moveable turrets, pivot guns were to be utilized. Neither vessel was completed because of the lack of iron armor. No monitor types were constructed in the Confederacy, although one to be built at Columbus, Georgia, was approved. The proposed vessel was apparently never laid down. Secretary of the Navy Mallory preferred the standard casemated ironclad. Less than two months before General Lee surrendered at Appomattox Court House, the secretary was writing, "for river, harbor, and coast defense, the sloping shield and general plan of armored vessels adopted by us . . . are the best that could be adopted in our situation. In ventilation, light, fighting space, and quarters it is believed that the sloping shield presents greater advantages than the *Monitor* turret."

The ironclads did contribute significantly to the Confederate war effort. They did not break or seriously challenge the Union blockade, but after the spring of 1862, this was not their primary objective. From then until the end of the war their real function was to defend the rivers, inlets, and ports. In this they had some success. Of the five seaports—Savannah, Charleston, Wilmington, Mobile, and Galveston—taken in the last six months of the war, two were taken by land forces from the rear, and two indirectly as a result of pressure from the rear. In all of the cities but one, Galveston, the Confederate Navy had ironclads as part of the harbor defense. Nevertheless, they suffered from serious defects in design and construction. The fundamental problems of weight, speed, seaworthiness, and mechanical inadequacies were never solved.

To a lesser degree the same was true of the Union armored vessels. Yet, they were superior in design and construction—not surprising, considering the available facilities and technological expertise in the North. This was particularly true of the monitors, which would remain the standard armored vessels in the United States Navy until the 1880s.

Like the Confederate ironclads the Union armored vessels played an important role in the Civil War. They were unsuitable for blockade duty, but in the amphibious operations along the coast and in the rivers and confined waters they proved their worth. Truly the Civil War was the ironclad era.

The USS Ozark *was unusual on the Mississippi. It carried a turret of Ericsson's design forward, and mounted four other cannons on the main deck.* (USAMHI)

A variety of less formidable ironclads and "tinclads" plied the Western rivers, boats like the USS General Grant, *shown here at Kingston, Georgia.* (NA)

David D. Porter had little good to say about any of the Mississippi ironclads. He was a devotee of the conventional Ericsson monitor design. (USAMHI)

Admiral Hiram Paulding backed Ericsson's original Monitor *design and worked hard to expedite its building and adoption by the navy. He succeeded.* (NYHS)

And so, obviously, was John Ericsson himself. Arrogant, egotistical, and painfully difficult to work with, he was still a genius of sorts, and the Union turned to him through most of the war for its monitor designs. (NHC)

Captain Francis H. Gregory, a hero of the era of iron men in wooden ships, superintended the construction of ironclads for Welles. (NYHS)

Chief Engineer Alban Stimers managed most of the construction of the original Monitor, *fought aboard her at Hampton Roads, and later lost his reputation with the unsuccessful* Casco *class of light-draft monitors.* (NHC)

Officers working under Gregory, like Chief Engineer James W. King, oversaw individual ironclads to completion. King supervised the Manayunk, Catawba, *and* Tippecanoe. *Later he built the* Ozark, Chickasaw, *and* Winnebago, *out west.* (LC)

The first turreted ironclads to follow the Monitor *were those of the* Passaic
*class, and they were the workhorse ironclads of the Atlantic coast. Here the
launch of the* Camanche *of that class. This launch took place in San Francisco,
California, where the vessel was shipped in parts and reconstructed. An 1864
photograph by C. E. Watkins.* (CHARLES S. SCHWARTZ)

The USS Catskill, *photographed in Charleston harbor in 1863, one of the most powerful—and most damaged—*Passaics. (USAMHI)

The anchor well of the Catskill. *Note how the anchor could be raised and lowered from within, without exposing men to fire.* (NHC)

An officer's cabin aboard the Catskill. *A beam of light enters through the skylight scuttle overhead. A watertight bulkhead door is closed behind the desk and above it on the bulkhead is a print of the original* Monitor *at sea.* (NHC)

The Catskill's turret machinery, the enormously heavy turret resting on and being turned by the massive vertical shaft at left. (NHC)

The engine room of the Catskill, showing part of the steam engine that powered not only the screw, but also the turret machinery. (NHC)

A similar, unpublished view of the engine room of the Camanche *while it was being reassembled in San Francisco.* (CHARLES S. SCHWARTZ)

The USS Nahant *undergoing repairs at Hilton Head, South Carolina, after being heavily damaged in the April 7, 1863, attack on Charleston, carried out largely by* Passaic-*class monitors like the* Nahant. (USAMHI)

Rear Admiral Samuel F. I. Du Pont commanded the fleet that attacked Charleston. Seeing the relatively low firepower of the monitors and seeing the heavy damage inflicted on them by Confederate batteries, he formed a poor opinion of monitors as offensive vessels. His entire monitor fleet fired 139 shots in the same time that it received at least 346 hits. (USAMHI)

The next step in improving monitor firepower was two turrets. The Onondaga *was commissioned in March 1864 and proved thoroughly reliable, though it saw very little action. Here it is in the James River, scene of most of its war service.* (USAMHI)

Next came the Miantonomoh *class, ships like the* Tonawanda, *shown here. Only one of them was finished in time to serve in the war, but they were far more seaworthy than their predecessors.* (P-M)

The Miantonomoh *itself actually steamed to Europe, proving the deep-sea capabilities of the monitor type. It appears here at the Washington Navy Yard in 1865. On the left is the USS* Montauk *of the* Passaic *class. In the distance is the light-draft monitor* Chimo *and, just visible behind it, the tall masts of the Confederate ironclad ram* Stonewall. *(NHC)*

Ericsson, meanwhile, turned his mind to much larger seagoing monitors, his Dictator *class. Only two were built, and neither was very successful. Here the* Puritan *peeks out of the shiphouse at the Continental Iron Works at Green Point, New York.* (NHC)

The launch of the USS Dictator, *December 26, 1863, at the Delamater Iron Works.* (THE MARINERS MUSEUM, NEWPORT NEWS, VIRGINIA)

Ready to slide down the ways, the Dictator *looms above the speakers' platform, flag-draped for the dedication ceremonies.* (NYHS)

Stimers's light-draft monitor Casco *on the James River. The* Casco-*type monitors were found to be ill-designed and barely awash, so their turrets were left off and they were turned into torpedo boats instead.* (USAMHI)

The launch of the light-draft USS Modoc, *photographed by the New York artist J. H. Beal in 1864.* (NHC)

James Eads designed powerful light-draft river "monitors" Osage *and* Neosho *to operate in barely four feet of water. Ungainly, they still proved effective against most enemy fire. Here the* Osage, *probably in the Red River in 1864.* (LC)

Soon after the Osage *and* Neosho *were begun, Eads started work on another class of light-draft river monitor, the* Winnebagos. *These included turrets designed by Eads, which were far superior to Ericsson's. They did good service on the Mississippi and at Mobile Bay and proved to be the spiritual progenitor of warships for a century to come. Here the USS* Milwaukee, *commissioned at Mound City in August 1864. It struck a "torpedo" on March 28, 1865, and sank.* (USAMHI)

The only three-turreted monitor built during the war, the USS Roanoke.
Originally a steam frigate, sister ship of the Merrimack, *which the Confederates
converted to the CSS* Virginia, *the* Roanoke *also was a conversion. Nearly
destroyed by the Confederate ironclad in the battle at Hampton Roads, it was
taken to the Brooklyn Navy Yard and the work of making it an ironclad
commenced barely two weeks after the battle. The result was not spectacular.
The* Roanoke *served two years with the North Atlantic Blockading Squadron,
but proved rather ineffective. This previously unpublished photograph shows it
at Brooklyn in mid 1865, the old ship-of-the-line USS* Vermont *in the left
background.* (NHC)

*By the end of the war, sights like these two
monitors lying off the Washington Navy Yard were
commonplace. The war gave rise to a whole new
generation of naval machines in the Union. An
unpublished image by Kilburn Brothers of New
Hampshire.* (USAMHI)

The Confederates looked to a different sort of ironclad, one more compatible with their limited technology and industrial facilities. No photographs of the Virginia *seem to have survived, but all subsequent Confederate ironclads followed the same general pattern originated by John Porter and John Brooke. Here the CSS* Chicora *in Charleston Harbor. On January 31, 1863,* Chicora *and its sister ship* Palmetto State *became the only Confederate ironclads to put to open sea when they steamed out and engaged elements of the blockading fleet successfully, then returned to port.* (OLD COURT HOUSE MUSEUM, VICKSBURG)

Nearly as famous as the Virginia, *the CSS* Albemarle *was equally as unwieldy and slow, yet managed to threaten Albemarle Sound most effectively, sink one enemy warship, and aid materially in the capture of Plymouth, North Carolina. To counter this threat, Lieutenant William B. Cushing attacked it on the night of October 27, 1864, with a torpedo mounted on the end of a spar projecting from a steam launch. The* Albemarle *sank almost immediately and is here shown at the Norfolk Navy Yard in 1865 after being raised by the Federals.*
(NHC)

In Georgia's waters, Confederates constructed this casemated ironclad, the CSS Jackson, only to find themselves so short of iron that it was never completed. The builders destroyed the ship before the Federals could capture it. This image may be by A. J. Riddle, who photographed the Andersonville prison camp in 1864. (TU, LOUISIANA HISTORICAL ASSOCIATION COLLECTION)

A remarkable unpublished view of the CSS Atlanta, *and perhaps the best illustration extant of the improvised nature of most Confederate ironclads. Taken after the war, this image probably shows the ship laid up at League Island, Pennsylvania, prior to its sale for salvage. It had been converted from the blockade runner* Fingal *in 1862, and the old* Fingal *hull shows clearly below the more streamlined additions that turned it into the* Atlanta. *This deep draft proved its undoing, for in its first engagement it ran aground and surrendered. The Federals later used it to patrol the James River.* (THE MARINERS MUSEUM)

The CSS Atlanta, *now the USS* Atlanta, *patrolling the James.* (USAMHI)

The CSS Tennessee *in Mobile Bay, after its surrender to Farragut. It was commanded in battle by Franklin Buchanan, who commanded the first Confederate ironclad, the* Virginia. (THE MARINERS MUSEUM)

The CSS Indianola, *formerly the USS* Indianola. *Captured from the Federals
and towed to Vicksburg, the* Indianola *was undergoing refurbishment into a
Confederate ironclad when its captors were forced to destroy it before the fall
of Vicksburg.* (USAMHI)

*A David class Confederate torpedo boat. These light-draft, semisubmerged
"ironclads" were well suited for harbor defense, stealing out in the night to
attack blockade ships. They enjoyed little real success, but created considerable
consternation among the Federals.* (NHC)

Mr. Cooley of Beaufort and Mr. Moore of Concord

A PORTFOLIO

Two of hundreds of unsung artists, these photographers captured South Carolina long before the Federals

THE WORK of two photographers, Samuel A. Cooley and Henry P. Moore, offers a remarkable view of South Carolina during this period.

Samuel A. Cooley represented that special class of quasi-official photographer, like George Barnard and Alexander Gardner, who sometimes did contract work for the government. Whenever possible, this group made private capital of their army contract work, implying that all of their work bore official sanction. Gardner called himself "Photographer to the Army of the Potomac." Cooley would use two titles—"Photographer Tenth Army Corps" and "U. S. Photographer, Department of the South." Perhaps it helped sales of their com-

mercial views. Certainly Cooley could offer an unusual range of images, for he operated permanent establishments in three South Carolina locations, Folly Island, Hilton Head, and Beaufort, and in Jacksonville, Florida. Houses, hospitals, camps, vessels, forts, landscapes, and everything else came before his lenses, and he sold stereo views of all of them.

By contrast, little is known of Henry P. Moore, of Concord, New Hampshire. He operated at Hilton Head in 1862–63, and probably came chiefly to take marketable views of the 3rd New Hampshire for the folks at home. His remarkable images speak for themselves.

SAMUEL A. COOLEY

The entrepreneur photographer. (USAMHI)

*"Cooley's" reads the sign in his Beaufort headquarters, and an unusual
"gallery" it is. Clothing, flour, hams, books, butter, stationery, oranges, baskets,
watches, and, of course, photographs, all could be bought over Cooley's
counter. He stands in the white jacket leaning against his wagon.* (USAMHI)

Another view of Cooley's Beaufort gallery, with a little less advertising visible.
(USAMHI)

*Cooley and assistants with his photographic wagon. Cooley himself stands
second from the right, his hand resting on one of his cameras.* (WRHS)

Cooley's favorite subject, Beaufort, South Carolina, seen from the river. The artist had a wonderful eye for the still-life possibilities of the camera. (USAMHI)

The Fuller House, one of Beaufort's showplaces, and now the headquarters of General Rufus Saxton. A sentry box stands outside the gates to the house.
(SOUTH CAROLINA HISTORICAL SOCIETY, CHARLESTON)

John S. Fyler's store and, next to it, the post office, one example of Cooley's sometimes extraordinary talent for still scenes that have life and seeming movement. (USAMHI)

A commissary storehouse, shot in October 1864, one of the contract images of government buildings made by Cooley. Right next door stands a fishing tackle and general provisions store. (SOUTH CAROLINA HISTORICAL SOCIETY)

*Bay Street in Beaufort, and J. W. Collins & Company's rather unusual clothing
store. In addition to coats, vests, pants, and caps, Mr. Collins also sold oats and
bran and, as advertised on the sign in his doorway, "cold soda." It certainly
seems to attract more customers than the dress shop next door.* (WRHS)

*The Beaufort Hotel and, on its right, the office of
the Adams Express Company, one of the early
private mail and package carriers in the country.*
(SOUTH CAROLINA HISTORICAL SOCIETY)

Another Beaufort post office, right next to the Adams Express. Since large sums of money often traveled in the post to and from the soldiers, the ground floor windows are barred with iron mesh to prevent burglary. (USAMHI)

Bay Street in 1862, another view of a typical Southern town. (SOUTH CAROLINA HISTORICAL SOCIETY)

The west side of Bay Street. (USAMHI)

*The Beaufort Hotel again and, to its left, the commissary storehouse and fishing
tackle shop. The dandies in front of the hotel may be Southern gentlemen who
demurred on soldiering, or they may be Yankee traders who followed the army
to sell to the soldiers.* (USAMHI)

A quiet street scene in Beaufort. (USAMHI)

A house used as a hospital for "contrabands," the slaves who gathered around the Union armies wherever they went, seeking freedom and protection. (SOUTH CAROLINA HISTORICAL SOCIETY)

*The one-time home of Dr. John A. Johnson, and now a hospital, with linen
and blankets airing on the balcony.* (USAMHI)

The Beaufort Arsenal on Craven Street. (SOUTH CAROLINA HISTORICAL
SOCIETY)

The United States Marine headquarters on Bay Point, rather a small headquarters, but then it was rather a small Marine Corps. (USAMHI)

The machine shops at Bay Point and, in the foreground, bits and pieces of the machinery they worked on here, mostly for maintenance on the ships of the South Atlantic Blockading Squadron. (USAMHI)

At right the saltwater condenser for purifying water, and in the background several vessels docked awaiting coal. (USAMHI)

A parade, the generals on their white chargers, the men and boys watching from the sideline. Cooley missed no opportunity to shoot a scene with a mass of men. The more subjects in an image, the more who might want to buy a print . . . and perhaps an orange or two from his gallery. (CWTI)

Hundreds of heavy guns passed through Hilton Head on their way to fight rebellion. They and their accoutrements lie here in some disarray. In the lower left corner, against the sand, can be seen the shadow of Cooley's camera. (USAMHI)

The headquarters of Major General David Hunter, now recovered from his Bull Run wound. Cooley did a much more brisk business at Hilton Head than at Beaufort. (USAMHI)

HENRY P. MOORE

Henry P. Moore, too, went to Hilton Head, where there was more bustle and activity than in sleepy Beaufort. The wharf looked over a bay jammed with warships, transports, tugs, and lighter craft. (USAMHI)

Here immense quantities of supplies for the army besieging Charleston were received. (USAMHI)

The Hilton Head signal station and, on the ground, several carriages for siege guns. (USAMHI)

Moore took his camera atop the signal station to photograph the hospital in the far distance and an ordnance storeyard in the foreground. Cannons and carriages lay awaiting shipment to the front. (USAMHI)

Another, larger, signal station was needed in 1863 on St. Helena Island. The engineers who built it based their tower on four existing trees still growing. (USAMHI)

And on Otter Island they built another, which Moore captured in the act of signaling to a ship out on the horizon. (USAMHI)

But at Hilton Head, Moore's best work was his portraits of the men in their camps, and particularly those of the 3rd New Hampshire. Here Lieutenant Colonel J. H. Jackson stands at left, his son Captain T. M. Jackson second from the right, and his servant Cyrus at right. (USAMHI)

Signal corpsmen, March 1, 1862. (USAMHI)

The 3rd New Hampshire's surgeon, A. A. Moulton, and his somewhat gothic-looking wife. (USAMHI)

Cook's galley of Company H. In the hut in back stand tin plates and cups for the mess. In the center foreground stands the cook, G. N. Wheeler, at his camp stove. The man seated on the small barrel is W. Blake, about to grind coffee beans in the grinder at his feet. In the right background an unknown New Hampshire officer peers from his tent to see what Moore is doing. (USAMHI)

The meal prepared, another cook looks on as the bandsmen of the 3rd New Hampshire dine, their drums and fifes set casually about the area. (USAMHI)

A nonchalant group of the New Hamphire boys pose for the artist, their table reflecting their leisure doings. It lies cluttered with books, a cigar, letters from home, cased ambrotypes of female loved ones, dominoes, and an ink bottle from which one man is writing his letter. The man seated on the other side of the table reads a page of crude cartoons from an issue of Harper's Weekly.
(USAMHI)

*The bandmaster's tent, with bandmaster G. W. Ingalls at left studying his
music while his servant polishes his boots. Sam Brown reads a New Hampshire
newspaper at the center of the table, while musician D. A. Brown on the right
does the same. Their horns lie on the table* (USAMHI)

*These New Hampshiremen added considerable decoration to their Hilton Head
quarters. Seashells, palmettos, cactus, driftwood, all contributed to a scene quite
out of the ordinary for Civil War camps. These musicians can enjoy their meal
in the most pleasant surroundings.* (USAMHI)

And the officers loved their dominoes. (USAMHI)

*The splendid plantation residence of John E. Seabrook on Edisto Island, in
1862. At far left is his library—at right, his wine cellar. Lying like a white
carpet on the lawn in front of the house is cotton captured aboard the blockade
runner* Empire *and spread out to dry in the sun.* (USAMHI)

*A closer view of the Seabrook mansion, now headquarters of Colonel
E. Q. Fellows and staff. The post adjutant, Martin James, stands under the
square marked on the image, his office indicated by the √ , and his sleeping
quarters by the ✳. Made by Moore on April 7, 1862.* (KA)

*Seabrook's fishpond, with his house in the distance at left. Bandmaster Ingalls
steers the boat.* (USAMHI)

H. P. Moore's images of the Seabrook plantation touched upon art. Here Seabrook's extensive garden as seen from the mansion house. One of Seabrook's slaves, a little boy, stands atop the sundial at right center. Standing with folded arms in the foreground is Colonel E. Q. Fellows, commanding the 3rd New Hampshire. It is early spring, April 7, 1862, and already the garden is verdant. Half a continent away, the second day's fighting at Shiloh is raging. (KA)

More cotton drying on Seabrook's grounds, being tended by freedmen who were once his slaves. In the distance at center stands the USS Pocahontas. (USAMHI)

Seabrook's library. (USAMHI)

*Men who died before Moore could catch them in life pose silent and still in
death. Almost all are of the 3rd New Hampshire—almost all died of disease.
Hilton Head could kill despite its tropical beauty.* (USAMHI)

And however easy it might have been to forget the war, they could not, and neither did Moore. Deceptive in its peacefulness, this scene could turn warlike at any time, and the soldier reading his letter beside the gun carriage in Fort Wells is certainly not far from his weapon. The sights atop the Rodman gun could fill with enemy vessels or blockade runners, and the tranquility of this image would vanish. Moore, for all his commercial instincts, knew as well that he was capturing a special part of the war for posterity. Thanks to him, these scenes will remain captive for all of time. (USAMHI)

The Peninsular Campaign

EMORY M. THOMAS

The first campaign going "on to Richmond,"
and the emergence of a general called "Granny" Lee

THE ARMY OF THE POTOMAC was awesome. In the spring of 1862 it was the largest, best equipped armed force ever assembled in the Western Hemisphere. From the masses of volunteers who had descended upon Washington, George B. McClellan had fashioned a mammoth war machine—150,000 men, plus the material to support and sustain this host. With such force McClellan confidently intended to deliver the *coup de grace* to the would-be Confederacy.

McClellan had taken command in the aftermath of the Union debacle at Bull Run in July 1861. He began at once to mold his army and endured pleas and pressure to commit to battle prematurely. Termed "Young Napoleon" by the press, McClellan believed he understood the complexity of "modern war." He first had to spar with ranking United States General Winfield Scott until the aged Scott finally retired from the service in November 1861; then McClellan suffered the "help" of his Commander-in-Chief Abraham Lincoln and other martial amateurs in the administration and Congress.

Having built so splendid an army and waited so long to employ it, McClellan could not afford to err; when he marched, he would have to win. As the campaigning season of 1862 loomed imminent,

Lincoln felt the need to rebuild his faith in "Young Napoleon." In frustration, the President issued his own General War Order Number One, which prescribed a "general forward movement" to begin on all fronts on February 22. Beyond this action, he and others in Washington could only chafe at McClellan's caution. Lincoln realized his administration had invested too much in McClellan to cut its losses now. Whatever "Young Napoleon" did or did not do would have to be Union strategy and policy.

Beyond the Potomac waited Confederate armies, the chief of which, commanded by Joseph E. Johnston, occupied the ground around Manassas near the battlefield of Bull Run. Johnston, who ironically held much the same low opinion of his President, Jefferson Davis, as McClellan did of Lincoln, had only some 40,000 troops. But he had 10,000 reinforcements nearby, and he had had all fall and winter to improve a position which had proven impenetrable the previous summer.

For the Army of the Potomac to emulate the tactics of First Bull Run and smash headlong into these waiting defenders seemed to McClellan artless and wasteful. Accordingly he determined to strike the Southerners elsewhere. He wanted to transport his army by water to the tiny port town

After Johnston and Magruder abandoned Yorktown, the Confederates found Norfolk untenable and evacuated on May 9. Before leaving they did their best to destroy the navy yard. Timothy O'Sullivan's December 1864 photograph shows how thoroughly they did their task. (P-M)

of Urbana on the Rappahannock and interpose the Army of the Potomac between Johnston's Confederates and Richmond. Johnston, however, foiled the Urbana approach by evacuating Manassas and moving to Culpeper Court House where he might counter attacks from the east and north with equal facility.

However sound was Johnston's movement, he acted in haste without fully apprising his President of his intentions. And he had had to destroy at Manassas enormous quantities of supplies his government had labored so diligently to collect. Davis, then, had doubts about Johnston nearly equal to Lincoln's about McClellan.

His Urbana landing scrapped, McClellan shifted to a strategic plan which was even more ambitious.

Now McClellan could pursue his original intention of campaigning up the Virginia Peninsula toward Richmond. Here he poses for a Brady camera with members of his staff including, standing at right, Van Vliet. (KA)

He proposed to transport the Army of the Potomac by water to Fort Monroe on the tip of the Virginia Peninsula between the York and James rivers. Union troops had maintained possession of the fort throughout the war, and McClellan planned to use this friendly perimeter as a staging area for an assault upon Richmond from the east. The combined army-navy operation and the eastern invasion route may have seemed complicated logistically, but it offered several advantages over a more direct

assault. The Peninsular approach would not compel the Federals to cross the many streams and rivers which crossed the direct route to Richmond. The advance would take place on the relatively flat, tidewater coastal plain. The James, York, and Pamunkey rivers would permit the Union Navy to support McClellan's army with both supplies and gunfire during the advance to Richmond. If Johnston or any other commander dared confront the Army of the Potomac on the Peninsula, he would risk the prospect of having a portion of the blue army landed behind him and thus encirclement and destruction. On the other hand, if the Confederates chose to give battle nearer Richmond, McClellan had the siege artillery with which to blast his way into the city and destroy the opposing army at the same time. Withholding McDowell's corps, Lincoln assented to the plan, and McClellan promptly moved his army to the Peninsula and began his month-long siege of Yorktown.

On April 14 in Richmond the Confederate high command met for fourteen hours to plan some response to McClellan's Peninsular approach. Johnston favored a concentration near Richmond because he thought the Federals too strong on the Peninsula. Robert E. Lee, the President's chief military advisor, and Secretary of War George W. Randolph contended that the Southern army would have to confront the threat somewhere and that the Peninsula was as good a place as any. President Davis feared losing his army and capital if the campaign produced siege operations in front of Richmond. Accordingly Davis instructed Johnston to move his entire force to the Peninsula. Johnston complied without enthusiasm and in the days which followed occupied the Yorktown line with 56,000 troops. He was all too aware that McClellan had nearly twice as many men on the other side of the thin curtain of earth. Thus Johnston, on the eve of the grand assault which would be the climax of McClellan's siege operations, determined to withdraw. On the night of May 3 the Confederates abandoned the Yorktown line and began retracing their steps up the Peninsula toward Richmond. Actually they stepped into seemingly bottomless mud—the result of an extraordinary amount of rain during April.

As Southern columns clogged the spongy roads westward, McClellan's Federals on May 4 rushed empty earthworks. To Washington McClellan announced a great victory at small cost. Then he set about directing the pursuit of his elusive enemy. Five Union divisions plunged into the Peninsular mud, by now well-churned by the retreating Confederates; four more divisions stood ready to move by water up the York to cut off the Southern withdrawal.

Johnston's rear guard (James Longstreet's division) first felt the pressure of the Federal pursuit near Williamsburg. Just east of the old colonial capital on May 5 a sharp fight ensued. The Southerners first stopped the Union advance, then counterattacked, and finally withdrew into the darkness. The Battle of Williamsburg was bloody, but inconclusive. Johnston gained the time he needed to make good his escape, but the Confederate counterattack was a costly failure.

McClellan, meanwhile, was trying to hasten Johnston's envelopment by water. William B. Franklin's division made a landing on the Peninsula opposite West Point, but encountered Gustavus W. Smith's Confederates soon after. The wily Johnston anticipated McClellan's move, and the engagement between Smith's and Franklin's troops on May 7 at Barhamsville (Eltham's Landing) convinced McClellan that his trap had failed. Thereafter he contented himself with a methodical pursuit of his quarry up the Peninsula.

The rival commanders each expressed satisfaction at the developments thus far. Johnston was pleased to have made good his escape, and McClellan took pride in his conquest of the Yorktown line and his pursuit of a fleeing foe. Both generals consumed themselves in cautious movement: Johnston to the vicinity of Richmond and McClellan to the vicinity of Johnston.

In the process both ignored their navies and a succession of military "dominoes" involved in the movement up the Peninsula. When Johnston evacuated the Yorktown line, he left the port city of Norfolk exposed and untenable. When Norfolk fell —the Confederates evacuated the city on May 9 —the Virginia became a ship without a port. When the Virginia's crew failed in their attempt to lighten the heavy-draft vessel sufficiently to steam up the James, they had to destroy the ironclad. This in turn opened the James all the way to Richmond to Union gunboats and troop transports.

Curiously, neither field commander appreciated this circumstance. Lee was the first Confederate to react; he hastened the work on gun emplacements, river obstructions, and "torpedoes" at Drewry's Bluff. McClellan was seemingly too preoccupied even to comprehend the city's vulnerability. Indeed, it was President Lincoln himself, while visiting Fort Monroe, who gave the instructions which led to Norfolk's capture. The Federal Navy then pressed the issue, and on May 15 two ironclads, the Monitor and Galena, led three wooden gunboats up the James toward Richmond. The small

*Lieutenant General Winfield Scott on
June 10, 1862, by Charles D.
Fredericks. Taken at West Point after
his retirement, it shows a man now
bitter at his treatment by the younger
McClellan. Two weeks from now,
however, "Little Mac" will begin to feel
his comeuppance on the Peninsula.*
(USAMHI)

fleet encountered little difficulty until it reached
Drewry's Bluff, which was only about seven miles
from the Confederate capital. There Southern batteries and channel obstructions halted the Union
advance. Had McClellan provided the expedition
with a supporting army column of any size, the
fight at Drewry's Bluff might have turned out quite
differently. As it happened though, this repulse
ended the Federal threat to Richmond by water.

Indeed water, in the form of rain, seemed to
plague instead of assist McClellan's campaign as
the Army of the Potomac advanced nearer Richmond. The Federal route lay up the northern half
of the Peninsula to take advantage of supply lines
from the York and Pamunkey rivers. At Cum-

berland Landing and White House the navy deposited massive amounts of supplies for transport
overland via road and the Richmond & York River
rail line to the troops. Throughout May unseasonal
amounts of rain hampered the movements of men
and supplies. Yet even though the Army of the Potomac seemed to ooze instead of march, it moved
nonetheless ever closer to Richmond.

As he neared the city McClellan recognized the
necessity to broaden his front and position his army
on the south as well as the north side of the
Chickahominy River, which bisects the Peninsula
near Richmond. Two Federal corps had crossed
the Chickahominy on May 30 when one of the
most violent rainstorms in memory descended upon

the area. The fresh rain turned the normally sluggish Chickahominy into a torrent which washed away bridges and left Erasmus Keyes's Union corps isolated from the rest of the army. Joe Johnston recognized his opportunity and determined to strike the exposed Federals with four Confederate divisions.

The Confederate attack appeared simple as long as it consisted only of lines drawn on a map. The lines, representing Southern troops moving along roads, converged at the village of Seven Pines, and there Johnston planned to attack a fraction of the blue army with masses of his own men. On the morning of May 31, however, Johnston's plan came unraveled. James Longstreet seemed most at fault; he took the wrong road and in so doing clogged the Confederate advance. As a result the

One of McClellan's commanders, Brigadier General Edwin V. Sumner, the oldest corps leader of the war. Born in 1797, he was called "bull head" because a musket ball supposedly bounced from his head in Mexico. During the coming campaign, however, he was wounded twice. (USAMHI)

supposedly coordinated attack degenerated into a series of single blows and an aborted Confederate opportunity. In the aftermath of the day's fighting Johnston fell wounded from his horse, leaving the Southerners not only confused, but also leaderless.

On June 1, after an unsuccessful attempt to salvage victory from the Battle of Seven Pines (or Fair Oaks), Robert E. Lee arrived to assume command and lead the march back toward Richmond. To this juncture, Lee had disappointed himself and others in the Southern cause. Possessed of splendid credentials at the outset of the war, he had directed a doomed campaign in the Kanawha Valley of western Virginia, presided over a retreat from the coast in South Carolina and Georgia, and served in the President's shadow as Davis's military advisor. In this last capacity, Lee had ameliorated somewhat the relations between Davis and Johnston; but of this, no one but Lee was aware. Thus, he took command of Johnston's army in the wake of a bungled battle in the midst of a desperate campaign with little reputation beyond those who knew him. And the first direction he gave to his troops was to dig holes in the ground—to shore up the defensive works in front of Richmond.

Those who crowned Lee with the sobriquet "Granny Lee" or "King of Spades," however, missed his intention. Lee threw up breastworks so that he might defend Richmond with as few troops as possible; with the bulk of his army he determined to attack.

If the new Confederate commander needed time to make Johnston's army his own following the battle, McClellan seemed to be in a cooperative mood. He moved, slowly and cautiously, to consolidate his position before Richmond. Completing his shift of troop units south of the Chickahominy, McClellan stationed four corps (Franklin's, E. V. Sumner's, Samuel P. Heintzelman's and Keyes's) directly east of Seven Pines about six miles from its limits and about one mile from the Confederate works. North of the Chickahominy were the 30,000 troops of Fitz John Porter's corps. McClellan was careful for good reason; his intelligence operatives and spies informed him that the Confederate Army numbered 200,000 men. The estimate, largely the product of Allan Pinkerton's civilian agents, was much exaggerated; Lee had perhaps 65,000 to 70,000 troops with which to confront McClellan's 90,000 to 100,000 at this point. Nev-

Some of McClellan's generals, on May 14, 1862. Seated from the right they are Brigadier General John Newton, Brigadier General William F. Barry, VI Corps commander Brigadier General William B. Franklin, and Brigadier General Henry W. Slocum. (NLM)

ertheless McClellan believed the Army of the Potomac was outnumbered, and he renewed his pleas for reinforcements.

While waiting for his government to appreciate his situation and support him as he believed necessary, McClellan brought up his big guns, 101 pieces of siege artillery. These weapons, he believed, would compensate for his numerical inferiority and enable the Federals to blast their way into Richmond. To his wife, McClellan explained that he planned to "make the first battle mainly an artillery combat." The artillery would "push them in upon Richmond and behind their works." Then he would "bring up my heavy guns, shell the city, and carry it by assault."

With uncanny insight into the mind of his foe, Lee wrote to Davis on June 5, "McClellan will

make this a battle of posts. He will take position from position, under cover of his heavy guns, and we cannot get at him without storming his works, which . . . is extremely hazardous." To counter the Union tactics, Lee proposed "to bring McClellan out," to make the Federals fight in the open, away from prepared fortifications and big guns. First he assured himself that his defensive works before Richmond were as strong as he could make them. Then he dispatched almost four brigades to the Shenandoah Valley to provide "Stonewall" Jackson with the strength to conclude his brilliant campaign there. Lee had need of the hard-hitting Valley Army at Richmond. Finally, he sent J.E.B. Stuart and 1,200 cavalry troopers to scout the Federal right flank.

Stuart left Richmond on the morning of June 12

and rode north twenty-two miles before making camp for the night. Next day the column turned east. The Confederates encountered slight resistance as they moved, and Stuart realized that the Union right flank was unsecured. Nevertheless, he pressed on—completely around McClellan's army and back into Richmond from the south on June 15. Stuart's "ride around McClellan" made him a hero and did wonders for Confederate morale; it also seemed to confirm McClellan's fears about Confederate strength. But most importantly the venture provided Lee with valuable information regarding the Federal flank.

During the latter half of June McClellan hesitated. He considered opening an additional supply route from Harrison's Landing on the James to supplement or supplant his bases on the Pamunkey. He contemplated an all-out assault on Richmond. Eventually he decided upon a limited advance to test Confederate defenses east of the city.

Meanwhile Lee was dreaming larger dreams. On June 23 he convened a meeting attended by Longstreet, D. H. Hill, A. P. Hill, and Jackson, and announced his plans. He would station 25,000 men commanded by Magruder and Benjamin Huger in the works to the east of Richmond; these troops would have to fend off the entire Union Army if Lee's plan miscarried. The divisions of Longstreet and the two Hills would mass on the Confederate left and strike the Union right at the village of Mechanicsville. And Jackson's Valley Army by rapid and secret marches would join Lee's force and strike the Federals in the rear of their right flank. If all went well, approximately 66,000 Confederates would assault Porter's 30,000 Federals from the flank and the rear. This would "bring McClellan out" of his works and, perhaps, destroy him. If, on the other hand, McClellan realized in time the weakness of the Confederate force covering Richmond, he was capable of blasting his way into the city. The stakes of Lee's gamble were high—victory or disaster.

Lee's campaign, known as the Seven Days Battles, began on June 25 when McClellan launched his limited attack upon the Confederate lines east of Richmond. Two Federal divisions advanced upon the Southern works, tested their strength, and then threw up field fortifications of their own. McClellan believed what Lee wanted him to believe—that the 25,000 Confederates were

Stewart Van Vliet, McClellan's chief quartermaster in the Peninsular campaign. (KA)

50,000. The same day McClellan also learned that Jackson's army was on the way down from the Valley. Immediately he sent a message to Washington announcing Jackson's presence and emphasizing his peril. "I am in no way responsible . . ." McClellan insisted, "I have not failed to represent repeatedly the necessity for reinforcements . . . if the result . . . is a disaster, the responsibility cannot be thrown on my shoulders; it must rest where it belongs." Then having prepared his government for the worst and exonerated himself, McClellan hastened to Porter's headquarters.

On June 26 Lee's three divisions formed for the attack on Mechanicsville. The commands of A. P. Hill, D. H. Hill, and Longstreet formed and waited. Nothing was supposed to occur until Jackson arrived, and Jackson was uncharacteristically late. Finally, at three in the afternoon, A. P. Hill could restrain himself no longer. Acting upon the assumption that Jackson must be nearby and poised for attack, Hill began the battle. The Confederates swept across the Chickahominy and through Mechanicsville. Then they crashed headlong into Porter's lines behind Beaver Dam Creek.

The Army of the Potomac at Cumberland Landing in May 1862, preparing for the push that will take it "on to Richmond." A Wood & Gibson photograph for Alexander Gardner. (LC)

Neither frontal assault nor flank attack could dislodge the Federals. The Confederates sustained 1,484 casualties against 361 Union losses and did precisely what Lee had not wanted to do—attacked the Unionists in their prepared works.

Darkness ended the day's fighting in the Battle of Mechanicsville, and still Jackson's troops had not arrived. Actually the Valley Army reached the vicinity at five o'clock in the afternoon; then Jackson, after being unaccountably late, became incredibly cautious. He made camp within the sound of the battle. The most rational explanation of Jackson's behavior focuses upon an irrational response to stress and exhaustion. He had ridden, fought, and marched too long with too little rest. And now a "fog of war" settled over him and clouded his otherwise clear mind. On the morning of June 27, Jackson finally found the battle. But the fact that the first shells fired by the artillery of the Valley Army landed among some of A. P. Hill's troops portended more confusion on Jackson's part.

Lee resolved to continue his attack on June 27;

he had little choice. During the previous night McClellan had removed Porter's troops to a new position near Gaines's Mill on Boatswain's Swamp. The Southerners attacked in the early afternoon, and again Porter's men withstood the assault. Jackson was supposed to send his troops crashing down upon the Federal flank, but once more he was late. At last, at seven o'clock in the evening, Lee was able to assemble his army for a concerted drive. In the face of this new attack, Porter's troops, who had been repelling piecemeal assaults for five hours, broke. Confederate infantry tore through the center of the Federal lines. In desperation Union General Phillip St. George Cooke, J.E.B. Stuart's father-in-law, ordered his cavalry to charge the oncoming Southerners. The charge only added to the general confusion, however, when it degenerated into a stampede to the rear in the face of Confederate rifle fire. At Gaines's Mill, at a cost of 8,750 Confederate casualties to 6,837 Union losses, Lee won his first clear victory. Yet during the night Porter was able to cross the Chickahominy and unite his battered men with the rest of the Army of the Potomac. McClellan's army was much alive and still a potent force.

McClellan himself was unnerved, however. Fearing for his supply lines to the Pamunkey and for the safety of his army, he determined to retreat to the James and open a new base of supply at Harrison's Landing. Some of his subordinates, notably Joseph Hooker and Phil Kearny, perceived that the Confederate forces directly before Richmond were as weak as they actually were. But McClellan rejected their counsel. He gave the order for his retreat and then vented his frustration upon his superiors in Washington. He dispatched a

One of Brady's assistants captures a scene at Cumberland Landing. Over 100,000 men await the order to advance against an enemy barely half their numbers. (LC)

A panorama showing the army at camp near Cumberland Landing. (CHS)

lengthy telegram in which he explained the situation as he understood it. In conclusion he placed the blame for this circumstance where he thought blame belonged. "If I save this army now, I tell you plainly that I owe no thanks to you or to any other persons in Washington. You have done your best to sacrifice this army." Fortunately for McClellan, the telegraph supervisor in Washington did not transmit these two final sentences to the President.

Satisfied that he had absolved himself of the responsibility for his "change of base," on June 28 McClellan set about saving his army. Confederates could see the smoke from burning supplies and wagons moving to the southeast. Nevertheless Lee had to act on less than confirmed intelligence when he committed his army to an all-out pursuit. Elements of the opposing armies fought on June 28, but the major effort to cut off and destroy the Army of the Potomac began the following day.

On June 29 Magruder was finally to have the chance for offensive, instead of defensive, action. Moving east, near the old battlefield at Fair Oaks, Magruder was in a good position to strike the retreating Federals. Jackson, too, had the opportunity to fall upon the Union rear. As it happened,

though, both Confederate generals failed to move fast enough or decisively enough. Jackson never really got his command into action, and Magruder advanced timidly until his troops encountered the Federals near Savage Station. There, late in the day, the Confederates attacked to no significant effect. Understandably Lee was concerned that he would lose the chance to reap the benefits of his hard-won victories thus far. Accordingly on June 30 he again exhorted his subordinates to press the pursuit. He planned to bring the troops of Longstreet, A. P. Hill, Magruder, Huger, and Jackson together for a climactic battle. Once more, however, Magruder and Jackson were slow, and Huger, too, was late. As a result, Hill's and Longstreet's divisions struck the center of the Federal Army in a battle variously named White Oak Swamp, Frayser's Farm, or Glendale. The combat raged in all three of these places, and more, and the Union line held firm amid fierce fighting.

On the morning of July 1 McClellan seemed to have made good his escape. Porter's corps and the huge wagon train of army supplies were safely at Harrison's Landing. The remaining four corps of the Army of the Potomac were drawn up on the slopes of Malvern Hill, the last position they would have to occupy before they reached Harrison's Landing and sanctuary. The Federal position seemed impregnable. Still, Lee hoped for total victory, and so he sent Longstreet to investigate "the feasibility of aggressive battle."

Longstreet believed he had discovered locations from which Confederate artillery might catch the Federals in a devastating cross fire. Lee gave the order to mass the guns where Longstreet indicated and instructed the infantry to charge in the wake of the artillery barrage. However, the Southern artillery never got completely into place or action. Hence Confederate infantry remained in place, and it seemed that there would be no battle.

Then in the middle of the afternoon the Federals began to move; they seemed to be withdrawing. Lee ordered an immediate attack. Southern troops charged up Malvern Hill to find the Army of the Potomac very much in place. The assault was slaughter. Union artillery raked the advancing ranks, and Federal infantry blazed away at the survivors. Yet the series of charges continued until dark. And in the night 8,000 casualties littered the field, 5,000 Confederate, 3,000 Union.

Lee had seized a last chance to destroy his foe and lost. Perhaps he sensed a moment of truth

which might not come again. Regardless of the reason the result was disaster.

Although no one knew it for sure at the time, the Battle of Malvern Hill was the last of the Seven Days Battles and the conclusion of the Peninsular campaign. The Army of the Potomac withdrew to Harrison's Landing to recuperate. The Confederates remained nearby for a time; then Lee left a token force and took the bulk of his army to Richmond. The campaign established Lee as savior of the Confederacy. When he took command, the Army of the Potomac was in the suburbs of Richmond; a month later the same army cowered inert under the protection of naval guns twenty-three miles away. Lee was lavish in his praise of his own army, the Army of Northern Virginia. Later in his official report, however, he admitted, "Under ordinary circumstances the Federal Army should have been destroyed."

Although out-generaled, the Army of the Potomac had fought well. The men who had stood firm against the furious Confederate assaults at Gaines's Mill, Malvern Hill, and elsewhere would be back. But McClellan, the "Young Napoleon" who molded this splendid army, had proven himself unable to command it.

*Two images by James F. Gibson almost form a panoramic view of troops at
Cumberland Landing on the Pamunkey River. The landing appears at right.*
(*left,* LC; *right,* USAMHI)

Another Gibson panorama of the camps on the Pamunkey. (USAMHI)

Probably Gibson's finest panorama. The enormity of an army on campaign is evident and overwhelming. (USAMHI)

*In mid-May McClellan moved his base to White House on the Pamunkey,
formerly the home of one of Robert E. Lee's sons. James Gibson photographed
the house on May 17, 1862.* (USAMHI)

*And G. W. Houghton, the Brattleboro, Vermont photographer, caught this
scene of the camps of the army at White House Landing.* (VERMONT
HISTORICAL SOCIETY)

Gibson's May 17 image of the destroyed bridge of the Richmond & York River Railroad over the Pamunkey. McClellan's people started the work of repair at once and . . . (NLM)

. . . soon it was rebuilt, though the steam engine here is on a barge. Tracks have not yet been laid on the bridge. And within a month, McClellan himself will have to destroy it once again when he retreats. (USAMHI)

George Washington was married in St. Peter's Church near White House. Now it is favored by touring Federals, including white-bearded General Sumner and his staff. (USAMHI)

Another view of St. Peter's, taken by a Brady assistant. (LC)

Contraband blacks flocked to the army's camps to become laborers and servants at White House Landing. (USAMHI)

And another sort of man gathered around the army, the romantic secret service men, the operatives and spies whose "intelligence" McClellan believed unquestioningly. The trouble was, their information proved consistently erroneous. Seated in the background, pipe in mouth, is the most unreliable of them all, Allan Pinkerton. Yet McClellan preferred to believe him since his reports of overwhelming enemy numbers confirmed "Little Mac's" own exaggerated fears. (NLM)

*On the march again. David Woodbury caught men of the 5th New Hampshire
and 64th New York at work on this military bridge over the Chickahominy in
the last days of May, as the Federals are on their way to Seven Pines.*
(USAMHI)

*On the battle line at Seven Pines, or Fair Oaks. Gibson's early June photo of
Fort Richardson, near the Quarles House.* (NLM)

Battery C of the 1st Pennsylvania Light Artillery, the extreme front line at Fair Oaks. (NLM)

Gibson's photo taken on the field at Fair Oaks, showing a fresh Union grave at left. (USAMHI)

Major General Gustavus W. Smith, center, and his staff. After the wounding of Johnston at Fair Oaks, Smith temporarily commanded the Army of Northern Virginia. (CHS)

*Two old frame houses, an orchard, and a well, near Fair Oaks, where over 400
dead Federals were buried after the battle.* (NLM)

*Union Fort Sumner near Fair Oaks, looking toward the Confederate lines,
taken by Gibson a few days after the battle.* (USAMHI)

Another view of the twin frame houses beside the orchard. A central main house was meant to connect the two wings, but it was never built. (USAMHI)

Battery A, 2nd United States Artillery, by Gibson, men who fought at Fair Oaks. (LC)

While the armies fought at Fair Oaks, Professor T. S. Lowe gained a true bird's-eye view of the fight from his balloon Intrepid. *Here it is being inflated on Gaines's Hill, June 1, 1862. Lowe stands at right with his hand resting against the balloon.* (KA)

Lowe replenishing the gas in his balloon Intrepid *from the* Constitution. *Brady's assistant made a series of images of Lowe and his apparatus.* (USAMHI)

"Your message received announcing the success of Balloon and Telegraph combined—the most wonderful feat of the age." So said Thomas T. Eckert of the Union's Military Telegraph. On June 1, 1862, during the Battle of Fair Oaks, a photographer working for Brady captured the scene that made Eckert so ecstatic. Professor Thaddeus Lowe's observation balloon, probably the Intrepid, *is grounded after an ascent. From his observations, telegrapher Parker Spring is sending a dispatch over the portable field key attached to the roll of wire. Lowe may be the man in the white hat seated below him. A third man sits with his back to the camera, sketching the scene on a pad. It was a blending of two new means of rapid communications, a historic moment. "Give my compliments to Prof Lowe and Spring," said Eckert after receiving the first telegram; "if they feel as proud over the enterprise as I do, they have been well repaid and will long be remembered."* (KA)

On his way to the heavens, an officer ascends in Lowe's craft to observe the fighting at Fair Oaks. His climb is controlled by the soldiers anchoring the balloon. (LC)

Brady's assistant captures Lowe's balloon during an ascent at Fair Oaks. (BRUCE GIMELSON)

Brigadier General David B. Birney, son of the abolitionist leader James G. Birney, commanded a brigade at Fair Oaks. He was charged with disobeying an order from his superior, . . . (USAMHI)

. . . Samuel P. Heintzelman, during the battle. Birney was acquitted. (CWTI)

Brigadier General Willis A. Gorman, former territorial governor of Minnesota, shown here with his wife, commanded a brigade in Sumner's corps and won acclaim from several superiors. (NA)

And General Oliver O. Howard, who fought at Bull Run, commanded a brigade at Fair Oaks. A bullet there cost him his right arm. He still had both arms in this Brady studio portrait. (USAMHI)

And Brigadier General John J. Abercrombie, born in 1798, was still active enough to lead a brigade at Fair Oaks at the age of sixty-four. Here he was wounded, and he left active service for the duration of the war. (USAMHI)

A house used by the Federals as a hospital after the battle. Image by Gibson in June 1862. (USAMHI)

Another view of the hospital, used by wounded from General Joseph Hooker's division. Even it did not escape the battle, as evidenced in the collapsed chimney and damaged wall. (LC)

The Quarles House near Fair Oaks. Many Federal dead were interred here after the fight. (USAMHI)

Gibson's photo of the house used as a hospital by General Philip Kearny's brigade. The nondescript looking lot of men here may well be walking wounded. (NLM)

For most of the men in McClellan's army, Fair Oaks was their first real fight. One of these was McClellan's chief of cavalry, Brigadier General George Stoneman, shown here in camp after the battle. He and his cavalry took little part, in fact. (USAMHI)

Stoneman, seated at right, and Brigadier General Henry M. Naglee. The dog is nearly as photogenic as the generals. (USAMHI)

On March 18, 1862, with the threat of McClellan coming up the Peninsula, President Jefferson Davis appointed a new Secretary of War, George Wythe Randolph of Virginia. He appears here in an unpublished portrait. One of the few war secretaries to attempt to exercise real control of the War Department, he only lasted in office until November. But he worked well with the man that he and Davis chose to replace the wounded Johnston at the head of the Army of Northern Virginia, . . . (UNIVERSITY OF VIRGINIA, EDGEHILL RANDOLPH PAPERS)

. . . General Robert Edward Lee. Until now, Lee's war service had been less than glorious. Some called him "Granny Lee," and some, like South Carolina Governor Francis Pickens, doubted that his heart was in the cause. The next month on the Peninsula would answer their fears. (SOUTHERN HISTORICAL COLLECTION, THE UNIVERSITY OF NORTH CAROLINA AT CHAPEL HILL)

Ironically, Lee's opposite number in the Confederate Navy on the Peninsula was his own brother Captain Sidney Smith Lee. "There will be no interference with the naval forces under your command by the land forces serving in conjunction with you," the general wrote to the captain, expressing the hope that "the two services will harmonize perfectly." Even among brothers the age-old rivalry between army and navy had to be resisted. (WILLIAM A. ALBAUGH)

The pace of the campaign quickened when, on June 12, Lee sent Brigadier General James Ewell Brown "Jeb" Stuart on a four-day reconnaissance around McClellan's army. Lee gained valuable information, but at the price of alerting McClellan that something was in the wind. (VALENTINE MUSEUM, COOK COLLECTION)

One of the cavalrymen with Stuart, the scout who led him on his ride around McClellan, Lieutenant John Singleton Mosby. Previously unknown, he established his reputation in this war. He appears in this unpublished portrait in the uniform of a colonel. (USAMHI)

Major General Fitz John Porter and his corps were dangerously isolated north of the Chickahominy River, and late in June Lee determined to attack. (USAMHI)

A group of staff officers on the eve of the fighting on the Virginia Peninsula.
The man lying at right with the dog is a twenty-two year old captain, George
Armstrong Custer. He too, like Mosby, made a name for himself in this war.
(LC)

Mechanicsville, Virginia, photographed in April 1865 by Gardner's assistant James Reekie. Here on June 26, 1862, was fought the second of the Seven Days Battles, when Lee attempted to strike Porter's exposed position north of the Chickahominy. (USAMHI)

Reekie's 1865 image of Ellison's Mill on the battlefield at Mechanicsville. The hottest of the fighting raged around and past this little structure as Porter successfully defended himself before withdrawing. (NA)

Confederate casualties at Mechanicsville ran high. Colonel Mumford S. Stokes of the 1st North Carolina Infantry took a mortal wound. (WRHS)

Brigadier General George Morell was instrumental in defending Porter's corps from Lee's attempted encirclement. (USAMHI)

Colonel Edward L. Thomas of the 35th Georgia took a bad wound at Mechanicsville. He recovered to become a fine brigade commander and, as pictured here, a brigadier general. (VM)

Faced with heavy numbers against him, Porter withdrew across the Chickahominy on bridges like this one on the Mechanicsville road. (LC)

Porter took a new position near Gaines's Mill, and here on June 27, 1862, Lee attacked again. Reekie's photo shows the destroyed mill in April 1865. (USAMHI)

The Gaines House. Less than two months before, Federal generals were posing for Houghton and others on this porch. Now it is Lee's headquarters. (MUSEUM OF THE CONFEDERACY, RICHMOND)

Brigadier General Andrew A. Humphreys served as McClellan's chief topographical engineer. Poor and inadequate maps plagued both sides on the Peninsula, where local traditions twist names and pronunciations. One road pronounced "Darby" was in fact spelled "Enroughty." (USAMHI)

*Brigadier General Arnold Elzey—whose real name was Jones—was a hero at
Bull Run. At Gaines's Mill he received a terrible wound which left him unfit
for field command for most of the rest of the war.* (DUKE UNIVERSITY, BRADLEY T.
JOHNSON PAPERS)

*Colonel James S. Connor, a veteran of Bull Run
and the Hampton Legion, took command of the
22nd North Carolina shortly before Gaines's
Mill. In this battle a rifle ball broke his leg.* (LC)

Major General Ambrose Powell Hill performed the greatest share of the fighting for Lee at Mechanicsville and Gaines's Mill. He became one of Lee's premier commanders. (FRANK DEMENTI)

James J. Archer, appointed a brigadier just before the fighting on the Peninsula began, commanded the Texas brigade at Gaines's Mill with distinction. (P-M)

William Dorsey Pender won promotion to brigadier for his service at Fair Oaks, and now led a brigade for A. P. Hill. One of the army's most brilliant young commanders, he died as a result of a wound at Gettysburg a year later. (USAMHI)

Vermont photographer G. W. Houghton found this tent wrecked after a Confederate shell fired during the Gaines's Mill fighting struck it. (VHS)

Part of the cost of Gaines's Mill. Federal soldiers buried hurriedly in shallow graves by their retreating comrades were exposed by later rains. Reekie found them like this in April 1865. (WRHS)

On June 29 the fighting moved to Savage Station on the Richmond & York River Railroad. It is shown here the day before the battle, photographed by James Gibson. (VM)

"Prince John" Magruder had been fighting holding actions south of the Chickahominy while Lee attacked Porter. Now Lee ordered him to attack McClellan's rear. He pushed the Federal advance back to Savage Station. (USAMHI)

In the subsequent fighting, over 1,500 Federals became casualties. Here some wounded from Gaines's Mill and earlier fights await transportation to the rear at Savage Station. (USAMHI)

Vermont soldiers particularly distinguished themselves at Savage Station. Here the Green Mountain Boys of the 6th Vermont's Company I at drill. (LC)

Sick and wounded of the 16th New York being tended at Savage Station, photographed by Gibson on June 28. (MHS)

McClellan retreated to White Oak Swamp where the forces joined battle again on June 30. There in furious fighting Brigadier General George G. Meade was wounded twice in almost the same moment. (USAMHI)

Brigadier General James L. Kemper, once speaker of the house in the Virginia capital, now led a brigade in the nightmarish morass of White Oak Swamp. (USAMHI)

John Sedgwick, now a brigadier, was once major of the 1st United States Cavalry, whose colonel was Robert E. Lee. Now he led a division in Sumner's corps, but a bullet at White Oak Swamp put him out of the war for several weeks. (NA)

Major General Erasmus D. Keyes, veteran of Bull Run, commanded McClellan's IV Corps without particular distinction at White Oak Swamp. One of his brigade commanders, . . . (USAMHI)

. . . Colonel Philippe Régis Denis de Keredern de Trobriand, was the son of a French nobleman. He became one of the Union's finest brigadiers. (USAMHI)

George M. Sauerbier's image of the "Westchester Chasseurs," the 17th New York on parade. They are among many regiments mauled in the Seven Days fighting and at White Oak Swamp. (NA, BRADY COLLECTION)

*The final battle came at Malvern Hill, where the retreating Federals made
their stand. On July 1, 1862, Lee attacked repeatedly and with heavy losses.
Regiments like the 4th Georgia, shown here in April 1861, could not move the
enemy.* (GEORGIA DEPARTMENT OF ARCHIVES AND HISTORY)

The 19th Georgia took part in repeated attacks. It was largely a family regiment. Standing at right is Lieutenant Colonel Thomas C. Johnson, and seated at right is Lieutenant William H. Johnson. The sergeant standing at back is R. A. Johnson, and the father of all three is seated second from the left. (EMORY UNIVERSITY, PHOTOGRAPHIC SERVICES, ATLANTA)

Despite heavy support from his artillery, commanded by Brigadier General William N. Pendleton, Lee could not break McClellan's line. Pendleton, an Episcopal clergyman, was often mistaken for Lee. When not fighting, he preached in the camps. This photo was probably taken in 1864 after the death of his son, thus the mourning band on his arm. (TONY MARION)

A remarkable J. D. Edwards image of Gaston Coppens's Louisiana Zouaves on parade in front of the general staff quarters at the navy yard at Pensacola, April 1861. Here was a real trouble regiment. "They are generally small," said a Richmond newspaper, "but wiry, muscular, active as cats, and brown as a side of sole leather." Mutinous, thieving, they never gave their superiors peace. One day's morning report a year from now would show only one man present for duty, the others being absent without leave or under arrest. But they fought like devils at Malvern Hill. The campaign almost destroyed the unit. (SOUTHERN HISTORICAL COLLECTION, THE UNIVERSITY OF NORTH CAROLINA AT CHAPEL HILL)

What stopped Lee at Malvern Hill was the massed guns of McClellan's artillery chief, Colonel Henry J. Hunt. He gathered a hundred cannons to repel enemy assaults. (P-M)

There were no birds perched on the rammers of the 1st Massachusetts Artillery when it took part in Hunt's massive barrage at Malvern Hill. (USAMHI)

The 15th New York Engineers assisted in emplacing the guns that Hunt brought together. (KA)

Captain August V. Kautz led a company of the 6th United States Cavalry at Malvern Hill, but there was little for the mounted arm to do in this largely infantry campaign. He later became a feared Federal cavalry raider. (AMERICANA IMAGE GALLERY, CUSTODIAN OF THE RINHART COLLECTION)

Lieutenant Colonel Louis Thourot had command of the 55th New York at Malvern Hill when his colonel, . . . (WRHS)

. . . Régis de Trobriand, took over a brigade. He stands at right holding a rammer, while members of the 55th New York look on. (AMERICANA IMAGE GALLERY)

Brigadier General John H. Martindale, seated here in 1864 with his staff, reportedly declared that he would sooner surrender than leave behind his wounded at Malvern Hill. A court of inquiry acquitted him of the charge. (LC)

Defeated in his purpose to take Richmond and unable to withstand Lee's attacks, McClellan finally withdrew to Harrison's Landing on the James River, thus ending the campaign. His troops occupied "Westover," once the plantation estate of William Byrd, a remarkable Virginia gentleman of a century before. For now the war must move elsewhere. (USAMHI)

In Camp with the Common Soldiers

BELL I. WILEY

The real story of the life of the Civil War soldier;
for every day in battle, fifty in camp

WHAT MOST YANKS AND REBS had in mind when they enlisted was to meet their foes in battle, and the sooner the better. Instead they learned after a while that fighting was to occupy only a small part of their army service. The long lulls between battles saw them occupied instead with drills, parades, inspections, and routine activities. However good or bad in the fight they might be, all Yanks and Rebs came to excel in "camp life."

Both in camp and on the march the first concern was food. At the beginning of the war the ration officially prescribed for both sides provided a daily allowance for each soldier of twelve ounces of pork or bacon, or twenty ounces of beef, fresh or salted; twenty-two ounces of soft bread or flour, or sixteen ounces of hard bread, or twenty ounces of corn meal; and to every one hundred rations: fifteen pounds of peas or beans and ten pounds of rice or hominy; ten pounds of green coffee, or eight pounds of roasted coffee, or twenty-four ounces of tea; fifteen pounds of sugar; four quarts of vinegar; three pounds and twelve ounces of salt; four ounces of pepper; thirty pounds of potatoes, when practicable; and one quart of molasses. This allowance exceeded that authorized in any European army. Even so, the Union government increased the allowance in August 1861 and the augmenta-

tion remained in effect until June 1864, when it was reduced to that provided at the beginning of the war. Experience had shown that the enlarged issue exceeded the needs of the soldiers and promoted wastefulness.

On the Confederate side authorities ordered a general reduction of the ration in April 1862, and later particular items were curtailed. In the autumn of 1863 Commissary-General Lucius B. Northrop reduced the bacon issue to one third of a pound, and the next year the flour or meal ration was cut to sixteen ounces. More often than not, owing to hoarding, bad management, and the breakdown of transportation facilities in the South, Johnny Rebs got considerably less food than that authorized by Northrop and his associates in Richmond.

In both armies the rations specified in regulations and the fare actually served in camp differed considerably. As a rule, Northerners enjoyed greater abundance and variety of food than did Southerners. Billy Yanks were never reduced to the low level of subsistence experienced by Rebs at Port Hudson and Vicksburg in the summer of 1863, but some of them experienced times of great hunger. Those who marched from Chattanooga to Knoxville and back late in 1863 had to subsist for

Where most of Civil War soldiering took place, the camp. Here the winter tents of the 40th Massachusetts Infantry at Miner's Hill, Virginia, in 1863. (USAMHI)

several days on corn gathered from the places where the horses fed and parched over the coals of their campfires. They experienced similar deprivation in Chattanooga before U. S. Grant and William "Baldy" Smith opened up the "cracker line" in October 1863. A Hoosier soldier wrote from Chattanooga on October 22, 1863, that for the past month he and his comrades had lived on "two meals per day and one cracker for each meal."

Mainstays of rations issued to both Rebs and Yanks were meat, bread (or the flour or meal with which to make it), and coffee. Meat was pork or beef, sometimes fresh from recently slaughtered animals, but more often salt-cured or pickled. Salt pork, widely known as sowbelly or sow bosom by the soldiers, was fried in skillets, boiled in pots, or broiled on the ends of sticks held above hot coals. It was also used as seasoning for vegetables cooked in containers suspended above campfires. Fresh beef was usually boiled. Pickled beef, commonly

called "salt horse," was sometimes putrid and so briny as to make it unpalatable. An Ohio soldier wrote from camp in Maryland in 1862 that "we drew meat last night that was so damd full of skippers that it could move alone; some of them is stout enuf to cary a musket." A Mississippi Reb stated that the beef issued to his company was so rotten that "the buzzards would not eat it." An Illinois Yank wrote, "Sometimes we draw sow belly and sometimes old bull. The old bull is very good . . . but the sow belly, phew!"

The bread most often served to Johnny Rebs was cornbread, though sometimes they drew loaves of flour bread and occasionally they had hardtack. When left to their own resources they often converted the flour into hoecakes or biscuits, which they baked on slanting boards placed near their campfires. Some Rebs preferred to wrap bits of dough around a stick or ramrod and convert them into rolls by rotating them above hot coals. Many

Southerners were surfeited on cornbread. A Louisianian wrote near the end of the conflict, "If any person offers me cornbread after this war comes to a close I shall *probably* tell him to—go to hell."

Yanks rarely ate cornbread. They much preferred flour loaves baked in field ovens or prepared by comrades or black servants who cooked for companies or messes. During seasons of active campaigning and sometimes during periods of inactivity the only bread issued to them was hardtack.

Hardtack were crackers $2\frac{1}{2}$ inches wide, $2\frac{7}{8}$ inches high, and $\frac{3}{8}$ inch thick. They weighed about $1\frac{1}{2}$ ounces and were so hard that soldiers referred to them as "teeth dullers," and said they were more suitable for the building of breastworks than for human consumption. They came packed in boxes or barrels stamped "B.C.," probably for Brigade Commissary, but some soldiers insisted that the abbreviation represented the crackers' date of manufacture. Consumers often increased the edibility of hardtack by pulverizing them with rocks or musket butts, or soaking them in water. Hardtack crumbs were sometimes fried in bacon grease or mixed with soup or coffee.

Coffee, boiled in large kettles for quantity distribution or prepared individually in small cans or tin cups which most soldiers slung to their belts while on the march, was one of the most highly cherished items of camp fare. Soldiers of both armies consumed it in vast quantities. When the genuine "Rio" became scarce in the South owing to the blockade, Rebs resorted to "Confederate coffee" brewed from parched particles of corn, sweet potatoes, peanuts, or rye. Lacking sugar, they added molasses for "long sweetening." Some Rebs professed a fondness for their coffee improvisations, but their tributes reflect more of patriotism than actuality.

White "army beans" and brown Boston beans were often issued to Billy Yanks. Southern counterparts were field peas, sometimes of the black-eyed variety but more often the speckled whippoorwills.

An unpublished photograph showing the camp of the New Orleans Confederate Guards, probably in 1861, a scene that would be unusual for its neatness and well-equipped appearance by 1863. (TU, LOUISIANA HISTORICAL ASSOCIATION COLLECTION)

The 5th Vermont in camp in 1861, a G. W. Houghton photograph. (LC)

Peas and white beans were usually mixed with chunks of pork and boiled in iron pots. New Englanders liked to bake their brown beans in submerged pans surrounded by smoldering coals.

Sweet potatoes, Irish potatoes, and dried fruit were consumed in large quantities in both Union and Confederate camps. Potatoes were often baked in their skins and dried fruit was sometimes stewed and used as filler for fried pies.

Soldier life was conducive to the development of hearty appetites. Private Daniel Peck of New York wrote his sister in December 1862, "I am well and tough and as hearty as ever. I can finish twelve tack a day, three quarts of coffee, one half pound pork or beef, some dried apples & beans. But the beans punish me so I don't eat them. The foretaste is better than the after-taste."

Yanks and Rebs supplemented commissary issues with boxes of edibles of all sorts sent to them by solicitous relatives and friends at home. Delays in transit often caused spoilage of perishables, and poor packing or rough handling frequently resulted in breakage. But enough of the foodstuff reached its destination in usable condition to keep recipients asking for more.

Foraging, an army euphemism for stealing, was another frequently used source of enrichment of soldier rations. Yanks, partly because they spent most of their time in "enemy" country, were the greater offenders, but Rebs when subjected to hunger, as they frequently were, foraged freely on fellow Southerners. Pigpens, poultry houses, orchards, watermelon patches, cornfields, vegetable gardens, smokehouses, and turkey roosts were rarely immune to soldier incursions in any locality occupied by either Yanks or Rebs.

Another source of ration supplementation was the sutler who set up shop in army camps. Yanks saw more of sutlers than did Rebs because of the dearth of money among Southerners. Sutlers stocked candy, pies, cakes, pickles, canned oysters, sardines, and other edibles, along with stationery, writing pens, books, beverages, and other articles sought by their clientele. Soldiers usually regarded the sutler's prices as exorbitant, and one of their favorite diversions was to raid the merchant's tent and clean out his stock. Civilians too, black and white, residing in areas near army camps often peddled provisions to military personnel. Favorite articles of sale were pies and cakes, which purchasers sometimes referred to as "pizen cakes."

Early in the war soldiers on both sides complained frequently about the quality of their fare. But as the struggle continued and provisions became scarcer, protests centered more on quantity. This was especially true of Confederates. During the Chattanooga campaign a famished Texan of Bragg's army declared that if he ever got home he was going "to take a hundred biscuit and two large hams, call it three days rations, then go down on Goat Island and eat it all at *one meal.*"

The culinary abilities of Yanks and Rebs improved as they adjusted to soldiering and many of them boasted to civilian friends and kin that the food they prepared in camp compared favorably with that served at home. They also bragged about the proficiency acquired in laundering their clothes. On the march they had to wash their garments in streams, lakes, and ponds, as opportunity afforded, and hang them on tree limbs while they lounged naked on the banks waiting for the apparel to dry. But when settled in camp for considerable periods of time, as they usually were in winter, Rebs and Yanks often observed weekly washdays. These resembled the same occasions known at home, except that the washing was done by males with whatever facilities were at hand. Water was usually heated in pots, and clothes were soaped and scrubbed in tubs fashioned from barrels. Sometimes the scrubbing was done on corrugated metal boards, such as those used by the homefolk, but in most instances the dirt was removed by repeated dousing and twisting. Ironing was dispensed with, owing to lack of equipment and the view that wrinkles were an acceptable part of camp life.

Of all the places remembered in afteryears, it is the camp tent with all its associations that soldiers will most clearly call to mind. Lieutenant J. B. Neill of the 153rd New York sits peacefully in his tent, pictures of his wife on the table with his books, his camp cot in the shadows. Arrayed on the shelf above him are the few simple items that he carries from one field to another in this war.

(USAMHI)

Colonel Henry Hoffman of the 230th New York at his camp table, cigar in hand, clay pipe on the table. And . . . (NA)

. . . his tentmate Major W. M. Gregg at the same table. The occupant of the bed is too tired—or shy—to sit for the camera. (WRHS)

Still, practices known at home were considered ideal and in their housing arrangements soldiers were inclined to approximate them to the fullest possible extent. The shelter tents, or pup tents, used during periods of active campaigning were too small to permit much "fixing up." But larger tents, whether the bell-shaped Sibleys, the A tents, or the wall tents, which provided protection from sun and rain during relatively mild seasons when troops were not on the move, gave Rebs and Yanks an opportunity to apply their homemaking instincts. Guns were neatly stacked in the center or near en-

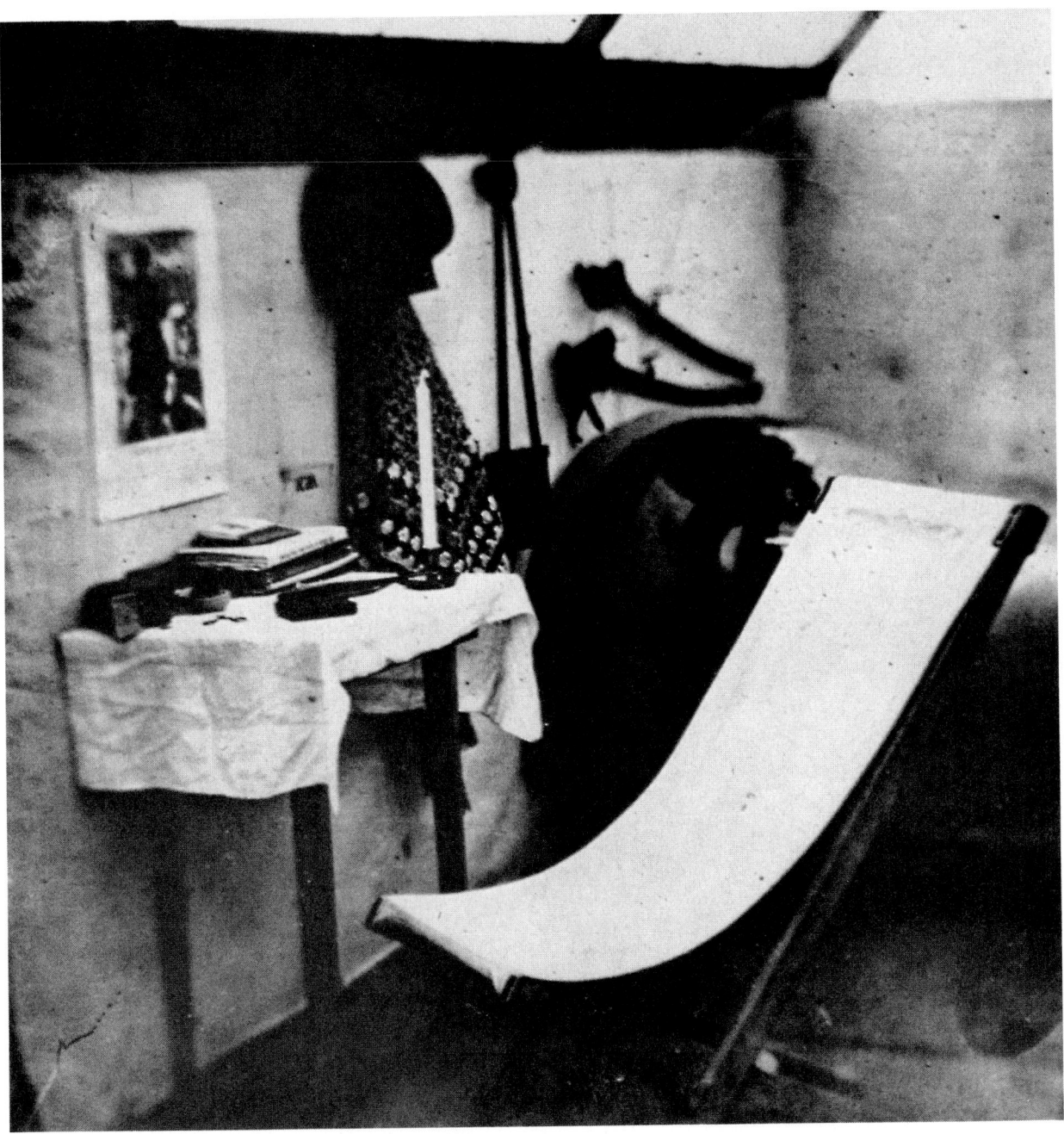

A typical officer's tent interior. Sabers, binoculars, a home-knitted shawl, a kepi, and a print adorn the canvas wall. On the table, a closed cased ambrotype, comb, candlestick, a few books, scissors, and a small sewing kit.
(NA)

Some officers enjoyed a bit more space and luxury. The same personal and military items hang on the wall. A plumed hat rests on the bed, and the table is set for a meal. There is almost a look of permanence here. (NA)

When winter came, permanence was necessary. The 1st Connecticut Heavy Artillery builds its winter quarters in 1864. (USAMHI)

trances of canvas abodes. Bunks fashioned of boards and filled with leaves, straw, or other soft materials and covered with blankets were placed around the interior to suit the taste and convenience of the occupants. When not used for reclining, bunks served as seats. Additional seating was improvised from kegs, barrels, and cracker boxes. Tables and writing desks were made of boards "liberated" from abandoned buildings or obtained from crates discarded by commissary or quartermaster. Canteens, cooking utensils, haversacks, knapsacks and other items of equipment were suspended from tent poles or stacked on the ground. Light came from candles stuck in bayonet sockets.

Homemaking proclivities were indulged to the fullest extent in cold weather when soldiers settled in winter quarters. Winter residences were frequently rectangular cabins made of logs cut from nearby trees, dragged to the building site, notched, and put in place by the soldiers. Slanting roofs

were made of boards or split logs covered with pine straw; spaces between the logs were filled with mud. A variation of the log hut was a hybrid structure part wood and part fabric, made by superimposing rectangular tents on log bases. These "winterized" or "stockaded" tents, like the log huts, were usually designed for four men. Sometimes the occupants increased roominess and warmth by excavating interiors to a depth of several feet. In some cases winter dwellings were warmed by stoves, which also were used for cooking, but more commonly heat for comfort and cooking was provided by fireplaces located usually at one end of the room. These were made of small logs chinked with mud and capped by chimneys made of the same materials. Draft was increased by topping chimneys with barrels, but these sometimes caught fire, routing soldiers from their bunks and threatening their abodes with destruction.

Some soldiers were content with floors of earth or

And moves in when they are completed. (USAMHI)

straw. Others, at considerable labor, covered the soil with split logs or with boards.

The average winter dwelling contained two bunks, one above the other, extending across the side or rear. The occupants made mattresses by filling cloth containers with pine needles, leaves, or straw. Ordinarily they placed knapsacks at the head of the bunks and suspended other equipment and extra clothing from nails or pegs driven into the walls. Seats, desks, and tables were made of logs, boxes, kegs, and barrels. Almost every company had a few fastidious members who insisted on providing their winter quarters with wallpaper and adding adornments in the form of mantelpieces, pictures, and fancy pieces of furniture.

When family or friends visited camp, as they sometimes did in the winter season, soldiers took great pride in showing off their homemaking prowess. Many described their comforts in letters to the folk at home. A Georgia private wrote his wife from camp near Fredericksburg in early March, 1863, "You would be surprised to know how com-fortable a place I have to live in, a white [from snow] hous and a good fire place and a box, chunk, or the ground wich are all used for seats hear. We all take our seats, some reading, som writing, some laughing, some talking, som set up sleeping and some thinking of home. . . . Finely [finally] Mr. A. begines to tell whare he herd his first bum and how bad it sceard him and Mr. B. not to be out don tells what dangers he has pased through. Mr. C. he tells his tale. . . . Mr. E. . . . says that he thinks that he is the man that ought to have the next furlow. . . . [After a lively argument over who had the best claim to a fur-lough] H. commenses singing home sweet hom, all the crowd joines in and the hole wood resounds with the music."

In both winter and summer officers generally lived better than their men, and the higher the rank, with some notable exceptions, the greater their comfort. In winter they had more com-modious huts, made usually by the soldiers whom they commanded, and when they lived in tents,

Whole cities of log huts dot the Southern landscape every war winter.
(USAMHI)

They are Confederate as well as Union. Here Confederate winter quarters of J. E. Johnston's army at Manassas in 1862. (USAMHI)

they normally had relatively spacious wall tents. Sometimes an officer had a dwelling all to himself, save perhaps for a black servant who performed menial duties. His furniture, clothing, and food usually were superior to that of the rank and file. Normally he had no difficulty in obtaining liquor, a commodity often denied to ordinary soldiers. However, most thirsty privates were able to circumvent the prohibitions when they had funds, but the stuff that they obtained on the sly was often the rotgut variety the imbibing of which was apt to result in sobering sojourns in the guardhouse.

Camp life at its best was apt to be monotonous and lonely. Daily drills, Sunday reviews, and periodic parades increased in onerousness with the passing of time. Marches in rain and mud or in heat and dust were irksome and exhausting, and when accompanied by poor rations and polluted water, as they frequently were, they became almost intolerable. Exposure, overexertion, undernourishment, and the ravages of insects and germs produced floods of sickness, and hostile missiles added countless others to the list of the disabled. In the American Civil War the sick and wounded

suffered most. Medicines and medical facilities fell far short of needs, especially on the Confederate side.

Both the ailing and the well sought diversion to combat their hardship and boredom. Music was a favorite pastime in both armies. Regimental and brigade bands often gave evening concerts at which they played sentimental, patriotic, and sometimes classical pieces. Occasionally bands would serenade officers, a practice which afforded pleasure to entire camps. General Lee, after listening to an informal band concert in 1864, stated, "I don't believe we can have an army without music." A Rebel private was prompted to remark at the conclusion of a stirring band concert in a Virginia camp, "I felt at the time that I could whip a whole brigade of the enemy." As a rule Billy Yanks, owing to the relatively greater number of musicians and instruments available in Northern units, enjoyed more and better band music than did Rebs. Some of the best music was provided by the Germans, about 200,000 of whom donned the Union blue.

In both armies the instrumental music heard

Built mostly from scavenged parts and ingenuity, these Confederate huts were good enough that Federals later used them. Manassas, 1862. (WRHS)

Union soldiers occupying once-Confederate winter houses at Centreville, Virginia. Winter, rain, and mud erased any care about who built them. "Corduroy" roads and walkways made of logs cross the mud. (LC)

most frequently was provided by individuals and small groups who brought violins, banjos, guitars, and flutes to camp with them and played informally for the entertainment of themselves and their comrades. A Mississippian wrote to a friend early in the war that he and his associates were experiencing lively times in camp. "Every night," he stated, "fiddlers are plentiful. . . . I wish you would happen in sometime while Will Mason is playing the violin & see some of his capers."

Many regiments had glee clubs who entertained fellow soldiers with a variety of songs. But, as in the case of instrumental programs, the most frequent, and probably the most appreciated vocal performances, were those given by informal groups brought together by the sheer love of music combined with a desire to entertain their comrades. A New York artillery captain wrote to a friend in

1863, "We have pretty lively times in the evenings, the Germans of my company get together and sing very sweetly and I try to join in with them."

Reading was another favorite diversion of Rebs and Yanks. What they enjoyed most was reading the letters of their homefolk. "Mail call" from company headquarters always brought throngs of eager soldiers rushing to claim missives from wives, children, parents, and friends. Arrival of mail was about the only incident that would cause men to interrupt their meals. Those whose names were called proceeded happily to some quiet spot to read and reread the latest word from home; those for whom no letters came slipped away in disappointment and envy to resume the drab routine of camp life. "Boys who will lie on their backs with hardly energy enough to turn over," wrote an Alabamian in 1862, "will jump up and hurry to

Winter quarters for some were far more luxurious. The 22nd Michigan at Camp Ella in Bishop, Kentucky, had regular barracks to withstand the cold. (GORDON WHITNEY COLLECTION)

the captain's tent to get it [mail]." A Texan wrote his wife in 1863, "I feel mightily down when the mail comes in and the other boys get letters and I don't." About the same time another Reb wrote his spouse that he "was almost down in histericks to hear from home." Yanks were less frequently disappointed than Rebs by nonreceipt of mail, because mail service in the North, owing to more and better rail and other communications facilities, was much better than in the South. Sometimes letters from rural areas of the South were not delivered in camp for several months. Slowness of Confederate postal service led correspondents to rely increasingly on personal delivery of letters by friends and relatives. Despite uncertainties and delays a large volume of mail reached its destination in both South and North. Unfortunately for the historian, only a small portion of correspondence received in camp was preserved, owing to the inconvenience of keeping it and fear on the part of recipients that it might fall into the hands of foes and become the subject of derisive comment.

Most soldiers enjoyed answering letters. A likely scene during any respite from camp duties was a Reb or Yank off to himself, with paper resting on stump, box, or knee "dropping a few lines" to the folk at home. Health was a favorite subject of comment and many a soldier complained to the homefolk of recurrent bouts with the "the sh-ts," a malady also known as "the Tennessee quick step." Correspondents almost always requested early responses and stressed a desire for information about the doings of children, the progress of crops, the condition of pets and livestock, and details of life in home and community. In the 165 extant letters that Robert M. Gill wrote to his wife Bettie in Mississippi before he was killed at Jonesboro, Georgia, August 31, 1864, one of his most frequent inquiries was about his little daughter, Callie. "Does she remember me?" he asked in one letter. "You must not whip her," he added, "I have a perfect horror of whipping children." The advice that innumerable Rebs and Yanks sent to their offspring was "mind your mother, say your prayers and don't neglect your books."

Next to letters, newspapers provided the most pleasure for soldier readers. Rebs had considerably less access to journalistic literature than did the men in blue because Southern papers did not approach those of the North in numbers, circulation, or coverage of events. Owing to scarcity of newsprint, deterioration of equipment, and inadequacy of financial resources most Southern newspapers declined in size and quality during the conflict, and some became casualties of war. The Memphis *Appeal* had to flee invading Federals so often that it came to be known as "the moving *Appeal*." Both this paper and the Chattanooga *Daily Rebel* devoted considerable attention to military affairs and were eagerly read by soldiers of the Western armies. The same could be said of the Richmond dailies and Rebs serving in the Army of Northern Virginia. These journals were not driven to use wallpaper for newsprint as were the Vicksburg *Citizen* and the Opelousas, Louisiana, *Courier*, but all of them had their troubles. Circulation in Southern camps suffered from various circumstances including scarcity of money among Johnny Rebs and their families. Papers that found their way to news-hungry Confederates were literally worn out as they passed from hand to hand.

The war created a great boom for Northern journalism, and as circulation increased, both at home and in the army, reporters, photographers, and artists frequented camps to gather news and illustrations, and news vendors regularly made the rounds of military units and hospitals hawking the New York *Tribune, Herald,* and *Times,* the Boston *Journal,* the Philadelphia *Inquirer,* the Cincinnati *Gazette,* the Chicago *Times,* and other metropolitan dailies. Both Yanks and Rebs gave a high rating to the illustrated weeklies that thrived during the war years, including *Leslie's* and *Harper's* and the Richmond-based *Southern Illustrated News.* County and town newspapers were not often sold in camps but soldiers, and especially Billy Yanks, frequently received issues of local journals sent through the mail by publishers or homefolk.

Sometimes regiments and other units issued their own papers, and in rare instances informal groups wrote out news sheets by hand. Both printed and manuscript newspapers contained military information, poetry, gossip, and jokes. After being read in camp they were usually sent to the folk at home.

Their officers' quarters even boasted a little bit of gingerbread trim. (GORDON WHITNEY COLLECTION)

*Wherever and whatever their accommodations, however, the soldiers enjoyed
winter. There was little or no fighting and, with some protection from the cold,
it was a peaceful time.* (USAMHI)

Magazines such as the *Atlantic* and *Southern Field and Fireside* had some circulation in camp. Books of fiction, literature, and history never lacked readers in either Northern or Southern camps, but Yanks, owing to better education, more money, and superior distribution facilities had considerably better opportunity to read them than did Rebs. On both sides, but far more often in Northern than in Southern camps, soldiers had access to cheap paperback novels and joke books. Religious organizations flooded camps with tracts, most of them warning readers against the evils of profanity, liquor, and gambling. Among Rebels especially, owing to a dearth of other materials, these tracts always found readers. The most widely read book among both Yanks and Rebs was the Bible.

Religious services provided diversion for many soldiers. Yanks and Rebs often spoke disparagingly of chaplains, and there is considerable evidence to indicate that the better ministers, owing to the poor pay and the great hardships endured by chaplains, preferred service on the home front to that in camp. But "Holy Joes of the Sixties" were often

sincere, dedicated individuals whose ministrations were much appreciated by the rank and file. In addition to attending Sabbath services, which usually featured the chaplains' sermons, religiously inclined soldiers often met on their own for prayer meetings led by one of their comrades. In the spring, when the season of active campaigning approached, revivals sometimes swept over the camps, but these occurred more frequently and on larger scale among Confederates than among Federals. This was due in part to the greater strength among Southerners of evangelistic denominations and to the greater religiousness of their officers, including such high-ranking leaders as Lee, Jackson, and Jeb Stuart. Interestingly, the largest and most fervent revivals experienced by Confederates came after 1862, when owing to the worsening of the military situation and the increasing prospect of exposure to death in combat, Southerners felt a greater need to seek spiritual guidance and comfort.

The religious activity that Yanks and Rebs probably enjoyed most of all was the singing of hymns. Favorites included "Sweet Hour of Prayer," "My

Faith Looks Up to Thee," "Rock of Ages," "All Hail the Power of Jesus' Name," "Amazing Grace," "On Jordan's Stormy Banks I Stand," and "There Is a Fountain Filled with Blood." Religious organizations encouraged singing by distributing pocket-size hymn books prepared especially for army use.

When opposing armies were stationed near each other much fraternization occurred. On these occasions Northern newspapers were swapped for those published in the South, and coffee was exchanged for tobacco. Sometimes trade was carried on by means of small boats equipped with sails set in

such a manner as to take the vessels across river, lake, or bay separating opposing forces. Throughout fighting areas, Yanks and Rebs swam together, drank together, and even gambled together. Friendly intercourse was sometimes interspersed with communication that was not so cordial. During the siege of Vicksburg, for example, Yanks would call out to Confederates, "Say, Rebs, how do you like your new general?" Southerners would respond, "What do you mean by new general? We've still got old Pemberton." The Federals would retort, "Oh, yes you have, General Starvation." Rebs would come back with the inquiry,

These Confederates of the 1st Texas at Camp Quantico, near Dumfries, Virginia, perform their camp chores with a casual air of contentment. They are the "Beauregard Mess," and this winter of 1861–62 they will be warm.
(ROBERT MCDONALD)

*Some even used civilian skills to build chimneys and fireplaces. They read books
and newspapers and letters from home, and they trained mascots like dogs and
birds.* (LLOYD OSTENDORF COLLECTION)

"Say, Yanks, have you got yourselves any nigger
wives yet? Do you suppose they will improve the
Yankee breed any?" The Federal taunt, "Say Reb,
haint you got any better clothes than them," once
provoked the response, "Who do you think we are,
a set of damn fools to put on our good clothes to
go out and kill damn dogs in." Then the shooting
would resume.

Clowning among themselves, horseplay, teasing,
and joking made soldiering more tolerable for
many. A person appearing in camp in any unusual
garb was almost certain to become the target of
much disparagement and ridicule, such as "Come
up outer them boots; I know you're in thar; I see
your arms sticking out." Or, "Look out, that parrot shell that you're wearing on your head is going
to explode." Unpopular officers were sometimes

subjected to groans or catcalls as they walked company streets or reclined in their bunks. Some Georgia soldiers once rode their colonel on a rail, letting
him dismount only when he promised better behavior.

A Federal officer stationed at Murfreesboro
wrote that in March 1863, when General Rosecrans and his staff rode through a camp of Yanks
living in pup tents they "were greeted with a tremendous bow-wow. The boys were on their hands
and knees, stretching their heads out of the ends of
the tents, barking furiously at the passing caval-
cade." The general, he added, instead of becoming
angry, laughed heartily and promised the barkers
better living accommodations.

Impromptu diversion was afforded by the appearance of a rabbit in camp or along the route of

Music occupied the time of many, as did cards. Here in the quarters of Dr. David McKay of the Army of the James, unusual luxury is evident. Ample space in an old occupied house, a fireplace, instruments galore, all combine to make the "5 Drons" and their "Fun & Fury" quarters more than habitable. (USAMHI)

march. Sometimes the excited animal was pressed so long and so hard by yelling soldiers as to be caught. Then an argument was apt to ensue as to what individual or mess was to have the pleasure of eating the captured hare. Hunting, with or without guns, and fishing, with hooks or seines, was always a welcome diversion, not only for the fun that it provided, but also for the enrichment that it gave to issues of hardtack and sowbelly.

Sports and games flourished during periods of leisure. Football was mentioned occasionally in the letters of both Yanks and Rebs but baseball, of the four-base or two-base "town-ball" variety, was a more popular exercise. The ball was often soft and in one version of the game the mode of putting out the runner was to hit him with the ball. Bats were frequently sticks or boards. Scores sometimes were very high. In a game at Yorktown, Virginia, in

*The average soldier and officer settled for much less, like the quarters of these
officers of the 1st Rhode Island Light Artillery, Battery E. But still they have
their books, their maps decorating the wall, and a well-stocked table.*
(USAMHI)

1863, the 9th New York Regiment beat the 51st
New York by a score of 58–19.

Holidays such as the Fourth of July and, in Irish
regiments, St. Patrick's Day, were celebrated by
horse races, boxing, wrestling matches, foot races,
leap frog, cricket, broad jumping, and free-for-all
scuffles. These festivities were often accompanied
by swigging of whiskey or beer on the part of participants and spectators, and at the end of the day
guardhouses might overflow with soldiers suffering
from black eyes, bruised limbs, and even broken
bones.

In winter, when the weather became cold
enough to coat lakes and ponds with ice, Yanks
found pleasure in skating. Rebs rarely had skates or
the skill of using them, but if soles were thick
enough they scooted awkwardly over the ice in
their shoes. Sleds, often improvised from boards or
tubs, carried soldiers down snow-covered hills and
merriment was enhanced by occasional spills.
Snowball battles were frequent occurrences. Sometimes participants would fight in regiments or brigades, commanded by the same officers who led
them in battle. Prisoners were taken and paroled,
and the wounded were attended by doctors or
nurses. Since contestants occasionally loaded their
snow pellets with cores of rock or metal, wounds
were sometimes more than superficial. Early in

Life in camp was not all relaxation. There were tasks aplenty to keep the men busy and fit. Chopping wood, sweeping, polishing boots, mending socks, and clowning all filled the idle hours. The denizens of "Pine Cottage" did their chores first, then dressed for the camera. (USAMHI)

The "Wigfall Mess" of the 1st Texas Infantry, chop their wood and carry water and wash their dishes. (THE MUSEUM OF THE CONFEDERACY, RICHMOND)

1863, near Fredericksburg, the 26th New Jersey Regiment and a Vermont unit formed a line of battle and pitched into each other with such fury that "the air was filled with white missles and stentorian cheers went up as one or the other party gained an advantage." After a series of charges and countercharges, each resulting in the taking of prisoners, "victory rested with the Vermonters and the Jersey boys surrendered the field." A Georgia Reb stationed near Fredericksburg wrote his wife in February 1863, "Some times the hole brigade formes and it looks like the sky and the hole elements was made of snow. . . . General Longstreet and his agitant took regs the other day and had a fight with snow balls but the Gen. charged him and took them prisners." A heavy fall of snow in March 1864, at Dalton, Georgia, led to a series of vigorous encounters among Rebs of the Army of

Tennessee. A participant in one of them wrote on March 24, "We had a Great Battle yesterday between the 63rd and 54th Va. Regt. It lasted some 2 or 3 hours. . . . [When] the 54th was like to drive us all out of camp . . . I . . . made a charge & drove them out, kept them out until we quit. The officers of the 54th invited me over after the fight . . . to drink with them, complimenting me for Bravery." He added, "I enjoyed the sport fine but it made horse [hoarse] on account of our great charges and cheering." Another Confederate wrote that in a snow fight involving members of New Orleans' Washington Artillery, "every man in our camp, both black and white," participated and that during the fracas, "Capt. C. H. Slocomb lost two front teeth, Lieut. Challeron [got a] black eye," and five privates came out with bloody noses. Among the captured property, he added, "is the flag of the Ga. Regiment, 8 or 10 caps and Hats, 1 frying pan and 4 or 5 pones of corn bread."

Less boisterous than snowball fights but equally enjoyable were the sham courts-martial, the minstrels, and the plays staged by Yanks and Rebs. In the simulated trials, enlisted men derived special pleasure from assigning officer roles to the rank and file and finding them guilty of such offenses as neglect of duty, drunkenness, immorality, and excessive harshness in discipline. Units such as the Richmond Howitzers and Boston's 44th Massachusetts Infantry formed dramatic associations and presented plays in a manner that won hearty applause from both soldiers and civilians. The 44th Massachusetts gave a program consisting of songs by a quartet, musical selections by the band, a scene from *The Merchant of Venice,* and a concluding drama entitled *A Terrible Catastrophe on the North Atlantic R.R.*

Minstrels and comedies were the most popular of all the shows presented in camp. The 9th New York Regiment's Zouave Dramatic Club in June 1862 gave a burlesque *Combastus De Zouasio,* which a soldier observing rated as well-performed. He liked the singing and dancing and the concluding farce *Box and Cox.* He reported that the theater was crowded with local aristocrats, soldiers, and officers, among them General John P. Hawkins.

Both individuals and units derived much pleasure from pets. George Baxter of the 24th Massachusetts Regiment wrote from camp in Maryland in December 1861, "Last night I was on guard. . . . Towards morning a little black kitten came purring around my feet, so I picked her up and put her on my shoulder and continued pacing my beat, with a rifle on one shoulder and a cat on the other." In December 1863 a correspondent of the Army of the Cumberland reported, "One of the boys has carried a red squirrel through thick and thin over a thousand miles. 'Bun' eats hard tack like a veteran and has the freedom of the tent. Another soldier has an owl captured in Arkansas &

The need for wood was endless. (USAMHI)

James F. Gibson's spring 1862 image of the servants of the Prince de Joinville doing his chores for him. (KA)

named 'Minerva'. Another has a young Cumberland Mountain bear; but chief among camp pets are dogs, riding on the saddle bow, tucked into a baggage wagon, mounted on a knapsack [or] growling under a gun. . . . A dog, like a horse, comes to love the rattle and crash of muskets and cannon." Colonel Lucius Fairchild of the 2nd Wisconsin Regiment wrote from near Fredericksburg in July 1862, "We have . . . a big half bull dog . . . named McClellan & stolen from a secesh. He attends all drills . . . is always at dress parade, sometimes marches up & down in front of the regt with the band & always marches to the center with his officers & up to the Col. All this is done with becoming gravity." A Union private wrote his homefolk from Hilton Head, South Carolina, in 1862, "Co. B has got 3 pets in the shape of yong aligators . . . captured . . . in the swamp. . . . Our little dog has a big time with them. . . . Co. A has a yong coon, Co. K has a crow."

Soldiers whiled away many hours at cards,

checkers, and dominoes, and almost every camp had a few chess enthusiasts. Meetings of Masons and other fraternal groups afforded diversion to a considerable number of men in both armies. Especially gratifying were the visits of wives and children, but these occasions were all too rare. The same was true of furloughs. A poor compensation for the lack of feminine association were the womanless dances at which soldiers and their bogus sweethearts whirled and stomped to fiddled renditions of such pieces as "Arkansas Traveler," "Billy in the Low Grounds," "The Goose Hangs High," "The Blue-Tailed Fly," and "Oh Lord God One Friday." These, like other social activities, sometimes were made more festive by copious draughts of "Oh Be Joyful," "Old Red Eye" and "Rock Me to Sleep Mother."

It is not surprising that many Yanks and Rebs sought relief from boredom in gambling. This was usually done with cards, and the most popular card games were poker, euchre, twenty-one, and faro. Soldiers used dice for craps and chuck-a-luck. They also gambled at keno, a game resembling bingo. Raffling was still another popular form of gambling. Rebel Sam Watkins stated that his comrades in the 1st Tennessee Regiment pitted vermin in trials of speed on tin plates. The owner of the louse that first vacated the plate was adjudged the winner. In one series of contests, one soldier's louse won so consistently as to arouse suspicion. An investigation disclosed that the winning Reb had been secretly heating his plate before each contest, thus giving his louse compelling reason to abandon it.

Gambling peaked in periods following payday. "Yesterday was Sunday," wrote a Mississippian shortly after a visit of the paymaster, "and I sat by the fire and saw the preachers holding forth about thirty steps off, and between them and me were two games of poker. . . . Chuck-a-luck and faro banks are running night and day with eager crowds standing around with their hands full of money. Open gambling has been prohibited but that amounts to nothing."

Visits to nearby towns and cities provided entertainment for many soldiers. Country lads derived special pleasure from these excursions. Zoos, large shops, tall buildings, and horse-drawn omnibuses were all new and exciting to men accustomed to a way of life devoid of all such attractions. Like soldiers of other conflicts, some of them freed for the first time from home restraints and knowing that the future was uncertain, yielded to the lure of a fling at the fleshpots. They visited grog shops and bawdy houses and in some instances paid a high price for their experimentation. The 10th Alabama Regiment, with a mean strength of 1,063, which went from the rural South in the early summer of 1861 to the environs of Richmond, had in July, according to the surgeon's report, a total of 62 new cases of gonorrhea and 6 of syphilis.

When visits to places beyond camp limits were made without leave, as they frequently were, apprehended offenders were subjected to punishment. Brief absences drew light penalties, prescribed by company or regimental commanders. These in-

The formal duties were ever-present in camp. Orderlies had to stand for inspection at the headquarters of the Army of the Potomac near Brandy Station in March 1864. (P-M)

Artillerists of the 1st Brigade of Horse Artillery, Brandy Station, in September 1863, studied their maps in off moments. (AMERICANA IMAGE GALLERY)

Signal corpsmen refined their skills, if somewhat lazily. A Brady & Company image from 1861. (CHS)

And there was always drill. (USAMHI)

cluded extra stints of guard duty, digging ditches, grubbing stumps, riding the wooden horse—a horizontal pole held aloft by two upright beams—standing in a conspicuous place on barrel, box, or stump, and cleaning company grounds. Unit commanders also punished other minor offenses such as petty theft, straggling on the march, excessive drinking, brawling, and neglect of duty. For these breaches of discipline Rebs and Yanks had to carry weights such as logs, rails, or cannonballs, wear placards specifying the offense, such as "I Stole a Shirt" or "I Am a Thief," promenade the parade ground in a "barrel shirt" with arms extending through holes cut in the sides, or wear a ball and chain, the ball being a cannonball weighing six to thirty-two pounds fastened to the ankle by a chain two to six feet long. One of the most painful penalties imposed by officers was to hang offenders by their thumbs from boughs or beams, with toes barely touching the ground for periods of time

varying with the gravity of the disciplinary breach. This was a common punishment for soldiers who spoke disrespectfully to their superiors. Another loathsome punishment often imposed for "back talk" to officers and for other insubordinate behavior was bucking and gagging. This consisted of seating the offender on the ground, tying a stick in his mouth, fastening his hands together with a rope, slipping them over his knees and inserting a pole between the arms and knees. Sometimes artillery officers strapped a recalcitrant with arms and legs extended in spread-eagle fashion to the extra wheel carried on the rear of a caisson. This punishment was cruel enough when the vehicle was stationary and the soldier's head rested at the top of the wheel; but if the wheel was given a half-turn and the caisson driven over rough ground, the pain was excruciating.

Punishments of the sort mentioned above were sometimes dispensed by regimental or garrison

And more drill. (MHS)

courts-martial instead of by unit commanders. These bodies consisted of three officers, and their jurisdiction was restricted to enlisted men and to noncapital cases. They could not assess fines greater than a month's pay or impose hard labor sentences of more than a month's duration.

The most serious offenses, such as murder, rape, arson, desertion, cowardice in battle, striking a superior, and sleeping on sentry post, were tried by general courts-martial, summoned by commanders of separate brigades, divisions, and larger units. They consisted of from five to thirteen officers, and their jurisdiction extended to all types of cases including capital crimes. Army regulations authorized them to issue sentences providing for death, life imprisonment, solitary confinement on bread and water, hard labor, ball and chain, forfeiture of pay and allowances, discharge from the service, reprimand, and, in case of noncommissioned officers, reduction in grade. General courts-martial

often specified a combination of legal punishments and sometimes they imposed penalties that violated the spirit if not the letter of the law, such as branding and shaving all or part of the head. The brand, stamped on with indelible ink or burned into the skin of hip, hand, forehead, or cheek, was usually the first letter of the victim's offense, such as "C" for cowardice, "D" for desertion, "T" for theft, and "W" for worthless. The Federals in August 1861 and Confederates in April 1862 enacted legislation prohibiting flogging, but these laws were sometimes ignored.

In both armies deserters, cowards, and other serious offenders who were sentenced to dishonorable discharge sometimes had their scalps shaved, had their buttons or insignia torn off, and were drummed out of camp to the tune of "The Rogue's March"—or in the case of Confederates, to the strains of "Yankee Doodle"—with soldiers fore and aft carrying arms reversed. Some capital offenders were hanged, but most Yanks and Rebs who paid the death penalty were shot by firing squads. Executions, which comrades of the condemned had to witness from a hollow square—a rectangle with one end open—made a tremendous impression. Private Thomas Warrick of Bragg's army wrote to his wife on December 19, 1862, "I saw a site today that made me feel mity bad. I saw a man shot for deserting there was twenty fore Guns shot at him they shot him all to pease . . . he went home and thay Brote him Back and then he went home again and so they shot him for that. Martha it was one site that I did hate to see But I could not helpe my self I had to do Jest as thay sed for me to doo." A Connecticut soldier reported that two of his comrades fainted while watching thirty executioners fire a fusillade that killed a deserter. Concerning an execution of six other deserters which he was forced to attend the next day, this soldier wrote that he stood within twenty feet of the victim sitting on the coffin nearest him. "They were all fired at the first time," he stated, "& 2 were killed instantly & 3 were shot the second time & the other one died while they were murdering the other three, for I call it murdering & I was not the olney one." Thomas Clark, a Pennsylvania Yank, registered no disapproval when in February 1864 he wrote his sister of the shooting of two deserters in Florida. "It was a great sight," he stated, "for it came on a Sunday and all of our regiment was out. . . . They where [were] hauled out in an opin wagon sitting on their coffins with a minister with each one of them and they looked and acted like they where going on an excursion. There was twelve men to shoot each one of them. The men was drawn up in a line nine paces from where the prisoners stood by their coffins. Four o'clock came and the order was given to fire and them and daylight was no more. There was nine balls went through one of their hearts and eleven passed through the other ones body. They did not live till the doctors came up to see if they were dead." If this report was accurate, the usual custom was not followed by loading only alternate rifles with live ammunition so that members of the firing squad might not know who fired the lethal shots. Clark attributed his indifference to the fact that the victims were recently recruited substitutes for whom "there was no pity."

Higher authorities on both sides showed a reluc-

And still more. The New York Excelsior Brigade. (USAMHI)

tance to approve death sentences. Apparently no Civil War soldier was executed for the capital offense of sleeping on sentry. Among Union forces totaling over 2,000,000 men, only 267 were executed and over half of these were deserters. Aggregate figures for Confederates are not available, but it is known that of 245 cases of court-martial convictions for desertion during the last six months of the conflict, mostly in the Army of Northern Virginia, death was prescribed in only 70 instances. President Davis's general amnesty of February 1865 set aside 31 of these sentences.

But death, by whatever means, became commonplace to Yanks and Rebs as the war progressed. Whatever respite they obtained from it came chiefly in the society and distinctly American character of their life in the camps. There the friendships were made, loyalties built, and memories indelibly imprinted on their minds. Here, at the fire, the tent, the mess table, men North and South displayed the true commonality of all Americans in all wars.

George N. Barnard caught this company drilling amid its own quarters, behind a decidedly decorative fence. (NA)

When the drill and the duties were done, however, then came the time for food. Every Civil War soldier was an expert at eating. Here Captain James W. Forsythe—later a brigadier general—sits on the staple of the soldier diet, a box of "Army Bread"—hardtack. (NA)

*Fresh bread came from the camp bakery, where the bakers let the dough rise in
the sun.* (INTERNATIONAL MUSEUM OF PHOTOGRAPHY)

They baked the loaves twenty at a time. (USAMHI)

And doled the loaves out to each mess's cook or servant, along with the ration of meat and vegetables. The meat was rationed by weight. (USAMHI)

No one was too bothered about sanitation. Keeping the bread in the same tent with the animal hay and letting a dog wander over both seemed not out of order. (USAMHI)

The armies brought their own herds with them, killing and butchering fresh beef daily when possible. These beef quarters have been salted and hung for drying. The salt residue lies on the boards below them. It would help preserve the beef—sometimes. (USAMHI)

Cutting the meat for the stew. Brady & Company published this image in 1861. (T. SCOTT SANDERS COLLECTION)

Doling out commissary stores at Camp Essex, weighing, carving, and—with the red tape so beloved of armies—recording who got how much of what and when. (MHS)

*Weighing beef on Morris Island, South Carolina. The more tropical the
climate, the more likely the soldier was to receive rancid meat—and eat it.*
(RONN PALM COLLECTION)

Boiled beef for the soldiers, cooked on the camp stove. (USAMHI)

Not the most nourishing meal, perhaps, but filling. Hardtack and butter on the plate, and bread in hand. Coffee would steam from the cup in good times. (LES JENSEN COLLECTION)

Like soldiers in all armies, Rebs and Yanks complained about their food. But they cooked and ate it nevertheless. (NA)

A few potatoes or other vegetables added variety to the salt pork and boiled beef. Always there was hardtack. A private of the 49th New York. (DALE S. SNAIR COLLECTION, RICHMOND)

Lieutenant Colonel F. M. Bache of the 16th United States Infantry and his mess in January 1864. He sits at left, with other members of the Army of the Potomac headquarters staff at Brandy Station. They dine well, served by a servant with a milk glass pitcher. Alexander Gardner's photograph. (USAMHI)

A noncommissioned officers' mess, Company D, 93rd New York, at Bealton, Virginia, August 1863. They dine with less style than the officers, but they still eat well. (MHS)

And the privates eat as they can, and as much as they can. Bread, hardtack, beef, and coffee are their staples. (COLLECTION OF MICHAEL J. MCAFEE)

After dinner, port and cigars for these men near Fort Monroe. (NYHS)

And now and then a picnic with sausages and bologna, cider, and sometimes chocolate. (COLLECTION OF MICHAEL J. MCAFEE)

The soldiers supplemented their uninteresting diet with delicacies bought from the sutlers—government-approved vendors—who followed the armies. Here a decidedly seedy-looking lot of them pose amid their wares of liquor and tobacco. (USAMHI)

They opened their stores wherever the tents and winter huts sprang up. Some, like A. Foulke, followed the same unit throughout the war. Brandy Station, Virginia, February 1863. (USAMHI)

The soldiers bellied up to the "bar" for their whiskey and beer. They bought Bibles and books at the same place. (USAMHI)

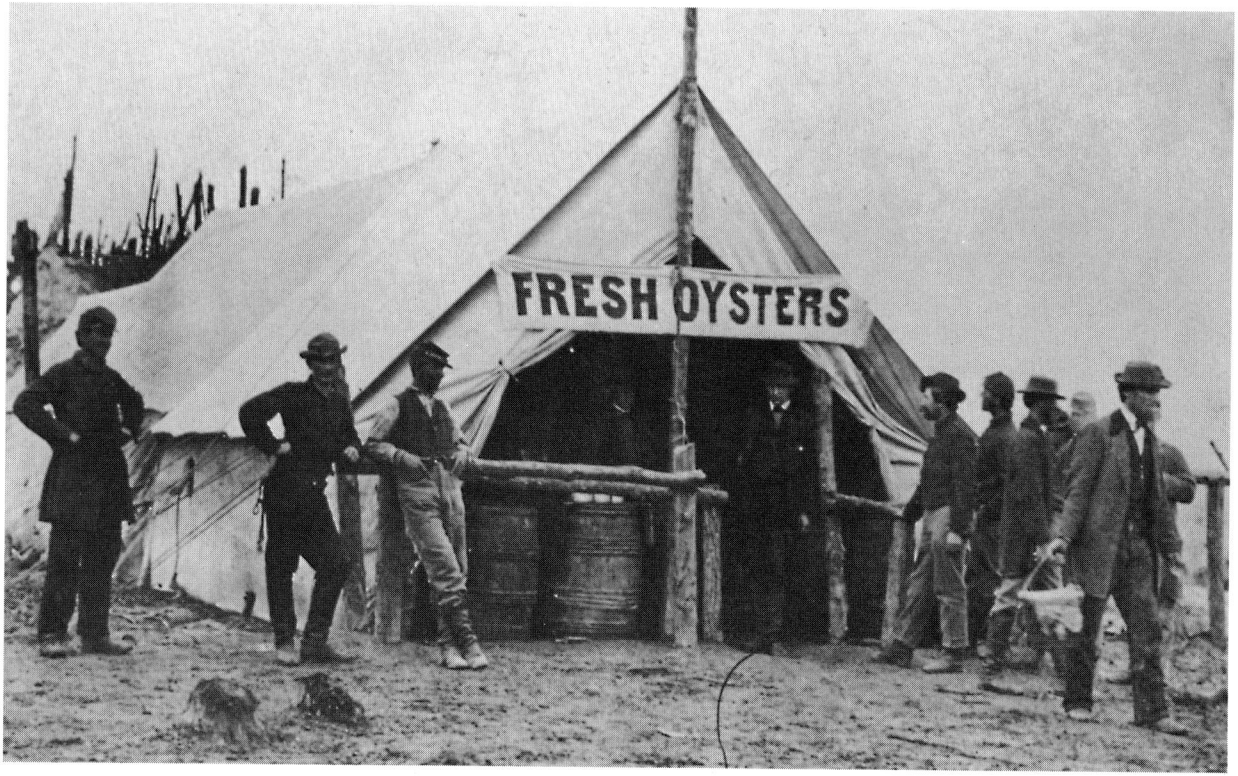

Fresh oysters were a real delicacy, and often not so fresh. Sutlers were frequently charged with selling rancid victuals. (USAMHI)

A "Fruit & Oyster House" in front of Petersburg in 1864. (USAMHI)

Some specialized solely in whiskey and tobacco, where the real money lay.
(USAMHI)

*Others created virtual shopping centers like this area at Petersburg in early
1865. Sayer's Oyster House sold pipes, cigars, oysters, and soda water. Next
door Mr. Shuz sold cakes, and his neighbor sold and repaired boots and shoes.
Up on the hill sat an "Eating House," while on the left a clothier sold "Ready
Made" army garments. In the center sits the wagon of Bates of New York City,
who attached himself strictly to the 7th New York, and behind him stands a
wholesale and retail condensed milk "depot." Behind that sits an outhouse.*

(LC)

Both armies also relied heavily on "foraging," officially sanctioned theft from local farmers who were sometimes—but by no means always—paid in government scrip. G. W. Houghton captured this foraging expedition, decidedly ambitious, leaving to scour the Virginia countryside for edibles. (VHS)

More common was the individual foraging soldier, though there was certainly nothing at all common about this grinning lad, Billy Crump of Company I, 23rd Ohio Infantry. He was orderly to Colonel—later President—Rutherford B. Hayes. In February 1863 he borrowed Hayes's horse and pistol and set off from camp near Gauley Bridge in West Virginia. He traveled twenty miles in two days and came back laden with fifty chickens, two turkeys, one goose, twenty to twenty-five dozen eggs, and between twenty-six and thirty pounds of butter. Here was a good provider. (USAMHI)

*Their hunger satisfied, the soldiers passed their leisure time as best they could.
Reading was a favorite in both armies, and literacy was much higher than
usually supposed. Those who could not read liked being read to. Gardner
caught these news vendors in October 1862. (LC)*

*A. P. Muben, a somewhat gaily bedecked news
vendor, with some of the New York illustrated
weeklies so popular with the soldiers. (LC)*

*In Chattanooga, Tennessee, at the quarters of the 1st Engineers and
Mechanics, they read and wrote letters.* (MICHIGAN DEPARTMENT OF STATE,
STATE ARCHIVES)

*The small building in the middle, just left of the tent, is the 13th
Massachusetts' library in their camp at Williamsport, Maryland. Few other
regiments could boast such an establishment, yet many of the Bay State
regiments were almost aggressively literate.* (USAMHI)

In the camp of the 5th Georgia they wrote their letters. (JOE CANOLE, JR.)

*Field post offices operated with most of the Federal armies, handling a huge
volume of soldier mail. Here an unidentified brigadier general hands a letter to
the postal clerk.* (NA)

*In winter quarters such as Brandy Station in February 1864, there were more
permanent postal establishments, like this post office with a clerk perched on a
mail bag.* (USAMHI)

Neither snow nor rain nor gloom of night—not even the enemy—could stay the delivery of the mail to the soldiers. It was one of the single most important factors in preserving morale. Brandy Station in April 1864. (USAMHI)

Religious revivals frequently swept through the camps even faster than the mail. Devotion, as many soldiers confessed, helped fill idle hours, and sometimes local belles attended as well. Here the 50th New York Engineers built their own church before Petersburg. (P-M)

A group of IX Corps chaplains pose before their "Baltimore Cotton Duck Extra" tent, near Petersburg. (LC)

Mass at Camp Cass for the largely Irish 9th Massachusetts Infantry. Only the officers attend this service. (LC)

At Camp Griffin, Virginia, the 49th Pennsylvania worships as Chaplain Captain William Earnshaw uses stacked drums for an altar. (LLOYD OSTENDORF COLLECTION)

Father Thomas H. Mooney performs Sunday Mass for the 69th New York. Its colonel, Michael Corcoran, stands with folded arms just left of the cleric. Both North and South claimed divine endorsement. (LC)

When chaplains like this one found themselves conducting services in the presence of shot and shell and weapons of destruction, some were inclined to question whether the deity could possibly condone either side. Fort Darling in April 1865, the chaplain's quarters of the 1st Connecticut Heavy Artillery, photographed by J. Reekie. (LC)

With reading and religion exhausted, the soldiers turned to sport. Many opted for something cerebral like chess, but most, like those at the left, preferred cards. (USAMHI)

Gambling filled the long hours of boredom, and not a few pockets as well.
Officers of the 82nd Illinois in camp at Atlanta, Georgia, in 1864 gambled
with ease and comfort. Outrageous pipes, often handmade, were also the rage
in the Western army. (CHS)

For the common soldiers, a blanket and a deck of cards were the only
necessities. These sergeants belong to the 56th Massachusetts. (USAMHI)

A cockfight could also provide entertainment of a gruesome sort, and plenty of money changed hands on a rooster's feet. Even the brass took part. Brigadier General Orlando B. Willcox affects disinterest, looking at a letter, but he cannot help glancing at the start of a fight staged by former slaves George, on the left, and John, and their chickens. Taken at Petersburg in August 1864. (USAMHI)

When gambling failed there was always horseplay, often at the expense of the poor freedman. (LC)

A friendly spar for the camera was a favorite picture to send home. Boxing in camp, however, did not enjoy wide popularity. There was too much real fighting to be done. (DON W. MINDEMANN)

Their funning could take a macabre turn at times. Being so close to death, it helped to make fun of it. (T. GORDON, JR.)

Shamming for the camera was a favorite, and drinking seemed always the chosen topic, perhaps because it was so important a release for the soldiers. An excellent series ranging from the first toast in "Here is to the gal I love," to "Over the Bay," "Going Home," and finally "Good Night." Taken probably by H. Skinner of Fulton, New York, in 1862. (COLLECTION OF WILLIAM WELLING)

*Whenever possible, however, camp life was mostly for relaxation. It was a
picture that did not change no matter the year, the place, or the army. J. D.
Edwards caught these men of the Perote Guards at Pensacola drinking,
reading, drawing, gambling. It was a never-ending scene.* (TU)

Edwards found the same scene with the 9th Mississippi in April 1861.
(MUSEUM OF THE CONFEDERACY, RICHMOND)

*General Robert O. Tyler and his staff presented much the same image two
years later in Virginia. Tyler stands second from the right.* (USAMHI)

*Many fortunate officers North and South were joined in winter quarters by
their wives, adding a dimension of domestic tranquility denied to most soldiers.*
(P-M)

Wives and daughters quickly became a focal point for attention, many men vicariously paying favor to loved ones at home through women with the armies. (USAMHI)

Many read and wrote letters for illiterate soldiers. Some, like the lady on the porch, even brought their babies. Hers has moved during the exposure, causing the blur with feet in her lap. (USAMHI)

The women's presence helped their men forget for a time that they were at war, especially when they had quarters like these in a casemate at Fort Monroe. (USAMHI)

The younger and prettier maidens became the belles of the armies, the object of every single officer's suit. This young lady attracts a host from an Illinois battery at Chattanooga in 1865. (CHS)

For one of these soldiers of Company G, 95th Illinois Infantry, camp life was more than exotic. It was a constant tension as he attempted to conceal a perhaps scandalous secret. For the soldier on the right, Private Albert Cashier, is in fact a woman. Born in Ireland, her feminine name was Hodgers, but all her life she was known as Albert J. Cashier. She not only successfully maintained her pose, serving well particularly at Vicksburg, but she eluded detection until 1911 when an automobile caused her hospitalization. It took a twentieth-century machine to expose the life-long sham of a patriotic woman who for so long fooled the men of her own century. (SPENCER H. WATTERSON, PONTIAC, ILLINOIS)

*The soldiers made their camps as much like vacation spots as they could. The
quiet moments were the best, like this one caught by Gardner in 1865.* (P-M)

*Intimate friendships made in camp lasted for life. Brevet Major General
Charles H. T. Collis sits at left with a friend. He won the Medal of Honor for
Fredericksburg.* (NYHS)

Confederates like these of the 1st Texas at Camp Quantico, Virginia, in the winter of '61, formed especially firm associations, bound tightly together by the shared hardships of the later war years. This recently discovered image is published here for the first time. (ROSENBURG LIBRARY, GALVESTON, TEXAS)

The fellowship . . . (TONY MARION)

. . . *the outrageous sense of fun* . . . (KA)

. . . *and the smiles of friends made the most memorable of war experiences. Smiling soldiers like Lieutenant John G. Hecksher of the 12th United States Infantry, at left, are rare indeed in Civil War photographs. The men preferred the more somber—nay, glum—aspect of his friend Captain William Sergeant.* (P-M)

Camp life was for the generals, too, and they usually enjoyed it even more than their men. Brigadier General George Stoneman sits astride his charger watching men build their winter quarters—or his. (USAMHI)

Major General John Sedgwick, left, sits with Brigadier General George Washington Getty, seated at right, at their Brandy Station tent. (USAMHI)

Major General Israel B. Richardson and servant pose in the summer shade in 1862. (USAMHI)

Brigadier General John A. Rawlins, Grant's chief of staff, was joined at City Point, Virginia, by his family in 1864. (USAMHI)

Brigadier General Marsena R. Patrick lived alone, as befitted Grant's chief policeman, provost-marshal general of the Army of the Potomac. (P-M)

Brigadier General Thomas W. Sherman lived in tropical tranquility on Hilton Head, South Carolina, when H. P. Moore took this image on March 8, 1862.
(USAMHI)

Brigadier General Edwin V. Sumner was not so old he could not enjoy paying court to a young belle visiting camp. (LC)

And their entertainments were much the same as those of the men they commanded, including even an occasional sleigh ride. Here at Port Hudson, Louisiana, in January 1864, Brigadier General Cyrus Hamlin—son of Vice President Hannibal Hamlin—sits with a companion in the small one-horse sleigh at left. Behind him are the officers of the black regiment he was raising. (USAMHI)

Music proved a pleasant diversion for all. Here a member of the band of the 26th North Carolina Infantry, with his horn. (DALE S. SNAIR COLLECTION, RICHMOND)

Members of the band of the 26th North Carolina, missing only their
compatriot of the previous image. Taken at Salem, North Carolina, around
1862. (MORAVIAN MUSIC FOUNDATION, INC.)

This Tennessee fiddler could enliven the coldest
winter camp with the "Bonnie Blue Flag" or
"Dixie." (TENNESSEE STATE MUSEUM)

Now terribly faded, this image of members of the Washington Light Infantry of Charleston once revealed the words "Music Hall" on the tent wall. A bugler stands at left and the soldier seated second from the right cradles a violin in his lap. This March 1861 photograph is ample evidence that music went to the camps with the very first Confederates. (WASHINGTON LIGHT INFANTRY, CHARLESTON, SOUTH CAROLINA)

Special ensembles like this group, with tambourine, banjo, guitar, violin, triangle, and bells, sprang up informally from among the members of several regiments. (T. SCOTT SANDERS COLLECTION)

The bands played for all sorts of occasions, the saddest being funerals and farewells to favorite generals being transferred to other commands. The band at left here serenades Major General Frederick Steele as he leaves Arkansas for another post, probably at the end of the war. Steele is standing second from the left between the columns immediately behind the band. (RONN PALM COLLECTION)

*A typical Federal regimental band, this one composed of Pennsylvanians,
photographed by S. R. Miller.* (RONN PALM COLLECTION)

*A concomitant to music was dramatics. This engineer battalion formed its own
theatrical club, the "Essayons Dramatic Club," giving performances in a
theater of their building at Petersburg in 1864.* (USAMHI)

Photographers McPherson & Oliver took this image in Baton Rouge in 1863.
It shows an improvised theater which at the moment is advertising a "Benefit
to Lieutenant M. W. Morris" and presenting the Lady of Lyons *and a Favorite*
Farce. (ILLINOIS STATE HISTORICAL LIBRARY)

Fraternal orders, chiefly the Masons, came with the army. Here Samuel
Cooley photographs an improvised "temple" on Folly Island, South
Carolina. (USAMHI)

*Building and elaborate decoration occupied some, especially the
ever-industrious 50th New York Engineers, who made their Petersburg
headquarters a virtual arbor.* (USAMHI)

*The men trained pets, like the nationally famous
"Old Abe," mascot of a Wisconsin regiment with
whom it lived through the war. In battle the eagle
would fly from its perch and remain aloft until the
fighting subsided.* (LC)

Dogs were the favorite. This one is supposed to be saying, "I am the dog that went through the army with the 25th Iowa Infantry." (CHICAGO PUBLIC LIBRARY)

And, of course, with idle time on their hands, the men would misbehave. That is where the provost came in. Here the Army of the Potomac's provost marshal's camp at Bealton, Virginia, in August 1863. (P-M)

Wherever the army went in numbers, so the provost went also. Mostly the men drank too much or disobeyed orders. (NA, U. S. WAR DEPARTMENT GENERAL STAFF)

When they did, the provost guard spirited them away to the guardhouse. Here the guard for the Army of the Potomac headquarters at Petersburg in 1865. Behind them is the picketed fence of their stockade. (USAMHI)

Minor offenders were fined pay or made to ride the wooden horse and other such essentially humiliating punishments. (ROBERT L. KOTCHIAN)

More serious cases spent time at hard labor in the heavy stockades like this United States Military Prison yard at Chattanooga. (NA, U. S. WAR DEPARTMENT GENERAL STAFF)

The worst cases went before courts-martial like this one meeting at Concord, New Hampshire. (USAMHI)

Another court-martial, at Chattanooga. If the offense was grave enough . . .
(TERENCE P. O'LEARY, GLADWYNE, PENNSYLVANIA)

. . . *so was the punishment. Troops stand drawn into a three-sided square to witness a hanging near Petersburg in 1864. The mounds of earth right of the gallows mark the grave of the condemned already dug.* (LC)

And like soldiers everywhere, the men of blue and gray loved to celebrate holidays. Here a Christmas feast appears ready for the men who will tightly jam the benches. Turkeys sit on the tables as well as relishes. The hot vegetables will be brought out and served, and every plate has a slab of bread or cake. (NA)

Another wreath-bedecked hall for Christmas. These diners will be a little less crowded. (USAMHI)

Washington's birthday, February 22, was a holiday in both North and South, and here the "New Forage House" ballroom in Beaufort, South Carolina, stands ready for an 1864 observance. (WRHS)

The speakers' stand for the Beaufort celebration, with flags and bunting aplenty. (USAMHI)

The Fourth of July was the greatest of all in the Union armies, and even some Confederates celebrated the day. Here the 50th New York Engineers revel in the day on July 4, 1864. Joining them, and seated at the extreme left, is Charles Francis Adams, Jr., historian, grandson of President John Quincy Adams, and future president of the Union Pacific Railroad. (USAMHI)

The Conquest of the Mississippi

CHARLES L. DUFOUR

The great river spawned great men to contest her waters

THE USS *Brooklyn* dropped anchor off the mouth of the Mississippi at 2 P.M. on May 26, 1861, and the Union conquest of the great river, so vital to the Confederacy, was underway.

It was the first implementation of General Winfield Scott's "Anaconda Plan," the purpose of which was not only the military envelopment of the Confederacy but its economic strangulation as well. As early as May 3, Scott had discussed his plan with General George B. McClellan, pointing out that a powerful Union movement, by land and by water, down the Mississippi together with an effective blockade of the river's mouth would "envelop the insurgent States, and bring them to terms with less bloodshed than by another plan."

The effectiveness of the Union blockade was almost immediately felt in New Orleans, the Confederacy's greatest city. On May 30, 1861, a ship loaded with Brazilian coffee was captured by the *Brooklyn* and the next day another New Orleans-bound vessel carrying foodstuffs was seized. From the moment the blockade was established, not a single ship reached the Confederate city until Farragut's attacking fleet ran past Fort Jackson and Fort St. Philip in April 1862. Although the Union blockading vessels prevented ships from entering the Mississippi, the river's five passes into the Gulf

of Mexico offered avenues of escape to blockade-runners from New Orleans and several did make it to sea. The most significant escape was that of the Confederate raider *Sumter* commanded by Raphael Semmes, later of *Alabama* fame, which eluded the blockade on June 30 to prey relentlessly on American commerce vessels for more than six months.

The Confederate government was slow to realize the defenselessness of New Orleans and the absolute necessity of making an all-out effort to prepare the city for invasion. Four months after Louisiana seceded from the Union, a general officer had not yet arrived in New Orleans to take command. During that time, the city had been drained of troops; they had been ordered to Pensacola to reinforce Braxton Bragg. On April 10, two days before the guns sounded at Charleston, Governor Thomas O. Moore of Louisiana complained to Confederate authorities, "We are disorganized, and have no general officer to command and direct." Seven weeks went by before seventy-one-year-old General David E. Twiggs, veteran of more than half a century in the United States Army, reached New Orleans to take command.

Although the Common Council of the City of New Orleans praised Twiggs's "integrity, sagacity,

The USS Brooklyn, *the first ship to go on blockade off the mouth of the Mississippi. The warship and the river were to see a lot of each other in the years to come.* (NA)

and nerve so essential to a commander," it soon became evident that the enfeebled septuagenerian general was not the man to defend the South's greatest city from Federal attack. President Davis had already received complaints of the "infirmities of General Twiggs," when Governor Moore's plea for "an officer . . . who, with youth, energy and military ability, would infuse some activity in our preparation and some confidence in our people," reached Richmond in September. In closing this appeal to Davis, Moore begged that "this city, the most important to be preserved of any of the Confederacy, and our coast, the most exposed of all the states, be no longer neglected."

President Davis finally conceded that General Twiggs "has proven unequal to his command," but he shifted the blame for Twiggs's appointment to the people of New Orleans: "As in his selection I

yielded much to the solicitation of the people of New Orleans, I think they should sooner have informed me of the mistake they had made."

When Major General Mansfield Lovell was assigned to New Orleans, Twiggs got the implied message and prevented an awkward situation by asking, on October 5, to be relieved from duty for reasons of health. Before leaving for New Orleans, Lovell conferred with both President Davis and Secretary of War Judah P. Benjamin and, with almost prophetic insight, declared that the only proper defense of New Orleans would require a unified command. He argued, but in vain, that the employment of naval as well as army forces should be under his direction. Fearing that Lovell had not fully understood the definition of his command responsibilities, Davis hurried off a letter to him stating, "The fleet maintained at the port of New

Major General Mansfield Lovell would never be fully appreciated in the Confederacy for his talents. Rather, he would be remembered as the man who lost New Orleans. (USAMHI)

Orleans and its vicinity is not a part of your command." This decision would prove fatal.

Lovell reached New Orleans on October 17 and found, as he reported to Richmond, "great confusion, irresolution, and want of system in every thing administrative." New Orleans was "almost entirely stripped of everything available in the way of ordnance, stores, ammunition, clothing, medicines etc." There existed a frightening shortage of powder, Lovell reported. So he established two powder mills in New Orleans, and moved a third mill from the Mississippi coast to the city.

Before leaving Virginia, Lovell met with his old army friend General P. G. T. Beauregard, a native of New Orleans who, for ten years before the war, had been in charge of the defenses of Louisiana. Beauregard reiterated to Lovell what he had told Louisiana authorities many months earlier, that Forts Jackson and St. Philip, miles downriver from New Orleans, could not prevent steam vessels from passing unless an obstruction in the river held the ships under the cross fire of the forts for half an hour. Such a barricade, talked about in February

but not constructed until the summer, had been in place about a month when Lovell reached New Orleans. After inspecting this so-called raft, Lovell undertook to strengthen it.

On arrival, Lovell heard much of a recent Confederate naval victory at the Head of the Passes where a bold attack on a Yankee squadron routed it in what David Dixon Porter later described as "the most ridiculous affair that ever took place in the American Navy."

The heroes of this exploit were Commodore George Hollins and the ironclad *Manassas*, popularly known in New Orleans as the "Turtle." The latter, originally the twin-screw tugboat *Enoch Train*, had been purchased by a syndicate of businessmen for conversion into an ironclad to operate as a privateer against the blockaders. The cigar-shaped *Manassas*, covered with railroad iron three quarters of an inch thick, mounted one gun, which operated through a trapdoor forward. It had a

David D. Porter did heavy duty on the Mississippi. At the outset of the war, however, he ridiculed the Confederate success at Head of the Passes as a "ridiculous affair." (USAMHI)

*Commodore George N. Hollins, who led the
successful Confederate attack on the little Union
squadron at Head of the Passes.* (LSU)

modore Hollins seized it for the Confederacy against the protests of the syndicate.

On the night of October 11–12, 1861, Hollins's little flotilla, consisting of the *Manassas, McRae, Ivy, Calhoun, Tuscarora, Jackson,* and *Pickens*—New Orleanians called it the "mosquito fleet"—attacked a Union squadron of four warships under Captain John Pope at the Head of the Passes, where the various mouths of the Mississippi leave the main stream.

What followed was a comic opera of naval warfare. The *Manassas* rammed the *Richmond,* and the ten-knot impact disabled the Confederate ironclad while causing panic aboard the Union flagship. In the confusion and darkness, three Union ships, *Vincennes, Preble,* and *Waterwitch,* on signals from Captain Pope, slipped their cables and began steaming down Southwest Pass, and the *Richmond* followed. A running fight of no actual consequence ensued, but the aftermath was farcical after the *Vincennes* ran aground on the bar. Commander Robert Handy, believing erroneously that Pope had ordered him to abandon ship, did so after ordering the lighting of a slow fuse to the magazine. Fortunately, a Union quartermaster, after lighting the fuse, cut off the burning end and tossed it into the river, and the *Vincennes* was thus saved. "Pope's Run" as the incident became known, was later characterized by Admiral Alfred T. Mahan as "a move which brought intense mortification to himself [Pope] and in a measure to the service."

Fully believing that he had sunk a Union vessel (he announced it as the *Preble*) in this weird affair at the Head of the Passes, Hollins hurried back to New Orleans with the morale-building news of a great victory. But the expedition had little significance beyond creating popular enthusiasm. Elise Ellis Bragg, writing her husband, General Braxton Bragg, said, "Our 'Turtle,' alias *Manassas* made a grand charge and would have done wonders if it had not been disabled. All these things make a sensation, but I fear they help our cause but little, and a dark and gloomy winter seems closing around us."

When General Lovell arrived, New Orleanians were still talking enthusiastically about the action at the Head of the Passes and also of the two giant ironclads *Mississippi* and *Louisiana,* which were under construction just above the city, and which were expected to be in operation in January.

heavy cast-iron prow, which extended below the waterline so that the vessel could operate as a ram.

Although the project was supposedly a secret one, reports of the "formidable instrument of destruction" the Confederates were building at New Orleans slipped into the Northern press. Fantastic stories, born of imagination and misinformation, told that the *Manassas* was equipped with a powerful auger which could bore holes in a ship below its waterline and that this "hellish engine" had twenty-four hoses with which boiling water could be played upon the crew of an enemy ship. The "Turtle" was, in fact, much more formidable in the Northern press than it proved in the water. Nevertheless, its owners had high hopes that, operating as a privateer, the *Manassas* would reap a rich harvest of prize money by capturing Union blockade vessels. But hardly had the *Manassas* been launched and given its trial runs than Com-

The CSS McRae, *part of Hollins's "fleet."* (NHC)

The USS Richmond *was rammed by Hollins's ironclad* Manassas, *an action that did more damage to the ironclad than to the Federal warship. The* Richmond *served continually on the river in the years to come.* (NHC)

Ironclads were of interest to the Union naval authorities on the Mississippi. Captain John Rodgers was sent by the Navy Department to supervise the construction of the Benton-*class gunboats at Cairo, Illinois.* (NA, U. S. WAR DEPARTMENT GENERAL STAFF)

Meanwhile, the first Union preparations on the upper Mississippi had been made on August 2, when James B. Eads of St. Louis was authorized to construct seven ironclad gunboats of a new type for use on the western rivers. Three river steamers, the *Tyler, Lexington,* and *Conestoga,* had been converted into gunboats, and they became the nucleus of the Union naval forces on the Mississippi until Eads's ironclads were completed.

On October 7, the gunboats *Lexington* and *Tyler,* on a reconnaissance from Cairo, steamed toward Lucas Bend, Missouri, to engage Confederate shore batteries at Iron Bluff, not far from Columbus, Kentucky. On October 12, the same date of the ignominious "Pope's Run" from the Head of the Passes, the *St. Louis,* first Federal ironclad, was launched at Carondelet, Missouri.

Initial land operation by Union forces on the Mississippi proved abortive. On November 7, Brig-

adier General U. S. Grant descended from Cairo with 3,000 troops on transports supported by two wooden converted gunboats. Landing on the Missouri side, Grant seized the village of Belmont, across the river from Columbus, Kentucky. Grant held Belmont until Confederate reinforcements from Columbus crossed the river, and then he regained his transports and steamed back to Cairo.

Before 1861 ended, the first significant operation concerned with the conquest of the Mississippi occurred when 1,900 Union troops under Brigadier General John W. Phelps landed on Ship Island, in Mississippi Sound, twelve miles off the mainland and sixty miles from the mouth of the Mississippi.

With the coming of the new year, Union efforts on the upper Mississippi were stepped up. On January 14, three Union gunboats descended to the vicinity of Columbus and shelled Confederate encampments along the river. After the fall of Forts Henry and Donelson early in February, 1862, Columbus became the prime Union objective in the West. The Confederate government, recognizing its extreme vulnerability, ordered the evacuation of Columbus on February 20. Withdrawal of troops, guns, and material began at once and by March 2 the evacuation was completed. All but two of Columbus's 140 guns were moved south to Island No. 10 and its adjacent batteries. The next day, as Federal troops occupied Columbus, another force under General John Pope laid siege to New Madrid, Missouri. After a heavy bombardment of their works on March 13, the Confederates slipped out of New Madrid the next day and retreated to Island No. 10, leaving behind a substantial amount of guns and supplies.

Island No. 10, so named because it was the tenth island in the Mississippi south of its confluence with the Ohio, was assumed by the Confederates to be impregnable. Situated in Madrid Bend, between Tennessee and Missouri, Island No. 10 commanded the river in both directions. Earthworks, constructed for two miles along the banks, made Island No. 10 formidable for an attacking fleet, while virtually impassable swamps made a land attack on Island No. 10 unfeasible.

When Pope seized New Madrid, the Confederate naval force—six gunboats under Commodore Hollins—found itself much outgunned and withdrew to Tiptonville, thirty miles below Island No. 10 by river, but less than five miles by land. The

Naval stations at places like Mound City, Illinois, were organized and readied to construct new ships as well as to refit and repair those already in service. (WRHS)

Mound City remained in a bustle of activity during most of the war. (LC)

stage was now set for a combined army and navy operation against Island No. 10, with Pope attacking by land while Commodore Andrew Foote's flotilla, headed by Eads's formidable ironclad *Benton,* most powerful warship on the Mississippi, engaged the Confederate bastion from the river. While Pope was impatient to begin operations against Island No. 10 as soon as New Madrid fell, it was not until March 14 that Foote's flotilla left Cairo for the fifty-mile run down to Island No. 10. With seven gunboats and ten mortar vessels, and transports carrying troops to occupy Island No. 10 after its capture, Foote dropped anchor two miles from the Union objective on the morning of March 15. The next day, Foote's mortars opened fire on the Confederate works and on March 17 the *Benton* and Foote's other ironclads went into action, at a range of 2,000 yards.

Meanwhile, Pope had realized he needed transports to get his troops across the Mississippi if the joint operation were to be successful. In an official request, he promised that if Foote were to ". . . run past the batteries of Island No. 10 with two or three gunboats and reach here, I can cross my whole force and capture every man of the enemy at Island No. 10 and on the mainland." Foote immediately rejected Pope's proposal.

Pope's chief engineer, Colonel Josiah W. Bissell, then proposed that a canal be dug through the overflowed swamps to bypass Island No. 10. Pope approved the project when Bissell assured him that he could open a way for vessels of light draft to cut across the neck of land. He authorized Bissell to employ his entire regiment to open the canal. Working feverishly for nearly three weeks, Bissell cut a twelve-mile-long channel, fifty feet wide.

Before Bissell's canal was ready, Foote had a change of mind when Henry Walke, commander of the *Carondelet,* volunteered to run his ship past Island No. 10's batteries. In a thunderstorm on the night of April 4, the *Carondelet* ran the fiery gauntlet and reached New Madrid at midnight, a few hours after Bissell's engineers had completed the last stretch of the canal. Three nights later, during another storm, the *Pittsburg* ran past Island No. 10's guns and anchored at New Madrid. The same night, four shallow-draft steamers passed through Bissell's canal to provide Pope with the transports he needed to get his troops across the river to assault Island No. 10 from the rear.

Island No. 10 had been subjected to constant fire from Foote's ships, and a bold Union raid on April 1 by soldiers landing from small boats had succeeded in routing a Confederate guard and spiking six guns—driving soft nails into their touchholes so they could not be fired. Now, with a two-pronged all-out attack imminent, the Confederates began the evacuation of Island No. 10 on April 7. Retreat, however, was futile and seven thousand Confederates, including three generals, hemmed in by Union troops and the swamps, surrendered. On the same fateful date that Island No.

10 fell, the Confederate Army at Shiloh, having been repulsed in the second day's fighting, was preparing its retirement back to Corinth.

With Island No. 10 in Union possession, the only Confederate stronghold on the Mississippi above Memphis was Fort Pillow in Tennessee. Situated on bluffs about eighty miles upstream from Memphis, Fort Pillow consisted of a line of fortifications extended for seven miles along the river. Foote lost no time in putting Fort Pillow under fire and on April 14 he shelled the Confederate works as a preliminary to what he expected to be another combined operation. To Foote's surprise, however, Pope's troops were ordered to Pittsburg Landing, thus making impossible a joint army-navy movement against Fort Pillow.

Meanwhile, at the lower end of the Mississippi, Flag Officer David Glasgow Farragut was readying his campaign against New Orleans. Listed at thirty-seventh among navy captains, Farragut, a vigorously active sixty-year-old, had been in the service for more than half a century. As a boy, he

Its shops and ways echoed to the sounds of machinery and workmen. Here, in the foreground, blocks and tackle and lines are visible on the bank where ships were hauled out of the water for hull-scraping and repair. (USAMHI)

Tugboats like the little Daisy *plied the river constantly off Mound City.* (NHC)

was a midshipman in the War of 1812, and in the Mexican War he served on blockade duty. Secretary of the Navy Gideon Welles was impressed with Farragut, finding him "modest and truthful . . . self-reliant and brave," and decided he was the man to capture New Orleans. He summoned Farragut to Washington from a desk job in New York in December 1861 and offered him command of the New Orleans expedition.

Early in April, forty-seven days after he reached Ship Island to organize his expedition, Farragut had installed himself at the Head of the Passes with a formidable fleet of 17 warships with a total of 154 guns; a mortar flotilla of 20 schooners, each with a 13-inch mortar and a total of 30 guns; and 7 steamers with 27 guns. Difficulties in getting some of his larger ships over the bar caused exasperating delays, but by April 8, Farragut was nearly ready to strike.

Once in the river, Farragut was tireless in his preparations, overlooking no detail needed for success. He sent a geodetic survey team up the river to establish ranges to Forts Jackson and St. Philip from points where David Dixon Porter's mortar

boats would be stationed. He had the hulls of his ships smeared with the tawny mud of the river as camouflage; he ordered bags filled with sand to strengthen bulwarks and protect the engines and other machinery; he had gun carriages and decks whitewashed to make easier the location of firing implements in the dark; he ordered iron-link cables suspended on the sides of the ships in the line of the engines; he had nettings made with large ropes spread above the decks to prevent injury from falling timber. Thus Farragut, by his energy, ingenuity, enthusiasm, and confidence not only prepared his ships superbly for the coming ordeal of passing the Confederate forts, but also infused into his officers and crew a high morale.

While confidence prevailed in the Union fleet at the Head of the Passes, New Orleans, with attack imminent, had become a jittery city. Spy fever, which had raged for weeks, was followed by an epidemic of wild rumors which the New Orleans press charged were circulated by "gossip-mongers or evil-disposed persons." The *Picayune* noted that "every day they hear one thousand alarming rumors," while the *Commercial Bulletin* complained that "every possible idea that could enter the head of credulous people seems to have been hatched up and enlarged."

General Mansfield Lovell had more serious matters than hunting spies and dispelling rumors to worry him. Although he was to have no control over the employment of the powerful warships *Louisiana* and *Mississippi*, he recognized them as integral to the defense of New Orleans and he viewed with considerable concern the way progress on the two ships was dragging.

Promised for service by January 1862, it was not until February 6 that the *Louisiana* was launched, with still considerable work left to be done in sheathing the vessel with armor and installing the machinery. The *Mississippi*, which had also been promised for January, was still on the way. Its woodwork was completed and its boilers were installed, but it lacked armor and machinery and the central shaft, which was slow in coming from Richmond's Tredegar Works.

Lovell, his hands already tied by Richmond's continued refusal to allow him to head a unified army-navy command, protested on being stripped of 5,000 troops which he was ordered to send to

Columbus. To his complaint, Confederate authorities, seemingly totally oblivious of the threat to New Orleans posed by the Union naval build-up at Ship Island, replied that "New Orleans will be defended from above . . . the forces withdrawn from you are for the defense of your own command."

As if in compensation for withholding from Lovell command of the Confederate Navy at New Orleans, the War Department ordered him to seize fourteen steamboats for a River Defense Fleet, "not to be a part of the Navy . . . [but] subject to the general command of the military chief." This peculiar arrangement, with the steamboat captains in command of their vessels, was startling to Lovell.

New Orleans' morale sagged when word of the fall of Forts Henry and Donelson reached the city, to be followed shortly by the news that Albert Sidney Johnston's Kentucky line had collapsed with the evacuation of Columbus. Criticism of Confederate leadership, both in Richmond and in the field, was widespread among citizens and in the press. New Orleans was on the verge of panic when Lovell, acting on orders from Richmond, declared martial law in effect on March 15.

And frequently an entire fleet of ironclads and "tinclads" appeared at anchor in midstream. The USS St. Louis *rests in the center of the image, while in the distance behind its stern can be seen what is probably the USS* Tyler.

(USAMHI)

Brigadier General Johnson Kelly Duncan, who commanded at Forts Jackson and St. Philip, New Orleans' principal defenses, seventy-five miles downstream from the city, worked his officers and men to the point of exhaustion in preparing the bastions for Farragut's certain attack soon to come. Nearly 1,000 troops garrisoned the forts, which had 115 guns of various calibers—69 at Fort Jackson and 46 at Fort St. Philip.

The barricade, or raft, which had been made more secure by Lovell shortly after his arrival, was supported by enfilading fire from the forts. However, accumulated driftwood and the strong current proved too much for the barrier early in March. The main chains snapped, and the obstruction, so needed to hold enemy ships under the fire of the forts, ceased to exist. A makeshift barrier of parts of the original raft and some schooners,

anchored and linked by chains, was hurriedly improvised. The schooners were anchored bow upstream, chained together stem, stern, and midships, with their rigging and cables trailing astern to be hazards to the propellers of enemy ships.

Nervous New Orleans received disheartening news from Shiloh's second day after exulting in the Confederate victory of the first day. The news of the fall of Island No. 10 followed fast, and the city then learned that a storm on April 9 and 10 had again dismantled the raft below the forts. Once more improvisation of a barrier was rushed.

To all of Lovell's worries there was added the continued incomprehensible unawareness in Richmond of the acute danger to New Orleans from Farragut's fleet at the Head of the Passes. Orders had come to send the still uncompleted *Louisiana* up the river, where President Davis and Secretary

Specialized craft like the hospital boat Nashville *were also needed to serve both the navy and the armed soldiers fighting along the river.* (LC)

Another hospital ship, the R. C. Wood, *on the wharf at Vicksburg in 1863.*
(OLD COURT HOUSE MUSEUM, VICKSBURG)

of the Navy Mallory amazingly believed the gravest danger to New Orleans lay. To Governor Thomas O. Moore's protest that "the *Louisiana* . . . is absolutely a necessity at the forts for the safety of New Orleans, and that it is suicidal to send her elsewhere," President Davis telegraphed back on April 17 the astonishing message: "The wooden vessels are below; the iron gunboats are above. The forts should destroy the former if they attempt to ascend. The *Louisiana* may be indespensible to check the descent of the iron boats."

This was not the only instance of Richmond's inexplicable blindness to the danger to New Orleans from the Union fleet in the river. When Commodore George N. Hollins, commander of the Confederate flotilla at Fort Pillow, asked permission on April 9 to steam down to New Orleans to participate in its defense, Mallory telegraphed back an emphatic refusal. Hollins, not waiting for Mallory's reply, however, reached New Orleans in the *McRae* and promptly urged by telegram that his fleet join him. Richmond's reply was a summons to Hollins to report at once in the Confederate capitol to head a board examining midshipmen. Thus was the best fighting man in the Confederate Navy

on the Mississippi shelved at the most critical moment for New Orleans.

On April 18, Porter's mortar ships began their concentrated fire on the forts and for five days and nights, from a sheltered bend in the river, 13-inch shells were lobbed into Forts Jackson and St. Philip at regular intervals. General Duncan estimated that the Union mortar boats had thrown more than 22,000 shells at the forts before Farragut made his move.

When it became evident that the *Louisiana*, without its motive power in operation, could not go up the river as ordered, Commander W. C. Whittle, navy commander of New Orleans, finally responded to the importuning of Lovell and Duncan to have the ironclad towed down to the forts to serve as a floating battery. Despite the remonstrances of Duncan, the ironclad's captain refused to place the *Louisiana* below the barrier, where it could enfilade the Union mortar boats. He anchored it just above Fort St. Philip where it remained inactive against them. The same day that the *Louisiana* went down to the forts, the *Mississippi,* still far from completed, was launched.

On the night of April 20, Farragut sent Captain

Cairo, Illinois, also hosted an important naval station. Here its wharf boat lies moored on the shore. (USAMHI)

Henry Bell with two gunboats to sever the barrier and open a way for the ships to pass through. Bell succeeded in his mission and Farragut, never enthusiastic about the mortar ships' ability to silence the forts, determined to make his run on the night of April 23–24.

Everything was in readiness at the Head of the Passes, but disorganization prevailed among the Confederate defenders. That strange War Department instrument, the River Defense Fleet, refused to take orders from the navy; the navy showed no inclination to cooperate with General Lovell's defense plans; and, to top it, New Orleans was a city verging on panic.

At 2 A.M. on April 24, the *Cayuga* raised its anchors and steamed off into the moonless night, the vanguard of Farragut's attacking fleet. One by one, the warships followed. At 3:30 A.M., the *Cayuga* passed noiselessly through the breach in the barrier, unchallenged by any Confederate vessel and unthreatened by the fire rafts which were supposed to have been illuminated and sent down the river. Immediately, the guns of Fort Jackson

and Fort St. Philip opened up as Farragut's other vessels moved into range, firing their broadsides at the forts. The flashes of their guns and the arching course of mortar shells lit the river in a spectacle of awesome grandeur. Three of Farragut's gunboats failed to make it through the breach in the barrier. The *Kennebec* entangled itself in the raft and the *Winona* suffered the same fate, and both freed themselves with difficulty and drifted out of action. The third, the *Itasca*, was badly crippled by gunfire from Fort Jackson and it retired downriver.

At the first fighting, the Confederate River Defense Fleet hurried off ingloriously, but three Rebel ships fought with valor. Hopelessly outgunned and outnumbered, the *Manassas* ("Turtle"), *McRae*, and *Governor Moore* were in the thick of the melee, each drawing the concentrated fire of several Union ships at various stages of the battle. The forts laid down tremendous barrages, but fourteen of Farragut's ships ran the fiery gauntlet successfully, although his flagship, the *Hartford*, was set ablaze by a fire raft while it was aground off Fort St. Philip. For a while, it was touch and

A river fleet at anchor off Cairo in 1865. (AMERICANA IMAGE GALLERY)

go for the *Hartford,* but discipline and engine power prevailed: The fire was extinguished by the crew and the flagship shivered and shook as it freed itself from the mud and steamed out of range of the forts.

At the peak of the battle, the roaring and flashing of the guns created a spectacular scene. One of General Benjamin Butler's officers wrote, "Combine all that you have heard of thunder, add to it all that you have ever seen of lightning, and you have, perhaps, a conception of the scene." To an officer on the *Hartford,* "it was like the breaking up of the universe with the moon and all the stars bursting in our midst." Farragut himself described it: "It was as if the artillery of heaven were playing upon the earth."

The *Manassas,* which had rammed the *Brooklyn* and *Mississippi* and fought at close quarter half a

dozen other Union ships, was finally disabled and scuttled by its crew. The *McRae,* just as active in the unequal fight, had its tiller ropes shot away and made it with difficulty to the protection of Fort Jackson. The *Governor Moore* engaged the *Varuna* in a running battle, rammed the Union ship twice and sank it—Farragut's only loss in the passage of the forts. Beverly Kennon, commander of the *Governor Moore,* fired his ship, threw his sword overboard, and surrendered himself as half a dozen Union gunboats descended upon his horribly cut-up craft. The dead on the *Governor Moore* totaled fifty-seven—nine more than the combined dead in Farragut's fleet and in the two forts.

The *Louisiana,* still anchored above Fort St. Philip, received heavy firing at close range as Farragut's ships passed up the river, but the ironclad was practically undamaged. David Dixon Porter

At Cairo, soldiers boarded transports like the USS Brown *for the journey to the front at New Orleans or Vicksburg or Port Hudson.* (USAMHI)

noted in his journal that had Commander Mitchell, captain of the *Louisiana*, "possessed the soul of a flea, he could have driven us all out of the river."

The next day, April 25, Farragut pushed up the river to New Orleans. He was amazed at the sight that met his eye: "The levee of New Orleans was one scene of desolation, ships, steamers, cotton, coal, etc., were all in one common blaze," he wrote. "The *Mississippi*, which was to be the terror of the seas, and no doubt would have been to a great extent . . . soon came floating by us all in flames, and passed down the river."

Demands that the city surrender met with a scornful refusal by Mayor John Monroe, who

pointed out to Farragut that as Lovell had evacuated his militia troops, New Orleans was defenseless and "the city is yours by the power of brutal force."

Meanwhile, down at the forts, mutiny broke out on April 27, compelling Duncan to surrender to Porter. During the signing, the *Louisiana* came drifting by ablaze, and moments later it blew up. All Confederate resistance below New Orleans was now ended. When the news reached Farragut he sent a party ashore to haul down the flag of Louisiana from the city hall flagpole and raise the American flag.

On May 1, Major General Benjamin F. Butler landed his occupation troops and New Orleans' days in the Confederacy were over. Mary Baykin Chesnut prophetically recorded the bitter fact in her diary: "New Orleans is gone, and with it the Confederacy! Are we not cut in two? The Mississippi ruins us if it is lost."

After Butler occupied New Orleans, Farragut was faced with a dilemma: What to do in the light of his original orders. These read: "If the Mississippi expedition from Cairo shall not have descended the river, you will take advantage of the panic to push a strong force up the river to take all their defenses in the rear. You will also reduce the fortifications which defend Mobile Bay and turn them over to the army to hold."

Farragut sent Porter and the mortar boats to Mobile Bay and dispatched Commander S. P. Lee with the *Oneida* and several smaller gunboats up the Mississippi, while he remained at New Orleans with the greater part of his fleet. Baton Rouge and Natchez, both undefended, were captured and the American flag was raised above their public build-

ings. At Vicksburg, however, Lee's demand for surrender was answered defiantly: "Mississippians don't know and refuse to learn how to surrender to an enemy. If . . . Farragut or . . . Butler can teach them let them come and try." Lee gave Vicksburg twenty-four hours to remove its women and children to safety, set up a blockade of the city, and awaited orders from Farragut.

When Farragut learned what was happening upriver, he was anxious to push up the Mississippi with his full command. On May 10, one of the few fleet actions of the war had taken place above Fort Pillow at Plum Run Bend when a much-outgunned Confederate flotilla of eight ships—the Confederate River Defense Fleet—with more valor than judgment attacked seven Union ironclads. With four of his ships disabled by the superior fire power of the Yankees' ships, Captain James Montgomery broke off action and retired downstream to Memphis. On May 23, Farragut's fleet, accompanied by 3,200 troops under Brigadier General

And packet boats carrying mail, like the Golden Era, *shared the stream with gunboats like the USS* Tyler *in the crowded waters off Cairo. Shipbuilder James B. Eads first used his skills to convert a steamer into the gunboat* Tyler. (CHS)

Thomas Williams, reached Vicksburg. Two days later, Colonel Charles Ellet's nine rams and two floating batteries, completed for the War Department in only forty days, made liaison with the Western Flotilla, now commanded by Captain Charles H. Davis, who had succeeded the ailing Commodore Foote.

Davis's reaction to Ellet's arrival was politely uncooperative. Ellet informed Davis that he was going to operate against Fort Pillow and asked for one gunboat to accompany him. Failing this, he invited Davis to assign some navy observers to the rams for this "daring and patriotic enterprise." Davis's reply reflected the age-old rivalry between military services: "I decline taking any part in the expedition . . . I would thank you to inform me how far you consider yourself under my authority; and I shall esteem it a favor to receive from you a copy of the orders under which you are acting." Ellet's reply was conciliatory: "No question of authority need be raised." But to Secretary of War

Stanton he wrote, "Commodore Davis will not join me . . . nor contribute a gunboat . . . nor allow any of his men to volunteer . . . I shall therefore . . . go without him."

The fall of Corinth on June 3 made the Confederate evacuation of Fort Pillow inevitable and exposed Memphis to serious threat. At Memphis, the Confederates were building two powerful ironclads, the *Arkansas* and *Tennessee,* and their seizure was a Union objective. Two of Ellet's rams drew sharp fire from the works at Fort Pillow on June 3, but the Confederates had already begun evacuation, and during the night of June 4 it was completed. The only Confederate defense now between the Union vessels and Memphis was a weak Confederate flotilla at that city.

Union gunboats attacked this flotilla on the morning of June 6 in another of the rare fleet actions on the Mississippi. People of Memphis lined the bluffs to watch the battle when Commodore Davis sent five Union ironclads and four rams—a

And he did the same with the USS Lexington. *These gunboats were not very effectively armored, but they were a start.* (USAMHI)

Far more effective was the USS St. Louis, *launched at Carondelet, Missouri, the first Federal ironclad.* (NA, U. S. WAR DEPARTMENT GENERAL STAFF)

total of sixty-eight guns—against Montgomery's inferior flotilla of eight makeshift vessels mounting only twenty-eight guns. In the unequal struggle, which featured ramming and close-quarter fighting, the Confederates were decimated. Three Rebel ships were destroyed and four were captured, with only the *Van Dorn* escaping. The Union Navy now controlled the entire Mississippi, except at Vicksburg, Mississippi, and at Port Hudson in Louisiana.

The principal concern of the Union fleet on the Mississippi was the uncompleted Confederate ironclad, *Arkansas,* which, when Memphis was under threat, had been sent downriver to safety.

In the late summer of 1861, the Confederate Navy Department authorized the building of four powerful ironclads, easily the most formidable gunboats on the Mississippi. Devastating to the Confederate cause was the policy of "too little and too late" that prevailed with its gunboat building projects. The *Louisiana* and the *Mississippi,* as was stated earlier, were to have been completed at New Orleans by the end of January 1862. But neither was finished when Farragut attacked the forts

below New Orleans in April, and the *Louisiana* was blown up and the *Mississippi* set afire.

About the time that work was begun on the *Louisiana* and *Mississippi* in New Orleans, two other formidable ironclads were started in a Memphis shipyard, the *Arkansas* and the *Tennessee.* Patterned on the *Louisiana* and *Mississippi* and perhaps even more formidable, the Memphis ironclads were to be ready by the end of December 1861.

The descent of the Mississippi by the Union fleet found work on both the *Arkansas* and *Tennessee* lagging, and on April 25, the same day Farragut's warships appeared at New Orleans, the *Arkansas* was launched. It was floated 300 miles down the Mississippi to the Yazoo River above Vicksburg and then was towed 200 miles up the Yazoo to Greenwood, where it was expected to be finished shortly. On orders from Richmond, the *Tennessee* was destroyed before launch.

A shortage of workmen, tools, equipment, timber, and other materials needed to complete the *Arkansas* resulted in interminable delays, despite the vigorous efforts of the ship's commander, Lieu-

Active operations on the Mississippi really begin with Brigadier General U. S. Grant, shown here as a major general. His attack on Belmont was staged from Cairo. (LC)

tenant Isaac Brown, who was charged with the *Arkansas*'s completion. Launch day finally came on July 4, but more than six months late, and the *Arkansas* steamed to Yazoo City.

It was Lieutenant Brown's intention to drive his ironclad through the entire combined Union fleet—Farragut had run Vicksburg's fortifications, and had joined Davis above the city—and anchor the *Arkansas* under the protection of the Confederate batteries.

Major General Earl Van Dorn, commanding at Vicksburg, impatiently awaited the *Arkansas*, which he expected to prove a formidable factor in defending the city. It was due on July 14, but it developed that a defective powder magazine admitted steam which dampened the powder. Lieutenant Brown lost a full day drying his powder on canvas spread along the bank. Underway once more, the *Arkansas* ran aground in the darkness.

Instead of reaching the Mississippi by daylight, the *Arkansas* was still in the Yazoo when Brown picked up in his glass three Union vessels steaming toward him. They were the ironclads *Carondelet* and *Queen of the West* and the gunboat *Tyler*.

At 6:20 A.M. the *Carondelet* began to fire on the *Arkansas* at less than half a mile away, then turned and headed down the Yazoo, followed by the other two Union vessels. Stern guns opened on the pursuing *Arkansas* as the chase got underway and the Confederate ironclad was badly cut up. Lieutenant Brown was mistakenly believed to have been seriously wounded when struck in the head by a rifle ball. But the *Arkansas*'s guns had severely punished the *Carondelet,* shattering its steering equipment and cutting steam-escape, exhaust, and cold-water pipes. The *Carondelet* limped to the bank and did not return the *Arkansas*'s broadside and stern guns' fire as the Rebel ironside swept past, still in pursuit of the *Tyler* and the *Queen of the West.* The latter had fled hastily and its com-

The first real Union success came at Island No. 10, when Brigadier General John Pope cooperated with Foote's flotilla to force the Confederate bastion to surrender. (NA, U. S. SIGNAL CORPS)

In both defense and offense, cannons mounted on rafts and floated into position were used frequently on the river at places like Island No. 10. (NHC)

mander, James M. Hunter, was later denounced in the *Tyler's* log for his "cowardly and dastardly" behavior. But the *Tyler,* in retreating, kept up its fire as the running fight brought the two vessels into the Mississippi and on toward Vicksburg.

Suddenly, on rounding a bend, the *Arkansas* came upon the combined fleets of Farragut and Davis—thirty-three ironclads, gunboats, rams, river steamers, and mortar boats—and quickly was furiously engaged. Lieutenant Brown reported later, "The shock of missiles striking our sides was literally continuous, and . . . we were now surrounded without room for anything but pushing ahead . . . I had the most lively realization of having steamed into a real volcano, the *Arkansas* from its center firing rapidly to every point of the circumference, without the fear of hitting a friend or missing an enemy."

For about two hours, the *Arkansas* fought its way through the Union fleets and at ten minutes before nine o'clock on July 15 it tied up at the Vicksburg wharf, "smokestack . . . shot to pieces . . . much cut up . . . pilot house smashed and some ugly places through our armor," as Lieutenant Brown later reported.

Elation in Vicksburg was unbounded and General Van Dorn, who had watched the fight from the top of the courthouse, said in his report that Brown "immortalized his single vessel, himself, and the heroes under his command by an achievement the most brilliant ever recorded in naval annals."

Farragut, not sparing himself in his criticism, wrote Davis, "We were all caught unprepared for him, but we must go down and destroy him. . . . We must go close to him and smash him in. It will be warm work, but we must do it." That night, Farragut made his run. Mortar fire on Vicksburg opened the action at 6 P.M. and forty-five minutes later the fleet was underway. At 8:20 P.M. it had passed the Vicksburg batteries and anchored below the city. But Farragut had not destroyed the *Arkansas;* in fact, only one of his ships, the *Oneida,* actually saw the Rebel ironclad. However, the *Arkansas* did not escape damage, for a shot passed through its armor, penetrated the engine room, and disabled the engine and also caused a severe leak. More casualties were added to the morning's toll of ten killed and fifteen wounded.

All efforts to destroy the *Arkansas* failed during the ensuing days—mortar fire directed at the Rebel craft, a direct assault by the *Essex* and *Queen of the West*. Captain Ledyard Phelps of the *Benton* summed it up in a letter to Andrew Foote: "The whole thing was a fizzle. Every day we heard great things threatened only to realize fizzles." Van Dorn, in a telegram to Jefferson Davis, characterized the attack on the *Arkansas* as a "failure so complete that it was almost ridiculous."

Farragut, chagrined, parted company with the *Arkansas* when he was ordered by the Navy De-partment to return to New Orleans with his fleet. Departing with Farragut was General Williams's force, which was so riddled with illness that barely a fourth of the 3,000-odd troops was ready for duty. Williams retired to Baton Rouge. With only his gunboats left at Vicksburg, Davis deemed it wise to steam upriver to the mouth of the Yazoo. For more than two months—sixty-seven days—Vicksburg had frustrated the efforts of two powerful Union fleets and more than 3,000 land forces.

Henry Gurney's image of the mightiest ironclad on the river, the USS Benton, *another of Eads's conversions. Foote made it his flagship. This photo was taken at Natchez in 1863 or later.* (JOAN AND THOMAS GANDY, NATCHEZ, MISSISSIPPI)

The 20,000 to 25,000 shells hurled at the city left Vicksburg undaunted.

Captain Brown took advantage of the respite to visit Granada, Mississippi, where he fell ill. Lieutenant Henry Stevens, left in command of the *Arkansas,* worked feverishly to repair the engines and to increase the ship's armor. General Van Dorn ordered Stevens to take the *Arkansas* down the river to Baton Rouge to support an attack on that city by Major General John C. Breckinridge.

On August 3 at 2 A.M. the *Arkansas* moved from the wharf and headed for Baton Rouge.

Commander Henry Walke, a Virginian by birth, ran his Carondelet *past No. 10's batteries to assist Pope's land assault.* (LC)

Throughout the day, the ironclad's engines functioned efficiently and an eight-knot speed was maintained. But shortly before midnight, the starboard engine broke down, and the *Arkansas* tied up while repairs were made throughout the night. At 8 A.M. on August 5, the *Arkansas* was apparently ready to participate in Breckinridge's attack, which was already underway. When the *Arkansas* was within eight miles of Baton Rouge, the engines went dead again. Once more repairs were rushed and once more the engines broke down. By 9:30 A.M. on August 6, the *Arkansas* seemed ready once again. At that time there appeared, steaming toward the *Arkansas,* four Union gunboats, the *Essex, Cayuga, Katahdin,* and USS *Sumter.* Stevens determined to make a fight of it, but the ironclad's port engine failed as the *Arkansas* headed to engage the enemy. A moment later the starboard engine gave way and the *Arkansas* drifted helplessly toward the advancing Union gunboats.

Both sides opened fire, but ineffectively, and Lieutenant Stevens realized he had no alternative to the destruction of the *Arkansas* to prevent its falling into the hands of the enemy. Ordering the crew ashore and commanding them to take off for the interior, Stevens, with seven officers and petty officers, prepared the *Arkansas* for its end and then abandoned ship, too. For an hour the *Arkansas* floated with the current, its loaded guns firing as the flames reached them, and shortly before noon, it blew up spectacularly.

"It was beautiful," recalled Stevens, "to see her, when abandoned by commander and crew and dedicated to sacrifice, fighting the battle on her own hook."

In a report to the Confederate Congress, Secretary of the Navy Mallory said, "Naval history records few deeds of greater heroism or higher professional ability than this achievement of the *Arkansas.*"

With the passing of the *Arkansas,* there passed also the last Confederate offensive challenge on the Mississippi. The Union now controlled the entire river except for the Rebel bastions at Vicksburg and Port Hudson, Louisiana.

Less than a year remained before these last two Confederate strongholds would fall, and the Father of Waters would again go, as Mr. Lincoln expressed it, "unvexed to the sea."

The USS Pittsburg *followed Walke's lead, and Pope's movement was ensured.*
(LC)

Captures included the Confederate ship CSS Red Rover, *a barracks ship which the Federals turned into the first hospital ship in the navy.* (USAMHI)

The CSS De Soto *was captured as well, to become the USS* General Lyon.
(NHC)

Flag Officer David G. Farragut will be much in evidence on the Mississippi, and nowhere more than in his reduction of Forts Jackson and St. Philip and the capture of New Orleans. (USAMHI)

Fort Jackson. The photograph was supposedly taken in 1862 but is probably early postwar. (WRHS)

The interior of Fort St. Philip looking toward the river, probably also a postwar image. The formidable command these forts exerted on river traffic is evident. (WRHS)

A front view of Fort St. Philip. (WRHS)

And here the much less known Fort Macomb, taken in 1863. The canal ran from Lake Borgne to Lake Pontchartrain in the rear of New Orleans. Colonel Francis Hesseltine and his wife stand with fishing poles in the foreground. (USAMHI)

Captain Napoleon B. Harrison commanded the USS Cayuga *when Farragut ran his fleet past the forts.* (USAMHI)

The mortar schooner USS C. P. Williams *took part with Porter's mortar fleet in the bombardment of the forts.* (WRHS)

And so did the USS Horace Beals. (USAMHI)

These monster mortars could throw a 200-pound shell from 3,000–4,000 yards. These were part of Farragut's fleet, later taken to rest here at the Philadelphia Navy Yard. (USAMHI)

To identify his ships from a distance in the confusion of battle, Farragut ordered numbers painted in letters six feet high on the stacks of each vessel. Number 2 was the USS Winona, which served two years on the Mississippi before joining the blockade off Charleston. (USAMHI)

Farragut's mighty flagship, the USS Hartford, its midships sides still showing the chains draped over them as protection from enemy shot during the passage of the forts. A. D. Lytle, the outstanding photographer of Baton Rouge, made this view shortly afterward. (CWTI)

Farragut and his executive officer Percival Drayton at the wheel of the
Hartford. (USAMHI)

Men and officers of the Hartford at the stern pivot gun, a massive Parrott rifle.
(USAMHI)

The gun deck of the Hartford, *looking aft.* (USAMHI)

The beautiful side-wheeler USS Mississippi, *built in 1839 under
the eye of Commodore Matthew C. Perry. She was his flagship in
the Mexican War and in his epic voyage to Japan in 1852.
Farragut would send it upriver to pass the enemy batteries at Port
Hudson the next year, and there it would run aground and be
destroyed by its crew. The executive officer was the future Admiral
George Dewey.* (USAMHI)

McPherson & Oliver's photograph of the crew of the USS Richmond *at quarters after the capture of New Orleans.* (USAMHI)

Brigadier General Morgan L. Smith, a native of New York, fought for the South and supervised New Orleans' defenses as well as leading troops there. (USAMHI)

The heart of the Crescent City, Jackson Square, showing St. Louis Cathedral and to the right of it, the Presbytère. The Andrew Jackson equestrian statue can be seen, and carved on its pedestal his declaration that the union "must and shall be preserved." (USAMHI)

Canal Street, running from Royal Street to the river. At the end can be seen the smokestacks of steamboats at the wharves. (USAMHI)

Chartres Street in the French Quarter. (USAMHI)

New Orleans' City Hall. Here Farragut raised the Union flag over the conquered city. (USAMHI)

*Looking down the levee from Canal Street. The busy traffic, once interrupted
by the war, now flows again. Bales of cotton await shipment.* (USAMHI)

*With the city taken, Major General Benjamin F.
Butler and his troops began their controversial
occupation. "Spoons" Butler they would call him,
after accusations that he stole silver from the
citizens.* (USAMHI)

Before long New Orleans would be designated the headquarters of the new Department of the Gulf. Here officers serving in the department from several services, army, navy, and marines, gather for a group portrait in March 1863. Seated from the left are Lieutenant Edward Terry of the Richmond, *Captain James Alden commanding the* Richmond, *and Brigadier General Godfrey Weitzel. The rest are staff officers.* (USAMHI)

Soon after the fall of New Orleans, Farragut's ships took Baton Rouge and, shown here, Natchez. Then it was time to try for Vicksburg. (USAMHI)

Commander S. P. Lee led the small fleet that first tried to force the surrender of Vicksburg, but unsuccessfully. (USAMHI)

Farragut soon moved north to join Lee, bringing with him the 3,200 men of Brigadier General Thomas Williams, an almost universally disliked commander. The soldiers would attempt nothing, being shattered by disease. Williams retired to Baton Rouge, and there on August 5 he was killed in the Confederate attack. (USAMHI)

On the way to Vicksburg, Farragut learned of the Union fleet victory at Plum Run Bend, a victory won over ineffectual Confederate ships by gunboats like the USS Carondelet. (USAMHI)

The USS Louisville, *too, shown here at Memphis, made light work of the
enemy River Defense Fleet at Plum Run Bend. It was, in fact, the largest fleet
engagement of the war.* (NHC)

Brigadier General John B. Villepigue commanded the defense of Fort Pillow as best he could, until forced to abandon and destroy his fortifications. (P-M)

Then the Union Navy moved against Memphis. The only thing in their way was a little fleet commanded by the flamboyant M. Jeff Thompson who, though never promoted brigadier general, dressed like one anyhow. (DAVID R. O'REILLY COLLECTION)

Thompson's flotilla was obliterated, all but one captured or destroyed. The Little Rebel was one of the captured, and it was later put into Federal service. (TERENCE P. O'LEARY, GLADWYNE, PENNSYLVANIA)

The CSS General Price *had been a cotton-clad—bales of cotton stacked on her sides for protection—when she was sunk at Memphis. Raised and remodeled she became the USS* General Price, *commanded by* . . . (USAMHI)

. . . *Acting Volunteer Lieutenant J. F. Richardson.* (ROBERT G. HARRIS)

One of the ships of Ellet's ram fleet that destroyed Thompson's little flotilla.
(NHC)

Alfred W. Ellet, later a brigadier general,
succeeded to command of the ram fleet when his
brother Charles died two weeks after the Battle of
Memphis. (USAMHI)

And now Memphis belonged to the Union again. The city is shown here viewed from the levee. (USAMHI)

Here the Memphis levee itself, with Federal shipping and barges crowding the shore. (USAMHI)

The Memphis Navy Yard, where the mighty CSS Arkansas *was constructed.*
(USAMHI)

Union Lieutenant John A. Winslow took command of the Memphis naval facilities, turning them to the purposes of Farragut's and Ellet's ships. (USAMHI)

Yet much of Memphis sat in ruins, the first Mississippi River city to feel the hand of destruction. (USAMHI)

Vicksburg became even more isolated. Its commander, the dashing Major General Earl Van Dorn, is shown here in an unpublished portrait. He expected the Arkansas to come and redeem the city, and he was not disappointed. (TU)

With Vicksburg secure, Van Dorn sent the Arkansas *downriver to cooperate with Breckinridge in the attack on Baton Rouge, the last real threat to Federal control of the lower Mississippi. Here the waterfront of Baton Rouge, with the state capitol to the right.* (LSU)

Brigadier General Halbert E. Paine commanded in Baton Rouge after Williams's death in battle, but refused to burn the city when ordered to do so by his superior, Butler. (LC)

Colonel Henry W. Allen was prominent in Breckinridge's attack on Baton Rouge until his leg was shattered by a bullet. He was crippled for the rest of his life. (LSU)

"Dirty Bill" Porter took his Essex after the Arkansas, and later claimed credit for destroying the feared Confederate ironclad. (USAMHI)

To be sure, the Essex *was a formidable ironclad. She appears here off Baton Rouge (which she helped defend) in March 1863. The* Richmond *and* Mississippi *can be seen off her stern.* (USAMHI)

A. D. Lytle's 1861 image of Baton Rouge, before the destruction of the war came to visit. (LSU)

Breckinridge was initially successful, but later he had to abandon Baton Rouge, which showed the effects of the battle. Most of this damage was done by Federal gunboats, chiefly the Essex, *as they attempted to support Williams's beaten troops.* (LSU)

Church Street in Baton Rouge, during the Federal occupation. (USAMHI)

Another view of Church Street. These views were made by the Baton Rouge firm of W. D. McPherson and his partner Oliver, whose first name is unknown. (USAMHI)

The Louisiana State House, taken by McPherson & Oliver. (USAMHI)

The Louisiana State Penitentiary, captured by Baton Rouge's other outstanding artist, A. D. Lytle. (USAMHI)

L. I. Prince's image of the Baton Rouge Arsenal. (ISHL)

Part of the arsenal grounds, by McPherson & Oliver. (USAMHI)

The courthouse as seen by McPherson & Oliver. It was turned into a barracks and later a hospital by the occupying Federals. (USAMHI)

Artillery covered as protection against rain on the grounds of the Jackson Barracks. (USAMHI)

Everywhere in the South, when the Union soldiers came, the slaves flocked to their camps. Here the headquarters of the contraband camps in Baton Rouge. (USAMHI)

General Williams's headquarters before the Battle of Baton Rouge. (USAMHI)

Here Farragut's fleet stands off the city in 1862, on its way north to Vicksburg.
The stern of the USS Mississippi *is just visible to the left of the wood pile. The*
USS Richmond *is in the center, and the USS* Winona *is to the left of it.*
(USAMHI)

The Baton Rouge coaling yard, with the Winona *at right, and the* Richmond
next to it. The other vessels are part of the mortar fleet. (LC)

Often erroneously identified as the Hartford, *this image shows the USS* Portsmouth *on the right and an unidentified warship astern of it.* (LC)

The Portsmouth *again, with one of the mortar schooners in the distance.* (LC)

Two of Porter's mortar schooners lie side by side against the bank at Baton Rouge, while a gunboat, perhaps the Tyler *or* Conestoga, *lies to the left with a damaged stack.* (LSU)

A similar view, showing the ruins of a factory at the water's edge. (CWTI)

The Hartford *lies off the Main Street levee in this McPherson & Oliver image.*

The same view, perhaps from Lytle's window, shows troops disembarking from the Sallie Johnson *in the spring of 1863.* (USAMHI)

The wharf boat at Baton Rouge, the Natchez, *operated as a warehouse, hotel, and even offered "Fresh Lake Fish" to the soldiers.* (USAMHI)

The Natchez *about to unload supplies from its "warehouse."* (USAMHI)

In March 1863 McPherson & Oliver photographed the Empire Parish *off Baton Rouge. Nathaniel Banks made the steamer his headquarters for a time.* (LSU)

A. D. Lytle's photograph of Federals at leisure on the Mississippi, apparently a celebration. (LSU)

Blacks drafted into service by the Federals worked within sight of the State House. (LSU)

And all around the city the white tents of the soldiers sprouted like mushrooms. (LSU)

Regiments drilled and reviewed constantly on the old arsenal grounds. (LSU)

And in front of the courthouse. (LSU)

And in front of the Jackson Barracks. (LSU)

And in a score of camps on the fringes of the city. Clearly, the Union was here to stay. (LSU)

One of the final acts of 1862 along the river was the Federal capture of Donaldsonville, Louisiana, in October. Unlike Baton Rouge, Donaldsonville suffered considerably from the fighting. Much of the town lay in ruins. Homes and businesses were burned or battered to pieces. (ISHL)

The Catholic church, damaged. (ISHL)

Everywhere scenes of destruction. (ISHL)

But the flag went up and the rebuilding began. (ISHL)

And by the dawn of 1863, nothing was more commonplace along hundreds of miles of Mississippi banks than the sight of Federal soldiers encamped, as here at Morganza, Louisiana. The Mississippi was truly conquered. Only Port Hudson remained, and Vicksburg. (NHC)

Jackson in the Shenandoah

ROBERT G. TANNER

A peculiar professor and a valley whose name meant "Daughter of the Stars"

IN THE SPRING OF 1862, the Union planned two invasions of Virginia. One is well known: McClellan's seaborne thrust to the Peninsula and Richmond. Less understood is the invasion that was to precede the Peninsula campaign and which was designed to make McClellan's campaign possible. That was the invasion of the Shenandoah Valley.

The Valley lay like a dagger across much of Virginia, running generally north and south between the James and Potomac rivers and bounded by the Blue Ridge and Allegheny mountains. At its northernmost rim, formed by the Potomac, the Valley was actually many miles north of both Washington and Baltimore, so that when Union commanders spread their maps to study the state they were always reminded that the Valley lurked behind them. Confederate forces occupied the northern portion of the Valley, from which they were always in position to thrust across the Potomac. The Baltimore & Ohio Railroad, one of the Union's main east–west highways, was severed by the northern tip of the Valley, as was the Chesapeake & Ohio Canal. The economic impact of the loss of those links was considerable. But worst of all was the fact that Winchester, headquarters of Rebel forces in the Shenandoah, was a scant sixty

miles northwest of the Union capital. Geography alone dictated that Confederate forces in the northern Valley must be removed before McClellan launched his Peninsula invasion.

It was initially assumed that ejection of the Rebels posed no significant problem to McClellan's operation. Indeed this was looked upon as an invasion promising major returns for nominal risks. Confederate forces in Winchester were believed to be weak and dispirited after hard campaigning during a savage winter. Federal intelligence reports estimated that Union forces should encounter little difficulty in crossing the Potomac at Harpers Ferry and pushing southward as far as Winchester to destroy Confederate forces there. To ensure success, it was decided that the Federal invasion force would be bolstered by additional thousands of men from McClellan's main army. Once the entire northern Shenandoah had been liberated, garrison forces would be left behind, and the remainder of the invading host would shift east of the Blue Ridge Mountains to take up covering positions around Washington. By protecting Washington these forces would free McClellan to transfer the main Union Army to the doorstep of Richmond.

The two invasions seemed, on paper, to form a sound and perhaps even brilliant plan. And yet, if

The men who saved the Valley. Stonewall Jackson and his staff in 1862. The photograph of Jackson was made in Winchester; the composite including all of the portraits is the work of Richmond's distinguished portrait artists Vannerson & Jones. (VM)

Major General Nathaniel P. Banks, the perennial loser. Jackson outmaneuvered, out-thought, and outfought him in the Shenandoah, costing Banks 30 percent of his troops in casualties. (LOUIS A. WARREN LINCOLN LIBRARY)

the invasion of the Valley were disrupted or delayed, the shift of forces eastward would likewise be retarded, which could endanger the Peninsular campaign. Rarely in military history has a major military operation such as the Peninsular campaign depended so substantially for its success upon a seemingly minor and far-removed initial assault.

Rarely, too, has any important military operation been entrusted to one so utterly inexperienced in warfare as Major General Nathaniel P. Banks. Banks was a skilled politician, an ardent abolitionist, and an influential member of the Republican party; during only his second term in the United States Congress he had become Speaker of

the House of Representatives. When South Carolina seceded he was retiring from the governor's mansion of Massachusetts; he knew virtually nothing of war, but unemployed governors had a way of finding themselves generals in the Civil War, and Banks was slated to lead the Union's drive into the Shenandoah.

That invasion began in February of 1862, as Banks's forces, totaling almost 40,000 men, spilled across the Potomac River and descended upon Winchester. The Federals advanced deliberately, brushing aside what seemed to be only token opposition. On the afternoon of March 11, 1862, Federal divisions converged upon Winchester from two different directions and found the Rebels drawn up in battle formation. A firefight ensued, and there was prospect of battle in the morning, but dawn found the Rebels gone and Winchester fell without a shot.

Banks trailed the Confederates southward from Winchester but was unable to bring them to a fight. They seemed, to Banks, to be running—just as had been anticipated. Within ten days the Rebels had moved far to the south, and Union forces were regrouping around Winchester. Thousands of Federals were already moving east of the Blue Ridge to take up their assigned positions around Washington. Banks even left the Shenandoah for a rest, a rest which was interrupted when, on the evening of March 23, 1862, the telegraph from the Valley began to crackle.

OPPOSING BANKS in the Shenandoah was the Confederate Valley Army, a force of perhaps 4,500 men rostered into three tiny infantry brigades, six small artillery batteries, and 600 poorly disciplined but splendidly mounted cavalrymen led by Colonel Turner Ashby. The Valley Army was commanded by Major General Thomas J. "Stonewall" Jackson, a West Pointer, retired United States Army Major, and former physics professor at Virginia Military Institute. Jackson was virtually unknown at this point of the war. Except for one brief hour of glory at the First Battle of Bull Run, he had contributed little to the Confederate struggle save a ruthless discipline of his men and a winter campaign in the Alleghenies that had killed or sickened hundreds of them.

But Jackson was full of fight, and that resolve was well adapted to his instructions. His task in the

Valley was to keep as many Federal soldiers pinned down there and as far away from McClellan as he could. It was the perfect mission for this fiercely stubborn man. Although outnumbered ten to one he had clung to Winchester even as Banks uncoiled around him; Jackson had even planned an attack on Banks for the night of March 11. He was prevented from striking only when his staff relayed his orders erroneously and moved the army out of position. Jackson retreated, but he left behind his cavalry commander Ashby to cover the rear and to search for openings to attack.

Ashby found an opening as Banks redeployed his forces east of the Blue Ridge to cover Washington in accordance with the overall Union strategy. His mounted scouts detected this eastward shift and relayed word to Jackson. Within hours, Jackson was pushing northward toward Winchester with the bulk of the Valley Army. On March 23, as Banks was reaching Washington for his rest, Jackson was nearing Kernstown, a hamlet three miles south of Winchester. His rapid march had left his troops exhausted and his ranks thinned by straggling; nevertheless, Jackson threw his men into the attack.

What followed was a confused stand-up soldiers' fight called the Battle of Kernstown. The Confederates made good initial headway, then were slowed by unexpected Federal strength. One Confederate wrote his father after the battle, "The crack of rifles and the whistling of balls soon told us what we must expect. Soon volleys of musketry seemed to shake the hills." When one of Jackson's aides reported sighting increasing Federal numbers, the General replied tersely, "Say nothing about it. We are in for it."

Jackson had blundered into at least 10,000 Federal troops under Brigadier General James Shields. Shields had kept most of his division hidden well enough to fool Ashby's scouts, and then fed them skillfully into the battle. His numbers allowed him to overlap the smaller Southern army on either flank, and by nightfall the Confederates were driven from the field in nearly total rout.

So the Battle of Kernstown ended as a Southern defeat—but a defeat which actually proved something of a victory. General Shields was impressed by Jackson's hard fighting; he believed that the Confederates had numbered at least 11,000 men who were the "very flower of the Southern Army."

Charlestown, Virginia, in 1862. Here and in the vicinity, the Federals who would face Jackson wintered and readied for the Valley campaign. (USAMHI)

The headquarters of Brigadier General Alpheus S. Williams, who commanded
a brigade under Banks in the Valley campaign, taken at Darnestown,
Maryland. (USAMHI)

Shields called for help from Northern forces moving east of the Blue Ridge after the battle; one large division was diverted back to the Valley at once. Shields's reports that the flower of the Southern army had emerged in the northern Shenandoah canceled plans for any further redeployment of Union forces from that area to Washington. Instead, the Union's invasion of the Valley had to begin anew.

Banks returned to the Shenandoah to handle operations there. His army was built up again to 25,000 men and he was directed to drive the Rebels as far south as Staunton. He would be assisted by Federal forces west of the Valley in the Alleghenies. Thus, Kernstown lured the Union to undertake an extended Shenandoah invasion. McClellan henceforth would be operating on one side of Virginia while Banks campaigned on the other; instead of one invasion of Virginia followed by another, the Union was now engaged in a dangerous two-pronged invasion. And every man who was in the Valley would be one man less for McClellan.

Confederate losses at Kernstown totaled almost 25 percent of those engaged; Jackson could not risk battle again for a month. During those weeks, while Federal forces were built up against him, he rebuilt his own battered army. Through March and April he retreated slowly southward up the Valley while he recruited, reorganized, and made his army ready for maneuvers.

In normal usage, because the top of a map represents the northernmost portion of the area depicted, to go *up* is to go *north* and, conversely, to go *down* is to go *south*. The idiom of the Valley is exactly the opposite because its streams drain generally northward and water routes were the principal early means of transportation. To go *down* the Valley is thus to go *northward* and, conversely, to go *up* is to go *southward*. The Shenandoah's *northern* region is the *lower* Valley, and the *southern* region is the *upper* Valley.

Before recounting these movements, a glance at the Shenandoah is essential. Up and down the middle of the region runs the great Valley Pike, a macadamized road which was one of the best highways of its time. Other roads in the area tended to be abysmal, so the principal towns clustered along the pike. From Martinsburg and Winchester in the north, the pike passed through Strasburg, New Market, Harrisonburg, and Staunton in the lower —northern—Valley. Staunton, which linked also with the eastern part of the state by the Virginia Central Railroad, served as Jackson's base of supplies. Another salient feature of the Valley is the great Massanutten Mountain. This is actually an interlocking system of ridges which rises precipitously just east of Strasburg and runs up the Valley for fifty miles. For this distance the Shenandoah is actually two valleys, the Luray Valley between the Massanutten and the Blue Ridge, and the Shenandoah proper between the Massanutten and the Alleghenies. There is only one pass through this tangled green wall, a winding and difficult road between New Market, in the Shenandoah, and the village of Luray, in the Luray Valley. From Luray a passable road ran northward to the little town of Front Royal and southward to the village of Port Republic. In the next few weeks Jackson would fight battles at both ends of that road.

While retreating southward after Kernstown, Jackson had not forgotten his primary mission of keeping Federal forces occupied in the Valley. Nevertheless, sheer Union numbers eventually forced Jackson to almost abandon the Shenandoah. By the end of April he had moved into Swift Run Gap, where he completed the reorganization of the Valley Army. He also received a major reinforcement from east of the Blue Ridge. This was the division of Major General Richard S. Ewell, a fine body of some 8,000 well-trained and well-equipped infantry. At the end of April Jackson and Ewell were concentrated within supporting range of each other in the vicinity of Swift Run Gap; their combined forces totaled 14,000 men.

The situation confronting Jackson was complex. Staunton, his base of operations, was threatened from two directions. Union Major General John C. Frémont—the "Pathfinder" of America's westward expansion to California—was approaching Staunton from the Alleghenies with an army of 10,000 to 15,000 men. His advance guard, under Brigadier General R. H. Milroy, was pressing forward vigorously against scattered Confederate

Camps of men of Banks's command at Darnestown. (KA)

strength. Banks, with 25,000 men, was located in Harrisonburg and threatened Staunton from the north. In simplest terms, Jackson's dilemma was how to keep Staunton secure and Fremont and Banks apart but still pinned down in the Valley. The resolution of that dilemma came through a series of dazzling marches and battles rarely equaled in military history.

On April 30, 1862, Jackson slipped out of his camps in Swift Run Gap and headed for Staunton. Ewell's division came across the Blue Ridge and occupied Jackson's camp, attempting thereby to conceal from Banks the start of a Confederate offensive. Winding in and out of the Blue Ridge, Jackson reached Staunton by May 3 with 6,000 men and then plunged westward into the Alleghenies. He soon linked up with the Confederate forces there and drove Frémont's vanguard back.

On May 8 Milroy turned to fight near the little mountain town of McDowell. Like Kernstown, the Battle of McDowell was a stand-up soldiers' fight. The mountainous terrain made it impossible to give much direction to the fighting, which broke into small groups of men banging away desperately at each other. Jackson managed to seize the high ground overlooking the Federal camp, and this proved decisive. Though the Rebels suffered heavier casualties than the attacking Federals, they repulsed all attacks, and the next morning found the Union retreat accelerating.

Movement now exploded all around the Valley. Jackson pursued Milroy through the Alleghenies for several days. Banks abandoned Harrisonburg and retreated northward to Strasburg, a signal that the Union again had decided that the Shenandoah invasion was over. Due to Jackson's earlier with-

Here in Williamsport, Maryland, the Federals also awaited the order to march south. No one yet knew much about this fellow Jackson. (USAMHI)

The men of the 13th Massachusetts shown here at Williamsport soon had to leave the comfort of their winter quarters. (USAMHI)

drawal to Swift Run Gap, the Union high command had decided the Shenandoah was secure and Banks could retire to defensive positions along its northern borders and dispatch one division out of the Valley. Unlike the situation in March, however, Banks's redeployment this time was not merely defensive. Instead, Banks was to send Shields's division to Fredericksburg to join forces assembling there which were, in turn, to march south and link up with McClellan outside Richmond. The first step in achieving this redeployment was Banks's withdrawal to Strasburg.

The race began. Jackson hustled his troops back down into the Shenandoah and surged northward after Banks. The movements were rapid; marches of twenty miles a day were typical. The movements were also secret. Jackson had a mania for secrecy and told his subordinates—and his superiors—almost nothing of his location and intentions. His army seemed to simply drop from sight.

That Jackson disappeared during much of the Valley Campaign was true in one literal sense. His movements were such that there is almost no pictorial record of them. Burdened with unwieldy and very heavy equipment, photographers of the day needed a more stationary subject than Jackson's army to bring their talents into play. He simply moved too fast for them to arrive in time to take photographs of his operations. Such pictures as we have are of battlefields and not of the actual battles or marches, with the result that what we know of this campaign comes not from the camera but from the written word.

During May 1862, those words grew increasingly fatigued. "We are very wearied by the march, in fact, virtually worn down. A night's rest appears to do us no good—just as sleepy and languid in the morning as when we sleep in the evening," one Rebel recorded in his diary. Those who had started from Swift Run Gap with Jackson on

The surgeons shown here before their quarters in Williamsport would have plenty of work, thanks to Jackson. (USAMHI)

A brigade headquarters in Banks's command at Martinsburg, Virginia, in March 1862. (USAMHI)

Officers of the 2nd Massachusetts in 1861. They and their regiment would feel the full sting of Confederate might in the Shenandoah. (USAMHI)

the last day of April had marched more than 250 miles, most of the way across mountains and over horrible roads. But by force of will and much hard work the Valley Army kept coming. Jackson passed through Massanutten Gap with his forces and those he had collected in the Alleghenies and united around Luray with Ewell's division. He thus assembled all of the Confederates in the Shenandoah, perhaps 17,000 men and 50 cannons. Without a day's rest he turned northward on May 22 and marched to within 10 miles of Front Royal. There would be battle in the morning.

ON THE MORNING of May 23, Banks's forces in the Valley were concentrated in two small bodies: 8,000 men at Strasburg, with 1,000 men twelve miles east in Front Royal. Banks's remaining strength was spread along the Manassas Gap Railroad east of the Blue Ridge and beyond supporting distance. Shields's division had completed its shift to Fredericksburg, where it was resting for the march southward to attack Richmond. The Shenandoah had supposedly been secured, a redeployment of forces out of the Valley had been completed, and all available Federal forces were prepared to move on to Richmond. As had happened after Kernstown, however, Union plans were disarranged.

Around midday on the twenty-third, Jackson's 17,000 men engulfed the Union garrison at Front Royal, comprised principally of the 1st Maryland Infantry. As it happened Jackson also had a regiment recruited in Maryland, and he used it as his shock troops. The Marylanders squared off in a brief but fierce skirmish, interrupted by arrival of a freight train that chugged into town between the opposing battle lines. The Rebels swept up the train, the town, and almost one thousand prisoners. Only a few dozen Federals escaped to bring Banks word of the onslaught.

Banks reacted to the situation poorly, first underestimating and then exaggerating Southern strength. His subordinates urged him to evacuate Strasburg at once, but he refused to do so until midmorning of the next day. He then ordered an immediate retreat, with the result that a near frantic collection of wagon trains, cavalry columns, and infantry poured down the pike for Winchester. The column was subjected to repeated Confederate cavalry raids and occasional shellings. Around Middletown the Federal column was severed, and hundreds of Yankees fled to the south and then the west as Rebels fanned out after them.

Banks, meanwhile, reached Winchester by evening with the bulk of his forces. He put them into line of battle on the hills south of Winchester and

Colonel John White Geary of the 28th Pennsylvania in an unpublished portrait by McAllister of Philadelphia. Formerly the first mayor of San Francisco and the governor of Kansas Territory, he was, like Banks, a politician turned commander. Unlike Banks, he proved to be a man of genuine military talent. In March 1862 he captured Leesburg before the campaign had fairly begun. (CWTI)

warehouses of urgently needed medical stores, herds of cattle, and tons of other stores had been captured from Strasburg to the Potomac. Confederates gloated that the Federal rout was more complete than that at Manassas; total Southern casualties from Front Royal to Winchester were less than four hundred killed and wounded. One Rebel veteran summarized this highlight of the war long after when he wrote, "We had no general engagement, and our loss was small; it being a kind of one-sided fight all the time. General Jackson 'got the drop' on them in the start, and kept it."

THE EFFECT of Jackson's onslaught was immediate. President Lincoln was seriously disturbed by events in the Shenandoah, and he responded with orders to capture or crush the Valley Army. Studying his map of Virginia, Lincoln noted that Jackson had moved dangerously north of both Frémont and the Union forces around Fredericksburg; the Rebels were, in fact, moving into a trap. Even as the Confederates were herding Banks out of the Shenandoah, Lincoln directed Frémont to drive into the Valley from the Alleghenies, while Shields was ordered to retrace the march he had just made and return to the Valley from the east with 20,000 men. Both halves of this pincer were to enter the Valley well south of Jackson so as to cut off his escape.

Lincoln's bold plan, which was, in effect, a third invasion of the Shenandoah, was purchased at the price of assistance to McClellan. With Shields leading 20,000 men back to the Valley, the remaining Union forces at Fredericksburg were too weak to lunge southward, which is just what Jackson desired. Jackson had fulfilled his mission to keep as many Federal troops as possible tied down in and around the Shenandoah. Overall, some 50,000 to 60,000 Federals across northern Virginia were concentrating on the Valley Army instead of Richmond.

Jackson, meanwhile, pushed northward to Harpers Ferry at the end of May and made a vigorous demonstration before a well-entrenched Union garrison hoping to multiply the shock value of his sudden appearance in the lower Valley. But his own situation was now critical. By May 30, Jackson learned he was almost surrounded by Federal columns from the west (Frémont), east (Shields), and north (Banks's reorganizing army

began to wire Washington frantically for reinforcements. But there was no time for help to arrive.

The Rebels hit again at first light on May 25, and Banks saw his army dissolve. Within two hours his brigades were swept from their positions in total rout. The Federal flight continued throughout the day, carrying them almost to the Potomac that night.

In two days of running battle, Banks had been swept out of the Valley. Three thousand Federals were prisoners. More than nine thousand rifles,

Harpers Ferry, Virginia, showing the remnant of the United States Arsenal.
Here Banks anchored his army at the outset of the campaign. (USAMHI)

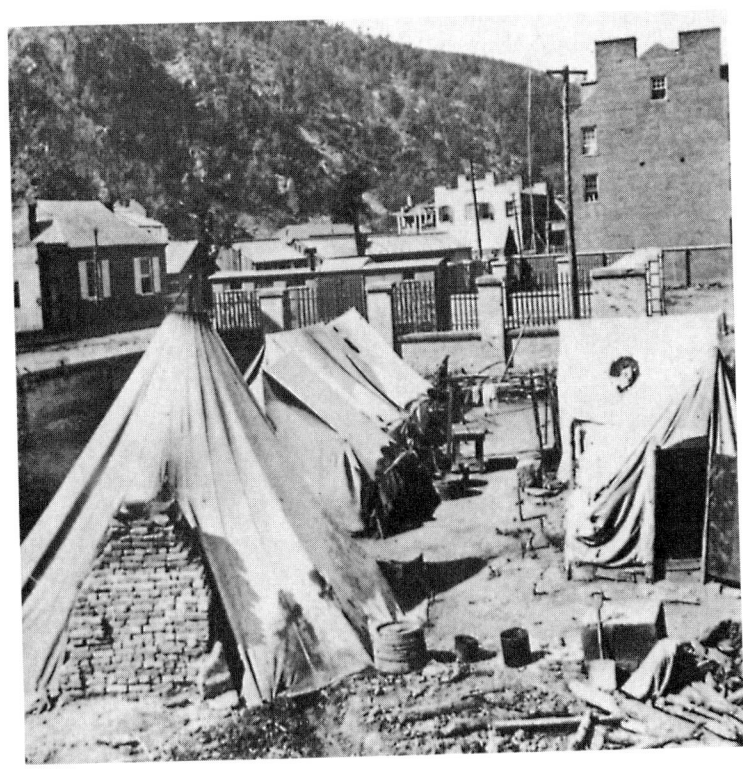

David B. Woodbury's October 1862
image of Federal troops camped on
ground which once held the armory
buildings. (USAMHI)

The charred remains of a canal boat and steam engine at Harpers Ferry, the scene of repeated destruction in 1862. (USAMHI)

and the garrison at Harpers Ferry). Jackson's response was calm and to the point: He ordered his men to turn around and march southward very fast. In two days of heroic effort he covered the fifty miles from Harpers Ferry to Strasburg with all his captured stores and prisoners. He collided with Frémont just outside of Strasburg and drove him back into the Alleghenies, clearing the way for the last of his stragglers to slip through the Union ring.

Throughout the first week of June, the Valley Army withdrew from Strasburg under terrific pressure. Frémont trailed the Rebels along the Valley Pike, while Shields pushed his divisions southward into the Luray Valley. Rain poured down in crackling streams. Units lost their wagon trains, officers lost their commands, regiments became intermingled, and confusion reached epidemic proportions. The courageous cavalry leader Turner Ashby was killed protecting the army's rear in a heavy skirmish. The retreat demanded the courage of a battle and was far more costly. The Valley Army had lost four hundred men fighting its way from Front Royal to Winchester; it lost thousands of stragglers and sick on this retreat. One Rebel wrote, "I never saw a Brigade so completely bro-

ken down and unfitted for service as our Brigade. . . . I am satisfied that the Brigade has lost at least 1,000 men broken down, left on the way and captured."

By June 7, Jackson had turned southeastward from Harrisonburg to slip around the Massanutten to the village of Port Republic. There he would stand between Frémont and Shields, and around this village were to occur scenes as thrilling as any of the Valley Campaign.

These events erupted on the morning of June 8, as a surprise Union cavalry raid stormed into Port Republic and almost captured Jackson and most of his staff. Other Union cavalrymen probed to within a few hundred yards of the huge Confederate wagon train. A courageous stand by a dozen sentries stalled the Union raiders just long enough to allow Jackson to move in reinforcements and eject them.

As if in echo, Frémont's guns began to pound Confederate positions west of Port Republic. Jackson feared that he was about to be struck from two sides at once and built up his positions around the village; he left the handling of Frémont to Ewell's division. Ewell did his job well. In what has be-

*Past this sawmill at Kernstown, Jackson advanced against Shields in the Battle
of Kernstown, first engagement of the campaign. An 1885 photograph.*
(USAMHI)

*Colonel John Echols was severely wounded leading
his 27th Virginia at Kernstown. Three weeks later
he was promoted brigadier, and would
become—though unsung—one of the finest
subordinates in the army. At 6 feet, 4 inches, and
weighing 260 pounds, he was a wonderful target.*
(USAMHI)

Jackson, with something of an affinity for stone walls, formed his line of battle on the near side of this one at Kernstown. (USAMHI)

Captain Pinckney D. Bowles led a company of the 4th Alabama in Jackson's army. Like many junior officers of talent, he gained from the ravages of the bullet, which gave him plenty of opportunity for advancement. He finished the war an unconfirmed brigadier. (USAMHI)

come known as the Battle of Cross Keys, Ewell sparred with Frémont throughout the day, repulsing every Union attack and driving the Federals back several miles by nightfall. During the day Shields's advanced guards showed themselves briefly to the east of Port Republic but made no advance.

Emboldened by Frémont's weak showing, Jackson planned the most ambitious battle of the campaign for the next morning. He would maneuver all available men across the two small rivers that joined around Port Republic to crush Shields's advance guard east of those streams, then return to rout Frémont. His timetable allowed only four hours to thrash Shields before he would have to rejoin the thin covering force he would leave behind to bluff Frémont. There was equally little time to prepare the attack; Jackson was able to span the river obstacles with only primitive temporary bridges, and this was to cost more valuable time.

Before dawn on June 9, Jackson's maneuver brigades were on the march, and things promptly began to go wrong. Delays were encountered crossing Jackson's hastily erected bridges, batteries came up without ammunition, and the Confederate attack began piecemeal about 7:00 A.M. It stalled at once and during the next several hours Jackson was outnumbered and on the defensive. Shields's men, recalling Kernstown, attacked furiously and at one point shattered the main Southern line. The dramatic arrival of Ewell with several fresh regiments reversed the flight, but more anxious minutes passed before Jackson finally assembled an overwhelming numerical superiority and drove Shields's forces back handsomely. Kernstown was revenged by the Battle of Port Republic but Confederate losses were severe, and Jackson abandoned any further hope of attacking Frémont. Instead, he coiled his forces along the slopes of the Blue Ridge out of enemy reach. He need not have worried, for both Frémont and Shields retreated the next day.

The Valley campaign comes to an end with those retreats. Jackson made preparations to join Lee around Richmond as soon as he learned of the enemy withdrawals. As he laid his plans, Jackson found himself something of a hero of the South. Since leaving Swift Run Gap on April 30, he had marched almost four hundred miles. He had inflicted approximately seven thousand casualties

It seemed almost unfair that with so much Confederate talent in the Shenandoah, the Federals enjoyed so little. A case in point is Brigadier General Robert H. Milroy. In 1863 he had almost an entire brigade captured in the Shenandoah, and he did little better against Jackson in the earlier campaign. (USAMHI)

on the Union, half of them prisoners, and captured enormous quantities of supplies. His own losses had been less than half of those of the enemy, light losses indeed when compared to the ghastly casualty lists from other encounters of this war. Most important of all, the Valley Army's weeks of marching had been weeks of victory which stalled the Union drive on Richmond. Jackson's successes reinspired a South parched for victory. Robert E. Lee expressed the feelings of the Confederacy when he wrote to Jackson, "Your successes have been the cause of the liveliest joy in this army as well as in the country."

A few days after Jackson's victory at Front Royal, a photographer caught these Confederate prisoners awaiting transport to prison. They keep a respectful distance from their guards and their stacked arms. (LC)

Brigadier General Alpheus S. Williams advanced from brigade to division command at the Battle of Winchester. Few Federals won laurels there. (P-M)

A street in Winchester showing Taylor's Hotel, the building with the columns, where Federal officers made their headquarters in April before the battle. Winchester changed hands in this war fifty-two times. (USAMHI)

Main Street in Winchester, probably taken after the war. Winchester saw more marching armies than any other town in the war. (USAMHI)

Brigadier General William B. Taliaferro, seated left, commanded a brigade for
Jackson. He had been in command of the Virginia Militia, as shown here, when
it mustered to put down John Brown's attack on Harpers Ferry. (MUSEUM OF
THE CONFEDERACY, RICHMOND)

Francis T. Nichols led the 8th Louisiana at Winchester, and there took a wound which cost him his left arm. Promoted to brigadier—as shown here—a few months later, he later lost a foot at Chancellorsville. (NYHS)

A ford on the Shenandoah River, crossed and recrossed by Jackson many times in the course of his campaign. (USAMHI)

A postwar view of the Massanutten Mountain, key to Jackson's brilliant success in the Shenandoah. (USAMHI)

Jackson's brilliant cavalry leader, Brigadier General Turner Ashby, made major contributions to the defense of the Valley. It cost him his life on June 6, 1862, just two weeks after he received his general's stars. The only known photograph of him in uniform is this one, taken in death. (CHS)

Colonel Beverly Robertson succeeded to command of Ashby's cavalry at his death, and three days later he was made a brigadier. (VM)

Brigadier General John P. Hatch commanded Banks's cavalry in the futile attempt to contain Ashby. Shown here in an 1865 portrait made in Charleston, South Carolina, he failed to distinguish himself. (USAMHI)

The battlefield at Cross Keys. (USAMHI)

The ever-present Brigadier General Louis Blenker had to make a torturous march with his division in March 1862, going from McClellan's army to join the Federals in the Valley. It took six weeks and the War Department forgot to supply him with anything. Cross Keys was his last battle. He fell from his horse during the war, and in October 1863 he died from the effects of the fall. (P-M)

Colonel Wladimir Krzyzanowski, a Pole by birth, led the 58th New York at Cross Keys. "Kriz" rose to brigade command within a year. (P-M)

Brigadier General George H. Steuart, called "Maryland Steuart," thanks to his birthplace, led a Virginia brigade and was badly wounded at Cross Keys. At Winchester he had declined to obey an order from Jackson because it did not come through the proper chain of command, and this may have cost the Confederates the chance to entirely destroy the Federals. (SOUTHERN HISTORICAL COLLECTION, THE UNIVERSITY OF NORTH CAROLINA AT CHAPEL HILL)

*Colonel Thomas T. Munford led the 2nd Virginia
Cavalry under Ashby and at Cross Keys. Like
many of these Virginians, Munford found that the
dashing Valley service appealed to the romantic in
him.* (CWTI)

*Brigadier General Arnold Elzey distinguished
himself and his brigade at Port Republic. His horse
was killed under him and he took a painful wound
in the head.* (VM)

Port Republic, in a photograph taken fifty years after the battle in which Jackson effectively completed the Valley campaign in victory. (USAMHI)

The Second Bull Run

DAVID LINDSEY

To Manassas once again, another battle, another defeat

AS UNION Major General George B. McClellan's Peninsular campaign sputtered out in the heavy fighting of the Seven Days Battles, the opposing armies drew apart. McClellan backed off his 100,000-man Army of the Potomac to a new base at Harrison's Landing on the James River, where Federal Navy control assured protection, supplies, and future mobility. The newly named commander of the 75,000-man Confederate Army, General Robert E. Lee, had succeeded in beating back the Union drive on Richmond. Both sides now paused, catching their breath, pondering how to proceed next.

From Washington a disappointed President Abraham Lincoln came in person to McClellan's headquarters to assess the situation. When McClellan handed him a lengthy note giving blunt advice on matters of policy, Lincoln kept his own counsel, while mulling over what to do with his balky general and the well-trained, well-equipped army. In a move to pump new blood and spirit into the eastern theater command, Lincoln now brought bewhiskered Major General John Pope from the west to command a newly organized Army of Virginia that combined the forces of Major Generals Nathaniel Banks, John Frémont, and Irvin McDowell. Pope's credits included some earlier victories in the west, strong antislavery views, and an aggressive attitude toward the enemy. He talked too much and had criticized McClellan's "indisposition to active movements." Also from the west came Major General Henry W. Halleck, clean-shaven and bug-eyed, whose large forehead inspired his nickname "Old Brains," to be installed as General-in-Chief of all Union armies.

Where McClellan fitted in the new command picture remained undetermined by Washington. Clearly "Little Mac" was extremely popular with his soldiers, one of whom wrote, "the real man of the army is Little Mac. No general could ask for greater love and more unbounded confidence than he receives from his men. . . . everywhere among his boys, as he calls them, . . . he is received with enthusiasm." For himself, McClellan says of his plans for midsummer 1862, "I would have crossed to the south bank" of the James River and seized Petersburg from which "I would have operated against Richmond and its communications from the west, having already gained those from the south." Perhaps. McClellan wrote this years later, knowing with hindsight that General U. S. Grant used precisely that approach in 1864–65. At least one of his soldiers thought it possible, agreeing with McClellan that the administration had not given adequate support, noting, "We want 300,000 men raised and sent down here immediately. We've been fooling about this thing long enough. . . . The army and the people demand such a vigorous prosecution of the war as shall give some hope of ending it."

But the Lincoln Administration decided otherwise by early August. On August 3 Halleck ordered McClellan "to withdraw your army from the Peninsula to Aquia Creek" on the Potomac, some thirty miles south of Washington. McClellan protested, arguing, "Here is the true defense of Washington; it is here on the banks of the James that the fate of the Union should be decided." But Halleck insisted McClellan get moving. But "Little Mac" as always moved with caution, sending first the wounded, followed by the able-bodied troops, on transports down the James, up Chesapeake Bay and the Potomac to Aquia Creek and Alexandria. All of this took time—too much time as it turned out.

During July Lee watched intently from Richmond seeking to fathom the next Federal move. He learned of Pope's taking command of the new

Then once again McDowell marched south into Virginia's heartland, past scenes remembered from his campaign of the year before, scenes like Falls Church. (USAMHI)

Octagon House in Arlington, Virginia, headquarters for Major General Irvin McDowell in the early summer of 1862, when Lincoln held his corps back from McClellan on the Peninsula. (USAMHI)

40,000-man Army of Virginia. If Pope should begin moving south toward Richmond and McClellan should punch again at Richmond from the east, the combined 140,000 Union force would put Lee in deep trouble. To remain inactive was to risk envelopment. Weighing the risks carefully, Lee decided on July 13 to move boldly by sending Major General Thomas J. "Stonewall" Jackson with 12,000 troops sixty miles northwest out of Richmond to Gordonsville. Here where the Virginia Central Railroad crossed the Orange & Alexandria Railroad was the critical point the Confederates had to hold—whether Pope decided to move south or Lee decided to move out from Richmond.

When the Federal command made no immediate response, Lee then sent Major General A. P. Hill's "light division" of 12,000 men forward to join Jackson, saying, "I want Pope to be suppressed." When Jackson probed forward north of the Rapidan he found a small advance Union force of about 8,000 men under Banks drawn up along a small stream near Cedar Mountain. Characteristically, on August 9 Jackson attacked immediately—probably too soon, since he had only about half his men in position. Banks's troops fought back fiercely, repulsing the first Confederate assaults and pummeling the celebrated Stonewall

Brigade (that had won Jackson his nickname at Bull Run a year earlier). But Jackson succeeded in rallying his men, hurried A. P. Hill's division into action, and drove the Federals from the field. After a brief pursuit Jackson withdrew south of the Rapidan.

In itself Cedar Mountain meant little. But overall it meant the military initiative was shifting away from the Federals, who only two months earlier were threatening Richmond. Now Lee, assuming the offensive, would step up pressure on Pope's army. On August 13, learning that McClellan's army was starting to embark from its James River position, he ordered Major General James Longstreet with 25,000 men forward to Gordonsville. Two days later he left some 25,000 soldiers to protect Richmond and he himself moved out to lead the Army of Northern Virginia in person.

General John Pope from his Culpeper headquarters fifteen miles north of the Rapidan River surveyed the military situation. Earlier on arriving from the west, he had issued some bombastic proclamations urging his army to fight tenaciously, not show their backs to the enemy, and not retreat. At mid-August Pope's command of about 55,000 men (including 8,000 of General Ambrose E. Burn-side's corps led by Major General Jesse Reno) were encamped north of the Rapidan with the Orange & Alexandria Railroad, their main supply route, running southwest from Alexandria some sixty miles distant. Pope was following Halleck's instructions to remain there until joined by the Army of the Potomac. Some 70,000 to 100,000 of McClellan's troops, withdrawing from the Peninsula via the Potomac and Aquia Creek, were expected shortly to line up alongside Pope's position. At that point, Pope thought, Halleck would come from Washington and take personal command in the field.

Seeking the weakness in Pope's position north of the Rapidan, with the Rappahannock in his rear, Lee calculated that fast-moving Confederate cavalry could knife swiftly across the Rapidan, drive north, and destroy the rail bridge over the Rappahannock, thus cutting Pope's supply line. But, Lee knew, the strike would have to be lightning fast because McClellan's troops would be reaching Pope within about ten days. On August 18 the Confederates tried it, but signals got crossed. Part of the cavalry missed an assignment. A river crossing was left unguarded, and a Federal patrol in a surprise raid south of the river just missed capturing Gen-

Photographer Timothy O'Sullivan's wagon on the road leading into Culpeper.
(USAMHI)

Culpeper's important railroad depot on the Orange & Alexandria. (USAMHI)

eral "Jeb" Stuart but did get his famous plumed hat and silk-lined robe. More important they seized a junior officer carrying Lee's orders. As a result Pope, now aware of Lee's strategy, pulled his troops back to the north bank of the Rappahannock and set strong units at each of the river's fords.

During the intermittent rains of the next few days Lee probed for a crossing of the Rappahannock and pushed farther upstream. Stuart's cavalry crossed after dark on August 22, snaked swiftly through the foothills, and then swinging eastward pounced on Pope's headquarters at Catlett's Station on the Orange & Alexandria Railroad. There Stuart seized a stack of Pope's military papers including an important dispatch book, took personal revenge for the loss of his plumed hat by carrying off Pope's uniform coat, and after trying in vain to fire the rain-soaked rail bridge, withdrew to the Confederate lines.

As the days passed, Lee saw his chance of a quick victory diminishing. From Pope's papers he learned that McClellan's V Corps under Major General Fitz John Porter, having landed at Aquia Creek, was marching to join Pope on the upper Rappahannock. Major General Samuel P. Heintzelman's III Corps was scheduled to follow shortly. Lee figured Pope had 70,000 troops within call on August 25 with more on the way. Already outnumbered, Lee would find attack futile if he postponed it even a few days. In fact, it was perhaps already too late for a pitched battle, unless Pope could be maneuvered off balance. Lee was willing to give it a try.

On August 25 Lee sent Jackson with 23,000 "foot cavalry" scurrying out on a long sweep west and north. This division of the army in the immediate presence of the enemy, contrary to all conventional military wisdom, posed a serious military risk. Had Pope pulled all his units together and

Inside Culpeper McDowell's soldiers made themselves comfortable for what they hoped might be a long stay. (USAMHI)

concentrated on Lee's force remaining south of the Rappahannock, the Rebels might have been badly whipped. But Lee took the gamble, counting on Pope not to move quickly while Jackson circled behind the Bull Run mountains out of sight and around Pope's right flank. If all went well, Jackson would swing in behind and cut Pope's supply and communication lines.

Shedding knapsacks and surplus paraphernalia, Jackson's men sliced swiftly north to Salem Village on the west side of the mountains, then turned east through Thoroughfare Gap in the Bull Run mountains. Having covered a remarkable thirty miles by evening of the first day's march, Jackson proudly watching his columns file forward was heard to murmur, "Who could fail to win battles with such men as these?" The gap, unguarded by Federal troops, was readily negotiated. From its eastern summit the Confederates surveyed the rolling farmland interspersed with woods stretching eastward, with Gainesville lying directly east on the main turnpike that ran northeast to Centreville and southwest to Warrenton. No Federal forces lay in sight on that road. Ten miles beyond lay the Orange & Alexandria rail line, Pope's supply artery and Jackson's target. Pouring out of the mountains, Jackson's troops pushed on swiftly and seized Bristoe Station by dusk on August 26. Capturing most of the astonished garrison, they destroyed the rail bridge over Broad Run, tore up the tracks, cut the telegraph wires, and wrecked two trains. But two trains escaped, one going north to Alexandria, the other south to Warrenton to spread the alarm. Jackson's two forward regiments captured Ma-

But they would not be there long. In August their wagons loaded to roll toward the enemy. (USAMHI)

nassas Junction by midnight, and he followed with the rest of his force by morning of August 27.

Manassas Junction, as the main Union supply depot, offered a rich harvest to the tired and hungry Rebels. Here were tons of supplies, hundreds of loaded freight cars, streets of bulging warehouses, fields filled with barrels, boxes, and piles of munitions. After the captured whiskey was carefully destroyed, Jackson's famished men—who had been on short rations for days—tore into the rich stores of food. An enormous picnic resulted as men gorged themselves not only on staples of bread, salt meat, and coffee, but also on canned lobster, oysters, boned turkey, pies, and other delicacies. Shoes, trousers, shirts, toothbrushes, combs, and more were appropriated. The revelry continued all through the day of August 27. Before the bloated

army marched that evening, torches were applied to the remaining, unconsumed supplies and munitions, which burned and exploded like fireworks all night.

Meanwhile General Pope with his troops on the north side of the Rappahannock found himself in a position that was both a risk and a challenge—it offered a good opportunity if Pope could seize it, but unless he managed well he would be in increasing danger. Of the three corps comprising his army at the outset, Pope saw McDowell's corps as the only one worth much. Major General Franz Sigel, he thought, was incompetent. Banks's corps, badly mauled at Cedar Mountain, with only 5,000 survivors, was of reduced effectiveness. From McClellan's army, one-armed Major General Phil Kearny brought a reliable division of Heintzelman's corps.

There was a new commander in Virginia, Major General John Pope, a hero from the western campaigns who promised he would lead this army to victory. He led the army first toward Cedar Mountain. Pope here appears as a brigadier. (LC)

Other troops were reported to Pope as at hand or nearby—Heintzelman's other division under Joe Hooker, Reno with most of Burnside's men, and John Reynolds's division from Porter's corps. The rest of Porter's command was reported moving to join Pope. This gave Pope over 70,000 men in the vicinity. If coordinated they could throw overwhelming power against Jackson. At the least they could plug Thoroughfare Gap and thereby prevent Lee and Longstreet's combined force of 30,000 men from using that route to come to Jackson's support. But to do these things, Pope would have

to get a good many separate units to do some fast marching under coordinated direction in conditions that would change as the movements of Jackson and Lee changed. Since Pope's wire dispatches to Washington were not reaching Halleck because Jackson had cut the telegraph, Washington had only a faint idea of what was happening in the countryside beyond Manassas Junction. Messages carried by mounted couriers were uncertain. Many slips were possible—Pope could misread enemy movements, his orders to subordinates could be misinterpreted or poorly obeyed, delay and confusion could set in. If any of these things occurred, Lee's gamble would pay off.

From John Buford's effective cavalry Pope learned of Jackson's march west of the mountains —but at first Pope somehow concluded that Jackson was heading for the Shenandoah Valley. Even when he discovered that Jackson's army was coming east through Thoroughfare Gap, Pope seemed unable to deal effectively with the information. Not that Pope was slow or lazy. If nothing else, he was a man of vigor. His response was understandably vigorous. When word reached him of Jackson's sacking of Manassas, Pope pulled his troops back from the Rappahannock to positions running roughly from Gainesville about five miles east of Thoroughfare Gap on the Alexandria–Warrenton turnpike to Warrenton Junction about twenty miles south on the Orange & Alexandria Railroad. This was a well-conceived move.

From Gainesville Pope sent James B. Ricketts's division of McDowell's corps west to cork the bottleneck at Thoroughfare Gap. But from this point forward Pope dispatched curious orders that were often incomprehensible or contradictory or self-canceling. Porter's corps, for example, was marched at top speed for ten miles under a broiling August sun only to be rushed back at the same fervid pace to the point it came from. Heintzelman's III Corps tramped eighteen miles to reach a point only three miles from where it started. Federal troops were being worn down by marching and countermarching on reduced rations, since the Manassas stores had been burned.

Pope pushed other Federal units forward to Manassas Junction to smash Jackson. There they found nothing but smoldering ruins. Leaving after dark the night before, Jackson had sent three columns forward—one across Bull Run and northwest toward Centreville, a second across Bull Run and northwest to Sudley Springs, the third up the west bank of Bull Run. Next day, August 28, he brought all three together near Groveton in a wooded area a short distance west of the Warrenton pike. Puzzled over the invisible Jackson, Pope concluded the enemy was heading north toward the Potomac and ordered troops forward to Centreville to head off such a move. But Jackson wasn't there either. Figuring Jackson was now desperately trying to escape, Pope determined to concentrate his forces on Jackson when he found him.

In making Jackson the sole target of his drive,

Pope somehow forgot about Lee and Longstreet. The Federal plug came uncorked from Thoroughfare Gap as Ricketts moved his men back from their forward position there. This was exactly the reverse of what was needed for a Union success. Ricketts should have been strengthened to thwart a juncture between Lee and Longstreet from coming through the pass and joining Jackson. Somehow Pope erroneously developed the notion that McDowell's unit, "ordered to interpose between" Jackson and the enemy's "main body . . . moving down through Thoroughfare Gap" had "completely accomplished" its mission by driv-

On August 9, 1862, the armies clashed at Cedar Mountain. That same day O'Sullivan caught this battery fording a tributary of the Rappahannock on its way to the fight. (USAMHI)

The battlefield at Cedar Mountain, taken a few days after the fight (NLM)

ing Longstreet "back to the west side" of the gap. This totally false impression led Pope into mistaken planning for the next day, August 28.

Arriving at Bristoe by dusk August 27, Pope convinced himself he had Jackson trapped. Out went orders to subordinates to march "at the very earliest blush of dawn" in order to concentrate forces between Gainesville and Manassas and "we shall bag the whole crowd. . . . Be expeditious, and the day is our own."

In pulling his forces away from Manassas Junction Jackson had ultimately chosen his position well. He brought his various columns together on the western edge of what had been the Bull Run battlefield of a year earlier, under the cover of a wooded area a short distance west of Groveton just off the Warrenton pike. His left was anchored on Bull Run at Sudley Springs, his right on a hill roughly two miles southwest toward Gainesville. His front was protected by a low wooded ridge and a steep embankment of an abandoned railroad line. Here he could rest his men concealed in the shade of the woods, but in a commanding position

difficult to assail and with a potential escape route via Aldie Gap in the mountains to his rear. And yet he was close enough for Lee and Longstreet to reach him when they passed through Thoroughfare Gap a dozen miles to the southwest. Here on August 28 Jackson waited in the woods and watched as units of McDowell's corps trudged along the pike to Centreville, past the Stone Bridge to Jackson's left.

Finally as evening approached Jackson determined to make Pope stand and fight rather than let him withdraw to a strong position on the Centreville side of Bull Run. The column of Rufus King's division approached along the pike in the late afternoon heat. "Stonewall" Jackson, after riding out in front of his hidden troops, eyed the Yankees through his glass, then wheeled, galloped back to the ridge, and barked an order. Confederate artillery batteries rolled out and began firing. From the woods Rebel troops charged "with a hoarse roar . . . like wild beasts at the scent of blood," red battle flags gleaming under the sinking sun. Forming the line of battle they started shooting.

On the Union side Brigadier General John Gibbon's four brigades took the initial shock of the enemy attack. Green, never under fire before, they should have panicked. Instead they wheeled about coolly into their own line of battle and stopped the Rebel attack. Joined by men from Abner Doubleday's brigade, 2,800 Federals faced nearly twice as many Confederates in one of "the hardest close-quarter fights of the whole war." The contending battle lines stood face to face "as if they were on parade awaiting inspection, and volleyed away at the murderous range of less than one hundred yards." For two solid hours the deadly firing continued until darkness closed in. By nine o'clock the lines drew apart. On both sides the losses had been staggering. Two of Jackson's generals, William Taliaferro and Richard Ewell, were carried from the field severely wounded. Gibbon's midwestern farm boys, already called the "Black Hat Brigade," won laurels that day and would soon be rightly known as the "Iron Brigade."

By nightfall August 28, Pope, now aware of Jackson's position, decided to destroy Jackson's force the next day. Again orders went to division commanders to move "at the earliest dawn." But as Pope moved his headquarters forward to a hill near the famous Stone House, well-remembered from the first Bull Run battle's intense fighting, he was still fuzzy on several crucial factors. For one, he did not know the current location of McDowell or that Ricketts had moved to Bristoe Station. He still held to his delusion that Lee and Longstreet had been repulsed at Thoroughfare Gap. In addition, his men, after much marching and little eating, were tired and sluggish.

From dawn on August 29 Federal artillery blasted away at Jackson's position in the woods just northwest of the Warrenton pike, while infantry units moved closer. Again, if Pope could get all his forces concentrated, he figured to outweigh Jackson's battered 20,000-man army by three to one. Chance for victory looked bright. Anxious to open the attack, Pope moved hastily while many of his units were still on the road and out of touch.

Cedar Mountain itself sits in the distance, seen here from the Union position.
(USAMHI)

Major General Nathaniel Banks. A failure in the campaign against Jackson in the Shenandoah that spring, he was defeated by Jackson again here at Cedar Mountain. (USAMHI)

After the artillery blasts drove in Confederate skirmishers, Sigel's 11,000 men were ordered to attack the center of Jackson's defense line. As a Confederate observer reported, "The Federals sprang forward with a long-drawn 'huzzah' ringing from their 10,000 throats. On they went until half the distance to the [railroad] cut and then the smoke, flash and roar of 4,000 well-aimed guns burst from the Confederate entrenchment, and a wild, reckless and terrifying Southern yell echoed and reechoed through the woodlands." Two more Yankee assaults were made on the center and repulsed.

The attack then shifted to Jackson's left where Pope sent Kearny and Hooker with 12,000 Army of the Potomac veterans aided by Reno's 8,000 seasoned veterans. But organization, timing, and coordination were lacking. Federal units went into action piecemeal, bit by bit, and the full effect of such a massive blow was lost. Besides, the Rebel

line here was defended by some of Jackson's best troops under A. P. Hill. The Confederate line bent and at one point snapped temporarily under the impact of six separate attacks, punctuated with vicious hand-to-hand bayonet fighting. Hill's ammunition supply was almost gone and his casualties were enormous, but he managed to hang on as dusk fell.

Meanwhile some 30,000 Union troops nearby had failed to get into action. These men under Porter and McDowell, moving from Manassas toward Gainesville to hit Jackson's right, sighted large clouds of dust ahead. Figuring that Confederate reinforcements were arriving, Porter and McDowell slowed, paused, and shifted course toward Groveton, beyond which fighting raged. Because of their slowness few of McDowell's and none of Porter's troops got into battle before the day's fighting ended. Porter would later be court-martialed and cashiered for holding back here.

Also sitting out the action of August 29 were Longstreet's 30,000 soldiers. They had emerged from Thoroughfare Gap early, marched forward, contacted Jackson's right by noon, and took position just south of the Warrenton pike by 3 P.M., where they blocked Porter's line of advance. Poised to attack the Federal left flank, Longstreet persuaded Lee to wait, arguing that his men needed rest after a long march and that delay might produce new Federal blunders. Toward evening Longstreet sent a reconnaissance unit forward on the pike only to clash with McDowell and to pull back to await the next morning. That night Lee reported to President Davis, "My desire has been to avoid a general engagement, being the weaker force, and by maneuvering to relieve a portion of the country."

That night at his headquarters on a hill close to the Stone House at the junction of the Warrenton pike and the Manassas–Sudley road, the husky Pope with the usual cigar in hand reviewed the day's action with some satisfaction. Jackson, as Pope saw it, was badly bruised, was cornered, and could be captured next day. Annoyed by Porter's failure to advance when ordered, he dismissed as nonsense Porter's claim that Longstreet barred his path with three times his numbers. Reporting optimistically, Pope told Halleck, "We fought a terrific battle . . . which lasted with continuous fury from daybreak until dark. . . . The enemy is still in our front, but badly used up. . . . The news just reaches me that the enemy is retreating toward the mountains."

On August 30 Pope's actions defy comprehension. During the morning he planned cautiously in the belief that Jackson, badly cut up, was pulling out of his position leaving only a rear guard—and of course that Lee and Longstreet were not in the vicinity. But if the Federals' task were simply to mop up the remaining Rebels, why wait until midday to start the process? True, Federal troops were tired after much marching and fighting and they had limited supplies; but the same applied to the enemy. As Pope eyed the situation, the railroad embankment, scene of yesterday's heavy fighting, seemed virtually empty, only a few Rebel sharpshooters replying to the Federal outposts' firing. (Jackson had his men out of sight getting some rest on the wooded hillslope above.) Systematically Pope disposed his units, pulling Porter's corps in on the left to close up with McDowell for a two-pronged drive along the pike, sending Heintzelman

to drive west from the pike against Jackson and "press him vigorously during the whole day."

As Pope was concentrating his forces, Lee kept Jackson firm on his left and had Longstreet fan his five divisions out on the right to form the lower mandible of a giant jaw. Into this maw Union troops were now marched. About noon Stuart reported to Lee that bluecoats were massing in front of Jackson. Lee forwarded the warning to Jackson, who alerted his men, but kept them concealed in the woods.

At noon without warning Federal troops charged forward in three waves—much heavier than the day before. Rebels rushed to man their line along the railroad bank and fought back doggedly. Determined Yankees slogging forward got within a few yards of the defense position. Confederates, running out of ammunition, began heaving rocks at their attackers. Hill's line wavered, broke, then reformed. Jackson signaled an appeal to Lee for reinforcements.

As Porter's units surged forward on the Union

The Robinson House near the center of the battlefield at Cedar Mountain.
Banks enjoyed some initial success on this line before Jackson smashed him.
(USAMHI)

*Brigadier General John White Geary, hand in blouse, stands with his staff at
Harpers Ferry. He fought well for Banks and took two wounds from the field.*
(LC)

left, Longstreet's men coming out from their forest
cover absorbed the first fury of the attack, then
began pivoting on a hinge close to Groveton and
positioned their artillery for enfilading fire. One
observer wrote, "gunners leaped to their pieces
. . . , bowling their shots along the serried rows
of Federals who up to now had been unaware of
the danger to their flank. The effect was instan-
taneous. Torn and blasted by this fire, the second
and third lines milled aimlessly, bewildered, then
retreated . . . whereupon the first line soldiers
[seeing] . . . their supports in flight, also began to waver and give ground." South of the
Warrenton pike two New York volunteer regiments
guarded the base of a knoll on which a six-gun
Union battery was stationed. As Longstreet swept
forward these men caught the brunt of the assault.
One regiment was quickly overrun. But the second
—Zouaves, nattily dressed with white spats, tas-
seled fezzes, blue jackets, and fancy scarlet trousers
—stood firm while the battery flailed the attackers
and then limbered—hitched the guns to their
teams—and got away, the New Yorkers then with-

drawing. The cost was enormous—of 490 Zouaves,
124 lay dead, 223 wounded when it was over.

By 4 P.M. Porter found his men fighting for their
lives on their front and left flank with a prospect of
being enveloped by Longstreet. A withdrawal
began with Longstreet in hot pursuit. As Porter
reeled backwards, Lee ordered his whole army to
advance—Jackson's units to drive east and south to
block Federal retreat along the Warrenton pike toward the Stone Bridge. Jackson's revived lines
surged forward down the embankment and out
onto the plain. Shrieking the Rebel yell, they
charged against the backdrop of the setting sun,
said a Northern observer, like "demons emerging
from the earth."

Federal forces rallied on the high ground of
Henry House Hill, where Jackson had won his
nickname thirteen months earlier. Sigel's and
Reno's troops joined Gibbon's "Black Hat" boys to
form a firm shield for the retreating Federal units.
Some feared the withdrawal might turn to panic
and rout, as it had in July 1861 on this very same
ground. Riding up to Gibbon, Phil Kearny, empty

sleeve flapping in the breeze, cried, "It's another Bull Run!" When Gibbon said he hoped not, Kearny replied, "Perhaps not. Reno is keeping up the fight. . . . I am not stampeded; you are not stampeded. . . . My God, that's about all!" At any rate, battling bluecoats on the hill held the charging Rebels long enough for Pope's army to reach and cross the Stone Bridge over Bull Run. The bridge was then blown up. As darkness and rain came on, these troops, grumbling about their inept leaders, slogged on four muddy miles to camp long after nightfall in positions on the heights of Centreville. These were entrenched fortifications left by Confederates from July 1861. What might have been a disastrous Union rout came off as an orderly withdrawal, quite in contrast to first Bull Run. As Pope saw it in his report that night to Halleck, "The battle was most furious for hours without cessation, and the losses on both sides very heavy. The enemy is badly crippled, and we shall do well enough."

But another observer assessed Pope's situation differently, pointing out he had been "kicked, cuffed, hustled about, knocked down, run over and trodden upon. . . . His communications had been cut; his headquarters pillaged; a corps had marched into his rear . . . ; he had been beaten and foiled in every attempt he had made to 'bag' those defiant intruders; and, in the end, he was glad to find refuge in the intrenchments of Washington."

That night Lee reported proudly if a bit inaccurately to Richmond, "The enemy attacked my left, under Jackson, on Thursday [August 28], and was repulsed. He attacked my right, under Longstreet, on Friday, and was repulsed; and on Saturday I attacked him with my combined armies, and utterly routed" the Federals "on the plains of Manassas."

Casualties on both sides were severe. Lee's losses included 1,481 killed, 7,627 wounded, 89 missing; Pope's, 1,724 killed, 8,372 wounded, 5,958 missing. Some 7,000 Federals appear to have been captured, not counting several thousand wounded left on the field. Over a three-by-five-mile stretch of the Manassas plain, dead and wounded men lay strewn, in some places in heaps. The day after the battle Longstreet's men worked to aid the wounded and bury the dead. Confederate surgeons were so busy with their own as to have no time for Yanks. Shortly Federal ambulances were permitted on the field. Some 3,000 Union wounded were brought to

Here the home of the Reverend Mr. Slaughter, an appropriate name for Cedar Mountain. Banks's losses were almost twice those of Jackson. (USAMHI)

makeshift facilities at Fairfax, where aides, doctors, and nurses were rushed from Washington. Clara Barton, seeking to get medicines and supplies there, estimated that 3,000 wounded men still lay on the straw-strewn ground at Fairfax a week after the battle. "All night," she wrote, "we made compresses and slings, and bound up and wet wounds, when we could get water, fed what we could. . . . Oh, how I needed stores on that field!"

As Pope's wounded were gathered at Fairfax, Union hope, which had been high only a few months before during the drive on Richmond, now lay dashed and broken. All the marching, maneuvering, fighting, dying, sickness, broiling in the Virginia sun had come to nothing by the end of August 1862. Federal troops were back where they had started—resentful, bitter, feeling betrayed and misled by military incompetents. Among Pope's soldiers, noted an officer, "Everyone had an unwashed, sleepy, downcast aspect . . . as if he would like to hide his head . . . from all the world." One newsman caught the mood: "We have been whipped by an inferior force of inferior men, better handled than ours."

From the Confederate viewpoint Lee had achieved a miracle—drawing a larger army than his own away from Richmond, running circles around the enemy and then administering a smarting defeat even in the face of superior Union numbers. Southern military fortunes were now at their highest as Lee plunged across the Potomac in early September to invade Union territory. Prospects for European aid to the Confederacy seemed brighter than before, even a possible European intervention that might assure Confederate independence.

In the North a crisis was at hand. Endless lists of wounded and dead filled newspaper pages. Morale sagged. Military leaders and Lincoln's administration were denounced by the surging political opposition. Prospects grew that Republicans would lose control of Congress in the upcoming midterm election, as voters tired of the war. Perhaps some kind of armistice leading to a negotiated peace, some thought, was preferable to continued slaughter and suffering. Obviously Lincoln's plans for wartime emancipation of the slaves—formulated in July—would have to be postponed. Gloom settled over a grim North as the people faced an uncertain future.

Yet Jackson, too, paid a heavy price. Brigadier General Charles S. Winder commanded Jackson's old division in the furious fighting, and in the battle a shell brutally mangled him. He died hours later in this house. (USAMHI)

Officers of the 10th Maine Infantry survey the field of battle some days later.
(USAMHI)

*The toll in animals, too, proved heavy. O'Sullivan caught this scene a few days
after the fight.* (USAMHI)

Simple homes became field hospitals, this one for Confederate wounded.
(USAMHI)

Men like Brigadier General Samuel W. Crawford—once the surgeon at Fort Sumter—saw their commands almost destroyed. Crawford's brigade suffered 50 percent losses. (NA)

The captured were taken back to Culpeper. Here O'Sullivan photographed several Confederates in their rather informal "prison" in Culpeper Court House. (LC)

The Union dead, 314 of them, were buried on the field, in sight of the mountain whose battle killed them. (USAMHI)

Though they lost the battle, the Federals held the field, and here at Cedar Mountain Pope and McDowell made their headquarters. In the background left of the house stands the field wagon for reporters of the New York Herald *who followed the army.* (LC)

On August 18, Pope began to move his army north of the Rappahannock to meet the threat posed by Lee. His engineers had to build several bridges to accomplish the movement. This one crosses the North Fork of the Rappahannock. (USAMHI)

The Hazel River, a tributary, afforded a crossing already in place and not destroyed by the Confederates. (USAMHI)

But most bridges had to be built. O'Sullivan took a series of fine images of Franz Sigel's corps crossing this bridge on August 19. (P-M)

Wagons and baggage cross. (LC)

Then horsemen and part of the army's beef herd. (USAMHI)

*Many of the Federals camped at Rappahannock Station, where they skirmished
with the enemy on August 23.* (LC)

*Meanwhile, at Catlett's Station, Lee's cavalry captured Pope's baggage,
including vital information on reinforcements coming to him from McClellan.*
(USAMHI)

*The pace of the campaign accelerated quickly. Jackson, occupying Manassas,
evacuated just as Pope was set to attack. All he found was ruins, some like these
dating to March 1862 and the first Confederate evacuation. George N.
Barnard photo.* (LC)

All that remained were enemy winter huts and earthworks, and at least one outhouse. (USAMHI)

The Barnard & Gibson views taken in March are almost all that survive to give a picture of Manassas. It looked much the same when Pope marched in. (USAMHI)

The fortifications were extensive. (USAMHI)

And so was the clutter and debris. The horse appears to have been hobbled
before it was killed, and several pieces of a steer are scattered about it.
(USAMHI)

Pope's Federals faced a big task just in cleaning up after the Confederates.
(USAMHI)

They occupied the old earthworks. (AMERICANA IMAGE GALLERY)

They restored and refurbished them. (WRHS)

O'Sullivan's July 1862 image shows the eastern range of earthworks at Manassas. (USAMHI)

And this photograph, probably taken by A. J. Russell, reveals Confederate Fort Beauregard. The Federals did not retain the name. (USAMHI)

Then Pope heard the enemy was at Centreville, and off he went, leaving behind some destruction of his own. Rolling stock of the Orange & Alexandria was burned to the wheels rather than be allowed to fall into Confederate hands. (USAMHI)

Engines were pushed over the railroad embankments. It would take a major effort to right this one. (USAMHI)

And then came another battle at Bull Run. Here Blackburn's Ford is shown on July 4, 1862, a few weeks before the battle. (USAMHI)

*Brigadier General William B. Taliaferro took a
bad wound in the preliminary fighting at
Groveton.* (USAMHI)

*Some familiar faces were here again. Major
General Richard S. Ewell played a minor role
at the first Bull Run. Here at the second he
was in the thick of the fighting and lost a leg.*
(VM)

William A. Wallace succeeded to the colonelcy of the 18th South Carolina on the field when its commander was killed. This later image shows him as a brigadier general. (USAMHI)

Major General David R. Jones, called "Neighbor" by friends, was a veteran of the first battle here. During the present campaign he made a major contribution to victory when he took Thoroughfare Gap. (SOUTHERN HISTORICAL COLLECTION, THE UNIVERSITY OF NORTH CAROLINA AT CHAPEL HILL)

And, of course, there was meandering Bull Run. Here the ruins of the Stone
Bridge, taken by Barnard & Gibson in March 1862. (USAMHI)

Stone Bridge and the heights beyond once
again shook with the sound of guns.
(USAMHI)

McDowell's engineers had to build bridges to span Bull Run a few days before the battle. (USAMHI)

At the southern end of the field, near Union Mills, the Orange & Alexandria crossed Bull Run. (USAMHI)

But the real fighting took place where it had before, around Henry Hill and along the Warrenton Road. Here a part of the battlefield. (USAMHI)

It must have seemed déjà vu *for McDowell. Another Bull Run, another defeat.* (USAMHI)

A. J. Myer, the signal officer who could not get his balloon aloft at first Bull Run, operated a more effective signal office for McDowell at the second. Here O'Sullivan's image of Myer in his headquarters in late August. (LC, H. J. MYER COLLECTION)

Sending intelligence to the front, though little good it did. (LC, H. J. MYER COLLECTION)

*The 2nd United States Sharpshooters, led by officers like
Lieutenant B. S. Calef, saw their first real action at Second
Manassas.* (USAMHI)

*Brigadier General Abram Duryée, formerly
commander of a flamboyant Zouave regiment, took
two wounds in the battle while he led a brigade.*
(USAMHI)

Reuben L. Walker fought with distinction at Second Bull Run, working A. P. Hill's artillery. (VM)

A face familiar to the fields along Bull Run, "Shanks" Evans, hero of the first battle. His command, called the "Tramp Brigade," seemed to be everywhere. A year from now his drinking would get him into trouble. (VM)

*The Stone House on the Warrenton Turnpike would be used as a hospital
again, as a year before, when the armies were done fighting around it.*
(USAMHI)

And the Widow Henry's house was no more. The war is simply too much for it.
(NA, U. S. SIGNAL CORPS)

Few of Pope's high commanders distinguished themselves in the fight. Franz Sigel, commander of a corps, almost never distinguished himself. (USAMHI)

Brigadier General Robert C. Schenck was an exception. He led a brigade in Sigel's corps with distinction until a bullet removed him from further field command. (WRHS)

Samuel P. Heintzelman ended his active field service with an unsuccessful attack on Jackson at Groveton in the opening of the battle. He was photographed here with his staff just a few weeks before the battle. (WRHS)

A new name attracting much attention was Joseph Hooker, called "Fighting Joe" by the Northern press after his performance on the Peninsula. He led a division for Heintzelman, and would shortly replace Sigel at the head of the I Corps. (USAMHI)

"Portici," the house that had been headquarters for Johnston in July 1861, saw the armies in its fields once again. (MANASSAS NATIONAL BATTLEFIELD PARK)

Another Manassas house, again the scene of encamped armies, this time Federals. (USAMHI)

Men of Second Bull Run. Company A, 10th New York Infantry. It was the first regiment hit by John B. Hood's Texans in Longstreet's attack on August 30. A year from now it would be so depleted by battle that it would be redesignated a battalion. (ROBERT MCDONALD)

The 21st Massachusetts. Its officers, like Lieutenant Henry H. Richardson of Company K, are there as well. (USAMHI)

The 73rd Ohio Infantry, shown here leaving Chillicothe in 1862, saw its first battle at Second Manassas. They would go on to march through Georgia with Sherman two years later. Photograph by J. A. Simmonds. (WRHS)

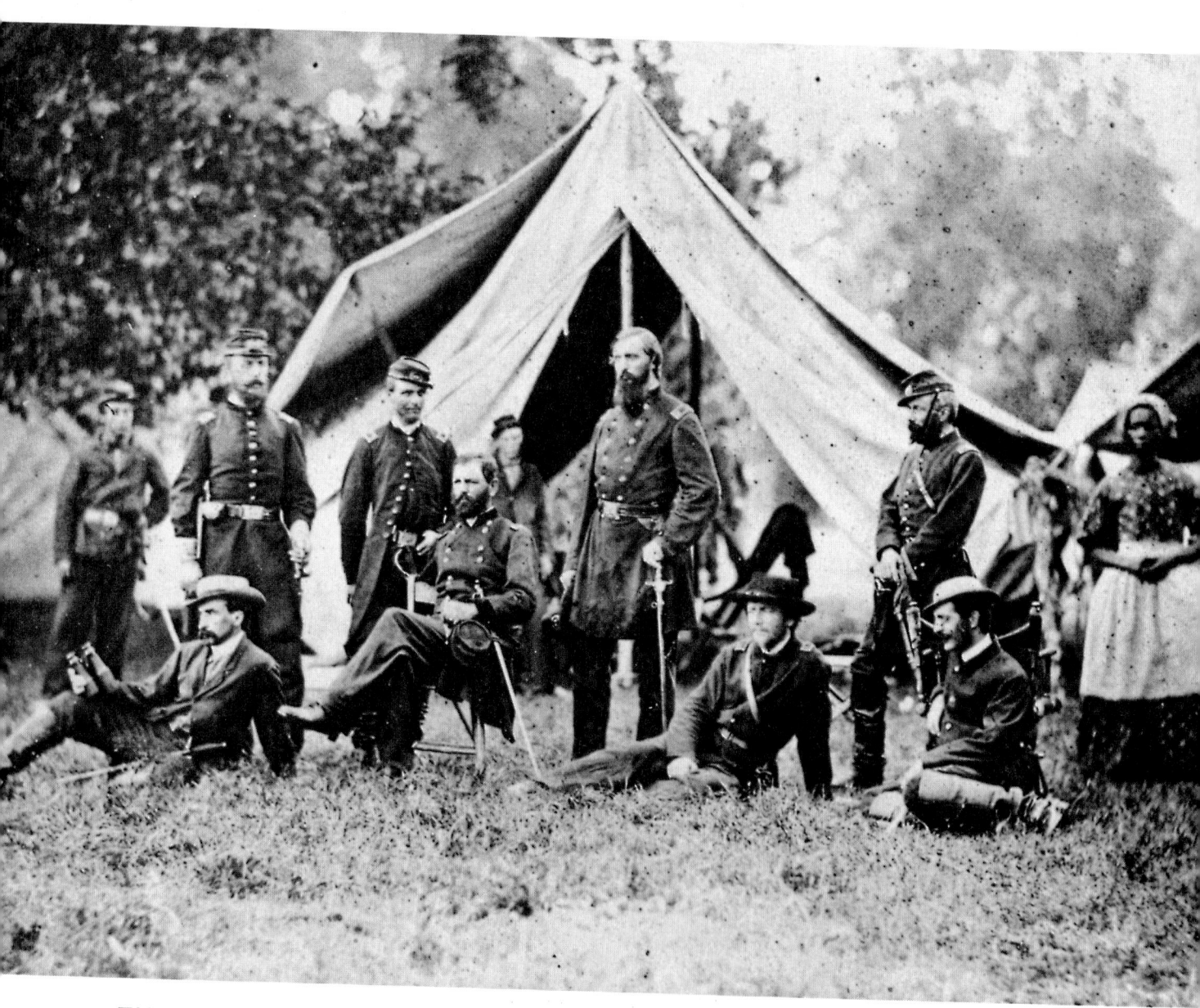

This battle was the undoing of Major General Fitz John Porter. Devoted to "Little Mac," he was used in Pope's vendetta against McClellan and charged with disobedience of orders and disloyalty. In January 1863 he was dismissed from the army. Exoneration did not come until 1886. He appears seated here on August 1, 1862, at Harrison's Landing, less than a month before the battle. (USAMHI)

Micah Jenkins had moved up since leading his 5th South Carolina at First Manassas. He is shown here as a colonel, but a severe wound at this second battle interrupted his career for several months. (LC)

Another promising younger officer, William Mahone, called "Scrappy Billy." Shriveled, dyspeptic, weighing less than one hundred pounds, and furiously combative, he was one of Lee's most active brigadiers. (USAMHI)

David A. Weisiger was officer of the day in Taliaferro's Virginia Militia at the hanging of John Brown. At Bull Run he led a regiment in Mahone's brigade. He was seriously wounded but recovered to become a brigadier as shown here. The Confederacy had no distinction of insignia among the various grades of general—brigadier, major, lieutenant, and full general. All wore three stars in a wreath. (USAMHI)

Colonel Jerome Robertson took a wound while leading his 5th Texas Infantry in its attack on the 10th New York. He became a brigadier a few months later. His son Felix also became a brigadier. A war criminal, accused of the murder of Negro soldiers at Saltville, Virginia, in 1864, Felix was to be the last surviving Confederate general, living until 1928. (P-M)

An unusual bearded portrait of Brigadier General Henry Slocum, promoted to major general just before the battle. He materially aided in covering Pope's retreat after the defeat. (NA)

There was a small engagement at Chantilly, the final echo of the Second Manassas battle, and there one of the Union's most promising officers, Brigadier General Philip Kearny, rode accidentally into enemy soldiers. While attempting to escape he was shot and killed instantly. Winfield Scott called him "the bravest man I ever knew." He lost his arm in the war with Mexico. (USAMHI)

Brigadier General Isaac I. Stevens, once governor of Washington Territory, head of the Breckinridge campaign in 1860, died after the Battle of Second Manassas was virtually done, at Chantilly, on September 1. The Union lost great potential in his death and Kearny's. It recognized the loss in the unusual act of promoting Stevens to major general posthumously. (USAMHI)

And so, defeated, Pope retreated to Centreville, and here he stood briefly. There was no rout this time. A Barnard photo from March 1862. (NLM)

*Six months before, jubilant Union soldiers had posed gaily here in the old
Confederate earthworks.* (USAMHI)

*Now these fortifications, designed to protect from an attack from the north,
were of little use to them against an enemy that might pursue from the south.*
(USAMHI)

The "Quaker guns" once used by the Rebels to fool the Federals were now a taunt. With the bitter memory of two defeats at Bull Run, Union soldiers were not saddened to continue their retreat to Washington. (USAMHI)

The War on Rails

ROBERT C. BLACK, III

Spiderlike the rails spread over the land, carrying the war
everywhere, and feeding its voracious appetites

THE IRON HORSE was not bred, on this continent, for war.

Indeed, American railroads have seldom been planned for military purposes. For over a century and a half they typically have been built to serve the economic convenience, either of the public, or of those interests which found it useful to associate their private aspirations with the public good. No railroad was ever designed to create a Southern Confederacy—or to save the Union. The original lines were established for local reasons; subsequent projects remained oblivious to the possibility of war. That such enterprises should have found themselves engulfed in the first significant railroad conflict in all history was as fortuitous as it was unexpected, and it was inevitable that the railroad facilities of 1861 should in few respects perfectly fulfill the wartime needs of either the United or the Confederate States.

At the dawn of the nineteenth century, Americans still thought of transportation in terms of waterways; even when facing inland, they sought out naturally navigable streams and lakes. Canals and steamboats, which came two decades later, were little more than elaborations upon the water concept. Highways were significant chiefly as land bridges, transcending inconvenient terrain between places of navigation. Railroads, when they appeared, were regarded as a special variety of highway, and they assumed for some time a kind of bridge role—Mohawk & Hudson; Baltimore & Ohio; Richmond, Fredericksburg & Potomac; Western & Atlantic—the western waters were meant. That railroads possessed the capacity to supersede waterways was understood at first by almost no one, and even at the outbreak of the Civil War the idea still lacked universal acceptance. As a result, American railroad enterprise was subject for a long time to local influences, frequently petty in nature, that did much to inhibit the growth of anything like a national *system;* indeed, neither of the famous sections, Northern or Southern, could boast of anything like a unified network.

There did exist, albeit in embryo form, a number of trans-Appalachian railroad routes that straggled across the map between the east coast and the Mississippi River. Three were unquestionably Northern: the New York Central (Albany to Buffalo) and its connections; the Erie (Piermont, New York, to Dunkirk, New York) and its connections; and the Pennsylvania (Philadelphia to Pittsburgh) and its connections. Another was of uncertain status—the Baltimore & Ohio (Baltimore to Wheeling, Virginia) with connections west, which

The railroad, like the camera, came of age just as the nation went to war. Even as the armies were ready to march, so were the routes and rolling stock ready to carry them. Here a locomotive of the Raleigh & Gaston Railroad in North Carolina, around 1850. The South lay far behind the North in its rail system.
(NORTH CAROLINA MUSEUM OF HISTORY)

ran so close beneath Mason's and Dixon's line that it found itself, during much of the Civil War, in a kind of no-man's-land; as a *carrier* it would serve the Union sometimes, the Confederacy never. Authentically *Southern* trackage, east to west, coalesced at Chattanooga into the single line of a single company, the Memphis & Charleston, a road destined to early fragmentation.

Though Northern superiority in terms of num-

ber of "routes" was clear, none of the routes could as yet be classified as trunk lines. The tradition of localism continued to be evident in even so fundamental a matter as the distance between the rails of a track. It is true that many Northern companies had adopted the classic British gauge of 4 feet, 8½ inches; moreover, there was an equally strong tendency in the South to use a gauge of 5 feet. But Northern practice could vary; the Erie was committed to an expansive 6 feet. The South contained considerable mileage of the British sort and in other places fancied an unconventional width of 5 feet, 6 inches. Connecting lines, even of an identical gauge, did not always represent unobstructed arteries. In many instances (but particularly in the South) there existed no physical contact between the roads that served a single city or town. Gaps of this sort were naturally cherished by hackmen and drayers, who saw to it that municipal ordinances discouraged their elimination.

The carriers themselves nursed restrictive notions. Many of them—and once more this was most conspicuous in the South—shrank from releasing their rolling stock to the lines of a "foreign" company. Even in the North, railroad execu-

. . . Herman Haupt, a near-genius who graduated from West Point at age eighteen and thereafter dazzled the railroad industry with his achievements. Stanton made him chief of construction of the United States Military Railroads with the rank of brigadier general. He worked wonders. (NA, U. S. SIGNAL CORPS, BRADY COLLECTION)

Secretary of War Edwin M. Stanton, learning from the bitter lesson of the First Battle of Bull Run, which was lost when the enemy used railroads to combine troops against McDowell, knew the vital role to be played by the railroads. As a result, soon after taking his portfolio, he brought to Washington . . . (USAMHI)

tives were happier when such interchanges involved the property of a third company—the germ of the car-line idea. North or South, the advantages of the through trains were as yet only dimly perceived.

Speaking very generally, it may be said that the railroad equipment of the Civil War period, both Union and Confederate, reflected a kind of American standard; that is, nearly all locomotives were of the 4-4-0 classification—two sets of four wheels front and center, and none under the cab—and burned wood; most rails were of wrought iron and weighed no more than 40 pounds to the yard; while the load limit of the average boxcar was established at about 16,000 pounds. This was only natural; most—though not all—of the engines and cars were manufactured in the North, while most —though not all—of the rails were rolled either in

*Tenuous lifelines, like this viaduct on the Baltimore & Ohio at Relay House,
Maryland . . .* (MHS)

the North or in England. But if the Confederacy
entered the Civil War with roughly similar patterns of railroad material, it typically possessed less
of everything. The South counted 9,000 line miles
of track; the North had 21,000. The Pennsylvania
Railroad—in 1861 it ran from Philadelphia to
Pittsburgh only!—owned more locomotives—220
—than did all the lines of secessionist Virginia.
The South Carolina Railroad possessed the greatest
number of cars of any Confederate property—849.
The leading company in the North was the Delaware, Lackawanna & Western with more than
4,000 cars.

Furthermore, if the Southern railroad plant was
deficient at the outset, its capacity to grow, or even

to maintain itself, was minimal. Confederate inferiority in the metallurgical arts and the steadily more
constrictive effects of the Federal blockage are
abundantly documented. But it must also be observed that these factors were rendered much worse
by an unimaginative public policy, which prevented the most effective use of what the Confederacy did have.

One must, of course, be fair. At the outset, the
United States authorities were as naïve with respect to the administration of railroads as were the
Confederate. Both opponents had sprung from a
common military background, and they now faced
each other with a common baggage of notions.
Prior to 1861, the steam locomotive had played a

scant role in American military activity; army transport had depended upon animal-drawn wagons, moving under the orders of commanders in the field and administered by a quartermaster organization whose traditions were as rigid as they were ancient. Enter the iron horse, offering greatly superior speed and almost unimaginable capacity. That the new beast would be useful was obvious, yet the wagon continued to afford an advantage that the boxcar could not match: it was not confined to a track and therefore, like its motorized descendant, provided a greater flexibility of movement. This flexibility had conditioned, over the centuries, the very *mores* of military transport. But now, whenever a field commander applied the tra-

ditional procedures to a railroad, the anticipated flood of supplies and reinforcements abruptly ceased. Official wrath would thereupon descend upon the railroaders concerned; "wretched" was an early and probably laundered epithet applied by General Joseph E. Johnston to the Confederate management of the Orange & Alexandria, and it is likely that other comments never saw official print.

The causes of such difficulties quickly became obvious to intelligent railroad men. One was understandable: military authorities were prone to dealing with train crews as if they were teamsters enlisted under the Articles of War, ordering them about without thought of the consequences. Another was inevitable: the temptation to regard rail-

. . . and the Orange & Alexandria here at Union Mills on Bull Run, were vital to supply and transportation for the armies. A March 1863 image by A. J. Russell. (USAMHI)

Sometimes they could be protected by a detachment of soldiers, as here near Union Mills in a G. W. Houghton photograph. (VHS)

road cars as convenient storehouses, and the disinclination of field units to unload and release them became notorious. Still another was the absence of any well-understood official relationship between the carriers and the military. None of these problems was ever to be perfectly resolved, but experience brought considerable improvement, especially on the Union side.

Of these principal difficulties, the absence of a formal railroad-army relationship was paramount. Until this was assured, there could be no dealing with the storehouses or the *ad hoc* train orders.

During the first year of the war, both adminis-

trations, Federal and Confederate, simply muddled through, relying largely upon quartermaster departments of the conventional kind. True, each side commissioned and inserted into the traditional structure certain knowledgeable railroad officials; the Pennsylvania's Thomas Scott and William S. Ashe of the Wilmington & Weldon are primary examples. But in neither organization were these men given appropriate authority: in the administrative bureaus their advice was overlooked; in the field it was flouted.

The Federal authorities finally moved, early in 1862, to attack the railroad problem in a serious way. First came a cleansing at the top: Edwin M. Stanton was appointed Secretary of War in place of the dubious Simon Cameron. Mr. Stanton has not enjoyed a universally favorable press; he could be an unpleasant colleague, and his political honesty remains cloudy to this day. But he was both intelligent and efficient, and he was devoted to the proposition that the Confederacy should be subjected to utter defeat. Shortly after Stanton's arrival, an administration railroad bill was pushed through Congress and received President Lincoln's signature on January 31, 1862. Its text was brief: it granted to the President of the United States the authority to assume, whenever the military situation warranted, full control over any railroad in the country. In the face of such a statute, the subordinate status of the railroad industry was clear.

To enact a law is one thing; to carry it out with imagination and dispatch is another. Even under Stanton an effective implementation required a lengthy period of trial and error. The substance of the act was published as a general order of the Adjutant General's office as early as February 4, and on the eleventh the widely respected general superintendent of the Erie, Daniel C. McCallum, was appointed military director and superintendent of railroads in the United States with very broad powers, based upon the statute and its derivative order. But the troubles persisted; they had penetrated so deep that their elimination would require not only an enlightened supervision but also Herculean labors in the field.

The labors were performed by Herman Haupt, a civil engineer of impeccable reputation, who was charged late in April with the restoration of reliable railroad service in the northern Virginia theater. Haupt was a humorless man, born to controversy. Although a graduate of West Point, he utterly lacked a sense of subordination, and his confrontations with certain braided martinets were memorable. He was, in fact, precisely the kind of man the situation demanded. His professional abilities were vast; they embraced every aspect of railroad construction, maintenance, and operation. He furthermore could usually depend upon the support of both McCallum and Stanton. Amid the Virginia disasters of 1862, he pounded out the fundamentals of an organization, the United States Military Railroads, divided specifically into construction and operating corps, and managed upon

carefully stated principles perfected by himself. In the course of his service Haupt underwent repeated fits of the sulks, and after the Gettysburg campaign he stamped home to Massachusetts for good. But his military railroad ideas would be enormously and, for the Federals, happily expanded. They would be much recorded by Yankee photographers.

Though the wartime railroad law conveyed sweeping powers to the Lincoln government, this did not mean that every carrier in the United States was subjected to seizure and operation by the Union Army. So Draconian a process was wisely reserved for emergencies—Gettysburg is an example—and was routinely applied only to occupied Confederate properties. The statute did, however, inspire a healthy cooperation by Northern companies.

Behind the Confederate lines, the railroad situation continued to be in woeful contrast to the improvements on the Union side. Underequipped for the burdens of wartime traffic, hard pressed even to sustain themselves, the Southern carriers were subjected, until nearly the end, to an official policy that can only be pronounced irresponsible. Nothing that was faintly similar to the establishment of McCallum and Haupt was ever achieved. Local, even private, rights were deemed sacrosanct; facts were brushed aside. The South possessed a wealth of natural waterways, especially in the West, but these tended, like the Mississippi, to run in directions favorable to the enemy. The South also enjoyed the means to develop a respectable system of wagon transport, but this was quite inadequate to the supply, over great distances, of the large defensive armies that had become necessary in the face of even larger enemy forces. These, in their turn, had been made possible by both the waterways and the new railroads! Nevertheless, Confederate rails did provide an imperfect skeleton of interior lines, and this just possibly might have been used to so prolong Confederate resistance that the Northern will to fight—always the *supreme* factor in this war—might have crumbled.

But the Southern leadership failed to make sophisticated use of what was available. It was not until December 1862 that the Richmond government went so far as to bring into its military structure a railroad man of a stature equivalent to that of McCallum and Haupt. This was William M.

But not always. Here, Barnard & Gibson's March 1862 picture of a ruined rail crossing near Blackburn's Ford on Bull Run. (USAMHI)

Wadley, who currently was associated with a half-finished enterprise in Louisiana, but who could look back upon a large and fruitful experience with a number of other companies in Georgia and Mississippi. He was, in a professional sense, probably the ablest railroad man in the Southern Confederacy. Wadley was noted for the brevity of his speech and, though not so brusque as Herman Haupt, was deficient in certain military niceties. His Southern loyalties were intense, but he had been born and raised in New England, a circumstance that aroused embarrassing suspicions. But his most serious difficulties were derived from the fact that he had been given rank—a full colonelcy—but no power over either the carriers or over any segment of the military. He tried earnestly to im-

prove matters, but he quickly found himself enmeshed in the thankless role of "ombudsman" between the railroads and the government, neither of which proposed to yield an inch to the other. He did contrive to organize, without clear authority, a quasi-independent Railroad Bureau, with informal lines of communication to a variety of Confederate points. He resigned his commission seven months later, when the Confederate Senate refused, for reasons unspecified, to confirm his appointment.

The activities, such as they were, of the Railroad Bureau were inherited by Wadley's principal assistant, Captain—later Lieutenant Colonel—Frederick W. Sims. Sims enjoyed neither the background nor the reputation of his predecessor, but he was by no means incompetent, and he was en-

Posing behind the embankment and pretending to defend the bridge after the fact was of little use. Other means, preventive means, had to be found.
(AMERICANA IMAGE GALLERY)

dowed with a happy ability to endure frustration. Like Wadley, he carried responsibility without authority, yet he served to the very end as the Confederacy's principal rail transportation officer, devising ineffective "miracles" and accomplishing nothing of lasting consequence. He was invested at last with the kind of power that he and Wadley should have received at the beginning, but the requisite legislation was approved, with open reluctance, by President Jefferson Davis only on March 9, 1865, precisely a month before Appomattox.

Yet the Confederates could sometimes demonstrate a certain brilliance in their use of railroads. On at least three occasions they managed to improvise a steam-powered mass transit system in order to accomplish a particular strategic purpose.

The first took place in the late spring of 1862, when the divisions of W. H. C. Whiting and Jackson were shunted in bewildering sequence between Richmond and the Valley of the Shenandoah and finally were concentrated upon Lee's left wing in the Peninsula. The episode involved at least 20,000 troops, and though they at times exceeded the capabilities of the Virginia Central Railroad, their commanders did achieve a commendable harmony with its operating personnel. The results, from the Confederate viewpoint, were satisfying.

The second occasion came a few weeks later. It witnessed the removal of the greater part of Braxton Bragg's army from Tupelo, in the northeastern part of Mississippi, and its reconcentration at Chattanooga, Tennessee. Like the Virginia episode

*Haupt built blockhouses, frontier-style forts to protect bridges in Virginia and
Tennessee. Here one overlooks the Orange & Alexandria crossing of Bull Run.*
(USAMHI)

it was locally conceived and executed—and was
carried out with a minimum of fuss. It was a
major undertaking; involved was the movement of
more than 20,000 men over the tracks of five railroads by a circuitous route through Mobile, Montgomery, and Atlanta. Yet it was completed in little
more than two weeks. The consequences were considerable: the disruption over many months of the
entire Federal offensive west of the Appalachians.

The third entailed the famous transfer, in September 1863, of Longstreet's corps from Lee's
army in Virginia to Bragg's command in northern
Georgia. It was a complex affair, organized under
difficult circumstances and carried out under the
general supervision of Sims's railroad bureau. Federal activities in eastern Tennessee denied to the
Confederates the logical routing via Knoxville, and
they were obliged to resort to a series of awkward
passages through the Carolinas and Atlanta; the

situation was further confused by certain unrelated
movements in the direction of Charleston. Nevertheless, the thing was brought off successfully. The
weather was pleasant, most schedules were kept,
and perhaps half the troops arrived in time to participate in the Battle of Chickamauga. The statistics of the operation remain uncertain; the best estimates suggest that the total number completing
the journey cannot have much exceeded 12,000.
But their presence undoubtedly contributed to the
Confederate victory and to a subsequent glimmer
of Confederate hope.

The most significant result of Chickamauga,
however, was the Union response to it. Hardly had
the plight of the defeated General Rosecrans, now
trapped in Chattanooga, become clear when plans
were being drafted to rectify the situation with
massive reinforcements. The most suitable available units were all in northern Virginia; they must

proceed by rail, beginning at once and upon an emergency basis, to the vicinity of Chattanooga. The substantive preparations were completed in a single day: General McCallum, President John Garrett of the Baltimore & Ohio, and Thomas Scott assumed the responsibility for specific segments of the route, which was necessarily long and roundabout. It passed through Washington, Benwood—on the Ohio River in West Virginia—then to Indianapolis, south to Louisville and Nashville, and then to Bridgeport, Alabama, on the Tennessee River. Needed cooperation was ensured by reminding participants of the railroad law of 1862, and behind the law stood a no-nonsense administration and a steadily growing U.S. railroad capability.

The first train puffed away from the Virginia encampments on September 25; the last crept down the winding grade into the Tennessee Valley on the evening of October 6. In eleven and one half days, 25,000 infantry, 10 batteries of artillery, and 100 carloads of miscellaneous equipment had been carried 1,200 miles over the lines of a half-dozen railroads without a single serious delay or notable interference by the enemy.

Although the reinforcing of Rosecrans at Chattanooga was the most spectacular incident of its kind over the whole course of the Civil War, it was not, in a technical sense, the most impressive. The United States Military Railroads organization was not to be presented with its supreme challenge until the following spring, when it was charged with the supply, over hundreds of miles of single track, of General William T. Sherman's Atlanta

Even this was not foolproof, as the same blockhouse, now burned,
demonstrates. (USAMHI)

But usually they were effective. Here a more elaborate blockhouse built on the East Tennessee & Georgia line to guard the Hiawassee bridge, largely from raiders like Nathan B. Forrest. (USAMHI)

campaign. This represented more than a rigorous exercise in logistics; thanks to the renewed activity of enemy guerrillas, very extensive portions of the route required constant rebuilding. The effort—physical and administrative—was staggering, but Sherman and his 100,000 men never lacked for rations or ammunition. Superintending the miracle were three officers of the Military Railroads—W. W. Wright, Adna Anderson, and E. C. Smeed. The Confederates were simply bewildered, and as they were thrust relentlessly back upon Atlanta they wondered aloud whether the Yankees were not carrying their bridges and tunnels with them in their knapsacks.

During all this, the officers of the United States Military Railroads were always pleased to have their accomplishments recorded photographically. This pleasant liaison between photographer and military railroader in the Civil War was a natural development; railroad gear "held still" frequently enough to serve as a subject for the slow and inconvenient emulsions of the day; moreover, railroad matters enjoyed, in the 1860s, a distinctive appeal to the picture-buying public.

The photographs that follow remind us of something more than the discussions in the text. They are nearly all *Northern* images and depict *Northern* activity. To suggest that there nowhere exists a photograph of an authentic *Confederate* railroad train would be taking a risk, but such a photo has yet to surface.

The South lacked boiler tubes for its locomotives. It also lacked developer and fixer. Consequently Confederate photographers could not undertake to record everything, and likenesses of loved ones must have always been more sought after than prints of the trains that carried them off to battle. Furthermore, the final catastrophe brought grievous disruption to Southern records in all categories. It was therefore inevitable that surviving views of Confederate railroads should be the work of Northerners and that they should portray scenes of occupation and ruin.

It is a fascinating coincidence that the American Civil War should have been the first conflict to encompass, in an extensive way, the techniques of both photography and railroading. And if railroads contributed to the victory of the Union, contemporary railroad photographs dramatically suggest the reasons.

*And here Barnard's 1864 image of a fortified bridge on the Louisville &
Nashville crossing of the Cumberland River. Giant fortress doors could close
each end of the bridge, turning it into a stronghold.* (LC)

It was men like Brigadier General John D. Imboden that Haupt sought to defeat. Though they were were usually troublesome to their superiors, on independent command they were skilled at destroying railroad equipment and installations. Imboden wreaked terrible damage on the Baltimore & Ohio in 1863 and 1864. (USAMHI)

So did Major Harry Gilmor and his 2nd Maryland Cavalry. On an 1864 raid on the B & O he not only stopped a train, but also robbed the passengers, a feat which got him suspended from command. This portrait was made in Columbia, South Carolina, by W. Weain. (USAMHI)

*The Baltimore & Ohio shops at Martinsburg, Virginia, a favorite target of
Confederate raiders. Probably an image from the 1850s. Shown are camelback
locomotives and several "iron pot" coal cars.* (BALTIMORE & OHIO RAILROAD)

*A somewhat retouched photo showing the junction of the Baltimore & Ohio
and Cumberland & Pennsylvania Railroads with the Chesapeake & Ohio
Canal at Cumberland, Maryland. The mules are moving the coal cars into
position to dump their contents into the canal barges. Another place
exceedingly vulnerable to Confederate raiders.* (B & O RAILROAD MUSEUM)

*Here the Chattanooga depot at Nashville, Tennessee, shows the effects of a
Rebel raid.* (HERB PECK, JR.)

And Manassas Junction, Virginia, is repeatedly disrupted by the passing of the armies. (USAMHI)

Keeping the U. S. Military Railroads running would be a massive task for the innovative Haupt. He proved equal to it. Here he paddles a small pontoon boat of his own design, used for inspecting bridge foundations. (USAMHI)

*Carrying out Haupt's instructions were engineers like these of the Construction
Corps, photographed with their tools in Chattanooga in 1864.* (LC)

*And commissioned to follow the railroads was one of the few officially
commissioned military photographers—perhaps the only one—Major A. J.
Russell. Here the headquarters of his operations at Petersburg, near City Point,
in the summer of 1864.* (ROY MEREDITH)

Haupt moved mountains of material over long distances to maintain old lines and build new ones as needed. Here Russell's image of tons of iron rails at Alexandria, ready to go where needed. (USAMHI)

*At Burnside's Wharf on Aquia Creek, the Construction Corps joined the rails
with the waters to transport supplies.* (NA)

*The lines of tracks seem endless. Haupt brought his rails to the very water's
edge on the James, below Richmond, in 1865. Photograph by Russell.*
(USAMHI)

Here, opposite Richmond, even locomotives were brought from ship to roadbed
at the war's end. (USAMHI)

In the summer of 1864 Russell captured this scene of the camp of the workers
of the Construction Corps at City Point, Virginia, their tents bordering the very
ties of their tracks. (USAMHI)

All along the vital arteries of supply Haupt's men could be found. One, at least, proved indifferent to the camera and, turning his back to it, had a mate shine his shoes. (ROY MEREDITH)

A Russell image of a Construction Corps camp on the outskirts of Richmond after the surrender. The Virginia state capitol appears on the skyline at left. (LC)

A Russell view of rolling stock and camps in Virginia. (NA)

Haupt's innovative mind produced many oddities, including the "shad belly" bridge, easily transportable, and speedily assembled. (ROY MEREDITH)

Here in 1863 one such bridge is tested. (ROY MEREDITH)

His "beanpole" bridges made him famous, attracting the admiration of President Lincoln. This bridge over Potomac Creek was built in forty hours, utilizing two old piers from its destroyed predecessor. An A. J. Russell image from May 1864. (USAMHI)

Two days before, this creek was an impassable barrier for trains. Now a train can cross in safety. (LC)

Russell's 1863 print of Bull Run and a bridge under construction in the distance. (KA)

The Bull Run bridge a-building. (LC)

And completed. The first train crosses. Russell took this scene in the spring of 1863. (KA)

Later there would be time to elaborate and refine the bridge, once it was passing traffic again. The makeshift undergirding of the previous photo is replaced by a sturdy "shad belly" superstructure, complete with ornamental eagle above the entrance. (SOUTHERN RAILWAY SYSTEM)

The same wonders were worked out West. The 1st Michigan Engineers, with Construction Corps help, built the Elk River bridge near Pulaski, Tennessee. It was 700 feet long and 58 feet high. (CHICAGO PUBLIC LIBRARY)

A similar "beanpole" bridge near Chattanooga. (MHS)

And a magnificent bridge built over the Tennessee at Chattanooga in 1864,
mighty Lookout Mountain brooding in the distance. (MHS)

The Howe Turn bridge over the Tennessee at Bridgeport, Alabama, a marvel of Construction Corps engineering. Here, in October 1863, it was just being rebuilt. (MHS)

And here it is almost finished, with still some temporary shoring at the old piles.
(USAMHI)

By January 24, 1864, it is complete, passing regular traffic, and something of a marvel. (MHS)

And at every major river and creek between Tennessee and Virginia, similar unheralded feats occurred regularly as Haupt kept the railroads running. (LC)

Conductors and engineers like these actually ran the trains. An A. J. Russell image. (USAMHI)

Their engines were frequently the best that the factories of the North could produce, splendid machines like the Gen. Haupt *built by William Mason of Taunton, Massachusetts.* (USAMHI)

Their engineers sometimes decorated their locomotives. (USAMHI)

And sometimes the Confederates did the decoration for them. In this Russell photo the men point to enemy shell damage in the stack and tender of the Fred Leach. (USAMHI)

*Most major cities soon got—if they did not have them already—major rail
yards. Alexandria, at the terminus of the Orange & Alexandria, became the
most important in the east by virtue of the O & A's necessary part in supplying
armies in Virginia.* (USAMHI)

*The roundhouse at Alexandria, shown in this Russell image, spun scores of
locomotives in the constant traffic moving south.* (USAMHI)

The offices of the Orange & Alexandria, photographed by Russell from the top of the roundhouse. (NEIKRUG PHOTOGRAPHICA, LTD.)

*Mountains of scrap collected at Alexandria for melting into new rails and
wheels.* (NA)

Nashville's Chattanooga depot acted as a principal link in the rail system supplying the Federals in the West. (KA)

Lesser depots like this one at Culpeper, Virginia, also played their part. (KA)

And always there was the constant motion of engines and cars. Here a puff of smoke and a blur give testimony to one of hundreds of iron horses at its task.
(KA)

A variety of special pieces of equipment came out of the needs of war. Here a private car sits on a siding at City Point in 1864. (ROY MEREDITH)

And here a more elaborate Presidential car, caught by Russell in the Orange &
Alexandria yard in 1865. It will take Lincoln home to Illinois, in his coffin.
(NA)

Iron boxcars like this one were built to safely haul ammunition over the
Baltimore & Ohio. (ARCHIVES OF THE B & O RAILROAD MUSEUM—CHESSIE
SYSTEM)

Car barges like these operated on the Potomac River, shifting trains where
bridges could not cross. (NA)

Improvised rail splices like this made quick repairs to old or sabotaged track.
(NA)

Haupt was not the only innovator, either. The Confederates, with far more limited means, are believed to have created this railroad battery near Petersburg. Such quickly mobile armored artillery could be very useful, if only the rails went to the right places. (USAMHI)

The Union, too, put guns on rails, and none greater than the mighty 13-inch mortar "Dictator." It weighed 17,000 pounds and performed well at Petersburg. Only rails could move the behemoth gun. (SOUTHERN RAILWAY SYSTEM)

It is unfortunate that so little survives to illustrate the role of Confederate railroads in the war. What does remain is from the cameras of Union photographers, like this tranquil image of an engine of the Atlantic & North Carolina line. Behind it is a "conductor's car." (USAMHI)

And here at Port Hudson, Louisiana, McPherson & Oliver caught two dilapidated pieces of equipment of the Clinton & Port Hudson Railroad. As in so many other areas, the South simply could not compete with the North's industry in railroading, and as shown, was hard pressed to maintain what it already had. (ISHL)

The Embattled Confederacy

The *Onondaga*, a workhorse twin-turreted monitor on the James River.
Only two double-turreted monitors saw service during the war, and when
Admiral David D. Porter stripped the James fleet for the attack on Fort
Fisher in North Carolina in 1864, the *Onondaga* was left to defend the river
almost alone.

(NO CREDIT GIVEN)

The Embattled Confederacy

The Bloodiest Day: Antietam

JAMES I. ROBERTSON, JR.

Lee the gambler and McClellan the slow
do terrible battle in Maryland

SEPTEMBER 2, 1862, found Virginia virtually free of Federal armies for the first time since the Civil War began. Major General George B. McClellan's huge Army of the Potomac had abandoned the Peninsula east of Richmond following Robert E. Lee's counterattacks in the Seven Days Campaign. A second Federal Army under Major General John Pope had just been all but routed at Second Manassas by the combined forces of Lee and "Stonewall" Jackson. The North's principal assault forces, now sullen and disillusioned, were filing into the fortifications around Washington. The war had returned to where it had begun sixteen months earlier.

Lee then decided on one of his most audacious moves. He would launch an invasion of the North. Based on historical hindsight, this decision appears questionable. Yet less desirable alternatives at the time seemed to justify Lee advancing into enemy territory with a numerically inferior army.

Washington, the North's king in the great chess game of war, was too powerfully defended to be attacked. On the other hand, Lee could not keep his destitute army at Manassas for any length of time. The northern counties of Virginia had been ravaged by war and could not sustain the Confederates. Lee's third choice was to retire to a more defensible site in the Shenandoah Valley or south of the Rappahannock River; but to do so would surrender everything that had been gained at Second Manassas. That left invasion as the most workable alternative, with a number of factors seemingly pointing to success.

The Federal armies were disorganized at the moment and posed no immediate threat. Maryland was a sister state of the South; and if the Army of Northern Virginia could "liberate" the state from Federal occupation troops, Maryland might then cast her lot with the Confederacy—which would have the spontaneous effect of leaving the Northern capital surrounded by seceded territory. An invasion by Lee would also draw the Federals' attention away from Virginia and enable the Old Dominion's farmers to gather the fall crops unmolested. A blow inside the North might trigger widespread demands on Washington for peace. Lastly, such a successful excursion could draw England or France into the Civil War on the side of the South; and foreign recognition seemed the one thing that could most assure victory for the Confederacy.

Therefore, in the pre-dawn darkness on September 4 Lee's columns began wading across the Potomac at the shoals near Leesburg. The Army of

*The gambler. General Robert Edward Lee took an enormous chance by
deciding to invade the North. It was characteristic of the man and of his army.
An image from 1862, the year of Antietam.* (CIVIL WAR TIMES ILLUSTRATED
COLLECTION)

Northern Virginia was weaker than it would be at any time during the war, save at Appomattox. Thousands were absent because of wounds, sickness, and exhaustion. Untold others had balked at invasion on the grounds that they had enlisted only to defend their beloved South, and they had simply walked away from the army. The 40,000 ragged Confederates who advanced into Maryland represented barely two thirds of Lee's force. Most of them were barefoot. (Of 300 men in a South Carolina regiment, fewer than 100 were wearing anything akin to shoes.) Yet they were the strongest, the hard core of the Confederacy's main army, and they appeared to one writer as "the scarecrow multitude of lean, vociferous, hairy men who reminded even noncombatants of wolves."

Lee's plan was to strike northward for Harrisburg, Pennsylvania. Capturing that point would break the dual arteries of the Pennsylvania Railroad and the Susquehanna River, thereby isolating the Federals' eastern and western theaters of operations from one another. At the same time, the inva-

The ruins of the Potomac River bridge at Berlin, Maryland. Here and elsewhere in the vicinity Lee began crossing into the North on September 4, 1862. Here the crossing appears a month later, with a Federal pontoon bridge in place. (U. S. ARMY MILITARY HISTORY INSTITUTE, CARLISLE BARRACKS, PA.)

An early postwar view of Frederick, Maryland. On September 6 "Stonewall" Jackson's troops occupied this much-troubled city. It changed hands several times during the war. (USAMHI)

sion had to be benevolent in tone. The necessity of winning converts in Maryland was such that Lee repeatedly urged his men to show exemplary behavior. That they did so, in the face of raggedness and hunger, is one of the remarkable incidents of the war.

On the morning of September 7 the Confederates paused at Frederick, Maryland. The army was subsisting—as it would throughout the first three weeks of September—on green corn, apples, and an occasional ration of potatoes. Lee himself

was in pain. A couple of days earlier he had slipped while mounting his horse. The fall to the ground had broken one hand and badly sprained the other. Yet no time existed for personal discomfort or rest. The army had to move. Maryland had not responded with support for the Confederates. Straggling was on the increase as hard roads tortured already raw feet. Even worse, Lee had received reports that a Federal army was now in pursuit.

Indeed, McClellan had been given a second

chance. In the latter stages of the Second Manassas Campaign he had found himself at Alexandria, Virginia, a general without an army. Yet Lincoln could not shelve McClellan, whether the President wished it or not. The salvation of the Union at the moment was the Army of the Potomac, and the only general who could make that army respond with any degree of effectiveness was McClellan. So, early in September the dapper little commander once again mounted his black charger, Daniel Webster, and rode to the head of his troops.

The 90,000 men that he greeted at Rockville, Maryland, were not all members of the old Army of the Potomac. Some units had been transferred from Pope's defeated Army of Virginia, while other regiments were entering the field for the first

time. Federal soldiers cheered the return of "Little Mac" and morale in the ranks climbed overnight. However, the march north and west in search of Lee was characteristic of McClellan: excruciatingly slow and methodical. In this instance McClellan was not entirely to blame. Scores of false reports relative to Lee's whereabouts poured into his headquarters. Worse, General-in-Chief Henry Halleck provided no stability. One day he would warn McClellan that if the Federal Army moved too far northward, Lee could veer around its right flank and threaten Washington. That same day, or the next, Halleck would warn McClellan that if the Federals advanced too far westward, Lee could lunge unmolested into Pennsylvania.

The self-doubts always lurking in McClellan

As Lee marched north, another gambler sat in the Executive Mansion in Washington pondering what seemed to be an unending succession of threats and reverses. Lincoln had little time to enjoy the grassy lawns being manicured here in a Brady & Company image from 1862. He had to stop Lee, and the only man who might do it was a high risk . . . (LIBRARY OF CONGRESS)

Major General George B. McClellan. He failed Lincoln badly on the Virginia Peninsula earlier that year and passively contributed to the defeat at Second Manassas. Yet Lincoln offered and "Little Mac" accepted. (USAMHI)

and they could be an impediment to a Southern withdrawal into the Shenandoah Valley. The possibility also loomed large that units from Pennsylvania's huge contingent of militia might move into the valley west of the first range of mountains and present a second front to the depleted Confederate Army.

What Lee decided to do became one of the most daring pieces of strategy in the Civil War. Jackson's fourteen brigades, in three different columns, would march southwestward to Harpers Ferry and overwhelm its defenders. Lee, with nine brigades,

But before he could get to Lee, McClellan had first to pass this stubborn, combative, highly opinionated Confederate, Major General Daniel H. Hill, shown here as a brigadier. At the South Mountain passes this brother-in-law of Jackson's held up the Federal advance for precious hours. (LC)

now festered. He wasted days in reorganizing his army, shifting generals here and there, insuring that supply trains, ammunition wagons, and the like were precisely where they were supposed to be. As a result—and during six critical days when the Army of the Potomac should have been in rapid, concentrated pursuit—it advanced a grand total of thirty miles.

In contrast, it took Lee a day at Frederick to analyze his problems and formulate his strategy. He had expected a Federal garrison at Harpers Ferry to abandon that post when the Confederates swept into Maryland. The garrison was still there. It had to be captured, for its 11,000 Federals lay across Lee's line of communications back to Richmond,

An early postwar view of the Wise House on South Mountain, near Fox's Gap.
Out in that field Major General Jesse Reno, commanding the Federal IX
Corps, took his mortal wound in the fierce fighting of September 14. (USAMHI)

would move due west across South Mountain and concentrate at Hagerstown to counter a potential threat from Pennsylvania militia. Daniel Harvey Hill's five brigades would advance only to Boonsborough so as to block both a Federal retreat from Harpers Ferry and a Federal advance toward the South Mountain passes.

These dispositions were spelled out precisely in Special Orders No. 191, which was issued to each of Lee's division commanders, and at dawn on September 10 the Confederates filed out of Frederick. Lee was taking a tremendous gamble: dividing his small army into five parts, with a river separating three of the parts from the other two. Secrecy was imperative for the success of the campaign. However, for the first time in the war, fortune was about to betray Lee.

On September 12, two days after Lee abandoned Frederick, McClellan's army fanned out in the fields surrounding the town. The 27th Indiana was relaxing in a campground formerly occupied by the Confederates when Corporal Barton W. Mitchell spied three cigars wrapped in a piece of paper on the ground. Tobacco was one of the most coveted commodities in the Union armies. Hence, it was a few minutes before Mitchell paid any attention to the wrapping. It was a copy of Special Orders No. 191, and within an hour it was at McClellan's headquarters. The Federal general was a beneficiary of the greatest security leak in American military history.

McClellan now knew precisely where Lee's army was, what Lee was doing, and what he was likely to do. The massive Federal Army at that moment was nearer each of the Confederate wings (Lee and Jackson) than they were to each other. McClellan would have to move promptly, for the orders were already four days old; and Lee was not one to waste time or to fall behind schedule. If McClellan took advantage of good roads, balmy weather, and advanced rapidly enough, he could annihilate the fractured Army of Northern Virginia. Yet the Federal commander again fell victim to gnawing uncertainty and self-doubt. Were Lee's "orders" purposefully left to be found? Was Lee where he said he would be? Was it all a trap?

Despite the fact that he outnumbered Lee by more than two to one, McClellan was not willing to take risks. With Jackson at Harpers Ferry, Lee at Hagerstown, and only Harvey Hill's division in his front, McClellan nevertheless began a slow

Colonel Rush Hawkins, organizer and commander of the 9th New York—Hawkins's Zouaves—was more fortunate than Reno. He lived through South Mountain to fight at Antietam. His first love, though, was old and rare books. (NATIONAL ARCHIVES)

movement westward. Throughout Saturday, September 13, the Federals crawled forward. Hill abandoned Boonsborough and began erecting hasty defenses at the passes atop South Mountain. This eminence, the key to the entire Confederate Army, was a long, irregular range of hills that began at the Potomac and continued some thirty-five miles northeastward. The two main passes—Crampton's and Turner's gaps—were about five hundred feet above the valley floor.

Hill had no time to reflect that this was his first independent command involving large numbers of troops. He was a dyspeptic, blunt, and caustic general; but as he looked down from the mountain at endless Federal brigades moving toward him, he confessed that he never felt so lonely in all his life. All of the world's soldiers seemed to be coming toward him. However, McClellan's continuing reliance on Allan Pinkerton's unreliable estimates of Confederate strength caused McClellan to conclude that Hill had five times more than the 6,000 Southerners digging in on the mountaintop.

McClellan therefore made careful, cautious plans that consumed a full day. Not until 9 A.M. on September 14 did the Federal columns start up the slopes. Union troops performed gallantly in scaling the mountainside in the face of sheets of musketry, but the Confederates were just as heroic in holding their position against tremendous odds. It was Thermopylae all over again. It was also the kind of battle that Harvey Hill fought best: hard, close-in combat, with firepower and determination rather than finesse and strategy being the major ingredients. On a more personal note, Hill had no way of knowing that day that one of the Federal brigade commanders assaulting his position was Brigadier General John Gibbon, who had been best man at Hill's wedding a few years earlier.

Intense conflict raged throughout the day as the bulk of two Federal corps swept repeatedly up the mountain, only to be driven back by concentrated fire from thin lines of Southerners massed above. Powder flashes blazed through the battle smoke; hand-to-hand fighting occurred in crevices and along ledges; bodies caromed down the mountainside. One observer likened the Army of the Potomac that day to "a monstrous, crawling, blue-black snake, miles long, quilled with the silver slant of muskets at a 'shoulder,' its sluggish tail writhing slowly up over the distant eastern ridge, its bruised

Alexander Gardner's October 1862 image shows some of the chief culprits in McClellan's consistent failures. These are men of the secret service corps at McClellan's headquarters. Standing, in a checked shirt, just left of the tent pole is Allan Pinkerton. A Scot with a considerable reputation as a detective before the war, he was an utter failure at gathering and evaluating military intelligence. He consistently exaggerated the enemy's numbers, making a cautious McClellan even more timid. (COURTESY OF THE CHICAGO HISTORICAL SOCIETY)

head weltering in the roar and smoke upon the crest above . . ."

Around 5 P.M. the Federals gained a momentary toehold at Crampton's Gap before Confederate reinforcements sent them scurrying down the ridge. The battle of South Mountain ended at sundown. Hill had suffered 40 percent casualties in a vicious fight that tactically was a draw. Yet the stand at South Mountain had given Lee a full day to react to McClellan's advance; and, as events were to prove, time was a critical factor.

On the Sunday that Hill made his reputation at South Mountain, "Stonewall" Jackson closed in on

the Federals defending Harpers Ferry. Jackson was still sore due to a fall from his horse a week earlier, but his concentration, as usual, was totally on the military situation at hand. Six divisions—the largest force Jackson had ever led—methodically took their positions on the mountains overlooking the Ferry. The tiny Federal garrison was caught in a trap. Late in the afternoon of the fourteenth Jackson's batteries began an uncontested bombardment. At dawn the following day Confederate smoothbores and rifled guns opened a concentrated barrage from three different directions. The cannonade lasted barely an hour before aged and ail-

Alexander Gardner's view of Main Street in Sharpsburg, Maryland, taken September 21 or 22. Here Lee came to a halt, his northern invasion stopped. Forced to the defensive, he now had to fight for his army's very life. (LC)

ing Colonel Dixon S. Miles realized the hopelessness of his situation and ordered his command to strike its colors. Miles was subsequently killed in the final shelling from Jackson's guns.

The Confederates bagged 11,500 prisoners, 73 cannon, 13,000 small arms, 200 wagons, and tons of equipment needed by a Southern army that was as destitute as it looked. A Union correspondent at Harpers Ferry noted that Jackson's appearance "was in no respect to be distinguished from the mongrel, bare-footed crew who follow his for-

tunes." That same reporter then added grudgingly: "I had heard much of the decayed appearance of the rebel soldiers, and yet they glory in their shame."

Jackson, now alerted by Lee to the necessity of rapid concentration, left Ambrose Powell Hill's division to secure Harpers Ferry while he headed northward to rejoin the other units of Lee's army. Meanwhile, Lee had weighed his options. During the fourteenth, with Jackson not in control of Harpers Ferry and Harvey Hill waging a no-win contest at South Mountain, Lee had contemplated withdrawal to Virginia. Then came news early on the fifteenth of Jackson's capture of the Ferry. Lee quickly decided to bring the fragments of his army together on the high ground at Sharpsburg, a village midway between Hagerstown and Harpers Ferry. Throughout that day, therefore, Southern brigades converged on Sharpsburg from the north, east, and south. McClellan could have assailed Lee's columns at any time with 60,000 men—which was far more than Lee could have mustered—but he vacillated too long before moving cautiously down the west face of South Mountain.

Lee's decision to stand and fight at Sharpsburg was, with the exception of Gettysburg, the most controversial decision he made during the war. It was bold, since he was weaker in terms of numbers, with the Potomac to his back and only one major avenue of escape. Yet boldness was characteristic of Lee, and boldness was also the only chance for success that the Confederacy possessed.

So the units of the Confederate Army hastily made for Sharpsburg. Major General James Longstreet opposed the site as a battleground; Jackson just as sternly endorsed it. Sharpsburg was a village three miles from the winding Potomac River. Only

Hall Street in Sharpsburg. At the moment that Gardner made his image, St. Paul's Lutheran Church, in the center background, was filled with wounded from the bloodiest day of the war. Gardner's photographic wagon is in the foreground. (LC)

*The Federals had been here before. In August 1862, in more placid days along
the Antietam, Colonel W. W. Averell of the 3rd Pennsylvania Cavalry sat with
fellow officers for the camera. (USAMHI)*

a ford at Shepherdstown offered escape. What attracted Lee to the site was a formidable defense
line: a low, crescent-shaped ridge that extended
from northwest to southeast of the town. The Confederate left would rest on the Potomac itself; the
right would anchor on Antietam Creek, a sluggish
north-south stream too deep for the passage of artillery. Hence, the few bridges over it would be of
great strategic importance.

Lack of time and tools prevented the Confederates from preparing elaborate entrenchments at
Sharpsburg. Brigades arriving on September 15
and 16 simply threw up what defenses they could.
It became a truly remarkable battlefield; the three-
mile Confederate line was so compact that from a
number of vantage points its entire length was visible.

September 16 was the day that McClellan lost

But now the whole Federal Army was here, McClellan making his headquarters in the Pry house. Alexander Gardner made this image within a day of the battle. (LC)

his opportunity. Lee was at most disorganized and at the very least off balance. Fully half his forces were still not on the field. Absenteeism and straggling had put the whole army in the weakest condition it had ever been in. Lee had barely 40,000 men to contest more than twice that number. Never was the opportunity for Federal victory greater. If McClellan had hurled the mighty Army of the Potomac against the improvised and under-manned Confederate line on the sixteenth, it undoubtedly would have snapped, with perhaps fatal consequences. Yet McClellan spent the day perfecting his own lines, getting cannon into proper position, reconsidering moves, and weighing risks. Thus, while skirmishers bickered and artillerists tested their aim, Jackson's men made a hard march and in the late afternoon were reunited with Lee's army at Sharpsburg.

The 93rd New York served at Antietam as the headquarters guard for the Army of the Potomac. It kept them from facing the terror of battle with the rest of the army, but they were happy to face Gardner's camera early in October. (USAMHI)

Through a night of drizzling rain the two armies sat and waited nervously for the battle that would come with the dawn. Jackson's brigades formed Lee's left, Harvey Hill held the center, and Longstreet commanded the right. Movements late on the sixteenth gave ample indication that the battle would begin in Jackson's front, a mile north of Sharpsburg. There, on the west side of the Hagerstown Turnpike, stood a patch of trees known as the West Woods. The area was two hundred to three hundred yards wide and surrounded, on three sides, the white, boxlike Dunker Church standing on a slight knoll. Immediately across the

turnpike from the West Woods was another clump of trees. Known as the East Woods and similarly about two hundred yards in width, it extended a quarter of a mile eastward. Between the two woods, adjacent to the east side of the road, was a forty-acre cornfield with green stalks head-high at that time of the season.

McClellan's battle plan seemed logical enough, given the preponderance of troops at his disposal. The I and XII Federal Corps would spearhead an assault on Lee's left flank. Two additional corps would act in support. This heavy attack would cause the Confederate left to collapse onto the cen-

From this site on Elk Mountain McClellan's signalmen watched Lee's movements in his lines along the Antietam. This signal tower was built after the battle. (USAMHI)

ter and block any further Southern advances toward Hagerstown. Simultaneously, the IX Corps on the Federal left would assail Lee's right flank and turn Lee from his escape route. Then, while the two-pronged attack acted as a vise against Lee's army, McClellan would advance with his remaining divisions and crush the Confederate center.

It was an excellent plan, multifaceted but simple.

It depended only on superior numbers and coordination—and McClellan failed on both accounts. Wednesday, September 17, 1862, became the bloodiest single day of the Civil War, in large part because the Federals attacked piecemeal, thus allowing a critically outmanned Lee to utilize his inner lines of defense to maximum advantage. Antietam Creek (or Sharpsburg, as the battle is also called) consisted of three heavy engagements piled one atop

The Potomac crossing at Harpers Ferry. Lee wanted the Federal garrison there eliminated to protect his rear. (USAMHI)

the other. It was a headlong, daylong explosion of combat, void of memorable tactics—concentrated violence in which thousands of soldiers blazed away in fiery collisions stretching across woods, fields, hillsides, and bottomland. American soldiers never fought harder. Death became commonplace as acts of heroism on one side matched gallantry on the other.

The rain stopped shortly before dawn that morning, and a wet mist quickly gave way to clear skies and the promise of a hot day. In command of the first attack (as well as the Federal I Corps) was handsome and ambitious Major General Joseph Hooker, a hard-fighting, hard-living officer. Thirty-five Federal cannon raked the Confederate positions as an overture. Then, at 6 A.M., ten bri-

gades from the I Corps charged down the Hagerstown Turnpike. Opposing this assault by 12,000 Federals were less than 7,000 Confederates under Jackson. Billy Yanks fought their way through the woods and the cornfield. Confederate musketry took a heavy toll; men fell to the ground with each passing second. Yet Hooker's troops almost reached the Dunker Church and the valuable high ground that was the key to Lee's left flank. A Confederate staff officer wrote of the action: "Such a storm of balls I never conceived it possible for men to live through. Shot and shell shrieking and crashing, canister and bullets whistling and hissing most fiend-like through the air until you could almost see them."

As Jackson called for reinforcements, the

McClellan then turned to Nathaniel Banks's veterans from the 1862 Valley Campaign. Reorganized as the XII Corps, these soldiers were under the command of Major General Joseph K. F. Mansfield. He was a red-faced, white-haired old regular who had graduated from West Point in 1822—before most of his men were even born. Mansfield rushed his brigades forward into action and was among the first to suffer a mortal wound when a bullet tore through his stomach. His men

One of those sent with Jackson to take Harpers Ferry was Brigadier General Ambrose R. Wright, a Georgian who would be seriously wounded at Antietam following the capture of Harpers Ferry.
(VALENTINE MUSEUM)

cornfield became a vast slaughter pen. It was a ghastly sight, bloodred now from the carnage. Never in the history of the Army of Northern Virginia were so many high-ranking officers knocked out of action so quickly. At one point a Confederate colonel was in command of a division because all of his superiors were either dead or wounded. Just as Jackson's line seemed on the verge of snapping, fresh troops under Generals Harvey Hill and John B. Hood rushed on the scene. This new Southern attack a Union officer likened to "a scythe running through our line." Around 7:30 A.M. the battered I Corps slowly withdrew from the field. A fourth of its number, including Hooker, were casualties; and the remainder were mentally up to nothing more that day.

Colonel Dixon A. Miles of the 2nd United States Infantry commanded the Federals at Harpers Ferry. Accused of drunkenness during the First Manassas fighting, Miles was relegated to a post of lesser importance—lesser, that is, until Lee invaded the North. He stayed longer than he should have and finally surrendered to Jackson. One of the very last shots fired killed him. (USAMHI)

*Antietam Bridge, taken by Gardner on September 22. In fact, relatively little
happened here, but the photographer found it an alluring subject for his
camera.* (WAR LIBRARY AND MUSEUM, MOLLUS-PENNSYLVANIA, PHILADELPHIA)

continued their assault and managed to regain part
of the East Woods and the cornfield. Fighting was
vicious every foot of the way. Hooker later observed that "every stalk of corn in the northern and
greater part of the field was cut as closely as could
have been done with a knife, and the slain lay in
rows precisely as they had stood in their ranks a
few moments before. It was never my fortune to
witness a more bloody, dismal battlefield."

This second wave of assaults by Mansfield's
corps came in from the northeast, lasted ninety
minutes, and also proved fruitless. Confederates
firing as rapidly as they could load their guns

forced the Federals to relinquish the ground. Had
the corps of Hooker and Mansfield attacked in
concert and in a concentrated fashion, the outcome
would probably have been different. Yet concerted
effort and concentration on the part of the Federal
Army was lacking throughout the battle.

At 9 A.M., after three hours of killing, McClellan
resumed the offensive with a third major attack
over the same ground. He ordered the 18,000
troops in the II Corps to assail Jackson from the
east-northeast. In command of this corps was
Major General Edwin V. "Bull" Sumner, an old
Indian fighter with a booming voice and an obses-

sion with rigid discipline. Jackson, meanwhile, had readjusted his lines so that they formed a rough northward-facing arc with the outer points firmly planted.

Sumner's three divisions dashed forward and promptly fell out of alignment, with the result that the sharp point of the attack was blunted before it could pierce the Confedrate lines. Major General John Sedgwick's lead division of 5,000 men lumbered into the battle web that Jackson had spun. Half of those Federals were casualties in less than twenty minutes. Sedgwick himself received three wounds that put this superior combat officer out of action for five months.

A lull in the fighting then gave Jackson a chance to launch an attack of his own, with the three fourths of Lee's army now under his command. Shouting Confederates rushed for the cornfield and were almost at the north end when they came under a withering cross fire from fifty cannon concealed several hundred yards away. The Southern ranks were shredded instantly. Jackson called off the assault; this order brought an end to the four-hour fight on the left. Three Federal corps had gone into action one after another. Two were shattered and the third was broken. Federal losses included over 5,000 men. The extent of Southern casualties can be gauged from the fact that after the battle New England soldiers scouting near the Dunker Church chanced upon 146 Confederate bodies lying in a neat, soldierly line. The celebrated Stonewall Brigade, reduced to 250 men by the Second Manassas Campaign, had 88 new holes in its ranks.

The Dunker Church on the Antietam battlefield, taken after the battle damage had been repaired. For the thousands of men who contested the ground around it, this simple structure came to symbolize the bloody horror of Antietam.
(USAMHI)

Antietam Bridge again, this time looking northeast. McClellan's headquarters in the Pry house was not far distant, and he used this crossing frequently in sending troops into the battle line. (USAMHI)

Around 10 A.M. the battle shifted southward to what was the Confederate center. This second stage of Antietam Creek would likewise last four hours. Like the rest of McClellan's strategy, this second stage lacked the coordination necessary for total success. The middle of Lee's line at that moment consisted of little more than two brigades (those of Robert Rodes and G. B. Anderson) in Harvey Hill's division. They were posted in a sunken road that ran eastward along a ravine for a thousand yards, then jackknifed southward for the same distance. The Confederates were frantically placing fence rails along the road as defenses when Federals appeared in force on the hilltop above them.

These columns were part of two divisions from Sumner's II Corps (the third division in that corps had literally been wrecked at the Dunker Church). Confederates massed in the road watched in awe as line after line of Federals advanced in paradelike fashion down the hill toward them. "Their gleaming bayonets flashed like burnished silver in the sunlight," a Southern officer noted, and they marched "with the precision of step and perfect alignment of a holiday parade." However, the two Federal divisions actually attacked in what that day was typical disjointed fashion.

The lead division was under Major General William H. French, a hot-tempered, hard-drinking commander whose habit of shutting his eyes tightly when talking caused the men to nickname him "Old Blinkey." French's first wave of troops simply

The Boonsborough Pike crossed the Antietam at the bridge as it ran from Elk Mountain to Sharpsburg. Behind Newcomer's barn, on the left, Lee laid his first line of defense on the ridge on September 15, awaiting McClellan.
(USAMHI)

melted away as a result of a heavy volley of musketry from the road. A second wave met the same fate as Federals struggled with the additional obstacle of getting over and around bodies sprawled across the hillside. A third attack produced more casualties for French's battered ranks. Billy Yanks seized whatever protection they could find along the hill; both sides rushed in reinforcements; and a Union officer reported that for three hours "the battle raged incessantly, without either party giving way."

Major General Israel B. Richardson's division then entered the contest in support of French's men. Richardson was a tough veteran of frontier fighting, an unpretentious man who had no use for such military frills as a uniform. He personally led his brigades into action, and he used his sword both to wave his lines forward and to drive skulkers from cover as his profane voice thundered above the action. At one point Richardson shouted: "Where's General ———?"

From the ranks came the reply: "Behind the haystack!"

"God damn the field officers!" Richardson bellowed as he raced downhill into the battle smoke.

Around 1 P.M. some of Richardson's men succeeded in capturing the high ground near the road's sharp bend. Federals poured an enfilading fire into the 300-odd Confederates still fighting defiantly. The Southerners could not withstand this

Newcomer's Mill on Antietam Creek, by Gardner. (USAMHI)

new fire. Weary, battle-blackened men fell back to a new position. The sunken road was thereafter known as Bloody Lane—and for good reason. A Federal officer who viewed the bodies strewn in the lane commented that a man could walk as far down that road as one could see without stepping on the ground. On the other hand, gaining that road had involved a staggering cost to the Federals. The divisions of French and Richardson suffered combined losses of 509 killed, 2,254 wounded, and 152 missing. Among the slain was Richardson, who died of infection resulting from a bullet wound.

With Lee's center all but broken, the situation was critical. Colonel E. Porter Alexander, a Con-

federate artillery commander, observed: "Lee's army was ruined, and the end of the Confederacy was in sight." How desperate things were for the Army of Northern Virginia is apparent from two personal incidents. Harvey Hill rounded up 200 stragglers, grabbed a musket, and led a pitiful counterattack that withered in the face of concentrated firepower from the Union lines. Major General James Longstreet, heavyset and somber, was hobbling that day in a carpet slipper because of an infected blister on his foot; nevertheless he helped exhausted gunners man an artillery piece. Yet these acts of devotion did not stop the Federal breakthrough from being complete. Astoundingly, McClellan did that. "It would not be prudent" to deliver another assault, he told Major General William B. Franklin, whose fresh VI Corps—along with Fitz John Porter's entire V Corps—stood poised for the final blow. After the four bloodiest hours to which that day would be witness, McClellan again changed directions and ordered attacks from a different sector. The conflict now moved to its third and final stage.

To the south of the battlefield was a stone bridge that spanned Antietam Creek. The road approaching it from the east ran parallel to the stream, then turned abruptly at the bridge and plunged into a funnel-like valley before crossing the bridge. Immediately at the western end of the structure the road veered sharply to the north because of a ridge sev-

eral hundred feet high that came to within a short distance of the creek's bank. Atop that hill some small Georgia regiments were entrenched under blustery Brigadier General Robert Toombs.

Commanding the Federal left was Major General Ambrose E. Burnside. A heavily bewhiskered Rhode Islander, he was well liked by all, especially the men in his IX Corps. His four divisions should have acted as a huge sledgehammer against Lee's right. However, instead of employing them en masse against the weak Confederate defenses, Burnside sent them piecemeal into battle that morning. He insisted that the regiments go one at a time across the stone bridge; and as they did, concentrated musketry and canister from the hilltop

The ruins of the Samuel Mumma house three days after the battle. Here the real fighting in the Battle of Antietam began as the Union I Corps swept against Ewell's and D. H. Hill's Confederates positioned here and nearby. (LC)

raked the lines and easily forced each column back from the arched span. Around 1 P.M., as the fight at Bloody Lane came to an end, Federal batteries opened a heavy bombardment at the bridge. The 51st New York and 51st Pennsylvania dashed across the span and established a bridgehead on the west bank of the Antietam. The Georgians, having waged a Thermopylae-like struggle throughout the morning, grudgingly retired from the crest of the hill.

For the Union Army the opportunity again existed for a decisive and fatal thrust into Lee's lines. Yet McClellan was tardy in ordering a concerted attack, Burnside was clumsy in executing it,

Brigadier General George L. Hartsuff led a brigade in Hooker's I Corps in the first attacks against the Confederates, falling with a wound that put him out of action for months. (USAMHI)

and coordination was once more lacking. Burnside consumed two hours in reorganizing his numerically superior forces, and it was midafternoon before thousands of Federals began moving across the rolling country toward the vulnerable Confederate flank. Long lines of Billy Yanks brushed aside what remained of Toombs's Georgians, then slammed into D. R. Jones's four brigades—which was all that was left of Lee's army south of Sharpsburg.

Lee quickly shifted artillery pieces and fragments of units southward to meet this powerful assault. Longstreet wrote of that moment: "We were already badly whipped and were holding our ground by sheer force of desperation." Indeed they were. By 4 P.M. Sharpsburg was in flames; wounded and demoralized Confederates filled the streets and added a mood of near panic to the frenzy of battle roaring across the countryside; Federal flags were waving in triumph as Burnside's men advanced to within half a mile of Lee's sole escape route. Less than nine hundred yards separated the Union from complete victory against Lee.

Then occurred one of those rare, dramatic moments that history never forgets. The Federal brigades were so intent in pushing northwestward against Lee's flank that apparently no one saw a column of dust rising in the air to the south. Beneath that dust was the Confederate "Light Division" of Major General A. Powell Hill, a hard-driving Virginian who sometimes wore red shirts in battle as if to underscore his disdain for danger. After Jackson had captured Harpers Ferry, he had left A. P. Hill's division behind to secure the post. The sound of battle early on September 17 told Hill that he was badly needed elsewhere; so late that morning he got his troops on the road and started northward. Hill pushed the men hard. Johnny Rebs too exhausted to maintain the pace collapsed along the roadside in droves. Yet Hill urged the men forward, sometimes with the point of his sword. No more than 3,000 of his 5,000 troops reached Sharpsburg; but they marched seventeen miles in seven hours and turned the tide of battle.

Confederates gasping for breath ploughed into Burnside's exposed left flank. Hill himself led the attack, obviously enjoying every second of the intense fighting (though he was the meekest of men away from battle). Many of his Confederates were wearing blue uniforms captured at Harpers Ferry.

Appearing almost asleep, this dead horse, probably belonging to Colonel Henry Strong of the 6th Louisiana, himself killed in the battle, lies peacefully near the East Woods where Hooker launched his attack. (LC)

This added to the confusion in the unexpected onslaught; shrill screams of the "rebel yell" brought a frightening dimension to weary Federals trying to cope with Hill's attack. It was no use. The conflict in Burnside's sector turned around in a matter of minutes. Federal columns ground to a halt, recoiled, then fell back to the cover of artillery along Antietam Creek. This withdrawal marked the last major action of the day. Night came at last; and when it was impossible to fight any longer, the opposing lines drew apart by mutual consent. In the ensuing darkness there slowly arose a new, more chilling sound: thousands of screams and moans from soldiers too maimed by war to do anything else.

Vicious combat had raged for fourteen hours. Over 100,000 men and 500 artillery pieces had fought a fierce struggle along a 3-mile front. After the long holocaust, Lee's left had been forced back a mile, while his right had retreated half a mile. Those were the day's gains; they paled to insignificance when compared to the losses. The Army of the Potomac suffered 12,410 casualties, including 3,000 dead. Lee's losses amounted to 10,700 men. That figure is smaller, to be sure, but it constituted fully a fourth of the Confederate Army. The extent of damage that the Army of Northern Virginia had suffered became obvious that night when Lee held a council of war. All of his lieutenants voiced discouragement. General Hood stated that he simply had no more men left.

"Great God!" Lee exclaimed. "Where is that splendid division you had this morning?"

"They are lying on the field where you sent them," the dejected Hood replied. "My division has been almost wiped out."

Brigadier General William E. Starke fell early in the fight with three separate wounds. He lay dying even as the Federals were pushing his division out of the West Woods. (USAMHI)

Displaying stubborn determination, however, on September 18 Lee waited for McClellan to renew the assaults. Lee had only 30,000 ill-equipped men at hand, while McClellan could boast of more than three times that number. On the field were two Federal corps that had seen no action in the slaughter of the previous day. Yet the hills and dales around Sharpsburg remained deathly still for hour after hour that Thursday. The stench of death fouled the air for miles as the two armies eyed each other warily. Meanwhile McClellan weighed his risks, gathered reports, conferred with his generals, awaited reinforcements, and made vague plans for an attack the next day, or the next, or the next. Across the way Lee's position became more untenable as the day passed, particularly

with Federal reinforcements fast approaching. Shortly after sundown bone-tired Confederates slipped away from their lines and painfully started southward toward Virginia. An abandoned battlefield greeted McClellan the following morning.

Permitting the Army of Northern Virginia to escape was the worst of McClellan's many failures at Antietam Creek. On the other hand, he must be given some credit in this campaign. He assumed command of demoralized forces early in September; and in the short space of three weeks he had restored morale, reorganized an army, strengthened Washington's defenses, fought two major engagements, forced Lee's retreat to Virginia, and swept Maryland clean of Confederate troops. McClellan felt quite justified in boasting, after Antietam Creek: "I feel that I have done all that can be asked in twice saving the country." Therein lies the tragedy of this general. He never talked of defeating the Confederacy; his only concern was in protecting the Union.

A disappointed Lee found pride in his men as compensation for defeat. "This great battle," he stated, "was fought by less than 40,000 men on our side, all of whom had undergone the greatest labors and hardships in the field and on the march. Nothing could surpass the determined valor with which they met the larger army of the enemy, fully supplied and equipped, and the result reflects the highest credit on the officers and men engaged."

Antietam Creek was not the decisive Union victory that Lincoln had hoped to see, but driving Lee from the North was success enough to prompt Lincoln into an action he had long been considering. On the Monday following the battle, September 22, the President summoned his Cabinet together and announced his intentions of issuing a preliminary emancipation proclamation. The base of the war would thereafter be broadened and its ends appreciably heightened.

Other than Lincoln, few persons at that time sensed that the war's high-water mark may have been reached. Another individual who possibly, and ironically, arrived at the same conclusion was Jefferson Davis. To his Secretary of War shortly after the battle, the Confederate President observed: "Our maximum strength has been mobilized, while the enemy is just beginning to put forth his might."

Truman Seymour, a brigadier general, led a brigade in Hooker's corps that distinguished itself and him, at Turner's Gap; it continued to perform well at Antietam. Among his regiments was . . . (USAMHI)

Colonel Hugh W. McNeill's 13th Pennsylvania Reserves, the "Bucktails." McNeill's own bucktail shows in his kepi. He was killed the day before the battle. (USAMHI)

Many fell. Many died. In the fierce fighting along the Hagerstown Pike beside the West Woods and just north of the Dunker Church, hundreds of Confederates of Starke's command sought shelter behind this rail fence. It did them little good. Two days later Gardner found them lying singly . . .
(USAMHI)

. . . in groups . . . (LC)

. . . and heaped in piles, their Louisiana blood soaking the soil of Maryland.
(LC)

*After Hooker's initial attack calmed, Major
General John Sedgwick led his division of the fresh
II Corps against the Hagerstown Pike and the
Confederates in the West Woods.* (NA)

Captain Joseph Knap's Battery E, Pennsylvania Light Artillery, joined Sedgwick in his attack, taking a position near the Dunker Church. Gardner photographed them two days later, with the open ground between the East, West, and North Woods beyond. (LC)

Men and colors of the 34th New York, Sedgwick's division. Antietam put more than one tear in their tattered banners. (COURTESY OF MICHAEL J. MCAFEE)

The fighting raged for hours, the casualties falling in rows. Near the Dunker Church, with the West Woods behind it, these Confederate artillerymen died defending their battery, probably Captain W. W. Parker's battery of Virginia Light Artillery. (USAMHI)

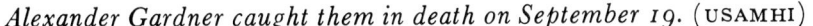

Alexander Gardner caught them in death on September 19. (USAMHI)

Brigadier General Roswell Ripley led a Confederate brigade posted behind the Mumma house. He ordered it burned to prevent its affording shelter to attackers, then later fell wounded himself in the fighting in front of the West Woods. (LC)

Brigadier General Samuel Garland also led a brigade that tried to resist Sedgwick's advance. He could not. He was not with them, having been killed in the fight for Fox's Gap three days before. (MUSEUM OF THE CONFEDERACY)

Brigadier General John B. Hood was in the fighting early, his brigade suffering terrible losses. The 1st Texas under his command lost 82.3 percent of its men as casualties, the greatest loss in any unit in either army during the war. (VM)

The division of Lafayette McLaws was rushed toward the West Woods as Sedgwick attacked. One of McLaws's brigade commanders was a man who, two years before, sat in President Buchanan's cabinet. Howell Cobb of Georgia, once Secretary of the Treasury and a prominent candidate for Confederate President, was now a brigadier general. (UNIVERSITY OF GEORGIA LIBRARY)

Brigadier General John G. Walker's division came to the West Woods, too. He served in the United States Army during the Mexican War, and appears here as a lieutenant in a photo from the 1850s. (TULANE UNIVERSITY)

The converging Confederates caught Sedgwick and shattered his command, forcing him back to the support of the rest of the II Corps, led by Major General Edwin V. Sumner, the oldest corps commander in the Union Army. (CWTI)

Here the Confederates counterattack, driving Sedgwick and Sumner back.
(NATIONAL LIBRARY OF MEDICINE)

Colonel Turner G. Morehead led his 106th Pennsylvania in Oliver O. Howard's brigade of Sedgwick's division. In the rout of Sedgwick, Morehead's horse was shot from under him. Retreating on foot, he ran back into the face of the advancing enemy to recover his sword. "I am not going to let them damned rebels get it," he exclaimed. (LC)

Brigadier General Winfield Scott Hancock was a brigade commander in the II Corps. After Sedgwick's repulse, he and others were ordered forward to take possession of ground east of the West Woods. The Confederates met them at a sunken road later to be called Bloody Lane. (P-M)

The hours of bloody fighting for that road took hundreds of lives, among them that of Hancock's division commander, Israel Richardson, seated at center. Hancock succeeded him. (LC)

The lane ran along the property of the Roulette farm. Richardson advanced past the farmhouse to hurl his brigades against the Confederates. (USAMHI)

William Harrow, as colonel of the 14th Indiana, fought his regiment for four hours against Bloody Lane, losing half of his numbers. (P-M)

Regular artillerymen from Fitz John Porter's otherwise unengaged corps aided in the attack on Bloody Lane. Captain James M. Robertson led two batteries of the 2nd United States Artillery in the assaults. He stands at right of center. He will become a general after the war. (P-M)

Among the Confederate defenders of the lane, Colonel John B. Gordon of the 6th Alabama took a wound in the head and was only saved from drowning in his own blood by the bullet hole in his hat. (TU)

Confederate dead in the Bloody Lane, taken by Gardner two days after the battle. (LC)

Dead North Carolinians awaiting burial in Bloody Lane. (USAMHI)

After the fighting on the right and center of McClellan's line, he finally sent Major General Ambrose Burnside forward to attack Lee's right flank. Burnside appears here as a brigadier. (KEAN ARCHIVES)

Despite low water that would allow wading the Antietam at several points, Burnside sent his command, brigade by brigade, across this stone span. It would later be called Burnside's Bridge. Here it is viewed from the position of the Confederates who defended it . . . (LC)

. . . and here is how it looked to the attackers who tried to cross it in the face
of a wall of fire from Confederates on the ridge beyond. (LC)

The Sherrick farm buildings just west of Burnside's Bridge. Confederates
swarmed all around the farm, and when Joseph Sherrick left to escape the
battle, he hid $3,000 in gold in his stone wall. He got it back after the battle.
(LC)

Once Burnside finally crossed, his men steadily drove back the Confederate defenders. They left their dead, like these on the Sherrick farm, behind them.
(LC)

Finally forced to leave the field to the enemy, Lee retired from Sharpsburg on September 19. Brigadier General James H. Lane commanded the rear guard as the Confederates withdrew. (VM)

The 139th Pennsylvania arrived on the field on the evening of September 17, too late for the battle. With more Federal reinforcements coming up, Lee would have been foolish to remain. (WESTERN RESERVE HISTORICAL SOCIETY)

The day after the fight. Alexander Gardner began the work of photographing the field. One of his first views was taken from near McClellan's headquarters, showing reserve artillery east of the Antietam. Long thought to be an actual "battle" image showing fighting taking place on the right, the picture actually shows only soldiers lounging in the lowland on the right, while artillery stands idle at left. (LC)

With the threat of dismissal from the army hanging over him as a result of charges about his conduct at Second Manassas, Fitz John Porter sat out the battle on the Antietam, his V Corps being held in reserve. (USAMHI)

Part of Porter's corps, however, did pursue Lee after the Confederates began
their withdrawal. The 2nd Maine, shown here in camp at Hall's Hill, Virginia,
crossed the Potomac and skirmished with the enemy on September 20. (WRHS)

And cavalry units, which sat out most of the main battle along the Antietam,
managed to snipe at Lee's heels as the Confederates crossed at Shepherdstown.
Here, standing in the center, is Colonel David M. Gregg and his officers of the
8th Pennsylvania Cavalry. (LC)

*Shepherdstown on the Potomac, where McClellan's feeble attempt to pursue
Lee made its only real challenge.* (LC)

*While part of the army pursued, much of it bled. Back on the Antietam the
Federal surgeons set up their makeshift hospitals. Many sprouted in barns like
Dr. Otho Smith's place near Keedysville, taken here by Gardner on September
20.* (USAMHI)

Huts were built of straw to provide temporary shelter from the sun. (USAMHI)

Dr. Anson Hurd of the 14th Indiana cared for the wounded from Confederate commands in a hasty field hospital. (USAMHI)

*Then there were the dead to bury, the men
who really purchased this field of blood.
They lay everywhere.* (USAMHI)

*On September 19 Gardner captured burial details working with Federal dead
near the North Woods.* (USAMHI)

And here is the lonely grave of John Marshall of Company L, 28th Pennsylvania, near the West Woods. (USAMHI)

And the land itself had to recover. St. Paul's suffered heavy damage from artillery fire on both sides. (LC)

And the Federals had time to rest after their greatest test yet in the war. Army blacksmiths had to tend to shodding new stock to replace the hundreds of horses killed. (COURTESY OF THE OAKLAND MUSEUM)

Soldiers like these relaxed in the calm of the waters beside Antietam Bridge, forgetting the pain of just a few days before. (LC)

The home of Stephen Grove became headquarters for Fitz John Porter. An officer of his staff could leisurely pose for Gardner in front of the house and headquarters tents. (USAMHI)

And dignitaries could visit to compliment the army and futilely urge McClellan to further action. On October 3 President Abraham Lincoln came to the army. McClellan stands facing him to the left. Just to the right of Lincoln, his hand on his sword, is Porter. To the far right, almost as if not a part of the group, is an aide on McClellan's staff, Captain George Armstrong Custer. (MINNESOTA HISTORICAL SOCIETY)

Talking to a general who would not listen. Gardner's October 4 image captured a historic scene as the President patiently tried to persuade "Little Mac" to go after Lee. McClellan was content with his battle trophies, like the Confederate battle flag lying on the ground at left. A month later the President would relieve McClellan of his command and continue his search for a general to bring him victory. (LC)

The Fury of Fredericksburg

PETER J. PARRISH

In a war of mistakes, this battle is the most senseless;
even the victor regrets it

THE SMALL VIRGINIA TOWN of Fredericksburg lay in the midst of the fiercely contested hundred miles of territory between the Union and Confederate capitals, almost exactly a halfway house between Washington and Richmond. A quiet town dating from the seventeenth century, with a population of some three or four thousand, it had watched the contending armies swirl around it for more than eighteen months, but the full horror of war had hitherto stopped short of its red-brick houses and cobbled streets. However, on November 21, 1862, a Union officer brought to the mayor and Common Council of Fredericksburg a letter from Major General Edwin V. Sumner, commanding the Right Grand Division of the Army of the Potomac. He demanded the surrender of the town; if his request was refused, sixteen hours would be allowed for the evacuation of the civilian population before a bombardment began. The arrival of Confederate troops on the high ground behind the town soon altered the situation, but Fredericksburg now found itself in the no-man's-land between two armies readying themselves for battle.

The arrival of the war at Fredericksburg's doorstep followed directly from the first major decision taken by the new commander of the Army of the

Potomac, Ambrose E. Burnside. When Lincoln had relieved George B. McClellan of the command of that army early in November 1862, he had surprised many observers by the choice of Burnside as his successor. Sensing his own inadequacy, Burnside accepted the appointment only with the greatest reluctance. But the President's range of choice was extremely limited. If the field of candidates was to be confined to corps commanders in the Army of the Potomac, Lincoln did not want to choose a confirmed disciple of McClellan's, such as William B. Franklin, nor an outspoken critic, such as Joseph Hooker. Despite his poor showing at Antietam, Burnside seemed to have much to commend him. He had shown promise in an independent command in North Carolina and courage and loyalty in the Army of the Potomac. He was in many ways an attractive figure, tall and striking in appearance, honest and straightforward in manner. However, his own self-doubt was amply justified; behind the imposing facade lived a man of limited capacity and limited horizons, as the next few weeks were to show. Like many other officers on both sides, Burnside could perform courageously and creditably up to a certain point, but he was quite incapable of effective command of an army incomparably larger than anything for which West

In the wake of Antietam, on October 4, 1862, Lincoln posed with Allan Pinkerton and Major General John McClernand at McClellan's headquarters. The President's patience with "Little Mac" was wearing thin. There was pressure for a new commander. (NA)

A month later Lincoln appointed one: Major General Ambrose Burnside. He was a man with great self-doubts that proved to be well justified. (USAMHI)

Point training or wartime experience had prepared him. Furthermore, whatever he did, he had little hope of satisfying both the defenders of the deposed McClellan and those who assumed that McClellan's removal would be followed by instant success.

When Burnside took command, the bulk of his army was in the area of Warrenton, just east of the Bull Run Mountains. He organized his huge force of over 120,000 men into three Grand Divisions (each comprising two corps), commanded by Sumner, Franklin, and Hooker. His redoubtable opponent, Robert E. Lee, had also reorganized his much smaller army, now numbering some 80,000

men, into two corps of four divisions each, commanded by James Longstreet and "Stonewall" Jackson. With characteristic audacity Lee had separated the two corps of his much smaller army by a distance of some fifty miles, with Longstreet at Culpeper Court House, to the south of the Union position, and Jackson still in the Shenandoah Valley.

Burnside quickly decided that he wished to transfer the operations of his army some thirty-five miles to the southeast, in the vicinity of Fredericksburg. This was Burnside's answer to the dilemma which faced all Northern commanders in Virginia. Operations near the coast offered the great advantage of secure supply lines by water but faced the obstacle of a series of rivers obstructing any advance. Operations farther inland faced less serious natural obstacles but depended on a fragile and lengthening supply line. Indeed, Burnside believed that he could not rely upon the rickety, single-track Orange & Alexandria Railroad to sustain his army; he therefore preferred to move farther east, with a view to moving upon Richmond from Fredericksburg. Neither General-in-Chief Henry Halleck nor the President cared much for this plan. Halleck visited Burnside and seems to have succeeded only in confusing both Burnside and himself about the specific movements which the former intended. On November 14 Lincoln finally gave his grudging consent to the plan, adding, in all too accurate words of warning, that "it will succeed if you move very rapidly, otherwise not."

Time was indeed the crux of the matter. If Burnside was to have any chance of success, it was essential that he should get his forces south of the Rappahannock River at or near Fredericksburg before Lee could concentrate his army to resist him. Burnside set his army in motion on November 15 and ordered pontoons to be sent to Falmouth, just across the Rappahannock from Fredericksburg, for use in the river crossing. On November 17 his leading contingent, under Sumner, arrived at Falmouth. The railroad from Falmouth to the landing at Aquia Creek was being repaired and supplies were beginning to arrive, but they included no pontoons. Sumner was anxious to cross the river without them, drive out the handful of Confederates in Fredericksburg, and seize the high ground beyond. However, Burnside thought the risks too great, and as the rest of the army came up, it

*But Burnside took his new command and showed a disposition to act. He
would turn Lee's flank on the Rappahannock by crossing and taking
Fredericksburg, shown here in an 1863 Timothy O'Sullivan image.* (USAMHI)

joined Sumner's troops in awaiting the pontoons.
They did not arrive until November 25, but by
then the opportunity to seize the key positions beyond the Rappahannock without opposition was
gone for good. From November 21, Longstreet's
corps of Lee's army was digging itself in on the
heights behind Fredericksburg, and on November 30 Jackson's corps completed its longer march
to the same area.

Before any serious fighting occurred, Burnside
had already lost his best opportunity. The blame
for the failure to deliver the pontoons on time may
have rested with Halleck—or, more generally, it
may have reflected the creaking organization and
unreliable communications of the Union Army.
The responsibility for the delay in crossing the river
was essentially Burnside's, and it is permissible to
speculate whether the pontoons would have mat-
tered so much if his army had made its sideways
move along both sides of the Rappahannock instead of only on its northern side.

With his usual skill in divining the intentions of
his opponents, Lee foresaw that Burnside might
move towards Fredericksburg, but he could not be
sure what would happen next. It was late in the
season for further campaigning in northern Virginia, and the weather had already turned wet and
cold. Indeed, the battle which was to take place at
Fredericksburg in December was the first great
winter battle of the war. At first Lee suspected that
Burnside's move to Falmouth and the Aquia Creek
base might be no more than a prelude to a return
to the Peninsular strategy, or even to a waterborne
attack at some point farther down the coast, perhaps in North Carolina. However, by the end of
November he was convinced that the next great
clash between the two armies was to be in and
around Fredericksburg.

Lee fully understood the strength of the defensive position which he occupied behind the town,
although it had not been his first choice to make a
stand there. He appreciated the force of the argu-

Major General Edwin V. Sumner was ready to cross part of his corps before
the Confederates reached Fredericksburg, but Burnside mistakenly withheld his
permission—a costly error. Sumner stands at the top, surrounded by members
of his staff, at Warrenton, Virginia, just days before his move to
Fredericksburg. (USAMHI)

ment presented by Jackson and others, namely, that while the position could be made defensively impregnable, it offered no scope for a counterattack. Even after the repulse of a Union attack, any Confederate attempt to seize the initiative and cross the river under the guns of the Union Army on the heights beyond would invite disaster. Jackson was all too accurate a prophet when he said that "we will whip the enemy but gain no fruits of victory." Lee would have preferred to fall back to

a position on the North Anna River which offered almost equally good defensive possibilities but also much greater opportunity for a counterstroke that might shatter the Union Army. But this would have meant the abandonment of another slice of Virginia territory and would have brought the war dangerously close to Richmond once again. For reasons which were political and psychological rather than purely military, therefore, Lee felt obliged to abandon the idea of a withdrawal to the

North Anna. He would stand—and he would win —at Fredericksburg, but what would that really achieve?

At Fredericksburg, as on so many Civil War battlefields, topography shaped the struggle. The setting was dramatic enough to inspire Lee's oft-quoted words as he watched the spectacle unfolding before and below him: "It is well that war is so terrible. We should grow too fond of it." The Rappahannock River, more than 150 yards wide at this point, swings sharply to the southeast just above Fredericksburg and flows through a fertile plain between low hills on either side. The Stafford Heights on the left bank gave Burnside's army a position from which its guns could command the river and the town beyond. However, the Heights, which ran in an irregular arc behind Fredericksburg on the right bank, were, for most of their

Burnside wanted to make a major crossing in force with the bulk of his army. On November 10, a week before Sumner reached Fredericksburg, Burnside posed at his Warrenton headquarters with several of his generals. Those seated are, from the left: Brigadier General Henry J. Hunt, Brigadier General Winfield S. Hancock, Major General Darius N. Couch, Brigadier General Orlando B. Willcox, and Brigadier General John Buford. Those standing are, from the left: Brigadier General Marsena M. Patrick, Brigadier General Edward Ferrero, Brigadier General John G. Parke, an aide, Burnside, Brigadier General John Cochrane, and Brigadier General Samuel D. Sturgis. (USAMHI)

length, far enough back from the river and the town to be beyond the range of the Union artillery. For considerable stretches, particularly south of Fredericksburg, these "heights" were no more than gently rising ground. As at Gettysburg, such heights or ridges have become clearer in the mind's eye from innumerable maps and battle narratives than they appear from the lie of the land itself. At all events, they were prominent enough to present to the trained military eye an excellent defensive position, and Lee's men had dug themselves in securely by early December.

Faced with this formidable barrier, Burnside saw three main choices. He could defer any new move until spring and then perhaps seek new ground, but this would be politically unpopular, and Burnside had made up his mind to act. He could cross the river and pit his men head on against the Confederate defenses, but the war had already offered its lessons in the futility of such frontal assaults on prepared positions. The third option, either in

place of the second or in conjunction with it, was to attempt a river crossing farther upstream, where there were several fords, or farther downstream, where there were several possible crossing points and where Union gunboats might offer some support. After visiting Burnside on November 26–27, Lincoln himself had outlined such a plan for diversions on both flanks in conjunction with a frontal attack, in the hope of trapping Lee's army as it was forced to abandon its prepared positions. But Halleck and Burnside both thought that such a plan was too complicated and would take too long to prepare. Lee expected an attempted crossing downstream; Burnside did, in fact, prepare for one at Skinker's Neck, some ten miles below Fredericksburg, but he abandoned the idea when Confederate troops moved in to resist any such landing.

Burnside now had nothing else to offer but the idea of a direct frontal attack. Like other and better generals on both sides before and after him, having missed good opportunities and spoiled

Surrounding the gathering of the generals was Burnside's headquarters guard, the men of the 93rd New York, and, shown here, Company G. (USAMHI)

Burnside had his headquarters in the quiet village of Warrenton. (USAMHI)

promising plans by delay, he succumbed to the temptation of the one remaining, and infinitely less promising, option. As a partial explanation, but not an excuse, for Burnside's decision to make a direct assault, it has to be said that his thinking was based upon inadequate information and misleading assumptions about Lee's dispositions. Union scouting had been poor and Burnside's observation balloons did not provide him with a full and balanced picture. He acted on the assumption that Lee's forces, and particularly Jackson's corps holding the southern part of the line, were much more scattered than they actually were. He totally failed to appreciate the high level of concentration of forces which Lee had achieved. In fact, at Fredericksburg the Army of Northern Virginia enjoyed the rare luxury of having several men to defend each yard of its line. In launching his attack on the heights behind Fredericksburg, Burnside thought that he was threatening the left wing of a quite widely dispersed army rather than the concentrated

strength of a tough and battle-hardened foe. The mistake was inexcusable, but it explains a good deal of what followed.

Burnside's plan was to use pontoons to establish bridgeheads at two points across the river, one in the town of Fredericksburg itself and the other two miles downstream. Such a division of forces added to the enormous hazards of a river crossing in the face of the enemy, for once across the river the two Union forces, separated by Deep Run and Hazel Run, would have to act independently. Many of Burnside's subordinate commanders were deeply distrustful of the whole plan—and with good reason—but after all the delays and frustrations of the previous month Burnside's mind was made up.

The crossings began on the night of December 10. There was no significant resistance to the crossing of Franklin's Grand Division downstream, but things were somewhat different at Fredericksburg itself, where Sumner's Grand Division was to establish itself. The sixteen hundred men of Briga-

Its empty streets and sleepy aspect belied the fact that a great army marshaled here for a great battle to come. (USAMHI)

dier General William Barksdale's Mississippi brigade held the town itself, and their fire repeatedly drove off the bridge builders. Even a heavy artillery barrage on the morning of December 11 failed to dislodge Barksdale's brigade. Eventually Union troops crossed the river in boats and cleared the town. By evening the two bridgeheads were firmly established, and on December 12 the great bulk of Sumner's and Franklin's men crossed the river without opposition.

Lee had quite deliberately chosen not to contest the river crossing. As he himself explained:

> The plain on which Fredericksburg stands is so completely commanded by the hills of Stafford, in possession of the enemy, that no effectual opposition could be offered to the construction of the bridges or the passage of the river, without exposing our troops to the destructive fire of his numerous batteries.

Furthermore, Lee was quite content to let his enemy come at him on ground of his own choos-

ing. Looking down upon the Union host assembling below, he had ample time to prepare for the coming assault.

His army occupied an immensely strong position. To the south of Deep Run Jackson's corps was drawn up along a low ridge on the edge of the forest, which had concealed so much of its activity from Burnside's airborne observers. His troops looked down an open and gentle slope over which Franklin's men would have to advance. If there was a weak spot in the line, it was created by a coppice jutting out from the rest of the forest. Jackson had concluded that this wood and the swampy ground within it were impenetrable, and had left a gap of some six hundred yards in his line at this point. The northern half of the Confederate position, behind Fredericksburg on Marye's Heights, was held by Longstreet's corps. Here the natural strength of the position was even greater than on Jackson's front. The Heights completely dominated the open ground below. Once the Union troops advanced, they would be at the

Its value to Burnside lay in the slender iron rails that linked Warrenton with Washington. An August 1862 image by O'Sullivan. (P-M)

mercy of the Confederate guns and beyond the protective cover of the Union artillery across the river. "A chicken could not live on that field when we open on it," said E. P. Alexander, commanding the artillery on Marye's Heights. To make matters worse for Burnside's men, two other features obstructed any advance towards Marye's Heights. On the outskirts of the town itself the troops had to cross a deep ditch by the only two available bridges, both already damaged to the extent that the soldiers could only pick their way across in single file. Much more serious was the superb defen-

sive position offered below Marye's Heights by a sunken road, on the town side of which was a stone wall, shoulder-high, with earth banked against it. Brigadier General T.R.R. Cobb's brigade, sheltering behind that wall, was to wreak havoc upon successive waves of Union soldiers who knew that they would have to get across that road if they were to achieve anything at all.

Having safely crossed the river, Burnside had no precise idea of how best to tackle the enemy in front of him. His oral orders the night of December 12 and his written orders the next morning

Perhaps the first casualty of the Fredericksburg Campaign never even saw the battlefield. Brigadier General Francis E. Patterson, the son of the Robert Patterson who so failed in the First Manassas Campaign, had made an error in judgment early in November, and an investigation was impending even as Burnside commenced moving his Grand Divisions. On November 22 he shot himself in the head. (USAMHI)

were equally vague and did not always tally with each other. Apparently still under the impression that his foe was widely dispersed, he seemed to think that modest attacks by one division on each of the two main sectors would compel Lee to abandon his position.

Thick fog hung over Fredericksburg at dawn on December 13. As it gradually rolled away, the Confederates had a grand view of 80,000 Union troops deploying on the plain below. It was on Jackson's front that the first assault came, but it was launched by only a single division under Major General George G. Meade. Its initial advance was held up by fire on its flank from the two rifled guns of Major John Pelham, commanding Jeb Stuart's horse artillery. When Pelham was at

last obliged to withdraw, Meade resumed his advance to the accompaniment of a furious artillery duel between the two sides. He was probing towards the weak spot in Jackson's line in the area of the projecting woodland. His men slogged their way through the marshy undergrowth which Jackson had thought impenetrable. Briefly Meade's men appeared to threaten the heart of Jackson's defenses as they bore down on Brigadier General Maxey Gregg's brigade. Gregg himself was fatally wounded, but two of his regiments held firm. No adequate support arrived to back up what Meade's Pennsylvanians had achieved, and heavy fighting had reduced their numbers by half to around 2,000. Confederate reinforcements came up quickly and turned the tide. Soon the Union troops were in flight, with the Confederates in hot, if unorganized, pursuit. The counterattack eventually ran out of steam—and into Union artillery fire—and the survivors of Meade's division rallied on the riverbank. The Union Army had suffered 5,000 casualties in the fighting on this front. General Franklin was so discouraged by what had happened that he failed to respond to orders from Burnside to renew the attack, although a large part of his force had not yet been engaged. There was no further heavy fighting in this area after 2:30 P.M.

The Union attacks on the right, towards Marye's Heights, ended in even more costly failure. Partly because of the fog which blanketed the terrain (and no doubt also because of the fog which enveloped Burnside's mind) the first assault on this front did not begin until 11 A.M. At intervals during the remaining five or six hours of daylight, wave after wave of Union attacks spent themselves against the combined strength of the Confederate artillery on Marye's Heights and the infantry in the sunken road below. There was no subtlety, no attempt at deception or diversion, and precious little variety as one frontal attack followed another. Division after division slowly crossed the ditch just outside the town, thus presenting a massed target for the Confederate artillery, and then marched up the wide open slope into a storm of fire.

One Union general, Darius N. Couch, surveying this appalling scene, later recalled that he had cried out: "Oh, great God! See how our men our poor fellows, are falling!" His recollections continue:

Finally Burnside brought his army to Fredericksburg, and from this height he stared across the Rappahannock at his objective. A. J. Russell's image was made the following May. (USAMHI)

I remember that the whole plain was covered with men, prostrate and dropping . . . I had never before seen fighting like that, nothing approaching it in terrible uproar and destruction . . . As they charged, the artillery fire would break their formation and they would get mixed; then they would close up, go forward, receive the withering infantry fire . . . and then the next brigade coming up in sucession would do its duty and melt like snow coming down on warm ground.

In his account of the battle from the other side, General Longstreet used a similar figure of speech: "The Federals had fallen like the steady dripping of rain from the eaves of a house."

There was never any real prospect of breaking the Confederate line. When Lee, momentarily impressed by the incredible persistence of the enemy attacks, expressed some anxiety, Longstreet reassured him:

General, if you put every man now on the other side of the Potomac on that field to approach me over the same line, and give me plenty of ammunition, I will kill them all before they reach my line.

It was a terrible but truthful assessment.

As the light began to fade, the attacks were at last called off. There was no Confederate counterattack on this front, and the threatened counterattack by Jackson's corps to the south eventually developed too weakly and too late, and was beaten off by Union artillery. Even when victory on the field of battle was so complete, the winning army was not prepared or organized for a counterstroke. Lee probably did not immediately realize the scale of his success; in any event, like Jackson he had known from the outset that their position, however admirable for defense, offered no springboard for counterattack.

Lee hoped that his opponent would renew the

Artillery was first employed to soften the Confederate resistance. Here O'Sullivan posed the 5th United States Artillery, Battery D, much as it appeared during the bombardment. (LC)

attack the next day. Overnight Burnside's mood swung between black despair and determination to continue the fight. He even talked of personally leading a new assault the next morning, but his subordinate commanders dissuaded him from this wild scheme or from any other plan for a further assault. Indeed, his fellow officers had lost all confidence in their commander, and the Army was in no state for further immediate action. On December 14 and 15 Burnside's army stayed in position under the eyes of the victorious Confederates. Only on December 15 did Burnside send a flag of truce to arrange for the burial of the dead. The ground in front of Marye's Heights was littered not only with the Union dead—often stripped of their heavier clothing by shivering and ill-clad Confederates—but with hundreds upon hundreds of wounded, many of whom lay untended through the two freezing nights which followed the battle.

Total Union casualties—killed, wounded, and missing—were around 12,500, half of them at the foot of Marye's Heights alone. Lee's casualties were less than half that number, a little over 5,000.

On the night of December 15, under cover of a howling storm, the Union Army withdrew back across the Rappahannock without losing another man or scarcely an item of equipment. It was an ironically efficient end to a tragically ineffective operation. Once again the two armies faced each other from the high ground on either side of the river. There they remained until the spring, when another general would launch a very different but equally unsuccessful attack upon Lee's position.

For the North Fredericksburg was perhaps the most humiliating and inexcusable defeat of the war. It triggered one of the deepest crises in the four-year struggle—not exclusively or essentially a military crisis but a test of Northern morale, of the

The only real damage done was to the town itself. This May 1864 image shows the effect of Federal artillery on three houses. (USAMHI)

Northern will to fight on and win. Army morale slumped and thousands of men went absent without leave. Lincoln distributed a message to the troops, congratulating them upon their courage and offering the nation's thanks. "Although you were not successful, the attempt was not an error nor the failure other than an accident," he wrote in an attempt to defy the plain facts as valiant and unavailing as the Army's attacks on Marye's Heights. The senior officers of the Army waged a war of words among themselves. Some, like Hooker, plied friendly congressmen with their complaints and their gossip; others, like Sumner and Franklin, wrote directly to Lincoln suggesting a return to the James Peninsula; still others, like Brigadier Generals John Newton and John Cochrane,

called on Lincoln at the White House to report on the demoralization of the Army as they saw it. Lincoln restrained Burnside from further action and had to face a crisis of command and confidence in the Army during January 1863, until, after charge and countercharge among its senior officers—and the fiasco of the "mud march" up the Rappahannock in another attempt to turn Lee's flank—Burnside was finally removed and replaced by Hooker.

But the crisis was by no means confined to the Army. Coming on top of Republican setbacks in the midterm elections, Fredericksburg raised the curtain on a major political crisis in which Republican senators demanded that Lincoln should reconstruct his Cabinet on more radical lines and prosecute the war more vigorously. Lincoln warded

Several others bare their wounds. (USAMHI)

off the challenge to his authority, but he badly needed military success to lift Northern morale from one of its deepest depressions. The final Emancipation Proclamation, to be issued on January 1, 1863, would scarcely inspire confidence, coming in the wake of electoral reverses, a Cabinet crisis, and a military disaster.

However, Northern morale and Lincoln's pertinacity did survive Fredericksburg, as they had survived so much else. If Confederate victory on the Rappahannock could not break the Northern will to win, it could not achieve much else. The Army of the Potomac would soon be restored to full strength. It continued to enjoy an overwhelming preponderance of men and materiel over its

Confederate opponents, and its soldiers had already given ample proof of their resilience and power of recovery in the face of the worst which blundering leadership, faulty organization, and battlefield reverses could inflict upon them. If the North retained the will, it certainly retained the means to fight and win the war. If the South had the ability to win battles, it was already sorely troubled by the depletion of manpower and resources. Battles like Fredericksburg, it was now clear, could not by themselves decide the war. The paradox of Fredericksburg was that it resulted in a victory which revealed the limitations of the victors and a defeat which revealed the strength of the defeated.

A home made almost uninhabitable. (P-M)

There was no question of the Phillips family reoccupying their house.
(USAMHI)

A whole city block is ravaged by the rain of iron. (USAMHI)

Fredericksburg much as it appeared to Sumner when he first arrived.
(USAMHI)

Shown here just four days before he reached Fredericksburg, Sumner made his headquarters at nearby Falmouth on November 17. (USAMHI)

The Lacey house in Falmouth became Sumner's center of operations. (P-M)

Leading his Tiger Bayou Rifles of the 14th Louisiana, R. W. Jones looks resplendent in saber, sash, and plumed hat. He will command the regiment by war's end. (TU)

Colonel Davidson B. Penn, 7th Louisiana, one of scores of regimental commanders who tried to stem Meade's advance. (VM)

But other great fighters will not last out the battle. Brigadier General Maxey Gregg and his brigade saved the weak spot in Jackson's line, but it cost Gregg his life. (USAMHI)

I Corps veterans like the 30th Pennsylvania, called the 1st Reserves, fought with Meade in the desperate attack on the Confederate left. The Pennsylvanians appear here several months after their Fredericksburg blooding. (USAMHI)

Unfortunately, William B. Franklin, commanding the Left Grand Division, did not support Meade's attack, thereby losing the fruits of Meade's division's bloody advance. Franklin is here shown as a brigadier. (P-M)

Meade's corps commander, Major General John F. Reynolds, a fellow Pennsylvanian, was with him in person during the attack but did not fully employ the rest of the corps. (USAMHI)

While Meade fought doggedly on the Federal left, Major General William F. Smith and his VI Corps spent December 13 mainly waiting in support instead of being used to further the advantage Meade almost secured. Smith stands in the center with his staff. (WRHS)

Men and officers of the 96th Pennsylvania were largely idle with the rest of
Smith's corps. Here they cluster around two field guns, the one on the right an
unusual repeating gun. (LC)

A company of the 139th Pennsylvania shows what the average infantry
company looked like when formed in line. Smith did not engage them. (LC)

Nor did the 67th New York enter the fray. (P-M)

Major General John B. Hood and his division held the long center of the Confederate line yet were barely engaged. This gallant soldier, with his sad, doleful eyes, chaffed at being inactive. Never a brilliant commander, he had the instincts of a born battler. (MUSEUM OF THE CONFEDERACY)

Following Meade's unsuccessful assault, Burnside directed the right of his line to attack through Fredericksburg. The Federals had to advance up these slopes. (NA)

In full view of Confederates posted along these heights behind earthworks. An 1864 image. (USAMHI)

Their destination was the high ground around Marye's house, called Marye's Heights. The bullet scars on the house testify to the fighting that took place. An 1865 image. (USAMHI)

Here and there houses and outbuildings provided shelter for the advancing bluecoats on their way up the slope. (USAMHI)

But the earthworks at the top gave the defenders excellent cover from which to pour a murderous fire on their attackers. This image of Marye's Heights, probably taken in May 1864, shows well the defenses and the damage left after the battle. (USAMHI)

And here the most deadly spot of all, the stone wall at the foot of Marye's Heights. From behind this wall Longstreet's Confederates delivered death to hundreds of their enemies. (USAMHI)

Lieutenant General James Longstreet, "Old Pete" to his men, solid, dependable, indomitable in defense. He commanded the left half of Lee's army and bore the brunt of the fighting at Fredericksburg. It was while viewing his work that Lee declared that he was glad war was so terrible, else they should grow too fond of it. (USAMHI)

One of Longstreet's premier brigade commanders, Brigadier General Joseph B. Kershaw, the flamboyant South Carolinian from First Manassas, felt that that battle should not be called "Bull Run" because it was such an undignified name. (USAMHI)

John R. Cooke had just been promoted to brigadier before the battle. He had taken seven wounds by the time of Fredericksburg, but surely the greatest wound of all was that his father was even now a major general in the Union Army. (VM)

George T. Anderson became a brigadier the same day as Cooke. He, too, commanded a brigade in Longstreet's corps. This Georgian was known to his men and friends as "Tige," and he could fight like a tiger at that. (VM)

Following Sumner in the attacks on Marye's Heights was Major General Joseph Hooker, already being called "Fighting Joe." Time after time he hurled his divisions against the stone wall and earthworks, and just as many times they were repulsed. He never entirely forgave Burnside for ordering his assault. Already given to politicking in the army, Hooker would soon start campaigning against Burnside. (USAMHI)

Daniel Sickles commanded Hooker's old division in the III Corps and took his promotion as major general just two weeks before the battle. He appears here as a brigadier. He proved to be a good fighter for a general with no qualifications for command other than political influence. (USAMHI)

Another good fighter, though a man intemperate in speech and habits, was Brigadier General Thomas Meagher, the fiery Irishman. He virtually destroyed his famous Irish Brigade in its brutal assaults on Marye's Heights. After the war he would drown when he fell overboard from a river steamer while drunk. (USAMHI)

Men like this dandy from a New York regiment had their finery ripped away in their desperate battle for the Heights, and for life, at Fredericksburg. (NA)

Baxter's Zouaves, the 72nd Pennsylvania, fought for Sumner even when he ordered them into the face of death itself. Seldom was greater heroism more foolishly wasted than at Fredericksburg. (COURTESY OF TERENCE P. O'LEARY)

Hawkins's Zouaves, too, and their colonel, Rush Hawkins, standing second from the left, bloodied their fancy uniforms in repeated attacks on Marye's Heights. (NA)

Their attacks availed them nothing. The battle ended, Burnside could only sit and look across the Rappahannock, and send flag-of-truce parties, like the one shown here, to bury the dead. It had been a wasted battle. (USAMHI)

*The armies would face each other across the water for some time. The
cameramen could even capture the enemy that had evaded the generals. One
set his instrument up at the end of a destroyed railroad bridge while
Confederates gaily posed for him at the other end. This war could be civil at
times.* (NA)

*A year or more later, in May 1864, the Union finally controlled the
Rappahannock at Fredericksburg, and its wagons and soldiers could cross these
pontoon bridges unimpeded, Marye's Heights no longer being a place of terror.
But that was in the future, and seemingly much farther off than anyone could
see through the smoke of Fredericksburg.* (USAMHI)

Strangling the South

JAMES M. MERRILL

*Improvised, often ineffective, the blockade
required the building of a new navy*

ON THE AFTERNOON of August 22, 1864, the Confederate blockade-runner *Lilian,* hauled away from the cotton press at Wilmington, North Carolina, glided down the Cape Fear River, exchanged signals with the forts at the entrance, dropped anchor, and waited. At nightfall she got under way, her helmsman steering a course due east for the open sea. A shout came from the darkness: "Heave to, or I'll sink you!" Instantly the pilot of the *Lilian* ordered the helm hard to port and attempted to ram the Federal picketboat. The Union craft began firing signal rockets simultaneously with her bow gun. Shells crashed over the *Lilian* without damage, and within an hour she had left all but one of the Federal blockaders far behind. She had barely eluded this vessel when she ran into a cross fire from Yankee steam frigates. After three hours of "frightfully accurate" firing, the Union ships took the badly damaged *Lilian* as a prize and its officers and crew as prisoners of war.

Three years earlier, at the outset of the Civil War, the Union Navy, its ships rotting in dry dock or scattered across the seas at foreign stations, shouldered the task of blockading the Confederate coast from Virginia to Texas. Despite a lack of fighting power in April 1861, the Navy Department dispatched all available seaworthy vessels to Southern ports. The steam frigate *Minnesota* and the sail frigate *Cumberland* anchored at Hampton Roads, the chief base for the North Atlantic Blockading Squadron.

As Lincoln's administration increased the purchase and construction of naval gunboats, the blockading squadrons were materially strengthened. With only 2 ships, in May 1861, guarding the entire coast of North Carolina, a year later 58 craft policed this sector, and at the end of the war the total had reached 142.

In the beginning the Union fleet was obviously unable to make its blockade effective, and as late as 1864 there was still much running of supplies into the South, but Secretary of the Navy Gideon Welles justly believed that his ships were cutting off the Confederacy's trade in most heavy goods.

If the only naval operation during the war had been to blockade the principal ports of the Confederacy, the work of the Navy would have been comparatively easy. However, the outer coastline from the northern boundary of Virginia to Mexico is more than three thousand miles in length; this exterior shoreline along the Atlantic seaboard is merely the outer edge of a series of islands, behind which there are sounds, rivers, and connecting channels and canals, thus forming a protected and

*Headquarters of the North Atlantic Blockading Squadron, Fort Monroe,
Virginia. Through this sally port passed thousands of soldiers and seamen
whose single task it was to deny to the Confederacy the succor of foreign
shipping, to assist in the conquest of the Southern coastline.* (USAMHI)

*Deceptively peaceful, the parade ground at Fort Monroe swarmed during the
war as ships and fleets outfitted and repaired for the arduous duty of patrolling
the Confederate coastline, the inlets, harbors, and rivers of rebellion.* (USAMHI)

*Surprisingly, considering its vital importance as headquarters of the North
Atlantic Blockading Squadron and as a jumping-off place for several
expeditions into the South, Fort Monroe was very little photographed during
the war. This image is the only one known that captures even a substantial part
of the old masonry fortification. Called Fortress Monroe for years, its name was
officially shortened to "Fort" a few years before the war.* (NA)

almost continuous inland waterway from Virginia
to Florida that is navigable for small vessels. Along
this outer shoreline there are countless inlets or
openings connecting the Atlantic Ocean with the
interior waterways. This peculiar topography constantly hampered the Federal blockaders throughout four years of war. Although a major port could
be effectively policed by Union ships, blockade-
runners and Confederate privateers could steal
through some inlet many miles above or below a
principal port and steam unmolested along the
sounds to their destinations within the Confederacy. An active coastal commerce, involving the

transport of men and supplies to the Southern armies in the field, was carried on in these protected
sounds, bays, and rivers, while far out to sea Union
blockaders patrolled off the main harbors.

To create an efficient blockade the United States
Navy either had to station ships off all the inlets
and establish an extensive ship-to-ship system of
supply or seize the inlets and suitable areas for
bases by means of amphibious attack. Obviously
the latter plan of using seaborne forces was more
practical and was adopted early by the Navy Department. The sea arm of the Union, commanding
Confederate waters, was in a position to execute

The wood and coaling yard at Fort Monroe. Here the fleet replenished its constant need for fuel to keep the warships patrolling the Southern coastline. A huge mound of coal is just visible through the archway at left center. (NA)

major amphibious assaults against Rebel shore installations. Since the Confederates lacked any semblance of a seagoing Navy, the Federals could concentrate an army in home ports and transport it unmolested to any area along hundreds of miles of enemy coastline.

The building, purchase, or chartering of additional vessels, their conversion for the blockade, and the finding of crews for them became Welles's greatest immediate task, in which time was a major factor. By mid-July 1861 the Navy Department had contracted for the building of 23 gunboats and had purchased or chartered 21 steamers and 3 sailing vessels of various descriptions. These were dispatched to the shipyards in New York and Boston for overhaul.

The early commanding officers of the North Atlantic Blockading Squadron, Commodores Silas H. Stringham, Louis Goldsborough, and Samuel Phillips Lee were careerists with long, spotless, but not brilliant naval dossiers, and they were well schooled in the techniques of the old Navy. Although they did not balk at the use of steam and, on occasion, used it to good advantage, their minds were not elastic enough to permit them to take full advantage of the revolution in naval science (e.g., the transition of sail to steam, wood to iron, and smoothbore to rifled cannon). They resisted employing the newly developed armored vessels to the best tactical advantage and clung tenaciously to the worn-out doctrines of the War of 1812, when ship dueled ship and boarders poured over the sides with cutlasses and engaged in hand-to-hand combat.

Thrust into positions of great responsibility, these officers followed the rule book of the old Navy. Their experience on routine assignments had not demanded of them a quick grasp of tactical advantage or imbued them with the imaginative intelligence necessary to the solution of new problems. They were men who had already established their professional reputations, and fear of tarnishing

And while the ships were supplied, so, too, were the tens of thousands of sailors and soldiers campaigning in Virginia and North Carolina. This view shows just one of the streets lined with quartermaster warehouses that crowded around Fort Monroe. (NA)

their good names made them overly cautious. They hesitated when they should have pushed their advantage. Initial victories were not followed up because they refused to assume personal responsibility for the risks involved.

David D. Porter, who was later to command the North Atlantic Blockading Squadron, does not belong in this category. Younger and more vigorous, he possessed a brashness which the others lacked. His mistakes were not prompted by a lack of confidence or an unwillingness to venture forth. On the contrary, in his first amphibious attack against the North Carolina coast in 1864 his failure was attributable to his overly optimistic evaluation of his own position.

Although the commanders can be criticized,

they should not be categorically condemned. Despite their shortcomings, they were competent administrators, and their abilities were equal to organizing and executing their routine blockade assignments. Despite the scarcity of ships and supplies in the beginning, they—especially Stringham, who inaugurated the blockade—should be commended for the way in which they handled their policing duties.

In early April 1861 Commodore Silas Stringham took command of the *Minnesota* and awaited further instructions. New orders called upon him to organize the Atlantic Blockading Squadron "to protect our commerce, suppress piratical or illegal demonstrations . . . guard the public interests," and to proceed to establish the blockade of Southern ports. His squadron's command extended from the capes of the Chesapeake to the southern extremity of Florida.

Since this was far too large an area for one command, a group of naval specialists, working in Washington, suggested to Secretary Welles in July 1861 that the Atlantic Blockading Squadron should be divided in two. This would be advantageous to the efficiency of the blockade since different portions of the Atlantic seaboard possessed differing topographical features and required distinct treatment. They pointed out that the northern, or upper, section was characterized by islands—some small, some large, some narrow, some wide—which separated the sounds and bays from the ocean and were divided at irregular intervals by openings or inlets through which the ocean tides ebbed and flowed. The southern, or lower, section was distinguished by ordinary ports and bays. The North Atlantic Blockading Squadron was to extend from Cape Henry, Virginia, to Cape Roman, South Carolina, a distance of about 370 miles; the South Atlantic Blockading Squadron was to stretch from Cape Roman to St. Augustine, Florida, covering about 220 miles. This recommendation was carried out.

At once Stringham saw that an obstacle to the effectiveness of the North Atlantic Blockading Squadron was the protection afforded Southerners by their coast, much of which was supplied with a

Part of the backbone of the North Atlantic Blockading Squadron was its armament, much of it tested here at Fort Monroe. Several fifteen-inch Rodmans lie mounted and dismounted here, either before or after testing, while at the far right appear the remnants of a cannon which was tried and failed.

(NA)

Mighty cannon like this one stared out from the casemates of the fort, awaiting anyone foolhardy enough to challenge Monroe's dominion over Hampton Roads. This Rodman smoothbore rests on an experimental carriage being tested by the government. (NA)

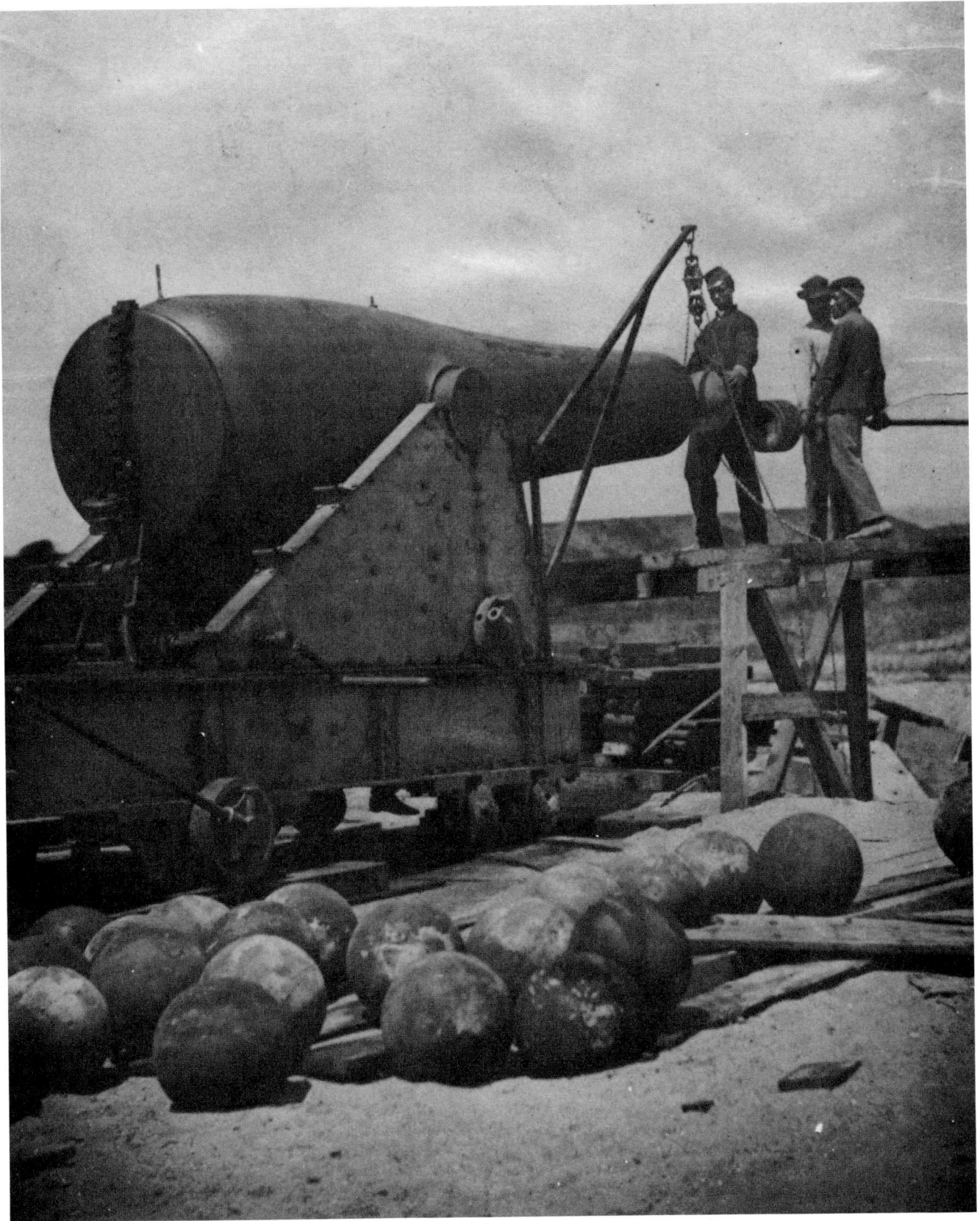

Another fifteen-inch Rodman rests heavily on Fort Monroe's parapet, showing the apparatus required to load its mammoth projectiles. (NA)

Captain Hiram Paulding suffered the first major naval loss for the Union Navy when he had to give up the Norfolk Navy Yard in Virginia in April 1861. With it he lost tons of ordnance, hundreds of cannon and spare ships' parts, and the hulk of the Merrimack, *soon to be used against the Union as the CSS* Virginia. (NA)

double shoreline. Small vessels from Carolinian ports sneaked along the inside passage until they reached an outlet and then dashed for the open seas. Hatteras Inlet was such an obstacle. "The Swash," as the inlet was referred to, was a long, sandy barrier off the coast of North Carolina, six miles south of Cape Hatteras and about ninety miles by water from New Bern, North Carolina. Confederate ships passed from North Carolina cities through internal waterways to Hatteras or neighboring inlets, and then headed for the open seas.

Secessionists recognized these advantages. Fortifications of these outlets were begun, and by the middle of June 1861 the major work had been accomplished on Fort Hatteras, located an eighth of a mile from the channel entrance. Nearby, a second bastion, Fort Clark, was ready for service in late July. The two redoubts, located about three fourths of a mile from one another on the same island, secured a cross fire upon the entrance to Hatteras Inlet.

Other fortifications were quickly marked off and built at Ocracoke and Oregon inlets, two neighboring outlets to the sea. Confederate privateers operating from Hatteras Inlet took their toll of Union merchantmen, especially when blockading vessels were patrolling other areas. The marauders would "dash out," bewailed a Union naval officer, and be "back again in a day with a prize." A large brig and three schooners were a week's catch during July 1861. Blockade-runners continued to use the North Carolina inlets. In Washington naval strategists concluded that the ports of Norfolk and Richmond could not be successfully blockaded until the Atlantic entrances to Pamlico and Albemarle sounds in North Carolina were shut.

After digesting reports and suggestions from various sources, Assistant Secretary of the Navy Gustavus Vasa Fox worked out plans for an offensive thrust against Hatteras Inlet. Naval vessels cooperating with a military unit would capture Forts Hatteras and Clark and, accepting the strategists' recommendation, obstruct the channel entrance by sinking schooners loaded with stone. The island was not to be held permanently.

In late August 1861 the expedition got under way for Cape Hatteras. Besides the Army transports filled with 860 soldiers commanded by Major General Benjamin Butler, the convoy included the stream frigates *Minnesota* and *Wabash*, the gunboats *Monticello* and *Harriet Lane*, the steam sloop *Pawnee*, the tugboat *Fanny*, the sailing frigate *Cumberland*, and a retinue of small vessels. On the morning of August 27 Cape Hatteras Light was sighted, and after rounding the shoals the squadron dropped anchor. The Federal assault on Hatteras Inlet commenced at 6:40 A.M. on August 28. Because of the heavy breakers along the beach only 320 soldiers were put ashore. Fort Clark was under heavy bombardment from the *Wabash*, *Cumberland*, and *Minnesota*. The Union ships passed repeatedly, belching round after round at the fort while remaining out of range of Confederate guns. The side-wheeler *Susquehanna*, returning to Hampton Roads after her tour of duty with

The steam frigate USS Minnesota, *flagship of the North Atlantic Blockading Squadron, anchored at Hampton Roads at the war's start. Just four years old in 1861, she would figure prominently in the war, almost being lost to the Confederate ironclad* Virginia *before being saved by the* Monitor *in March 1862.* (MHS)

the West Indian Squadron, steamed upon the scene and joined the bombardment.

Brutally pasted by naval gunfire, with Yankee troops only three miles away and ammunition nearly exhausted, the Confederates fell back to Fort Hatteras. Federals hoisted the Stars and Stripes over Fort Clark. The *Minnesota, Wabash,* and *Susquehanna,* together with the *Monticello,* which had already started firing, opened up on Fort Hatteras.

When darkness arrived the firing ceased. At 5:30 A.M. the following day the squadron weighed anchor and stood towards shore. Warned not to fire upon Fort Clark, the ships steamed in and opened fire on Fort Hatteras.

The ineffective range of Confederate guns, lack of ammunition, and casualties convinced Confederate officers to run up the white flag. Fort Hatteras was surrendered at 11:07 A.M. About 600 Confederates together with their wounded were

To begin building the Navy for combat against the enemy, Secretary Welles refitted many ships at the New York and Boston navy yards. Here several naval mortars await being placed on the decks of ships in Boston. (USAMHI)

herded on board a Union transport. Southern casualties numbered 7 dead and 30 wounded.

That evening Stringham and General Butler decided not to level the forts and block the channel as their orders had stated. They recognized that Hatteras would be invaluable as a depot for the blockading squadron, a safe refuge in all types of weather for the coasting trade, and a staging area for future operations against North Carolina and Virginia. To hold the inlet troops and a naval force remained behind. The following day, August 30, the squadron headed northward.

The seizure of Hatteras was successful because of the squadron's accurate fire, with its smothering effect on the forts. But had there been more troops, an adequate plan of attack, and aggressive leaders, the Hatteras expedition could have pushed into North Carolina and created considerable havoc. A Confederate naval officer confided that the enemy erred in not taking possession of the sounds immediately after capturing Hatteras: "There was nothing to prevent it."

Rear Admiral Silas Stringham was the first commander of the North Atlantic Blockading Squadron. Sixty-four years old, a fifty-two-year veteran of the service, he was loyal, though out of date for the war at hand. Gideon Welles found that "whilst there were doubts and uncertainty on every hand as to who could be trusted, I knew Commodore Stringham to be faithful." (COURTESY OF THE NEW-YORK HISTORICAL SOCIETY)

The sidewheel frigate USS Susquehanna *joined Stringham's blockaders early in the war, and fought well with him in the attack on Hatteras Inlet. Here her officers pose on deck in 1864. The paddlewheel box is visible behind the standing rigging.* (NYHS)

Secretary Welles, terming the failure to capitalize on the attack "a misfortune," later pointed out, however, that the victory was the "first effective blow struck by the Navy," and that it was the "commencement of that series of coast movements which from step to step . . . [was to wrest] almost every port on one long line of sea coast from the insurgents and . . . [drive] them to the interior." The capture of Forts Hatteras and Clark was timely for the Union cause, exclaimed a naval commander, as it was "the first substantial [Federal] victory of the war." Coming soon after the disaster at Bull Run, it raised Union spirits and gained prestige for the Navy.

The Hatteras expedition not only quickened Northern morale but caused alarm in North Carolina and dejection throughout most of the South. The rendezvous area quashed, Confederate marauders from Hatteras no longer preyed upon Union cargo ships plying the coast of North Carolina. In September 1861 fortifications at another inlet, Ocracoke, were captured without a struggle by bluejackets sent from Hatteras. Schooners loaded with stone were sunk at Ocracoke, closing this inlet completely to Confederate commerce and raiders.

Blockade procedures continually varied as the North and South tried to outwit each other. With each passing year blockade and blockade-running techniques became more sophisticated. Swift gray steamers with telescoping funnels glided in and out of Confederate ports. Southern and British mariners, navigating the sea-lanes between Rebel coasts and nearby neutral ports—especially Nassau—traded Southern cotton for English cannon.

Once a runner was safely moored in Wilmington, stevedores dumped her freight on the dock and quickly began hauling cotton on board. Dock

This is what Stringham was after: sleek blockade-runners seeking to penetrate his curtain of ships to bring supplies to the Confederacy. The ship to the right is the British steamer Giraffe *in dry dock at Glasgow, Scotland, fitting out as a blockade-runner. Renamed the* Robert E. Lee, *she would run the blockade in 1863.* (MARINERS MUSEUM)

workers stuffed the bales so closely together in ships' holds that "a mouse could hardly find a room to hide." After the hatches were battened down, a tier of bales was secured fore and aft in every available spot on deck, leaving space only for approaches to the cabins, engine room, and forecastle. A vessel loaded in this way resembled a huge cotton bale with a mast stuck upright at one end.

If blockade-running was "rollicking good fun" for British and Confederate skippers, it was "perfect hell" for Yankee seamen who tried to stop it. For hours crews stood wearily at the guns, waiting, watching, cursing, until the order came to secure.

"We go below," grumbled one officer, "and throw ourselves, clothes and all, on the bunk—only to be startled by another gunshot."

Roanoke Island, North Carolina, was recognized by most North Carolinians and a few authorities at Richmond as being of vital importance to the defense of the Old North State and to the Confederacy. Albemarle and Pamlico sounds, strategic to the interior water commerce, connect the Atlantic Ocean and the inlets with the rivers and coastal towns of the North Carolina mainland and with the canals, which lead to Norfolk and Richmond. Located in Croatan Sound, forty-five miles above Federal-held Hatteras Inlet, Roanoke Island commands this chain of sounds, inlets, and rivers. Possession of the island by Union troops would give them undisputed command of the sounds, the seacoast towns, the rear door to Norfolk and, possibly, to the railroads running northward into Virginia.

Realizing the strategic importance of Roanoke Island, Confederate officials hustled a regiment southward from Virginia to occupy and fortify it. Governor Henry T. Clark of North Carolina, sensing the strategic value of the island to the eastern counties, dispatched a disorganized regiment of state troops. Defensive preparations crept forward.

After the fall of Hatteras, naval strategists in Washington recommended that the sounds of North Carolina be occupied permanently by gunboats to break up the foreign and interior trade. At Hampton Roads an expedition of the North Atlantic Blockading Squadron was slowly fitted out.

Two more steamers at Glasgow destined to be blockade-runners. The vessel at right is the Juno. (MARINERS MUSEUM)

In Bristol, England, more blockade-runners were born. Here the Old Dominion
*undergoes her conversion for the swift service. Telescoping funnels and
smokeless coal, the low lines, and swift speed all worked to her advantage.*
(CHS)

Captain Louis M. Goldsborough, recently assigned to command the squadron, met with President Lincoln and his Cabinet in October to discuss naval tactics in the sounds.

Early in November 1861 Brigadier General Ambrose Burnside, who was then at Annapolis equipping a force for Chesapeake waters, was summoned to Washington, where, in the presence of Lincoln, Secretary of State William Seward, General-in-Chief George B. McClellan and Goldsborough, he was told that his division's objective had been switched to North Carolina. Cooperating with the Navy, his force was to strike such points as would give the Union complete control of Al-

Captain Smith of the Old Dominion *and his officers adopted Confederate naval dress even though their ship was never formally part of the Southern Navy.* (COURTESY OF MICHAEL J. MCAFEE)

Lieutenant McClellan of the Old Dominion. (COURTESY OF MICHAEL J. MCAFEE)

bemarle and Pamlico sounds. Once the thrust into North Carolina was decided upon, Goldsborough returned to Hampton Roads and Burnside to Annapolis. Early in December the naval commander insisted on the capture of Roanoke Island. Troopships, cargo schooners, and Staten Island ferryboats arrived at Hampton Roads during the evening of January 10, 1862. On January 11 the attack force, totalling seventy vessels, slid down the channel from Hampton Roads. Orders were explicit. The first objective was Roanoke Island; then, in rapid sucession, New Bern, Beaufort, Fort Macon, and, possibly, Wilmington. On January 13 the fleet anchored in the comparative shelter of Hatteras Inlet.

Goldsborough and Burnside held several "full and free consultations" to work out details for the assault on Roanoke Island. With everything in readiness on February 5, the attack force headed northward toward Pamlico Sound, led by fifteen gunboats and followed by eight of the Army's armed vessels and forty-seven transports with 7,500 men. Foul weather prevented the execution of battle plans on February 6, but at 9:55 A.M. the next day the fleet got under way and steamed toward the narrow opening to Croatan Sound. Slowly the vessels threaded their way through the passage out into the sound. Union and Confederate guns boomed. Goldsborough's vessels hurled "every conceivable kind of projectile" into the Confederate fort. Four thousand Union soldiers disembarked from the transports and waded ashore. Due to heavy rain, operations came to a halt. Burnside

A stopping place for the runners before their final journey through the blockade was the British ports in Bermuda. Here the naval dockyard shows a British fleet at anchor during the Civil War. Most are old line ships, sailing vessels on their way to becoming receiving hulks like the one in the foreground.
(U. S. NAVAL HISTORICAL CENTER)

and Goldsborough mapped out work for the next day.

A half hour before sunrise on February 8 Union soldiers moved forward. A small naval force maneuvered northward in the sound, removed obstructions, and widened the channel. From the clatter of gunfire on the island, Burnside's position was noted. Once assured that he was not in the line of their fire, other gunboats steamed up and salvoed. After severe fighting, the Confederates surrendered Roanoke Island at 5:25 that afternoon.

News of Roanoke Island thrilled the victory-starved North. This success, coupled with those of General Grant in the west at Forts Henry and Donelson, infused the Union with a spirit, more pronounced than at any time since Bull Run, that the war was soon to be over. During the days which followed the Confederate surrender, Union

troops at Roanoke Island improved roads, cleaned up the forts, campgrounds, and hospitals, and built a wharf at Park Point to facilitate the loading and unloading of troops and supplies. Once ammunition ships arrived from the north, the Union force was ready to move. On March 14, 1862, New Bern fell to a Union assault. The port town of Beaufort and nearby Fort Macon succumbed to another effort of the Federal Navy and Army in April 1862. Beaufort, one of the best harbors on the southern coast, was converted into a much-needed coaling station and supply base for the North Atlantic Blockading Squadron for its blockade against Wilmington, the only Confederate port of any significance remaining open north of Charleston.

Minor operations in the sounds proceeded without interruption. Union vessels obstructed the entrances to the Dismal Swamp and the Albemarle-Chesapeake canals. The North Carolina towns of Elizabeth City, Edenton, Washington, Winton, and Plymouth were temporarily occupied by Union soldiers and sailors. The back door to Norfolk had slammed shut. The proposed assault against Wilmington was not carried out. The Yankees now held so many points and so long a stretch of coastline that it was impossible throughout May and June 1862 to spare troops for any additional operation, although Goldsborough boasted that he could take the city without the Army's help. The successes of the Goldsborough-Burnside expeditions at Roanoke Island, New Bern, Beaufort, Fort Macon, and other coastal towns impaired the war effort of the Confederacy and North Carolina. Blockade-runners which, prior to March 1862, could pick and choose among several inlets and North Carolina ports had to converge on Wilmington.

In March 1862, after nearly a year of strife, Northerners totaled their successes and discovered that it was the Navy alone, or the Navy acting in conjunction with the Army, that sustained the Union with victories in the eastern theater of operations. Starting from a state of extreme unpreparedness in April 1861, after ten months of struggle the Navy was welded into a potent offensive as well as defensive force. Speaking of the Army, the editor of *Frank Leslie's Illustrated Newspaper* remarked that the successes in the East, "although neither few nor unimportant, have been, for the most part, gained in conjunction with the Navy, which has, not undeservedly, obtained the larger share of the credit . . . against these successes, our land forces have had reverses at Big Bethel . . . Bull Run, and Ball's Bluff."

Early in 1862 the importance of the ironclad warship was underscored in the famous Hampton Roads naval duel. The Confederates had seized the

The harbor at Hamilton, Bermuda, saw scores of the runners pass through. Here the British steamer Dee *appears in 1863. On February 5, 1864, she ran ashore off Masonboro Inlet, North Carolina, and was destroyed by the USS* Cambridge *the next day. Her image was captured aboard the blockade-runner* Don *when she was captured by the USS* Pequot *off Wilmington on March 4, 1864.* (USAMHI)

The former Giraffe *as she appeared as the* Robert E. Lee *shortly after her capture. The Union Navy refitted her and renamed her* Fort Donelson. (LC)

powerful steam frigate the *Merrimack*—sunk by the Yankees during the evacuation of the Norfolk Navy Yard and quickly raised by the Rebels—and a cast-iron ram had been added to her bow. On March 8, 1862, this powerful ironclad, renamed the *Virginia,* steamed down the Elizabeth River to attack the Union blockading squadron in Hampton Roads. With ease the *Virginia* rammed and shelled the *Cumberland.* The *Congress* was then destroyed by hot shot with heavy casualties. Southerners were jubilant as their newspapers predicted the raising of the blockade and the reduction of Washington.

Secretary of the Navy Welles, however, had early in the war contracted for several new types of ironclads; one of these, the *Monitor,* now made her appearance in Hampton Roads. Although the *Monitor* presented a simple appearance, like a "cheese box on a raft," its construction revealed advanced engineering techniques. Her distinguishing features were her small size, her low, flat hull hung a few inches above the waterline, and

her central revolving gun turret, which proved impregnable against ten-inch shot at close range.

On March 9 the *Virginia,* returning to attack the *Minnesota* and the rest of the blockading squadron below Fort Monroe, was challenged by the *Monitor.* There followed a hotly fought duel at close quarters in which the *Monitor* protected the *Minnesota* from the onslaught of the Confederate ironclad. Neither vessel did much damage to the other, and after several hours of fighting both quit as if by mutual agreement.

In May 1862, during the Peninsular Campaign, George B. McClellan and his troops marched toward Richmond. They captured Yorktown on May 4, 1862. When Norfolk fell to Union hands, the James River lay open. Goldsborough, still commanding the North Atlantic Blockading Squadron, realized that there was a good chance of the Navy reaching Richmond. The Union ironclad *Galena* drew too much water to reach the Confederate capital, but the approach of the *Monitor* and wooden gunboats might render the city untenable.

Unfortunately for the Union, the ironclads *Galena* and *Monitor*, accompanied by wooden gunboats, were halted by Confederate batteries at Drewry's Bluff, near Richmond. The *Galena* was riddled. Besides severe damage to the hull, she lost thirteen men and eleven were badly wounded. The *Monitor* was uninjured, but due to the comparatively long range at which she fired, her nonrifled guns made little impression on the Confederate works. The engagement at Drewry's Bluff was an undoubted tribute to Confederate energy and ingenuity but a discouraging reverse for the Union Navy. It meant that Army cooperation was essential to take Richmond or any other well-defended port. The Goldsborough-Burnside work in the North Carolina sounds was itself finally halted in early July 1862 when a defeated General McClellan recalled the Army unit to the James River in Virginia.

In fact, the trickiest shoreline to blockade on the Atlantic Coast was that of the Cape Fear River sector, for the river leading to Wilmington had two navigable outlets forty miles apart, both of which were guarded by forts and coastal batteries. As the war continued, the North Atlantic Blockading Squadron began lining up its gunboats in two rows off each of these entrances. The sluggish, barely seaworthy vessels were stationed near the beach, with orders not to chase the blockade-runners out to sea but to flash their position to the swifter Union gunboats farther out. The course the runner was steering was indicated by rocket signals (e.g., one rocket and a white light meant northwestward, and so forth). During the daylight hours in clear weather, when conditions were unsuitable for a runner's escape, the blockading steamers anchored, enabling the captains, officers, and men to sleep. Half an hour before sunset the inshore patrol boats hoisted anchor, got under way and, as twilight fell, moved in toward the beach, keeping a taut watch

The blockade-runner A. D. Vance *shortly after her 1864 capture. She, too, entered the Federal service as the USS* Frolic, *remaining in commission until 1883.* (NHC)

The runner Teaser *photographed off Fort Monroe in December 1864, following her capture. Damage to her paddle box and waterline is clearly evident. Most blockade-runners surrendered without a fight when challenged, having virtually no protection against Federal fire.* (LC)

on Rebel coastal batteries. The speedier Union vessels operating off Wilmington policed an area that extended forty miles offshore. They chased and picked off British and Confederate freighters, signaling the inshore blockade regarding inbound runners.

One afternoon the men on board the blockader *Florida* had their fishing interrupted by a shout: "Sail ho! two points off the port bow." The officer of the deck sang out to the captain, "That's an Englishman, sir, sure as there's snakes in Virginny." The *Florida* got under way as the captain bellowed to the chief engineer, "Give her all you can." The *Florida* trembled. "The welcome relief from the monotony of months, that had nearly driven men crazy, had come at last," a seaman noted. Changing courses frequently, the *Florida* shortened the distance to the runner until she was within range. Yankee guns blazed. One shot

splashed close to the runner's bow. She surrendered.

Approaching the British freighter, the crew of the *Florida* saw sailors jettisoning cargo and papers and preparing to abandon ship. "Train the two pivots on her," the captain of the *Florida* ordered, running out to the bridge and hailing the Britisher: "Throw one more thing . . . overboard and I'll send a broadside into you, and let you go to the bottom . . . I shan't pick up a single man." A prize crew was placed on board the runner *Calypso,* and her passengers were transferred to the *Florida.*

Except for such actions, most Civil War duty at sea was monotonous. Some bluejackets who served on board the blockaders described shipboard routine as "pretty stupid." Although the work in the Navy involved neither the degree of peril nor the amount of privation that attended the military

Another view of the Teaser, *extensively damaged.* (NA)

campaigns, the awful boredom was broken only by exposure to the elements and blockade-runners dashing out for the open sea. At night no lights or noises were permitted on board the Yankee gunboats, hatches were covered, and lanterns were dimmed with casings. Expecting to sight enemy craft at any minute, crews stood ready to slip cables and man the guns; steam was kept up; officers slept half dressed, with their sidearms within easy reach. A naval lieutenant declared in a letter to home that he was "being used up so fast by the anxieties and climate together" that if he should spend more time on blockade duty he would not be "worth a damn."

Characteristic of any navy at any time, complaints by Union bluejackets increased as the Civil War lengthened from months into years. The men grumbled about everything from the daily routine, hard work, and heat to food, homesickness, and the absence of girls. Journals, letters, courts-martial proceedings, and newspaper accounts all attest that the commonest grievance of the sailor in the North

Atlantic Blockading Squadron concerned monotony. "During the last week," a seaman wrote home, "I have seen enough of the sea. I am not sea sick, but I am sick of the sea." On board the *Florida,* off Wilmington, a sailor penned the following in his diary:

> I told my mother, she could get a fair idea of our 'adventures,' if she would go on the roof of the house, on a hot summer day, and talk to half a dozen hotel hallboys, who are generally more intelligent, and agreeable, than the average officer.
>
> Then descend to the attic and drink some warm water, full of iron-rust. Then go on the roof again and repeat this 'adventurous process' at intervals, until she was tired out, and go to bed, with everything shut down tight, so as not to show a light.
>
> Adventure! Bah! The blockade is the wrong place for it.

For those "raging lions" who believed that wars

Captain R. H. Harper of the blockade-runner Hallie. *He and his fellow captains ran a dangerous business* . . . (WILLIAM A. ALBAUGH COLLECTION)

. . . but the rewards could be enormous, which is what attracted men like Captain A. G. Swaszey to risk the run in his ship Ella. (WILLIAM A. ALBAUGH COLLECTION)

were won by firing cannon, the quiet and usually uneventful work of the blockade seemed to accomplish nothing.

As the war wore on, the North Atlantic Blockading Squadron, bolstered with more ships and men, executed hit-and-run commando raids along the hostile shores. Assistant Secretary of the Navy Fox recommended to the commander of the squadron, then Admiral Samuel P. Lee, that Union sailors sneak up rivers and destroy runners, arsenals, and saltworks. In late February 1864 a lieutenant effected a daring plot against an installation up the Cape Fear River. Twenty Federal sailors in two boats rowed up the river one cloudy night and disembarked directly in front of a Smithville hotel. Posting a guard for the boats, three officers and one seaman crept up to the commanding general's headquarters, gained entrance, and captured the chief engineer of the river defenses. To their disappointment the Union sailors discovered that the general had gone off to Wilmington. His chief

aide, hearing the rumpus and thinking that the 1,000 soldiers in a nearby barracks had mutinied, scampered into the woods and neglected to turn in the alarm. The Federals, meanwhile, hauled away their prisoner so quietly that the Rebel sentries failed to notice. The Yankees were out of the harbor before the chief engineer was missed.

Such activities, although minor in importance, roused the anxiety of the Confederate troops in North Carolina. More men were shuttled to coastal areas. Officers reasoned that if boat expeditions could go up to Smithville unnoticed, Unionists could load barges with troops, land on the beaches, and destroy the forts guarding the Cape Fear River.

Besides such hit-and-run raids, the spirits of Union bluejackets were buoyed by the prospects of prize money from captured blockade-runners. Profits from the sale of a prize vessel were first split equally among the captors and the United States

And for the Federals it meant a routine of constant vigilance: standing at the rail, glass in hand, ever watchful for the thin wisp of smoke or the rakish gray hull nearly blending into the horizon that meant a blockade-runner. (USAMHI)

Government and, after a 5 percent cut to the squadron commander, the blockader's portion was divided up into twenty equal shares. The skipper took three for himself; the lieutenants, masters, and warrants took four; midshipmen and petty officers took six; and the sailors received the remaining seven.

Competition was keen. Some captains dipped into their own pockets and awarded $50 to the first man spotting a runner, while Congress authorized a $200 bounty to each sailor on board a Yankee gunboat that sank or destroyed an enemy of "equal or superior force" and a $100 bounty for each enemy ship of "inferior force."

When the little tug *Aeolus* pounced on the *Hope* off Wilmington in October 1864, the master won $13,164; the assistant engineer $6,657, or more than four years' pay; the seamen over $1,000 apiece; and the cabin boy $532. Nine days later the *Aeolus* assisted in taking the *Lady Sterling,* which, with her cargo, sold for $509,354.64. Each

seaman on board the tug reaped $2,000 from the sale of the Britisher, making $3,000 in prize money for ten days' work.

Officers sitting out the war on the beach bitterly condemned the prize money system for obvious reasons. Admiral Porter also complained that such laws weakened a strict blockade since each man was more interested in looking out for his own interests than in cooperating with his flotilla. Although later in the war Porter condemned the system, when he commanded the North Atlantic Blockading Squadron it was dubbed the "prize money command." Among Union officers, Admiral Lee, who was chief of this squadron for several years, piled up the single largest chunk of prize money, netting $109,689, while the disapproving Porter, running a close second, banked $91,528.

From the beginning of the Atlantic coastal war, Secretary of the Navy Gideon Welles wished to close the port of Wilmington to Confederate commerce. The task was not easy. Natural conditions

Captain Louis M. Goldsborough came of an old Maryland family with strong naval ties. Though fifty-six years old in 1861, he still succeeded Stribling in command of the squadron and led it in the attack on Roanoke Island. He would be promoted to rear admiral in a few months, but, like Stribling, would eventually ask to be retired in the face of heavy criticism from the press. (USAMHI)

forced the Yankee squadron to post ships at both openings of the river; because of the weather its gunboats were often in danger of being driven ashore. "Cape Fear River," wrote Welles, "is more difficult to blockade than any other port [entrance] on the coast of the United States." The Richmond *Dispatch* claimed that it was "a matter of absolute impossibility" for the Federals to stop Southern blockade-running at Wilmington.

The capture of the Florida sounds in 1862, the closing of Savannah as a port, and the continuous bombardment of Charleston in 1863 by the South Atlantic Blockading Squadron turned the attention of blockade-runners toward Wilmington on the

Cape Fear River. By August 1863 the Confederate officer in charge of the blockade-running could report that Wilmington had become the chief supply center of the Confederacy. Forts Fisher and Caswell guarded the approaches to Cape Fear. For one reason or another, plans for an assault against these forts were shelved. In the fall of 1864, however, it seemed necessary, more than ever, to Union strategy that Wilmington should be taken. Secretary Welles confided that the closing of this harbor and the cutting off of communications with Richmond was paramount and "more important, practically, than the capture of Richmond."

Plans for an amphibious assault against Fort Fisher were worked out. In early December 1864, 6,500 troops commanded by General Butler were assigned to the expedition for the assault. Admiral Porter, now commanding the North Atlantic Blockading Squadron, amassed "the most formidable armada ever" and hoped to hand over Fort Fisher "to the Government as a fitting Christmas present." During those early December days Butler and Porter failed to work out any coordinated attack doctrine.

In late December 1864 the army transports, tenders, and small craft—eighty-five in all—steamed out of Hampton Roads. Off the Cape Fear River Porter calculated that Butler and his troops would arrive so that they could land before 8 A.M. on December 24. But at 8 A.M. the transports were nowhere to be seen. Porter waited until shortly before noon and then decided to start the bombardment against Fort Fisher without the troops. At 11:30 A.M. Porter signaled the squadron to start the attack, with the *New Ironsides* and the monitors *Monadnock, Canonicus,* and *Mahopac* leading the forty-six wooden ships.

Guns blazed from the fort and the fight became general. After an hour and a half the Confederates ceased firing, but Porter's ships maintained the barrage. At sunset a few of Butler's transports came into view, but it was now too late to effect a landing. That night, on board Porter's flagship, Major General Godfrey Weitzel, who was to lead the attack, arrived to discuss the next day's operation. Porter and Weitzel decided that while the Navy attacked Fort Fisher, the Army would land and assault under the cover of twenty-seven gunboats.

On Christmas Day the *New Ironsides,* the moni-

In his efforts to enforce the blockade, Goldsborough used fine new gunboats like the USS Kansas . . . (LC)

tors, and the wooden gunboats steamed into position and commenced pounding the fort. By midafternoon 2,000 soldiers had landed. What General Weitzel saw when he came up made him shiver. Fort Fisher was the strongest bastion that he had "ever seen or heard of." Noting that the fort had not been "materially injured" by naval gunfire, the general withdrew, boarded a dispatch boat, and reported to Butler that "it would be butchery to order an assault." Five hundred advanced troops had moved to within "150 paces" of Fort Fisher, and had sent back word to move up reinforcements, but a messenger arrived with orders to retreat and re-embark.

Porter was incensed. He accused the Army of "cowardice," Weitzel of "having no backbone," and Butler of being "a failure."

When news reached Washington, Northerners wanted to know who was responsible for the failure. *Harper's Weekly* declared that someone had blundered and pointed its finger at Butler, while the New York *Herald* termed the military phase of the expedition "a ridiculous fizzle." In Washington naval strategists "toasted confusion" to Butler and to all "civilian generals."

The lack of harmony between Army and Navy was partially responsible for the failure at Fort Fisher. Neither Porter nor Butler had been vested with overall authority and responsibility for the operation. The attack conclusively demonstrated the defects of a joint command, where neither branch of the service had final responsibility. This deficiency was fortunately rectified in the final amphibious assault of the war.

. . . and converted army transports like the side-wheeler USS Fulton, *shown here on June 20, 1864.* (NA)

Three days following the Fort Fisher defeat Admiral Porter, who was still with his squadron off North Carolina, jotted a note to Assistant Secretary Fox. The repulse "is only temporary," Porter said, "for we can take it [i.e., Fort Fisher] at any time —Don't give it up, we will have it yet." On December 30 General Grant at City Point, believing that the Confederates had been lulled into a sense of false security, urged Porter to hold his position, promised an increased force "without the former commander," and took steps to collect more transports.

Porter was happy over Grant's renewed interest. The admiral suggested that the troops rendezvous at Beaufort, North Carolina, where by this time most of his squadron was engaged in loading coal and ammunition. At City Point preparations were being made to get the troops ready for the expedition. Major General Alfred Terry was placed in command of 8,000 troops, most of them veterans of the first Fort Fisher Campaign. Grant told Terry that it was desirable that "a most complete understanding" should exist between him and Porter, and that he should consult with the admiral freely and "get from him the part to be performed by each branch of the public service" so that there would be "unity of action." Grant told Terry to defer to Porter "as much as is consistent with your own responsibilities." Acting on the lesson learned, the army chief was unofficially suggesting that

Terry regard Porter as the commander of the joint operation.

On January 8, 1865, Porter and his commanders spied the troopships heading toward Beaufort. They were quickly coaled. Four days later the Federal expedition, composed of 53 naval vessels and 19 transports, started for Fort Fisher. By evening the expedition was off the Confederate stronghold, which Rebel commitments elsewhere had reduced to a force of only 800.

At daylight on January 13, 5 ironclads and 48 wooden vessels steamed to their positions. Headed by the *Brooklyn,* a detachment of vessels maneuvered to within 600 yards of the beach to assist landing operations. *New Ironsides* and the monitors were ordered to anchor 1,000 yards from the fort and "pour in their fire." At 8 A.M. the *New Ironsides* and the monitors opened fire, while a half hour later troops landed up the beach under the

command of the Navy. The first 500 soldiers waded ashore unopposed.

In a dense forest a short distance away a Rebel division, numbering 6,000, under General Braxton Bragg had just arrived from Wilmington. It watched the Federal landing, but due to an intervening swamp and "the heavy metal of the fleet," it refused to budge from its hiding place. Bragg rationalized that not even "Grant's army could . . . storm and carry the fort." Without firing a musket, the division retreated when it later learned that "everything at Fort Fisher was in confusion."

The landing proceeded. The beach was "black with men with their bayonets glittering in the sunshine and their regimental flags fluttering in the breeze." By 3 P.M. 8,000 Federal soldiers had landed. As soon as they dried out, Terry's main force moved inland toward Fort Fisher, located five miles away. During the entire day Porter's fleet

Converted New York ferryboats like the USS Morse *took part in the operations at Hatteras Inlet and Roanoke, covered troop landings up the Virginia rivers, and assisted in the blockade patrol.* (USAMHI)

Others, like the USS Shawsheen, *scoured the rivers and harbors for "torpedoes," submerged mines that could quickly sink a wooden-hulled vessel.* (WRHS)

pounded the fort. To remedy the miserable showing his ships had made on the previous assault, the admiral had issued detailed firing instructions.

Urgent pleas went out from the beleaguered fort for reinforcements. In the midst of the bombardment, area commander Major General W.H.C. Whiting arrived at the fort, shook hands with the commanding officer, Colonel William Lamb, and said, "Lamb, my boy, I have come to share your fate. You and your garrison are to be sacrificed."

At nightfall Porter ordered the wooden vessels to haul off and the monitors to keep up their firing. On the beach darkness also overtook the military, who were forced to halt for the night. As January 14 dawned, the wooden vessels took their positions next to the monitors and fired until sundown.

Porter now regarded the fort as "reduced to a pulp." His calculation was correct. Every Confederate gun on the land front had been knocked out, all defensive barriers had been torn up, and not a man had dared "show his head" in that "infernal storm" of shellfire. The Army, meanwhile, was still in the process of unloading its field artillery and was forced to wait throughout the day at a distance of nearly two miles from Fort Fisher.

That evening on board the *Malvern* Terry and Porter decided to attack the following day, January 15. The naval bombardment was to continue and the assault was scheduled for 3 P.M. The soldiers were to attack the rear of the fort, while armed sailors were to strike the eastern side, or sea face.

In the early morning hours of January 15 the Federal squadron moved in once again and by 10 A.M. it was pounding the fort. The naval assault force, composed of 1,600 sailors and 400 marines, landed two miles up the beach from the bastion. At precisely 3 P.M. a long blast on the *Malvern's* steam whistle signaled the assault. Naval vessels ceased the bombardment of the stronghold. On board sailors watched their shipmates on the shore jump up, cheering, and run down the open beach. The Rebels, seeing this assault, thought it was the main attack, and nearly the whole force lunged for the sea face. In an instant the entire front wall was "one dense mass of musketeers" who poured a "hot fire" into the advancing bluejackets.

Some Federals reached the parapets of the fort but were mowed down and "slaughtered unmercifully." The wounded limped or crawled out of range, while the dead and dying lay strewn along the beach. The naval charge, though unsuccessful,

acted as a decoy for the main military assault and allowed the first detachments of Terry's men to reach the rear parapets unmolested. Army officers were the first to admit that had there been no naval attack, their losses would have been severe. While the attention of the fort was focused on the sea front, the first brigade of soldiers effected a lodgment on the rear parapets and fired into the backs of the Rebels. The defenders turned, but the Federals had already gained their initial footing. Other Union brigades rushed forward to support the first.

There was desperate fighting on the parapets. By 5 P.M. the Union soldiers possessed half the land front of Fort Fisher. The fighting for each traverse continued until nearly 9 P.M., when the Confederates, seeing that further resistance was useless, fled from the stronghold. Across Cape Fear River Confederates blew up their remaining installations. The Union had captured Fort Fisher.

And there were little vessels, like the Seth Low, *which had a special duty. On March 6, 1862, the* Seth Low *left New York with an unusual ship in tow, the USS* Monitor. *Both were on their way to Hampton Roads, the* Virginia, *and the* Monitor's *destiny.* (USAMHI)

Commander John Worden commanded the
Monitor. *It was his first ship of the war, he being
the first officer to have charge of this new type of
warship. He nearly lost his sight thanks to one of
the* Virginia's *shots.* (USAMHI)

On board the gunboat *Gettysburg* an officer
assessed the situation: "I firmly believe the Rebels
will feel the loss of Fort Fisher more keenly and
that our victory here will do more towards the return of peace than anything that has yet been done.
We stop supplies." Porter agreed, for he considered
the victory "the death blow to the rebellion." To
William T. Sherman Porter declared: "The door
through which the enemy was fed, is closed on
them, and all we have to do, is to watch them
starve."

By mid-February 1865 Porter and the military
units captured Wilmington. Thousands of Tarheels
slipped away from the Confederate armies and
went home. Late in February General Robert E.

Lee declared that the despair of the North Carolinians was destroying his army and that desertions
were becoming frequent. The blockade-running
bases in the West Indies were hit hard. After the
fall of Wilmington one sea captain reported that
speculators in Nassau saw that "the bottom had
fallen out," and that all of them were in the
"depths of despair." Even the stevedores and laborers bewailed the misfortune, for they knew that
"the glory of Nassau had departed forever." By
March 1865 the blockade-running captains had
shifted their base to Havana for the run to Galveston, Texas, and minor ports on the Gulf Coast
which still remained open. Except for maintaining
the blockade and clearing Confederate harbors of
mines, the amphibious assault against Fort Fisher
in early 1865 signaled the end of naval operations
along the Carolina seaboard.

To accurately gauge the North Atlantic Blockading Squadron's efficiency or its influence on the
final collapse of the Confederacy is extremely
difficult. Owing to the secrecy required in blockade-running, British and Confederate shipowners
and merchants either failed to keep or burned, lost,
or completely destroyed cargo statistics, arrival and
departure reports, and lists of vessels engaged in
the traffic. Years later a historian poring over Confederate newspapers and other documents wrote
several articles in *The American Neptune* during
the 1940s. Although he neglected to divide the operations of the North and South Atlantic Blockading Squadrons, he concluded in his article on the
blockade of the Carolina ports that between 1861
and 1865 more than 2,054 attempts were made to
penetrate the Yankee squadrons, a daily average of
one and a half runs. Eighty-four percent of the
known attempts were successful.

The measure of the blockade's effectiveness,
however, lay not in the number of ships seized but
rather in the number of cargoes rotting on Liver-
pool docks and the number of British vessels that
never got under way for Nassau. Shipowners who
ordinarily would have deposited freight at Carolina
wharves were deterred by nightmares of capture,
resulting in bankruptcy and, possibly, the poor-
house. Better by far that the Confederacy should
starve than that they should as well. Paper blockade though it might be, the Union's naval embrace
of the Southern coastline proved effective against
many of its suitors.

Acting Volunteer Lieutenant Louis N. Stodder served aboard the Monitor, *helping work her turret during the epic fight on March 9.* (USAMHI)

The officers of the Monitor *on July 9, 1862. The turret of the prototype warship rests behind them. Unfortunately no photograph of the entire ship is known to exist.* (USAMHI)

Seated on the chair at right is Lieutenant Samuel D. Greene, who took command of the Monitor *when Worden was wounded. Years later Greene would take his own life, reputedly in frustration over an article he was preparing on the* Monitor-Virginia *battle, making him the fight's last "casualty." (USAMHI)*

The officers in yet another pose. Paymaster William Keeler, standing wearing spectacles, was with the ship on her last voyage. When she was sinking, he stuffed money and some valuable papers in one of the cannon barrels. A cat jumped into the other. (USAMHI)

Men of the Monitor *lounge on deck. The two seamen in the right foreground play backgammon. On the turret behind them some of the slight damage done by the* Virginia *is evident.* (MARINERS MUSEUM)

The cook's fire smoking away, men of the Monitor *await a midday meal.* (USAMHI)

James Gibson caught this image on July 9, 1862, of two officers surveying the turret. At the edge of the deck just to the right of them can be seen a plate slightly loosened where the Virginia *attempted to ram the ironclad but glanced off instead. The pilothouse, the pyramidal object behind the turret, was originally rectangular. Worden was injured there.* (USAMHI)

Worden's successor in command of the Monitor, *the largely unpopular Lieutenant William N. Jeffers, seated before the turret. He commanded the ship in the ill-fated attack on Drewry's Bluff.* (USAMHI)

Lieutenant Catesby Ap R. Jones was executive officer of the Virginia, *a man from an old and honored naval family. When Franklin Buchanan was wounded on March 8, Jones commanded the Confederate ironclad in its battle with the* Monitor *the next day.* (NHC)

Lieutenant John Taylor Wood, grandson of President Zachary Taylor and a career naval officer, served one of the Virginia's guns. He would later become a dreaded commerce raider. (PRIVATE COLLECTION)

Midshipman Henry H. Marmaduke of Missouri was badly injured when the muzzle of his gun was shot away aboard the Virginia. (COURTESY OF JON NIELSON)

Midshipman Hardin B. Littlepage served another of the Virginia's *guns in the epic contest.*
(COURTESY OF ALVAN C. MACAULEY)

Commodore Gershom Van Brunt commanded the USS Minnesota *in the battle at Hampton Roads, running the vessel aground on March 8. She remained immobile the next day while the* Monitor *successfully kept the* Virginia *away from her.*
(USAMHI)

Commander George U. Morris valiantly fought his ship, the USS Cumberland, *both before and after she was rammed by the* Virginia. *Some of the sinking ship's guns were kept in action until the rising water reached their muzzles.* (USAMHI)

Not so fortunate was Lieutenant Joseph B. Smith, commanding the USS Congress. *In the hot fighting before his ship was destroyed by the Confederates, he was killed instantly when a shell carried away his head and shoulder. His father had a premonition of his son's death the same day.* (USAMHI)

Brother against brother meant something to Paymaster and Lieutenant Commander J. McKean Buchanan aboard the Congress. *His brother was Franklin Buchanan, commanding the CSS* Virginia. (USAMHI)

Other ironclads did not always prove as impervious to enemy shells as the Monitor. *In the abortive attack on Drewry's Bluff the USS* Galena *suffered severe damage, as shown in Gibson's June 1862 image. She was never an effective ironclad warship.* (LC)

Once portions of the rivers were taken from the Confederates, the ships of the squadron had to patrol them to prevent Rebel crossings and maintain supply and communications. Here at White House, on the Pamunkey River in Virginia, several of these smaller craft go about their tasks. (USAMHI)

One of the converted New York ferries, the Commodore Morris *spent its entire war career on the rivers of Virginia. The ferryboats were unsuited to operations on the ocean. (USAMHI)*

Officers aboard one of the "Commodore" class ferry-gunboats. (CHS)

The USS Commodore Barney *patrolled the James River and the inland
waterways of North Carolina.* (USAMHI)

The Commodore Barney's *officers on her foredeck. Cannon and shot now line the deck once used by commuters to New York City.* (USAMHI)

Larger ships like the USS Maratanza, *a side-wheeler gunboat, ventured out of the rivers to take the occasional blockade-runner or Confederate naval vessel. This ship engaged the Rebel gunboat* Teaser *on July 4, 1862, when the* Teaser *tried to run down the James to launch an observation balloon following the Seven Days battles. James Gibson made his image the same day.* (LC)

Gibson's image of the deck of the Teaser *after her capture. In the background stands her captor, the* Maratanza. (LC)

The Teaser's *bow gun, a thirty-two-pounder with reinforced breech, was no match for the* Maratanza, *which put a shot into the Confederate's boiler early in the engagement.* (LC)

The Teaser's *stern gun, a ten-pounder Parrott rifle, did no better. This first "aircraft carrier," complete with silk balloon, was abandoned by its crew.* (LC)

The tugboat Clyde *on the James River. All vessels great and small had work to do in the North Atlantic Blockading Squadron.* (NA)

Most captivating of all the ships patrolling the Southern rivers for the squadron were the monitors. The photographers fell under their spell; more images were made of them than any other class of vessel. Here pose the officers of the USS Sangamon, *like most monitors named for a river.* (USAMHI)

The seamen of the Sangamon, *too, stand for the camera. The iron
"breastwork" above the turret was intended to protect lookouts from small
arms fire.* (NA)

One of the favorite iron monsters on the James, the USS Saugus. *Shown here
with a torpedo boom and net in front, it spent nearly its entire career on the
James. At war's end, however, it went to Washington to become a temporary
prison for the conspirators in the Lincoln assassination. On the hill in the
distance behind it is the "crow's nest" signal tower.* (USAMHI)

Officers of the Saugus. The varying width of the white stripes on the turrets of this and other monitors was for identification from a distance. (NA)

The men of the Saugus, or at least a few of them. Monitor crews were not large because of the cramped quarters below decks. (NA)

The Saugus *in the lead, as a fleet of monitors and other craft patrol the James. The boom across the river in front of the* Saugus *is intended to catch mines that the Confederates would put in the river to float down against Federal ships. The* Sangamon *is just behind, and to its right, in the distance, sits the* Mahopac. *At far left is the twin-turreted* Onondaga. *Between it and the* Sangamon *is the* Atlanta, *once a Confederate ironclad but now in Federal service.* (USAMHI)

The Onondaga, *a workhorse twin-turreted monitor on the James. Only two double-turreted monitors saw service during the war, and when Porter stripped the James fleet for the attack on Fort Fisher, the* Onondaga *was left to defend the James almost single-handedly.* (USAMHI)

The Onondaga *on the James, with the USS* Mackinaw *partially hidden at left.*
(USAMHI)

The Onondaga, *pound for pound perhaps the finest monitor built during the war.* (USAMHI)

Besides the monitors, special double-ended gunboats, like the USS Mendota,
*were also built. Possessing reversible engines, they could steam up or down a
narrow river or channel without turning around. She is shown here at Deep
Bottom on the James in 1864.* (USAMHI)

The officers of the Mendota. *Commander E. T. Nichols, in white trousers, is
seated in the right foreground.* (USAMHI)

The crew of the Mendota *on the foredeck, a Parrott rifle aimed over the starboard side.* (USAMHI)

The view from the crow's nest, with the Saugus *at left and the* Sangamon *at right.* (USAMHI)

*On patrol on the James. An unknown gunboat appears in the foreground, and
the* Mahopac *is visible in the distance.* (COURTESY OF BRUCE GIMELSON)

The little monitor Casco *on the James, near Dutch Gap, in early 1865. Three
side-wheel gunboats and another monitor lie astern.* (NA)

The Saugus, Sangamon, *the former Confederate ironclad* Atlanta, *and the* Onondaga *make one of the endless patrols on the James in the final months of the war.* (NA)

The Mackinaw *and the* Saugus *on the Appomattox River in the summer of 1864.* (USAMHI)

One of the dangers facing these rivercraft of the North Atlantic Blockading Squadron was the torpedoes made by Confederate engineers. Here, late in 1864, Federal engineers disarm enemy mines near Dutch Gap on the James. One such mine rests at the feet of the officer with the long pipe. At the right of the image is the portable darkroom and boxes of equipment of the photographer, Egbert G. Fowx. (LC)

Lieutenant Hunter Davidson, once commander of the ill-fated Teaser, *took charge of the development of the dreaded torpedoes, thus exacting his measure of revenge, for the mines sank more Federal ships than did Confederate guns.* (NHC)

More torpedoes fished out of the James River. (USAMHI)

The squadron did more than simply patrol rivers. Daring men and ships engaged the Confederates frequently. More than once they launched raids against the Rebel ironclads that often protected the harbors and upper reaches of the rivers. On October 27–28, 1864, Lieutenant William B. Cushing led a courageous expedition up Albemarle Sound, North Carolina, to destroy the dreaded ironclad CSS Albemarle. (USAMHI)

With a torpedo mounted at the end of a spar on his steam launch, Cushing drove it against the submerged hull of the Albemarle *under darkness and sank her immediately. Here she lies as photographed shortly afterward by Plymouth photographer W. B. Rose. The Federals later raised her.* (NHC)

The Federals put another captured Confederate ironclad, the CSS Atlanta, *into service patrolling the James. She was captured by the monitor* Weehawken *in Wassaw Sound, Georgia, on June 17, 1863, in her first and only battle. Here her new Union officers pose on the foredeck. The characteristic slope-sided casemate of a Confederate ironclad rises behind them.* (USAMHI)

Commander John Newland Maffitt, shown here in a damaged and faded old photograph never previously published, enjoyed three Confederate careers. Besides being commander of the commerce raider CSS Florida, *he also proved a nuisance to the North Atlantic Blockading Squadron as a captain of several blockade-runners, and then, for a time, served as commander of the ironclad* Albemarle. *His adventuring did not stop with the war. He went on to serve foreign governments and Cuban revolutionaries before retiring to North Carolina.* (TU)

While the Confederates could never mount much of a fleet on the rivers, they did emplace batteries along the James and other streams to interdict the passage of Federal traffic. Batteries like this Federal emplacement near Fort Brady on the James commanded a clear field of fire against any hostile vessels, and often had to be taken from the land side before ships could pass. (USAMHI)

Admiral Raphael Semmes, the commander of the James River fleet for the Confederates at the close of the war, was a man already famed for his high seas adventures. Once captain of the feared commerce raiders Sumter *and* Alabama, *he finished the war in Richmond. He destroyed his fleet rather than see it captured with the fall of the capital, and then accompanied the fleeing Confederate government.* (VM)

*Rear Admiral Samuel P. Lee replaced
Goldsborough in command of the North Atlantic
Blockading Squadron and intensified efforts
against blockade-runners.* (USAMHI)

Lee's flagship was the USS Agawam, *shown here on the James.* (USAMHI)

She was a powerful ship. Here her crew poses with a massive one hundred-pounder Parrott rifle. (NHC)

Lee continued the capture of hostile shipping, and his sailors continued to share the prize money. The Lady Sterling, *also called the* Hornet *and the* Cuba, *brought over half a million dollars in prize court. She is photographed here by C. W. Yates in Wilmington, North Carolina, in 1865, while serving as the USS* Hornet. (NHC)

Moral support for the blockading squadron came from across the Atlantic, from the czar. The Russian frigate Osliaba *came into the harbor at Alexandria, as did other Russian vessels in New York and San Francisco. They were old ships, not terribly useful in a sea battle should the British or French enter the war on the side of the Confederacy, but their presence was nevertheless a symbol of the czar's support for Lincoln. A. J. Russell made this image.* (LC)

Eventually Lee, too, was replaced by Admiral David D. Porter. The latter appears here at left, seated beside Major General George G. Meade, in an image taken in May 1865. Though he often conspired against his brother, David G. Farragut, still Porter rose in fame and accomplishment and deserved the new command. He earned it in the operations to take Fort Fisher. (USAMHI)

From his headquarters at Fort Monroe Porter built his armada for the assault on Fort Fisher. Thousands of men and seamen passed over this wharf. The Hygeia Dining Saloon fed hundreds of them. (USAMHI)

Porter called his command "the most formidable armada ever." Here several ships of his fleet ride out a storm off Hampton Roads in December 1864, before leaving for the attack on Fort Fisher. (USAMHI)

Porter himself made his headquarters aboard the USS Malvern. *Here he poses with his staff in December 1864. Standing at far left is William B. Cushing, destroyer of the Albemarle. Porter is in the center with his hand across his chest.* (USAMHI)

Cushing was now a commander, promoted in recognition of his exploits against the Albemarle. At Fort Fisher he would risk his life for over six hours in a small boat as he sounded and marked the channel for the larger ships to approach the fort. Then he would lead an assault against the ramparts of the fort itself. Here he is only twenty-two years old. His brother, Alonzo, also aged twenty-two, was already killed at Gettysburg. (USAMHI)

Porter's fleet included Lee's old flagship, the Agawam. (CHS)

The ironclads were organized into a separate division, commanded by Rear Admiral William Radford. (USAMHI)

There are familiar ships here, like the Saugus, *shown in the James River a few months later.* (USAMHI)

Her officers can look to more action, indeed, more than they have yet seen in their river service. (USAMHI)

Steamers like the USS Rhode Island *will tow some of the ironclads to North Carolina waters, since the monitors are unstable in rough seas. Indeed, the* Rhode Island *was towing the original* Monitor *when the little ironclad went down in two hundred feet of water off Cape Hatteras in December 1862.* (NA)

The sloop of war Mohican, *shown here off the Washington Navy Yard, joined the burgeoning fleet.* (CWTI)

So did smaller monitors like the Canonicus. *She was towed by the* Rhode Island, *experiencing better fortune than the* Monitor. *Here a coaling boat refuels the single-turreted monitor.* (CHS)

And the Mahopac *will go along.* (USAMHI)

Acting Assistant Paymaster Henry M. Meade of the USS Mattabessett *went along. He was General Meade's nephew.* (P-M)

So did the USS Santiago de Cuba. *She was a merchant side-wheeler at the war's opening, and was then purchased by the Navy Department. With a fine sense of diplomacy, the Navy sent her to patrol the waters around Havana, Cuba, in search of blockade-runners. It was a nice touch, having a ship named for a Cuban city assigned to her shores, especially since the Cubans were rather disposed to favor the Confederacy.* (USAMHI)

Porter's great "armada," lying off Hampton Roads and ready for the Fort Fisher expedition. Timothy O'Sullivan is probably the artist responsible for this vivid view. Only one of the ships can be identified, the workhorse ironclad **New Ironsides**. *She rests at anchor, the third ship to the right of the vessel in the center of the image. Her bow slopes downward toward the water rather than outward from it.* (LC)

Porter's objective, Fort Fisher. O'Sullivan captured these images after the fort was taken on Porter's second try in January 1865. This is the view of part of the face of the earthworks seen from the shore. (USAMHI)

An assault from the ocean would first have to send troops against and over the wooden obstruction, right in the face of cannon fire from the fort. (USAMHI)

The formidable nature of the fort is better seen from the inside. This view of the first three traverses shows the heavy protection afforded each gun. (USAMHI)

Another traverse, now in ruin after the naval bombardment. (USAMHI)

O'Sullivan's image of "The Pulpit," the heavily protected bombproof dug right into the earth face of the fort. The calm aspect of the Federal soldiers hardly betrays the excitement and frenzy of the day of their attack. (CHS)

A British Armstrong gun in place. This is one of many heavily reinforced seacoast guns that the Confederacy obtained from Great Britain despite England's supposed neutrality. (USAMHI)

An interior view of "The Pulpit." Accommodations were, to say the least, spartan. (USAMHI)

*An interior view of the first six traverses on the seaward face of Fort Fisher.
Littering the sand are cannon shot, probably misses fired by Porter's fleet as
they pounded the traverses.* (USAMHI)

*Another Armstrong. The carriage has imprinted upon it "Sir W. G. Armstrong
& Co. Newcastle-Upon-Tyne." It is a 150-pounder cannon with an 8-inch
bore, one of the most formidable guns in the South.* (USAMHI)

A banded rifle broken at the muzzle by the heavy fire from the Federal fleet.
(USAMHI)

*The land side of the fort was less built up since the Confederates only
anticipated an attack from the sea.* (USAMHI)

*Several ruined carriages and dismounted cannon lie amid
these three traverses.* (USAMHI)

*Another columbiad now peering silently out upon a
seascape that is undisputedly Union territory. Once stilled,
the mighty guns of Fort Fisher, once the most feared
Confederate fortress on the Atlantic, never spoke again.*
(USAMHI)

A columbiad with its muzzle blown away by a direct hit from one of Porter's ships. (USAMHI)

Another cannon, its carriage completely shattered, lies, like Fort Fisher itself, the helpless captive of Northern might. (USAMHI)

The entrance to the fort is at left, next to the first traverse. The two dismounted cannon lying at the water's edge are columbiads, with the remains of their carriages next to them. Either the Confederates never had time to get them up on the traverse and mounted or else the Federals' fire cast them back down into the sand and mud. (USAMHI)

The shot furnace at the fort, used for heating solid shot until it was red-hot. Fired against wooden ships, hot shot could start disastrous fires and detonate magazines. (NA)

For Major General William H. C. Whiting Fort Fisher ended a troubled Confederate career. Almost abandoned by the War Department, lent no aid by nearby General Braxton Bragg, he was forced by overwhelming numbers to surrender on January 15 after the bombardment and assault. He himself took a wound and died less than two months later as a prisoner of war, perhaps the final casualty of Fort Fisher and of the last major engagement of the North Atlantic Blockading Squadron. (VM)

Meanwhile the Yankee ships kept on at their work. Ships like the USS Hunchback, shown here on the James, *maintained their ceaseless vigil on the Southern rivers and coastline, seeking to do the Navy's part in putting an end to the Civil War.* (NA)

New Bern in North Carolina

A PORTFOLIO

One peaceful Southern town that looked far,
far away from the conflict

*The quiet streets of a lovely Southern town to which war has come. New Bern,
North Carolina, was much contested during the war, commanding as it did the
North Carolina Railroad linking Raleigh with the sea, as well as the Neuse
River. Yet somehow it always managed to look peaceful, more a Southern still
life than a town at war. Its quiet streets rarely betrayed the conflict of which it
was a part.* (USAMHI)

The headquarters of Major General John G. Foster in New Bern as it looked in 1862 or early 1863. Foster himself stands in front of the second pillar from the left. Private residences like this one bustled with military activity as officers rented or occupied rooms. (SOCIETY FOR THE PRESERVATION OF NEW ENGLAND ANTIQUITIES)

Foster and his staff posed yet again for the camera in front of their decidedly plush headquarters. While active field generals—even Grant, Lee, and Sherman—lived in tents, officers with comfortable occupation assignments like New Bern enjoyed rare amenities. (USAMHI)

Now and then even the men in the ranks enjoyed some of the pleasures of this sedentary duty. They are not gone soft on garrison duty, yet there is an informal, relaxed atmosphere in their jaunty pose. The constant threat of battle and death does not trouble them—or New Bern. The town and its conquerors look comfortable with each other. (USAMHI)

Another peaceful home now host to the men in blue. (USAMHI)

General Foster actually made his residence in this modest dwelling. (USAMHI)

A brigade headquarters at the corner of a New Bern street. The proud colonels stand on the porch, their horses awaiting. In fact, they really had nowhere to go. (SOCIETY FOR THE PRESERVATION OF NEW ENGLAND ANTIQUITIES)

Company H of an unknown regiment, probably from Massachusetts, traded
their tents for this fine house. There were servants available for tiny sums,
pleasant weather, pretty ladies, and rather little military excitement. Most of
the time in New Bern the Yankee soldiers could almost forget the war.
(SOCIETY FOR THE PRESERVATION OF NEW ENGLAND ANTIQUITIES)

Company I of the 44th Massachusetts spent nine months in the Union service,
almost all of it at New Bern. They appear here on September 25, 1862, at
Readville, Massachusetts. Their uniforms will be little soiled in their months in
North Carolina. (USAMHI)

*Five comrades of Company F, 44th Massachusetts.
They proved gentlemanly occupiers.* (COURTESY OF
MICHAEL J. MCAFEE)

*Major J. L. Stackpole sits on the steps of his home, surrounded by his family
and a few fellow officers. It could be a scene from back home in Massachusetts:
the peaceful street; the carriage lazily awaiting; the shy lady, unwilling to come
outside, who sits in the window at right.* (SOCIETY FOR THE PRESERVATION OF
NEW ENGLAND ANTIQUITIES)

And here "Company E" watches the war pass them by. (SOCIETY FOR THE
PRESERVATION OF NEW ENGLAND ANTIQUITIES)

*The New Bern photographer found artful contrasts in light and shade, as well
as in shapes and lines, in the town's homes and inhabitants.* (USAMHI)

The town's public buildings became warehouses. (USAMHI)

Its little restaurants, like this one, bulged with hungry soldiers. (USAMHI)

While great battles like Fredericksburg and Chancellorsville raged in Virginia, and while Vicksburg starved under siege, New Bern passed along in its tranquil path through the war. (USAMHI)

The occupiers seemed to be everywhere, yet the lack of tents and stockades
made them seem less threatening somehow. They hung their blankets out of
windows to air just like the citizens. They chopped their firewood and cooled
themselves in the breezes just like the civilians. (SOCIETY FOR THE
PRESERVATION OF NEW ENGLAND ANTIQUITIES)

Thousands of placid scenes greeted the eyes of New Bern's considerate
conquerors. (USAMHI)

The backyards and gardens. (USAMHI)

The former slaves gathered for the camera, their hopes of freedom written on their faces. (USAMHI)

Even faces no longer visible in New Bern could still be seen. When the Confederates left the town, a photographer left behind several images of Southern officers in his gallery. There were old men . . . (USAMHI)

. . . rather bemused-looking men . . . (USAMHI)

. . . those resplendent in their homemade finery
*. . . (*USAMHI*)*

. . . and the fully professional-looking soldiers, like
Colonel J. K. Jordan of the 31st North Carolina.
A host of such faces of their enemies peered out at
the Federals when they took the town. (USAMHI)

Yet the occupiers' presence still was felt. They brought with them the United States Sanitary Commission to help tend the soldiers' medical and spiritual needs. (USAMHI)

To be sure, they brought a few tents with them. The officers of the 43rd Massachusetts made their headquarters under canvas. (USAMHI)

They built some earthworks as a defense against possible attack. After all, New Bern was still in enemy country. Here Fort Totten appears as it did in August 1862, being garrisoned by the 3rd New York Artillery. (USAMHI)

They brought their heavy guns to the ordnance yard on Craven Street, where many of them remained unused. (USAMHI)

Meanwhile, New Bern, like so many other small towns in the South under occupation, enjoyed the luxury of being out of the way of the devastating armies. Escaping the death and destruction of the terrible war, New Bern and its people, Northerners and Southerners, lived out an existence somehow out of keeping with the terrible conflict raging all around. They learned of the war by reading of it, by going to F. W. Beers's book and stationery shop to buy Elements of Military Art & History *or* The Mounted Rifleman. *There was no good war, but for New Bern in North Carolina this one was not such a bad one.* (USAMHI)

Slaves No More

DUDLEY T. CORNISH

Negroes, slave and free, had to fight just to take part

De massa run? Ha, ha!
De darkey stay? Ho, ho!
It mus'be now de kingdom comin'
An' de year ob Jubilo!

—HENRY CLAY WORK, 1862

FOR NEGROES our Civil War was the great divide between slavery and freedom, however limited and partial that freedom turned out to be. Even before the white songwriter had penned his prescient lyrics, Negroes sensed the fundamental meaning and promise of the war. Frederick Douglass, the foremost Negro leader of nineteenth-century America, read the future accurately as early as May 1861 and, with characteristic candor and eloquence, called for the recruitment of a Negro liberating army "to march into the South and raise the banner of emancipation among the slaves." If this proposal seemed as extreme as John Brown's fatal venture less than two years earlier, Douglass was convinced that circumstances in the rousing spring of '61 justified it: "The South having brought revolution and war upon the country, and having elected and consented to play at their fearful game," the Maryland ex-slave reasoned, "she has no right to complain if some good as well as calamity result from her own act and deed."

During a brief foray into historical biography in the 1920s, a white American novelist asserted that "American negroes are the only people in the history of the world, so far as I know, that ever became free without any effort of their own . . . [The Civil War] was not their business." So far as *he* knew, and his knowledge did not run far. From the very beginning of the war it *was* their business, and they were involved, North and South, East and West, from beginning to end. Negroes knew what the war was about even before Alexander H. Stephens of Georgia, Vice-President of the Confederacy, had clarified the issue in his "corner-stone speech"; they, however, saw in the war the final solution of the slavery controversy that had rent the Union. Even as their grandfathers found meaning in Thomas Jefferson's electric declaration—"all Men are created equal" and are "endowed by their Creator with certain unalienable Rights,"—so Frederick Douglass's generation felt in its bones that the year of Jubilo had arrived. Tens of thousands of Negroes were eager to help move toward what Abraham Lincoln later called "this great consummation." Hundreds of thousands of others were caught up in the tides of war as the "peculiar institution," of which they were the essential working parts, buckled, strained, and

The Negro began the Civil War little better off than he had been two centuries before. Though the foreign slave trade was abolished and much internal slave trafficking had been curtailed, all too many Negroes, at one time or another, still passed through slave pens like this one at Alexandria, Virginia, the establishment of Messrs. Price & Burch. (USAMHI)

finally collapsed, crushed to death by the tightening coils of Winfield Scott's "Anaconda Plan." To suggest that Negroes saw the war only from the sidelines, as spectators, is to deny the facts and miss the heart of the conflict.

Certainly the American conflict officially began as a "white man's war" on both sides. It was only a matter of time, however, before the logic of the struggle extended its own parameters. It was simply impossible for the 3,953,760 slaves and their 488,070 free brothers and sisters (250,787 in the slave states at that) to ignore the struggle or to be ignored for long in the course of that struggle. President Lincoln made it clear that his primary war aim, indeed, his only war aim for the first eighteen months after the fall of Sumter, was the preservation of the Union. President Jefferson Davis made it just as clear that his primary war aim was the establishment of Southern inde-

pendence, with slavery (Alexander Stephens's cornerstone) intact. Accordingly, from the opening rounds of the war Union generals offered to help border state governors put down slave insurrections "with an iron hand." Union troops served occasionally as "slave-catchers" in that same early phase. Spurred by protests, both civil and military, the Union Congress moved to halt both practices in the second spring of the war.

Ironically, Benjamin F. Butler, political general from Massachusetts, based his pragmatic solution to the problem on Confederate use of Negro labor to build fortifications within his field of observation. With the irritating logic that was his hallmark, Butler called fugitives from such military labor "contraband of war" and so added a new word to the American language, a new argument for congressional debate, and a new dimension to the war. Scarcely two weeks after First Bull Run

It was not a pleasant place. (USAMHI)

the Union Congress passed its First Confiscation Act, providing for the seizure of all property used "in aid of the rebellion," including slaves. Despite all efforts to ignore slavery as a war issue, Negroes by their very presence—a mobile presence at that —helped make slavery an important issue. Before the war was a full year old slavery had been abolished in the District of Columbia and in all Federal territories, and an additional Article of War prohibited the military "rendition" of fugitives to Confederate masters.

Another political general, John C. Frémont of "Pathfinder" fame, commanding Union forces at St. Louis, stole a march on Lincoln on August 30, 1861, by declaring martial law in Missouri and freeing the slaves of every Rebel in the state! Despite much Northern applause, Lincoln, concerned for border state loyalty, modified Frémont's order to make it conform to the First Confiscation Act. Negroes, and not a few white Unionists, were dismayed at Lincoln's action; James Russell Lowell spoke for a growing minority when he asked, "How many times are we to save Kentucky and lose our self-respect?" Several weeks later Major General David Hunter replaced Frémont in command of the Western Department; as a regular officer and graduate of the U. S. Military Academy at West Point, Hunter was presumed to be safely conservative.

From the first weeks of the war Negroes begged for permission to join the Union forces. Applications, proposals, and requests reached the War Department from Boston, New York, Philadelphia, Pittsburgh—even Cincinnati and Cleveland; all were uniformly rejected. Secretary of War Simon Cameron told Jacob Dodson of Washington, when the war was only a fortnight along, that "this Department has no intention at present to call into the service of the Government any colored soldiers." Cameron's personal intention had changed by the end of that year, with the result that Edwin M. Stanton replaced him, and Cameron went to Russia, in part because he had advocated arming the Negro to help save the Union. Meanwhile, articulate Negroes—editors, preachers, teachers, prominent leaders in their communities—agitated the question, arguing that they had a stake in the war, indeed, a greater stake than their white brethren. For the time being, however, John Brown's soul marched in almost exclusively white company; a few hundred light-skinned Negroes actually did enlist in a variety of Union regiments, and not only as cooks and waiters. Those whose racial identity was discovered were uniformly discharged.

From the first weeks of the war other Negroes took advantage of Union incursions into their neighborhoods and began to make their way to Union lines, away from plantations no longer secure and across the bridges leading from Virginia to Washington. Union field commanders first encountered the Negro refugee problem in substantial numbers in Virginia and North Carolina. But the first major disruption of the slave system came at the very end of 1861, when a powerful Army-Navy expedition led by Commodore Samuel F. Du Pont and Brigadier General Thomas W. Sherman descended on the coast of South Carolina and established a beachhead at Port Royal. This beachhead, a sword in the side of the Confederacy, was steadily extended, year after year, down the fringe of the Sea Islands all the way to Florida. Here came the first fatal shock to the peculiar institution—and the first large-scale Union effort to deal with totally unprecedented problems.

With the death of slavery, what was to be done for, to, and with the thousands of slaves whose masters, hearing the guns of Du Pont's squadron smashing the forts at Port Royal, abandoned their rich tidal plantations and headed for safety inland? Under that First Confiscation Act those slaves were

*Much more pleasant were the quarters slaves often enjoyed on the better
plantations in the South. H. P. Moore of New Hampshire captured this image
of the slave quarters of John E. Seabrook's plantation on Edisto Island, South
Carolina, on April 7, 1862.* (KEAN ARCHIVES)

the property and responsibility of the Union, and
Yankee ingenuity outdid itself in developing
schemes and projects suitable to the opportunity.
Here began, in Willie Lee Rose's happy phrase, a
"rehearsal for reconstruction" which continued
throughout the war, with results as various as the
programs. While the Union Army had primary responsibility in the Department of the South (and
both Army and Navy employed large numbers of
former slaves at minimal wages), the Treasury Department got the job of organizing and operating
the abandoned plantations; this was a dual assignment with the potential for intramural disputes.
Whatever the practical problems of operation,
whatever the quarrels between Treasury agents
sent down to make cotton and military officers
more concerned with making war, what resulted
was a curious variety of activities revolving around

this first major experiment to apply a wage system
to slave labor, the first large-scale effort to shift
from the forced labor of the plantation to a semblance of economic self-interest. Responsible for
the social and economic well-being of the population on the Sea Islands as well as for the extension
of Union military and naval operations in the
Department—Port Royal became a major base for
the Atlantic Blockade—Union officials, both civil
and military, had their work cut out for them.

To counter the abysmal ignorance of the Sea Island population, isolated from the mainland plantations for generations, Edward L. Pierce of Boston, in charge of Treasury Department enterprises,
recruited scores of young men and women from
the North to establish and operate schools for the
freedmen and their families. Negro reaction to this
unprecedented opportunity was instant and over-

The slaves of James Hopkinson on Edisto Island also lived a comfortable existence compared to many of their brethren in less lavish surroundings. (USAMHI)

whelming; letters and reports from "Gideon's Band," as the teachers were soon called, were rich in references to an eagerness to learn, from toddlers to grizzle-headed grandparents. To enrich the Port Royal experiment even more, several New England and New York entrepreneurs came down to put the abandoned plantations on a paying basis, for the most part with promising results. In those Sea Islands off South Carolina and Georgia began the first extensive, imaginative, and, on the whole, encouraging efforts to move a whole people from the old slavery basis of working for "Massa" to the new Yankee basis of working for wages and—though the promise was never quite achieved—on land of their very own. Former slaves worked directly to establish a degree of economic independence for themselves and indirectly against the very underpinning of "Massa's" struggle for political independence. From the start of the Port Royal experiment, Negro men and women (as well as

children) began to learn, besides reading and writing and the beginnings of arithmetic, their first lessons in freedom and responsibility, which were both new and frightening. Many of the New England plantation superintendents had to learn new lessons in cotton culture from the former slaves, particularly those who had been captains and drivers in former times. In that same Department of the South, in the late spring of 1862, came another, more startling experiment, one designed to make direct and military use of that "sable arm" of whose strength Frederick Douglass liked to boast.

Meanwhile, across the South, other Negroes found their lives disrupted in many ways as the military needs of the beleaguered Confederacy took precedence over the orderly routine of plantation life. Fortifying the South, including Southern cities, forts, and ports, required prodigious pick-and-shovel work, the felling of trees, and the building of redoubts and gun emplacements. Military leaders requisitioned and even impressed free and slave labor to erect mile upon mile of fortifications—some fifteen miles at Fort Donelson alone. The longer the war continued, the more unpopular these military demands on the Negro population of the South became, especially to slave owners concerned for the health and safety of their people and for the neglected crops back home. Add to this constant problem another that tended to disrupt plantation life even more: the slow but steady advance of Union forces as Scott's "Anaconda Plan" began to uncoil and move down the Atlantic Coast, past Hatteras and Port Royal, on down around Florida to Ship Island off the mouths of the Mississippi, and even up that great river in the second spring of the war. At the same time, Union forces in the west were moving down. Brigadier General U. S. Grant won the first significant land victories of the war with the capture of Forts Henry and Donelson in February 1862, followed, with remarkable swiftness, by the fall of Nashville, the first Confederate state capital to welcome Yankee troops. As Union lines extended, slave owners

either lost considerable numbers of their "property" or moved them to the interior, out of harm's way. Plantation records from the spring of 1862 on, from Kentucky down through Tennessee to the Gulf, show the gradual collapse of the planters' economy in such poignant entries as "Big Joe went off with the Yankees," followed, say, two weeks later by "Big Joe seen driving Army wagon in N. Orleans." Tens of thousands of Big Joes went off to drive army wagons—and for other reasons.

Lincoln's favorite solutions to the slavery problem were compensated emancipation (financial aid to states which would free their slaves) and colonization, a variety of projects developing from the American Colonization Society after 1817. The first oft-repeated proposal fell on deaf ears even as late as the second year of the war, when the demise of the institution seemed imminent. The second met with very mixed responses, as it had from the founding of Liberia during the presidency of James Monroe. Some prominent Negro leaders, including Henry Highland Garnet and Martin R. Delany, began to advocate emigration to Haiti during the

Joseph E. Davis, brother of the Confederate president, owned these slaves, shown standing in front of the library on Hurricane Plantation, south of Vicksburg, Mississippi. (OLD COURT HOUSE MUSEUM, VICKSBURG)

The Negro cabins on General Thomas F. Drayton's plantation on Hilton Head, South Carolina, in 1862. A genuine little community existed on many of these larger farms, though, in fact, most slaves in the South belonged to masters who had only a handful of chattels. (USAMHI)

1850s, especially after the Dred Scott decision doomed their hopes of anything like equality of treatment in the United States. Negroes were divided in their attitudes. Dr. John Rock of Boston spoke for the opposition in 1860: "This being our country, we have made up our minds to remain in it, and try to make it worth living in." A Washington Negro, on the other hand, argued: "Let us emigrate to Hayti, where we shall be free from the white man's contumely, and where we can secure for ourselves and our children after us, a home, a farm, and all the rights which citizenship confers." In June 1861 Fred Douglass came out strongly against emigration: "We are Americans, speaking the same language, adopting the same customs, holding the same general opinions . . . and shall

rise or fall with Americans." By mid-1862 most Negro responses to proposals of colonization took the form of angry denunciations. The New York *Anglo-African* called Lincoln's Central American scheme a message "to stir the hearts of all Confederates" and went on to propose an appropriation "to expatriate and settle elsewhere the surviving slaveholders." Lincoln's one colonization venture was a disastrous failure: Some 450 Negroes from Virginia went to Ile à Vache (off Haiti) in May 1863 to endure smallpox, mutiny, and starvation before the President sent a ship to bring home the survivors in February 1864. Most Negroes, says one historian, "were determined to stay in their native land and struggle their way to equality."

Impatient with the hesitating evolution of Union

policy, David Hunter, commanding the Department of the South in May 1862, declared the slaves of South Carolina, Georgia, and Florida "forever free." This had the Frémont ring, and it got the Frémont treatment. Lincoln reacted immediately (he had learned about the proclamation through the newspapers!) and called Hunter's decree "altogether void." Even before word of Lincoln's action reached him, Hunter took another radical step: He began to recruit a regiment of former slaves, lamentably using methods little better than impressment. This activity stirred interest throughout the country, stimulating debate in Congress and the press. In the Sea Islands the immediate results were deplorable: Edward Pierce's plantation superintendents penned reports protesting the breakup of families and the disruption of agricultural labor. Undeterred, Hunter pressed his project (and more recruits), selecting noncommissioned officers from the white regiments in his command as company officers to drill the new men and make soldiers of them. In response to congressional inquiries about his regiment of fugitive slaves Hunter explained that his men were not fugitives —their *masters* were fugitives, and the former slaves had expressed eagerness to overtake their masters in the most effective way—as Union soldiers. This occasioned gales of laughter in the House, particularly since Charles Wickliffe of Kentucky had offered the resolution of inquiry. Meanwhile, George B. McClellan had begun his ill-starred Peninsular Campaign, and Union manpower needs were greater than ever. Despite this military circumstance, Lincoln viewed Hunter's program with profound disfavor, and his War Department declined either to commission the new regiment's officers or to pay its troops. Frustrated, Hunter was forced to let the men go back to their plantations, except for Company A, which remained in camp awaiting better times.

Throughout our military history white Americans have shown much reluctance, even antipathy, to arm Negro men—until harsh military necessity in the form of manpower shortages outweighed other considerations. So it was in the colonial wars and in the American Revolution, with Negro men eventually taking up arms against the French, Indians, and the British—in every American war except the Mexican, when a few Negroes bore arms but the majority went along in their more

traditional menial roles. In 1862, however, Union manpower needs finally began to outweigh "other considerations." Hunter needed more soldiers than the War Department could provide in his slowly expanding Sea Island beachhead. Other Union commanders—in Louisiana after the Navy had captured New Orleans, and along the bloody Kansas-Missouri border—needed more fighting men and, like Hunter, elected to follow Fred Douglass's advice and "call on Africa." Probably no one ever put the basic premise more bluntly than Kansas Senator James H. Lane. A Negro, he asserted, "might just as well become food for powder [i.e., cannon fodder] as my son." If Con-

George S. Cook of Charleston captured this blurred yet starkly contrasted image of a slave "mammy" with the master's child entrusted to her care. The sense of family between white and black was widespread, one of the few happy circumstances of slavery. (COURTESY OF HERB PECK, JR.)

On Cockspur Island, Georgia, this Negro cabin provides a closer look at the life of the average slave. (USAMHI)

federates object to being killed by Negroes Lane continued with what passed for humor on the frontier, "let them lay down their arms." Despite War Department orders to the contrary, Lane persisted in recruiting both Negroes and Indians, secure in the knowledge that he was a thousand miles from Washington.

Down in Louisiana Benjamin Butler reached the same conclusion by a more circuitous route. At first opposed to Negro enlistments, Butler even drove a subordinate, Brigadier General John W. Phelps, out of the Army for advocating that course. Phelps had begun recruiting Negroes and had drawn up an imaginative program to "organize and train our African levies." In early August Butler rejected Phelps's proposal and ordered him to put his Negroes to work, arguing legalistically that only the President had the authority to employ Negro soldiers under the Second Confiscation Act of July 17, 1862. Claiming that he was no slave driver, Phelps resigned and started for his Vermont home. Long before Phelps saw the Green Mountains,

Butler had done a complete about-face: He invited Negro recruits on August 22, using as legal cover his authority to enlist former Confederates who had seen the error of their ways. Among the defenders of New Orleans had been "a military organization known as the 'Native Guards' (colored)," and Butler made it clear that his invitation applied only to it. Thus, Butler temporarily escaped the opprobrium of having armed slaves. Contemporary observers claimed that Butler's recruiting officers asked few questions, with the result that "the boldest and finest fugitives have enlisted, while the whole organization is known as the Free Colored Brigade." Helping to persuade Butler to this new position and practice, besides his demonstrable manpower shortages, were advices from Secretary of the Treasury Salmon P. Chase and Mrs. Butler, both of whom had pointed out that anti-Negro soldier sentiment in the North and West was abating and that the time was ripe for action. Chase put it well: "And who better to begin the work than my friend Gen. Butler." Results? Three Negro regiments were mustered into the Union Army in September, October, and November 1862, regiments which Butler called, with his usual flair, "Louisiana Native Guards." Their cadres had come from that formerly Confederate "military organization," and the vast majority of their company officers were "free men of color."

Thanks, in large measure, to military necessity (McClellan's adventure on the Peninsula had turned into a costly failure, and John Pope's fumbling Second Bull Run campaign made the situation even worse) and to congressional authority to arm Negroes under the Second Confiscation Act, Secretary of War Stanton not only blessed Butler's work but also empowered Brigadier General Rufus Saxton, on August 25, 1862, to raise 5,000 Negro troops in Hunter's Department of the South. Using that stubborn Company A as a nucleus, Saxton went to work to build the 1st South Carolina Colored Volunteer Infantry. He invited a young Harvard captain in a Massachusetts infantry regiment to come south as its colonel. So Thomas

Wentworth Higginson, certifiable abolitionist and personal friend of the late John Brown, began to collect material for his Civil War classic, *Army Life in a Black Regiment*.

Lane's recruiting grounds were not nearly so ripe for the harvest as Hunter's or Butler's. The census of 1860 showed only 2 slaves in Kansas territory, plus 625 free Negroes—hardly enough for a Civil War regiment of 1,000 men. Lane, a Jayhawker of the first water, was blessed with a fertile imagination and an acquisitive instinct. Selecting his recruiters from abolitionists come West to make Kansas free, he procured sufficient men for the 1st Kansas Colored Volunteer Infantry among fugitives from Missouri and Arkansas. Like Hunter, he selected officers from the noncoms of white regiments. This first Negro regiment to be raised in a free state was mustered into Union service on January 13, 1863. Even before then, in late October, five companies of the 1st Kansas Colored had seen action against bushwackers in Missouri. A week earlier Saxton's "Fust Souf" saw its first action in a

For many, in fact, living space was so rudimentary as to be barely habitable. Here in Fredericksburg, Virginia, a slave family stands before its house, so ramshackle that cold winds could blow through it unimpeded. (USAMHI)

Slavery had its brutal side as well, when men had absolute power of life and death over their property. Wilson Chinn, a slave from Louisiana who also bore brands on his flesh, poses with instruments of punishment used on unruly Negroes. Such photographs were used during the war to inflame Northern passions and firm resolve against the slaveholders; they helped to exaggerate greatly the stories of cruelties against slaves. (USAMHI)

long-range raid up the Bell and Sapello rivers, destroying nine saltworks and carrying off lumber and other supplies. That was Company A's reward for patience.

It remained for President Lincoln to put his seal of approval on the war's new dimension. This he did in his Emancipation Proclamation of January 1,

1863: "Such persons of suitable condition, will be received into the armed service of the United States to garrison forts, positions, stations, and other places, and to man vessels of all sorts in said service." With this presidential blessing, however limited, the movement Fred Douglass had advocated in the first month of the war got under way in earnest. The war became a revolution.

At first enterprising states, like Massachusetts and Rhode Island, and ambitious individuals, like Daniel Ullmann of New York and James Montgomery of Kansas, secured War Department license to raise regiments, even brigades. Montgomery, frozen out of competition in Kansas, became colonel of the 2nd South Carolina Colored Volunteers. Ullmann recruited a cadre of white officers in New York and then shipped to Louisiana to find his men. There he found Nathaniel P. Banks, Butler's replacement in the Department of the Gulf, already raising his own Negro brigade.

Most enterprising were the efforts of Massachusetts and her abolitionist governor, John A. Andrew. A well-organized recruiting committee sent agents across the North who found volunteers as far west as Chicago and Milwaukee. Douglass joined in the work, giving his full editorial support and two sons. So effective were these tactics that the 54th Massachusetts Infantry soon filled up, and the overflow was enough to form a sister regiment, the 55th. To lead the 54th Andrew selected a young captain, Colonel Robert Gould Shaw, who went to glory six months later on the bloody parapet of Fort Wagner, outside Charleston. The Confederates "buried him with his niggers" with instant effect on the whole Union.

The War Department put the movement on a sound and organized basis in the spring of 1863 by two distinct moves. In late March Stanton sent Adjutant General Lorenzo Thomas out to the Mississippi Valley, where raw material was plentiful, to push the organization of Negro regiments. In May Stanton set up the Bureau for Colored Troops within his department to centralize activities, monitor officer selection, and provide administrative support. A year later the "African levies" were redesignated as regiments of United States Colored Troops: Higginson's "Fust Souf" became the 33rd U.S.C.T.; Montgomery's 2nd Carolina became the 34th U.S.C.T., and the 1st Kansas Colored became the 79th. Native Guard, Corps d'Afrique, and African Descent regiments lost their picturesque names to become United States forces with no state identity.

Lorenzo Thomas was so diligent in his efforts that he had begun a score of regiments in Arkansas and Louisiana before returning to Washington. He made it plain to reluctant Union commanders that he spoke for the President, and he successfully reduced anti-Negro sentiment among Union troops by offering opportunities for commissions in the new regiments. By the end of 1863 Stanton could report fifty Negro regiments in existence, some of them even in action.

More significant than mere numbers, Stanton could demonstrate that the new auxiliaries had proved their mettle. In three actions in May, June, and July of 1863 Negro regiments showed themselves capable of more than the garrison roles Lincoln had initially assigned them. At Port Hudson on May 27 the 1st and 3rd Regiments, Corps d'Afrique—Butler's 1st and 3rd Native Guards—attacked a strong Confederate position; while they failed to dislodge its defenders after five attacks, they stood up well under fire despite heavy casualties. At Milliken's Bend on June 7 the 9th and 11th Regiments of Louisiana Volunteers of African Descent, both begun by Thomas, stood off Rebel attack, with timely support from a Union gunboat. The third engagement was the July 18 assault on Fort Wagner by Shaw's 54th Massachusetts. That was a military failure, since the Confederates repelled the attack, but only after a hand-to-hand struggle on the very parapet. Shaw died with his leading companies, but the news of his death—and especially of his burial in a ditch with his troops—made him a martyr to the cause. Cabinet officers, congressmen, generals, and journalists thereafter linked the three actions as significant in reducing popular antipathy to permitting Negroes to join the war.

Out on the far frontier on July 17—the day before the 54th Massachusetts won immortality outside Charleston—the 1st Kansas Colored established its military reputation at Honey Springs in present-day Oklahoma. In a "sharp and bloody engagement of two hours duration," as part of Major General James G. Blunt's Army of the Frontier, the Kansas regiment fought well and even captured the colors of a Texas regiment! Of greater importance was the effect of their perform-

But some stories were not exaggerations. J. W. Mercer, assistant surgeon of the 47th Massachusetts, examined 400 runaway slaves in Baton Rouge, Louisiana, in the summer of 1863, and found many "to be as badly lacerated as the specimen presented in the enclosed photograph," taken on April 2, 1863. The whip could be brutal in the hands of cruel men. This slave, Gordon, later became a corporal in the Union Army.
(USAMHI)

ance on western sentiment. Blunt stated the case tersely: "The question that negroes will fight is settled; besides they make better soldiers in every respect than any troops I have ever had under my command." Another less dignified but even more expressive comment came from an officer of the 3rd Wisconsin Cavalry who was identified as an Irish Democrat: "I never believed in niggers before, but my Jasus, they are hell for fighting."

The Federals soon dubbed as contrabands the flocks of slaves who escaped from their masters to seek refuge with the advancing armies. Camps for them were set up wherever the columns of the Union advanced. Here a wagonload of contrabands fords the Rappahannock in August 1862, following Pope's army. Timothy O'Sullivan made the image. (P-M)

Early in 1864 another Irish officer, Confederate Major General Patrick R. Cleburne, urged the training of "the most courageous of our slaves," arguing that "half-trained negroes have fought as bravely as many other half-trained Yankees." The idea was anathema to most Southerners; Howell Cobb of Georgia found it "the most pernicious idea that has been suggested since the war began . . . You cannot make soldiers of slaves . . . If slaves will make good soldiers our whole theory of slavery is wrong." Too late, in January 1865, Robert E. Lee himself sanctioned the policy of arming slaves: "We should employ them without delay." A month before Appomattox President Davis signed a "Negro Soldier Law" authorizing slave enlistments. Too late.

Some 200,000 Negroes served in the Union armies, some as volunteers, some as paid substitutes, some drafted, others ruthlessly impressed from the hordes of contrabands swarming Union camps and columns. They came from New England and New York, Pennsylvania, and all across the North, as well as from every Southern state. What did they do for the Union Army? Everything its white commanders asked them or would let them. They fought in over four hundred engagements, in every theater of the war: from Deep Bottom and Hatcher's Run and Petersburg in Virginia to Poison Spring and Jenkins Ferry in Arkansas; from Olustee in Florida to Brice's Cross Roads in Mississippi; from Fort Fisher, North Carolina, to Fort Blakely outside Mobile. They fought under Major General George H. Thomas at Nashville in the last weeks of 1864; he remarked, as he rode up Overton Hill after the victory: "Gentlemen, the question is settled; negroes will fight." They also dug miles of trenches before Richmond and around Petersburg; they guarded prisoners at Point Lookout and Rock Island and on the Dry Tortugas. They learned to read in company schools, even hiring teachers out of their small pay. For much of the war Negro troops got only ten dollars per month, as against the thirteen their white comrades drew—and officers held back three of the Negro soldier's ten for his uniform. One Negro sergeant was executed for mutiny because he refused to allow his company to be paid at the discriminatory rate. Too often Negro troops were issued inferior weapons and horses discarded by white cavalry regiments. Their fate, if captured, was potentially hard: the Confederacy declined to recognize them as soldiers, choosing to consider them as "slaves taken in arms." Some 54th Massachusetts troops, free Negroes from the North, became prisoners at Fort Wagner, and some of them were sold into slavery. "Indiscriminate slaughter" of Union Negroes at Fort Pillow and Poison Spring (both called massacres by the Union) had an ironic effect on their morale: They seldom surrendered after those engagements in the spring of 1864, and they seldom took any Rebel prisoners.

Rough, even barbarous, as were the trials of Negro soldiers, wherever they served the ordeals of the fugitives were worse. Despite the best efforts of army officers, chaplains, and a host of church and civic organizations who sent doctors, nurses, and teachers to the camps, thousands of fugitives found ultimate freedom from disease and even starvation in death. An estimated 200,000 Negro laborers toiled for the Union field forces, driving wagons, digging fortifications, cooking, chopping wood and even cotton on abandoned plantations. Their wages were minimal (and not always paid), whether in South Carolina, Tennessee, or Louisiana, but their efforts helped in at least two ways: to assist the progress of Union arms and to maintain themselves and their families, even at a subsistence level. How many hundreds of Negro scouts and guides helped Union forces—or escaped Yankee prisoners—find their way to safety or a hidden route toward their objective cannot be determined.

It is safe to say that Negroes, both men and

Contrabands congregated on the plantation of General Drayton once it came under Federal dominion. (USAMHI)

women, worked for the cause of the Union—and for their own freedom—in every way imaginable. Susie King Taylor of Savannah escaped to Union lines to become a teacher of the freedmen, a laundress, a nurse, and the bride of a Negro soldier. William Tillman, cook and steward aboard the Yankee schooner *S. J. Waring,* recaptured his ship after she had been made a Confederate prize and brought her safely to New York. Robert Smalls of Charleston, assistant pilot of the steamer *Planter,* ran out to deliver her to Union blockaders; he won half the prize money—and during Reconstruction he became a congressman from his native state. Roughly one fourth of the Union Navy were Negroes; an estimated 29,000 by war's end. This was not revolutionary; Negroes had never been barred from naval service, although custom kept them in the lowest ratings—except for an occasional Negro pilot like Smalls, who even became skipper of his own ship—by right of conquest.

Thousands of other Negroes served the Confederacy, although hardly ever as soldiers. They made up the bulk of the South's labor force and worked in virtually every craft: carpenters, foundry workers, coal miners, even drivers of railroad loco-motives and canal barges. They were totally involved in the war, chopping cotton, cutting sugar cane, raising corn, protecting the plantation while the white men were "away," bringing their fallen masters home from the front, and even sweating as iron puddlers in the furnaces of Shelby County, Alabama. They sang and they mourned, they struggled against all manner of handicaps and dangers, and they endured, praying for the sweet chariot to swing low, and waiting for Jubilo.

A great American scholar, Benjamin Quarles, the dean of black historians, has summed up the story eloquently: ". . . the war, with all its bloodshed and sorrow, was an emancipating and uplifting national experience. Its most striking achievement was not its battle conquests on sea and land, but in the momentum it gave to the ideals of the freedom and dignity of man. It made easier every subsequent battle for human rights."

> De whip is lost, de han'cuff broken,
> But de massa'll hab his pay;
> He's ole enough, big enough, ought
>   to know better
> Dan to went an' run away.

There they continued to harvest and gin the cotton, only now it was for their own benefit rather than that of their onetime masters. (USAMHI)

At Follie's farm, near Cumberland Landing on the Pamunkey River in Virginia, the contrabands posed for James Gibson while McClellan campaigned on the Peninsula. (USAMHI)

At Williamsport, Virginia, in 1862 contrabands attached themselves to the 13th Massachusetts. Often whole families came. At first uncertain what to do with the Negroes, the armies frequently turned them to laboring and other service-oriented tasks. (USAMHI)

These two tattered lads, called "intelligent contrabands," quite probably found their way into service as servants for a soldiers' "mess" or in an officer's tent. (USAMHI)

An unidentified cavalry unit with some of the contrabands who followed them and tended to their needs, including washing and cooking. Many contrabands simply exchanged one form of servitude for another. (COURTESY OF RONN PALM)

Timothy O'Sullivan captured these Negroes at rest outside a cook tent at Culpeper, Virginia, in November 1863. (LC)

Lieutenant W. B. Sears of the 2nd Rhode Island Infantry poses with his servant boy, shown leaning against a camp chair. (USAMHI)

The Freedmen's Bureau attempted to cope with the ever-swelling numbers of ex-slaves flocking to the Union armies—and did so rather effectively, providing some education and training, as well as spiritual guidance. Here one sees a Freedmen's office at Petersburg, Virginia, late in the war. (USAMHI)

And here is another Freedmen's office, this one in South Carolina, as photographed by Cooley. (NA)

Whole "Freedmen's Villages" like this one at Arlington Heights, Virginia, appeared. Here the inhabitants all pose with books, which many of them probably could not yet read. Perhaps they are bibles, hymnals, or fundamental readers. Whatever, they represented a first step in the noble cause of raising the Negro up from slavery. (USAMHI)

Feeding the thousands of Negroes fell to the Freedmen's Bureau as well. Here, at Beaufort, South Carolina, rations are issued to Negroes. (USAMHI)

Old churches used by the slaves were maintained and new ones were opened. (USAMHI)

And, most important, schools were opened. Here the first schoolhouse built for the instruction of freedmen, at Port Hudson, Louisiana, is the backdrop for several Negro soldiers who are now fighting for their brothers' freedom. (CHS)

The Freedmen's school at Beaufort. (USAMHI)

And the Freedmen's school on Edisto Island, with several of the teachers posing in the doorway. (USAMHI)

Often called Gideonites, the Yankee teachers who went south to educate the former slaves were a dedicated, idealistic band. Whole families devoted themselves to the work. Three Chase sisters pose here with other schoolteachers at Norfolk, Virginia, in 1865. (WRHS)

A group of Gideonites in Beaufort or Port Royal, as captured by the camera of Samuel Cooley. The southern climate seems to have had a softening effect on the normally dour visage of the Yankee schoolmarm. (WRHS)

Five little children at New Bern, scrubbed and ready for school. Even with their education they face a hard road ahead. (USAMHI)

Negro soldiers pose with their teachers, their books resting in their laps.
Reading alone will not be enough to prepare them for the years of struggle
before them. For now they are content to struggle just for their freedom. (LC)

Happy scenes take place for freedom. At Brierfield, the Mississippi plantation
home of Jefferson Davis, the Fourth of July in 1864 was cause for decoration
and a Freedmen's picnic. (OLD COURT HOUSE MUSEUM, VICKSBURG)

And here, at Emancipation Oak near
Beaufort, a tax collector named
Brisbane first read Lincoln's
Emancipation Proclamation to the
Negroes of South Carolina. It was a
hallowed place. (USAMHI)

Negroes did more than just study and work. Thousands saw in the war their chance for a blow against the institution that had enslaved them for centuries. A slave, Robert Smalls, together with eight other Negro men and several women, captured the Confederate ordnance transport Planter *in Charleston and steamed her out to the blockading fleet on May 13, 1862.* (USAMHI)

The steamer Planter, *photographed at Georgetown, South Carolina, with several hundred bales of cotton aboard. Smalls was made a navy pilot for his exploit and later became captain of the vessel. Years later he served five terms in Congress.* (NHC)

To Douglass's voice were added those of influential white statesmen and military figures. James H. Lane, the abolitionist firebrand of Kansas, spoke fervently for Negro regiments as a United States Senator. An unstable man, he was to take his own life in 1866. (USAMHI)

The ex-slaves wanted to be armed to fight, and no one advocated their cause more strongly or effectively than Frederick Douglass, surely the most articulate and widely respected free Negro of his day. (NA)

White-haired Brigadier General Lorenzo Thomas, Federal adjutant general,
shown standing, went West to promote the organization of Negro regiments
once their raising was approved. (COURTESY OF DAVID D. FINNEY)

Prominent officers like Brigadier General Cyrus
Hamlin, son of Vice-President Hannibal Hamlin,
early advocated the use of Negroes in the fighting
army, and later commanded the 80th United
States Colored Infantry. (CWTI)

Charles Hamlin, like his brother Cyrus, led Negro troops in the war. Many officers did so out of simple conviction. For others, taking a commission in a Negro unit was a speedier way to rise, since finding officers for them was not always easy. (CWTI)

Colonel Robert Gould Shaw felt genuine conviction about Negro soldiers. He gave his life fighting at the head of his regiment, the 54th Massachusetts, at Charleston. Contemptuous Confederates "buried him with his niggers." (LC)

Brigadier General Edward A. Wild, whose name fitted his temperament, lost an arm at South Mountain. In 1863, at New Bern, North Carolina, he raised "Wild's African Brigade." He and his men saw wide service in 1864 and 1865. (USAMHI)

Brigadier General Rufus Saxton raised the 1st South Carolina Colored Infantry and spent the better part of the war recruiting Negro regiments. After the conflict he went into the Freedmen's Bureau. (USAMHI)

Writing under the pen name "Private Miles O'Reilly," Lieutenant Colonel Charles Halpine advocated the inclusion of Negroes in the army for his superior, David Hunter. He wrote the poem "Sambo's Right to be Kilt," and carried out Hunter's first order to organize Negro soldiers. (USAMHI)

Officers of the 4th United States Colored Infantry at Fort Slocum in April 1865. The officers, with rare exception, were white, and "Sambo" is little in evidence. The Negroes might fight, but real equality was another matter. (USAMHI)

"Contraband Jackson" looks much like the other young Negroes who flocked to the Union banners. He soon became . . . (USAMHI)

. . . "Drummer Jackson" of the 79th United States Colored Troops. These photographs were widely circulated as propaganda to encourage Negro enlistments and white support of the Negro regiments. (USAMHI)

Photographs like this one were used as the basis for recruiting posters. "Come and Join Us, Brothers," reads the broadside featuring these well-equipped soldiers. (COURTESY OF JAMES D. SPINA)

In towns all across the country the sable regiments mustered. Here one sees the 127th Ohio, renamed the 5th United States Colored Troops, on Sandusky Street in Delaware, Ohio. (OHIO HISTORICAL SOCIETY)

Guard mounting, probably by the 1st South Carolina Colored Troops at Beaufort. The photographer's shadow is evident in the right foreground. (USAMHI)

*Men of Company E of the 4th United States Colored Troops in Fort Lincoln
in the defenses of Washington.* (USAMHI)

*Out West Negro soldiers paraded in captured Vicksburg under their white
officers.* (OLD COURT HOUSE MUSEUM, VICKSBURG)

*Battery A of the 2nd United States Colored Artillery practiced its gun drills
with the Army of the Cumberland.* (CHS)

In Tennessee in 1864 this battery posed all of its members at the gun, standing in pride. It was a long way from a time when Negroes were not trusted with weapons of any sort. Now they had cannon. (COURTESY OF JOSEPH M. BAUMAN)

The 1st United States Colored Artillery; in fact, it was probably an artillery battery attached to the 1st South Carolina Colored Troops at Beaufort. (WRHS)

A Corps d'Afrique battery at Port Hudson, Louisiana. (USAMHI)

Negro soldiers looked as smart on parade as their white counterparts, the white officers standing before them. (NA)

Negro soldiers lived a life similar to that of their white comrades, only for less pay and often with inferior equipment. They were not always the best soldiers, but, given the chance to fight, they did. (COURTESY OF ROBERT MCDONALD)

They had their bands, like this one of the 107th United States Colored Troops, as they appeared in November 1865. The bandmaster, of course, was white. (USAMHI)

And they had their unruly men, like all armies in all times. The 107th also had its own guardhouse and provost guard, shown here at Fort Corcoran in the Washington defenses. (USAMHI)

The ill-behaved were punished, put in the guardhouse, and made to ride the wooden mule, as shown here at Vicksburg. The dovecote atop the guardhouse seems somehow incongruous with the scene. (USAMHI)

And when they transgressed seriously, they faced commensurate punishment. The worst crime a Negro soldier could commit was the molestation of a white woman in occupied territory. A Negro soldier named Johnson allegedly did so, and the scene shown here was the result. With men of his regiment and other spectators drawn up before the gallows, a noose is slipped over his head . . .
(USAMHI)

. . . and the trap is dropped. It is June 20, 1864.
(USAMHI)

But for every case of ignominy there were tens of glorious stories of Negro heroism. Martin R. Delany became one of the very first Negro officers in the army's history when he was made major of the 104th United States Colored Troops. He and several other Negroes were awarded the Medal of Honor for their bravery. (USAMHI)

Thousands served in the Union Navy, as shown here aboard the USS Vermont,
off Hilton Head, in 1863. (USAMHI)

Wherever the war went, they went as well, sometimes fighting, more often digging and carrying, freeing the white soldiers for the battle. (OHIO HISTORICAL SOCIETY)

*But they carried their battle flags proudly, and carried as well the torch of
freedom and dignity for the generations of their blood to follow. The color
sergeant of the 108th United States Colored Troops leaves little doubt that he is
a soldier, and a free man by his own right.* (COURTESY OF MICHAEL J. MCAFEE)

Washington at War

A PORTFOLIO

A panoramic view of a divided city trying desperately
to cope with its own growth

Washington in 1863. Symbolically the city and the Capitol that looms over it are, like the Union, not yet complete. Barracks and troop tents below the Capitol show that this is a city at war. Taken from the Smithsonian central tower in 1863. (COURTESY OF THE UNIVERSITY OF ROCHESTER)

The northeast view from the Smithsonian. (COURTESY OF THE UNIVERSITY OF ROCHESTER)

Looking north up Tenth Street. The large Grecian porticoed building in the right background is the Patent Office. To its front right stands the General Post Office. On Tenth Street itself, about half way up on the right side, stands a large building where President Lincoln occasionally attended a play—Ford's Theater. (COURTESY OF THE UNIVERSITY OF ROCHESTER)

Turning the camera to the northwest and continuing his panorama of the capital, the photographer captured the State and Treasury departments in the large building at right center. Just left of it stands the Executive Mansion, now coming to be called the White House. (COURTESY OF THE UNIVERSITY OF ROCHESTER)

Looking due west, the camera sees the still unfinished Washington Monument. On the Virginia shore in the distance, at right center, nearly on the crest of the ridge, is the faint image of the Custis-Lee mansion, called Arlington House, until 1861 the home of Robert E. Lee. (COURTESY OF THE UNIVERSITY OF ROCHESTER)

The Long Bridge crosses the Potomac, leading to Alexandria, southwest of Washington. (COURTESY OF THE UNIVERSITY OF ROCHESTER)

Looking south from the Smithsonian tower. The point of land jutting into the Potomac at left center is Greenleafs Point; the buildings on it are known as the Washington Arsenal. (COURTESY OF THE UNIVERSITY OF ROCHESTER)

Completing the panorama, the camera looks southeast. Unseen, the Eastern Branch provides a waterway leading from the Potomac to the Washington Navy Yard, marked by the tall smokestacks and the long workshop just under the horizon at left center. (COURTESY OF THE UNIVERSITY OF ROCHESTER)

The Treasury Department, where the massive effort of financing and maintaining the Union war effort had its heart. (COURTESY OF AMERICANA IMAGE GALLERY)

The "cash room" inside the Treasury building. By the end of the war the conflict was costing nearly four million dollars a day. (LC)

The nerve center of Mr. Lincoln's army, the War Department. Here Secretary of War Edwin M. Stanton forged the mighty weapon that sought to defeat the Confederacy. The broadside on the tree at left advertises a then popular drama, Guerillas on the Potomac, *a problem much on Stanton's mind, as a matter of fact.* (COURTESY OF LLOYD OSTENDORF)

The Navy Department, where Gideon Welles built a navy and a blockade. The bureaucracy both here and at the War building quickly outgrew the premises. (LC)

The "mall" around 1864. The Smithsonian Institution stands at left amid the park-like plantings along Independence Avenue. The Capitol, its dome near completion, looms in the background. (USAMHI)

The incomplete monument to Washington. Like the Almighty, Washington was invoked as being on the side of both North and South. Clearly, Washington's work, like his monument, was yet undone. (NA)

The Cabin John Bridge over the Chesapeake & Ohio Canal northwest of the city. Built when Jefferson Davis was Secretary of War in the 1850s, his name was removed from the dedicatory plaque in 1861 as a symbolic gesture. (KA)

Signs of war came early to Washington. Often they came in the persons of those who sought to save the Capitol from the threat of the Confederate presence on the Virginia side of the Potomac. Fiercely loyal Kentuckian Cassius M. Clay raised a company of volunteers in the spring of 1861 to stand guard in the city before the first volunteer regiments arrived. He would become a brigadier general and, later, minister to the court of the czar. (NA)

Civilian residences and boardinghouses all over the city bulged with military personnel. Here one sees the headquarters of Brigadier General Martin D. Hardin, in command of the defenses of Washington from 1864 to the war's end. He is just to the left of the tree at the corner, missing the left arm he lost in a guerrilla ambush. (USAMHI)

Men of Company K, 150th Pennsylvania Infantry. Nicknamed Bucktails because of the ornaments worn in their caps, they formed the President's bodyguard in Washington. In a "modern" war it was assumed that the chief of state needed protection. (COURTESY OF RONN PALM)

Private homes became hospitals. Here is "Minnesota Row," three homes on New Jersey Avenue at I Street. The corner home is that of Stephen A. Douglas. The center house belonged to John C. Breckinridge, and the one on the left belonged to Henry M. Rice of Minnesota, for whom the block was named. By May 1864 Douglas was dead, Breckinridge was a Confederate general, and Rice no longer sat in the Senate. Their homes are now the Douglas Hospital. Breckinridge's house would become a residence for General U. S. Grant after the war. (USAMHI)

Timothy O'Sullivan's view of the Armory beef yard, with the Treasury and Executive Mansion in the background. Washington smelled of livestock for four years. In the hot summer months Lincoln had to go to the Soldiers' Home on the outskirts of the city to escape the odors. (COURTESY OF AMERICANA IMAGE GALLERY)

Troops had to eat. Here just one of scores of government mess houses and, to the left, one of many impromptu boardinghouses advertising "sleeping rooms."
(USAMHI)

Feeding the troops defending the capital required an office for the quartermaster at the Seventh Street wharf, shown here in May 1865.
(USAMHI)

An April 1865 image of the mess house at the U. S. Government Stables.
(USAMHI)

Armory Square, down Constitution Avenue from the Capitol, had its own
chapel, complete with onion-shaped bell tower. (USAMHI)

A. J. Russell made this 1864 view of the Washington Arsenal on Greenleafs Point. In the distance is the Long Bridge. (USAMHI)

The Arsenal stored, shipped, and put into service the bulk of the ordnance used in the Union armies. Here one sees the cannon and rolling equipment of several batteries of the Excelsior Brigade. (USAMHI)

*At any one time the Arsenal yard could always sprout neatly arranged rows of
cannon, caissons, limbers, disassembled carriages, and gun tubes. (CHS)*

*Brigadier General Christopher C. Augur
commanded the Department of Washington in the
final two years of the war, helping with its defense
against Jubal Early's 1864 campaign toward the
capital. (KA)*

Men of the 10th Rhode Island, Burnside's Zouaves, posing with bayonets fixed. They spent the war as part of the capital defense forces. (COURTESY OF THE RHODE ISLAND HISTORICAL SOCIETY)

A member of Burnside's Zouaves, taken in Providence before he went to war. (COURTESY OF THE RHODE ISLAND HISTORICAL SOCIETY)

The Federals ringed Washington with a formidable series of defenses. Here Fort Carroll, just across the Eastern Branch from the Arsenal, guards the capital's Maryland approaches. (KA)

Completely on the other side of the city, near Silver Spring, Maryland, sat Fort Stevens. Here is where Early attacked in 1864, facing guns like this 6.4-inch Parrott rifle mounted on a seacoast carriage. (LC)

Fort Richardson sat on the Virginia side, in advance of the approach to the Long Bridge. On this side of the Potomac passes into the defenses always had to be checked, as is being done here by members of the 1st Connecticut Heavy Artillery. (WRHS)

Fort Lyon, considerably more ambitious than many Washington forts, guarded Alexandria from the south, the southernmost major outpost in the Virginia line of defenses. (USAMHI)

Here men of the 34th Massachusetts pose beside a cannon aimed toward the still frequently hostile northern Virginia landscape. (USAMHI)

Fort Slemmer sat north of the city. The men of the 2nd Pennsylvania Heavy Artillery stand in their best warlike pose despite the fact that the fort saw no action. (WRHS)

A. J. Russell's 1864 image of Battery Rodgers in Alexandria. Its fifteen-inch Rodman smoothbore dominates the parapet, though it never fired in anger. (NA)

Officers of the 3rd Massachusetts Heavy Artillery pose at their brigade headquarters in Fort Lincoln, not far from Bladensburg, Maryland. (USAMHI)

Fort Foote, opposite Alexandria, was one of the largest fortifications in the whole defensive chain. Any attack on the capital by water would first have to pass this mighty bastion. (CHS)

Fort Haggerty, just across the Potomac from Georgetown, was one of the smaller installations, yet it still had the sting of four large smoothbores. The man in the left foreground wears the sash of the officer of the day. (COURTESY OF ROBERT J. YOUNGER)

Just east of Fort Haggerty stood the much larger Fort Corcoran, the major defense on the road from Washington to Falls Church, Virginia. (USAMHI)

George Barnard caught this image of guards examining a pass at the ferry landing on Mason's Island opposite Georgetown. (LC)

An image, probably by Russell, showing Alexandria, with Washington in the distance, in the winter of 1864–65. With hostile Virginia just across the Potomac, the defenders of the capital had to take special precautions to guard access to the city. (USAMHI)

The Navy Yard bridge over the Eastern Branch, with Uniontown in the distance. A small guard stands post, yet people could get through. John Wilkes Booth was to cross this bridge after shooting Lincoln. (USAMHI)

The Aqueduct Bridge over the Potomac, taken from Fort Corcoran, showing Georgetown in the distance. (USAMHI)

Another view, by Russell, of the Aqueduct Bridge. (P-M)

The Chain Bridge, which crossed the Potomac three miles upriver from Georgetown, was one of the most heavily protected spots. Here a guard box stands at the right, while the guards themselves lounge for the camera. (KA)

William Kunstman of Pennsylvania brought his camera to capture this image of the Chain Bridge. (J. FREDERIC KNECHT COLLECTION)

He stayed to photograph the bridge guards. (J. FREDERIC KNECHT COLLECTION)

The bridge itself, with two soldiers feigning a spar as they perch on the rail.
(J. FREDERIC KNECHT COLLECTION)

The men on the Maryland side waited with small smoothbores to repel any
assault across the bridge. (J. FREDERIC KNECHT COLLECTION)

Another photographer caught the men practicing; some are standing with cartridges in their hands, the fuses in place, and lanyards in hand as if ready to fire. (LC)

An old tree was pressed into service for a signal station above the Chain Bridge. (USAMHI)

*Kunstman took his camera to nearby Fort Marcy, there to be met by this stern-faced young Horatio of Company A. (*J. FREDERIC KNECHT COLLECTION*)*

*The interior of Fort Marcy in a damaged old stereo view by Kunstman. A young Negro soldier, perhaps a servant, stands alone in the center. (*J. FREDERIC KNECHT COLLECTION*)*

Fort Marcy's parade ground, with the men drawn into ranks for review and inspection. Two carriages of spectators look on. (J. FREDERIC KNECHT COLLECTION)

A mighty Parrott rifle looks out over the Virginia countryside from its emplacement in Fort Marcy. (J. FREDERIC KNECHT COLLECTION)

The men defending Washington enjoyed some luxuries denied to their brothers marching with the armies. One was the much greater opportunity to have families with them or nearby, as with these wives and children who posed with their husbands for Kunstman's lens. (J. FREDERIC KNECHT COLLECTION)

Quarters for the guard on the Virginia side of the Chain Bridge. At far left is the signal station in the tree. (J. FREDERIC KNECHT COLLECTION)

The view from the signal tree. Many of Kunstman's photographs survive in poor condition, the glass negatives having been stored away and forgotten for over a century. (J. FREDERIC KNECHT COLLECTION)

Hunting Creek, near Alexandria, and a long bridge with a blockhouse at midstream. (USAMHI)

A closer view of a blockhouse in winter. Most Civil War bridges were defended at both ends. This one, with the defense in the middle, may be unique. (USAMHI)

The entrance to the Long Bridge, the major artery from Washington to Alexandria. "Walk Your Horses" reads the sign on the right. (KA)

The Long Bridge in May 1865. With the parallel railroad bridge visible to the left, this span could accommodate enormous traffic. It was the capital's chief link with the armies in Virginia. (USAMHI)

Colonel D. C. McCallum, director of the United States Military Railroads, sits in the center of the group at right, with the railroad span of the Long Bridge before him. (USAMHI)

*The Alexandria side of the Long Bridge looked like a virtual stockade,
controlling access for horse and pedestrian alike.* (KA)

*Richard Wallach's election as mayor of
Washington was a loud declaration of Union
sentiment toward the capital despite its largely
Southern population.* (USAMHI)

Brigadier General John H. Martindale served as military governor of Washington in 1863 and early 1864. It was an unenviable task for a soldier because of the constant interference of politicians and the wide Southern sentiment in the city. He left to return to field command. (NA)

But Washington could also be pleasant duty. The officers of the United States Treasury Battalion, here shown posing in April 1865, could display uniforms unsullied by hard service. (USAMHI)

Soldiers, civilians, and dignitaries could enjoy the scenic loveliness of the Potomac, as is evident here on the pontoon bridge linking Georgetown with Analostan Island. (USAMHI)

There was fishing and lounging in the shade along the banks of the Potomac near the Aqueduct Bridge. (USAMHI)

*Officers like Brigadier General Daniel Sickles, on leave, could leisurely inspect
the Wiard guns at the Washington Arsenal.* (USAMHI)

*And when Sickles was on leave again, following the loss of his leg at
Gettysburg, he could visit with other shelved field officers like Major General
Samuel P. Heintzelman, now commanding part of the capital defenses.*
(USAMHI)

Though war did not come to the heart of the city, still destruction visited from time to time. Here the Smithsonian has burned on January 24, 1865.
(SMITHSONIAN INSTITUTION)

But the Smithsonian, like Washington itself, went onward. When Lincoln won re-election in 1864, the safety of the Union was secured. Three years later U. S. Grant became Chief Executive. At heart always a loyal city, the citizens of Washington turned out in record numbers to witness the parade and ceremonies for his inauguration in March 1869. A city at war for four years, it looked confidently toward peace. (LC)

Chancellorsville, Lee's Greatest Triumph

FRANK E. VANDIVER

The greatest gamble, the greatest success;
Lee's last victory in open campaign

WINTER CAMPS had been fairly comfortable for both the Army of the Potomac and the Army of Northern Virginia. And as spring came in 1863, stirrings began in Blue and Gray lines.

Lee's army had been extensively refitted following the December 1862 Battle of Fredericksburg. "Stonewall" Jackson's II Corps, stretching along the Rappahannock from near Marye's Heights to below Hamilton's Crossing, had recruited and refurbished well; Jackson himself by now shared international renown with Lee. James Longstreet's I Corps had also rebuilt, and the bluff general, with several of his divisions, lingered in North Carolina scavenging and harassing Federal coastal raiders. In the old Fredericksburg lines, made nearly impregnable by months of digging, Lee counted almost 60,000 men.

Across the river the Army of the Potomac also had filled and burnished and had said farewell to yet another luckless leader, Ambrose E. Burnside.

Joseph Hooker came to command at some cost to honor but none to self-esteem. Dapper, often dashing, considered very brave by his troops, Hooker always chafed in subordination. Under Burnside his frustration had been almost overwhelming, and the backwash of Fredericksburg and the so-called "mud march" of January 1863

had fueled Hooker's anger. He had argued with Burnside, complained, and finally openly criticized his commander. Loud and intemperate, Hooker's complaints ran all the way to Washington. When Lincoln at last determined to relieve Burnside, he searched the rolls for a successor. Hooker's reputation for fighting attracted a president longing for aggressive generals. In selecting Hooker, Lincoln weighed his virtues against his carping. The results were conveyed to Hooker in a masterful appointment letter:

> Executive Mansion
> Washington, January 26, 1863

Major General Hooker:

General

I have placed you at the head of the Army of the Potomac. Of course I have done this upon what appeared to me to be sufficient reasons. And yet I think it best for you to know that there are some things in regard to which, I am not quite satisfied with you. I believe you to be a brave and skillful soldier, which, of course, I like. I also believe you do not mix politics with your profession, in which you are right. You have confidence in yourself, which is a valuable, if not an indispensable quality. You are ambitious, which, within reasonable limits, does good rather than harm. But I think that during General Burnside's command of the Army, you have taken counsel of your ambitions, and thwarted him as much as you could, in which you did a great wrong to the country, and to a most meritorious and honorable brother officer. I have heard, in such way as to believe it, of your recently saying that both the Army and the Government needed a Dictator. Of course it was not *for* this, but in spite of it, that I have given you the command. Only those generals, who gained successes, can set up Dictators. What I now ask of you is military success, and I will risk the Dictatorship. The Government will support you to the upmost of its ability, which is neither more nor less than it has done and will do for all commanders. I must fear that the spirit which you have aided to infuse into the Army, of criticizing their Commander, and withholding confidence from him, will now turn upon you. I shall assist you as far as I can, to put it down. Neither you, nor Napoleon, if he were alive again, could get any good out of an Army, while such a spirit prevails in it.

And now, beware of rashness. —Beware of rashness, but with energy, and sleepless vigilance, go forward, and give us victories.

Yours very truly,
A. LINCOLN

Piqued but hardly daunted, Hooker boasted loudly that he would mold a winning army, and throughout the winter he made an impressive beginning. Attention to such vital things as socks, good food, and lodging endeared the general to his troops. Reorganization into traditional divisions and corps, some command adjustments, won approval from veteran commanders. When April brought fighting weather to northern Virginia, Hooker counted some 130,000 men in his ranks, most of them in good spirits and under competent leaders.

Hooker took the initiative. He learned old lessons well and consequently wisely planned to flank Lee's formidable lines by crossing upriver from Fredericksburg, moving rapidly through Virginia's Wilderness, and getting between Lee and Richmond. If his plan worked, Lee would have to fight where Hooker wanted.

Lee's pickets reported long blue lines moving on April 29, 1863. Jeb Stuart's outriders watched the Rapidan and Rappahannock fords—United States, Germanna, Ely's. These were good ones that offered access to various roads penetrating the heavily forested Wilderness.

With the first reports of Yankee movement, Lee reacted by dispatching R. H. Anderson's division toward Chancellorsville. Anderson must watch for the enemy vanguard and hold them back. With luck he might prevent Hooker's emergence from the entangling woods. At any rate, the enemy would be surprised and unable to flank Confederate positions.

Hooker knew he had thought of all contingencies. As his heavy columns marched off toward the river crossings, he kept 40,000 men under Major General John Sedgwick in the Fredericksburg lines to hold Lee's attention. Despite last-minute problems which appeared to fuddle Hooker a bit, the general pushed his advance and himself went to cross the Rappahannock on April 30. Caution lifted as action neared. Hooker boasted to a newsman: "The rebel Army . . . is now the legitimate property of the Army of the Potomac. They may as well pack their haversacks and make for Richmond; and I shall be after them . . ."

Optimism tinged with experience colored Rebel thoughts. Lee balanced force ratios and remained hopeful. If Longstreet, with the rest of his corps, were at hand, hope would have been brighter. Even so, there seemed a good chance that a detachment could hold Fredericksburg's entrenchments while Lee and Jackson followed Anderson toward the Wilderness.

Wilderness trails were never especially easy, and now, after hard rains, they were boggy and hard on infantry. Hooker's men encountered environmental resistance as soon as they were south of the Rappahannock. Roads were really sluices, narrow and darkened by dripping trees. Federal maps were not entirely accurate. Hooker had intended to move briefly south to the Old Turnpike, near Melzi Chancellor's Farm, and then turn east and clear the trees.

Intentions wavered once Hooker entered the woods. Although his subordinates, especially

In the aftermath of the Fredericksburg fiasco, President Lincoln faced the same crisis that had confronted him since the war's beginning. Somewhere he must find the right general for the Army of the Potomac. Fredericksburg had shown that Burnside was not the man. There were many who felt themselves capable, and some loudly proclaimed their self-confidence. The President could confide his private reservations to his secretaries—John G. Nicolay on the left and John Hay on the right—but to the public he expressed only confidence in his new choice of a commander. (USAMHI)

George G. Meade and William B. Franklin, urged a speedy execution of the original plan, Hooker took refuge at the Chancellor House during the night of April 30 and ordered his men to halt where they were.

Some of Hooker's subordinates worried. They recognized loss of initiative and, with it, one of the greatest wasted opportunities of the war. With Longstreet's corps depleted, and with Jubal Early and his division detached at Fredericksburg, Lee appeared to be more vulnerable than ever before! But Hooker hesitated. And, truth to tell, the omens were bad. Trees dripped in a kind of dark foreboding. Sounds were magnified and specters frequent. Axes thudded, muffled and mysterious, as men in blue felled trees for entrenchments.

Near the Chancellor House, where he established his headquarters, Hooker tested the omens and balanced the odds in that strange way he had of arguing with himself. For weeks everything had been going his way and he had basked and boasted far and wide. Despite the gloomy landscape, recent moves would bring success. If George Meade pressed quickly along the Rappahannock's south bank, Lee would be flanked from the wicked works at Marye's Heights and his army might possibly be divided. In one of his moods of destiny, Hooker published success to his army on April 30, 1863, in the form of General Orders No.

47: "It is with heartfelt satisfaction the commanding general announces to the army that the operations of the last three days have determined that our enemy must either ingloriously fly, or come out from behind his defenses and give us battle on our own ground, where certain destruction awaits him."

Several Federal commanders must have been both irked and disturbed by this order—irked because of its bombast and disturbed because of its suddenly defensive tone. Where had the aggressiveness of earlier orders and speeches gone? Now, if Lee came out of his lines, the Army of the Potomac would receive attack. Clearly, as Stonewall Jackson guessed, Hooker's zest had gone. Why? What happened in the brooding, wet woodland as Yankee soldiers huddled around campfires and

Major General Joseph Hooker. Now just forty-eight, he had been one of the most highly commended young officers in the war with Mexico. As a result of an accident in a telegraph office, he was called "Fighting Joe Hooker" early in the war and the sobriquet stuck. He bitterly attacked Burnside behind his back, politicking blatantly, and finally won the army command. In giving it, Lincoln warned that the spirit of divisiveness that Hooker had fostered might well turn on him one day. (USAMHI)

wondered about the quirks of high command—especially when Hooker, on the afternoon of May 1, ordered some of his advancing units to retreat!

A long time later Hooker admitted what happened: "For once I lost confidence in Hooker." He did not realize it for a while and became extremely busy and distracted.

Jackson, too, became busy. With all his divisions, save Early's, which would man the Fredericksburg lines, Jackson marched toward the Wilderness shortly after midnight on May 1. By 8 A.M. he could hear firing from the west and soon found Anderson, who had entrenched a line facing west and northwest, guarding the Old Turnpike, the Plank Road, and the Old Mine Road. With six brigades (three of them from Lafayette McLaws's division) Anderson had skirmished with mysteriously hesitant Union units and kept them at bay. Stonewall became impatient; Hooker ought to be attacked while still clogged in the woods. Anderson, helped by McLaws, was ordered forward on the Old Turnpike. One of Anderson's brigades would lead Jackson's II Corps on the Plank Road—which seemed to offer manuevering room toward Hooker's rumored flank. Jackson urged his men forward and soon noted that Federals retreated before a determined Rebel advance. Lee joined Jackson about midday, approved plans for pressing the enemy's right, and galloped off toward his own right, where the enemy's line had not been fully discovered. Jackson rode on to his left, beyond the Catherine Furnace, topped a hill where Jeb Stuart stood watching his horse artillery in action, and the two surveyed the front. Trees clotted their vision; Stuart told of the roads he knew which led toward the Federal right rear. There might be others.

Late in the afternoon Jackson knew that a heavy Union force had entrenched near Chancellorsville; he had one further look at Federal masses and then rode to meet Lee at the Plank Road junction. Federal timidity convinced "Old Jack" that Hooker's

There were still many old familiar faces about the army headquarters despite the new general. Major General Daniel Butterfield became Hooker's chief of staff, a position he would retain for much of the war. (USAMHI)

The 93rd New York was still the headquarters guard for the Army of the Potomac. Here the regimental staff poses just three months after its one campaign with Hooker. (USAMHI)

offensive had fizzled and that all Yankees would be north of the Rapidan and Rappahannock by morning.

Something had gone wrong with Hooker's offensive—there was no doubt of that. But Hooker still concentrated near Chancellorsville, and his numbers were daunting: Scattered through the trees and clearings, dotted behind works, and clustered around guns were nearly 75,000 men and 208 guns. What could he do with such strength? Calling his commanders to a conference during the night of May 1, Hooker heard two propositions: Find good ground and dig in or attack Lee in the woods, where he was at an equal disadvantage. Retreat was not a real choice—too much boasting had been done and a victory-hungry President Lincoln dogged the Military Telegraph Office for news. The original plan had pretty well "gone up" now that Rebels were in the woods. Attack might be possible, as was a slide south, across Lee's front, toward Richmond, which might still put the Army of the Potomac between Lee's left and the Confederate capital. Hooker ordered General John Reynolds to bring his I Corps from Fredericksburg and then pondered his opportunities.

Lee and Jackson pondered too. Lee disagreed about Hooker's possible retreat during the night. He hoped Jackson was right but felt Hooker could not abandon so notorious an effort. Unless Hooker's right could be turned, things looked sticky—the entire Union left and center seemed firm and strong and attacks on them would likely crumble. If a way around the enemy right could be found, Lee plotted a pincers attack against Hooker's front and rear—Jackson would march around the Union Army and hit it from behind. All that kept "Old Jack" from his greatest opportunity was the need for a protected and secret road curving south and then north back to the Old Turnpike. Was there one? Jackson put the problem to an old chaplain friend, the Reverend Tucker Lacy, who knew the country, and to his trusted topographical engineer, Jedediah Hotchkiss. They vanished in the darkness as May 1 dwindled in camp light and in the odd closeness of killing hordes.

Rumors of numerous Rebel reinforcements—perhaps Longstreet's missing men—flickered through the woods and struck special nerves way out on the Union right, where the XI Corps,

Just one month after Chancellorsville, the 8th United States Infantry, provost guard for Hooker's army headquarters, stood for the camera. (P-M)

Oliver O. Howard commanding, rested in lines mostly facing south. This corps, full of German-Americans, was big but not lucky. It suffered often from xenophobic jokes in an army aggressively "American." Many of its officers, though, had Prussian training and knew much about war. Colonel Leopold von Gilsa was one such professional, and he worried increasingly about his brigade as he noted that Hooker's entire right flank was "in the air," unprotected by any natural or other man-made barrier. Masses of Rebels were reported by pickets on the western end of the Federal line, yet worries and reports from von Gilsa that passed upward through the chain of command were ridiculed and rejected. The story ran that the Confederates were all clustered to the east and were so outnumbered that they had already begun retreating. That was what everybody saw—the Rebel retreat! What so many Federals saw was "Stonewall" Jackson's corps marching southwest, down past the Catherine Furnace to the Brock Road.

Jackson made the decision to move early on the morning of May 2, when he received word from Lacy and Hotchkiss that a usable, well-screened road leading toward the Yankee right and rear existed. That news came after Jackson and Lee met at a Wilderness campfire—and both generals studied the route. Could Hooker be hit before he shook off his fears and resumed the attack? If Lee divided his force to strike the Federals front and rear, both wings of his army would be smaller than the enemy and each one might be smashed. If Hooker pushed Sedgwick to attack Fredericksburg, Early's force might be wrecked and the Confederates caught in a closing vise. In the firelight Lee looked at his trusted lieutenant and asked: "General Jackson, what do you propose to do?" Still gazing at the map, Jackson pointed to Hotchkiss's sketched route and answered, "Go around here." Lee considered this and queried, "What do you propose to make this movement with?" Jackson had the reply ready, confirmed by hours of thought: "With my whole corps." If the enemy's flank lay as exposed as it seemed, maximum advantage must be taken of the situation—decisive victory lay within the Confederate grasp. A bit surprised, Lee wondered, "What will you leave me?" "The divisions of Anderson and McLaws" came the swift reply—so Jackson would march with 28,000 men and leave Lee 14,000 men to face the bulk of Hooker's strength. Lee's daring matched Jackson's; the attack would be made!

At about 8 A.M. the march began in a warming sunlight. Veteran infantry moved easily and covered ground. Speculation ran through the ranks as to where they were going, but all the gray-clads in the II Corps knew "Old Jack" had a surprise in store for Hooker. Even when they came to an exposed hill and took random shelling, they were confident and happy.

"Old Jack" himself seemed content. At midmorning he sent Lee a request to attack Hooker's front when fighting began behind Chancellorsville, then joined a group of officers at the head of his column. Former cadets or colleagues at the Virginia Military Institute, the officers listened to their commander explain a serious Confederate problem: "The trouble with us has always been to have a reserve to throw in at the critical moment to reap the benefit of advantages gained. We have always had to put in all our troops and never had enough at the time most needed." Hooker, Jackson heard, had more men than he could handle. "I should like to have half as many more as I have today, and I should hurl him in the river!"

Hooker may have had more men than he could handle, but some of his senses were sound that day. Reports coming to him during the morning of a gray column marching southwest stirred speculation. Major General Dan Sickles thought the Rebels were retreating, but Hooker remarked that it was unlike Lee to fall back without fighting. He sent circulars to Major Generals Howard and Henry Slocum warning them to consider the possibility of a flank attack and to keep reserves handy just in case. At the same time, Hooker told Sickles to hit the passing column but to do so cautiously.

Sickles struck the enemy at Catherine Furnace at midafternoon, drove in their skirmishes, and reported the column large and burdened with wagons and guns. He could, Sickles told Hooker, reach the road and engage the whole gray force, but the commanding general still urged caution. Sickles strengthened his line and advanced to the

Lee still faced the Federals across the Rappahannock at Fredericksburg—now much more heavily fortified than the previous December—despite the peaceful aspect of the city in this February 1863 view. Hooker knew he could not launch an attack across the river against positions worse than those faced by Burnside. He would make a diversion here while he crossed most of his army upriver.

(USAMHI)

The terrain Hooker planned to cross was known in Virginia as The Wilderness,
a densely wooded, confused, sometimes impenetrable barrier that could confound
an army unfamiliar with it. This image, taken in the winter of 1865, shows
trees shattered by the battle that Hooker would fight here. (USAMHI)

road, where a sharp fight won him many Rebel prisoners—snappy-looking, husky men of the 23rd Georgia. Like most troops disgusted with being bagged, they tried taunting their captors, saying that they had come over to help "eat them eight-day rations." One grizzled Rebel listened to a Yankee boast, "We'll have every mother's son of you before we go away," to which he growled, "You'll catch hell before night." Another irked prisoner blurted, "You think you've done a big thing just now, but you wait until Jackson gets around on your right." Blusters from captives go pretty much unnoticed, especially when things are looking up.

Sickles reported that his men were in among Rebel wagons and with a little help could do large damage. Hooker told Howard to send Sickles a brigade. As it happened, when Howard took Francis Barlow's brigade toward the sound of battle, he stripped his corps of its only reserve.

While Hooker waited for good news, expectations ran dismally out on his right. Portents of trouble gathered against the Dutchmen in the XI Corps during the morning. The corps rested, arms stacked, through the lunch hour, but then an odd tension sifted through the ranks. Numerous commanders shook out curtains of skirmishes south of the turnpike on the corps's front. Reports came back of active gray cavalry ahead of parties of hostile infantry, and it looked as though great numbers of Rebels were moving off toward the Federal right. Reports back to corps headquarters earned wise comments about a reconnaissance in force to cover Lee's retreat.

Officers at headquarters were sharp and educated about all such high martial matters, but veterans in the ranks knew a retreat when they saw one—and they were not seeing one. The ranks grew restive as the day wore on and the portents became worse.

Several important things worked against the Dutchmen—in addition to Howard's leaving with their reserve. First, they were strung out in a mile-long line, for most of the distance only two ranks deep. They faced south and could probably cope with a frontal attack, but a flank attack from the west or northwest would roll them up in a gathering crowd of disaster. Second, by the height of the afternoon old hands knew the Rebels had flanked them. Third, confirmation of that suspicion led to a terrible mounting frustration as nobody high up would listen.

Everything about XI Corps's situation looked bad. It was, in fact, isolated, with its eastern end—where Sickles's had been—resting on open ground near Dowdall's Tavern, a designated strong point with rifle pits and gun emplacements facing south. Westward from there the corps line ran along the road through woods and finally came to an end. There, at the right end of Hooker's whole line, two guns stood in the road and two regiments faced west, each in heavy skirmish order—one rank of men spread thin.

Worst of all, there was political trouble in the corps's right division, with Brigadier General Charles Devens of Boston commanding. Out near the division's far right lay Brigadier General Nathaniel C. McLean's brigade. (McLean had been division commander and was bumped down to make way for Devens.) So, as McLean's men repeatedly reported gray masses moving west, Devens chose to regard them as frightened alarmists and lectured them on the fact that corps headquarters—surely steeped in the fullest wisdom—had sounded no warnings. One of McLean's regimental commanders went to corps headquarters only to be laughed out.

It happened that Leopold von Gilsa's brigade was out on the western end of things; consequently, it also happened that late in the afternoon that wily Prussian veteran received word from his picket line that what looked like the whole Confederate Army was massing and "For God's Sake, make dispositions to receive" them. Von Gilsa took the message to Howard's staff, where the news was

In March Hooker began his probes across the Rappahannock at points above Fredericksburg. Lee remained in the city, letting his cavalry guard his flanks. Colonel William Morgan, then a major, led his 1st Virginia Cavalry in repeated skirmishes with the Yankees, trying to halt their progress and divine their intent. (PRIVATE COLLECTION)

dismissed with the thought that the forest out to the west was too thick for a line of battle to pass. Vastly bothered, von Gilsa returned to his line to greet "Iron Pants" Dilger, coming over from Carl Schurz's front. He had been sent scouting by his general, who, though not a trained professional, shared the spreading alarm and had shifted part of his front near Wilderness Church to face west just in case. Captain Hubert Dilger, late of the Baden Mountain Artillery, could have saved Hooker.

Defying von Gilsa's warning not to go too far west lest he be captured, Dilger ran into a Rebel battle line, fled for his freedom, and skirted far north, almost to the Rapidan, before he reached Hooker's headquarters. There he failed to get past a supercilious major who showed considerable contempt for alarming words given in a heavy foreign accent. Hooker need not be bothered; go back to

XI Corps headquarters. Back there Dilger was berated for unauthorized scouting and was reminded that Lee's army was retreating. Back among his own guns, Dilger cautioned his men to keep the horses handy.

Skirmish firing picked up around 5 P.M., but it went unremarked by great leaders. That skirmish fire Jackson noted as he watched a massive gray battle line form slowly in the late afternoon light. Everything seemed to happen so slowly. The march from Catherine Furnace along Hotchkiss's fifteen-mile route had gone steadily, but heat and rain-sogged roads brought a kind of summer lethargy to his veterans. Sickles's attack had not really stalled the march, but its confusion caused problems for a while.

Jeb Stuart ranged ahead of Jackson's men to probe woods for usable roads. By midafternoon he

Meanwhile, Hooker marshaled his army in and around Falmouth. Many of the regiments had wintered here in now-abandoned winter huts like these. (USAMHI)

A campaign was coming, and as the army gathered at Falmouth, there was little place for solitude. A soldier took it where he could. (USAMHI)

realized the Brock Road would lead obliquely into the Union lines. Another must be found. The turnpike? Could it be reached in secrecy? Finding Jackson, Stuart rode with him to a knoll near the Brock Road that overlooked the western end of the enemy's lines; the two generals saw entrenchments, guns, and ready infantry. Jackson agreed his men must go farther. Stuart confirmed their road would lead to the turnpike, full aflank the Federals. "Press on, men, press on," Jackson urged. Knowing his customary impatience before impending success, his men marched in growing glee. They were out on "Fighting Joe's" flank, and they were going to ruin his reputation. Where would "Old Jack" put them? He put them across the turnpike in a line that stretched a mile, stretched as far as a man could see in the patches of trees and dense underbrush, and he put them in four divisional lines, clouds of skirmishers out in front. Ahead of them, they knew, lay the XI Corps, and on this second day of May 1863 that would be a corps of Flying Dutchmen.

Robert Emmett Rodes, a young and gifted brigadier, had charge of the forming Rebel lines. At 5:15 P.M. Jackson asked him if he was ready and Rodes said he was. "You can go forward then." The young general signaled his bugler, the notes rang through the woods, and the skirmishers ran forward. The big lines followed, slowly at first, then faster, with increasing momentum, and at last men were tearing through scant growth, running, running with their high, eerie Rebel yell floating on before them.

What the Dutchmen saw first were deer, rabbits, and other animals running at them, fleeing the skirmishers and the yelling. A few braced, but most fled when a long wave of gray dotted with reddened battle flags streamed out of the forest, washed over them, and rolled beyond.

That old muffling effect of the Wilderness trapped the noise of fighting. Hooker spent the afternoon awaiting news from Sickles and urging Sedgwick to take his VI Corps across the Rappahannock in pursuit of Lee's rearguard and trains. This message gave the impression that Hooker firmly accepted the notion of Lee's retreat. At about 6:30 P.M. that fiction dissolved. Hearing noises to the right, one of Hooker's staff walked out

Spirits rose once more as the pain of the defeat at Fredericksburg subsided. Looking to another "go" at "Bobby Lee," the men in blue could relax with horseplay. This time they would beat the Confederates—of that they were certain. (USAMHI)

in front of headquarters and saw a wild melee of men, horses, wagons, and bouncing guns streaming straight at him down the road. "My God—here they come," he yelled. Hooker and other aides scrambled on horses and rode to try to stem the stampede. "Vere ist der pontoon?" screamed some of the XI Corps's remnants; most just ran without thought. Hooker's little coterie charged the rout, but they were engulfed.

Jolted from his daylong reverie, Hooker came to life now that battle raged. Quickly he ordered trustworthy John Reynolds to get his I Corps forward. Sadly Reynolds reported that a lost dispatch bearer had delayed his move toward Hooker; his men were not yet across United States Ford. There was a hope. The "Old Hooker Division" had been kept close to headquarters. Hooker rode up to its commander, Hiram Berry, and shouted: "General

. . . throw your men into the breach—receive the enemy on your bayonets—don't fire a shot—they can't see you."

Hasty efforts to amass artillery at Fairview Cemetery, facing west, met some success. Howard, all bravery now that disaster loomed, collected some infantry, a few batteries, and put them with Berry's men in a line across the road, west of Hooker's headquarters. Schurz brought up a polyglot force and went to Berry's right; a division of the XII Corps prolonged the left. Guns behind this makeshift line poured shells into the Rebels. Hooker wanted to reinforce his right, but Lee demonstrated so strongly in front of Chancellorsville that an attack seemed imminent and Hooker dared not weaken Winfield Scott Hancock or George Gordon Meade.

Darkness settled over the Wilderness in an uneasy gloom. Sporadic flashes marked isolated fighting, cannonading shook the trees, but heavy encounters stopped. The impetus ebbed from the Rebel attack.

Success stalled Jackson's advance, success and darkness and stiffening resistance. "Old Jack" worked to unscramble units mixed in the headlong rush, bring fresh men forward, replenish munitions, and prepare another thrust. He hoped to crush Hooker between Lee and his own II Corps, perhaps slide a bit to his left, and get between Hooker and vital river crossings.

Reorganization proved complicated; Jackson hated the delay, which gave Hooker time to regroup. Ever eager to move forward, to know where the enemy was, Jackson took a small party of aides and rode ahead of the Confederate lines. Somewhere beyond lay the enemy. Where? Down a dark, shadowy lane he led his little detachment. Slowly, carefully they went until, at last, the clang of axes and voices was heard—the enemy was entrenching just ahead.

Pulling his horse, Little Sorrel, around, Jackson rode quickly back toward the Rebel lines. Rumors were running wild that night—Yankee cavalry roamed everywhere—they were coming down the road straight into a North Carolina regiment! Hasty challenges, quick volleys, and Jackson fell from his saddle, wounded in the left arm and right hand. Hastily put on a stretcher for transfer to the rear, Jackson and his bearers were caught in a terrific cannonade; several bearers fell and Jackson's stretcher crashed to the ground. Major General A. P. Hill, second in command, had just reached Jackson when the barrage struck; he, too, fell wounded. Command devolved, by rank, on Jeb Stuart. Stuart sent a messenger to Jackson's side at a field hospital, hoping to receive orders. His left arm amputated, "Old Jack" rose on his other elbow. The battle light gleamed in his shocked eyes and then faded. He said Stuart must do what he thought best.

Too much of Jackson's spirit pervaded the corps to give up the offensive. Stuart reorganized and planned to attack in the morning.

By morning Hooker had some chance not only for survival but even for success. Reynolds's I Corps was at hand to stabilize the right; Meade had put some of the V Corps in next to Reynolds, and Sickles held important high ground at Hazel

But the sober reality of war came soon enough. Hooker started to move late in April, and even before the full armies met, men began to die. Lieutenant George Busch of the 98th Pennsylvania was killed opposite Fredericksburg on April 30, 1863, days before the main battle. The horseplay ended abruptly. (USAMHI)

Grove. The way the Confederates had pushed their attack shoved their right flank out in front of Sickles and exposed their left to Reynolds. Boldness now might turn Lee's gamble into the loss of the war. Hooker looked at Sickles's position and pronounced it too exposed should Lee come up from the south. He told Sickles to retreat to Fairview.

Nothing worse could have been ordered save surrender. Rebels immediately put guns on this high ground, which could enfilade the Union right and left. By holding Hazel Grove the Rebels virtually connected their two wings. Hooker need not, should not, have withdrawn Sickles. With Reynolds at hand, he now counted 76,000 men and the

Awaiting Hooker's move was General Robert E. Lee, a man with a depleted army less than half the size of the Federals. In 1863 he posed in Richmond for the camera of the firm of Minnis and Cowell, his eyes alight with calm determination. Faced on two fronts, at Fredericksburg and by Hooker advancing in The Wilderness, he made a daring decision. (COURTESY OF DIMENTI STUDIO)

A big part of Lee's gamble would rest on this man, variously known as "Tom Fool," "Old Blue Light," and "Stonewall." Lieutenant General Thomas J. Jackson was to lead his corps in a bold flanking march around Hooker's unsuspecting right. Outnumbered two-to-one, Lee was splitting his army in the face of the enemy. (MUSEUM OF THE CONFEDERACY)

*Brigadier General Robert Rodes led the way as Jackson
threaded his way over a little-used side road to march around
Hooker. He had distinguished himself in every battle he fought,
and would continue to do so until a bullet cut him down in
1864.* (VM)

Confederates counted around 42,000, reduced by unknown numbers of casualties; and with Reynolds on the Rebel left, Union numbers were positioned to count. While Jeb Stuart rode along his line exhorting his troops by singing "Old Joe Hooker, won't you come out of the Wilderness," the Federal leader huddled in a mile square of shell-swept ground, waiting to be saved. He had ordered the harried John Sedgwick to speed toward Chancellorsville.

During the morning Hooker's men did well and the Union lines held—until a tactical blunder forced further contraction of the Federal position. Desperately Hooker waited for Sedgwick, who was having serious trouble cutting through from Fredericksburg.

About midmorning Hooker walked out on the south porch of his headquarters and a shell from a Rebel gun at Hazel Grove splintered a pillar of the Chancellor House; part of it struck Hooker on the head and knocked him down, stunned. Rumors flowed immediately that he was dead—some wish, perhaps, fathering the thought. He revived quickly, though in considerable pain. Shortly thereafter he gave General Darius Couch limited command of the army, with instructions to retire into a U-shaped tête-de-pont, open end toward United States Ford. By the morning of May 4 Hooker's

Brigadier General Alfred H. Colquitt, who came from Georgia, studied at the College of New Jersey in Princeton and served a term in Congress. On May 2 he led his Georgia brigade with Jackson in the flank march, then wildly attacked Hooker's ill-prepared and surprised right. (LC)

men were well dug in and waiting. Waiting ruined the last hope of crushing Lee.

Sedgwick had broken through Early's lines at Fredericksburg on May 3 and had pushed on toward Chancellorsville. But Lee noted Hooker's loss of nerve on the third, posted a force to watch Hooker, and took a big portion of his army toward Sedgwick at Salem Church. Early had skirmished and backed up, tired of retreating, when Lee arrived; together they drove Sedgwick to cover near Banks' Ford and threatened to capture over 20,000 bluecoats.

Lee's attack on the fourth began late and scrambled over difficult ground. Sedgwick held his front

until nightfall. Then he got his men across the Rappahannock. That piqued Lee, who had played a daring game of inserting his inferior force between two large enemy elements. He had, by most odds, been lucky to avoid destruction—and yet he always counted on boldness in stressful times. The original decision to let Jackson go around Hooker had been a gamble that paid high dividends; the decision on the third to go against Sedgwick was no less a gamble, and the Salem Church fighting had promised the elimination of an entire Union corps. It had escaped as a result of poor ground and sluggish reaction times in some of his units. This Lee thought a serious lapse, one that wasted another great opportunity. Returning to face Hooker's main body on the fifth, Lee planned to attack on the morrow—but Hooker's bedraggled columns crossed the Rappahannock at United States Ford during the night. His campaign had cost 17,000 Union casualties and achieved nothing save 13,000 Rebel casualties.

Lincoln reacted in anguish. "My God! My God! What will the Country say!" Horace Greeley put it this way: "God! It is horrible—horrible . . . ! 130,000 magnificent soldiers so cut to pieces by less than 60,000 half-starved ragamuffins!"

Historians have said much about Hooker's errors and his moral failure. They have said much, too, about the crowning achievement of Lee and Jackson, about a battle showing the value of maneuver and applied psychology.

Yet Chancellorsville was a Confederate victory fought at too high a price: On May 10, 1863, "Stonewall" Jackson died.

The road on which Jackson led his command in the flanking march. The "plank road" in the foreground, so called because it was paved with board planks, is here joined by the little byroad just beyond the two men in the center of the image. Jackson was riding up this little road when accidental shots fired by his own men felled him. (USAMHI)

Major General Oliver O. Howard, shown here as a brigadier, commanded Hooker's XI Corps. He detected Jackson's flank march but did not comprehend its significance. When "Stonewall" struck, Howard's corps was shattered. (USAMHI)

Howard's corps were largely Germans. Major General Carl Schurz, prominent German revolutionary in the 1840s, led a division which was routed by Jackson's attack. (P-M)

Commanding the 1st Division of the XI Corps was Brigadier General Charles Devens. His division utterly disintegrated, yet he was promoted for his service. Devens stands in the center, surrounded by his staff. (NA)

As Jackson's attack rolled back Howard's corps, the Federals and Confederates both passed by the unassuming little Wilderness Church. Almost exactly one year from now it would figure in a terrible battle once more, continuing the macabre irony of a war in which great battles seemed to be fought on the sabbath and simple churchyards became pastures of death. (USAMHI)

But the surprise came at a cost to the Confederates, too. That evening, after the surprise attack, "Stonewall" Jackson was riding on the south side of the Plank Road. When he reached this spot, his own men mistook him for an enemy and fired on him. Eight days later he would die. (USAMHI)

Howard made his headquarters at the home of George E. Chancellor, on the Plank Road. It would soon become a hospital, and its owner would give his name to Lee's greatest victory, as well as the nearby village: Chancellorsville. (USAMHI)

Samuel McGowan of South Carolina gallantly led his brigade in the heavy fighting that routed Howard's corps, but he himself took a serious wound in the fray. (VM)

Colonel Reuben L. Walker was chief of artillery in
A. P. Hill's division of Jackson's II Corps.
Chancellorsville was a nightmare for artillerists
because of the dense terrain. Only the Plank Road
allowed good movement of the guns, and it was
too often thronged with moving soldiers. This is a
heavily retouched portrait photograph. (VM)

Brigadier General Raleigh Colston led a dashing
life. Born in France, adopted by a Virginian, a
professor at the Virginia Military Institute, and an
observer at the March 9, 1862, duel between the
Monitor and the Virginia, he followed the war
with soldier-of-fortune service in the Egyptian
Army. At Chancellorsville he led a division under
Jackson. (VM)

Major General David B. Birney was the son of the famous antislavery leader
James G. Birney. Standing in the front row center, he commands the 1st
Division of Daniel Sickles's III Corps, posted next to Howard when the
Confederate flank attack strikes. This image, made toward the end of 1863,
shows the divisional banner with the battles of the unit emblazoned thereon.
Immediately to the right of the center square one can read the word
"Chancellorsville." It was a name hard won. (USAMHI)

Men like this unidentified zouave of the 114th Pennsylvania paid a high price to put that word on their division's flag. (COURTESY OF TERENCE P. O'LEARY)

Poor Francis R. T. Nichols. Only twenty-eight years old, he had already lost his left arm fighting with Jackson in the Shenandoah in 1862. Now a brigadier general, he saw his left foot torn off by a Federal cannonball at Chancellorsville, thus precluding further active service. (VM)

Brigadier General Hobart Ward, seated at left, led a brigade for Birney in the heavy fighting of May 2. A year later he would be relieved of command for alleged intoxication during another campaign in this same Virginia Wilderness.
(AMERICANA IMAGE GALLERY)

The 110th Pennsylvania Infantry posed at Falmouth on April 24, 1863, only a week before it went into the inferno of Chancellorsville. A. J. Russell caught the regiment, a part of Sickles's III Corps, anxious for the fight, unaware that Jackson would nearly destroy them. (LC)

Russell photographed Company C, of the 110th Pennsylvania, that same day. Some of the boyish faces would never smile again. "No braver or better troops" fought at Chancellorsville, said their brigade commander. For two hours the 110th held a position against superior odds. (MHS)

Sickles's artillery aided materially in staying, at least in part, the thundering advance of Jackson. Private Davis Shephard, shown here mounted next to one of the guns of his 11th New York Light Artillery, saw hard service at Chancellorsville as his three-inch ordnance rifles vainly tried to halt the Confederates. (COURTESY OF ROBERT MCDONALD)

On May 3 Confederate regiments battered ceaselessly against Hooker, while Lee turned his attention to Sedgwick at Fredericksburg. The 16th Virginia and its officers, once the regiment of General Raleigh Colston, fought in Richard H. Anderson's division, assaulted Hooker's center when Jackson struck Howard, and then, on May 3, turned to meet Sedgwick. (MUSEUM OF THE CONFEDERACY)

An artilleryman of the Salem Flying Artillery from Roanoke, Virginia. His battery moved with the 16th Virginia in the attack on May 3. (COURTESY OF DALE S. SNAIR)

On the day after Jackson's attack the fighting continued furiously around the Chancellor House and Chancellorsville. Here the ruins of a once-imposing structure testify to the fury of the fighting. This is an 1865 image. (USAMHI)

Major General Hiram G. Berry commanded a division that had once belonged to Hooker in the III Corps. On the morning of May 3, as the disorganized Federal Army tried to recover from the devastating blow dealt by Jackson, Berry took a mortal wound while fighting with his division. (USAMHI)

He led men like these of the 73rd New York. (USAMHI)

They fought in terrain like this, near and along the Plank Road. This image, taken two years later, shows gruesome reminders of the toll of Chancellorsville. (USAMHI)

Brigadier General Romeyn B. Ayres led a brigade in George G. Meade's V Corps. Briefly engaged on May 1, he enjoyed the luxury of being relatively idle during the rest of the battle. It did not appeal to the combative veteran of First Manassas. (KA)

Major General Winfield Scott Hancock, who seemed to appear prominently on every field of the Army of the Potomac, did no less so at Chancellorsville. When, finally, Hooker abandoned his position after a few days of idleness following the battle, Hancock covered the withdrawal against excessive odds, and did so successfully. (USAMHI)

But Chancellorsville was a two-part battle. The second part took place at Fredericksburg, an old battleground of 1862. There Hooker had assigned Major General John Sedgwick. (NA)

Repeatedly Sedgwick sent his men across the Rappahannock against Marye's Heights. A. J. Russell captured this image of Fredericksburg that very day from across the river. The thirty-two-pounders in the foreground are now idle, but earlier that day they spoke ferociously. (LC)

Indeed, while the fighting for Marye's Heights was going on, Russell operated his camera. The battle is in the far distance, with nothing visible to betray it except the line of smoke just below the horizon. (NEIKRUG PHOTOGRAPHICA, LTD.)

Units like the 31st Pennsylvania, shown here in camp, fought valiantly in repeated assaults before they finally broke through the Confederates' line and started to drive toward Lee's rear. (P-M)

*The fighting along the stone wall on Marye's Heights was particularly brutal.
Russell took his camera across the Rappahannock to capture the scene less than
twenty minutes after the Confederates were driven out. Brigadier General
Herman Haupt, chief of construction and transportation on the United States
Military Railroads, came with Russell. "I walked over the battle-ground, and
examined the heights beyond Marye's house. I then realized the great strength*

of the position and the impossibility of taking it, if properly defended, by a direct assault in front, as had been attempted by Burnside with disastrous results. My photographic artist, Captain Russell, was with me and secured several large photographic negatives—one very good one of the stone wall, with the rebel dead lying behind it." (USAMHI)

Brigadier General Albion P. Howe led his division of the VI Corps personally in its attacks on Marye's Heights. Two years later, to the day, he would act as an honor guard over the coffin of Abraham Lincoln. (P-M)

Company K of the 6th Vermont was part of the second regiment to crest Marye's Heights in the final successful attack. (LC)

As Sedgwick pursued the retreating Confederates, unaware that Lee would stop him in a few hours and end the battle as a Confederate victory, Russell anxiously moved his camera through the abandoned Southern camps. The briefly victorious Federals celebrated by ransacking the Rebel winter huts, finding liquor, blankets, and souvenirs that most would not have time to take with them. (CHS)

Russell's image of Haupt, at left, surveying the damage to an artillery battery's animals and equipment after the battle. (KA)

Brigadier General Robert F. Hoke would one day tell his North Carolinians that "the proudest day in all your proud careers was that on which you enlisted as Southern soldiers." In defending Fredericksburg he performed proudly, taking a serious wound. (VM)

This 1865 image shows part of the toll of the battle, with Federal dead buried in The Wilderness. Hooker and his campaign had failed despite his bravado. These dead paid the price for his failure. (USAMHI)

Some even escaped burial, or were so hastily interred that war's end found their bones shining in the sun. (USAMHI)

Hooker's supply base at Aquia Creek Landing became untenable as he withdrew his army. (LC)

There was no choice but to evacuate. In June 1863 Timothy O'Sullivan captured several images of the barges and steamers loaded with supplies and materiel for the successful withdrawal. As little as possible would be left for the Confederates. (LC)

Whole trains of cars were loaded on barges, as with the flatcars on the right. It was a massive operation. (KA)

For Hooker it was the only success of the campaign. In June, back in Falmouth, he would pose with his staff. Butterfield is seated at right, followed by Hooker, General Rufus Ingalls, and Major General H. J. Hunt. Within days the sober-looking "Fighting Joe" would be relieved of command even as Lee's Confederates were invading the North. (USAMHI)

But Lee's victory cost him dear. This early postwar view shows a house near Guiney's Station, a few miles from Fredericksburg. Here "Stonewall" Jackson was brought after he was wounded. His arm was amputated, the wound seemed to be healing, and then pneumonia grasped the great soldier. (DUKE UNIVERSITY LIBRARY)

And in this room, now filled with a shaving horse, rude anvil, planes, and barrel maker's tools, the mighty "Stonewall" died. He had "crossed over the river," and with him went much of the hope of the Army of Northern Virginia. (DUKE UNIVERSITY LIBRARY)

The South at War

CHARLES P. ROLAND

The tragic vision of decline, yet of seemingly indomitable determination

THE SOUTHERN POPULATION experienced war at close quarters during the conflict. For four years it raged in their midst. It stirred them to heroic sacrifice and endeavor, but in the end it consumed them. It left its mark in their abandoned homes and cities. It left a deeper mark in the graves of a quarter of the region's men of military age, and in the scarred faces and maimed bodies of countless others. Deepest of all was the mark it left on the heart of the South. A century later the memory of defeat and military occupation remained one of the major distinguishing characteristics of the Southern people.

Few Southerners foresaw the disastrous outcome of the struggle, and those who did foresee and warn of it were ridiculed. Spirits soared at the first call to the colors. The Yankees were too crass and mercenary to be good soldiers, Southerners told themselves, and the world's need for Southern cotton would overcome whatever weaknesses there might be in the regional economy. After traveling through the South in 1861, the English newspaper correspondent William Howard Russell wrote: "With France and England to pour gold into their lap with which to purchase all they need in the conflict, they believe they can beat all the powers of the Northern world in arms."

Lightheartedly the South prepared for war, mustering its state militia companies and forming its volunteer Confederate regiments. A rural and traditionally unregimented society, the South in the beginning supported the Confederate effort with a great spontaneous folk movement. Parties and balls, dinners and barbecues, lotteries and raffles, these and a dozen other forms of entertainment were used to raise money, clothing, and arms for "the cause." Patriotic oratory with a Southern accent and bias gave urgency to these occasions. Even the somberness of troop departures for the front was leavened with gaiety, feasting, dancing, and singing of martial airs, along with the sermons and prayers of the ever-present Southern preachers.

The hard days soon arrived as the Federal blockade isolated southern ports and caused shortages and deprivation of imported necessities. Prices quickly spiraled upward and the Confederate currency was devalued. By 1864 the people in Richmond were saying, with grim humor, that they once took money to the market in their wallets and returned with purchases in baskets; now they took money in baskets and returned with purchases in their wallets.

As the war ground on, the Southern masses underwent extreme hardship. Heads of families were not exempt from Confederate military service, and their wives and children were obliged to endure the travails of war alone. They did so with exemplary fortitude, tilling the land, harvesting the crops, and playing an indispensable role in sustaining the armies and keeping the crippled economy alive.

Those areas beyond the immediate reach of invading Federal armies usually had enough food, but such luxuries as sugar and coffee were soon gone. Salt, an almost essential preservative, was extremely rare. Most medicines were practically unobtainable, and the population had to fall back on outmoded home remedies.

Southern city dwellers experienced shortages more severe than those felt by their rural compatriots. This was the result of a rapid increase in the urban population to work in the war factories while at the same time the Southern transport system was taxed beyond its capacity in mobilizing and supplying the armies. Also, the slave labor force was disrupted by the struggle, thus reducing the region's supply of necessities. Whole families in Richmond and other cities lived in single rooms, using the fireplaces for both warmth and cooking, and subsisted on corn fritters, boiled potatoes, and beans.

The greatest suffering occurred in the wake of the grappling armies, and this ultimately covered most of the land. The Federals looted Southern food and supplies because, in part, they lived by foraging, and also because of a desire to inflict punishment for the sin of rebellion. The Confederates were to be feared almost as keenly as the invaders. A Louisiana sugar planter complained that Confederate troops had stripped his plantation of virtually every resource for day-to-day living. "From a condition of ease, comfort and abundance," he wrote, "I am suddenly reduced to one of hardship,

There were many Souths in 1861, but as the war progressed they melded more and more into one, struggling to cope with adversity and survive. There was the South of Richard Habersham's Port Royal plantation, pastoral and carefree . . . (USAMHI)

. . . and there was the South of busy seaports like Charleston and Savannah, bustling with commerce until the blockade left most of the wharves idle. (NA)

want & privation." At this time not a Federal soldier had set foot on his place. The population of Georgia late in the war came to dread the appearance of Confederate Major General Joseph Wheeler's cavalry about as much as they dreaded the approach of General Sherman's columns. Victims of friend as well as foe, countless Southern families were left at the door of starvation.

Recreation and entertainment suffered the effects of wartime shortages and of the absence of many of the men. Music and dancing still took place on plantations and in city mansions, but much of the conviviality was now gone. Food and drink became ever more scarce, and in the final months of the conflict "starvation parties" were held where nothing was served but water. Among the rural common people the usual diversions went on, for they cost but little. The chief differences now were the extreme youth of most of the boys

who were there to take part, or, sadly, the presence of young men with missing limbs or marred features. The folk amusements included square dancing and singing, picnics and barbecues, corn husking, quilting, and spinning bees. Religious revivals were also social occasions. Hunting and fishing, the oldest and most widespread of pastimes among Southern men and boys, remained favorites throughout the conflict and, at the same time, became increasingly important as sources of victuals. The urban poor were less fortunate than the rural poor. Ordinary Southerners living in the cities usually had to be content with such inexpensive activities as neighborly visits, church meetings, open-air band concerts, or military reviews. Ultimately life became too somber for frolics or frivolities anywhere in the stricken South.

As portions of the Confederacy fell to the Union armies, many of the inhabitants, especially among the planter class, left their homes and "refugeed" to Texas or some other temporarily safe place. Taking with them their slaves, valuables, and as many household belongings as possible, they jammed the roads with wagons and carts while the people themselves walked wearily along the edges. They traveled in groups and camped in the fields at night. Their hardships and heartbreak were beyond expression.

State and local governments appropriated funds for the subsistence of soldiers' families. Citizens formed benevolent societies to help the needy. City authorities set up charity markets to collect and distribute produce supplied by planters and farmers of the surrounding areas. Innumerable individuals aided the less fortunate with donations of goods and services. But these measures fell woefully short of the exigencies of the times, and the Confederate government itself attempted no systematic relief of the destitution that spread throughout the population as the war grew in fury.

Loneliness, anxiety, and grief became the constant companions of the people behind the lines. The Confederate postal service broke down almost completely late in the conflict, and the isolation and seclusion of the farms and plantations were maddening. When news did at last arrive, it often contained dread tidings of the death of a loved one in

There were scenes like this, captured by George Barnard in 1866, with the docks crowded with bales of cotton awaiting shipment to foreign ports. (KA)

Forests of masts betold the riches that lay in the precious fiber so entwined with the Southern economy and way of life—and with slavery. (SOUTH CAROLINA HISTORICAL SOCIETY)

camp or battle. A keen observer of the Confederate scene wrote that nearly as many Southern women died of grief and anxiety as did Southern men of Northern bullets.

The Confederacy had no propaganda department and attempted no organized mobilization of the region's cultural and intellectual resources. Yet because of Confederate patriotism and shared beliefs and values, most of the religious, literary, artistic, and educational leaders of the South lent their talents and energies to the Confederate war effort.

It has been said that the churches are perhaps the best places to look for the origins of cultural nationalism in the Old South. The region was overwhelmingly Protestant, and long before the coming of secession the Southern segments of the two largest national Protestant bodies—the Methodists and Baptists—had broken away and formed themselves into separate denominations. Southern churchmen provided the most telling argument in defense of the institution of slavery—the Biblical argument. Thus the Southern churches were also ideal sources of Confederate political nationalism and wartime morale. Southern preachers and theologians justified secession as a fulfillment of God's will and urged their followers to self-sacrifice in the Confederate cause. They condemned the North for its alleged atheism and materialism, and they believed the Lord would uphold the arms of His people of the South in their struggle for independence. Preachers "sounded the trumpets" that called the South to war.

With the coming of secession, the other major Protestant churches (Episcopal, Presbyterian, and Lutheran) broke into Southern and Northern wings. Southern Catholics could not follow this course, but they supported the Confederacy as if they had done so. The role of religion in the Confederate effort was to be seen in the lives of many of the Southern leaders. President Davis, reared in a Baptist family but never before formally a church member, became a convert to the Episcopal faith soon after the Confederate government moved to Richmond. He regularly attended services at St. Paul's Episcopal Church and was there on April 2, 1865, when he received General Robert E. Lee's fateful message saying the capital must be abandoned. Many of the chief military figures of the Confederacy were men of strong religious faith. Lee himself was a devout Episcopalian. His great subordinate, Lieutenant General Thomas J. "Stonewall" Jackson, was just as devout a Presbyterian.

Inland commerce, too, teemed before the war brought it to a near halt. Steamboats like these, photographed at the landing at Chickasaw Bayou, Mississippi, bore a carrying trade that practically disappeared when the Federal gunboats came. (CHS)

Thus were the Southern Cavalier and the Southern Puritan joined in the common cause of Southern defense.

The Reverend Robert Louis Dabney, a noted Presbyterian theologian, served on Jackson's staff, and Lee's chief of artillery, Brigadier General William N. Pendleton, was an Episcopal minister who prayed for the souls of his Northern enemies even as he killed them. When commanding a battery early in the war, Pendleton carried the religious-military theme to its extremity by naming his guns Matthew, Mark, Luke, and John. Apparently he was oblivious to the incongruity of identifying these engines of death with the apostles of peace. Lieutenant General Leonidas Polk, though a graduate of the United States Military Academy, had long been the Episcopal bishop of Louisiana when the war broke out. At various times during the conflict he reverted to his ecclesiastical role. Affected by the prospect of defeat, many other Confederate generals turned to religion late in the war. On the retreat from Sherman's advance through Georgia, the "Fighting Bishop" took time out from his military duties long enough to baptize Generals Joseph E. Johnston and John Bell Hood.

The Confederate government consciously sought to use religion to strengthen the will of the people. On many occasions throughout the war a day was set apart for special prayers and thanksgiving. Perhaps the most vehement Confederate sentiments ever expressed were those in a plantation overseer's prayer on one of these days. He wrote the following passage in the plantation journal:

This Day is set a part by presedent Jefferson Davis for fasting and praying owing to the Deplorable condishion ower Southern country is In My prayer Sincerely to God is that Every Black Republican in the Hole combined whorl Either man women o chile that is opposed to negro slavery as it existed in the Southern confederacy shal be trubled with pestilences & calamitys of all kinds & drag out the Balance of there existence in misry & degradation with Scarsely food & rayment enugh to keep sole & body to geather and O God I pray the to Direct a bullet or a bayonet to pirce the hart of every northern Soldier that invades southern Soil & after the Body has Rendered up its Traterish Sole gave

it a trators reward a Birth in the Lake of fires & Brimstone. My honest convicksion is that Every man women & chile that has gave aid to the abolishionist are fit Subjects for Hell I all so ask the to aide the Sothern confedercy in mantaining ower rites & establishing the confederate Government Believing in this case the prares from the wicked will prevailith much—Amen—.

Congregations held their own prayer meetings in behalf of Confederate success, and great revivals occurred in the armies as civilian missionaries and preachers circulated among the camps and added their voices to those of the chaplains. That religion played an important role in sustaining the fighting spirit of the Southern people, despite the ultimate outcome of the war, seems beyond doubt. Governor Francis W. Pickens of South Carolina said early in the struggle that the South had made it a holy war. A Confederate congressman said later that the clergy had done more than any other class for the Southern effort. "Not even the bayonets have done more."

This might also be said of the press. Journalism was the most vigorous and most widely read form of writing in the Old South. Many Southern newspapers played an important part in bringing on secession, and by the time the war began almost all Southern journals were behind the Confederate cause. But Southern editors were fiercely independent in their views, and they disagreed thoroughly in their attitudes toward President Jefferson Davis and his measures. Nathaniel Tyler's Richmond *Enquirer,* Richard M. Smith's Richmond *Sentinel,* and Richard Yeadon's Charleston *Courier* were so staunch in their support that they came to be looked upon as mouthpieces of the government. Other newspapers were just as strongly hostile. Edward Pollard and John M. Daniel of the Richmond *Examiner* accused Davis of incompetence and tyranny. Robert Barnwell Rhett, the so-called "Father of Secession," was relentless in his diatribes against Davis through the columns of his son's newspaper, the Charleston *Mercury.* Such critics probably would have been silenced in the wartime North, but the Confederate government followed a scrupulous hands-off policy that unquestionably allowed its detractors to cripple the popular morale.

It was a South of small country courthouse towns, towns like Warrenton,
Virginia, whose chief excitement until then lay in the occasional trial in the
courthouse. (USAMHI)

Southern creative writers turned out many works extolling the virtues of the people and their cause. Most of these writings were hastily done and too emotional and sentimental to be of lasting quality. But two South Carolina poets, Henry Timrod and Paul Hamilton Hayne, responded to the exaltation and tragedy of the times with verse of genuine merit. Hayne's best wartime composition was "The Battle of Charleston Harbor," which celebrated the heroic episode named in the title. Timrod, remembered as the poet laureate of the Confederacy, praised what he considered to be the peculiar virtues of his region in "The Cotton Boll" and "Ethnogenesis." His "A Cry to Arms" was a poetic bugle call. His most beautiful piece came after the war in his "Ode" to the Confederate dead buried in the Magnolia Cemetery at Charleston. Its opening lines were:

> Sleep sweetly in your humble graves,
> Sleep, martyrs to a fallen cause,
> Though yet no marble column craves
> The Pilgrim here to pause.
>
> In seeds of laurel in the earth
> The blossom of your fame is blown
> And somewhere, waiting for its birth
> The shaft is in the stone!

The most respected novelist of the Old South, William Gilmore Simms of Charleston, lived through the Civil War and supported the Confederate cause with some poetry and many vigorous

When the armies came to Warrenton in 1862, they found a sleepy market town which had never seen war before. (LC)

editorials. But the conflict seems to have blighted his genuine literary talents. He wrote no novel on the war. Indeed, little fiction came out of the Confederacy; perhaps there was not enough time for it to mature. Best known was the novel *Macaria; or, Altars of Sacrifice* by the popular novelist Augusta Jane Evans of Mobile. The hero of the story dies on a Civil War battlefield, thus fulfilling the author's theme that the people of the South, like the Greek heroine for whom the story is named, ought to lay down their lives in defense of hearth, home, and independence.

Not surprisingly, the Confederate literature of humor lacked the verve and color that distinguished the tales of the great prewar Southern humorists. Life now was too grim for that. Yet humor did survive the hardships of the war. The Confederacy's chief professional humorist, "Bill Arp" [Charles H. Smith of Georgia], entertained his readers with newspaper barbs addressed to "Mr. Abe Linkhorn." Nor did he neglect Confederate foibles. When the Confederacy became swamped in a confusing mass of treasury notes, he quoted the Secretary of the Treasury as saying he was not sure whether the notes in circulation amounted to six hundred million dollars or six thousand million dollars.

Far more suited to the modern ear was the spontaneous humor of many nonprofessional Southerners of the time. For example, take the bold headline in a Jackson, Mississippi, newspaper late in the war:

RAILROAD ACCIDENT
The 10:00 o'clock train
from Meridian
arrived on time today.

Or witness the naughty but clever poem written in response to a request by one John Harrolson of the Niter and Mining Bureau that the women of Selma, Alabama, save their chamber pot contents to provide lye for the manufacture of explosives. The last verse went:

John Harrolson! John Harrolson!
  Do pray invent a neater
And somewhat more modest mode
  Of making your saltpetre;
For tis an awful idea, John,
  gunpowdery and cranky
That when a lady lifts her shift
  she's killing off a Yankee.

Or take this gem of Southern feminine humor: A South Carolina minister preached a sermon on Joseph in Egypt, closing with the pronouncement that the young Hebrew slave, in refusing to be seduced by his master's wife, had resisted the greatest temptation known to man. At this point a young woman in the audience said in a stage whisper: "Fiddlesticks, everybody knows Old Mrs. Pharaoh was every day of forty." Humor remained a source of Confederate morale when most other sources were gone.

The most enduring of Confederate literature was not written as literature at all in the formal sense. This included the diaries and letters of Southerners describing the tumultuous events of the times and the emotions stirred by them. Most of the diaries were by women; they thus provide insights never before revealed into the hearts and minds of the feminine segment of the Southern population. The most celebrated of the diaries is that of Mary Boykin Chesnut of South Carolina, whose husband was a former United States Senator and served throughout most of the war as an aide to Jefferson Davis. Mrs. Chesnut was able to record with striking candor and freshness the affairs of society at the capital of the Confederacy. She was also able to discern the weaknesses of the short-lived republic. Late in the war she said the Confederacy had destroyed itself with internal dissension. One of the most comprehensive collections of family letters was left by the Charles Colcock Jones family of Georgia. They tell the story of Southern travail and heroism with unexcelled poignancy and intimacy.

The Confederacy inherited no strong tradition in the fine arts, nor did it have the time or opportunity to create one. Only in its architecture could the Old South boast of distinguished aesthetic accomplishments—in its great Georgian and neoclassical plantation houses, town houses, and public buildings. The war put an end to the construction of houses and destroyed or damaged many that were already standing. Yet the fine arts did not fail to serve the Southern cause. Theaters were active in all Southern cities, especially in Richmond and Charleston. Shakespearean plays and other classic works continued to be staged. But patriotic or comical themes with hastily contrived and banal plots tended to replace the old favorites. Popular productions of this nature included John Hill Hewitt's *King Linkum the First*, Joseph Hodgson's *The Confederate Vivandière*, and J. J. Delchamp's *Great Expectations: or, Getting Promoted*. Minstrels and other cheap comedy productions catered to the lower economic and social classes. All offered a means of escape from the terrible burdens of real life. Southern painters and sculptors also turned their talents to patriotic works, depicting war scenes or producing likenesses of well-known Confederate officers. Perhaps the most popular painting done in the Confederacy was William Washington's "The Burial of Latané," which captured the pride and pathos attending the funeral of a young officer killed during Jeb Stuart's daring ride around McClellan's army early in the war.

Music was the most popular and most sustaining art form of the South, being ideally suited to the martial spirit of the age. But the music that most distinguishes the region is its folk music, which at the time of the Civil War was not yet committed to formal composition. Ironically, the most stirring songs of the Confederacy were written by out-

Culpeper, Virginia, was much the same until the tented fields bespoke that warring armies had come to stay. (P-M)

siders: the "national anthem" of the Confederacy, "Dixie," by Daniel Emmett of Ohio, as a prewar minstrel tune; and "The Bonnie Blue Flag" by Harry McCarthy, an Irish immigrant. Many other songs caught the emotions of the Southern people at war. Among these were "Maryland, My Maryland," "The Yellow Rose of Texas," and "Somebody's Darling," a heartrending piece about a young soldier killed in the line of duty.

Southern schools were quick to feel the damaging effects of the war. Many of the region's most distinguished educators were from the North, and a number of them resigned their positions and left the South when the states where they were teaching seceded from the Union. Perhaps the outstanding example was the resignation of President Frederick A. P. Barnard of the University of Mississippi, who was later to become the president of Columbia College in New York City. A more memorable instance was that of the president of the Louisiana State Seminary and Military Academy, who left his academic post to become one of the most renowned leaders of the Union Army—William Tecumseh Sherman.

But many other college teachers were native Southerners who remained to support their region in the war. Some of them provided essential services to the Confederacy. For example, Professor John W. Mallet of the University of Alabama used his scientific knowledge to invent an improved artillery shell and to supervise the preparation of chemicals for the manufacture of explosives. The famed brother scientists from South Carolina, John and Joseph LeConte, placed their expertise at the disposal of the Confederate Niter and Mining Bureau.

Unable to purchase textbooks, as was the usual custom, from Northern firms, the South set about to supply its own, and soon a number of such volumes were on the market. Though they were inferior to the Northern books because of a lack of good paper and experienced editing, they pleased their readers with sound Confederate sentiments. M. B. Moore's *Geographical Reader for Dixie Children* pictured the South as a Christian land of benign masters and happy slaves. Even the arithmetic books were filled with Confederate indoctrination. They followed the lead of a book produced before the war by Daniel Harvey Hill, then a college mathematics professor and later a Confederate general. In his *Elements of Algebra* Hill included problems with illustrations of Yankee peddlers who allegedly mixed wooden nutmegs with the real ones they sold to unsuspecting Southern housewives. Hill's book also contained an illustration involving Indiana volunteers who ran away from the fighting in the battle of Buena Vista in the Mexican War. Johnson's *Elementary Arithmetic,* published during the Civil War, adopted a similar theme with such illustrations as: "If one Confederate soldier can whip 7 Yankees, how many Confederate soldiers can whip 49 Yankees?"

Southern schools soon lost many of their teachers to the armed forces, and before the war was over most of the college students were also gone. Those of conscription age were not exempt from service; even if they had been exempt, they probably would have volunteered because of their intense Confederate feelings. Ultimately most of the region's colleges closed down; those that remained in opera-

tion had a mere handful of faculty and students. Nor did the lower-level schools escape. Many of the region's private "academies," the mainstay of precollege education in the Old South, were obliged to close for lack of money. The public schools, which in a majority of the Southern states were weak at best, suffered from inferior teaching as unqualified women or old men replaced the regular teachers who were now in uniform. Only in North Carolina, where Superintendent Calvin Wiley was able to prevail upon Governor Zebulon Vance to keep the public schools in his budget, did they continue to operate in a fairly normal way. The Southern educational system barely survived the war. In many places it failed to do so.

Negro Southerners, especially the almost four million slaves who made up the vast majority of the group, received the greatest benefits from the Civil War: They gained their freedom. But during the course of the war they may have suffered more than anyone else. In the Confederate interior before the arrival of the Northern armies, the slaves

Dusty streets that had known only farmers' wagons became accustomed to the booted heels of the soldier, both friend and invader. (NA)

*Military wagons filled the streets, with prisoners of war and wounded often
billeted in the courthouses and churches, as shown here in Culpeper.* (MUSEUM
OF THE CONFEDERACY)

continued their labors almost as if nothing unusual
was afoot. True, their efficiency tended to drop
where no white man was still in charge, but generally their productivity remained high. Louisiana
slaves harvested and ground the greatest sugar crop
in the history of the industry during the first year
of the war. At the midpoint of the conflict, long
after the issuance of the Emancipation Proclamation, Union soldiers in Louisiana were astonished at the immensity of the corn crops they
found being grown by slave labor on plantations
recently converted from sugar. According to one of
them, the soldiers scoffed at the "ponderous articles" appearing in Northern newspapers saying the
Confederacy was about to be starved into submis-
sion. Virginia slaves were, to a marked degree, responsible for that state's great behind-the-lines
strength during the four years that most of its able-
bodied white men were in uniform.

As the Northern forces penetrated into the Confederacy, the slaves flocked away from the plantations and assembled around the Union encampments in a great "jubilee" of freedom. Torn from
their moorings and destitute of the means of livelihood, Negroes doubtless would have been ravaged
by starvation and disease had not the Union armies
provided rations and medical attention for them.
Many succumbed in spite of this assistance. A
Louisiana planter wrote in pity that the occupants
of a nearby runaway camp were living in "the
most abject misery Degredation & Filth," and that
they were dying by the hundreds. Such scenes
caused some Northern soldiers to predict the demise of the entire race in the South.

Perhaps the most remarkable thing about the behavior of Negroes was that they did not resort to
insurrection. The South, as always, seethed with
rumors of impending slave violence. Northern ab-

olitionists, as always, expected to see it. Joshua Giddings of Ohio was convinced that the appearance of a force of 40,000 freedom soldiers would set off an upheaval of cataclysmic proportions, a mistaken conviction that the Southern bondsmen were eager to rise like the rebellious slaves of ancient Rome. Southern authorities tightened the restrictions in their slave codes; patrols and home-guard military organizations exerted a vigilance not usually found in the lackadaisical South. There were scattered efforts among the bondsmen to stage an uprising. About 134,000 Negroes from the Confederate states were enlisted in the Union armies; large numbers died in uniform. Many individual Negroes committed deeds of sabotage against the Confederacy or otherwise rendered aid to the invaders. Sometimes the Negroes became fractious with their masters. On rare occasions the Negroes resorted to violence; they often pillaged, especially places that had been abandoned by the owners, for the slaves believed the Lord had authorized a latter-day "spoiling on the Egyptians."

But the Negroes did not rebel. Just why they did not do so is difficult to determine. Possibly they were unwilling to take the risk. One of them explained the conduct of his people fatalistically, saying, "I see no use of us going and getting ourselves into trouble. If so be it we are to get free, we get it anyhow . . . We think it betterer to stay home on the plantation, and get our food and our clothes. If we are to get freedom, dar we are! But, if we run away . . . where is we?" Probably many slaves refrained from violence because of genuine affection for kind masters. After the war, Mary Boykin Chesnut wrote that the "fidelity" of the Negroes was a principal topic of conversation in South Carolina. "There seems not a single case of a Negro who betrayed his master." Such statements of slave loyalty were gross exaggerations. Yet the slaves did not take advantage of the opportunity to revolt. Through the travail of invasion and the exultation of freedom the South was spared the horrors of a war of the races.

Southern women supported the Confederacy

The war disrupted the thousands of little railroad siding hamlets that dotted the South. (CHS)

with unexcelled devotion. They upheld the righteousness of a war for Southern independence, encouraged men to enlist, and shamed those who hesitated to do so. They formed "sulk and pout" clubs to indicate their displeasure with "unpatriotic" males; sometimes they sent them petticoats as tokens of contempt. The women vowed to take up arms and go forth into battle if need be to assure the success of the South. Northern soldiers believed them more militant than the men. Henry Timrod paid tribute to their zeal with these lines:

> Does any falter? let him turn
> To some brave maiden's eyes,
> And catch the holy fires that burn
> In those sublunar skies.
>
> Oh! could you like your women feel,
> and in their spirit march,
> A day might see your lines of steel
> Beneath the victor's arch.

The greatest contribution made by women to the Confederate effort was in filling the jobs left by the multitude of men who were under arms. In addition to managing plantations and working farms, the women made uniforms for the Quartermaster Department and cartridges for the Ordnance Department. They served as clerks in the government bureaus, taught school, and did hundreds of other tasks normally done by men. Doubtless the women of the Old South were never the delicate butterflies of popular legend. Certainly the women of the Confederacy were not. They played a vital role in supplying their cause with its "sinews of war."

A few Southern women entered the Confederate Army disguised as men. Others served glamorously and importantly as spies. The most famous of these, Belle Boyd, repeatedly came through the Union lines with information that was useful to the Confederate commanders. Mrs. Rose O'Neal Greenhow was drowned in an attempt to get through the Union naval blockade while on an official mission for the Confederacy.

Perhaps the most celebrated heroines of the Confederacy were the women who ministered to the sick or wounded soldiers. They helped to estab-

Everywhere the local calm gave way to the overpowering sense of change and displacement of war. (CHS)

Only the shantytowns on the fringes of the larger cities seemed unaffected.
Even the armies avoided slums like "Slabtown," located outside Hampton,
Virginia. O'Sullivan's camera did not. (USAMHI)

Here in "Slabtown" there was no room for the armies—and precious little for
the Southerners who lived there. (USAMHI)

The major Southern cities showed the marks of war in direct proportion to their proximity to the front. Alexandria was the first front, facing Washington across the Potomac. Streets were frequently barricaded to control traffic into and out of the Northern-held but pro-Southern city. (USAMHI)

Evidence of the Northern occupiers was everywhere. The provost's building in Alexandria had once been the Marine and Fire Insurance Offices. (WRHS)

*Military governors, like Brigadier General John P. Slough, seated at center,
ruled in Alexandria and other Southern cities. Many were kind, and most were
vilified.* (USAMHI)

lish the improvised hospitals of the early campaigns, often supplying food and medicine directly
from their own homes. At times they risked their
lives tending disabled soldiers under fire. Twice
wounded on the battlefield in this work, Mrs.
Arthur F. Hopkins earned from General Joseph E.
Johnston the title "Angel of the South." Ella King
Newsom became the "Florence Nightingale" of the
Confederate Army. Kate Cumming, Phoebe
Pember, and Louisa Susanna McCord were famous as hospital matrons. "Heaven only knows,"

wrote a foreign observer, "what the soldiers of the
South would have done without the exertions of
the women in their behalf."

Ultimately the fierce Confederate patriotism of
the Southern women yielded before the realities
of war. Their demoralization was a major cause of
Confederate collapse. Moved by the appeals of
countless women to have their men exempted from
conscription, a War Department official wrote:
"The iron is gone deep into the heart of society."
Letters from distraught wives were a major reason

None attracted greater condemnation than Major General Benjamin F. Butler. He so managed to antagonize the people of New Orleans that he was branded an outcast by Confederate authorities and was not entitled to the usual courtesies of war should he be captured. He and others like him made potent weapons for Southern anti-Yankee propaganda. (INTERNATIONAL MUSEUM OF PHOTOGRAPHY)

Brigadier General Richard Busteed had bitterly opposed Lincoln's election in 1860, but in 1862 he was entrusted with occupation duty protecting Fort Monroe in Virginia. He would later be a Federal judge in Alabama, and would be accused of fraud. (NA)

for desertion from Confederate ranks. Most of them described genuine destitution and a growing conviction that all the sacrifice was futile, that the war was irretrievably lost. Which soldier could resist such a letter as the following from his wife? "Before God, Edward, Unless you come home we must die. Last night I was aroused by little Eddie's crying . . . He said 'Oh, mamma, I'm, so hungry!' And Lucy, Edward, your darling Lucy, she never complains, but she is growing thinner and thinner every day."

The emotions of the Southern people at war surged and ebbed with the tides of victory or de-

feat on the battlefield. In the beginning the Confederates were gay and hopeful, naively believing the struggle would be quickly won by them. Brilliant early successes—bought, as they were, with heavy sacrifice of life—created a sense of mingled exaltation and grief that was akin to a religious experience in intensity. But enthusiasm waned as the conflict lengthened, the toll in casualties mounted, and the faith in ultimate victory disappeared. Late in the war a Louisiana planter expressed the prevailing mood in the following lines in his diary: "The days (emphatically days of darkness & gloom) succeed each other bringing nothing but despondency with regard to the future . . . The Lord help us. —Such is war, civil war."

The homes, great and small, of Southerners became fair game for Federal officers seeking headquarters. Dr. Murray's home in Fauquier County, Virginia, was captured in this image taken in November 1863 by O'Sullivan after it had been appropriated for the use of some Yankee brass. (P-M)

The Marye house behind Fredericksburg became a Federal office for a time after its bloody part in the battles of December 1862 and May 1863. Rifle pits are still evident in the left foreground of this May 1864 image. (P-M)

General Meade made his September 1863 Culpeper headquarters at the home of a Mr. Wallach. Generally the occupiers took scrupulous care of the properties thus appropriated, paying for damages done by them and their soldiers. (P-M)

In September 1863 these Federals occupied the home of John Minor Botts, a famous Culpeper resident who had been a congressman and bitter opponent of secession. The Confederates imprisoned him in Richmond for his disloyal sentiments. (P-M)

The Fauquier Springs Hotel in August 1862, as seen by O'Sullivan. It was occupied by the advancing Federals during the Second Manassas campaign. (P-M)

It was the same in the West, though generally on a less grand scale. Brigadier General Grenville Dodge had to make his divisional headquarters in Corinth, Mississippi, in this much less imposing home. (CHS)

Homes not made headquarters all too often became hospitals, like this home on the Manassas battlefield, caught in July 1862 by O'Sullivan. (LC)

The destruction and displacement caused by the war in the South was on a scale that no one could have anticipated. Tens of thousands of civilians, usually women and children, had to flee the advancing enemy for refugee havens in the interior. They took what they could with them, including granny's pipe. (LC)

Thousands of rural Southern scenes like this unidentified spot bore witness to the destructive force of the contending armies. Southern men in shirtsleeves and suspenders survey the wreckage of what was perhaps a store, a courthouse, or a home, now reduced to rubble, its foundation an echo of a place where Southerners once lived or worked. (CWTI)

Once beautiful places like Fauquier Springs were destroyed, leaving only haunting reminders of their former grandeur. (P-M)

Even churches bore the bullet and shot holes of the battle. This one in
Fredericksburg looks almost abandoned. (P-M)

Hampton, Virginia, lay largely in ruins after the early fighting of 1862.
(USAMHI)

George Barnard found the main entrance to Hampton Church on July 2, 1862,
as much a tombstone as the markers in its cemetery. (NLM)

It had been the oldest Protestant church in America. Now it was a hollow shell.
(NLM)

Industry, too, suffered in the South. Never well advanced prior to 1861, Southern industry was overtaxed by the war and was often the target of Union destructiveness. Small companies like the Schofield Iron Works of Macon, Georgia, were hard pressed to meet the demand for weapons and munitions. (COURTESY OF HERB PECK, JR.)

The Confederacy built some of its own industry, though on a very limited scale. The Augusta Powder Works in Georgia was one such plant. (LC)

It was the brainchild of Colonel George Washington Rains, an inventive and dedicated Confederate engineer. His brother was a brigadier general. (COURTESY OF THE AUGUSTA-RICHMOND COUNTY MUSEUM)

Yet there was also a quiet life in the South during the war, a few places seemingly untouched by the sword. Bowling Green Court House in Caroline County, Virginia, seems almost a still life. Restaurant bills of fare, a recruiting poster, and attorney's shingles crowd its pillars and trees. (P-M)

The market square in Norfolk, Virginia, bustles with the same trading activity as before the war. This image by the Kilburn brothers of New Hampshire may have been taken just after the war. (USAMHI)

Armistead and White of Corinth captured Southern laborers going about the same business that they had done for generations, only now sometimes under the watchful eye of a Federal officer. (CHS)

There were still quiet moments, as in this image of a man and a woman out shopping in Winchester, Virginia. (WINCHESTER-FREDERICK COUNTY HISTORICAL SOCIETY)

The people who were left behind carried on their lives much as they had before the war. A croquet match on the lawn at Patellus House in Virginia seemed entirely natural in the midst of war. (LC)

There was even the occasional idyllic scene. This is the Big Spring at
Huntsville, Alabama, in 1863. It seems more like a genre painting by George
Caleb Bingham than a photograph. All that betrays the wartime aspect of the
image is the fact that there are no young men, only old men and boys. The rest
are off to war. (USAMHI)

The rivers and lakes were still flooded in the spring, as seen here near
Huntsville. (CHS)

The Big Spring a year later, taken by Armistead and Taylor of Corinth. The Federals are much in evidence now, and they have considerably improved the spring house. (CHS)

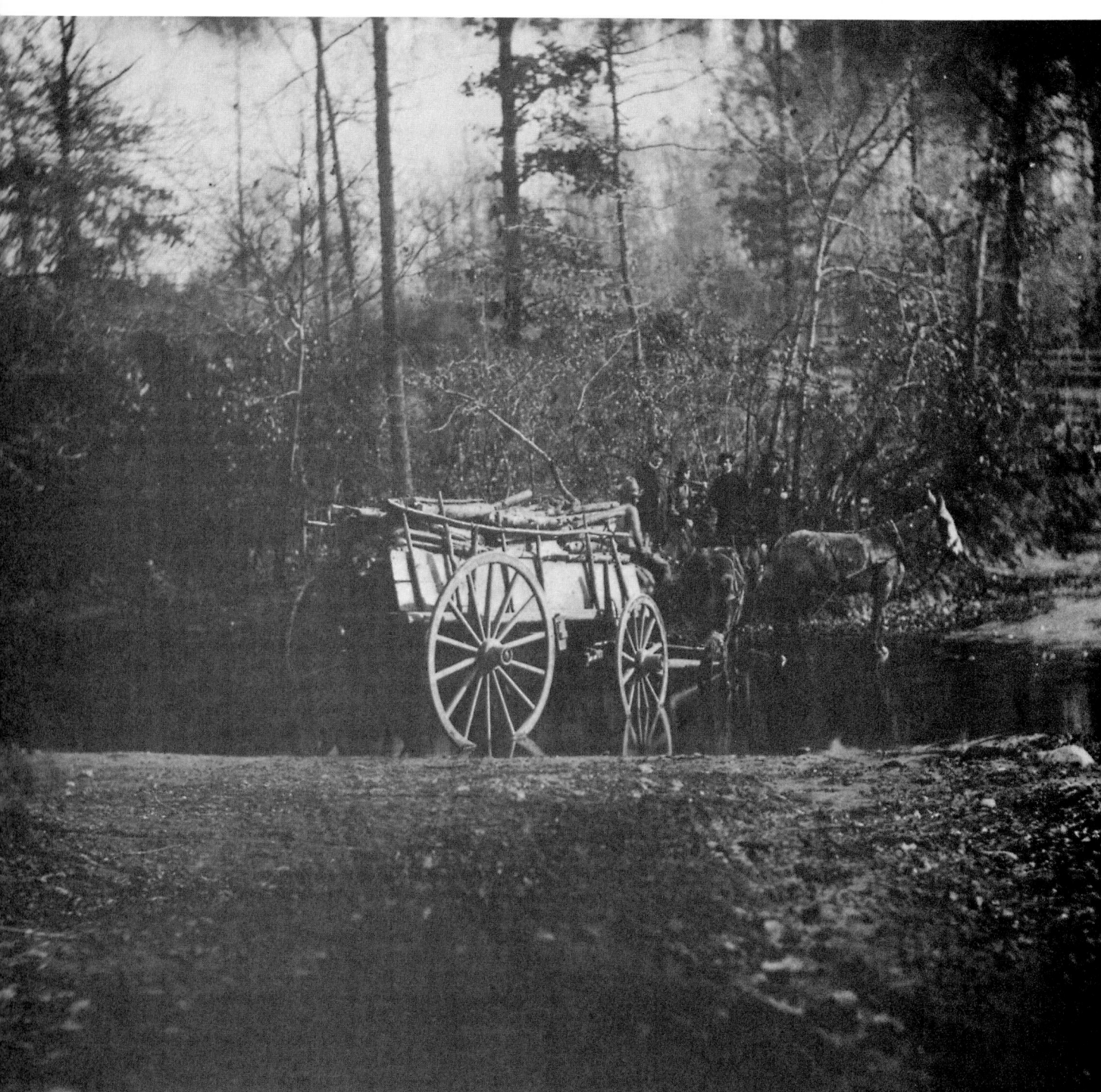

A lonely mule team could still be seen crossing a brook in Virginia. Some things never changed. (LC)

*People in marshy areas and in the Everglades of Florida still lived on the water
and traded on it as before, as in this scene not far from Jacksonville captured
by Shaw and Sons of Jacksonville.* (CHS)

*Confederate women still gathered with their children to talk over their sewing.
Here they do so outside the house where General Charles Winder died on
Cedar Mountain.* (LC)

*They met for play and picnics, though sometimes amid scenery that would
have seemed foreign prior to the war. Here, in South Carolina, women and
children play beside a Confederate "David" torpedo boat. One young man
pokes his head out through the top hatch.* (VM)

*In Florida people still enjoyed the shade of the
palm trees and coconuts.* (USAMHI)

The church, always important in Southern life, assumed new proportions. With
the Almighty on their side, Southerners met to fervently invoke His assistance in
the field. Christ Church in Alexandria heard more than one prayer for
Jefferson Davis and the Confederacy. (USAMHI)

Of course, not all the Southern clergy were so loyal
to the South. "Parson" William G. Brownlow of
Tennessee was an ardent pro-Union advocate, even
publishing a newspaper called the Whig and Rebel
Ventilator. (NYHS)

Education, already backward as compared to the rest of the nation, suffered a setback during the war, yet universities like the University of Virginia managed to continue to graduate students, though fewer and younger, as the war lured the young men from the classroom to the battlefield. Jefferson's rotunda is shown here in what is perhaps an early postwar image. (VM)

The legal machinery and state governments continued to function, even to flourish, in some places. Courthouses and state capitol buildings like this one all across the South continued to be centers of business and politics as they had been before the war. (CHS)

Military schools, always popular in the South, continued with their studies, though the boys tended to be younger than before. The Citadel in Charleston, shown here, sent many a young officer into the Confederate Army. (COURTESY OF JOHN A. HESS)

Public libraries struggled to maintain the literary tradition of the South, often against the greater demands of war. This public library in Beaufort, South Carolina, became a contraband hospital. (USAMHI)

The disruption of the labor force in the South, as slaves fled to contraband camps, left much work to be done by those unused to it—and much that simply remained undone. Here slaves on Joseph Davis's plantation near Vicksburg have set aside their tools to await freedom. (KA)

Yet even for the slaves much of life continued as normal: menial work for little
or no compensation. Only the promise of freedom gave them more cheer than
most of the their white Southern brethren. (ONONDAGA HISTORICAL ASSOCIATION)

It was a war that affected the young. Cadet
Private Thomas Jefferson, a relative of the
President and a student at Lexington's Virginia
Military Institute, went to war with the VMI
Cadets at the age of seventeen. In battle at New
Market, on May 15, 1864, he took a mortal
wound. (COURTESY OF NEW MARKET BATTLEFIELD
PARK)

And the war took the old. An old Rebel sits here with an Enfield musket, providing an eloquent comment on the strain on Southern society when the armed forces had to turn to the aged and the young for manpower. (COURTESY OF HERB PECK, JR.)

The war affected even the mighty and powerful. Vice-President Alexander H. Stephens saw his nephew go into the Confederate service and posed with him for the camera. (PRIVATE COLLECTION)

State governors and politicians like Milledge L. Bonham of South Carolina often had to lay aside their statesman's black broadcloth to don the Confederate gray in defending their states. (USAMHI)

*Families went to war. Corporal William H. Martin of the 7th Louisiana poses
with his father, James, a captain in the Algiers Battalion of the Louisiana
Militia. The father looks more like a Revolutionary soldier—and was nearly old
enough to have been one.* (LOUISIANA HISTORICAL ASSOCIATION)

Another elderly member of the Continental Guard, as it was sometimes called.
(THE HISTORIC NEW ORLEANS COLLECTION)

Families and friends often had to collect their tinware, old clothes, and other castoff items to salvage what could be used, as shown here on the Davis plantation. (KA)

Women, of course, bore the brunt of maintaining the home front, but a few would not settle for that and had to take a more active part in the war. Belle Boyd became a celebrated, if much overrated, female spy for the Confederacy. (CHS)

Phoebe Y. Pember left her comfortable home to spend the war working as a nurse in Richmond's overflowing hospitals, particularly the mammoth Chimborazo military hospital. (COURTESY OF FANNY U. PHILLIPS)

The children of President Jefferson Davis felt the pain of war. They are shown here in Montreal just after the surrender. There should have been a fifth child, the son who fell from the Executive Mansion balcony in 1864 and died as a result of the fall. Davis, called from a meeting to be told the news, steeled his nerves and, exhibiting iron self-control, returned to complete the important military conference. The sadness of war touched everyone. (LC)

The children grew up playing at war. John Y. Mason Anderson—son of Brigadier General Joseph R. Anderson, who managed Richmond's Tredegar Iron Works, makers of much of the South's ordnance—played in his little zouave suit of red kepi, pantaloons, blue tunic, and vest. (VM)

But, always, the most constant reminder of the war for those in the South was the wounded and maimed. Charles Rees of Richmond focused his camera to capture the image of an unidentified officer with his crutches. The war sapped the strength of Southern men and women at home as much as on the battlefield, leaving the entire section on crutches by 1865. It would require a long and painfully slow recovery from the wounds the war inflicted on an entire section of America. (VM)

The Guns at Gettysburg

WILLIAM A. FRASSANITO

A Pennsylvania summer is shattered
by the greatest battle of the war

BY THE END of May 1863, the war in the eastern theater was progressing well for the Confederacy. Having recently won two major battles at
Fredericksburg and Chancellorsville, Robert E.
Lee, in consultation with President Davis, determined that the time had once again arrived for a
bold thrust northward.

Despite high expectations, the immediate goals
for the 1863 invasion were nevertheless quite realistic. Of primary concern was the fact that northern
Virginia desperately needed a breathing spell. By
forcing the war out of Virginia and into enemy territory, a Southern invasion would almost certainly
disrupt Union offensive plans for the upcoming
summer months, thereby relieving pressure on the
Confederate capital at Richmond. Additionally,
Virginia farmers would thus be able to tend to
their much-needed crops without interruption.

If all went well, and a substantial penetration
into enemy territory was achieved, Lee's army
would be able to live off of the land, and by threatening and perhaps even capturing one or more
major Northern cities, the already downhearted
Northern populace might be convinced to support
a political peace settlement. Finally, Lee hoped
that the invasion might relieve pressure on the vi-
tally important Confederate city of Vicksburg,

Mississippi, then struggling for its very survival
against Union forces under General Grant.

With the advent of June, Lee's Army of Northern Virginia and Joseph Hooker's Army of the Potomac faced each other at Fredericksburg. Lee's
command totaled some 75,000 men. In the wake
of Jackson's much-lamented death the month before, it had been reorganized into three infantry
corps: I under A. P. Hill, II under Richard S.
Ewell, and III under James Longstreet. The cavalry was commanded by J.E.B. Stuart.

Numbering roughly 97,000, the opposing Army
of the Potomac was composed of seven infantry
corps: I under John F. Reynolds, II under
Winfield S. Hancock, III under Daniel E. Sickles,
V under George Sykes, VI under John Sedgwick,
XI under O. O. Howard, and XII under Henry
W. Slocum. The Union cavalry was commanded
by Alfred Pleasonton.

Under a veil of secrecy, Lee shifted his army
westward on June 3, 1863, first concentrating in
the vicinity of Culpeper and then moving into the
Shenandoah Valley, where he could march northward while using the mountains as a shield. His
cavalry protected the mountain gaps.

Initially unaware of Lee's intentions, Hooker
sensed that a major enemy movement was under

way following a severe cavalry engagement at Brandy Station on June 9. Urged on by the Lincoln administration, Hooker cautiously followed Lee northward, keeping his army east of the mountains and between Washington and the enemy. On June 15 the vanguard of Lee's forces overwhelmed a Union force under General Robert Milroy at Winchester and continued northward. By June 28 all three Confederate corps had crossed the Mason-Dixon Line; although widely scattered between Chambersburg, Carlisle, and York, they were nevertheless converging steadily on the Pennsylvania state capital at Harrisburg.

In the meanwhile, tension between Hooker and the Lincoln administration reached the breaking point due to Washington's increasing lack of confidence in the Union commander subsequent to the Battle of Chancellorsville. Finally, on June 28, George G. Meade replaced Hooker. June 28 was a critical date in the history of the invasion not only because of this last-minute change in Union commanders but also because it was on this date that Lee first received intelligence that the enemy had crossed the Potomac River and was closing in on his widely dispersed forces. This information came as a surprise to him, for he had been depending on Stuart to keep him informed of enemy movements. Unbeknownst to Lee, his cavalry commander, then involved in a bold raid east of the Union Army, had lost all contact with the main invading force.

Reacting swiftly to this latest intelligence, Lee ordered his detached elements to concentrate at Cashtown, a small hamlet located at the mountains between Chambersburg and Gettysburg. Here Lee would prepare to receive the advance of the Union Army. Thus, by the end of June 1863 Lee's forces, although converging on Cashtown, lay situated generally west and north of Gettysburg, while Meade's Army of the Potomac pressed northward in the direction of Gettysburg from points in the vi-

Another campaign is on the way, another battle to come, another meeting between the minions of North and South, and yet one more opportunity for the Army of the Potomac to retrieve its reputation after so many defeats. Perhaps this time there will be a victory. Here, at headquarters near Fairfax Court House, Virginia, in June 1863, the leaders watch and wait. (USAMHI)

Here, too, the leaders change. Even as the unvanquished Robert E. Lee is leading his Army of Northern Virginia on an invasion into Pennsylvania, the high command shifts in the Union Army. "Fighting Joe" Hooker will fight no more in Virginia. On June 28, 1863, his command passed to the steady, reliable, and cantankerous Major General George Gordon Meade, standing in the center of this group photographed at Culpeper, Virginia, three months later. The rest are members of his staff who served him well in the coming battle. (USAMHI)

cinity of Frederick, Taneytown, and Emmitsburg, Maryland. Neither army knew exactly where the other was on June 30, the day advanced Union cavalry units under General John Buford reached the borough of Gettysburg in search of the invading army.

Prior to that summer there was little to distinguish Gettysburg from countless communities of similar size throughout the nation. With a population of 2,400, and located just ten miles north of the Mason-Dixon Line, Gettysburg possessed a moderately thriving carriage industry which had

relied heavily on retail markets in Maryland and Virginia before the war. The borough's chief claim to fame, however, rested in its two institutions of higher learning, the Lutheran Theological Seminary and Pennsylvania College (Gettysburg College).

Having reached the town on the last day of June, Buford's cavalry established a picket line beyond the Lutheran Seminary to cover the approaches from the west. By chance a brigade of Confederate infantry under General John Pettigrew of Heth's division, Hill's corps, had been

Serving Meade as well were his headquarters guard, the 93rd New York.
Theirs was an easy service, for a headquarters guard rarely saw action. Here
Company E poses in August 1863 near the Rappahannock. (USAMHI)

sent to Gettysburg from the direction of Cashtown to secure supplies that same day. Upon sighting the Union pickets, Pettigrew retired westward to report the enemy's presence.

Early on the morning of July 1, 1863, two Confederate brigades, Archer's and Davis's (also of Heth's division), were dispatched toward Gettysburg to investigate. It was entirely possible that the Northern cavalrymen were nothing more than local militia. The skirmish that ensued quickly escalated into a heated encounter as Buford's troopers offered stiff resistance to the probing enemy reconnaisance.

General Buford, deciding that his position was tenable, and aware that the Union I and XI Corps were then situated just a short distance to the south (in the direction of Emmitsburg), chose to hold his ground and send for help. The Confederates did the same, and before long both armies marched toward Gettysburg in their entirety. Thus it was that a chance encounter between relatively small units ultimately decided the ground upon which the decisive battle of the campaign would be fought.

Prior to that morning neither Lee nor Meade had intended to fight at Gettysburg.

For nearly two hours the hard-pressed cavalrymen, fighting dismounted, held off repeated enemy assaults in the vicinity of the McPherson farm. Shortly before ten o'clock Buford's force was relieved by the arrival of Reynolds's I Corps. As elements of Wadsworth's division of that corps crossed an unfinished railroad cut north of the Chambersburg Pike and formed a line of battle to engage Davis's Confederate brigade, Archer's Confederates were renewing their pressure against McPherson's Woods, south of the Pike. Reynolds himself directed the Iron Brigade into McPherson's Woods when he fell to enemy rifle fire. Killed instantly, John F. Reynolds, second in command of the Army of the Potomac and the highest ranking officer from either side to fall at Gettysburg, ironically died during the earliest stages of the three-day battle.

With Reynolds's death, command of I Corps devolved upon Abner Doubleday, whose men continued to maintain their lines against heavy enemy assaults. In a subsequent maneuver against the railroad cut, elements of I Corps succeeded in capturing a large number of Mississippians of Davis's brigade.

At about midday a lull which extended into the early afternoon fell over the field. During this interlude Robert Rodes's Confederate division of Ewell's corps arrived at Oak Ridge, north of the Union line, and soon began to press the extreme right flank of I Corps, held by Baxter's and Paul's brigades of Robertson's division. This threat to the Union right, however, was reduced by the timely arrival of Howard's XI Corps, which, after marching through the streets of Gettysburg, formed a line of battle in the open fields just north of Pennsylvania College. Howard's line extended the Union right flank to a small hill known as Barlow's Knoll.

By 2 P.M. the fighting had resumed in earnest, as elements of Hill's and Ewell's powerful corps advanced against the Union I and XI Corps along a nearly two-mile arc traversing the western and northern approaches to Gettysburg. Unfortunately for the Army of the Potomac, Howard's corps was the last to reach the field in time to engage the enemy on July 1. For the Confederates the situation was just the opposite, and by midafternoon Southern reinforcements still arrived in large numbers. At about four o'clock General Jubal Early's newly arrived division of Ewell's Corps struck Union General Francis Barlow's division on the exposed right flank of the XI Corps. Within a short while Barlow's division, and then Howard's entire line, began to crumble.

Retreating into Gettysburg from the northern

The new campaign drew first blood well before Meade's accession, when the cavalry of Blue and Gray clashed at Brandy Station. Brigadier General Alfred Pleasonton, shown here less than two months before the fight, led the Federal cavalry in its first real victory over the Confederate horsemen, the first true cavalry battle of the war. Better yet, after Brandy Station the Yankee horse soldiers never again felt inferior. (USAMHI)

sector of the field, Howard's men were joined by retreating elements of I Corps, who had almost simultaneously succumbed to Confederate pressure in the vicinity of the McPherson farm. Unfamiliar with the streets and back alleys of the town, and falling back from two different directions, north and west, hundreds of Union soldiers became disoriented as they sought the shelter of Cemetery Hill, a predesignated reserve position located on the southern outskirts of town. In superior numbers the jubilant Confederates followed their distraught foe into the borough streets and succeeded in capturing not only the entire town but some 2,500 Union soldiers as well.

Lee's forces made no attempt to storm Cemetery Hill that evening. Instead, the Confederate commander, having established his headquarters across from the Thompson house on the Chambersburg Pike, began the task of consolidating his lines in preparation for the next day's battle. As the fighting on July 1 drew to a close, Cemetery Hill was fortified by Union forces with the intention of using that point as the nucleus for a new defensive line.

By the next morning Meade had arrived on the field, and the Northern lines were rapidly assuming what has since become known as the "fishhook" formation. Cemetery Hill, defended by the remnants of XI Corps, became the curve of the fishhook, while the heavily wooded Culp's Hill, located just to the east, was occupied by the recently arrived XII Corps. The latter hill became the hook, or right flank, of the Union line. The shank of the formation was eventually occupied by Hancock's II Corps and extended southward along the open fields on Cemetery Ridge. Sickles's III Corps would occupy the extreme Union left.

Little fighting, aside from the scattered fire of opposing skirmishers, occurred throughout the morning and early afternoon of July 2, as both sides prepared for the second day's action. Although it was Lee's design to strike both Union flanks at the same time, the attack was delayed for several hours as Longstreet attempted to maneuver his corps, undetected, into the line of battle on the southern extension of Seminary Ridge, located parallel to the Union positions on Cemetery Ridge.

As Longstreet marched and countermarched his troops behind the Confederate lines, Union General Sickles decided to advance his entire III Corps from its position in the vicinity of the imposing hill known as Little Round Top—the left flank, or eye, of the fishhook—to a more forward position located closer to the Confederate lines. By the time Longstreet was ready to attack, Sickles's new line extended northwestward from the enormous boulders in Devil's Den, through the Rose Woods and the Wheat Field, and then turned sharply northeastward at the Peach Orchard, where it continued along the Emmitsburg Road.

Birney's division held Sickles's left, while A. A. Humphreys's division held the right flank of the III Corps line, which at best was placed precariously and was difficult to defend. Not only did Sickles fail to connect his right flank to the left of II Corps, leaving an ominous gap between the two commands, but he also neglected to occupy the most important single terrain feature in his sector, namely, Little Round Top. Only the last-minute efforts of General Gouverneur Warren, Meade's chief of engineers, saved the hill from certain capture by vanguard elements of Longstreet's assaulting force.

The Confederate attack against the Union left began a short while after four o'clock on the afternoon of July 2. The first points to be struck were Little Round Top, which had been occupied by Union infantry just ten minutes before the arrival of Hood's division of Longstreet's corps, and Devil's Den, which fell to Hood's men after a bitter struggle lasting more than an hour. In successive waves the various brigades of Longstreet's corps stormed into the Rose Woods, the Wheat Field, and advanced against III Corps positions at the Peach Orchard and along the Emmitsburg Road.

As the sharp and often confused action progressed throughout the late afternoon hours, Sickles's battered line was reinforced and eventually relieved by elements of Sykes's V Corps, and then by a portion of II Corps. Sickles himself fell, severely wounded near his headquarters at the Trostle farm. Many desperate attempts by individual Union brigades, regiments, and artillery units to check the relentless Confederate tide failed, in-

Brigadier General Beverly H. Robertson, a troublesome subordinate whom Stuart neither liked nor trusted, nevertheless used his own initiative at Brandy Station and helped prevent the episode from being even more embarrassing to Stuart than it already was. (USAMHI)

cluding the noteworthy action of Edward Cross's Union brigade at the Wheat Field, the counterattack of Brooke's brigade against Semmes's Georgians at the Rose Woods, and the stand of the 9th Massachusetts Battery at the Trostle farmyard. But after nearly four hours of fighting, all Union positions on the initial III Corps line were ultimately overrun.

Indeed, only Little Round Top, the one key terrain feature which should have been occupied by Sickles earlier that afternoon but was not, remained to stem the Southern onslaught. At approximately 7:30 P.M., as the sun began to fall below the mountains on the western horizon, and as remnants of numerous Union commands streamed back toward the safety of Little Round

There were other commands moving in Virginia as Lee's campaign got under way. Down on the Virginia Peninsula the IV Corps stayed behind when McClellan left back in 1862. As Lee marched into Pennsylvania, the Federals there hoped to threaten Richmond and keep reinforcements pinned there instead of going to Lee. Major General Erasmus D. Keyes failed to show enough vigor in the enterprise and found himself put out of the war for good as a result. (WRHS)

Then, in June, as the Confederates marched toward the North, they swarmed over poor Major General Robert H. Milroy and his command at Winchester, Virginia. He managed to stay in the army but never outlived the shame of his defeat. (WRHS)

Top—closely pursued by their victorious but generally exhausted enemy—Crawford's fresh division of Pennsylvania Reserves charged down the slopes of the hill to punch the last gasp of air out of Longstreet's assault. With the onset of darkness, the final defensive line of the Union left flank had been secured.

Despite the limited Confederate successes in capturing Sickles's advanced positions, Lee's overall offensive on July 2 had failed, mainly because of a lack of coordination. Not only had Confederate pressure become piecemeal by the time of the advance of Wright's brigade of Hill's corps in support of Longstreet (against the Union center), but the Southern thrust against the Union right flank at Cemetery Hill and Culp's Hill—intended to commence simultaneously with the attack against the Union left—did not get under way until the heaviest fighting on the Union left had already terminated. In fact, it was roughly sundown when elements of two divisions of Ewell's corps began their assault against the hook and curve of the Union right flank.

After fording Rock Creek and moving through the darkening woods at the base of Culp's Hill, Johnson's division advanced up the eastern slope of the hill and soon became engaged with Greene's brigade of the Union XII Corps. Ironically, Greene's New Yorkers stood alone at this critical juncture in the battle, the bulk of the corps having been removed earlier from their Culp's Hill positions to support the Northern effort on the left flank. Thankfully for the Union forces, the hill had previously been fortified by an extensive line of earthworks, strengthened by felled trees and rocks.

Badly outnumbered, Greene's men used their earthworks to great advantage, and although Johnson was able to secure all the abandoned defenses on the southern slopes, he failed to dislodge Greene's line commanding the summit of the hill. Only darkness prevented Johnson from fully appreciating the value of the positions he had, in fact, occupied, which virtually left ajar the door to the Union rear.

Meanwhile, two Confederate brigades of Early's division met with even less success in their attempt to capture the barren and imposing Cemetery Hill. Initially breaking through XI Corps positions at the northern base at about 7:30 P.M., Avery's North Carolinians suffered severely from a devastating artillery enfilade from nearby Stevens's Knoll. As H. T. Hays's Louisiana "Tigers," who had likewise broken through the initial Union defenses, continued up the steep face of Cemetery Hill, Union reinforcements raced to the aid of the artillery batteries on the crest. After a bitter hand-to-hand struggle, and in the absence of any support from Confederate infantry units stationed near the southern outskirts of town, Hays's men were forced to relinquish their temporary foothold on the Union right. Thus ended the second day's battle, with Meade's basic fishhook formation remaining intact.

Later that night Meade held a council of war at his headquarters on the Taneytown Road to evalu-

As soon as he took his new command, Meade began marching toward Pennsylvania to stop Lee. By June 30 elements of the Army of the Potomac reached Emmitsburg, Maryland, a quiet little town of schools and churches.
(P-M)

*A few days later Alexander Gardner and his team of photographers came to
the little town. They found Mount St. Mary's College.* (USAMHI)

ate the progress of the battle thus far, as well as to determine whether or not the positions of the Army of the Potomac were worth maintaining for yet another day of fighting. They decided to hold the line.

With the return of the detached elements of XII Corps during the night, Johnson's tenuous opportunity for imperiling the Union rear vanished. Beginning at 4:30 the morning of July 3, XII Corps took the initiative by opening on the Confederate lines east and south of the hill. After an engagement lasting nearly seven hours, all of the Union earthworks lost the night before were recaptured. By 11 A.M. the Union right flank stood firmly secured.

For General Lee the failure of his attempts to crush the two Union flanks suggested strongly the tempting possibility that both Union flanks had been fortified at the expense of the Union center, held by Hancock's II Corps. By midday on July 3

the Confederate commander decided to make one last gamble at Gettysburg, a direct frontal assault against Cemetery Ridge. Lee's plan called for a concentrated artillery bombardment to cripple the Union line on the ridge, to be followed by the advance of elements of four infantry divisions: Pickett's, Heth's (now commanded by Pettigrew), Trimble's and Anderson's (in support). All told, the attacking force would number nearly 11,000 men, with Longstreet in overall command. Facing the Confederates across the open fields separating Seminary Ridge and Cemetery Ridge sat II Corps divisions of Alexander Hays, on the Bryan farm, and John Gibbon, near the Codori farm buildings. Supporting these divisions were portions of I Corps, the entire defending force numbering roughly half that of the attackers.

Shortly after one o'clock on the afternoon of July 3, 1863, more than 140 Confederate artillery pieces under the supervision of E. P. Alexander opened fire on the Union center. Upwards of 100 Union guns responded, and for the next two hours the greatest artillery exchange ever witnessed in the Western Hemisphere continued without interruption. As three o'clock approached and Southern artillery ammunition began to run low, orders were issued along Confederate lines to cease fire. The time for the infantry assault had finally arrived.

The subsequent gamble was destined to be far greater than Lee anticipated, for unbeknownst to virtually everyone on the Confederate lines, the majority of Southern artillery rounds completely overshot the main Union defenses. After two hours of bombardment Hancock's positions survived in surprisingly good order. As the dense clouds of smoke from the cannonade slowly drifted away, a few brief moments of anxious quiet descended upon the field.

Then at 3 P.M. an awesome formation of Confederate infantry one mile long abruptly emerged en masse from the woods on Seminary Ridge and began to march, as if on parade, eastward toward what the Confederates hoped would be the disorganized debris of the Union center. The distance between the two ridges averaged slightly less than a mile. In a matter of minutes, as the advancing forces approached the middle of the open fields, artillery batteries from the Union left and right unleashed their fury against both Confederate flanks. Closing their gaps, the advancing divisions continued to push eastward.

It was only when the forward brigades crossed the Emmitsburg Road, roughly two hundred yards west of Hancock's positions, that the main line of the Union II Corps opened fire—shattering the enemy's front ranks with terrible effect. Quickly recovering from this initial shock, the Southern brigades broke into a run and surged up the gentle slope of Cemetery Ridge under a veritable hail of fire, their command structure rapidly disintegrating every step of the way. The next ten or so minutes saw a slaughter rarely equaled in American history, for even before the Confederates reached the low stone wall on the ridge, the Union lines formed into a pocket—elements of Hays's command having swung around into the fields on the Confederate left, and Stannard's Vermont brigade having done the same on the Confederate right.

In the ensuing melee scores of high-ranking officers from both sides, together with literally hundreds upon hundreds of their men, were either killed or wounded. In Pickett's division alone all

And they found St. Joseph's Seminary, founded by Elizabeth Seton, one day to become America's first saint. (P-M)

But by the time Gardner found Emmitsburg, the armies had found Gettysburg.
(USAMHI)

three brigade commanders were hit: Garnett was killed; Kemper was severely wounded and captured; and Armistead, who led an estimated 150 men over the wall and into the mass of Union infantry surrounding Cushing's battery, was also killed.

Receiving fire from three directions, and with the hopelessness of their situation painfully apparent, vast numbers of trapped Southerners surrendered. Although several thousand members of the attacking force managed to escape to the safety of Seminary Ridge, Longstreet's assault, also known to history as "Pickett's Charge," ended in a dismal failure, with approximately two thirds of the Confederate infantrymen involved having been either killed, wounded, or captured. Casualties in many of the northern units had likewise been appalling, but at the conclusion of the struggle it was their line that held.

Earlier that day J.E.B. Stuart, who had finally rejoined Lee's army following his ill-conceived June raid, was directed to proceed far around Meade's right to harass the Union rear at the same time that Lee's infantrymen were striking the Union center. Three miles east of Gettysburg Stuart's cavalry ran into strong elements of Pleasonton's cavalry corps, and after a sharp encounter in which Union General Custer's Michigan brigade distinguished itself and Confederate General Wade Hampton was wounded, Stuart retired from the field, his lone effort at Gettysburg having been thwarted.

The next day, July 4, 1863, both armies remained on the battlefield, with Meade and Lee each waiting for the other to make the next move. When nothing of significance developed that day, Lee reluctantly concluded that his invasion had reached an impasse. Far from his base of supplies, running low on ammunition, and now facing an impregnable enemy line, Lee saw no alternative

It was Major General Henry Heth, a Virginian, who led his division toward Gettysburg after learning of the Federal presence there. On July 1 he clashed with them, beginning the bloodiest battle of the Civil War. Before the battle was done, Heth's own blood ran from a dangerous wound. (VM)

but to terminate the invasion. Two of his primary goals—the temporary relief of war-torn Virginia and the disruption of Union offensive plans for that summer—had already been achieved. The other, more wishful goals, which perhaps may have led to a peace settlement favorable to the South, would have to be postponed for another campaign. It was indeed ominous, however, that Vicksburg, Mississippi, would by coincidence fall to General Grant on that same July 4, 1863.

Lee's retreat from Gettysburg commenced late on July 4 and into the early morning hours of July 5. Technically the campaign ended with his successful recrossing of the Potomac River two weeks later. Not only had the Army of Northern Virginia survived the campaign intact but the invasion had so disrupted the Northern war effort in the eastern

theater that fully ten months passed before the Army of the Potomac was again able to launch a serious threat against Richmond.

Of the 150,000 soldiers who fought at Gettysburg, 51,000 became casualties during the three days of fighting. In terms of magnitude as well as significance, Gettysburg will forever be ranked among the greatest battles in American history. On November 19, 1863, slightly more than four months after the engagement, the name Gettysburg was further immortalized at the dedication of the Soldiers' National Cemetery when, from a speaker's platform on the summit of Cemetery Hill, Abraham Lincoln delivered his brief but fitting eulogy to those Union soldiers who fell on that field. His promise to them was of equal reassurance to those still living. They had not died in vain.

The first Federal infantry to arrive on the scene belonged to the I Corps, Major General John F. Reynolds commanding. Here, in this field in front of McPherson's Woods, the I Corps ran headlong into Hill's Confederates and fought desperately for hours to hold his position until Meade could come up. Finally the Southerners forced them back. This view, made two weeks later, shows the scene of the first fighting, with Mathew Brady surveying it. His assistants made this panorama from two separate images. (NA)

*The Federals who met Heth were cavalry, horsemen, men in the division
commanded by Brigadier General John Buford, a Kentuckian whose cousin
was a general in the Confederate cavalry. He held Gettysburg long enough for
Meade to begin sending up his army. Buford sits here among members of his
staff.* (NA)

*Wesley Merritt became a brigadier just two days
before he led his cavalry brigade in Buford's
desperate defense on July 1. His distinguished
career in the army continued for another
thirty-seven years after Gettysburg.* (P-M)

Heth was only the vanguard for the Confederate III Corps, led by the dashing yet peculiar Lieutenant General Ambrose P. Hill. All during the first day's fight Hill directed the battle as it gathered momentum. (OLD COURTHOUSE MUSEUM, VICKSBURG)

Reynolds did not live to see the retreat. As the fighting raged that morning, he looked back from his saddle toward anticipated reinforcements. A bullet coursed through his head. He was dead before he fell from the saddle. (P-M)

Upon Reynolds's fall, command of the I Corps devolved upon Brigadier General Abner Doubleday, who fired the first Federal shot from Fort Sumter and never had anything to do with the invention of baseball. (USAMHI)

Brigadier General James S. Wadsworth led one of the I Corps divisions that battled valiantly. The corps was more than decimated by the day's fight, and later disbanded. Wadsworth, seated at right, performed admirably, only to fall a year later with a wound almost exactly like Reynolds's. (NA)

Brigadier General Gabriel R. Paul led a New Jersey brigade on that dreadful first day's field. A bullet crashed into his right temple and passed out his left eye, leaving him almost totally blinded for the remaining twenty-three years of his life. (NA)

Francis Barlow was a young brigadier when he fought in the vain attempt to keep the Confederates out of Gettysburg. A bullet left him briefly paralyzed and so dangerously wounded that many believed him dead. Confederate General John B. Gordon personally comforted him as best he could, and years later they became devoted friends. (USAMHI)

The Confederates took losses, too. In the early fighting the Federals captured Brigadier General James J. Archer. He was mortified at being the first Confederate general captured on the field in over a year. When his old friend Doubleday offered his hand and said, "I am glad to meet you," Archer replied coolly, "I am not glad to meet you, sir." (USAMHI)

It was men like Shepherd Green Pryor of the 12th Georgia who finally forced the Federals back. (UNIVERSITY OF GEORGIA LIBRARY, ATHENS)

When the Yankees streamed back from the McPherson's Ridge line, they rushed across these fields into the town of Gettysburg, and from there to the summit of Cemetery Hill, marked by the tall tree on the right at the horizon. Two weeks later Brady's operatives made this view of the scene. (USAMHI)

The Federals retreated along the Chambersburg Pike, too, shown here while looking from the town toward the Lutheran Theological Seminary at the left. Hill's Confederates pursued them hotly, and after the day's battle was done they proceeded to remove the rails from the fences for firewood. F. Gutekunst of Philadelphia probably made this image. (KA)

The Lutheran Theological Seminary was at first used as a field hospital by the
Federals. From its cupola Reynolds had observed the enemy positions. After the
rout on McPherson's Ridge it became a Confederate hospital. (LC)

When Lee finally arrived on the field, he, too, probably used the cupola of the
Lutheran Theological Seminary as an observatory. (P-M)

The Rebels quickly occupied the town of Gettysburg, and a number of Federals were actually cut off from their commands and captured. One who escaped capture was Brigadier General Alexander Schimmelfennig. Isolated from his division, he took refuge in a small outbuilding which, among its other inhabitants, included a number of pigs. There he was forced to hide for two more days before emerging. Wags in later days referred to the shed as General Schimmelfennig's "headquarters." (P-M)

Classes actually began as usual at the Pennsylvania College on July 1, but the coming battle quickly disrupted the schedule. The buildings soon housed wounded and dying instead of students. (USAMHI)

*The Tyson brothers made an excellent set of views in August 1863, showing
the Hagerstown Road on the right. Hill's Confederates raced along it while
pursuing the retreating Federals. Here again they probably burned the fence
rails at their campfires during their stay in Gettysburg.* (P-M *left;* KA *right*)

Meade felt uncomfortable with Doubleday in command on the field and sent trusted Major General Winfield Scott Hancock ahead of the army to assume direction of the defense at Gettysburg. Hancock proved to be Meade's strongest arm in the dreadful battle. (USAMHI)

Late on July 1 the Confederacy's strongest arm, Robert E. Lee, finally reached the field. Now he decided to take the battle to the enemy and drive them from their high ground south of the town. This portrait is by the distinguished Richmond photographer Vannerson. (USAMHI)

When Lee reached the scene, he made his headquarters in a tent across from the home of the Widow Thompson. Brady's camera captured the Thompson house two weeks later. (KA)

The second day's fighting rested largely in the hands of Lieutenant General James "Old Pete" Longstreet, Lee's trusty South Carolinian leading the I Corps. He recognized the value of the two tiny mountains called Big and Little Round Top. (LC)

The Round Tops, Big Round Top on the right and Little Round Top on the left, as they appeared to Brady's assistants around July 15. Brady himself leans against the tree at left. Up these steep, rocky slopes the Confederates charged. (USAMHI)

Had the Southerners been able to take and hold the crest, their cannon could have driven Meade from the field. (USAMHI)

It was largely thanks to Meade's chief engineer, Brigadier General Gouverneur K. Warren, that the Confederates were denied Little Round Top. He saw its natural advantages and commandeered troops to man it just as Longstreet's divisions began their assault. (USAMHI)

During the nighttime hours immediately following the second day's battle, Union soldiers further strengthened the hill by constructing a network of stone walls in anticipation of renewed Confederate assaults the next day. Gibson's photograph shows a portion of these defenses as they appeared on July 6, 1863. (ROBERT J. YOUNGER)

Hastily erected breastworks on Little Round Top's crest gave the Yankees defenses behind which they would ultimately protect themselves from enemy sharpshooters on July 3. Timothy O'Sullivan brought his camera to the summit just four days later. (P-M)

Brady came there a week later. In the distance appears the ground on which the Union center was positioned. (LC)

Brigadier General Evander M. Law of Alabama was one of Longstreet's
Confederates. Seated here, in the center, with members of his staff, he led a
brigade and then a division in the attacks on Little Round Top. This
unpublished image was probably made a few months after the battle. (VM)

Up these dreadful slopes they charged. They came to call the ground below the slope the "Valley of Death." A James Gibson photograph taken on July 6, 1863. (LC)

Reinforcements rushed to the Little Round Top fight as quickly as Meade and Hancock could send them. Major General George Sykes brought his V Corps to the vicinity but found a greater threat on the way. (P-M)

Units like the 6th Vermont of John Sedgwick's VI Corps were present
to support Sykes. (LC)

As the dreadful slaughter was taking place around Little Round Top on
July 2, equally severe fighting raged among the boulders of a sharpshooters'
nest called Devil's Den. Here, at the foot of Big Round Top, lie several
soldiers, probably Confederates, who will not fight again. They lie about as
O'Sullivan found them on July 6. (USAMHI)

"The Slaughter Pen" was what they called the area at the foot of Big Round Top—and not without reason. (USAMHI)

And in Devil's Den itself James Gibson's camera caught the poignant scene of a young Confederate, hardly out of his teens, dead among the rocks toward which he had charged. (USAMHI)

Just before the struggle for Little Round Top commenced, Major General Daniel E. Sickles foolishly led his III Corps out in advance of the main Union line. Having failed to protect Little Round Top, he now failed to heed orders to come back into line. Instead, he led his corps to destruction in the Wheat Field and the Peach Orchard. He lost a leg in the inferno. (KA)

It was the Confederate division of Major General John B. Hood that struck repeatedly at Little Round Top and then at Sickles in the Wheat Field. Hood suffered a disabled arm in the repeated attacks. (VM)

The III Corps regiments like the 114th Pennsylvania, a zouave outfit, suffered heavily from the cross fire into which Sickles led them. (USAMHI)

Beyond the Wheat Field, at the southernmost edge of the Rose Farm, raged a heavy fight that left scores of dead Confederates behind. Seminary Ridge, the Southern main line, is in the far distance in this O'Sullivan view taken on July 5. (USAMHI)

After Sickles's wounding, Major General David B. Birney assumed command of the imperiled III Corps and led it ably in extricating itself from Sickles's folly. (USAMHI)

But many Union soldiers remained behind, never to move again. Short on supplies, the Confederates removed the shoes from these fallen Yankees. (USAMHI)

Major General Andrew A. Humphreys won a second star for his leadership of one of Sickles's divisions along the Emmitsburg Road. Soon thereafter he became Meade's chief of staff. He would return to field duty later in the war as one of the ablest corps commanders. (USAMHI)

Many of those attacking the Union center on July 2 were Georgians, and some of their regiments were family affairs. Here are six brothers, all of the 22nd Georgia and all named Jones. At least one of them fell in the fighting this day. (COURTESY OF LUCY C. MULCAHY, ATLANTA)

The 2nd Georgia Battalion served in the same brigade with the 22nd Georgia. They were so dispersed at the opening of the July 2 fight for Cemetery Hill that they ceased to function as a unit. Here are posed the men of "Mess No. 9," at Norfolk, Virginia, in 1862. Their servant, "Pink," stands at right. (NA)

When Birney took over the III Corps, Brigadier General J. H. Hobart Ward, seated at right, assumed command of his division, holding the vulnerable left between Little Round Top and the Emmitsburg Road. He did so admirably. But a year later his presumed drinking got him dismissed from the army. Forty years later he was run over by a train. (USAMHI)

Few stories are more ironic than that of the beloved Colonel Edward Cross of New Hampshire. He went into the Wheat Field fight leading his New Hampshire brigade. Hancock cheered him on, saying it would be the last time he fought without a general's star. "Too late, general," replied Cross. "This is my last battle." Minutes later he was dead. (USAMHI)

Everywhere the dead piled up. Here Confederates at the Rose Farm lie in a neat row, awaiting burial on July 5. (USAMHI)

*A farmhouse unfortunate enough to be in the path of the Confederate
advance on July 2 was Abraham Trostle's home. Timothy O'Sullivan
found it looking like this a few days later.* (P-M)

These horses were once the animals of the 9th Massachusetts Artillery.
(USAMHI)

*One of the most eloquent images of all, Timothy O'Sullivan's July 5
photograph shows a Georgia Confederate disemboweled and dismembered by a
Federal shell. O'Sullivan probably placed the shell and rifle in the picture,
but no artificial posing was necessary to present an eloquently brutal picture
of the terror of the war.* (USAMHI)

There seemed no end to the dead resulting from the terrible fighting.
(USAMHI)

*Portions of the V Corps soon went into the fight to assist the beleaguered III
Corps. Brigadier General Samuel W. Crawford, who had been a surgeon in the
garrison at Fort Sumter, led a division to the relief of Little Round Top.
Here he stands grasping the pole of his headquarters flag a year later.* (USAMHI)

Units like the 30th Pennsylvania, with Company A shown here, fought in those fields on their own home soil. Rarely did a Union soldier have that experience, which was commonplace among Southerners. (USAMHI)

The fighting on July 2 raged elsewhere as well, such as in the vicinity of Rock Creek, at Culp's Hill, where the XII Corps held Meade's extreme right. (USAMHI)

A major assault came at Cemetery Hill, the right center of Meade's line. As evening approached, Confederates swept across the fields in the distance of this Brady Company image to attack these slopes. (USAMHI)

The Tysons captured this image of the stone wall along the base of Cemetery Hill, looking toward Culp's Hill. The Confederates hurled themselves against the opposite side of this wall and into the guns of the Yankees. (KA)

Brady's men are believed to have made this view of the ground over which the Rebels attacked. They swept from the right of the picture to the left. (NA)

Their objective was the crest of the hill named for the cemetery at its summit. Here one sees a Brady Company view of the gatehouse to Evergreen Cemetery. (USAMHI)

Another view of the gateway, by the Tysons. Men hid behind the gravestones, visible in the background, while enemy bullets split and cracked them, showering splinters of marble over the once peaceful "bivouac of the dead." (P-M)

Federal gun emplacements on Cemetery Hill, showing the hasty defenses thrown up by the Yankee gunners. A photograph by F. Gutekunst. (KA)

Finally July 3 arrived, marking the last day of the battle and the most desperate. Attacks had failed to take Culp's Hill, Meade's extreme right, though places like the Taney farm, shown here in a Tyson photograph, did fall to the Confederates. (COURTESY OF WILLIAM C. DARRAH, GETTYSBURG)

Breastworks such as these played a vital role in the successful defense of Culp's Hill. Shown here are two of Brady's assistants, gazing in the direction from which the Confederate attacks were made on both the evening of July 2 and the morning of July 3. (ROBERT J. YOUNGER)

After the failures elsewhere on the Union lines, Lee now looked to a massive assault on Meade's center as his last hope of success. His chief of artillery, Colonel E. Porter Alexander, massed scores of guns to bombard the Yankee line on Cemetery Ridge. (VM)

Guns like this unusual Whitworth breech-loading rifle could throw a shell almost five miles, but with so little accuracy as to be useless. Lee had two of them at Gettysburg. (USAMHI)

Charles W. Squires, seated at left, served with the Washington Artillery of New Orleans. To these men fell the honor of firing the opening shots signaling the commencement of the cannonade. (COURTESY OF W.H.T. SQUIRES, HENDERSON, N.C.)

Behind the Federal lines on Cemetery Ridge Meade made his headquarters in the modest Leister farmhouse. Three days later Gardner made this view, the horses killed in the battle still littering the ground. (LC)

Here Meade held his council of war the night before and determined to stay and risk another day's battle. (P-M)

Now Major General George E. Pickett led his division, accompanied by two others of Hill's corps, for the grand infantry assault that forever after bore Pickett's name. Both Longstreet and Pickett believed it a mistake. (VM)

Brigadier General James H. Lane led his brigade in the charge and lost almost half of his command. (VM)

Up the slopes of Cemetery Ridge swept the Confederates. They raced past the modest home of free Negro Abraham Bryan, only yards from the crest. The clutter and damage from the fight is still evident in the Brady Company photograph made several days later. (USAMHI)

A dead and decomposed horse lies in Bryan's yard, while a very much alive photographer's assistant poses for dead several days after the fight in this unpublished Brady Company image. (P-M)

Over 1,500 artillery horses were killed in the battle. (USAMHI)

It was Hancock and his II Corps that formed the mainstay of the Cemetery Ridge line, with division commanders like Brigadier General Alexander Hays fighting admirably. (P-M)

The terrible losses to the Confederates could not be replaced. Brigadier General James L. Kemper, who was seriously wounded, fell within a few feet of the enemy line, only to be captured. (VM)

Richard B. Garnett had been one of Jackson's best commanders. He led his Virginia brigade in the charge, died in the furious smoke of the fight in front of Meade's line, and was buried with his men in a common grave. (USAMHI)

Supporting Garnett and Kemper was the brigade of General Lewis A. Armistead. With his color-bearer and a few others he actually penetrated the Federal line and just managed to touch a Yankee cannon with his hand before he received a mortal wound. He died a short time later. (VM)

There were heavy casualties in blue as well. Meade's horse, Baldy, took a bad wound, having already been wounded at both Bull Runs and at Antietam. This last injury put him out of field service for good, though the animal lived on until 1882. He marched in Meade's own funeral in 1872. (P-M)

And even a single civilian was killed on July 3. Miss Jennie Wade died instantly when struck by a sniper's bullet earlier that day as she baked bread in her sister's home in the town. (USAMHI)

Brigadier General Joseph R. Davis, nephew of the Confederate President, led his brigade in support of the great assault and helped cover its retreat when it failed. (USAMHI)

The commander of that brigade was Elon J. Farnsworth, a general for just four days. He died in the attack as it was repulsed. (P-M)

Only after the main Battle of Gettysburg was over did the nearby cavalry finally get involved. Brigadier General Hugh J. Kilpatrick led a division of Federal horse, and as the Confederates streamed back toward Seminary Ridge after the failure of the attack, he foolishly sent a brigade in to attack the enemy on another strongly held portion of the field. (COURTESY OF BARBARA CHEATELY, ONTARIO, CALIFORNIA)

A Confederate commander in the mounted fighting was Brigadier General Wade Hampton, who actually held his fire in a duel with a Federal enlisted man until the Yankee could reload his carbine. Then Hampton shot him, only to be wounded grievously himself a few minutes later. (MUSEUM OF THE CONFEDERACY, RICHMOND)

Colonel Laurence S. Baker's leadership of the 1st North Carolina Cavalry in Hampton's command won him promotion to brigadier a few weeks later. Few cavalrymen would boast of their performance in the Gettysburg campaign. (VM)

Three miles east of Gettysburg a larger and exclusively cavalry fight took place on the afternoon of July 3, as Stuart's attempt to penetrate Meade's rear failed. One of the Yankee brigades was led by another new brigadier, George A. Custer. (USAMHI)

Confederate field hospitals full of wounded were left behind by the retreating Lee and quickly surrendered to Meade. At the bottom of this hill the Black Horse Tavern and the barn in front of it contained wounded from Longstreet's corps, in the care of Surgeon Simon Baruch, father of Bernard Baruch. An early postwar view. (SOUTH CAROLINA RELIC ROOM AND MUSEUM, COLUMBIA)

The field hospitals for the Federal wounded grew rapidly as all the injured were brought in, and hundreds of humanitarians flocked from the North to tend them. Here the United States Christian Commission cares for men believed to be from the II Corps. (KA)

Photographer F. Gutekunst of Philadelphia came to make this image of more Christian Commission hospital tents for the II Corps. What had until recently been a cornfield was now a field of pain. (NATIONAL PARK SERVICE)

And everywhere, it seemed, there were men to bury. Here O'Sullivan caught Confederates being laid in shallow graves near the Rose Farm. For them, at least, the war was over. (USAMHI)

Meade finally pursued Lee's retreating army as it trudged back toward Virginia, but it was too late. In Emmitsburg, as Stuart's cavalry covered the retreat, the Southerners stopped long enough to briefly capture the Farmers' Inn and Hotel on July 5. With it they detained one of Gardner's photographers, as Gardner's team was just on its way to photograph the recent battlefield. (USAMHI)

Battery F of the 5th United States Artillery was one of the leading units in the delayed pursuit of Lee. They followed his tracks to the Potomac. (KA)

Yet finally Lee crossed the great river. On July 19 Meade was himself ready to cross in pursuit, but the bridge at Berlin had been destroyed two years earlier. (USAMHI)

Consequently the engineers threw pontoon bridges across the stream and over they went. But the campaign was done. (USAMHI)

Four months later people again flocked to Gettysburg, this time for the dedication of a national soldiers' cemetery. Hundreds toured the battlefield, itself still not recovered from the fight. Soldiers posed and feigned death in such hellish places as Devil's Den. (LC)

Several hundred spectators assembled to hear the dedication remarks by Edward Everett of Massachusetts and by President Lincoln. (NA)

*Lincoln's remarks proved so brief that he had finished and had sat down before
the photographer could capture the scene. Instead he caught the President a
few minutes later. (His head is encircled in this photograph.) He had spoken
of democracy and devotion, of freedom and sacrifice, of the good things in men
that must never perish from the earth. (NA)*

ABBREVIATIONS

AIG   America Image Gallery, Gettysburg, Pennsylvania

CHS   Chicago Historical Society, Chicago

CM   Confederate Museum, New Orleans

CSS   Charles S. Schwartz

CWTI   Civil War Times Illustrated Collection, Harrisburg, Pennsylvania

DAM, LSU   Department of Archives and Manuscripts, Louisiana State University, Baton Rouge

GDAH   Georgia Department of Archives and History, Atlanta

GW   Gary Wright

HP   Herb Peck, Jr.

ISHL   Illinois State Historical Library, Springfield

JM   Jack McGuire

JMB   Joe M. Bauman

KA   Kean Archives, Philadelphia

KHS   Kentucky Historical Society, Kentucky Military Museum, Frankfort, Kentucky

LC   Library of Congress, Washington, D.C.

LJW   Larry J. West

LO   Lloyd Ostendorf Collection

LSU   Louisiana State University, Department of Archives and Manuscripts, Baton Rouge

MC   Museum of the Confederacy

MHS   Minnesota Historical Society

MJH   Michael J. Hammerson

MJM   Michael J. McAfee

MM   Mariners Museum, Newport News, Virginia

NA   National Archives, Washington, D.C.

NHC   U. S. Naval Historical Center

NLM   National Library of Medicine, Bethesda, Maryland

NYHS   New York Historical Society, New York

OCHM   Old Court House Museum, Vicksburg, Mississippi

PHS   Pensacola Historical Society, Pensacola, Florida

P-M   Pennsylvania-MOLLUS Collection, War Library and Museum, Philadelphia

RJY   Robert J. Younger

RP   Ronn Palm

SCL   South Carolina Library, University of South Carolina, Columbia

SHC   Southern Historical Collection, University of North Carolina, Chapel Hill

TU   Louisiana Historical Association, Special Collections Division, Tulane University Library, New Orleans

USAMHI   U. S. Army Military History Institute, Carlisle Barracks, Pennsylvania

VHS   Vermont Historical Society

VM   Valentine Museum, Richmond, Virginia

WA   William Albaugh Collection

WCD   William C. Davis

WG   William Gladstone Collection

WRHS   Western Reserve Historical Society, Cleveland, Ohio

The Contributors

Robert C. Black is a retired professor of history at Colorado Women's College whose special interest has always been transportation. He is the author of *The Railroads of the Confederacy*.

Albert Castel has specialized in the war west of the Alleghenies in his books and articles, among them *General Sterling Price and the Civil War in the West, Kansas—A Frontier State at War,* and *William Clarke Quantrell.*

Dudley T. Cornish, professor of history at Pittsburgh State University, is the author of the classic work *The Sable Arm: Negro Troops in the Union Army, 1861—1865.*

Joseph P. Cullen served for many years as a historian with the National Park Service. The author of numerous articles on the Civil War, he also wrote the National Historical Society's *Concise History of the American Revolution and The Peninsula Campaign.*

Charles Dufour, past president of the Louisiana Historical Association and one of the founders of the Civil War Round Table, is a New Orleans native and retired newspaperman, and the author of eight books, three of which dwell on the Civil War.

William A. Frassanito, chief photographic consultant for this work, is one of the foremost historians and interpreters of Civil War photographs.

Warren W. Hassler, Jr., longtime professor of history at Pennsylvania State University, is a highly regarded and prolific historian in the field of American and Civil War military history.

Leslie D. Jensen, Curator of Collections at Richmond's Museum of the Confederacy, is a specialist in Confederate uniforms and equipment.

Virgil Carrington Jones has long been associated with the naval history of the war through his trilogy *The Civil War at Sea.*

Maury Klein is the biographer of General E. P. Alexander, Lee's chief of Artillery, as well as Jay Gould. He has also published works on the Louisville & Nashville Railroad and the Great Richmond Terminal.

David Lindsey, professor of history at California State University, Los Angeles, since 1956, is the author of numerous books, including *Americans in Conflict: The Civil War and Reconstruction.*

James M. Merrill, a Guggenheim and Mershon Fellow, served as a lieutenant in the United Sates Navy, which inspired his interest in Civil War naval and maritime operations. Among his books are *Battle Flags South: The Civil War on Western Rivers, Rebel Shore: Union Sea Power in the Civil War,* and *Sailor's Admiral,* a biography of William F. Halsey.

Peter J. Parrish, author of *The American Civil War,* is professor of modern history at the University of Dundee, Scotland.

Frederic E. Ray is art director of *Civil War Times Illustrated* and *American History Illustrated,* as well as serving as a photographic consultant for this work. His *Alfred R. Waud, Civil War Artist,* is one of the foremost biographies of the legion of battlefield artists who followed the armies.

James I. Robertson, Jr. has written and edited numerous books and articles on the Civil War years. He served as executive director for the United States Civil War Centennial Commission from 1961 to 1965. One of his outstanding contributions is the two-volume *Civil War Books: A Critical Bibliography.*

Charles P. Roland, professor of history at the University of Kentucky, served as assistant to the chief historian for the Department of the Army. Among his books are *Louisiana Sugar Plantations During the American Civil War* and *The Confederacy.*

William N. Still, professor of history at East Carolina University, Greenville, North Carolina, has written numerous articles as well as *Iron Afloat: The Story of Confederate Ironclads and Confederate Shipbuilding.*

W. A. Swanberg has written on a wide range of subjects in American History, from the Civil War to biographies of Jim Fisk and Theodore Dreiser. His Civil War works include *Sickles the Incredible,* a biography of General Daniel Sickles, and *First Blood—The Story of Fort Sumter.*

Robert G. Tanner, an attorney, is the author of *Stonewall in the Valley.* His main interests lie in the Shenandoah Valley campaign of 1862.

Emory M. Thomas is professor of history at the University of Georgia. Among his works on the Confederacy and Reconstruction are *The Confederacy as a Revolutionary Experience, The Confederate Nation, The Confederate State of Richmond: A Biography of the Capital,* and *The American War and Peace, 1860–1877.*

Frank E. Vandiver, president of Texas A&M University, was a recipient of the Harry S Truman award from the Kansas City Civil War Round Table and has written numerous books and articles on the Confederacy, most notably his biography of T. J. Jackson, *Mighty Stonewall.*

Bell I. Wiley was preeminent among Civil War historians, with more than fifty books to his credit. The story of the common people of that era was his chief interest, and his two works *The Life of Johnny Reb* and *The Life of Billy Yank* have become classics. He also served as chairman of the Board of Advisors of the National Historical Society.

T. Harry Williams achieved a reputation as one of the foremost American historians of our time. His biography *Huey Long* won him the Pulitzer Prize and the National Book Award. He was, however, best known for his work on the Civil War, including *Lincoln and the Radicals, Lincoln and his Generals, P. G. T. Beauregard, The Union Sundered,* and many more.

H

J